**FOURTEENTH EDITION AND
FORTIETH ANNIVERSARY EDITION**

Intercultural Communication

A READER

Larry A. Samovar
SAN DIEGO STATE UNIVERSITY,
EMERITUS

Richard E. Porter
CALIFORNIA STATE UNIVERSITY,
LONG BEACH, EMERITUS

Edwin R. McDaniel
JAPAN–U.S. COMMUNICATION
ASSOCIATION (JUCA)

Carolyn Sexton Roy
SAN DIEGO STATE UNIVERSITY

CENGAGE
Learning®

Australia • Brazil • Japan • Korea • Mexico • Singapore • Spain • United Kingdom • United States

CENGAGE
Learning®

Intercultural Communication: A Reader, Fourteenth Edition

Larry A. Samovar, Richard E. Porter, Edwin R. McDaniel, Carolyn Sexton Roy

Product Manager: Nicole Morinon

Product Director: Monica Eckman

Content Developer: Larry Goldberg

Content Coordinator: Alicia Landsberg

Product Assistant: Colin Solan

Media Developer: Jessica Badiner

Senior Marketing Brand Manager: Kara Kindstrom

Brand Manager: Ben Rivera

Rights Acquisitions Specialist: Alexandra Ricciardi

Manufacturing Planner: Doug Bertke

Art and Design Direction, Production Management, and Composition: Cenveo® Publisher Services

Cover Image: gettyimages®

Library of Congress Control Number: 2013941790

ISBN-13: 978-1-285-07739-0

ISBN-10: 1-285-07739-3

Cengage Learning
20, Channel Center Street
Boston, MA 02210
USA

Cengage Learning is a leading provider of customized learning solutions with office locations around the globe, including Singapore, the United Kingdom, Australia, Mexico, Brazil, and Japan. Locate your local office at: **international.cengage.com/region**

Cengage Learning products are represented in Canada by Nelson Education, Ltd.

For your course and learning solutions, visit **www.cengage.com**.

Purchase any of our products at your local college store or at our preferred online store **www.cengagebrain.com**.

Instructors: Please visit **login.cengage.com** and log in to access instructor-specific resources.

Printed in the United States of America
1 2 3 4 5 6 7 15 14 13

About the Authors

LARRY SAMOVAR, Emeritus Professor at San Diego State University, received his Ph.D. from Purdue University, where he taught for five years. He was also an invited scholar at Nihon University in Japan. Dr. Samovar was instrumental in defining the field of intercultural communication and delineating its major components. In this role he has been a guest speaker at many universities. In addition, Dr. Samovar has worked as a communication consultant in both the private and public sectors. He has written and/or edited 14 textbooks—totaling 45 editions. Many of his publications have been translated into foreign languages and are used in 11 countries. As an active researcher he has presented more than 100 scholarly papers and conducted seminars and workshops at international, national, and regional conferences. His publication list is extensive and encompasses books and articles on intercultural communication, small group communication, interpersonal communication, and public speaking.

RICHARD E. PORTER, Professor Emeritus in the Department of Communication Studies at California State University, Long Beach, received his Ph.D. from the University of Southern California. He developed his interest in intercultural communication in 1967 before there was an established field of study. His early work along with that of other pioneers in the field laid a basic structural foundation which has been used by many later scholars as the field developed and expanded. He created and taught undergraduate and graduate courses in intercultural communication for 30 years. Dr. Porter is the co-author and editor of 4 books with 24 editions that deal with the subject of intercultural communication.

EDWIN (ED) R. McDANIEL received his Ph.D. from Arizona State University. He is currently a Member-at-Large of the Japan–U.S. Communication Association and a member of the Thunderbird Educator Network at the Thunderbird School of Global Management. He is also a retired Professor of Intercultural Communication at Aichi Shukutoku University, in Nagoya, Japan, and has been a Japan ICU Foundation Visiting Scholar at the International Christian University in Tokyo. Dr. McDaniel has also taught at San Diego State University, CSU San Marcos, and Thunderbird. In May 2013, he was an invited speaker at the China Cultural Industry Forum (CIF) in Beijing. He is the co-author/co-editor of numerous books on intercultural communication. His articles and book chapters have been published in China, Germany, Korea, and Japan, as well as the United States. Before beginning his academic career, Dr. McDaniel was in government service for over 20 years, during which time he lived and traveled in more than 40 countries.

CAROLYN SEXTON ROY has been a member of the History Department at San Diego State University since 1989. Her doctoral studies in Colonial Latin American History were conducted at the University of California, Los Angeles. She is a well-practiced presenter of papers at regional, national, and international conventions, and has been published numerous times. She has traveled extensively in Latin America. A Fulbright Fellowship enabled her to conduct research for an extended period and salvage an archive in Parral, Chihuahua, Mexico. Her linguistic skills, particularly applied to Latin America, facilitate her high level of understanding of intercultural communication.

Contents

Preface

We begin, as we have in each edition, with an expression of appreciation to all the students and faculty who have seen us through thirteen prior editions. However, this time our gratitude is accompanied by a sense of pride, and a touch of ego, as we introduce this Fortieth Anniversary special edition. Our enthusiasm derives from two sources. First, we are reminded that during the last four decades, tens of thousands of readers have found something of value in earlier presentations. Second, this volume affords us the opportunity to offer a collection of essays from past editions that we believe are "foundational" to the field of intercultural communication. Since the first edition in 1972, *Intercultural Communication: A Reader* has presented approximately 600 essays. A great many of these helped introduce and define the discipline of intercultural communication.

The first few editions drew most of their selections from a variety of academic fields. The content was eclectic because intercultural communication was in its infancy and searching for a basic set of core principles at that time. Our early editions were interdisciplinary, allowing users to gain an understanding of various approaches to intercultural communication while observing the historical, philosophical, and theoretical evolution of the field. These same characteristics served as the overriding goals for this new edition. Hence, the essays in this present volume represent the best "core" essays from the last forty years. They also demonstrate how the field has altered and expanded its description of intercultural communication during this same period.

As noted, since our first edition the study of intercultural communication has, like most academic disciplines, expanded and evolved. This growth demanded that we offer readers access to contemporary approaches and theories in each new edition. The requirement to adapt to changes in the field, some temporary and others more enduring, forced us to omit scores of older selections to accommodate the new essays. Some of the foundational essays were supplanted by newer materials. Over the history of the book many of the reviewers, as well as numerous instructors who used the text, have requested that particular selections be revived and returned to the anthology. In most instances these have been articles that can be considered "foundational." In addition, we frequently received requests from professors who sought permission to use specific selections from earlier editions in their classes. We kept an informal record of these requests and have taken this opportunity to include many of these essays in this fourteenth edition.

A POINT OF VIEW

In this special edition we have endeavored to remain true to the central mission of the forty-year history of the book. We have traditionally attempted to accomplish two goals. First, we have taken a culture-specific approach to intercultural communication, focusing on national cultures, co-cultural groups, and ethnicities. Second, we have introduced broad theoretical concepts within our examination of these individual cultures. This dual approach has been especially germane in the contemporary era of globalization and changing demographics within the United States. Individuals are now living, working, and traveling in a more intercultural social environment, and globalization and diversity remain the themes of this new volume as well. We begin with globalization. This word can no longer be applied solely to international economic activities, but now connotes the existing state of interdependencies and interactions among all the world's nations and people across almost every context. Globalization has stimulated the growth of both developed and developing nations and significantly increased the economic, political, and in many cases, military aspirations of what are now called "emerging markets." Brazil,

Russia, India, and China are but a few nations that need to be examined by anyone interested in intercultural communication. This new cluster of nations now influences how world international financial systems are managed, how goods and services are shared, and how people participate in worldwide conversations. The influence of religious ideology, whether in the Middle East, Central Asia, or the United States, is an important consideration in global stability. Although the idea may be a bit hackneyed, it is true that what happens in one part of the world has the potential to influence the entire world.

The changes and challenges brought about by globalization are not limited to the international sphere. Within the United States, people from a host of diverse cultures are coming together by both chance and design. These "meetings" are taking place in workplaces, classrooms, health care facilities, tourist venues, and a multitude of other locales. Most encounters are positive and lead to productive relationships, but not all. Whether it be issues of immigration, race, gender or sexuality, religion, or political ideology, sometimes negative, even destructive, interaction occurs. We feel that those failures are partially due to a lack of effective intercultural communication. Developing an intercultural awareness and transforming it into understanding remains at the heart of this book. As a member of this multicultural globalized world, your ability to successfully engage in intercultural communication may be one of the most important skills you will ever develop. Now, more than ever, you are being challenged by a future in which you will interact with people from a wide range of dissimilar cultural backgrounds. You no longer compete on a local, regional, or even national level. Competition today is worldwide!

Developing effective intercultural communication skills will require you to develop new ways of perceiving, thinking, and interacting. This will not be easy. First, because your view of the world is shaped by the perspective of your own culture, it is often difficult to understand and appreciate many of the actions originated by other people, groups, and nations. Your cultural perceptions tend to condition you to see people and events through a highly selective lens. Second, to be a successful intercultural communicator you must be open to new and different communication

experiences, have empathy toward cultures different from your own, develop a universalistic, realistic worldview, and learn to be tolerant of opinions and behaviors that differ from your own. Although these communication characteristics are easy to read about, translating them into action is a very difficult task. Training in intercultural communication offers you an arena in which to work on these skills. In short, it is your ability to change, to make adjustments in your communication habits and behavior, that gives you the potential to engage in successful and effective intercultural contacts.

OUR APPROACH

Many aspects of our approach may well have trickled out by now. But let us be more specific about our orientation. The basic energizing motive for this book has remained the same since we became interested in the topic of intercultural communication over forty years ago. We believe that the ability to communicate effectively with people from other cultures and co-cultures is valuable to each of us as individuals. Effective communication has the potential to benefit the approximately seven billion people with whom we share this planet. We have intentionally selected materials that will assist you in understanding those intercultural communication principles that are instrumental to success when you interact with people of other cultures. Fundamental to our approach is the conviction that communication is a social activity; *it is something people do to and with one another.* The activity might begin with ideas or feelings, but these are manifested in our behaviors, be they verbal or nonverbal. In both explicit and implicit ways, the information and the advice contained in this book are usable; *the ideas presented can be translated into action.*

NEW FEATURES

As you have observed by now, the most significant new feature of this edition is the fact that we are presenting eight chapters containing the "foundational" essays of the last forty years. Because intercultural communication is a dynamic field in constant evolution, we also have included a chapter of five original articles we believe reflect some new directions for the field in the coming decade.

The title page reveals yet another new feature of this volume—the addition of another editor. We invited Carolyn Sexton Roy to be part of this new edition. A member of the History Department at San Diego State University, Ms. Roy earned the Candidate for Doctor of Philosophy Degree in Colonial Latin American History at the University of California at Los Angeles. She was also a Fulbright Fellow doing research in Parral, Chihuahua, Mexico. Having lived in Mexico and traveled extensively in Latin America, she is fluent in Spanish and Portuguese. Her major research and teaching focus has been the social and cultural history of Latin America and the United States.

THE SELECTION PROCESS

We have already made indirect references to the selection process. However, that procedure is important enough to warrant further explanation. Selecting the most significant papers for this special edition from a list of more than 600 essays was a challenging assignment. We spent months discussing which selections to include and which to exclude. Not wanting to be capricious or arbitrary, we established the following criteria to guide us during our deliberations. First, in nearly every instance we have selected essays that were *originally written for the Reader*. Implementing that condition meant that several foundational selections are excluded from this edition. Because many of these pieces are considered "classics," we urge you to seek them out in other sources. Some of these are the seminal works of scholars such as Edward T. Hall, Geert Hofstede, Dean C. Barnland, Julia T. Wood, Marshal R. Singer, Anne B. Pedersen and Paul B. Pedersen, Harry C. Triandis, Richard Brislin, Peter S. Adler, Shirley N. Weber, La Ray Barna, Edward Stewart, Thomas Sowell, Kathy Jankowski, and others.

Second, many of the essays that constitute our final collection are incorporated into this volume because of their *continued popularity*. This positive status took two forms. First, prior to each edition our publisher conducted detailed reviews and surveys of faculty members who had adopted the book. An assessment of that data helped us isolate which selections the users of the anthology found most beneficial. In many instances these essays had often been updated and were used in numerous editions. Many of them now appear in this special edition.

Third, when making our final selection, we wanted to include readings that had proved *instrumental in expanding the field of intercultural communication*. These essays were both new and innovative. Put in slightly different terms, we perceived that our book has been a conduit allowing various authors to stake out some new territory in the area of culture and communication. In this sense the anthology became a place where scholars could share their original ideas in a forum somewhat different from a traditional academic journal. By adopting this philosophy early in the history of this book, scholars such as Peter Andersen, Brian H. Spitzberg, Young Yun Kim, Stella Ting-Toomey, Edith Folb, Judith N. Martin, Mary Jane Collier, Mary Fong, Miike Yoshitake, Bernard Saint-Jacques, and Mira Bergelson, along with others, found an outlet for their pioneering ideas. We selected many of those essays for this commemorative edition.

Fourth, we would be less than candid if we did not reveal that in some instances we had to omit certain essays because we could *not secure a current permission*. In most of those instances the author was deceased, but had failed to make estate arrangements granting someone else the authority to permit the essay's republication. In a few cases, despite concerted efforts, we were simply unable to locate the author.

Finally, we conclude this section by offering our apologies to all those past contributors if we were compelled to omit your works from this current volume. Perhaps we will be able to include them in the Fiftieth Anniversary Edition.

UTILIZING THE BOOK

As in the past, we designed this anthology for the general reader who is interested in learning about intercultural communication. Therefore, we have selected materials that are broadly based, comprehensive, and suitable for both undergraduate and graduate students. Although the level of difficulty may fluctuate from essay to essay, we have attempted to select essays aimed at the level found in most textbooks directed toward college and university students.

Intercultural Communication: A Reader is designed to meet three specific needs. The first comes from a canon maintaining that successful intercultural communication is a matter of highest importance if humankind and society are to survive. Events during the past forty years have created a world that sees us becoming increasingly linked in a multitude of ways. From pollution to economics to health care, to world hunger to terrorism, what happens to one culture potentially happens to all other cultures. This book is designed to serve as a basic anthology for courses concerned with the issues associated with human interaction. Our intention has been to make this book both theoretical and practical so that the issues associated with intercultural communication can first be understood and then acted upon.

Second, the book may be used as a supplemental text to existing service and basic communication skills courses and interpersonal communication courses. Third, the text provides resource material for courses in communication theory, small group communication, organizational and business communication, and mass communication, as well as for courses in anthropology, health care, sociology, social psychology, social welfare, social policy, business, and international relations. The long list of possible uses only underscores the increased level of intercultural interaction that is characteristic of what is now often called the "global village."

ORGANIZATION

The book is organized into nine closely related chapters. In Chapter 1, "Approaches to Intercultural Communication," our purpose is twofold: We acquaint you with the basic concepts of intercultural communication as we arouse your curiosity and interest in the topic. Hence, the essays in this chapter are both theoretical and philosophical. The selections explain what intercultural communication is, why it is important, and how it operates.

Chapter 2, "Cultural Identity: Issues of Belonging," has essays that demonstrate how different cultural and ethnic identities influence role expectations,

perceptions, and intercultural interaction. The various selections will instill in you an appreciation for how a person's cultural identity helps shape his or her view of the world.

Chapter 3, "International Cultures: Understanding Diversity," describes the communication patterns of cultures from Northeast Asia, India, Russia, the Middle East, and Africa. In other chapters of the book we examine additional international cultures in health care, business, and educational settings.

Chapter 4, "Co-Cultures: Living in a Multicultural World," moves us from the international arena to domestic co-cultures within the United States. For many of you these will be the groups you interact with on a daily basis. Although space constraints have limited the total number of co-cultures we could include, we believe that through the selection of African Americans, women, the disabled, and homosexuals, you will get a summary of the cultural diversity found in those groups. As is the case with international cultures, other co-cultures are discussed in other chapters.

In Chapter 5, "Intercultural Messages: Verbal and Nonverbal Interaction," we study how verbal and nonverbal symbols are used (and vary) in intercultural interactions. We offer readings that introduce you to some of the difficulties that might be encountered when your intercultural partner uses a different verbal or nonverbal coding system. We look at how verbal idiosyncrasies and distinctions influence problem solving, speaking, perception, and understanding. As noted, this chapter is also concerned with nonverbal symbols and explains some of the cultural differences in movement, facial expressions, eye contact, silence, space, time, and the like.

Chapter 6, "Cultural Contexts: The Influence of the Setting," continues with the theme of how culture modifies interaction. This time, however, the interaction is examined within a specific context and environment. The assumption is that "rules" that influence how members of a culture behave in certain settings will fluctuate across cultures. To clarify this important issue, we have selected "places" where people of different cultures are most likely to be confronted with situations in which the "rules" of interaction differ from those found in the United States. More specifically, we look at settings related to business, groups, negotiations, health care, and education.

In Chapter 7, "Communicating Interculturally: Becoming Competent," the readings are intended to help you become a more competent intercultural communicator. The chapter highlights some inherent intercultural communication problems ranging from cultural differences in dealing with conflict to variations in interpersonal rituals. In addition, solutions are advanced to provide you with knowledge about and suggestions for responding to these and other difficulties you might face when communicating with "strangers."

Chapter 8, "Ethical Considerations: Changing Behavior," presents essays that deal with ethical and moral issues as well as future directions and challenges of intercultural communication.

Chapter 9, "New Perspectives: Prospects for the Future," contains five new, original selections based on the simple premise that intercultural communication evolves, as do all academic disciplines. Change is difficult to calculate because by its very nature it involves the future, so we invited several leading intercultural communication scholars to help us discern the future trajectory of the field.

Finally, we ask that you not conclude your study of intercultural communication with the reading of a single book or the completion of one course. We believe that the study of intercultural communication is a lifelong endeavor. Each time you want to share an idea or feeling with someone of another culture, you face a new and exhilarating learning experience.

ASSISTANCE

As in the past, many people have helped us rethink and reshape this project. We express appreciation to Content Developer Larry Goldberg. Larry saw to it that the manuscript was free of problems as he guided it through each phase of the production process. We also thank Alexandra Ricciardi who was instrumental in securing permissions for selections in this Anniversary edition. Since some of the permission releases reached back over forty years, her task was not a simple one. And, as we do with each edition, we call attention to our first editor, Rebecca Hayden. Becky had enough courage and insight four decades ago to decide that intercultural communication should and would become a viable discipline. We also recognize the contribution of our publisher Cengage Learning, who has been consistent in the determination to produce and market a quality textbook.

A special note of thanks is owed to the many instructors who have adopted previous editions of this reader over the past forty years. Their continued confidence in our ability to provide a useful pedagogical tool is especially gratifying. We would also like to thank the reviewers for their helpful comments and suggestions: Katie Dunleavy, La Salle University; Vicki Karns, Suffolk University; Jaesub Lee, University of Houston; Carmen Mendoza, Trinity International University; Dante Morelli, Suffolk County Community College; Karri Pearson, Normandale Community College; Kipp Preble, Chaffey College; Natalie Rybas, Indiana University East; Miki Thiessen, Rock Valley College; and Jonathan Watt, Geneva College/Ref. Pres. Theological Seminary. We conclude by expressing our gratitude to those hundreds of scholars who allowed us to share their work with so many readers. Without all of your articles this collection would never have survived for forty years. You know who you are. Thank you.

Approaches to Intercultural Communication

I will say at the outset that there is only one world, and although we speak of the Old World and the New, this is because the latter was lately discovered by us, and not because there are two.

GARCILASO DE LA VEGA, FROM *ROYAL COMMENTARIES OF THE INCAS, AND GENERAL HISTORY OF PERU* (1690)

It is not our differences that divide us. It is our inability to recognize, accept, and celebrate those differences.

AUDRE LORDE, AMERICAN POET

This fourteenth edition of *Intercultural Communication: A Reader* is in some ways a historical perspective on the growth and evolution of intercultural communication. Therefore, it is appropriate to consider some of the societal dynamics behind that growth and how they have been reflected in past editions. When the first edition was published in 1972, the world was locked in the grip of the Cold War, dealing with two contending ideologies, led by the United States on one side and the Union of Soviet Socialist Republics (USSR) on the other. Both nations possessed nuclear weapons capable of total destruction. That awareness stimulated the need to increase understanding and communication between peoples holding varied worldviews. On the domestic scene, the civil rights movement of the 1960s had given minorities a voice, and understanding those voices required knowledge of nondominant communication styles.

The recognition that society was becoming more mobile was also highlighted in the early editions. This mobility was facilitated by technological advances in transportation and communication, which gave rise to significantly increased levels of international business. The time and distance barriers that had historically impeded cross-border interactions were rapidly being eroded. By the mid-1980s, selections in the *Reader* reflected the significance of the growing numbers of refugees coming to the United States to escape political oppression and wars in their homelands. In addition to discussions on ethnic minorities, editions from the 1980s and 1990s began to include essays about the varied communication styles of U.S. social minority groups, such as women, gays, and the disabled.

The advancement of transportation and communication technologies continued unabated during the late twentieth century, enabling U.S. audiences to experience historical international events—such as the Tiananmen Square protests and the fall of the Berlin Wall—in near real-time. The collapse of the Soviet Bloc also enabled the many cultures of Eastern Europe and Central Asia to become active on the international stage. Continued internationalization of the economy increased the presence of U.S. commercial representatives abroad and promoted a growing number of international workers in the United States.

Essays in the *Reader* gave evidence of the increased importance of intercultural communication competency at the beginning of the twenty-first century. The influence of globalization became a theme in many of the selections. Additionally, the influence of culture in the health care setting, the increasing number of international marriages, and issues of ethnic identity were noted. Concurrently, articles discussing the importance of intercultural communication competence and ethical considerations in a globalized society were presented. This fourteenth edition offers a retrospective of those earlier articles, all of which illustrated the vital role of intercultural communication at the time they were first published and serve to remind us of the increased requirement to be able to communicate across cultures in today's contracted global society.

Our exploration of intercultural communication begins with four varied articles that (1) provide a foundation for further study of the discipline, (2) examine the impact of globalization on intercultural communication, (3) introduce a non-Western worldview and its role in perception, and (4) discuss the role of theory and research. As was done for each of the previous thirteen editions, the first essay in Chapter 1 is written with two objectives in mind—to motivate you to study intercultural communication and to provide the basic structure needed to conduct that study.

With this in mind, the essay "Understanding and Applying Intercultural Communication in a Global Society: The Fundamentals" is divided into two parts. Part 1 offers an overview of several selected historical eras in which intercultural communication played a primary role in social development on a grand scale. Part 2 provides you with an appreciation of the philosophy underlying our concept of intercultural communication and describes the fundamental components of communication, culture, and intercultural communication. After discussing the objective of communication, we define and preview its characteristics. Next is an overview of culture, to include what it is and how it guides our behaviors. Some of the specific dimensions of culture that are relevant to intercultural communication are explained. To assist you in understanding what transpires during communicative interactions between people with varied cultural backgrounds, we examine several major variables—perceptual elements, cognitive patterns, verbal and nonverbal behaviors, and social contexts. The essay promotes insight into what the study of intercultural communication entails and establishes a foundation for understanding subsequent essays.

Today, globalization is a frequent referrent in discussions of geopolitics, international business, or almost any other contemporary topic. As you are now aware, the forces of globalization have created an environment where cross-cultural awareness and intercultural communication competence are daily necessities. This is the reason our next essay remains relevant.

Bernard Saint-Jacques examines the impact of globalization on the study of culture and intercultural communication. First, he critiques pre-globalization-era theoretical concepts of culture and proposes a new approach. Saint-Jacques contends that events over the past several decades have changed the way we should consider culture because globalization has created a "mixture of cultures and people within each culture." Thus, earlier cultural concepts, such as Hofstede's model of individualism–collectivism, are dated and no longer reflect contemporary societal complexity. Saint-Jacques contends that any theory of culture in the globalized social order must address "three basic facts: (1) Cultural Predestination! (2) Individual Values, and (3) a Set of Dynamic Processes of Generation and Transformation." These three constructs are then integrated to form the basis for his proposed theoretical approach to culture. Japan is used as a case study to illustrate how culture is being transformed by the continued growth of the global community.

The impact of globalization on identity is also discussed in the essay. Saint-Jacques sees people in modern society as "living at the same time within particular cultural settings on the one hand, and between different cultural environments on the other one," which results in multiple identities. In the second part of the essay, he proposes an approach to teaching intercultural communication in a globalized society. His method involves viewing culture as "ways of thinking, beliefs, and values," and a greater incorporation of language into the instruction.

This essay remains important because it shows that there are multiple ways of viewing culture, and these ways should not become static. Culture and communication are influenced by societal changes, and those changes need to be acknowledged in theoretical development, practical application, and classroom instruction.

We elected to include "'Harmony without Uniformity': An Asiacentric Worldview and Its Communicative Implications" because it introduces and examines a different cultural perspective, one particularly relevant to the growing Asian presence on the world stage. Yoshitaka Miike proposes that conflict arises not from cultural difference itself but from an unawareness of that difference. Moreover, as global citizens, not only must we appreciate cultural diversity, we must learn from that diversity. According to Miike, too frequently cultural difference is viewed through the lens of one's own worldview, but to appreciate and learn from another culture, "we must understand the worldview of the culture and its impact on the forms and functions of communication."

The essay purports that much of the research underlying the intercultural communication discipline has imposed a European worldview on other cultures, producing a critical examination instead of an investigation designed to gain "insight and inspiration." To commence the process of learning *from*, rather than merely *about*, other cultures, Miike suggests that you need to (1) understand your own worldview, (2) understand the worldview of other cultures, and (3) understand how your culture is perceived by other cultures. The latter recommendation is particularly relevant to the success of relations in a globalized society.

The second half of the essay discusses an "Asiacentric worldview and its communicative implications in local and global contexts." Miike offers five Asiacentric communication propositions, which reflect his interpretation of the Asian worldview. These include (1) circularity, (2) harmony, (3) other-directedness, (4) reciprocity, and (5) relationality. Awareness and understanding of these propositions provide greater insight into Asian cultures and offers an alternative to the Eurocentric worldview. The essay posits that the processes of globalization have heightened the requirement to not only learn *about* other cultures but to find ways that promote and facilitate intercultural *learning*.

In this chapter's final article, "Relevance and Application of Intercultural Communication Theory and Research," written more than twenty years ago, Felipe Korzenny highlights three significant aspects of intercultural communication, all of which remain relevant today. He begins with a discussion of the synergistic relationship between culture and communication, explaining how each is necessary to construct and support the other. Next, Korzenny highlights the role theory and research have had in shaping the actual practice of intercultural communication. The final section describes nine important reasons to engage in the study and practice of intercultural communication, all of which remain as relevant today as they were twenty-plus years ago. These benefits range from increasing self-understanding to the possible prevention of war. Particularly prescient among these benefits is Korzenny's discussion of how people from varied cultural backgrounds may interpret the same information differently. This is an especially important consideration in view of the global reach of contemporary media sources.

Understanding and Applying Intercultural Communication in the Global Community: The Fundamentals

EDWIN R. MCDANIEL

LARRY A. SAMOVAR

Y ou are no doubt already familiar with terms such as "globalization," "global village," "culture," "communication," and "cultural diversity," all common expressions today. Perhaps you have even heard or read something about "intercultural communication," but it is less likely that you have been exposed to an in-depth examination of what it is, how it works, and why it is important. Answering those questions is the purpose of this chapter.

Our exploration begins with a brief overview of the role that intercultural communication has played in some of the notable eras of world history. We then provide a summary of how intercultural communication has developed as an academic discipline over the past seventy years. This historical review will help you realize that intercultural communication is not a new phenomenon, but rather a process that has long been an integral part of human interactions. Following the two historical synopses, the chapter examines what are considered the fundamentals of intercultural communication. Understanding these basic concepts will facilitate your study and appreciation of how prevalent, and important, intercultural communication is in contemporary society.

INTERCULTURAL COMMUNICATION IN HISTORICAL PERSPECTIVE

The Beginnings

The history of intercultural interactions is as old as humankind. The migration of peoples, whether seeking new homelands, engaging in trade, or bent on physical or ideological conquest has brought people from different cultural backgrounds into contact. Often these interactions have proven beneficial, but sometimes they have led to disaster. Let us look at a few examples of how intercultural communication has been instrumental in shaping sweeping global changes.

Consider for a moment how two of the world's great religions originated in the Middle East and subsequently spread globally. Christianity began its journey from a small area in what is today Israel and Palestine, and over a couple of centuries spread across the globe to become the world's largest religion. A few hundred years after the rise of Christianity, Islam was founded in the desert of modern-day Saudi Arabia and ultimately spread across the Middle East, Northern Africa, Central Asia, and South Asia. It is now the world's second largest religion. During the Seventh Century, Buddhism arose in contemporary northeast India and over the next several hundred years spread eastward throughout Southeast Asia, China, Korea, and Japan. Today, it is the world's fourth largest religion. The ability to promulgate, establish, and sustain the religious philosophy of each of the faiths across such a diversity of cultures and languages required competent intercultural communication.

Commerce is another context that easily lends itself to demonstrating the historical and enduring effect of intercultural communication. Let us reflect on just two very early examples—the Phoenicians and the Silk Road. The Phoenicians were an ancient trading civilization located in the coastal area of what is now Syria and Lebanon. By the late 800s BCE, they had established trading routes, outposts, and colonies along the southern Mediterranean coast and ventured into the Atlantic along the peripheries of Spain and West Africa. The Phoenicians focused on maritime trade rather than territorial conquest, which obviously required a keen appreciation for different cultures and languages. Their legacy remains evident today in the word "Bible," which the Greek's derived from Byblos, the name of an ancient Phoenician city (Gore, 2004).

Reference to the "Silk Road" often conjures up a Hollywood based romantic image of caravans transporting exotic goods across Central Asia between China and the West. In actuality, however, there were numerous roads, or routes, linking China with the west, beginning late in the first millennium BCE and lasting until the fifteenth century CE. These tracks passed through Central Asia, South Asia, along the coast of the Arabian Peninsula, and through today's Middle East. In addition to the many tradesmen, the routes were traveled by explorers, religious prelates, philosophers, warriors, and foreign emissaries. New products, art works, technology, innovation, and philosophical ideas traveled in both directions to consumers in the east and west, as well as those in between. These overland conduits passed through the domains of many different cultures. Thus a successful transit required the knowledge and ability to effectively interact with peoples instilled with contrasting worldviews, possessing varied cultural values, and speaking a multiplicity of languages.

These several examples from the distant past illustrate two important factors. First, globalization is not new. Peoples from other lands and diverse cultures have been interacting across the span of time. The advent of new technologies has simply accelerated the process. Second, these historical vignettes demonstrate the instrumental role intercultural communication has played in the establishment of today's global social order. We will next look at the development of intercultural communication as an academic discipline.

Intercultural Communication as an Academic Discipline

Despite a lengthy historical legacy, intercultural communication as an academic discipline is relatively new, commencing only about 70 years ago. A focused examination of culture and communication arose out of a need to understand allies during World War II and to better carry out the post-war reconstruction of the many nations destroyed by that conflict. The continued growth of international commerce in the 1970s and 1980s created a need to understand how to effectively interact with, and manage, people from other cultures. As a result, scholars became interested, launched research projects, and began offering classroom courses treating different contexts. The end of the Cold War, in the early 1990s, coupled with technological advances in transportation and communication made intercultural competence a necessity. Suddenly, there were unprecedented levels of interaction among people from different national, ethnic, and religious backgrounds. Commercial and social organizations realized the importance of communicating across cultures on both an international and domestic level. This heightened the demand for increased scholarly inquiry and topic specific literature, which continued unabated into the new century. Post 9/11 conflicts in Iraq and Afghanistan demonstrated a need for cultural awareness training among U.S. forces.

Today, the rapidly globalizing social order has made the study and practice of intercultural communication a requisite for success in both the international and domestic arena. Now, an appreciation of cultural differences is needed in order to succeed in almost any endeavor. The essays in this text are designed to help you achieve that awareness and assist in acquiring the ability to become a more skilled intercultural communicator. Each chapter introduces you to a topic considered critical to acquiring and improving intercultural competence.

Before moving further into the study of culture and communication, however, we need to specify our approach to intercultural communication and recognize that other people investigate quite different perspectives. For example, some scholars who examine mass media are concerned with international broadcasting, worldwide freedom of expression, the premise of Western domination of media information, and the use of electronic technologies for instantaneous worldwide communication. Other groups study international communication with an emphasis on interactions among national governments—the communication of diplomacy, economic relations, disaster assistance, and even political propaganda. Still others are interested in the communication needed to conduct business on a global basis. Their concerns include such issues as cross-cultural marketing, negotiation styles, management, and conflict resolution, as well as daily communication within domestic, multinational, and transnational organizations. And scholars who apply critical theory seek to demonstrate how communication can be used as a means of domination.

Our focus, however, relates to the more personal aspects of communication: What happens when people from different cultures interact face to face? Thus, our approach explores the interpersonal dimensions of intercultural communication across different contexts. The essays we have selected for this edition focus on the variables of culture and communication that are most likely to influence an intercultural communication encounter—those occasions when you attempt to exchange information, ideas, or feelings with someone from a culture different from your own.

With this in mind, we adhere to the following definition: *Intercultural communication occurs whenever a person from one culture sends a message to be processed by a person from a different culture.* Although this may seem somewhat simplistic, it requires a thorough understanding of two key elements—communication and culture. Therefore, in the following section we begin by examining communication and its various components, after which culture is explained. Finally, we explore how these two concepts are fused into the components of intercultural communication.

UNDERSTANDING COMMUNICATION

Communication is inescapable. It is something we have to do and something we enjoy doing, and in the Digital Age, we do a lot of it. Think about the many different ways that you engage in communication every day—watch TV, listen to music, talk to friends, listen to a class lecture (well, at least pretend to), daydream, send and receive messages through e-mail, Facebook, and Twitter, search for something new on YouTube, wear a suit to an interview, and in many, many other ways.

These are but a few of the communication events you participate in on a daily basis. To function in today's data rich society, one cannot avoid communicating. Moreover, we seem to have an innate need to associate with, and connect to, other people through communication. Thus, the motives for entering into

any communicative interaction can be categorized under one of three broad classifications. When people communicate, regardless of the situation or context, they are trying to (1) persuade, (2) inform, or (3) entertain. In other words, when you communicate, you do so with a purpose, an objective.

Explaining Communication

It should be intuitively evident that communication is fundamental to contemporary daily life. But what exactly is communication? What happens when we communicate? In answering those questions, we will first define and then explain the phenomenon.

Communication has been defined variously, and each definition is usually a reflection of the author's objective or of a specific context. Often the definition is long and rather abstract, as the author tries to incorporate as many aspects of communication as possible. In some instances, the definition is narrow and precise, designed to explain a specific type or instance of communication. When studying the union of culture and communication, however, a succinct, easily understandable definition is in everyone's best interest. Thus, for us, *communication is the management of messages with the objective of creating meaning* (Griffin, 2005). This definition is somewhat broad, yet is precise in specifying what occurs in every communicative episode. Nor does it attempt to establish what constitutes successful or unsuccessful communication. Success is actually determined by the involved participants, can vary from one person to another, and is frequently scenario dependent. The only qualifiers we place on communication are intentionality and interaction. In other words, if communication is considered to be purposeful—to persuade, inform, or entertain—then we communicate with an intention, and we achieve our objective only by interacting with someone.

The Framework of Communication

Employing the definition of communication provided above, let's now examine the eight major structural components used to manage messages and create meaning. The first and most obvious is the **sender**— the person or group originating the message. A sender is someone with a need or desire, be it social, work, or public service, to communicate with others. In completing this desire, the sender formulates and transmits the message via a channel to the receiver(s).

The **message** consists of the information the sender desires to have understood—the data used to create meaning. Messages, which can be verbal or nonverbal, are encoded and transmitted via a **channel** to the receiver. The channel is any means that provides a path for moving the message from the sender to the receiver. For example, an oral message may be sent directly when in the immediate presence of the receiver or mediated through a cell phone, a conference call, or a YouTube video. A visual, or nonverbal, message can be transmitted directly by smiling to indicate pleasure or mediated through a photograph or text. Today, websites such as YouTube, Facebook, or LinkedIn provide channels offering senders a means to reach millions of receivers through mediated messages.

The **receiver(s)** is the intended recipient of the message and the location where meaning is created. Because the receiver interprets the message and assigns a meaning, which may or may not be what the sender intended, communication is often characterized as *receiver based*. You may text a friend, but for a variety of reasons, such as lack of nonverbal cues or insufficient context, the receiver may misinterpret the message and feel offended. After interpreting the message and assigning a meaning, the receiver may prepare a **response.** This is any action taken by the receiver as a result of the meaning he or she assigns to the message. A response can be benign, such as simply ignoring a provocative remark, or, at the other extreme, a physically aggressive act of violence.

The **feedback** component of communication is related to, yet separate from, the response. Feedback helps us to evaluate the effectiveness of a message. Perhaps the receiver smiles, or frowns, after decoding our message. This offers a clue as to the meaning the receiver assigned to the message and helps the sender adjust to the developing situation. Depending on the feedback, we may rephrase or amplify our message to provide greater clarity, ask whether the message was understood, or perhaps even retract the statement.

Every communicative interaction takes place within a physical and contextual **environment.** The physical environment refers to the location where

the communication occurs, such as a classroom, coffee shop, business office, or on an airplane. The contextual, or social, environment is more abstract and exerts a strong influence on the style of communication employed. Think about the different styles of communication you use during an interview or when applying for a student loan, asking a stranger for directions, visiting your professor's office, or apologizing when late meeting a friend. We alter our communicative style in response to the occasion and the receiver—the contextual environment.

Noise, the last component of communication, concerns the different types of interference or distractions that plague every communication event. *Physical noise* is separate from the communication participants and can take many forms, such as two people chatting in the back of the classroom during lecture, someone talking loudly on the subway, the sounds of traffic coming through the window of an apartment, or static on your cell phone.

Noise that is inherent to the people participating in the communication episode can take a variety of forms. Suppose during a Friday class you find yourself concentrating more on plans for a weekend road trip than on the lecture. Perhaps you are in a funk after learning your car needs an expensive brake job, or you might be worried about a term paper due next week. These are examples of *psychological noise* that can reduce your understanding of the classroom communication. *Physiological noise* relates to the physical well-being of the people engaged in the communication activity. Coming to class with too little sleep, dealing with a head cold, or simply feeling too hot or cold in the room will interfere with your ability to fully comprehend the classroom activity.

The final type of noise often occurs during intercultural communication and can easily produce misunderstandings. For effective communication in an intercultural interaction, participants must rely on a common language, which usually means that one or more individuals will not be using their native tongue. Native fluency in a second language is very difficult, especially when nonverbal behaviors are considered. People who use another language will often have an accent or might misuse a word or phrase, which can adversely influence the receiver's understanding of the message.

This type of distraction, referred to as *semantic noise,* also encompasses jargon, slang, and even specialized professional terminology (Wood, 2013).

Collectively, these eight components provide an overview of factors that facilitate, shape, and can hamper communication encounters. But there is also another influential factor that normally plays a role in communicative interactions. Our *culture* provides each of us with a set of standards that govern how, when, what, and even why we communicate. However, you must first understand the concept of culture itself in order to appreciate how it impacts communication.

WHAT IS CULTURE?

Culture is an extremely popular and increasingly over-used term in contemporary society. Expressions such as *cultural differences, cultural diversity, multicultural-ism, corporate culture, cross-culture,* and other variations continually appear in the popular media. Culture has been linked to such diverse fields as corporate man-agement, health care, psychology, education, public relations, marketing, and advertising. You may have heard that before deploying to Afghanistan U.S. troops receive training about the local culture and language. The pervasive use of the term attests to the increased awareness of the role that culture plays in our everyday activities. Seldom, however, are we provided a defini-tion of just what constitutes culture or exactly what it does. This section will provide that information.

Explaining Culture

As with communication, the term culture has been the subject of numerous and often complex, abstract definitions. What is frequently counted as one of the earliest and most easily understood definitions of cul-ture, and one still used today, was written in 1871 by British anthropologist Sir Edward Burnett Tylor, who said culture is "that complex whole which includes knowledge, belief, art, morals, law, custom, and any other capabilities and habits acquired by man as a member of society" ("Sir Edward," 2012, para 1).

Ruth Benedict offered a more succinct definition when she wrote, "What really binds men together is their culture—the ideas and the standards they have in common" (1959, p.16). A more complex explanation was provided by Clifford Geertz, who said culture is "a historically transmitted pattern of meaning embod-ied in symbols, a system of inherited conceptions expressed in symbolic forms by means of which men communicate, perpetuate, and develop their knowl-edge about and attitudes toward life" (1973, p. 89). Contemporary definitions of culture commonly mention shared values, attitudes, beliefs, behaviors, norms, material objects, and symbolic resources (e.g., Gardiner & Kosmitzki, 2010; Jandt, 2012; Lustig & Koester, 2012; Martin & Nakayama, 2010; Neuliep, 2011; Samovar et al., 2012). Indeed, the many and varied definitions attest to the complexity of this social concept called culture.

We propose an applied and hopefully more simpli-fied explanation of culture. Stop for a moment and think about the word *football*. What mental picture comes to mind? Most U.S. Americans will envision two teams of eleven men each in helmets and pads, but someone in Montréal, Canada, would imagine twelve men per team. A resident of Sydney, Australia, might think of two eighteen-men teams in shorts and jerseys competing to kick an oblong ball between two uprights, while a young woman in São Paulo, Brazil, would probably picture two opposing teams of eleven players each attempting to kick a round ball into a net. In each case, the contest is referred to as "football," but the playing fields, equipment, and rules of each game are quite different.

Try to think about how you would react in the fol-lowing situations. Following your successful job inter-view with a large Chinese company, you are invited to dinner. At the restaurant, you sit at a round table with other people, and plates of food are continually being placed on a turntable in the table's center. Peo-ple are spinning the table, taking food from different places, talking with each other, and urging you to try items you are completely unfamiliar with. *How do you feel*? At a later date, one of your close friends, whose parents immigrated from Mumbai, India, invites you to his home for the first time. There, you are intro-duced to your friend's grandfather, who places his palms together in front of his chest as if praying, bows, and says, "*Namaste*." *What do you do*? In each of these examples perhaps you felt unsure of what to do or say, yet in China and India these behaviors are routine.

These examples illustrate our applied definition of culture. Simply stated, *culture is the rules for living and functioning in society*. In other words, culture provides the rules that socially organize a collective of people (Gudykunst, 2004; Yamada, 1997). Because the rules differ from culture to culture, in order to function and be effective in a particular culture, you need to know how to "play by the rules." We learn the rules of our own culture as a matter of course, beginning at birth and continuing throughout life. As a result, our culture rules are ingrained in the subconscious, enabling us to react to familiar situations without thinking. It is when you enter another culture, with different rules, that problems are encountered.

What Culture Does

If we accept the idea that culture can be viewed as a set of societal rules, its purpose becomes self-evident. Cultural rules provide a framework that gives meaning to events, objects, and people. The rules enable us to make sense of our surroundings and reduce uncertainty about the social environment. Recall the first time you were introduced to someone you were attracted to. You probably felt some level of nervousness because you wanted to make a positive impression. During the inter- action you may have had a few thoughts about what to do and what not to do. Overall, you had a good idea of the proper courtesies, what to talk about, and generally how to behave. This is because you had learned the proper cultural rules of behavior by listening to and observing others. Now, take that same situation and imagine being introduced to a student from a different country, such as Jordan or Kenya. Would you know what to say and do? Would the cultural rules you had been learning since childhood be effective, or even appropriate, in this new social situation?

Culture also provides us with our identity, or sense of self. From childhood, we are inculcated with the idea of belonging to a variety of groups—family, com- munity, church, sports teams, schools, and ethnicity— and these memberships form some of our different identities. Our cultural identity is derived from our "sense of belonging to a particular cultural or ethnic group" (Lustig & Koester, 2006, p. 3), which may be Chinese, Mexican American, African American, Greek, Egyptian, Jewish, or one or more of many, many other possibilities. Growing up, we learn the rules of social conduct appropriate to our specific cultural group, or groups in the case of multicultural families such as Vietnamese American, Italian American, or Russian American. Cultural identity can become especially prominent during interactions between people from different cultural groups, such as a Pakistani Muslim and an Indian Hindu, who have been taught varied values, beliefs, and different sets of rules for social interaction. Thus, cultural identity can be a significant factor in the practice of intercultural communication.

Culture's Components

While there are many explanations of what culture is and does, there is general agreement on what consti- tutes its major characteristics. An examination of these characteristics will provide increased understanding of this abstract, multifaceted concept and also offer insight into how communication is influenced by culture.

Culture Is Learned. At birth, we have no knowledge of the many societal rules needed to function effectively in our culture, but we quickly begin to internalize this information. Through interactions, observations, and imitation, the proper ways of thinking, feeling, and behaving are communicated to us. Being taught to eat with a fork, a pair of chopsticks, or even one's fingers is learning cultural behavior. Attending a Catholic mass on Sunday or praying at a Jewish Synagogue on Saturday is learning cultural behaviors and values. Celebrating Christmas, Kwanza, Ramadan, or Yom Kippur is learn- ing cultural traditions. Culture is also acquired from art, proverbs, folklore, history, religion, and a variety of other sources. This learning, often referred to as encul- turation, is both conscious and subconscious and has the objective of teaching the individual how to function properly within a specific cultural environment.

Culture Is Transmitted Intergenerationally. Spanish philosopher George Santayana wrote, "Those who can- not remember the past are condemned to repeat it." He was certainly not referring to culture, which exists only if it is remembered and repeated by people. You learned your culture from family members, teach- ers, peers, books, personal observations, and a host of media sources. The appropriate way to act, what to say, and things to value were all communicated to the members of your generation by these many sources. You are also a source for passing these cultural expectations to succeeding generations, usually with little or no variation. Culture represents our link to the past and, through future generations, hope for the future. The critical factor in this equation is communication.

Culture Is Symbolic. Words, gestures, and images are merely symbols used to convey meaning. It is the ability to use these symbols that allows us to engage in the many forms of social intercourse used to construct and convey culture. Our symbol-making ability facilities learning and enables transmission of meaning from one person to another, group to group, and generation to generation. In addition to transmission, the portability of symbols creates the ability to store information, which allows cultures to preserve what is considered important, and to create a history. The preservation of culture provides each new generation with a road map to follow and a reference library to consult when unknown situations are encountered. Succeeding generations may modify established behaviors or values, or construct new ones, but the accumulation of past traditions is what we know as culture.

Culture Is Dynamic. Despite its historical nature, culture is never static. Within a culture, new ideas, inventions, and exposure to other cultures create change. Discoveries such as the stirrup, gunpowder, the nautical compass, penicillin, and nuclear power are examples of culture's susceptibility to innovation and new ideas. More recently, advances made by minority groups, the women's movement, and gay rights advocates have significantly altered the fabric of contemporary U.S. society. Invention of the computer chip, the Internet, and the discovery of DNA have brought profound changes not only to U.S. culture but also to the rest of the world.

Diffusion, or cultural borrowing, is also a source of change. Think about how common pizza (Italian), sushi (Japanese), tacos (Mexican), and tandoori chicken and naan bread (India) are to the U.S. American diet. The Internet has accelerated cultural diffusion by making new knowledge and insights easily accessible. Immigrants bring their own cultural practices, traditions, and artifacts, some of which become incorporated into the culture of their new homeland, for example, Vietnamese noodle shops in the United States, Indian restaurants in England, or Japanese foods in Brazil.

Cultural calamity, such as war, political upheaval, or large-scale natural disasters, can cause change. U.S. intervention in Afghanistan is bringing greater equality to the women of that nation. For better or worse, the invasion of Iraq raised the influence of Shia and Kurdish cultural practices and lessened those of the Sunni. International emergency relief workers responding to the earthquake and tsunami disaster in Japan brought their own cultural practices to the situation, some of which no doubt became intermingled with the cultural practices of the local Japanese.

Immigration is a major source of cultural diffusion. Many of the large U.S. urban centers now have areas unofficially, or sometimes officially, called Little Italy, Little Saigon, Little Tokyo, Korea Town, China Town, Little India, etc. These areas are usually home to restaurants, markets, and stores catering to a specific ethnic group. However, they also serve to introduce different cultural practices to other segments of the population.

Most of the changes affecting culture, especially readily visible changes, are often topical in nature, such as dress, food preference, modes of transportation, or housing. Values, ethics, morals, the importance of religion, or attitudes toward gender, age, and sexual orientation, which constitute the deep structures of culture, are far more resistant to major change and tend to endure from generation to generation.

Culture Is Ethnocentric. The strong sense of group identity, or attachment, produced by culture can also lead to ethnocentrism, the tendency to view one's own culture as superior to others. Ethnocentrism can arise from enculturation. Being continually told that you live in the greatest country in the world or that the United States is "exceptional," or that your way of life is better than those of other nations, or that your values are superior to those of other ethnic groups can lead to feelings of cultural superiority, especially among children. Ethnocentrism can also result from a lack of contact with other cultures. If exposed only to a U.S. cultural orientation, it is likely that you would develop the idea that your way of life was superior, and you would tend to view the rest of the world from that perspective.

An inability to understand or accept different ways and customs can also provoke feelings of ethnocentrism. It is quite natural to feel at ease with people who are like you and adhere to the same social norms and protocols. You know what to expect, and it is usually easy to communicate. It is also normal to feel uneasy when confronted with new and different social values, beliefs, and behaviors. You do not know what to expect, and communication is probably difficult. However, to view or evaluate those differences negatively simply because they vary from your expectations is a product of ethnocentrism, and an ethnocentric disposition is detrimental to effective intercultural communication.

INTEGRATING COMMUNICATION AND CULTURE

There are a number of culture related components important in the study of intercultural communication. These include (1) perception, (2) patterns of cognition, (3) verbal behaviors, (4) nonverbal behaviors, and (5) the influence of context. Although each of these components will be discussed separately, you must keep in mind that in an intercultural setting, all become integrated and function at the same time.

Perception

Every day we encounter an overwhelming amount of varied stimuli that we must cognitively process and assign a meaning. This procedure of selecting, organizing, and evaluating stimuli is referred to as perception. The volume of environmental stimuli is far too large for us to pay attention to everything, so we select only what is considered relevant or interesting. After determining what we will attend to, the next step is to organize the selected stimuli for evaluation. Just as in this book, the university library, media news outlets, or Internet web sites, information must be given a structure before it can be interpreted. The third step of perception then involves evaluating and assigning meaning to the stimuli.

A common assumption is that people conduct their lives in accordance with how they perceive the world, and these perceptions are strongly influenced by culture. In other words, we see, hear, feel, taste, and even

smell the world through the criteria that culture has placed on our perceptions. Thus, one's idea of beauty, attitude toward the elderly, concept of self in relation to others, and even what tastes good and bad are culturally influenced and can vary among social groups. For example, Vegemite is a yeast extract spread used on toast and sandwiches that is sometimes referred to as the "national food" of Australia. Yet, few people other than those from Australia or New Zealand like the taste, or even the smell, of this salty, dark paste spread.

As you would expect, perception is a critical aspect of intercultural communication, because people from dissimilar cultures frequently perceive the world differently. Thus, it is important to be aware of the relevant socio-cultural elements that have a significant and direct influence on the meanings we assign to stimuli. These elements represent our belief, value, and attitude systems and our worldview.

Beliefs, Values, and Attitudes. **Beliefs** can be defined as individually held subjective ideas about the nature of an object or event. These subjective ideas are, in large part, a product of culture, and they directly influence our behaviors. Bull fighting is generally thought to be cruel and inhumane by most people in the United States but many people in Spain and Mexico consider it part of their cultural heritage. Strict adherents of Judaism and Islam believe eating pork is forbidden, but in China, pork is a staple. In religion, many people believe there is only one god but others pay homage to multiple deities.

Values represent those things we hold important in life, such as morality, ethics, and aesthetics. We use values to distinguish between the desirable and the undesirable. Each person has a set of unique, personal values and a set of cultural values. The latter are a reflection of the rules a culture has established to reduce uncertainty, lessen the likelihood of conflict, help in decision making, and provide structure to social organization and interactions. Cultural values are a motivating force behind our behaviors. Someone from a culture that places a high value on harmonious social relations, such as Korea and Japan, will likely employ an indirect communication style. In contrast, a U.S. American can be expected to use a more direct style, because frankness, honesty, and openness are valued.

Our beliefs and values push us to hold certain **attitudes,** which are learned tendencies to act or respond in a specific way to events, objects, people, or orientations. Because culturally instilled beliefs and values exert a strong influence on attitudes, people tend to embrace what is liked and avoid what is disliked. Someone from a culture that considers cows sacred will surely take a negative attitude toward your invitation to have an Arby's roast beef sandwich for lunch.

Worldview. Although quite abstract, the concept of worldview is among the most important elements of the perceptual attributes influencing intercultural communication. Stated simply, worldview is what forms an individual's orientation toward such philosophical concepts as God, the universe, nature, and the like. Normally, worldview is deeply imbedded in one's psyche and usually operates on a subconscious level. This can be problematic in an intercultural situation, where conflicting worldviews can come into play. As an example, many Asian and Native North American cultures hold a worldview that people should have a harmonious, symbiotic relationship with nature. In contrast, Euro-Americans are instilled with the concept that people must conquer and mold nature to conform to personal needs and desires. Individuals from nations possessing these two contrasting worldviews could well encounter difficulties when working to develop an international environmental protection plan. The concept of democracy, with everyone having an equal voice in government, is an integral part of the U.S. worldview. Contrast this with Afghanistan and parts of Africa where the worldview holds that one's tribe or clan takes precedence over the central government.

Cognitive Patterns

Another important consideration in intercultural communication is the influence of culture on cognitive thinking patterns, which include reasoning and approaches to problem solving. Culture often produces different ways of knowing and doing. Research by Nisbett (2003) has demonstrated that Westerners use a linear, cause-and-effect thinking process, which places considerable value on logical reasoning

and rationality. Thus, problems can be best solved by a systematic, in-depth analysis of each component, progressing individually from the simple to the more difficult. In contrast, Nisbett's research disclosed that Northeast Asians (Chinese, Japanese, and Koreans) employ a holistic thinking pattern. They see problems as much more complex and interrelated, requiring a greater understanding of, and emphasis on, the collective rather than focusing separately on individual parts.

A culture's normative thought patterns will influence the way individuals communicate and interact with each other. However, what is common in one culture may be problematic in another culture. As an illustration, in Japanese-U.S. business negotiations, the Japanese have a tendency to reopen previously discussed issues that the U.S. side considers resolved. United States negotiators find this practice to be frustrating and time-consuming, believing that once a point has been agreed upon, it is completed. From the Japanese holistic perspective, however, new topics can have an influence on previously discussed points (McDaniel, 2000). This example demonstrates the importance of understanding that variant patterns of cognition exist and the need to learn how to accommodate them in an intercultural communication encounter.

Nonverbal Behavior

Another critical factor in intercultural communication is nonverbal behavior, which includes gestures, facial expressions, eye contact and gaze, posture and movement, touch, dress, silence, the use of space and time, objects and artifacts, and paralanguage. These nonverbal activities are inextricably intertwined with verbal behaviors and often carry as much or more meaning than the actual spoken words. As with language, culture also directly influences the use of, and meanings assigned to, nonverbal behavior. In intercultural communication, inappropriate or misused nonverbal behaviors can easily lead to misunderstandings and sometimes result in insults. A comprehensive examination of all nonverbal behaviors is beyond the scope of this chapter, but we will draw on a few culture-specific examples to demonstrate their importance in intercultural communication exchanges.

Nonverbal greeting behaviors show remarkable variance across cultures. In the United States, a firm handshake among men is the norm, but in some Middle Eastern cultures, a gentle grip is used. In Mexico, acquaintances will often embrace (*abrazar*) each other after shaking hands. Longtime Russian male friends may engage in a bear hug and kiss each other on both cheeks. People from Japan and India traditionally bow to greet each other. Japanese men will place their hands to the side of the body and bow from the waist, with the lower-ranking person bowing first and dipping lower than the other person. Indians will perform the *namaste,* which entails holding the hands together in a prayer-like fashion at mid-chest while slightly bowing the head and shoulders.

Eye contact is another important culturally influenced nonverbal communication behavior. For U.S. Americans, direct eye contact is considered a necessary part of making a good impression during an interview. However, in some cultures, direct eye contact is considered rude or even threatening. Among some Native Americans, children are taught to show adults respect by avoiding eye contact. When giving a presentation in Japan, it is common to see people in the audience with their eyes shut, because this is thought to facilitate listening (try it…you may be surprised). How a person dresses also sends a strong nonverbal message. What are your thoughts when you see an elderly woman wearing a *hijab* or a Jewish child with a *yarmulke,* or a young black man dressed in hip hop style.

Nonverbal facial and body expressions, like language, form a coding system for constructing and expressing meaning, and these expressions are culture bound. Through culture, we learn which nonverbal behavior is proper for different social interactions. But what is appropriate and polite in one culture may be disrespectful or even insulting in another culture. People engaging in intercultural communication, therefore, should try to maintain a continual awareness of how body behaviors may influence the interaction.

Contextual Influences

We have defined culture as a set of rules established and used by a group of people to conduct social interaction. These rules determine what is considered correct communicative behavior, including both verbal and nonverbal elements, for both physical and social (situational) contexts. For example, you would not normally attend a funeral wearing shorts and beach sandals or talk on your cell phone during the service. Your culture has taught you that these behaviors are disrespectful (i.e., contextually inappropriate).

Context is also an important consideration in intercultural communication interactions, where the rules for specific situations usually vary. What is expected in one culture is not necessarily correct in another. As an example, among most White U.S. Americans, church service is a relatively formal occasion, but among African American congregations, services are traditionally more demonstrative, energetic gatherings. In a restaurant in Germany, the atmosphere is usually somewhat subdued, with customers engaging in quiet conversation. In Spain, however, the conversation will be much louder and more animated. In U.S. universities, students are expected to interactively engage the instructor, but in Japan the expectation is that the instructor will simply lecture, with limited or no interaction.

In these examples we see the importance of having an awareness of the cultural rules governing the context of an intercultural communication exchange. Unless both parties in the exchange are sensitive to how culture affects the contextual aspects of communication, difficulties will most certainly arise and may negate effective interaction.

CONCLUSION

We began with a discussion of how intercultural communication has been a constant factor in human interactions throughout history. We end with a reflection on the requirement and urgency for greater tolerance of cultural differences generated by this new globalized, interdependent world order.

The world's population, as well as U.S. domestic demographics, continues to move toward a pluralistic, multicultural society at a quick-step pace. The social, economic, and political forces behind this movement will not easily or soon subside. The resulting cultural mixing requires that everyone, both individually and as a society, become more tolerant of the varied beliefs, worldviews, values, and behaviors of people from other cultures. Acceptance or tolerance may not be appropriate in every situation, nor is universal, unquestioning acquiescence to every difference advocated. We do, however, have to be willing to "live and let live" on a broader scale. That we do not yet seem able or prepared to do this is demonstrated by ongoing international and domestic struggles.

The international community is beleaguered with violence and strife arising from ideological, cultural, ethnic, and historical differences. As we write this chapter, conflict between religious factions in Iraq appears to be resurging. The long-standing Israeli-Palestinian conflict remains unresolved and there is little promise of a solution in the near future. The dispute between India and Pakistan continues over who should control the Jammu and Kashmir Province in the Himalayas. Japan is at odds with China and the Republic of Korea over two different sets of uninhabited islands. The indigenous Tibetan population continues to resist what they consider an oppressive domination by the Chinese government. Iran is at odds with most of the Western world over the issue of becoming a nuclear power. The global war on terrorism, a product of variant ideological and cultural perspectives, continues with little prospect of a final solution. Disagreement over what constitutes human rights remains a source of tension among many nations, but especially the United States, China, and Russia.

Intolerance of differences is also a continuing issue within the United States, where we are divided over a seeming multitude of culturally based issues, many of which fall along a conservative vs. liberal ideology divide. The demands of coping with diverse customs, values, views, and behaviors inherent in a multicultural society are producing increased levels of personal frustration, social stress, and often violence.

As tides of immigrants and refugees continue to arrive in the United States and other economically developed nations, we will be confronted with increased cultural diversity. If we continue to aver that cultural diversity is a valuable, desirable asset and embrace the concept of a global village, we must quickly learn to accept and tolerate the resulting differences. Your authors do not profess to have the solution to these problems. However, as a means of better preparing you for life in the global village, requiring frequent interactions with people who perceive and experience the world differently from you, we do hope to stimulate thought and discussion about the advantages and difficulties of multiculturalism and the need for effective intercultural communication.

References

Benedict, R. (1959). *Patterns of culture* (Sentry Edition). Boston: Houghton Mifflin.

Gardiner, H. W., & Kosmitzki, C. (2010). *Lives across cultures* (4th ed.). Boston: Pearson Education.

Geertz, C. (1973). *The interpretation of cultures*. New York: Basic Books.

Griffin, E. (2005). *A first look at communication theory* (6th ed.). Boston: McGraw-Hill.

Gore, R. (2004, October). Who were the Phoenicians? *National Geographic*. Retrieved December 29, 2012, from http://ngm.nationalgeographic.com/features/world/asia/lebanon/phoenicians-text/1

Gudykunst, W. B. (2004). *Bridging differences* (4th ed.). Thousand Oaks, CA: Sage.

Jandt, F. E. (2012). *An introduction to intercultural communication* (7th ed.). Thousand Oaks, CA: Sage.

Lustig, M. W., & Koester, J. (2006). The nature of cultural identity. In M. W. Lustig & J. Koester (Eds.), *Among us: Essays on identity, belonging, and intercultural competence* (2nd ed., pp. 3–8). New York: Longman.

Lustig, M. W., & Koester, J. (2012). *Intercultural competence: Interpersonal communication across cultures* (7th ed.). Boston: Pearson.

Martin, J. N., & Nakayama, T. K. (2010). *Experiencing intercultural communication: An introduction* (4th ed.). Boston: McGraw-Hill.

McDaniel, E. R. (2000). *Japanese negotiation practices: Low-context communication in a high-context culture*. Unpublished doctoral dissertation, Arizona State University.

Selected Sources of US Domestic Division

• Stem cell research	• Assisted suicide
• Gay rights	• Same sex marriage
• Affirmative action	• Illegal immigration
• Right to life vs. Freedom of choice	• Government involvement in healthcare issues
• School prayer	• School voucher program
• Legalization of drugs	• Sex education
• Death penalty	• Gun control
• Role of government	• Environmental issues

Neuliep, J. W. (2011). *Intercultural communication: A contextual approach* (5th ed.). Boston: Thousand Oaks: Sage.

Nisbett, R. (2003). *The geography of thought.* New York: Free Press.

Samovar, L. A., Porter, R. E., & McDaniel, E. R. (2012). *Communication between cultures* (8th ed.). Boston: Wadsworth-Cengage.

Sir Edward Burnett Tylor. (2012). In *Encyclopædia Britannica*. Retrieved December 29, 2012, from Encyclopædia Britannica Online: http://www.britannica.com/EBchecked/topic/611503/Sir-Edward-Burnett-Tylor

Wood, J. T. (2013). *Interpersonal communication: Everyday encounters* (7th ed.), Boston: Wadsworth-Cengage.

Yamada, H. (1997). *Different games, different rules: Why Americans and Japanese misunderstand each other.* New York: Oxford University Press.

Concepts and Questions

1. Do you believe that most people are prepared to engage in intercultural communication? Explain.
2. How often do you find yourself in situations where an increased facility in intercultural communication would be useful? What are some of those occasions?
3. How can knowledge of the basic principles of communication be useful in daily life?
4. How do the authors define culture? What is another definition of culture that might help you to understand intercultural communication?
5. What is the purpose of culture?
6. What is meant by the statement, "Culture is learned"?
7. What are some instances in your life that demonstrate how culture is learned?
8. What are cultural values? How do they relate to individual values?
9. Distinguish several ways in which verbal behavior might differ between cultures.
10. What role does context play in communication? How does context affect intercultural communication?
11. Think of five different situations in which an understanding of culture and communication behaviors would be beneficial.

Intercultural Communication in a Globalized World

Bernard Saint-Jacques

A NEW APPROACH TO A THEORY OF CULTURE

Introduction

Intercultural communication is based on intercultural understanding. Intercultural understanding cannot be realized without an objective and up-to-date understanding of the notion of culture. Globalization, however, has changed the notion of culture. Culture can no longer be described as the property of a single nation. Globalization has changed the concept of culture (Ogura, 2004, 23). Globalization stands for the overlapping of global and local factors (Robertson, 1997). Human beings are living at the same time **within** particular settings on the one hand, and **between** different cultural environments on the other one. This is nothing new. One lives **between** one's home in a family on the one side, and also situated in the daily life world—going to school, working in one's professional life on the other. This has been happening for thousands of years. In a culturally globalized world, **between-situations** are becoming essential for any understanding of culture. There were three stages in globalization. The first one was political, the founding of the United Nations in 1945. The second one was the economic globalization, the spread of free-market capitalism in virtually every country of the world since 1980. The third one is... cultural globalization, which has an essential function for the efficient working of the political and economic globalizations of the world. In fact, the economic and political globalizations have given rise to the problematic triangle "identity-culture-communication" in international relations (Wolton, 2005). As the technology for worldwide transmission of information continues to progress, attempts by some countries to restrict this transmission are becoming more and more ineffective (McPhail, 1989). The debates on globalization have focused on economic and political issues, but the powerful impact of globalization on culture has not been sufficiently analyzed and researched.

Globalization provides a good opportunity to reflect on the efficiency of the tools which the intercultural enterprise so far has developed to promote intercultural understanding (Kalscheuer, 2002). Thomas's (1996) definition of culture as a system that is valid for all members of a society or nation, as well as Hall's (1984) and Hofstede's (1980, 1991, 1997) "cultural dimensions," fixed sets of polar attributes (collectivism vs. individualism, monochronic vs. polychronic, high power distance vs. low power distance, high context culture vs. low context culture, etc....) obtained with questionnaires to very small groups of participants of a given society, are not any more adapted to research in intercultural understanding. Cultures are not homogeneous and stable entities. Recent cultural theory takes into account the increasing mixture of cultures and people within each culture, and emphasizes the hybrid nature of culture (Bhabba, 1994, Pieterse, 1994, Shweder & Sullivan, 1990). Welsch (1999) stresses the reciprocal influences of cultures.

Three Decades Have Passed

It is essential to recall that three decades have passed since Hofstede proposed his cultural dimensions and his classification of countries. During that time, there were many reviews of Hofstede's work expressing several important caveats in dimensionalising cultural values. A large number of questions remains as to how exactly these concepts work in real-life relationships. These concepts suffer from the same weakness as the concepts of culture in that they are too readily used to explain everything that occurs in a society (Kim, Triandis, Kagitcibasi, & Choi, 1994). Concerning individualism versus collectivism, the multidimensional nature of these concepts has been frequently discussed. We can be both individualistic in some situations and collectivistic in others (Kim et al., 1996). In a recent paper, Chirkov, Linch, and Niwa (2005), examining the problems in the measurements of cultural dimensions and orientations, raised three basic questions: (1) "The operationalization of individualism/collectivism assumes a high degree of cultural homogeneity of the surveyed countries across geographical regions and across different life domains. This assumption however is far from reality, especially in multiethnic countries" (p. 472). (2) Moreover, this operationalization of cultural dimensions ignores the fact that different cultural values and practices may be internalized by people to different degrees, thus demonstrating high interpersonal variation in their endorsement (D'Andrade, 1992). (3) Measuring culture-related constructs to average individual's scores on, for example, an individualism–collectivism self-report scale, across samples taken from different countries is wrong. "This does not make sense because culture is not an attribute of a person, nor is it the main value of some aggregate of individuals" (p. 473). Further, quoting Fiske (2002), Chirkov et al. (2005) conclude that "taking the mean of a group of individual scores does not make such variables into measurements of culture" (p. 473). Moreover, the expressed cultural values of many intercultural surveys and questionnaires are not necessarily the same as behaviors. The sample and the participants used in intercultural surveys have often been criticized as not representative of the culture of a given country being studied. In many cases, the participants were college or university students, and sometimes surveyed outside of their country of origin, without taking into account the cultural influence of the country in which they had been international students for some years. Visser, Krosnick and Lavrakas (2000) have emphasized the non-probability and the non-representative sample of participants in most cross-cultural studies. These authors warned social and cross-cultural psychologists that "social psychological research attempting to generalize from a college student sample to a nation looks silly and damages the apparent credibility of our enterprise" (p. 237, quoted in Chirkov et al., 2005).

In Goodwin's book *Personal Relationships across Cultures* (1999), one can find interesting discussions of Hofstede's classification. In the introduction,

Goodwin writes: "I will try to demonstrate how many of our cherished views of other cultures are becoming less relevant and less accurate—If, indeed, they were ever accurate at all" (1999, p. 1). What is also striking is that data from a reexamination of Hofstede's country classifications, conducted twenty-five years after the original research, suggest "significant shifts in value classifications in some countries" (Fernandez et al., 1997, p. 52). In an interview in Canada published in the *InterCultures Magazine,* Oct. 2006, when asked, "Between the time that you were first analyzing the IBC data and now, has your definition of culture changed at all?" Hofstede answered:

> No, not really. Of course, you have to realize that culture is a construct. When I have intelligent students in my class, I tell them: "One thing we have to agree on: culture does not exist." Culture is a concept that we made up which helps us understand a complex world, but it is not something tangible like a table or a human being. What it is depends on the way in which we define it. So, let's not squabble with each other because we define culture slightly differently; that's fine.

From this interview, it is quite clear that Hofstede's "cultural dimensions" are not at all the rigid and universal fixed sets of polar attributes that several scholars are still using in their intercultural research.

For instance, in a recent paper by Sasagawa, Toyoda, and Sakano (2006, p. 337), I was astonished by their grouping Australia, Belgium, Canada, England, France, Germany, Italy, Scotland, Spain, and the United States as individualistic countries, and China, Colombia, Ecuador, Egypt, India, Indonesia, Hong Kong, Kazakhstan, Korea, Malaysia, Mexico, Saudi Arabia, Morocco, Singapore, Panama, Paraguay, Peru, Philippines, Thailand, Turkey, United Arab Emirates, The Netherlands, South Africa, [and] Switzerland as collectivistic. The three Japanese authors of this paper must have regretted their allegiance to this rigid dichotomy "individualistic versus collectivistic," because their results show that "students returning from so-called collectivistic countries were more individualistic than returnees from so-called individualistic countries" (p. 340). Moreover, these 141 Japanese students had sojourned in 39 different countries, which as a sample per country means only 3.6 participants! One more example of this traditional

approach to the study of culture and intercultural understanding can be found in a study by Merkin (2006) that reports data tending to confirm the following in Hofstede's hypotheses:

[H1]: Members of strong uncertainty-avoidance cultures are more likely to communicate ritualistically than members of weak uncertainty-avoidance cultures,

[H2]: Members of strong uncertainty-avoidance cultures are less likely to use harmonious facework strategies than members of weak uncertainty-avoidance cultures,

[H3]: Members of strong uncertainty-avoidance cultures will be more likely to respond to face-threatening acts with aggression than members of weak uncertainty-avoidance cultures. These confirmations are based on the following data: 658 college students (442 women and 216 men) representing the following six countries: Japan, Sweden, Israel, Hong Kong, Chile and the United States. The samples from each country were not equal, the United States having the largest number—241 students, and Hong Kong only 32. From this data, one can have serious doubts about the scientific value of these confirmations of the Hofstede hypotheses which read "Members of strong Uncertainty-Avoidance cultures...," when in this paper "members" is restricted to college students who in 5 of the 6 countries represent a very small number of participants. As mentioned before, any social psychological research attempting to generalize from a college sample to a nation has no scientific basis.

Several other examples could be given. It is quite clear, however, that intercultural research based on the traditional cultural dimensions is certainly not the key for intercultural understanding. From now on, research dealing with cultures can no longer be satisfied with the approach which consists only in trying to apply to all cultures so-called universal "cultural dimensions" or fixed sets of polar attributes.

Three Basic Facts for a Theory of Culture and Intercultural Understanding

Any theory of culture in this globalized world must address the following three basic facts: (1) Cultural Predestination!, (2) Individual Values, and (3) A Set of Dynamic Processes of Generation and Transformation.

Some aspects of these facts are not new and have been discussed by scholars in the past; these basic facts, however, have often been disregarded by those doing research in intercultural communication, resulting in very dubious affirmations about the nature of various cultures and people living in these cultures. The pragmatic integration of these three facts in intercultural research represents the essential basis for the new approach to a theory of culture proposed in this paper.

Cultural Predestination!

Cultural comparisons should avoid overstressing differences because it leads to overemphasizing the features of a given culture, as if it were a unique attribute. It is quite clear that in the past, in order to make comparisons more striking, people have been tempted to exaggerate differences, leading to a focus on a given country's distinctive features at the expense of those characteristics it shares with other societies. Yamazaki (1994, p. 3) writes: "Human beings seem to like to give themselves a sense of security by forming simplistic notions about the culture of other countries." Stereotypes are then often created. It is essential to research distinctive features in the light of features which are common to other cultures. To put it in Yamazaki's words: "Commonalities are essential if comparisons are to be made" (Yamazaki, 2000, p. V). Cultures are not predestined to have some immutable distinctive characteristics. Yamazaki uses the expression "cultural predestination" (2000, p. 9) and Demorgon (2005, p. 170) emphasizes the same idea: "The absolute distinctiveness of cultures is a problematic notion." The reason for this is quite simple: cultures influence each other and often there is a process of fusion. How can one attribute at a given moment distinctive features to a culture which is in perpetual development and change? This point will be developed to a greater extent in the section dealing with the dynamism of cultures.

Individual Values

A nation or an ethnic group cannot be considered as a single unit. Nations are not culturally homogeneous. Within the same nation, social classes, age, gender, education, religious affiliations and several other factors constitute the self-awareness and self-consciousness which become the markers of cultural identity, subcultures within a national culture. There are, within a nation, regional cultures, cultures of towns and villages, small group cultures, and family cultures which form cultural units. Renan's 1882 famous definition of nation, "L'essence d'une nation est que tous les individus aient beaucoup de choses en commun" [The essence of a nation is that the individuals of this nation have many things in common] has to be extended to the various groups which constitute cultural units in a nation. The members of these groups also have many things in common. Nations are not culturally homogeneous. Individuals within a given nation are not always identical and their cultural behavior might be different. Several studies, for instance, Kim (2005), and Kim et al. (1996) have emphasized this point. Very often, individual values rather than cultural values will be better predictors of behavior (Leung, 1989, Leung & Bond, 1989, Triandis, 1988). It is quite evident in the modern world that culture-level generalizations or national-culture generalizations are no longer adequate for intercultural research. It is sufficient to consider the vast number of countries in the world which are multicultural and multilingual and where there is considerable immigration. Canada, where you have English-Canadians and French-Canadians, First Nations, and another 35 percent of the population which is neither from British nor French origin but coming from forty different countries, is only one example. It is also the case for the United States, all countries of the European Union, South American countries, and most Asian and African countries. Here, one cannot resist quoting some passages of a very recent article by James B. Waldram (2009): "Anthropologists began to appreciate the artificial nature of their notion of 'cultures' as distinct, bounded units harbouring culturally identical citizens. . . . We began to appreciate 'culture' as a live experience of individuals in their local, social worlds" (p. 173). In addition, he adds: "Cross-cultural psychology has retained the broad generalizations and essentializations rejected by anthropology, to continue to assign research participants to groups as if there were no significant intra-cultural variability, and then engage in primarily quantitative comparisons" (p. 174).

It is now more than evident that serious cultural research cannot apply anymore the absolute and general dimensions of individualism versus collectivism, high-context versus low-context and other similar dimensions to most countries in the world.

Culture Is a Set of Dynamic Processes of Generation and Transformation

The third fact which must be considered in intercultural research is that culture is not static, it is a dynamic process. In his recent book, Demorgon (2005) insists that cultures are not static phenomena; they change constantly and are indefinitely renewable. Yamazaki makes the same point: "Culture is by no means a fixed entity, but a set of dynamic processes of generation and transformation" (Yamazaki, 2000, p. 119). To affirm the singularity of culture is questionable, insists Demorgon (2005, p. 21), how indeed can one label a culture as unique and coherent when it is in constant development? Different cultures influence each other, occasionally fusing. It is necessary therefore to direct attention from narrowly defined culture theory and seek not for the attributes present in specific cultures, but for the fundamental principles that precede and give rise to all cultures. These pre-cultural principles are subliminally present in every culture. According to Yamazaki, cultural fusion, therefore, is not a matter of one culture assimilating features of another but something in the other culture stimulating the full flowering of aspects already present in the first. One of these pre-cultural principles is individuation. The tendency toward individuation represents the drive to preserve individual units of life. This principle is antecedent to culture. The concept of individuation relates to the modern notion of individualism but precedes it (Yamazaki, 2000, p. 13).

Following several authors, Waldram (2009) argues that the concept of acculturation has outlived whatever usefulness it may have had, and that scholars should focus on the process of enculturation, or culture learning. For Waldram, culture learning is "the process of learning to be cultural in a given real world context" (Waldram, 2009, p. 174). He concludes that a new paradigm for culture is needed: "one that is theoretically and conceptually driven, rather than methodologically driven".... This, of course,

represents quite a shift in thinking from the classic emphases on contact involving "autonomous cultural systems" (Waldram, 2009, p. 175).

Moreover, it has to be strongly emphasized that globalization is not a factor of homogenization but of diversity. In a recent paper, Bhawuk (2008, p. 316) writes: "Creating new knowledge using concepts and ideas from indigenous cultures will help increase the diversity of theories and models which may be necessary for the global village.... Quality cross-cultural research demands that models and theories that question the contemporary values, beliefs, and models be welcomed.... Globalization is not about homogeneity but about diversity.... It is hoped that researchers will contribute to the differentiation of knowledge base rather than force homogeneity for defending monocultural theories."

Individualism–Collectivism, the Case of Japan

In relation to the individualism-collectivism dimension, many scholars have disregarded the three facts mentioned above. A typical example is the Japanese culture. During the last 30 years, drastic changes have taken place in one aspect of Japanese culture: the group orientation. *Jiko tassei*, the promotion of the individual, is no longer a taboo subject. Individualization has been making strong inroads in the Japanese society. For the young generation, self, the individual, has become more important than the group. Recently, in a white paper, the Japanese government described these changes, giving examples. An example is the young salary man who refuses to work late at night or during weekends because he wants to relax or do things that he likes. Or again, the young salary man who refuses to be transferred to another city, thus giving up a promotion, because he wants to be with his family. The lifetime employment, which is the lifetime commitment between corporations and their employees, is also under siege (Abegglen, 2003). According to a survey by the Management and Coordination Agency, in the one-year period ending February 1989, about 2.5 million Japanese switched jobs. Seventy-three percent said they changed jobs to seek better working conditions for themselves. Gakusei Engokai in 1989 conducted a survey among young salary men aged between 20 and 30 in the Tokyo and Osaka areas: Seventy-four percent declared that their own personal work and happiness were more important than the company which employs them. Ninety percent of these same salary men also believe that in the future even more salary people will change jobs (Saint-Jacques, 2005). In a recent paper, Shigeyuki writes:

> Around the year 2000, personnel managers began talking about how the latest recruits had a whole new outlook. They said that the new employees were narrowly focused on their careers, interested only in themselves, and lacking loyalty to the company. (2006, p. 20)

The seniority-based wage systems and promotion systems are giving way to performance-based systems, and companies are looking for talented individuals who would be an asset for the company from day one.

This new "individualism" tendency also influenced the most basic group underlying all other groups: the family. The rate of divorce has climbed to previously unknown heights. Japanese women marry later and have fewer children. Many women now decide not to marry. In the 2005 census, about 60 percent of women in their late twenties and 30 percent in their early thirties reported they were single. In comparison with the 1975 census, the first figure has roughly tripled and the second quintupled.

In his recent book, *The New Japan,* Matsumoto, quoting his own research and that of several other scholars, makes the statement that "there is no support for the claim that Japanese are less individualistic and more collectivistic than Americans" (2002, p. 41). He makes the distinction of two groups in Japan, the young generation being more individualistic and the older generation still attached to the importance of the group. He proposes the concept of "individual collectivism," that is, a society which can celebrate cultural diversity in thought and action, that is, individualism, while maintaining core values related to the importance of the group and hierarchy, that is, collectivism. Robert Christopher was more than prophetic when in 1983 he wrote: "To an extent unmatched by the inhabitants of any other nations, the Japanese succeeded in marrying the social discipline that is the chief virtue of a strong collective consciousness with individualism" (Christopher, 1983, p. 328). Moreover,

it should be remembered, as Tanaka points out in his 2007 paper "Cultural Networks in Premodern Japan," that the Japanese of the Edo period were not nearly as group-oriented (collectivism) as most people are inclined to believe. The Japanese of the Edo period did not have the group mentality in the sense in which this concept is generally understood: that is, a strong tendency for the individual to conform to group norms in respect to education, values, skills, fashions and lifestyle (Tanaka, 2007). It is quite evident that Japan cannot simply be classified as a collectivistic culture.

Identity

Closely related to the concept of culture are the notions of individual, social and national identities. Identity, particularly in the age of globalization, is never a fixed reality, a pre-given identification; it is a dynamic and evolving reality. "Cultural identity is a matter of becoming as well as being. It belongs to the future as much as to the past. It is not something which already exists, transcending places, time, history and culture. Cultural identities come from somewhere, they have histories. But like everything which is historical, they undergo constant transformation" (Hall, 1990, p. 225). "Identity is never *a priori,* not a finished product" (Bhabba, 1986, p. xvi). "Things fall apart, the centre cannot hold" ("Yeats"). This famous quotation from Yeats, which he wrote in the aftermath of the First World War, has often been used to highlight the current sense of cultural fragmentation and dislocation of the individual in the new world dominated by globalization. In this new world, individual identities, group identity, cultural and ethnic identity, as well as national identity are no longer clearly defined concepts to which individuals and groups can relate and find their own identification. Identity is no longer conceptualized as a given but rather as something which is constantly negotiated and struggled over (Saint-Jacques, 2002, p. 13). In this world, the individual's activity has been diversifying and group membership becomes more pluralistic; belonging to a number of groups means that the individual will have several identities or multiple identities. The case of immigrants is a good example. In a recent article, Van Oudenhoven, Ward and Masgoret write that immigrants may give up parts of their cultural heritage without giving up their cultural identity (2006, p. 647). Hybridity and multiple identities (whether affirmed or negated) are part of the human condition, and we should begin considering them as "normal" (Boyland, 2005). In their recent paper, Bhatia and Ram (2009) rightly make the point that acculturation and immigrant identity is not only an individual process: "We call for a shift from conceptualizing acculturation and immigrant identity as an individual process to a more broad, contextual, and political phenomenon" (p. 141). Their research shows clearly that the acculturation experiences of Indian immigrants living in the diaspora in the United States "are constructed through a dynamic, back-and-forth play concurrently between structure and self, being privileged and marginalized, caught in the web of socio-political and historical forces" (p. 147). Human beings are living at the same time within particular cultural settings on the one hand, and between different cultural environments on the other one. Bayart (2005) argues that identities are fluid, never homogenous and sometimes invented. Fixed cultural identities never exist.

Globalization can be a profoundly enriching process, opening minds to new ideas and experiences, and strengthening the finest values of humanity. "The homogenizing influences of globalization that are most often condemned by the new nationalists and by cultural romanticists are actually positive: globalization promotes integration and the removal not only of cultural barriers but of many of the negative dimensions of culture. Globalization is a vital step toward both a more stable world and better lives for the people in it" (Rothkopf, 1997). This new approach to intercultural understanding might help intercultural communication.

HOW TO TEACH MULTICULTURAL COMMUNICATION

Multicultural or intercultural communication cannot be learned without intercultural understanding, which is based on the knowledge of culture. The word "culture" has four different meanings: (1) High culture, the achievements of a society in terms of the most esteemed forms of literature, art, music. (2) Culture as behavior, the ways people agree to behave, act, and respond.

(3) Culture as ways of thinking: modes of perception, beliefs and values. (4) Culture as language, the close link between language and culture. The second meaning of culture, that is, culture as behavior, is related to clothing, food, architecture, transportation, appearance and so on, it is usually called "overt culture" or, in the "iceberg model of culture," what is above the waterline and therefore easily observable. Culture as behavior is subject to constant changes and is easily learned. The third meaning of culture, modes of perception, beliefs and values, [is] not easily observable and [is] often out of our own and others' awareness, it is called "covert culture" and, in the "iceberg model of culture," what is below the waterline. In our search of how to teach and learn intercultural understanding and communication, we shall be dealing with meanings three and four of culture.

Culture as Ways of Thinking, Beliefs and Values

Culture is first of all perceptions concerning our system of values, our ways of thinking, our beliefs, our psychological orientations. Intercultural understanding is therefore the ability to understand the perceptions concerning one's own culture and the perceptions of the people who belong to another culture, and the capacity to negotiate between the two. The Greek philosopher Socrates had chosen for himself the following maxim: "*gnôthi seauton*," "Know Thyself." The same is true for intercultural understanding. The first step for intercultural understanding is to have a clear idea about one's own culture and about our personal perceptions of this culture. This is not an easy task, however. Perceptions about one's culture are mostly unconscious. When asked to describe one's culture, a person might have very vague answers or often provide certain social generalizations which are stereotypes about one's culture. There are two important facts concerning perceptions of one's culture: First, nations are not culturally homogeneous, individuals in a nation might have different perceptions about their culture. These perceptions will vary according to social class, age, education, gender, experiences in life and many other factors. Second, cultures are not static, they change constantly. These two facts are true for all cultures.

Does this mean that it is practically impossible to find out the perceptions a person has about her or his own culture or the perceptions a person of a different culture holds about her or his own culture? No, it is quite possible through questioning, debates, discussions, reflective writing **about one single cultural aspect,** thus allowing the person to reflect about her or his own perception about one cultural aspect, often linked to other aspects of the culture. Thus, the door to one's perception of one's culture has been opened. The types of questions and discussions in this approach will vary according to the age and background of students. Let's say that we are dealing with university students. If a student or a person of another culture is present, this is an ideal situation because that person can also answer the same question and then a lively discussion can take place. When it is not possible, however, answers for a question can be found in books dealing with a variety of cultures. Here are some examples of questions that students have to answer, and statements they have to qualify: strongly agree, agree, no opinion, disagree, or strongly disagree[1]:

- Men in my country usually expect women to prepare and serve food.
- A married man should help around the house, doing cleaning, ironing and cooking.
- In my country, it is common for a man to give up his seat to a woman on public transport.
- In my country, it is not typical for women to speak their minds and contradict men.
- Do you think that both husband and wife should contribute to the household income?
- How normal is "going Dutch" (when each pays half of the costs) when a man and a woman go out?
- If a man and a woman are having dinner together, is it OK for the woman to pay the bill?
- Is it OK for a man to give a woman a pat on the backside to show he likes her?
- Is it proper for a man to hold a door open for a woman?
- Whenever a mixed group of people (male/female) come together the men always sit together.

- If you are a student at school and you received a mark that seemed not to reflect your knowledge, is it proper to talk to the teacher about it?
- If children do well at school, parents should reward them with a present or pocket money.
- Do students in your country treat what the teachers and textbooks teach as something final and unquestionable?
- Faithfulness is the most important factor for a successful marriage.
- In English, the terms stewardess (or steward for men) have been replaced with the gender-neutral term "flight attendant." Can you give examples of such changes in your language?

These are only a few examples. Statements and questions could be prepared dealing with all aspects of life, but only one cultural aspect at a given time. After discussions, students can be asked to do some reflective writing, for instance, describe what YOU think of marriage. It is quite possible that students of the same culture have different perceptions about several cultural aspects.

Pictures and videos showing daily life scenes of people (for instance, ways of greeting between two men, two women or between a man and a woman) from one's country and other countries are also excellent indirect ways to start fascinating discussions about differences in cultures and students, reactions about these differences. This approach is the first step to the understanding of one's perception about one's culture and absolutely essential for apprehending the perceptions of a person of another culture, that is, intercultural understanding and communication.

Culture as Language: The Close Link Between Language and Culture

It is quite evident that the teaching and learning of a second language could be an excellent way to access another culture and therefore to improve intercultural understanding and communication. This, however, is possible only if this learning and teaching begin with the idea that language and culture learning are fundamentally interrelated and that this interrelationship constitutes the centre of the teaching and learning processes. A language is a window into the culture of people speaking this language. For instance, the teaching of personal pronouns **I** and **You** in languages like French, German, Spanish, and Japanese is an excellent opportunity to enter various aspects of the cultures of these languages, such as the social relations between two persons talking together: How well do they know each other? Is one superior to the other because of age, sex, position, or the social group to which one belongs? In these languages, there are choices of personal pronouns which have to be selected according to the reference points mentioned earlier. In French, for **You, tu or vous,** in German, **du or Sie,** in Spanish, **tu or usted.** In Japanese, for **I,** (to mention only a few) **ore, boku, watakushi, watashi,** for **You, omae, kimi, anata** (Saint-Jacques, 1971). In the English language, the speaker does not have to worry about these various points of reference: the personal pronouns **I** and **You** are the only pronouns. However, in these other languages, the teaching of these pronouns provides a unique opportunity to observe language as an essential and closely integrated element of social behavior. In these languages, the wrong choice of pronouns can have disastrous effects for the speaker. Recently, a German driver who was arrested for speeding was so mad that he forgot the basic rules of pronouns in his mother tongue: the pronoun **du** is not to be used with people who are not close friends. He was fined for using **du** to the officer who arrested him! Intercultural learning involves developing an understanding of one's own language and culture in relation to an additional language and culture (Liddicoat, Scarino, Papademetre & Kohler, 2003, p. 43). Traditional language teaching and learning with the sole emphasis on phonetics and syntax cannot produce speakers who have acquired some understanding of one's own language and culture in relation to an additional language and culture—necessary conditions for intercultural understanding and communication.

Moreover, there is also another important reason to link the teaching and learning of a language together with the culture of the people speaking this language. To learn a language, whether it is a first or second language, two basic conditions are essential: motivation and the opportunity to use this language. These two facts are closely related to each other, if there is no opportunity to use a language, motivation also ceases to exist, that is, the learner's motivation to

learn the language will become weaker and eventually disappear. The opportunity or necessity to use a language is a fundamental law of language learning. A language which is not used for frequent communication will slowly disappear, first on the active level, speaking and writing, and eventually on the passive level, listening and reading. Does it mean that the teaching and learning of a second language is a waste of time? The various benefits of second language learning usually identified in the defense of language education fall into two categories: (1) the practical and tangible benefits of being able to communicate in a second language, and (2) the broader benefits of expanding one's intellectual experience, the improvement of cross-cultural awareness and a better understanding of other cultures. A language is like a window to the world of another culture (Saint-Jacques, 2006). Even if a person loses the active and even the passive knowledge of a second language, the learning of this language is a very enriching and beneficial process. Sakuragi (2006), in a recent paper, gives the example of second language teaching in the United States: "While the practical benefits of language learning in the United States are sometimes questioned due to the increasing dominance of English in international communication, the argument that language study helps students develop a sense of being a 'world citizen' remains cogent" (p. 20). There are many second language learners who will never become fluent in their second language because of the lack of opportunity to use the language for communication. Even for them, in the cultural perspective, the study of languages is very beneficial. There are many countries in the world where a great majority of citizens does not have the necessity or opportunity to use another language for communication. The learning of languages, however, is part of the curriculum in schools and universities because it can provide students with a better understanding of other cultures as well as their own culture.

Note

1. Some of these questions were inspired by *Developing Intercultural Understanding: An Introduction for Teachers*, Australian Government Department of Education, 2005.

References

Abegglen, J. (2003). Kaisha missionary. *International House of Japan Bulletin,* 23(2), 2.

Bayart, J. F. (2005). *The illusions of cultural identity.* Chicago: University of Chicago Press.

Bhabba, H. (1994). *The location of culture.* London: Routledge.

Bhatia, S., & Ram, A. (2009). Theorizing identity in transnational and diaspora cultures: A critical approach to acculturation. *International Journal of Intercultural Research,* 33(2), 140–149.

Bhawuk, D. (2008). Globalization and indigenous cultures: Homogenization or differentiation. *International Journal of Intercultural Research,* 32(4), 305–317.

Boyland, P. (2005). Keynote talk at the sixth annual IALIC conference, Brussels, Belgium, December 11, 2005.

Chirkov, V., Linch, M., & Niwa, S. (2005). Application of the scenario questionnaire of horizontal and vertical individualism and collectivism to the assessment of cultural distance and cultural fit. *International Journal of International Relations* D.S., 29(4), 469–490.

Christopher, R. C. (1983). *The Japanese mind: The goliath explained.* New York: Linden Press/Simon & Schuster.

D'Andrade, R. G. (1992). Schemas and motivation. In R. G. D'Andrade & C. Strauss (Eds.), *Human Motives and Cultural Models* (pp. 23–44). Cambridge: Cambridge University Press.

Demorgon, J. (2005). *Critique de l'interculturel.* Paris: Anthropos.

Fernandez, D. R., Carlson, D. S., Stepina, L. P. & Nicholson, J. D. (1997). Hofstede's country classification 25 years later. *The Journal of Social Psychology,* 137(1), 43–45.

Fiske, A. (2002). Using individualism and collectivism to compare cultures—a critique of the validity and measurement of the constructs. *Psychological Bulletin,* 128 (1), 78–88.

Goodwin, R. (1999). *Personal relationships across cultures.* London: Routledge.

Hall, E. T. (1984). *The dance of life: The other dimension of time.* Garden City, NY: Anchor.

Hall, S. (1990). Cultural identity and diaspora. In J. Rutherford, (ed.) *Identity, community, culture, difference* (pp. 223–237). London: Lawrence & Wishart.

Hofstede, G. (1980). *Culture's consequences. International differences in work-related values.* Newbury Park, CA: Sage.

Hofstede, G. (1991). *Cultures and organizations: Software of the mind.* London: McGraw-Hill.

Hofstede, G. (1997). *Lokales Denken, globales Handeln. Kulturen, Zusammernarbeit und Management.* München: Beck.

Kalscheuer, B. (2002). *Ein Schritt vor und einer zurück: Über die neue Praxis der Kulturellen Grenzziehung in der Interkulturalitätsforschung.* Vortrag im Rahmen dem 6 internationalen Kongress der Neuen Gesellschaft für Psychologie, Berlin, February.

Kim, M. S. (2005). Culture-based conversational constraints theory: Individual- and culture level analyses. In W. B. Gudykunst (Ed.) *Theorizing about intercultural communication* (pp. 93–117). Thousand Oaks: Sage Publications.

Kim, M. S., Triandis, H. C., Kagitcibasi, C., & Choi, S. C. (1994). *Individualism and collectivism: Theory, method and applications.* Thousand Oaks, CA: Sage.

Kim, M. S., Hunter, J. E., Miyahara, A., Horvath, A-M, Bresnahan, M., & Yoon, H. J. (1996). Individual versus cultural level dimensions of individualism and collectivism: Effects on preferred conversational styles. *Communication Monographs,* 63, 29–49.

Leung, K. (1989). Cross-cultural differences: Individual-level versus cultural-level analyses. *International Journal of Psychology,* 24, 703–904.

Leung, K., & Bond, M. H. (1989). On the empirical identification of dimensions for cross-cultural comparisons. *Journal of Cross-Cultural Psychology,* 20, 133–151.

Liddicoat, A. J., Scarino, A., Papademetre, L., & Kohler, M. (2003). *Report on intercultural language learning.* Canberra: Commonwealth Department of Education, Science and Training.

Matsumoto, D. (2002). *The new Japan: Debunking cultural stereotypes.* Yarmouth (Maine): Intercultural Press.

McPhail, T. (1989). Inquiry in international communication. In K. A. Asante & E. Gudykunst (Eds.), *Handbook of international and intercultural communication* (pp. 47–66). London: Sage.

Merkin, R. (2006). Uncertainty avoidance and facework: A test of the Hofstede model. *International Journal of Intercultural Relations,* 30(2), 213–228.

Ogura, K. (2004). Japan's new cultural diplomacy. *International House of Japan Bulletin,* 24(2), 17–28.

Pieterse, J. N. (1994). Globalization as hybridization. *International Sociology,* 9(2), 161–184.

Renan, E. (1882). Qu'est-ce qu'une nation? In H. Psichari (Ed.), *Oeuvres Complètes de Etrnst Renan. Paris: Calman-Lévy.*

Robertson, R. (1997). Glokalisierung, homogenität und heterogintät in raum und zeit. U. Beck (Hg.) *Perspektiven der Weltgesellschaft.* Frankfurt am Main: Suhr-kamp, 87–124.

Rothkopf, D. (1997, Summer). In praise of cultural imperialism. *Foreign Policy,* 107, 38–53.

Saint-Jacques, B. (1971). *Structural analysis of modern Japanese.* Vancouver: University of British Columbia Press.

Saint-Jacques, B. (2002). Identity and communication. *Intercultural Communication Studies,* 5, 13–23.

Saint-Jacques, B. (2005). The new Japan: A model for other societies. In J. F. Kress & H. Lansdowne (Eds.). *Why Japan matters* (pp. 241–248). Victoria: University of Victoria Centre for Asia Pacific Initiatives.

Saint-Jacques, B. (2006). The paradox of English learning in Japan: Problems and policies. International Political Science Association Fukuoka Congress, July 9–12.

Sakuragi, T. (2006). The relationship between attitudes toward language study and cross-cultural attitudes. *International Journal of Intercultural Relations*, 30(1), 19–31.

Sasagawa, S., Toyoda, H., & Sakano, Y. (2006). The acquisition of cultural values in Japanese returnee students. *International Journal of Intercultural Relations*, 30(3), 333–343.

Shigeyuki, J. (2006). End of the road for the seniority system. *Japan Echo*, 33(5), 18–22.

Shweder, R., & Sullivan, M. (1990). The semiotic subject of cultural psychology. In L. A. Pervin (Ed.), *Handbook of Personality*. (pp. 399–416). New York: Guilford Press.

Tanaka, Y. (2007, April). Cultural networks in premodern Japan. *Japan Echo*, 34(2), retrieved from http://www.japanecho.co.jp/sum/2007/340217.html

Thomas, A. (1996). Analyse der Handlungswirksamkeit von Kulturstandards. In *Psychologie interkulturellen Handelns*, Göttingen, Germany: Hogrefe (pp. 107–135).

Triandis, H. C. (1988). Collectivism and individualism: A reconceptualization of a basic concept in cross-cultural psychology. In Verma & Bagley (Eds.), *Personality, Attitudes and Cognitions* (pp. 60–95). London: Macmillan.

Van Oudenhoven, J. P., Ward, C., & Masgoret, A. M. (2006). Patterns of relations between immigrants and host societies. *International Journal of Intercultural Relations*, 30(6), 637–652.

Visser, P. S., Krosnick, J. A., & Lavrakas, P. J. (2000). Survey research. In H. T. Reis & C. M. Judd (Eds.) *Handbook of Research Methods in Social and Personality Psychology* (223–252). Cambridge: Cambridge University Press.

Yamazaki, M. (1994). *Individualism and the Japanese: An alternative approach to cultural comparison*. Trans. Barbara Sugihara, Trans. Tokyo: Japan Echo, Inc. (Originally published as M. Yamazaki, 1990, *Nihon bunka to kojinshugi*, Chuo Koron Sha.)

Waldram, J. B. (2009). Is there a future for "culture" in acculturation research? An anthropologist's perspective. *International Journal of Intercultural Relations*, 33(2), 172–176.

Welsch, W. (1999). Transculturality: The puzzling form of cultures today. In M. Featherstone & S. Lash (Eds.), *Spaces of Cultures* (pp. 194–213). London: Sage.

Wolton, D. (2005). *Il faut sauver la communication*. Paris: Flammarion.

Yeats, W. B. (1991). *Selected poetry*. Harmondsworth: Penguin.

Concepts and Questions

1. Saint-Jacques says we are living "*within* particular settings" and concurrently "*between* different cultural environments." Explain this assertion using examples from an international context.

2. How do you think that "identity–culture–communication" could be a problem in international relations for a globalized society?

3. Can you think of situations where you act in an individualistic manner and others where you take a more collectivistic approach? Explain.

4. Do you agree or disagree with Saint-Jacques's opinion that "research dealing with cultures can no longer be satisfied with the approach which consists only in trying to apply to all cultures so-called universal 'cultural dimensions' or fixed sets of polar attributes"? Why?

5. Explain the term "cultural predestination" as used in this essay.

6. According to Saint-Jacques, "nations are not culturally homogeneous." Explain this statement using the United States as your context.

7. Do you think globalization is making the world more homogeneous or more diverse? Why?

8. For Saint-Jacques, identity in the age of globalization "is never a fixed reality, a pre-given identification; it is a dynamic and evolving reality." Explain this statement. How does it apply to your identity?

9. Why is understanding one's own culture an important part of intercultural communication?

10. What do you think Saint-Jacques means when he writes, "language and culture learning are fundamentally interrelated"?

"Harmony without Uniformity": An Asiacentric Worldview and Its Communicative Implications

Yoshitaka Miike

We may speak of many civilizations in human history, some dead, others living. But human civilization should also be viewed as a grand old tree with many branches, flowers, and fruits, nurtured by the same earth, water, air, and human ingenuity. There is a clear unity in diversity.

Majid Tehranian (2007, p. 46)

In response to Samuel Huntington's (1993, 1996) proposition that the world would be divided by "the clash of civilizations," Tu Weiming (2006) tersely states, "Civilizations do not clash. Only ignorance does" (p. 12). Indeed, ignorance of cultural diversity, not cultural diversity itself, is a source of disharmony and conflict in the global village. To be sure, as Chesebro (1996) notes, "multiculturalism is a symbolic issue, a question of how we understand ourselves, how we understand our heritages, and how we understand our futures to be" (p. 13). Hence, it does sometimes radically challenge our basic sense of identity, community, and humanity. And yet, we must learn to appreciate all cultural traditions as valuable resources for humanity because diversity is vital to human survival and flourishing (Tu, 2001a). It is counter-productive to see difference as an obstacle to "progress" in the age of intercultural encounters. Our task as global citizens is not to "liberate" different

people from their "primitive" and "uncivilized" traditions, but to learn from different people *with* their respective traditions about alternative visions of humanity and communication.

In this essay, I will share my thoughts on the what and the how of culture learning to achieve mutual understanding and dialogue, and discuss, as an illustrative example, how Asians and non-Asians alike may be able to benefit from an Asiacentric worldview and its implications for communication. I will re-interpret Molefi Kete Asante's (1993) idea of "multiculturalism without hierarchy" (i.e., the co-existence of many cultures alongside) in the global context and apply the Confucian ideal of "harmony without uniformity" (i.e., the balanced integration of different elements) to the contemporary world. Wisdom is a precious gift to humanity. Every continent, every community, and every culture has accumulated indigenous wisdom, from which we can learn a great deal about how we should relate to one another, nature, and the spirits in the universe (Miike, 2004). It is my argument in the succeeding discussion, therefore, that, if we are to remain hopeful for a prosperous and peaceful world and to realize unity in diversity in the global society, we ought to reflect earnestly on the question of humanity and the way of communication from different local knowledges in different cultures.

CULTURES IN HIERARCHY AND CULTURES ALONGSIDE

Asante (2003b) claims that difference alone does not create a problem, and that it is the assigning of hierarchical value to difference that creates a problem. His idea of "multiculturalism without hierarchy" thus pinpoints how cultures should relate to one another in the context of diversity. He implies that, if multiculturalism is defined as the co-existence of many cultures, there are two ways of cultural co-existence: (1) cultures in hierarchy and (2) cultures alongside. *Cultures in hierarchy* is the form of cultural co-existence in which we see one culture above others so that we learn a frame of reference from one culture and view others through the single cultural standpoint.

Cultures alongside is the form of cultural co-existence in which we see all cultures equal so that we learn different outlooks from different cultures and view all cultures through their respective cultural lenses. Asante (1993) refers to the second form of cultural co-existence as pluralism without hierarchy and hegemony. He believes that, when we bring together local knowledges from all cultures, we will have a truly global knowledge about people in the world and move toward a truly transcultural understanding of humanity, diversity, and communication. In this section, using Satoshi Ishii's (1997) conceptualization of culture, I will envision the ideal of culture learning that enhances "multiculturalism without hierarchy." My premise here is that, in order to appreciate any culture, we must understand the worldview of the culture and its impact on the forms and functions of communication.

Worldview as the Mental Layer of Culture

Ishii (1997) proposes a three-layer-structure model of culture (see Figure 1). According to him, culture consists of three layers—material, behavioral, and mental. The most external, overt, and visible layer of culture is the material one, which is represented

Figure 1 *Satoshi Ishii's Model of Culture*

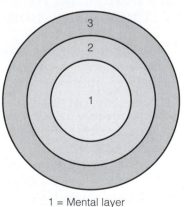

1 = Mental layer
2 = Behavioral layer
3 = Material layer

by various artifacts (e.g., food and clothing) produced, operated, and controlled by the behavioral layer. The semi-overt layer of culture is the behavioral one, which is [composed] of verbal and nonverbal behaviors as symbols (e.g., words and gestures) and reflects the mental layer. The most internal, covert, and invisible layer of culture is the mental one, which functions in the form of values, beliefs, and attitudes. Ishii (1997) is of the opinion that "understanding the mental layer is the most important in intercultural communication situations because it is the core of culture which operates and controls the two outer behavioral and material layers" (p. 321). The mental layer of a culture is, in a nutshell, a cultural worldview that answers ultimate questions about humanity and the universe—the tri-world of humans, nature, and the supernatural (Ishii, 2001)—and their relationships (e.g., Who are we? Where have we been before birth? Where will we go after death? For what do we live? What should we do in this secular world? How should we relate to other humans, nature, and the spirits?)

Samovar, Porter, and McDaniel (2010) define a worldview as "a culture's orientation toward God, humanity, nature, the universe, life, death, sickness, and other philosophical issues concerning existence" (p. 150). A worldview should be regarded [as] neither completely static nor completely fluid. It is always evolving and transforming and yet maintains the contours of the culture. Different portions of the worldview are instilled in the minds of different members of the culture. Given that it is the deep structure of communication (i.e., the mental layer), we may or may not be aware of its profound impact on the surface structure of communication (i.e., the behavioral and material layers). Because the mental layer of a culture is the most internal and invisible, we can only guess what it is like by comprehensively interpreting the linguistic, religious, philosophical, and historical foundations of the culture. As Ishii, Klopf, and Cooke (2009) comment, a worldview is, more often than not, "implicit and symbolically implied but not explicitly expressed.... How it is formed, therefore, is a significant matter of speculation" (p. 30).

Learning About and From Cultures

Learning *about* cultures is one thing. Learning *from* cultures is another. We can be very arrogant and ethnocentric, but we can still learn about other cultures. Learning from cultures, on the other hand, requires us to be humble and modest to understand and appreciate other cultures (Miike, 2008a). The former approach is an attempt to describe, interpret, and evaluate a different culture through the worldview that is *not* derived from the culture. In other words, we use the mental layer of our own culture to analyze the material, behavioral, and mental layers of other cultures. In this approach, cultural critique, rather than culture learning, is prone to take place because we tend to treat other cultures like texts for criticism and their members like objects for analysis. I call such an approach "centrism." For example, if we use the mental layer of European cultures to understand African cultures, our Eurocentrism (*not* Eurocentricity) will most likely distort the cultural realities of the African world from an outsider's point of view (see Figure 2). When we consciously or unconsciously presume that independence, individualism, and freedom are better than interdependence, communalism, and obligation without reference to the African worldview, we are tempted to view African and European cultures in hierarchy, not alongside, and fail to acknowledge the *ubuntu*-based humanity in the African context

(see Kamwangamalu, 2008). Indeed, we relate only to African cultures in a *hierarchical* way.

The latter approach is an attempt to describe, interpret, and evaluate a different culture through the worldview that is derived from the culture. To put it in another way, we use the mental layer of the culture to understand its material and behavioral layers. In this approach, culture learning and cross-cultural self-reflection are likely to take place because we tend to view other cultures as resources for insight and inspiration, and their members as willful agents. I call such an approach "centricity." For instance, if we use the mental layers of African and Asian cultures to understand the material and behavioral layers of African and Asian cultures, our Afrocentricity and Asiacentricity (*not* Afrocentrism and Asiacentrism) will more accurately capture the cultural realities of the African and Asian worlds from an insider's point of view (see Figure 3). It goes without saying that it is often difficult but critically important for us to engage in learning from, not about, cultures if we wish to broaden and deepen the understanding of culture-specific thought and action, and to expand the notion of humanity in cultural context. This ideal form of culture learning undoubtedly helps us achieve multiculturalism without hierarchy and facilitate dialogue among civilizations (Miike, 2008a).

Figure 2 *Eurocentrism*

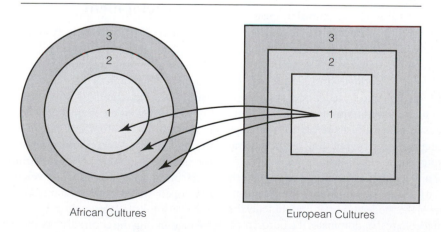

African Cultures   European Cultures

Figure 3 *Afrocentricity and Asiacentricity*

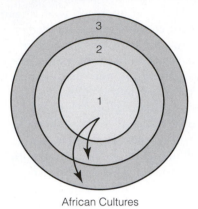

African Cultures

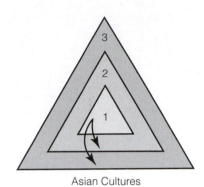

Asian Cultures

HUMANITY AS AN EXPRESSION OF EUROCENTRISM

What is problematic in many intercultural studies is that the mental layer of European cultures is frequently used to analyze the behavioral and material layers of non-European cultures, which decontextualizes them and obscures their nexus with the mental layer of non-European cultures (Miike, 2003a, 2010b). Because it is the mental layer of culture that explains why these symbolic behaviors and material artifacts are of immense value, such analyses will not result in the deeper appreciation and better understanding of behavioral and material layers of non-European cultures. Consequently, those descriptions, interpretations, and evaluations present them as exoteric, irrational, and backward and, hence, ultimately create the image of "the Other." In other words, they impose the Eurocentric vision of humanity on other versions of humanity. I contend that we should begin to rethink the role of non-Western worldviews in comprehending non-Western behaviors and in redefining and reconceptualizing humanity and communication. I reiterate that we must see all cultures as central resources for humanistic insight and inspiration, not peripheral targets for ethnocentric analysis and critique.

The nature and ideal of humanity have often been delimited by the Eurocentric worldview. The Enlightenment mentality of the modern West is undoubtedly the most powerful ideology that dominates the Eurocentric worldview. Its core values are instrumental rationality, individual liberty, calculated self-interest, material progress, and rights consciousness (Tu, 2002, 2007). Although aggressive individualism, excessive scientism, and self-destructive anthropocentrism may result in the isolated self, the fragmented community, and the over-exploited earth, these values have served as Eurocentric criteria from which to scrutinize and judge non-European versions and visions of humanity. They have shaped false dichotomies such as the civilized and the primitive, the modern and the traditional, the progressive and the backward, the developed and the developing, and the humane and the inhumane.

Rethinking Civilization and Development

Tehranian (2007) persuasively argues that, if civilization is defined not as modernization but as "the pursuit of peace with peaceful means," it is an "unfinished journey." All nations and regions are civilized in some ways and uncivilized in other respects. Tehranian (1990, 1999) also convincingly demonstrates that, if we rethink development not in terms of the living standard (e.g., economic growth) but in terms of the quality of life (e.g., human warmth), all societies and communities are both developed and underdeveloped. In his "communitarian" eyes, each country and every culture is struggling to achieve a sustainable balance among the contradictory themes of individual freedom, social equality, civil order, benevolent community, and sacred nature in the conflict-ridden waves of globalism, regionalism, nationalism, localism, and spiritualism (Tehranian, 1993). These themes are perennial concerns and yet intractable issues facing both the local community and the global society.

The indigenous *Sarvodaya* movement in Sri Lanka, for instance, is based on this holistic philosophy and practice of development (see Dissanayake, 1984, 1991). According to Tu (2007), China's major challenge today is "to embrace the market economy without turning the whole country into a market society. It would be disastrous if academic institutions, mass media, city organizations and even families were eventually to be totally marketized" (p. 12). The painful realization of many well-informed citizens in materially over-developed environments is that modernization can liberate us from material poverty, but it can also enslave us to spiritual poverty. Without the bonds of fellowship and community, we can be easily driven to the world of psychological alienation, status anxiety, social envy, relentless acquisition, and conspicuous consumption (Tehranian, 1990, 1993).

In spite of criticisms of the aforementioned invalid binaries, Eurocentric constructions of humanity have led to Eurocentric critiques of other non-Western views of humanity. They have also made [us] oblivious to . . . the past and potential contributions of non-European cultures to human civilization. As Rogers (1976) cautions, therefore, it is very easy for us to "forget that India, China, Persia, and Egypt were old, old centers of civilization, that their rich cultures had in fact provided the basis for contemporary Western cultures" (p. 216). In retrospect, Rogers (1978) goes on to say that, "even if their family life displayed a warmer intimacy and their artistic triumphs were greater, *that* was not development. It could not be measured in dollars" (p. 65). Looking at the non-Western world only with a Eurocentric *critical* eye and looking at the West only with a Eurocentric *uncritical* eye, nonetheless, poses a serious problem in approximating and appreciating the fullest potentials of humanity, civilization, and communication. This is especially so when the Eurocentric vision of humanity, heavily influenced by the Enlightenment in the West, is undermining the human condition (Tu, 2002).

Being a Teacher and Being a Student

Asante (1998) posits . . . "Any interpretation of African culture must begin at once to dispense with the notion that, in all things, Europe is teacher and Africa is pupil" (p. 71). There is a persistent and pervasive tendency to approach European cultures from a student's perspective and non-European cultures from a teacher's perspective in the study of culture and communication. As discussed earlier, much cross-cultural and intercultural research deals with non-European cultures as targets for analysis and critique, but not as resources for insight and inspiration. Therefore, it promotes a teacher's perspective on non-European cultures, which decenters and dislocates non-European people. It should be kept in mind, however, that we do not appreciate cultures when we always analyze and critique them. We appreciate cultures when we learn from them. We must be diligent students of non-Western learning and abandon the role of being teachers from the West all of the time (Miike, 2006). Tu (2008), for example, duly insists on the value of seeing African cultures from a student's point of view:

> If we consider ethnic, cultural, linguistic, and religious diversity as a global asset, Africa should not be characterized by the HIV epidemic, poverty, unemployment and social disintegration alone. It should also be recognized as a rich reservoir for human spirituality and the wisdom of elders. The African Renaissance, symbolized by the geological and biological diversity of the tiny area around Capetown (said to be comparable in richness to the vast area of Canada) ought to be a source of inspiration for a changed mindset that addresses social development as a global joint venture. (p. 331)

Three Steps to Cross-Cultural Dialogue

With "a global mindset by which we try to see things through the eyes of others and add their knowledge to our personal repertoires" (Chen & Starosta, 2000, p. 1), we can perhaps take three steps to cross-cultural dialogue. The first step is to understand the mental layer of our own culture and its impact on the behavioral and material layers. The second step is to understand the mental layer of other cultures and its impact on the behavioral and material layers. The third step is to listen to others' perspectives on our culture and share our perspectives on other cultures in order to reflect on what it means to be human in both local and global contexts and how humans should relate to one another, nature, and the spirits. In this step, we must engage in intercultural dialogue with Asante's (2006) spirit of mutual respect and learning: "As creators of our own societies, we have valuable experiences to share, not to impose, which might be examined and adapted in a spirit of sharing and dialogue. This is the real meaning of intercultural interaction" (p. 154). Tu (2008) echoes Asante's position by saying that "the celebration of cultural diversity, without falling into the trap of pernicious relativism, is profoundly meaningful for global stewardship" (p. 331).

Centricity in the first step of cross-cultural dialogue is the beginning and basis of equality and mutuality in intercultural communication (Miike, 2008a). It prevents our interactions with people from different countries and cultures from becoming a mere imposition–imitation encounter. This point should be well taken, especially by non-Westerners who wish to have sincere and serious conversations about intercultural cooperation and collaboration with Westerners on an equal footing. As Asante (2009) elucidates, centricity urges us, first and foremost, to inquire about our own identities, cultures, and histories as a way of contributing to the grand flow of the entire humanity without being imitators who blindly follow others. Paradoxically, in this soul-searching process, we may discover that the development of our own culture is, in fact, indebted to other cultures, and that the nature of human civilization is truly multicultural and synergic. In any case, imitation is not intercultural (Miike, 2008a).

ASIACENTRIC WORLDVIEW AND COMMUNICATION

In this section, I will draw on my previous writings (Miike, 2003a, 2004, 2007) based on the principle of Asiacentricity (see Miike, 2006, 2008b, 2010a, 2010b) and outline an Asiacentric worldview and its communicative implications in local and global contexts. More specifically, I will discuss five Asiacentric propositions on human communication. They are *propositions, not truths,* in the sense that they reflect my interpretation

of the *invisible* mental layer of Asian cultures and my intent to tap into Asian cultural wisdom both for an Asiacentric understanding of Asian communication and for dialogue among civilizations. Hence, they do not capture the whole profile of the Asian communicator and the entire picture of Asian communication. Every scholarly investigation must "make certain simplifying assumptions about complex realities that it studies" (Rogers, 1990, p. 261). The present inquiry of Asiacentricity is no exception in this regard. My discussion here is based on the five elements of an Asiacentric worldview that I have identified from the existing literature on the psychology and practices of Asian cultures and communication (e.g., Chen & Miike, 2003; Dissanayake, 1988; Kincaid, 1987; Miike, 2009a, 2009b; Miike & Chen, 2006, 2007; Nordstrom, 1983): (1) circularity, (2) harmony, (3) other-directedness, (4) reciprocity, and (5) relationality. These recurring themes collectively paint an Asiacentric picture of humanity and communication.

Communication as a Reminder of Non-Separateness

The first Asiacentric proposition is that *communication is a process in which we remind ourselves of the interdependence and interrelatedness of the universe.* This proposition can complement the Western dominant thinking that communication is a process in which we demonstrate our independence and express our individuality. The two Asian themes of relationality and circularity have much to do with the ontological belief that the universe is a great whole in which everyone and everything are interrelated across space and time. No one and nothing in the universe exists in isolation (Chen, 2006; Jung, 2009; Miike, 2003a). Asian religions and philosophies illuminate the interpenetrated nature of the self, family, community, society, nation, world, and cosmos.

Confucius (551–479 BCE) remarks in the *Analects* (6: 30) that "if you wish to establish yourself, you have to help others to establish themselves; if you wish to complete yourself, you have to help others to complete themselves." Similarly, in the words of Suzuki (2006), Buddhism teaches: "So to save oneself we have to save others. . . . By helping others, I may be able to save myself. My salvation and others' salvation are so intimately involved, connected together, that we can never save ourselves just by ourselves. We must always be saved together" (p. 19). More interestingly, the Hindu notion of *Virat Purusha* [Cosmic Person] views each individual as the manifestation of the cosmos itself. The universe is "a single body where each element lives for all and all live for one . . . [T]he weal and woe of one individual affect another" (Saral, 1983, p. 54). It is the teaching of Hinduism that "the world of distinct and separate objects and processes is a manifestation of a more fundamental reality that is undivided and unconditioned" (Jain, 1991, p. 80).

The Asian worldview demands that we constantly communicate with fellow humans, nature, and the world of spirits in order to escape from the illusion that we are independent individuals in a particular place at a particular time (Miike, 2007). For humans are prone to engage in a present-oriented and lifeworld-centered way of thinking. It comes as no surprise, then, that Asian patterns of small group and organizational communication correspond especially to this ideal of communication as a reminder of . . . non-separateness with a view to strengthening group or organizational unity, loyalty, and harmony. The Indonesian *musyawarah-mufakat* performance and the Japanese *nemawashi* practice, for instance, allow group members not only to exchange ideas but also to increase the sense of interdependence and interrelatedness (Saito, 1982).

The Asian worldview essentially defines communication as an endless process in which we continuously locate and relocate ourselves in an ever-expanding network of relationships across space and time. This ancient yet radical Eastern idea of communication must be taken seriously now that the global village has never been so divided by wealth, power, technology, and influence in world history, and [now] that we have polluted the air we breathe and poisoned the water we drink to the extent that we risk our own lives (Tu, 1998, 2002). Social disintegration is also becoming a worldwide phenomenon in modern societies. As Asante (2005) observes, "The lack of connectedness creates insensitivity to others, harshness, abrasiveness, and arrogance" (p. 135). Yum (2000) further points out that "[a]lthough individualism has its own strength as a value, individualism that is not accompanied by commitments to large entities

eventually forces people into a state of isolation, where life itself becomes meaningless" (p. 71). We must learn about communication as a way to realize that our well-being is inextricably and inescapably intertwined with [the well-being] of other members of the human family, nature, and even the supernatural.

Communication as Ego-Reduction and Self-Cultivation

The second Asiacentric proposition is that *communication is a process in which we reduce our selfishness and egocentrism*. This Eastern viewpoint makes a sharp contrast to the Western presumption that communication is a process in which we enhance our self-esteem and protect our self-interest (Yin, 2009; Yin & Miike, 2008). Dogen (1200–1253), the founder of the Soto Zen school in Japan, writes at the very beginning of his 13th-century book *Shobogenzo* [*Treasury of the Eye of the True Dharma*]: "To study the Way is to study the self. To study the self is to forget the self. To forget the self is to be enlightened by ten thousand things." What he meant was that removing all the divisions and distinctions of self and other renders it possible to form an ultimate unity with everything. According to Dogen, intrapersonal communication, in which we reduce selfishness and ego-centrism, can lead to ultimate communication with the whole universe (Saito, 1970). Likewise, the Confucian way of learning to be human is to engage in ceaseless self-cultivation and creative self-transformation by crafting the self as *a center* of myriad relationships, not *the center* of all things. The point of departure in quest of our authentic identity is, paradoxically, to overcome selfishness and egocentrism (Tu, 2002). What is intriguing about Buddhist and Confucian epistemologies is that we need to reduce our selfishness and egocentrism through communication and then become better communicators as a result of self-discipline and self-cultivation.

It should not be misunderstood, however, that Asian traditions of thought discourage the values of autonomy and agency. Confucian thought, for example, enunciates the view that "the reciprocal interplay between self as center and self for others enables the self to become a center of relationships. As a center, personal dignity can never be marginalized and, as relationships, the spirit of consideration is never suppressed" (Tu, 2001b, p. 26). While they recognize the importance of individuality in collectivity and independence in interdependence, Asian religious-philosophers, especially Buddhist thinkers, are critically aware that humans are by nature self-centered and egocentric. Therefore, their teachings impel humans to discipline and cultivate themselves so that they can experience the oneness of the universe and harmoniously coexist with fellow humans, nature and the world of spirits. In the Asian worldview, communication is conceptualized as central to this process of self-discipline, self-cultivation, self-development, and self-realization. In such a line of thinking, the Asian way of knowing is grounded on the elimination of excessive and aggressive ego as a primary source of mental suffering and perceptual barriers (Ishii, 2004).

Asian daily experiences appear to concertedly indicate that interacting with other humans, nature, and the spirits facilitates the process of disciplining and cultivating ourselves. Asians may be truly touched and highly motivated to discipline themselves and work harder when they listen to, or simply observe, individuals who possess sophisticated skills through their years of practice or people who are struggling against all odds in their lives. Moreover, reducing selfishness and egocentrism means increasing connection and cooperation not only at the interpersonal level but also at other levels. From the perspective of Zen Buddhism, "An awareness of 'oneness' develops from emptying oneself and accepting the other" (Saito, 1970, p. 17). Encountering fellow humans, nature, and the spirits in a way that we reduce our selfishness and egocentrism enables us to rise above nepotism, parochialism, ethnocentrism, and anthropocentrism as well as egocentrism.

In such a sense, this second communicative proposition is, once again, in consonance with the two Asian themes of relationality and circularity. In this increasing ego-driven world, the time is right to turn our attention to the role of interpersonal communication as an ego-reduction and self-decentering practice. For, as Chen (2005) understands, in order for us to fully unfold our potential as co-creators of the whole universe with heaven and earth, our self must be "ceaselessly edified, constantly liberated, and perpetually purified" (p. 7) in intercultural encounters with the other.

Communication as Sensing and Feeling

The third Asiacentric proposition is that *communication is a process in which we feel the joy and suffering of all sentient beings.* This proposition is linked particularly with the Asian theme of other-directedness. As the Chinese concept of *renqing,* the Japanese concept of *ninjo,* and the Korean concept of *jung* imply, emotional sensitivity, not instrumental rationality, occupies a central place in being and becoming fully human in the Asian worldview. To feel through sensitivity, rather than to analyze through rationality, is one of the "habits of the heart" in Asian communication (Chen and Starosta, 2003). Such a feature manifests in many trans-Asian premises and practices of communication. The Filipino *pahiwatig-pakikiramdam* dynamics (Maggay, 1999; Mansukhani, 2005; Mataragnon, 1988), the Japanese *enryo-sasshi* style (Ishii & Bruneau, 1994; Miike, 2003b, 2010c), and the Korean *saryo-nunchi* anticipation (Choi & Choi, 1992; Robinson, 2003), for example, underscore and underline the importance of communicative sensitivity to the joy and suffering of fellow human beings. This preponderance toward affection instead of cognition does not mean that Asians are not rational and do not rely on reason (Chen, 2006), but feelings and emotions are equally, or even more, valued as essential qualities in the Asian version of humanity and communication.

Asian religions and philosophies also endorse this communicative proposition. Confucianism delimits the cardinal concept of *ren* [human-heartedness] in light of sympathy and empathy. Buddhism likewise emphasizes the development of compassion, which literally means "feelings in common." Tu (2001a) accounts for the centrality of emotional sensitivity in Buddhist and Confucian visions of humanity:

[B]oth Confucianism and Buddhism maintain that sympathy, empathy and compassion are at the same time the minimum requirement and the maximum realization of the human way. According to Confucian and Buddhist modes of thinking, human beings are sentient beings. Sensitivity, rather than rationality, is the distinctive feature of humanity. We feel; therefore we are. Through feeling, we realize our own existence and the coexistence of other human beings, indeed birds, animals, plants and all the myriad things in the universe.

Since this feeling of interconnectedness is not merely a private emotion but a sense of fellowship that is inter-subjectively confirmable, it is a commonly shareable value. (pp. 83–84)

It is important to note that the Asian worldview does not encourage speaker-centered affective communication where individuals explicitly disclose their emotions to one another. According to the Asian experience, because "[r]elational emotions that bind and bond individuals together, not the private and narcissistic emotions, are emphasized" (Kim, 2001, p. 67), emotional convergence in communication is often possible when the ego-decentered and other-directed listener attempts to sense and read the speaker's emotional dynamics. Thus, to be communicatively active in the Asian sense is to be perceptive, receptive, and introspective to *feel together* with fellow humans, nature, and the spirits (Miike, 2007). The desirable profile of such a sensitive Asian communicator is close to what Gordon (2009) has in mind as an "attuned communicator": "To develop sensitivity to the importance of 'fine-turning' to the other, to sensing who they are, where they've been, what they believe and value, and feel what they need, what their style is, what their rhythms are, this is the work of an 'attuned' communicator" (p. 13).

Buddhist theories postulate that the development of compassion parallels the increased degrees of the awareness of interdependent interrelatedness and egoless altruism. As the first and second Asiacentric propositions suggest, then, communication can augment such an awareness and egolessness, which, in turn, helps us develop empathic sensitivity to communicate and feel togetherness and interdependence. This Asian portrait of communication may be pressed into service so as to extend the affective and altruistic aspect of humanity in the global community.

Communication as Reciprocal Duty and Responsibility

The fourth Asiacentric proposition is that *communication is a process in which we receive and return our debts to all sentient beings*. Many Asian religious-philosophical teachings as well as everyday practices highlight the fact that our existence is dependent on all other beings. The Buddhist doctrine of *pratitya samutpada*

[dependent co-arising] is a case in point (see Chang & Holt, 1991; Dissanayake, 1983; Ishii, 1998). It is the idea that "the existence of every being in the universe is made possible only by Buddhist *engi* or pre-determined cooriginations and corelationships with all other beings" (Ishii, 2001, p. 7). Implicit in this Asian worldview is that we must be grateful to our fellow humans, natural environments, and ancestral spirits for our blessings and have ethical obligations to return something to them. We owe our debts of gratitude to our ancestors, parents, siblings, neighbors, teachers, friends, animals, oceans, rivers, mountains, and plants. Confucianism and Hinduism similarly accentuate the primacy of obligatory reciprocity in embodying supportive and cooperative interdependence and in nurturing loyal and long-term relationships (Chen & Chung, 2000; Saral, 1983; Yum, 2000). The Asian theme of reciprocity comes into play here.

Daisetsu Suzuki (1870–1966), perhaps the most renowned scholar of Zen Buddhism in the West, once advocated the importance of *shujo-no-on* [the debt of gratitude that we owe to the universe for our existence] for humanity (Sato, 1959). In traditional Japanese culture, people ought to feel obligated to remember and repay the *on* [debt of gratitude] that they had received from all contacts in the course of their life. In particular, four types of *on* were emphasized: *on* from parents as life givers, *on* from teachers and mentors, *on* from lords, and *shujo-no-on*. From a Buddhist viewpoint, *shujo-no-on* is the ultimate *on* of interdependence based on our awareness and appreciation of the support of the universe with which we are living on the earth. It is age-old wisdom similar to the emerging and evolving philosophy of "ecopiety" about the self-defeating humanity and the endangered earth (see Jung, 2009). Suzuki in Sato (1959) explicates this concept as follows:

It rains and the ground becomes wet. It is the *on* of rain; it is the virtue of rain. The earth absorbs the rain, and sends it to the roots of trees and grasses, and then to their buds. This is the *on* of the great earth. They are helping each other, loving each other; it is *on*. I receive *on* from others, at the same time I extend *on* to others.... It is love and the action of love we feel as *on* for each other. To understand *shujo-no-on* means to get rid of the world of power-domination, to enter into the area of loving each other and helping each other. *"Okage-sama"* means literally "appreciation of the protection of the tree under its shade," but the implication can be extended to our existence on the earth in the solar system, in this Universe. Indeed, true meaning of human existence lies in realizing this relationship. (p. 244)

Other Asian concepts in Asian languages such as the Filipino concept of *utang na loob* and the Thai concept of *bhunkun* also allude to communication as the process of reciprocating love and kindness. These cultural practices ideally enhance our deep affection and thoughtful consideration toward others. It is noteworthy that this communication process of receiving and returning debts of gratitude often goes beyond here-and-now reciprocity. As Ho (1993) attests, the Asian worldview stresses an extended and circular perspective on space and time in the need to repay our debt of gratitude. That is, if we are unable to pay in our present life, the debt may be passed on to the next and future generations. Or it may also be assumed in our next life. "In a sense," Yum (2000) writes, "a person is forever indebted to others, who in turn are constrained by other debts" (p. 66). Such an Asian perspective on communication as assuming responsibilities, not as asserting rights, may be perceived as a challenge to individual freedom, but it can project duty-centered character building and ethical intelligence in the age of global exploitation (Yin, 2009; Yin & Miike, 2008).

Communication as Moralizing and Harmonizing

The fifth Asiacentric proposition is that *communication is a process in which we moralize and harmonize the universe*. This proposition concerns itself with the Asian axiological emphasis on the social order and, ultimately, the order of the universe. It is also pertinent to an Asian criterion by which to evaluate communicative conduct. In Asian cultures, generally speaking, communication is positively evaluated when it attempts to actualize the moral integrity and harmony of the universe, while it is negatively evaluated when it aims to pursue our own individual self-interest. Like the African worldview, "humaneness is characterized by how well people live in harmony

with each other and nature. To be inhumane is to live poorly in relationship to your fellow human beings and nature" (Asante, 2005, p. 135). Hence, ethics and morality revolve around harmony from the intrapersonal level to the cosmological level. In the Asian worldview, harmony is the end rather than the means of communication (Chen, 2004, 2006). As Chen and Starosta (2003) clarify, harmony in Asian communication processes "represents a kind of ethical appeal that can induce a sense of duty for cooperation with the other party, not by the communicator's strategic words but by the sincere display of whole-hearted concern with the other" (p. 6).

The Asian de-emphasis on speech has been stereotypically exaggerated in the culture and communication literature to the extent that it gives the impression that Asians traditionally have not valued the act of speaking at all. But speaking for the benefit of others, not for the sake of self-interest, "is much cherished in Asian traditions of thought." Dissanayake (2003), for instance, explores the Buddhist teaching of *samma vaca* [right speech] and its moral implications in human communication. There are four primary guidelines for right speech: (1) right speech should be de-linked with falsehoods of any sort; (2) right speech discourages slander and calumny leading to friction and hostility among people; (3) right speech presupposes the absence of, and refraining from, harsh language; and (4) right speech encourages speakers to desist from frivolous and idle chatter and to embrace purposeful and productive speech. There is also much to learn from Confucius's teaching of "humble talk and moral action" (see Chang, 2008) and Gandhi's nonviolent philosophy of *Satyagraha* (see Pandikattu, 2001; Starosta & Shi, 2007) about moralizing and harmonizing styles and strategies of communication.

"An exemplary person seeks harmony but not uniformity," Confucius opines in the *Analects* (13:23). This ideal of "harmony without uniformity" can be an ultimate goal of communication both in Asian societies and in the global village. In Confucius's mind, a global citizen is a person who can fully recognize diversity as the basis for harmony and take the moral responsibility to make the best out of it. To such a citizen, intercultural communication is a means of integrating differences without creating the sameness.

Tu in UNESCO (2006) articulates the critical relationship between harmony and diversity:

> Harmony is predicated on diversity and difference. The opposite of harmony is sameness. The "great unity" is diametrically opposed to homogenized unity. The greatness of the "great unity" lies in its convergence, confluence, integration and harmonization of different colors, sounds, tastes and experiences. Harmony embraces difference. Without difference, harmony is impossible. If we do not mix spices, we cannot make tasty soup. Without different sounds, there is no music. Without different colors, there are no paintings. Geodiversity and biodiversity are preconditions for human survival, and linguistic and cultural diversity is congenial to human flourishing. (p. 181)

Asiacentric Communication Ethics and Competence

Asia is diverse and dynamic. It is a region of cultural complexity, continuity, and change, although the term signifies a certain geographical location in the world, designates a common historical and political struggle against Western imperialism and colonialism, and implies shared religious-philosophical foundations and cultural heritage (Miike, 2003a). Asian nations are plural societies. They "have a dominant community and a number of minority communities divided on the basis of language, religion, caste, and ethnicity living together under a single polity" (Goonasekera, 2003, p. 368). Chen and Starosta (2003) vividly depict such a place of remarkable variety and vitality:

> Indonesia is largely Muslim, yet it contains a large Hindu enclave in Bali. Indians were also imported to parts of Malaysia, and Buddhism, started in India, [but] can hardly be found there now, except [as] a political reaction to casteism. Instead, it has taken root in China, Sri Lanka, and elsewhere. Shintoism thrives in Japan, but maybe nowhere else. Asia has some massive cities, but 80% of some Asian countries are rural. India and China have 800 language varieties or dialects. (p. 1)

Obviously, therefore, all Asian communicators do not subscribe to the above-discussed five propositions. These propositions do not necessarily reflect the way Asians actually communicate in real-life situations.

Nevertheless, they serve as theoretical lenses from which to see an Asian version of humanity and to view Asian thought and action. They are designed to provide much food for thought in rethinking the nature and ideal of human communication in Asia and beyond from an alternative vantage point.

For example, the advent of the global village and the crisis of the human condition have made it compelling to ruminate on communication ethics and competence in intercultural contexts (Chen, 2005; Miike, 2009b; Tehranian, 2007). There have been extensive discussions on Eurocentric biases in the definitions and components of these key concepts (e.g., Chen & Starosta, 2008; Ishii, 2009; Shuter, 2003; Xiao & Chen, 2009). We can reexamine current conceptualizations of communication ethics and competence from the five Asiacentric propositions. They suggest that an ethical communicator can (1) remind herself or himself and others of interrelatedness and interdependence through communication, (2) discipline and cultivate herself or himself without being overly self-centered through communication, (3) develop her or his altruistic sensitivity to the sufferings of others, (4) feel her or his obligation to remember the debts that she or he has received and to try to return them in one way or another, and (5) speak up for greater harmony and morality.

Just like many proponents of Asian values who are often misunderstood by Western conservative intellectuals (Mahbubani, 2002), I am *not* asserting that these Asiacentric viewpoints on humans communicating are superior to Eurocentric ones, but I am protesting that they are not inferior to them. They are rooted in the Asian worldview and yet may be sharable along with those rooted in, say, the African worldview toward what Tu (2006, 2007) calls "a dialogical civilization" or what Sitaram (1998) calls "a higher humanity." In Sitaram's (1998) view, such a truly human civilization "is not an extension of any one culture; rather it would be the essence of all cultures of the entire humanity" (p. 13). Hence, there is room for Asiacentric, as well as Afrocentric and other non-Western, contributions. As Asante (1993) avers, there is also "space for Eurocentricity in a multicultural enterprise so long as it does not parade as universal. No one wants to banish the Eurocentric view. It is a valid view of reality where it does not force its way" (p. 188).

"Cherishing the Old to Know the New"

It was my intention in this essay to argue that learning from, not about, cultures for self-reflexivity is a *sine qua non* for cross-cultural dialogue and to illustrate how Asians and non-Asians can benefit from an Asiacentric worldview and its implications for communication in local and global contexts. Tu (2001a) propounds two propositions on globalization. First, globalization can be hegemonic homogenization without cultural diversity and sensitivity, but through dialogue it may lead to a genuine sense of global community. Second, the search for identity can degenerate into extreme ethnocentrism and exclusion, but through dialogue it may lead to an authentic way of intercultural communication and to a real respect for diversity. It is then up to us whether we will further risk our lifeboat by imposing the ethnocentric version of humanity on others and dividing the world with the clash of ignorance, or we will engage in mutual dialogue with the principle of "multiculturalism without hierarchy" toward "harmony without uniformity." In either case, Mahatma Gandhi's statement that "this world has enough for all of us but not enough for the greed of a single person" (Tehranian, 1999, p. 191) now sounds soberer than ever before.

Asante (2003a) asseverates that innovation and tradition are key to humanizing the world. He contends that "The generation of the new, the novel, is basic to the advancement of cultural ideas but also is the maintenance of the traditional" (p. 78). His contention is in perfect resonance with the Confucian spirit of "cherishing the old to know the new" (*Analects*, 2: 11). It is indeed imperative for us to study and apply old wisdoms both locally and globally in order to respond to new situations in the changing world (Miike, 2004). Tu (1998) aptly describes where we stand in search of global ethics and humanistic values:

> The problematique of the viability of the human race . . . is that having transformed ourselves into the most aggressive and self-destructive animal the evolutionary process has ever witnessed, we have now added ourselves to the long list of endangered species. This is the magnitude of the human dilemma today. We are urgently in need of a new way of perceiving, a new mode of thinking, even a new form of life, which

is predicated on a radically transformed attitude and worldview. Paradoxically, our determined effort to move away from militarism, materialism, aggression, conflict, and destruction may be a new discovery, but it is also a return to the spiritual roots that have provided the ground for humans to survive and flourish for centuries. In this sense, our humanity is at a crossroads. (p. 3)

References

Asante, M. K. (1993). Multiculturalism without hierarchy: An Afrocentric response to Diane Ravitch. In F. J. Beckwith & M. E. Bauman (Eds.), *Are you politically correct? Debating America's cultural standards* (pp. 185–193). Buffalo, NY: Prometheus Books.

Asante, M. K. (1998). *The Afrocentric idea* (Rev. ed.). Philadelphia: Temple University Press.

Asante, M. K. (2003a). *Afrocentricity: The theory of social change* (Rev. ed.). Chicago: African American Images.

Asante, M. K. (2003b). Education for liberation: On campus with a purpose. In V. L. Farmer (Ed.), *The Black student's guide to graduate and professional school success* (pp. 162–169). Westport, CT: Greenwood Press.

Asante, M. K. (2005). *Race, rhetoric, and identity: The architecton of soul*. Amherst, NY: Humanity Books.

Asante, M. K. (2006). The rhetoric of globalization: The Europeanization of human ideas. *Journal of Multicultural Discourses, 1*(2), 152–158.

Asante, M. K. (2009). *Erasing racism: The survival of the American nation* (2nd ed.). Amherst, NY: Prometheus Books.

Chang, H.-C. (2008). Language and words: Communication in the *Analects* of Confucius. In M. K. Asante, Y. Miike, & J. Yin (Eds.), *The global intercultural communication reader* (pp. 95–112). New York: Routledge.

Chang, H.-C., & Holt, G. R. (1991). The concept of *yuan* and Chinese interpersonal relationships. In S. Ting-Toomey & F. Korzenny (Eds.), *Cross-cultural interpersonal communication* (pp. 28–57). Newbury Park, CA: Sage.

Chen, G.-M. (2004). The two faces of Chinese communication. *Human Communication: A Journal of the Pacific and Asian Communication Association, 7*(1), 25–36.

Chen, G.-M. (2005). A model of global communication competence. *China Media Research, 1*(1), 3–11.

Chen, G.-M. (2006). Asian communication studies: What and where to now. *Review of Communication, 6*(4), 295–311.

Chen, G.-M., & Chung, J. (2000). The "Five Asian Dragons": Management behaviors and organizational communication. In L. A. Samovar & R. E. Porter (Eds.),

Intercultural communication: A reader (9th ed., pp. 301–312). Belmont, CA: Wadsworth.

Chen, G.-M., & Miike, Y. (Eds.). (2003). Asian approaches to human communication [Special issue]. *Intercultural Communication Studies, 12*(4), 1–218.

Chen, G.-M., & Starosta, W. J. (2000). Communication and global society: An introduction. In G.-M. Chen & W. J. Starosta (Eds.), *Communication and global society* (pp. 1–16). New York: Peter Lang.

Chen, G.-M., & Starosta, W. J. (2003). Asian approaches to human communication: A dialogue. *Intercultural Communication Studies, 12*(4), 1–15.

Chen, G.-M., & Starosta, W. J. (2008). Intercultural communication competence: A synthesis. In M. K. Asante, Y. Miike, & J. Yin (Eds.), *The global intercultural communication reader* (pp. 215–237). New York: Routledge.

Chesebro, J. W. (1996, December). Unity in diversity: Multiculturalism, guilt/victimage, and a new scholarly orientation. *Spectra: Newsletter of the Speech Communication Association, 32*(12), 10–14.

Choi, S.-C., & Choi, S.-H. (1992). The conceptualization of Korean tact, *noon-chi*. In S. Iwawaki, Y. Kashima, & K. Leung. (Eds.), *Innovations in cross-cultural psychology* (pp. 49–61). Amsterdam: Swets & Zeitlinger.

Dissanayake, W. (1983). The communication significance of the Buddhist concept of dependent co-origination. *Communication, 8*(1), 29–45.

Dissanayake, W. (1984). A Buddhist approach to development: A SriLankan endeavor. In G. Wang & W. Dissanayake (Eds.), *Continuity and change in communication systems: An Asian perspective* (pp. 39–51). Norwood, NJ: Ablex.

Dissanayake, W. (Ed.). (1988). *Communication theory: The Asian perspective*. Singapore: Asian Mass Communication Research and Information Center.

Dissanayake, W. (1991). Ethics, development, and communication: A Buddhist approach. In F. L. Casmir (Ed.), *Communication in development* (pp. 319–337). Norwood, NJ: Ablex.

Dissanayake, W. (2003). Asian approaches to human communication: Retrospect and prospect. *Intercultural Communication Studies, 12*(4), 17–37.

Goonasekera, A. (2003). Communication studies in Asia: Theoretical and methodological issues. In A. Goonasekera, L. C. Wah, & S. Venkatraman (Eds.), *Asian communication handbook* 2003 (pp. 358–369). Singapore: Asian Media Information and Communication Center.

Gordon, R. D. (2009). *On becoming an attuned communicator.* Bloomington, IN: iUniverse.

Ho, D. Y. F. (1993). Relational orientation in Asian social psychology. In U. Kim & J. W. Berry (Eds.), *Indigenous psychologies: Research and experience in cultural context* (pp. 240–259). Newbury Park, CA: Sage.

Huntington, S. P. (1993). The clash of civilizations? *Foreign Affairs, 72*(3), 22–49.

Huntington, S. P. (1996). *The clash of civilizations and the remaking of world order.* New York: Simon & Schuster.

Ishii, S. (1997). Tasks for intercultural communication researchers in the Asia-Pacific region in the 21st century. *Dokkyo International Review, 10,* 313–326.

Ishii, S. (1998). Developing a Buddhist *en*-based systems paradigm for the study of Japanese human relationships. *Japan Review, 10,* 109–122.

Ishii, S. (2001). An emerging rationale for triworld communication studies from Buddhist perspectives. *Human Communication: A Journal of the Pacific and Asian Communication Association, 4*(1), 1–10.

Ishii, S. (2004). Proposing a Buddhist consciousness-only epistemological model for intrapersonal communication research. *Journal of Intercultural Communication Research, 33*(2), 63–76.

Ishii, S. (2009). Conceptualizing Asian communication ethics: A Buddhist perspective. *Journal of Multicultural Discourses, 4*(1), 49–60.

Ishii, S., & Bruneau, T. (1994). Silence and silences in cross-cultural perspective: Japan and the United States. In L. A. Samovar & R. E. Porter (Eds.), *Intercultural communication: A reader* (7th ed., pp. 246–251). Belmont, CA: Wadsworth.

Ishii, S., Klopf, D., & Cooke, P. (2009). Worldview in intercultural communication: A religio-cosmological approach. In L. A. Samovar, R. E. Porter, & E. R. McDaniel (Eds.), *Intercultural communication: A reader* (12th ed., pp. 28–36). Boston, MA: Wadsworth Cengage Learning.

Jain, N. C. (1991). Worldview and cultural patterns of India. In L. A. Samovar & R. E. Porter (Eds.), *Intercultural communication: A reader* (6th ed., pp. 78–87). Belmont, CA: Wadsworth.

Jung, H. Y. (2009). *The way of ecopiety: Essays in transversal geophilosophy.* New York: Global Scholarly Publications.

Kamwangamalu, N. M. (2008). *Ubuntu* in South Africa: A sociolinguistic perspective to a pan-African concept. In M. K. Asante, Y. Miike, & J. Yin (Eds.), *The global intercultural communication reader* (pp. 113–122). New York: Routledge.

Kim, U. (2001). Culture, science, and indigenous psychologies: An integrated analysis. In D. Matsumoto (Ed.), *Handbook of culture and psychology* (pp. 51–75). New York: Oxford University Press.

Kincaid, D. L. (Ed.). (1987). *Communication theory: Eastern and Western perspectives.* San Diego, CA: Academic Press.

Maggay, M. P. (1999). *Understanding ambiguity in Filipino communication patterns.* Quezon City, Philippines: Institute for Studies in Asian Church and Culture.

Mahbubani, K. (2002). *Can Asians think? Understanding the divide between East and West.* South Royalton, VT: Steerforth Press.

Mansukhani, R. (2005). *Pakikiramdam:* A critical analysis. In R. M. Gripaldo (Ed.), *Filipino cultural traits: Claro R. Ceniza Lectures* (pp. 185–202). Washington, DC: Council for Research in Values and Philosophy.

Mataragnon, R. H. (1988). *Pakikiramdam* in Filipino social interaction: A study of subtlety and sensitivity. In A. C. Paranjpe, D. Y. F. Ho, & R. W. Rieber (Eds.), *Asian contributions to psychology* (pp. 251–262). New York: Praeger.

Miike, Y. (2003a). Beyond Eurocentrism in the intercultural field: Searching for an Asiacentric paradigm. In W. J. Starosta & G.-M. Chen (Eds.), *Ferment in the intercultural field: Axiology/value/praxis* (pp. 243–276). Thousand Oaks, CA: Sage.

Miike, Y. (2003b). Japanese *enryo-sasshi* communication and the psychology of *amae:* Reconsideration and reconceptualization. *Keio Communication Review, 25,* 93–115.

Miike, Y. (2004). Rethinking humanity, culture, and communication: Asiacentric critiques and contributions. *Human Communication: A Journal of the Pacific and Asian Communication Association, 7*(1), 67–82.

Miike, Y. (2006). Non-Western theory in Western research? An Asiacentric agenda for Asian communication studies. *Review of Communication, 6*(1/2), 4–31.

Miike, Y. (2007). An Asiacentric reflection on Eurocentric bias in communication theory. *Communication Monographs, 74*(2), 272–278.

Miike, Y. (2008a). Advancing centricity for non-Western scholarship: Lessons from Molefi Kete Asante's legacy of Afrocentricity. In A. Mazama (Ed.), *Essays in honor of an intellectual warrior, Molefi Kete Asante* (pp. 287–327). Paris: Editions Menaibuc.

Miike, Y. (2008b). Toward an alternative metatheory of human communication: An Asiacentric vision. In M. K. Asante, Y. Miike, & J. Yin (Eds.), *The global intercultural communication reader* (pp. 57–72). New York: Routledge.

Miike, Y. (2009a). "Cherishing the old to know the new": A bibliography of Asian communication studies. *China Media Research, 5*(1), 95–103.

Miike, Y. (Ed.). (2009b). New frontiers in Asian communication theory [Special issue]. *Journal of Multicultural Discourses, 4*(1), 1–88.

Miike, Y. (2010a). An anatomy of Eurocentrism in communication scholarship: The role of Asiacentricity in de-Westernizing theory and research. *China Media Research, 6*(1), 1–11.

Miike, Y. (2010b). Culture as text and culture as theory: Asiacentricity and its *raison d'être* in intercultural communication research. In R. T. Halualani & T. K. Nakayama (Eds.), *The handbook of critical intercultural communication.* Oxford, UK: Wiley-Blackwell.

Miike, Y. (2010c). *Enryo-sasshi* theory. In R. L. Jackson (Ed.), *Encyclopedia of identity.* Thousand Oaks, CA: Sage.

Miike, Y., & Chen, G.-M. (2006). Perspectives on Asian cultures and communication: An updated bibliography. *China Media Research, 2*(1), 98–106.

Miike, Y., & Chen, G.-M. (Eds.). (2007). Asian contributions to communication theory [Special issue]. *China Media Research, 3*(4), 1–109.

Nordstrom, L. (Ed.). (1983). Communication—East and West [Special issue]. *Communication, 8*(1), 1–132.

Pandikattu, K. (Ed.). (2001). *Gandhi: The meaning of Mahatma for the millennium.* Washington, DC: Council for Research in Values and Philosophy.

Robinson, J. H. (2003). Communication in Korea: Playing things by eye. In L. A. Samovar & R. E. Porter (Eds.), *Intercultural communication: A reader* (10th ed., pp. 57–64). Belmont, CA: Wadsworth.

Rogers, E. M. (1976). Communication and development: The passing of the dominant paradigm. *Communication Research, 3*(2), 213–240.

Rogers, E. M. (1978). The rise and fall of the dominant paradigm. *Journal of Communication, 28*(1), 64–69.

Rogers, E. M. (1990). Communication and social change. In G. L. Dahnke & G. W. Clatterbuck (Eds.), *Human communication: Theory and research* (pp. 259–271). Belmont, CA: Wadsworth.

Saito, M. (1970). Learning to communicate. *General Semantics Bulletin, 37,* 14–18.

Saito, M. (1982). *Nemawashi:* A Japanese form of interpersonal communication. *ETC: A Review of General Semantics, 39*(3), 205–214.

Samovar, L. A., Porter, R. E., & McDaniel, E. R. (2010). *Communication between cultures* (7th ed.). Boston, MA: Wadsworth Cengage Learning.

Saral, T. B. (1983). Hindu philosophy of communication. *Communication, 8*(1), 47–58.

Sato, K. (1959). The concept of *on* in Ruth Benedict and D. T. Suzuki. *Psychologia: An International Journal of Psychology in the Orient, 2*(4), 243–245.

Shuter, R. (2003). Ethics, culture, and communication: An intercultural perspective. In L. A. Samovar & R. E. Porter (Eds.), *Intercultural communication: A reader* (10th ed., pp. 449–455). Belmont, CA: Wadsworth.

Sitaram, K. S. (1998). Introduction: Multiculturalism for a higher humanity. In K. S. Sitaram & M. H. Prosser (Eds.),

Civic discourse: Multiculturalism, cultural diversity, and global communication (pp. 1–14). Stamford, CT: Ablex.

Starosta, W. J., & Shi, L. (2007). Alternate perspectives on Gandhian communication ethics. *China Media Research, 3*(4), 7–14.

Suzuki, D. (2006). *Daisetsu speaking on Zen: Three lectures in English that impressed the world* (in Japanese and in English, S. Shigematsu, Trans.). Tokyo: Art Days.

Tehranian, M. (1990). Communication, peace, and development: A communitarian perspective. In F. Korzenny & S. Ting-Toomey (Eds.), *Communicating for peace: Diplomacy and negotiation* (pp. 157–175). Newbury Park, CA: Sage.

Tehranian, M. (1993). Ethnic discourse and the new world dysorder: A communitarian perspective. In C. Roach (Ed.), *Communication and culture in war and peace* (pp. 192–215). Newbury Park, CA: Sage.

Tehranian, M. (1999). *Global communication and world politics: Domination, development, and discourse.* Boulder, CO: Lynne Rienner Publishers.

Tehranian, M. (2007). *Rethinking civilization: Resolving conflict in the human family.* London: Routledge.

Tu, W. (1998). Mustering the conceptual resources to grasp a world in flux. In J. A. Kushigian (Ed.), *International studies in the next millennium: Meeting the challenge of globalization* (pp. 3–15). Westport, CT: Praeger.

Tu, W. (2001a). The context of dialogue: Globalization and diversity. In G. Picco (Ed.), *Crossing the divide: Dialogue among civilizations* (pp. 49–96). South Orange, NJ: School of Diplomacy and International Relations, Seton Hall University.

Tu, W. (2001b). The global significance of local knowledge: A new perspective on Confucian humanism. *Sungkyun Journal of East Asian Studies, 1*(1), 22–27.

Tu, W. (2002). Beyond the Enlightenment mentality. In H. Y. Jung (Ed.), *Comparative political culture in the age of globalization: An introductory anthology* (pp. 251–266). Lanham, MD: Lexington Books.

Tu, W. (2006). The Confucian ethic and the spirit of East Asian modernity. In UNESCO (Ed.), *Cultural diversity and transversal values: East-West dialogue on spiritual and secular dynamics* (pp. 7–13). Paris: UNESCO.

Tu, W. (2007). Toward a dialogical civilization: Identity, difference and harmony. In D. Zhao (Ed.), *Dialogue of philosophies, religions and civilizations in the era of globalization* (pp. 11–14). Washington, DC: Council for Research in Values and Philosophy.

Tu, W. (2008). Mutual learning as an agenda for social development. In M. K. Asante, Y. Miike, & J. Yin (Eds.), *The global intercultural communication reader* (pp. 329–333). New York: Routledge.

UNESCO. (Ed.). (2006). *The forum of reflexion: What UNESCO for the future?* Paris: UNESCO.

Xiao, X., & Chen, G.-M. (2009). Communication competence and moral competence: A Confucian perspective. *Journal of Multicultural Discourses, 4*(1), 61–74.

Yin, J. (2009). Negotiating the center: Towards an Asiacentric feminist communication theory. *Journal of Multicultural Discourses, 4*(1), 75–88.

Yin, J., & Miike, Y. (2008). A textual analysis of fortune cookie sayings: How Chinese are they? *Howard Journal of Communications, 19*(1), 18–43.

Yum, J. O. (2000). The impact of Confucianism on interpersonal relationships and communication patterns in East Asia. In L. A. Samovar & R. E. Porter (Eds.), *Intercultural communication: A reader* (9th ed., pp. 63–73). Belmont, CA: Wadsworth.

Concepts and Questions

1. How does the essay describe worldview? In what ways is this different from or similar to the previous essay?
2. Differentiate between learning *about* other cultures and learning *from* other cultures.
3. What is meant by "cultures in hierarchy"? Is this considered a negative or positive perspective? Why? Is there a better way of viewing cultures?
4. Describe and provide examples of the core values underlying the Eurocentric worldview.
5. Are there any dangers to exploring other cultures from a strictly descriptive perspective? Will simply analyzing and critiquing another culture help or hinder intercultural understanding and communication?
6. Describe and discuss the three steps to cross-cultural dialogue.
7. Summarize, with examples, the five Asiacentric communication propositions.
8. According to the essay, "the Asian worldview stresses an extended, circular perspective on space and time...." How is this similar or different from the worldview structure discussed in the previous essay?
9. What are some ways that a culture's worldview could influence communication style? How could these create difficulties during an intercultural communication interaction?
10. Do you think Westerners can obtain any benefits from the Asiacentric worldview? If not, why? If yes, what are they?

Relevance and Application of Intercultural Communication Theory and Research

FELIPE KORZENNY

Theory and research in culture and communication are essential for self-understanding, the development of relationships, the conduct of business, and ultimately for the preservation of our species and habitat. This paper will first examine the relationship between communication and culture. Second, the reader will find a section that addresses the influence of intercultural theory and research on practice. Third, and to conclude, this paper will point to several reasons the study of communication and culture is important.

CULTURE AND COMMUNICATION

In a general and abstract fashion, the study of culture can be said to be the study of communication. Communication is said to be the glue of society. In a planetary metaphor, communication is the gravitational force that keeps the planets in a certain relation to each other. Culture, in a parallel fashion, is the mechanism that allows human beings to make sense of the world, and to deal with it. Culture is a mix of manifest and latent patterns of behavior and relationships among human beings, patterns that allow humans to function and strive in the pursuit of order and survival. Culture is a social product and is the

 The major concepts in this paper were presented at the Spotlight Program "Why Study Culture?" at the Sixth Annual Intercultural and International Communication Conference at the University of Miami, Florida, February 1989. Felipe Korzenny Professor of Advertising and Integrated Marketing Communication and Director of the Center for Hispanic Marketing Communication at Florida State University.

result of humans originating interaction, that is, communication processes. While it is true that not all cultural manifestations are communication expressions *per se*, the factors that lead to cultural manifestations must be communication processes.

In the practice of human communication, then, we create, change, and/or reinforce culture. Journalists, broadcasters, artists, speech writers, producers, directors, communication teachers, and all of us who interact with others influence culture, although to different extents and for different reasons. It is clear, however, that the modification of culture is a relatively slow process. Cultural change is usually slow because the acquisition of generally accepted ways of doing things requires widespread acceptance; once a cultural pattern has been widely communicated and adopted, however, it becomes relatively stable. We humans have the tendency to cling to our culture as to our clothing—we fear being naked. Our culture is like a security blanket; it is that with which we are familiar and comfortable. The culture one identifies with has been infused in one's being since early in life, and to each person it seems to be the most logical, consistent, and appealing way of life. Our culture constitutes an important set of tools that enables daily living, providing us with assumptions and established routines that reduce the need for constant reinvention and, in so doing, allowing for what we call progress. Culture, however, runs in the background, and it seldom makes itself explicit. The practice of intercultural communication, therefore, may entail the modification of culture for more adaptive living, making culture explicit so individuals may better understand themselves and others in a particular context.

THE INFLUENCE OF THEORY AND RESEARCH ON PRACTICE

Communication is an essential part of culture and a condition for it. Intercultural communication, a very broad umbrella title for the study of communication and culture, has made great progress in the past twenty years. The field proper is only about that old. Perhaps the most important contribution of intercultural communication theory and research has been an agenda-setting function.

Currently it is acceptable and understandable to speak of intercultural training for those who need to interact with other cultures; it is unquestionable that teachers need to have intercultural skills to succeed in the most challenging task of educating a multicultural student body; and it is now in vogue to speak of training for a multicultural work force. Journalists today seem to accept the notion of cultural sensitivity and respect in covering and reporting culturally diverse communities. Advertising and marketing specialists dedicate large budgets and attention to culturally different markets. Diplomatic efforts are beginning to explore and utilize such intercultural communication constructs as *face, uncertainty reduction*, and *high- versus low-context communication*. In the United States, we have long assumed a common traditional past, involving the notion of an undifferentiated melting pot, but this assumption has been replaced with the image of a multicultural society. In this latter image, cultural differences need to be addressed rather than ignored, and the professionalization of intercultural practice is a necessity. The large number of bibliographic contributions in the past twenty years, as well as the emergence of intercultural communication divisions, interest groups, and associations, have contributed to making intercultural communication practice a universal need.

Academic interest and pursuit, in this case, has led and played an important role in the awakening of the need for practice, and this has not been easy. In contrast to other areas of endeavor, intercultural communication practice faces human barriers of great magnitude, such as the following:

1. *Natural but endemic ethnocentrism* which, below the surface, negates the importance of intercultural practice. This ethnocentrism is manifest in such statements as: "I already know that! I am not a racist! I know how to deal with those people." It is very difficult for most of us to accept the fact that we naturally give preference to the in-group over the out-group. It is, however, an innate tendency of humans to attribute increased importance to those who are closer to the self. Perceived similarity along multiple dimensions, including ethnic background, values, beliefs, customs, and patterns of relationships, is the basis for evaluating others. We are most likely to attribute positive traits to those similar to us, but because to do so is, paradoxically, a societal taboo, we deny it. The denial of ethnocentrism may be one of the most crucial barriers to intercultural communication because such denial prevents confrontation, clarification, and acceptance. Accepting that ethnocentrism is natural and endemic should be an important first step in the realization that in this turbulent period, when space and time are dramatically shrunk, we must overcome ethnocentrism for survival.

2. *Assumed similarity.* Culture is like water for the fish: We are in it and are part of it but we do not see it. A great temptation exists to assume that others are just like us, and if they are different it is because they have not developed, or because they are defective (or of a superior kind, whatever the case may be). The external manifestations of culture—food, buildings, dress—are too obvious to ignore. Implicit or subjective culture is invisible, but it is the dimension of culture that is most likely to affect human interaction. The values, beliefs, attitudes, behavioral patterns, and role relationships that different cultures hold dear are difficult to detect by members of each culture as well as by those who are alien. Making culture explicit will therefore help us understand ourselves in contrast to others. The expertise to make culture explicit does not come easily, and that is a role that intercultural communication professionals can assume.

3. *Lack of immediate rewards.* In the field of diffusion of innovations, preventive innovations are known to face important difficulties—they do not have obvious consequences; for example, if you use a seat belt you do not observe yourself being safer. One of the main difficulties of the application of intercultural communication theory and research is that few, if any, rewards are immediate, and it is difficult for most of us to delay gratification. For instance, it takes a long time to detect the benefits of an intercultural communication workshop. Intercultural communication skills and sensitivity are likely to be rewarded in the long term through better understanding and consequent good will, as well as material gains. Reports of the "bizarre," on the other hand, are readily rewarded with attention and money. Showing short-term profits, for example, is seen as true accomplishment

by scattered shareholders. Currently, therefore, in our economic system, we have seen dramatic shortsightedness in business; meaningless take-overs appear to be more important than the cultivation of long-term business strategies. In contrast, intercultural communication training and research would be most likely to reward long-term strategies in the cycle of economic productivity.

4. *Cost and effort beyond expectations.* It is usual to assume that intercultural communication skills and practice are easy to come by. Books and cultural "capsules" exist that provide "quick-and-easy" pre-scriptions, but intercultural communication is just not that easy, unfortunately. In the first place, the multivariate and complex nature of intercultural communication makes effective, fast-and-easy solutions very difficult to find. It is important to remember that research and development projects in the physical sciences are frequently funded at the level of several million dollars. In the social sciences in general, and communication in particular, it is difficult to find research and development projects funded at the $100,000 level. The implication can thus be drawn that electronic components are more important and complex than humans. The temptation is to get rid of the "human problem" quickly so that we can proceed with business. In truth, however, human behavior is highly complex, and it is not until we acknowledge its importance in the productive cycle of our social system that we will be realistic in our expectations.

THE IMPORTANCE OF THE STUDY OF CULTURE AND COMMUNICATION

There are several benefits derived from the study of culture and communication. The following generalizations and assertions highlight the importance of intercultural communication for practitioners.

Intercultural communication provides remediation of the cultural filter that information processors impose on the content. Culture in this role is of extreme importance since only limited effects of the media can be expected, due to selective exposure, attention, perception, and recall. Clearly, a large part of these phenomena are culturally mediated. One of the main findings in media research within a "plural" perspective has been that media effects are highly dependent on the background and social context of the receivers, or, better stated, processors of information. This fact is seen in current attempts at revitalizing American pragmatism in communication through symbolic interactionism, coordinated management of meaning, and other means. The way diverse cultural groups interpret information is not straightforward. For example, the reason black viewers seem to be more lenient about drug-related issues and crime, as my research shows, can very well be due to the meshing of the context of the blacks as processors with the media portrayals observed. In other words, people are likely to interpret information according to the circumstances of their immediate lives. My research on international news effects has clearly demonstrated that there is no monolithic media impact but a diversity of interpretations. This lack of homogeneity contradicts the claims of many mass-oriented scholars, who have traditionally argued that the U.S. media is homogenous and that consequently it homogenizes its audiences. The conceptualization of communication processors, and the recognition of audiences as plural collections of individuals and not masses, should prove useful in future pragmatic endeavors.

Cultural understanding avoids the pitfalls of early development communication research. Early development communication efforts ignored the value and usefulness of other cultures: It was assumed that only Western life styles were "modern" or "productive." With that bias, the application of stereotyped remedies became an obsession, and the outcome was frequently failure. "Just make those people more modern, more rational" seemed to be the motto. Only recently has the understanding of social information processing modes and information needs resulted in well-tailored efforts geared to alleviate social problems. Examples are Radio Netherlands, rural journalism programs in Ecuador, where rural journalists are trained to serve their own communities, and integrated farming and research systems, where farmers contribute to their own agricultural research. When one is able to understand the function of cultural traits for the members of a culture, one is able to appreciate those traits. The idea that Western values are held by all people is now being questioned by academics and increasingly by practitioners.

The study of culture helps us understand ourselves. If we accept the premise that we learn by contrast, then intercultural communication research and theory provides us with the mirror that projects an image, which can be pleasing or displeasing but which sets us in the context of human interaction. We must believe that we are only able to "know," to understand, ourselves in the context of other social beings and the diversity that now pervades our world. How can we evaluate our actions or beliefs without a point of comparison? Literature dealing with communication and culture has been largely anecdotal. Currently, as more research becomes available, contrasts of different ethnic groups and nationalities are being substantiated or negated. My research on cross-cultural comparisons of Anglo-Americans, Hispanics, Asians, and blacks has confirmed or disconfirmed many of those anecdotal accounts, and I believe that this type of comparative research serves as a mirror in which we can find ourselves in comparison to others. We are different, but understanding the differences may allow us to appreciate them, and, consequently, to be able to better tailor our messages and strategies to promote understanding. As our differences become evident, our "selves" thus become more knowable to us, and we become less prejudiced.

Prejudice in the media is a manifestation of the beliefs of those who are in charge. Intercultural communication theory and research can assist in allowing individuals to become aware of their own prejudices. A prejudiced media, however, can only reinforce the status quo. The realization of prejudice does not eliminate it but provides individuals with the departing point for managing ethnocentrism, and, indeed, perhaps the acceptance and recognition of prejudice is the best point of departure for its effective social management. As previously discussed, a view of the world that contains wider categories for the classification of cultural experiences may assist in the promotion of collaboration among culturally diverse individuals. These sensitizing efforts can best be achieved by communication professionals who have themselves been trained in intercultural communication theory and research. The media, with its ample power of message distribution, may, under the proper management, begin to help audiences question prejudice.

Communication rules are seldom explicit; they must be uncovered. As the fish in the water is unaware of the water, we are unaware of the cultural rules that dictate patterns of interaction. Cross-cultural understanding, then, requires that the rules of cultural "others" and "our own" be made explicit. Edward T. Hall[1] has made an important contribution in arguing that "going beyond culture" is necessary for communication to take place among the culturally diverse, but to go beyond culture, it is necessary to first know it. Once we are able to transcend culture, we are in the position to strive toward convergence in achieving understanding. It is as if open confrontation functions as a prerequisite for harmony among the culturally diverse. But the confrontation of orientations must be planned for, with the intention of achieving cooperation.

Establishing an intercultural relationship requires attention to the subtle aspects of culture. Advertising, marketing, counseling, teaching, public service, and news coverage require the cultural sensitivity that only truly bicultural/multicultural individuals can have. So, more than being understood, for successful practice culture needs to be lived. This is easier said than done, however. Those catering to the tastes and needs of diverse cultural groups need to immerse themselves in those cultures, obtain the collaboration of cultural informants, and sincerely attempt to serve the needs of those individuals. Lip service and pro forma research are not successful long-term alternatives. The provision of services and products to culturally different persons entails the communication positioning of that service or product in terms that address the reality of the other culture. Selling expensive hotel rooms to individuals who culturally prefer to stay with friends and family when traveling, for example, is simply absurd. Bicultural or multicultural individuals are in the best position to serve as bridges, but these intercultural persons are difficult to find and training for these skills is not readily available. Our understanding of intercultural communication should provide the means to produce these needed cultural interpreters.

Although knowledge of a culture provides the cognitive tools for understanding, only acting in a culture can provide the tools for appropriate emotional and motor responses. While we are in a different cultural environment, we are operating in a distorted psychological space and do not know it. It seems as if continuous bumping against the walls of the new culture is one of the most effective learning processes. Studying a culture in books or movies may not be enough, because motor behavioral shaping takes place independently from verbal behavior. In a book I may learn that "those different" people value individualism, and I may be able to describe such a value. Most likely, however, I will not feel comfortable with individualism until I incorporate it into my behavioral repertoire in particular contexts—that is, until I experience the reward of individualism in a particular situation. To be able to function within a culture, therefore, one has to experiment within it. Basically one needs to approach cultural learning with reserved optimism, as one needs to learn how to accept failure, and this learning can be seen as a benefit of cultural shock, if one is prepared for it. It is better to know in advance that the task of intercultural communication will be difficult, because then the encounter with reality will be less severe than if one expects no difficulties.

The study of culture and communication will become more important, but the nature of the individual culture and the problems analyzed will be different. Customized cultures are likely to evolve as individuals become increasingly isolated from traditional human contact and their choices of channels multiply dramatically. The media choices available will enable subsets of individuals to share with each other a culture or cultural domains that do not resemble cultures of the past—these will be electronic cultures. As humans increasingly have more and more choices of media channels, their ability to control the cultural inputs will be greater. New cultures will emerge that encompass individuals who may have never been with each other physically. Other, older cultures may be reinforced through the availability of multiple cultural manifestations on recorded media. As interpersonal contact decreases, a new diversity may emerge that needs to be understood. Further, it looks like there is no going back, although perhaps in the relatively distant future a knowledge navigator will re-enable human interaction and return individuals to the idyllic global village envisioned by Marshall McLuhan.

The study of communication and culture can prevent war. Appropriate interpretations of actions can certainly lead to the reduction of tensions. Faulty attributions of intention, on the other hand, tend to be dominant causes of friction and stress across nations and cultural groups. How do individuals from different cultures reduce uncertainty in negotiation? What are the face-saving strategies common to different cultures? What are the conflict styles that characterize diverse cultures? Are there universal human principles that can provide a framework for mediation and understanding? How can international negotiators become intercultural persons? These and other questions, likely to be answered through the study of intercultural communication, are perhaps the most ambitious practical contribution that this field can make.

Note

1. Hall, Edward T. (1967). *Beyond culture.* Garden City, NY: Anchor Books.

Concepts and Questions

1. What does Korzenny mean when he says culture is a "social product"?
2. According to Korzenny, culture is like a "security blanket." Give an example of how culture provides a sense of security. What is a context or situation in which culture can produce insecurity?
3. Explain the relationship between culture and communication.
4. What is meant by the claim that natural, but endemic, ethnocentrism is a barrier to intercultural communication?
5. Do you think the study of intercultural communication can lead to a better self-understanding? Explain.
6. Korzenny indicates that an academic appreciation of culture is insufficient to make you culturally competent—you need to actually experience the culture. How does living in a culture create a greater understanding of that culture?
7. The United States is considered to be a pluralistic, multicultural society. What are five advantages and five difficulties of living in a multicultural society?
8. Korzenny's essay is more than twenty years old. Do you think it is still applicable? Explain.

Cultural Identity: Issues of Belonging

*The value of identity of course is that so often
with it comes purpose.*

RICHARD R. GRANT

*Identity would seem to be the garment with
which one covers the nakedness of the self:
in which case, it is best that the garment
be loose, a little like the robes of the desert,
through which one's nakedness can always be
felt, and, sometimes, discerned.*

JAMES BALDWIN

*Identity is a concept of our age that should
be used very carefully. All types of identities,
ethnic, national, religious, sexual or whatever
else, can become your prison after a while.
The identity that you stand up for can enslave
you and close you to the rest of the world.*

MURATHAN MUNGAN, CONTEMPORARY TURKISH POET

It wasn't until some of the more recent editions of this anthology that we decided to add a chapter on identity. It had become obvious that we are living in an era of dramatic social transformations. One of those transformations involves identity. Forces of globalization and new immigration patterns are creating enormous pressures on the established nation-state geopolitical order. New institutions are creating an environment in which electronic labor, capital, and media content flow almost seamlessly across national borders. And within these borders waves of immigrants are leaving their homelands in search of greater opportunities in other countries and regions. International political and economic integration in the form of alliances and trade agreements have become common practice. Collectively, these conditions represent powerful agents of social change and create a dynamic milieu affecting the formation and maintenance of both self-identity and cultural identity. As a result of these evolving contemporary social conditions, it has become essential to understand the role of identity and how culture forms and preserves identity. Our concern is not only for immigrants but also for those who are members of various co-cultures. These individuals are attempting to embrace their co-culture identity while also being members of the dominant culture. These two groups, immigrants and members of co-cultures, became the main focus of a chapter first introduced into our book twelve years ago.

Perhaps the most central function of identity is to provide meaning for each individual by serving as a source of self-definition. In other words, we organize meaning around our self-identity (Castells, 1997). Identities serve as a foundation for meaning in part because of their origins, which can stem from a variety of influences including geography, history, fantasies, religion, and many, many more. Identity takes various time- and scenario-dependent forms. People can, and often do, align themselves with nations, states, regions, religions, ethnic groups, gender, and professions. Regardless of the identity that motivates the individual, one thing is evident—one's identity helps determine how a person views the world and behaves in that world.

A common trait influencing identity formation and maintenance is culture. Identities are socially constructed through a cultural lens, employing the medium of communication. We identify with our initial cultural in-group as a function of enculturation, and later expand to other cultural groups or social institutions as a product of interaction (Castells, 1997). This results in a culturally bound concept of which type of identity is socially appropriate. For example, in the individualistic culture of the United States, army recruits are urged to be an "Army of One," which emphasizes self-determination, independence, and individual achievement. This emphasis contrasts remarkably with that of a collectivistic culture in which identity is strongly connected to, and dependent on, in-group membership.

As previously noted, in a world where multicultural interactions are increasingly unavoidable, and where sojourners often live and work for extended periods in other cultures, the influence of, and effects on, identity must be understood. For this reason we offer six essays dealing with different aspects of culture and identity. The first essay, which was one of the early articles to link cultural identity and intercultural communication directly, focuses on how people come to identify themselves with their various general and specific cultural membership groups. In "Cultural Identity and Intercultural Communication" Mary Jane Collier examines the connection between culture and identity by considering symbols and meanings, cultural norms, cultural history, types of culture based on national and ethnic considerations, as well as gender, profession, geographic location, organization, and physical ability or disability. As part of her overview, Collier seeks to answer the following four questions about identity and intercultural communication: (1) What is cultural identity? (2) How are multiple cultural identities created and negotiated with others? (3) How can knowledge of the cultural identity approach help you become more competent when dealing with persons who are taking on an identity different from yours? (4) What are the benefits of such an approach to intercultural communication for research, training, and practice?

Our second essay was first chosen because it offered a unique approach to the subject of identity. In "An Alternative View of Identity" Guo-Ming Chen advances an alternative interpretation of identity. To place his line of reasoning into a context, Chen begins with an overview of contemporary approaches to the study of identity. In this essay you are introduced to an interdisciplinary overview of the principal theories related to contemporary identity study. In addition, Chen links his approach to four major Eastern religious and philosophical doctrines that demonstrate an alternative to the Western view of identity.

As mentioned, Chen offers a historical review and critique of several identity theories and also provides a thorough discussion of identity theory and social identity theory. The essay then moves to the field of communication, where the study of identity has been largely the province of intercultural communication scholars. He explains that the bulk of this work has arisen from four approaches: (1) intergroup, (2) cultural, (3) critical cultural, and (4) postcolonial. Following a brief explanation of each approach, Chen puts forward an alternative for considering self and identity by suggesting an Eastern perspective.

In explicating his proposal, Chen examines the foundational Eastern religions and philosophies of Confucianism, Hinduism, Buddhism, and Taoism. This is followed by a more comprehensive discussion of Taoism and how it offers an alternative to the Western perspective on identity and self. Chen concludes the essay by pointing out that identity in the West focuses on the individual, but in an era of increasing multiculturalism, this attitude could facilitate misunderstanding by highlighting differences rather than bringing out similarities among people(s). Taoism, on the other hand, "advocates the importance of attending to the self and the other simultaneously by fitting in and being harmoniously interdependent with each other."

We follow these two theoretical essays with a selection that explores the concept of identity as it applies to a single co-culture. This essay, by Steven B. Pratt, Merry C. Pratt, and Lynda D. Dixon, examines an American indigenous population. Specifically, the authors are concerned with American Indians. They focus on three topics: (1) how American Indians are defined, (2) problems related to researching American Indian issues, and (3) contemporary identity issues of American Indians that help explain the role of identity in the lives of American Indians. They first bring to your attention the idea that American Indians are often asked to "prove" their ethnic heritage in one way or another, whereas, most other U.S. groups need only state their cultural identity. The authors indicate that while manifestations of identity are not an overt requirement for members of the majority culture, this often becomes an explicit part of daily life among American Indians. Furthermore, in the United States, American Indians need a federally issued Certificate of Degree of Indian Blood to prove they are Indian. Other ethnic groups, however, usually need only voice their cultural affiliation.

The essay also discusses how American Indians' traditional connection to their tribe has been eroded by modernity. This has brought about a lessening of *tribal-ness* and a movement toward increased *Indian-ness*. The authors then discuss the media's influence on the formation and transmission of the image most people hold of American Indians, pointing out that these images are often based on misinformation, characterized by stereotypes, and tend to aggregate all Indians into a single, homogeneous grouping.

Although the American Indian has been the subject of study across many academic disciplines, the authors point out that little research has been devoted to Indian communication practices. The essay also explains the difficulties related to researching this topic due to issues of discerning what constitutes cultural competency and an inability to generalize cultural traits across all American Indians. Pratt and his associates advocate an approach to studying Indian communicative behaviors that breaks away from the theories and approaches used to examine communication among European Americans.

We suggested earlier the idea that identity can take a variety of forms and is generated from a number of experiences. Two of those forms are gender and ethnicity, the focus of the next two essays in this chapter. In the first of the two, Judith Martin, in a selection titled "Understanding Whiteness in the United States," looks at the question of what it means to be a white person in the United States. We have included Martin's contribution in this special edition because the topic of whiteness as an ethnic group is often overlooked. Yet, nearly twenty years ago Martin introduced this topic to the field of intercultural communication when she made the case that whiteness is an identity category worthy of study. In her pioneering essay she provides insight into how ethnic identities—including that of a white European American—are (1) negotiated, (2) co-created, (3) reinforced, and (4) challenged through communication. By making comparisons to other co-culture and ethnic identities, Martin is able to reveal the distinctness of white ethnic identity in order to help you better understand both the notion and uniqueness of ethnic identity.

Perhaps we should call the next essay, "What's in a name?" Or even more appropriate might be, "Why so many different names?" Since this piece first appeared over thirty-five years ago, scholars, as well as laypeople, have been unable to agree on a single word or phrase to employ when speaking of the ethnic group that resides in the United States, yet has roots in Mexico and other regions of Latin America. Over the years phrases such as Chicano/a, Hispanic, Latino, and Mexican American have been proposed. One of the problems is that there is not only confusion outside of this ethnicity, but members within the group disagree over what label to use. This disagreement is at the heart of our next essay by James Steven Sauceda. The author writes, "I have come to the conclusion that most researchers have completely misunderstood the essential mechanisms of Chicano/a ethnicity." To help explain some of the misunderstanding, in "Chicano/a Ethnicity: A Concept in Search of Content," Sauceda examines many of the terms in question and proposes a solution. Although his analysis, and even his use of terms, might seem outdated by today's classifications, Sauceda does place this argument in an interesting historical context. In many ways his essay was instrumental in framing the positions that propel the discussion even today.

To begin, the author reviews some of the words and phrases we alluded to in the previous paragraph. He then moves to a discussion of how traditional definitions of these terms have contributed to the misperceptions of this co-culture and hampered progress toward self-identity. First, Sauceda believes that "the definition of Chicano/a ethnicity rests upon the psychological constructs of identification and acceptance, *not* upon any genetic, socioeconomic, historical, or demographic features." You may not share Sauceda's attitude concerning membership and identity, but the strident language of his second argument offers you a window into intercultural relations in the 1970s. Sauceda writes that membership in this co-culture is created by "racist intolerance and stereotypic classification imposed by the mainstream American society." Reading Sauceda's essay can assist you in understanding how this intolerance and stereotyping, at least in the 1970s, influenced members of this co-culture to strengthen their ethnic identity.

We conclude this chapter with a selection that asks an important question: How do sojourners maintain their identities as they travel from one culture to another... often staying for extended periods of time? The question is important on two counts. First, one of the major themes of this book is that people are moving between countries and cultures in increasingly larger numbers. Second, we stress throughout this book that being a competent intercultural communicator means being able to adjust to a variety of cultures. You probably know from personal experiences that when you travel to foreign locations circumstances can be puzzling and confusing. Your ability to interact effectively in a new cultural environment depends on your ability to adjust to what often appear to be "strange" occurrences. However, the process of adapting not only relates to your traveling to another culture, but also to how you readjust to your "home culture" once your journey is completed. In this age of abundant travel opportunities, increased numbers of business executives, students and teachers, missionaries, and government and military personnel are experiencing extended stays in places far removed from their home culture. Regardless of the length of the "visit" or the motivation behind this movement and travel, in nearly every instance the sojourner eventually returns "home." This phenomenon is so widespread that a new phrase, *cultural transients,* has been coined to describe those involved in this movement. The identity problems faced by these "transients" is the theme of the final article in this chapter, "Straddling Cultural Borders: Exploring Identity in Multiple Reacculturation," by Chuka Onwumechili, Peter O. Nwosu, and Ronald L. Jackson II.

Since the early 1950s scholars have been looking at the question of how people adjust to the problems associated with entering a new "host culture" and what happens when they return "home." Most of their findings have indicated that the adjustment pattern begins with a period of euphoria and then often advances to culture shock, recovery, and eventually adjustment. Upon returning home the person is likely to go through a similar pattern. Researchers have also been concerned with the impact of cultural identity as people experience foreign cultures. In an attempt to update the research on cultural transients, Onwumechili, Nwosu, and Jackson have added some new key variables to the challenges facing the person whose living arrangements bridge multiple cultures.

The authors believe that not all acculturation and reacculturation situations are the same. They see four types of transient activity: (a) short-term socioeconomic/political transients, (b) long-term socioeconomic/political transients, (c) short-term service/employment transients, and (d) long-term service/employment transients. In each instance the authors are concerned with the cultural effects on the transient's cultural identity. Blending the transient's identity with the processes involved with moving in and out of two or more cultures demands that the transient, regardless of amount of time in the host culture, decide on a personally comfortable contact style. The authors describe three of the most common strategies utilized by experienced transients. The first is called a *ready to sign* approach. In this instance transients decide that they are comfortable with their cultural identity and hence experience little need to adjust their personal perceptions. Second, the *quasi-completed* method of contact is often called the "middle ground." Here the transient is open to merging parts of the identity of both cultures. The third type of cultural adaptation is called the *co-created contract*, in which "cultural identity is fully open to negotiation." The importance of this final essay is not in the details involved in each of the contact methods, but rather in the realization that when you move from one culture to another you must be attentive to the fact that you will have to reaccess your identity as part of the transient experience. Onwumechili, Nwosu, and Jackson help explain that process.

Reference

Castells, M. (1997). *The power of identity*. Malden, MA: Blackwell.

Cultural Identity and Intercultural Communication

MARY JANE COLLIER

Several useful approaches that can help you understand and improve the quality of your intercultural communication encounters are included in this book. One option you have for understanding why you and others behave in particular ways and learning what you can do to increase the appropriateness and effectiveness of your communication is to view communication from the perspective of cultural identity enactment.

This article presents an approach to culture that focuses on how individuals enact or take on one or more cultural identities. Questions that are answered here include the following: (1) What is a cultural identity? (2) How are multiple cultural identities created and negotiated with others? (3) How can knowledge of the cultural identity approach help you become more competent when dealing with persons who are taking on an identity different from yours? (4) What are the benefits of such an approach to intercultural communication research, training, and practice?

CULTURE

We approach culture here in a very specific way. **Culture** is defined as a historically transmitted system of symbols, meanings, and norms (Collier & Thomas, 1988; Geertz, 1983; and Schneider, 1976). Notice the emphasis placed on the communication process in the definition. Notice also, that culture is *systemic*, meaning it comprises many complex components that are interdependent and related; they form a type of permeable boundary.

Symbols and Meanings

The components of the system are the patterned symbols such as verbal messages, nonverbal cues, emblems, and icons, as well as their interpretations or assigned meanings. Culture is what groups of people say and do and think and feel. Culture is not the people but the communication that links them. Culture is not only speaking a language and using symbols but interpreting those symbols consistently; for example, traffic lights in South Africa are called "robots" and in England elevators are called "lifts." In urban areas, gang members change the items of clothing that denote gang membership periodically so that only in-group members know who is "in" and who is "out."

Norms

Another major component of the system of culture is normative conduct. **Norms** here are patterns of appropriate ways of communicating. It is important not only to speak with symbols that are understood, or to use nonverbal gestures or modes of dress so that the cues will be understood consistently, but also to use the symbols at acceptable times, with the appropriate people, with the fitting intensity. Japanese Americans may send their children to Japanese school and speak Japanese at home, but they may speak English at work and use direct and assertive forms of communication in business or educational settings. Malay women may wear traditional Muslim dress and show respectful silence to elders in the family, but they may be assertive and use a louder tone of voice among women in social settings.

History

The cultural system of communication is historically transmitted and handed down to new members of the group. Groups with histories include corporations, support groups, national groups, or civil rights groups. History is handed down when new employees are trained, "ground rules" are explained to new members of groups such as Alcoholics Anonymous, or dominant beliefs and the value of democracy are taught to U.S. American children in school.

We learn to become members of groups by learning about past members of the group, heroes, important precepts, rituals, values, and expectations for conduct. We are taught how to follow the norms of the group. In this way we perpetuate the cultural system. When a person becomes a college professor and joins a particular academic institution, she or he is taught about the mission of the institution, past academic heroes (faculty who have won awards, published prestigious works), the importance of "publish or perish" versus the importance placed on effective instruction, the role of sports or liberal arts in the institution, commitment to multiculturalism, and so on. The symbols and norms change over the life of the system, but there is enough consistency in what is handed down to be able to define the boundaries between systems (universities) and distinguish cultural members of one system from members of another.

Types of Cultures

Many groups (though not all) form cultural systems. Examples of many types of groups have already been included. In some cases, shared history or geography provides commonality of worldview or lifestyle which helps create and reinforce a cultural system of communication.

To create a culture, groups must first define themselves as a group. This definition may be made on the basis of nationality, ethnicity, gender, profession, geography, organization, physical ability or disability, community, or type of relationship, among others. We will discuss many of these groups later.

Once the group defines itself as a unit, a cultural system may develop. For instance, U.S. Americans define themselves as a group based on use of English as a shared code; reinforcement of democracy through political discussion and action; individual rights and freedoms of speech, press, religion, and assembly being explicitly described in the Bill of Rights and enforced in the courts; and so forth. Attorneys or sales clerks or homemakers may be linked by similarities in daily activities and standard of living. Friends may see their group as including persons who like the same activities and support one another.

National and Ethnic Cultures. To better understand the many different types of cultures, we can categorize them from the more general and more common, to those that are more specific. National and ethnic cultures are fairly general. These kinds of groups base membership on heritage and history that has been handed down among several generations. Their history is based on traditions, rituals, codes of language, and norms.

Persons who share the same nationality were born in a particular country and spent a significant number of years and a period of socialization in that country. Such socialization promotes and reinforces particular values, beliefs, and norms. Because many people contribute to the creation of a national culture's symbols, meanings, and norms, "national culture" is fairly abstract, so predictions about language use and what symbols mean can only be generalized. Japanese national culture, for instance, has been described as collectivistic, high context, high on power distance, and other-face oriented (Gudykunst & Ting-Toomey, 1988). Yet, not all Japanese people follow these norms in every situation. But when comparing Japanese to Germans, the Japanese, as a group, are more group oriented and emphasize status hierarchies more than the Germans as an overall group (Hofstede, 1980).

Ethnicity. Ethnicity is a bit different—ethnic groups share a sense of heritage and history, and origin from an area outside of or preceding the creation of their present nation-state of residence (Banks, 1984). Ethnic groups, in most but not all cases, share racial characteristics and many have a specific history of having experienced discrimination. In the United States, ethnic group members include African Americans, Asian Americans (Japanese Americans, Chinese Americans, Vietnamese Americans, Korean Americans, and so on), Mexican Americans, Polish Americans, Irish Americans, Native American Indians, and Jewish Americans, just to name a few examples.

Remember that national and ethnic cultures are the *communication systems* that are created by persons who share the same nationality or ethnicity. From this perspective, culture is the process of creating a perceived commonality and community of thought and action. Culture is based on what people say and do and think and feel *as a result* of their common history and origins.

Gender. Many subcategories of gender cultures exist. Groups create, reinforce, and teach what is interpreted as feminine or masculine. Groups also reinforce what is appropriate or inappropriate for a good husband, wife, feminist, chauvinist, heterosexual, gay, or lesbian. Mothers and fathers, religious leaders, teachers, and the media all provide information about how to be a member of a particular gender culture.

Profession. Politicians, physicians, field workers, sales personnel, maintenance crews, bankers, and consultants share common ways of spending time, earning money, communicating with others, and learning norms about how to be a member of their profession. Health care professionals probably share a commitment to health, to helping others, and to improving others' quality of life. They also share educational background, knowledge about their aspect of health care, and standards of practicing their profession.

Geographical Area. Geographical area sometimes acts as a boundary, contributing to the formation of a cultural group. In South Africa the area surrounding Cape Town has its own version of spoken Afrikaans, has a higher population of Coloreds (those of mixed race), and is viewed by many as the most cosmopolitan area in South Africa. The South in the United States has its own traditions, historical orientation, and southern drawl. Rural communities sometimes differ from urban communities in political views, values, life styles, and norms.

Organization. Large corporations such as IBM, Nike, or Xerox create the most common type of organizational culture. In this culture members are taught the corporate symbols, myths, heroes, and legends, and what it means to be an employee. The proper chain of command, procedures and policies, and schedules are also taught. Finally, they learn the norms in the corporation—who to talk to, about what, at which particular moment. Some corporations value "team players" while others value "individual initiative." Some corporations have mottos like "Never say no to an assignment" or "never be afraid to speak up if you don't have what you need."

Support groups have their own version of organizational culture. Alcoholics Anonymous, Overeaters Anonymous, and therapy and support groups, among others, form their own sets of symbols, interpretations, and norms. "Let go and let God" is an important requirement in the Anonymous groups; relinquishing individual control to a higher power is a tool in managing one's addictions. Social living groups, such as sororities and fraternities, international dormitories, and the like, often create their own cultures as well.

Physical Ability or Disability. Groups form a culture based upon shared physical ability or disability. Professional athletic teams teach rookies how to behave and what to do to be an accepted member of the team. Persons who have physical handicaps share critical life experiences and groups teach them how to accept and overcome their disability, as well as how to communicate more effectively with those who do not have the disability (Braithwaite, 1991).

CULTURAL IDENTIFICATION AS A PROCESS

Each individual, then, has a range of cultures to which she or he belongs in a constantly changing environment. Everyone may concurrently or simultaneously participate in several different cultural systems each day, week, and year. All cultures that are created are influenced by a host of social, psychological, and environmental factors as well as institutions and context.

Consider African Americans in the United States. In the last 40 years, myriad factors have all affected what it means to be an African American in the United States including: civil rights marches, leaders such as Martin Luther King, Jr., affirmative action, racism, the resurgence of the Ku Klux Klan, television shows such as "*Roots*" and "*Cosby*," films by Spike Lee, Anita Hill's testimony in the hearing of Supreme Court nominee Clarence Thomas, and the riots among African Americans and Hispanics in South Central Los Angeles following the Rodney King verdict.

Cultures are affected not only by changing socioeconomic and environmental conditions, but by other cultures as well. A person who is a member of a support group for single mothers in her community is influenced by other cultural groups such as feminists, conservative religious groups, or the Republican party members who made family values and two-parent families an important issue in the 1992 presidential campaign. The important questions from a cultural identity approach may be things like, "What does it mean to be a single mother who is Euro-American, Catholic, out of work, and living in a large city in the Midwest? How does that identity come to be and how is it communicated to others? How does it change across different contexts and relationships?"

CULTURAL IDENTITY

Diverse groups can create a cultural system of symbols used, meanings assigned to the symbols, and ideas of what is considered appropriate and inappropriate. When the groups also have a history and begin to hand down the symbols and norms to new members, then the groups take on a *cultural identity*. **Cultural identity** is the particular character of the group communication system that emerges in the particular situation.

A Communication Perspective

Cultural identities are negotiated, co-created, reinforced, and challenged through communication; therefore we approach identity from a communication perspective. *Social psychological perspectives* view identity as a characteristic of the person and personality, and self as centered in social roles and social practices. A *communication perspective* views identity as something that emerges when messages are exchanged between persons. Thus, identity is defined as an enactment of cultural communication (Hecht, Collier, & Ribeau, 1993). Identities are *emergent;* they come to be in communication contexts. Since you are being asked to emphasize a communication perspective, what you study and try to describe and explain are identity patterns as they occur among persons in contact with one another. Although we have noted that such factors as media, literature, and art influence identity, our focus is directed at the interaction between people. Identities are co-created in relationship to others. Who we are and how we are differs and emerges depending upon who we are with, the cultural identities that are important to us and others, the context, the topic of conversation, and our interpretations and attributions.

Properties of Cultural Identity

As students and researchers in intercultural communication, we can apply our knowledge about how cultural identities are enacted and developed in order to explain and improve our understanding of others' conduct. We outline the properties or characteristics of cultural identities and then compare the properties across different cultural groups. These comparisons ultimately help us build theories of cultural and intercultural identity communication.

The first property we outlined is self-perception; this addresses both avowal by the individual and ascription by others. Second, we note modes of expressing identity. Identities are expressed through core symbols, labels, and norms. The third property focuses on the scope of the identity, and whether the identity takes an individual, a relational, or a communal form. A fourth property examines the enduring, yet dynamic, quality of cultural identity. Fifth, affective, cognitive, and behavioral components of identity provide us with a means of contrasting what groups think, feel, say, and do. Sixth, we describe the content and relationship levels of interpretation in messages revealing cultural identity. Content and relationship interpretations allow us to understand when power and control issues contribute to conflict or when friendships and trust can be developed. Seventh, salience and variations in intensities characterize useful identity in new or unusual settings. Being the one who stands out in an otherwise homogeneous group causes us to be conscious of and perhaps alter the intensity with which we claim our identity.

Avowal and Ascription Processes. Each individual may enact various cultural identities over the course of a lifetime as well as over the course of a day. Identities are enacted in interpersonal contexts through avowal and ascription processes. **Avowal** is about the self an individual portrays, analogous to the face or image she or he shows to others. Avowal is the individual saying, "This is who I am."

Ascription is the process by which others attribute identities to an individual. Stereotypes and attributions communicated are examples of ascriptions. In part, identity is shaped by others' communicated views of us. For example, a black Zulu female's cultural identities in South Africa are not only shaped by her definition and image of what it means to be a black Zulu female but also by the white Afrikaners for whom she works, her Zulu family and relatives, the township in which she lives in poverty, her white teachers who speak Afrikaans and English, and so forth.

Another way of thinking about this is to say that cultural identities have both subjective and ascribed meanings. In Japan, a philosophy and practice known as *amae* is common. **Amae** signifies an other-orientation or group-orientation, and a sense of obligation to the group. An individual is expected to sacrifice individual needs and give to others; others are expected to reciprocate, thereby maintaining the harmony and cohesiveness of the group (Doi, 1989; Goldman, 1992).

Amae represents the interdependence of subjective and ascribed meanings in relationships. The meanings may not be shared across cultural groups, however. To many Japanese, such a complex, long-term, obligatory relationship with members of in-groups is a functional and revered system of relational maintenance. To U.S. Americans, such rules and obligations to others may appear to be unnecessary, threaten individuality and choice, and therefore be unacceptable.

Information about avowal and ascription can be useful in understanding the role others play in developing your own cultural identities. If a particular group has low self-esteem or a high need for status, those aspects of identity may be influenced by the stereotypes or conceptions held and communicated by other groups.

Modes of Expression: Core Symbols, Labels, and Norms.

Cultural identities are expressed in core symbols, labels, and norms. **Core symbols** tell us about the definitions, premises, and propositions regarding the universe and the place of humans in the universe that are held by members of the cultural group. They are expressions of cultural beliefs about the management of nature and technology and such institutions as marriage, education, and politics. The symbols point us to the central ideas and concepts and the everyday behaviors that characterize membership in that cultural group.

Sometimes these core symbols can be summarized into a set of fundamental beliefs; sometimes a particular mode of dress, gesture, or phrase captures the essence of a cultural identity. Carbaugh (1989) analyzed transcripts of the popular television talk show, "Donahue." After doing a content analysis of the comments made by audience members, he proposed *self-expression* as a core symbol of mainstream U.S. identity.

Authenticity, powerlessness, and expressiveness were identified as three core symbols among African Americans (Hecht, Ribeau, & Alberts, 1989; Hecht, Larkey, Johnson, & Reinard, 1991). These core symbols were posited after African Americans were asked to describe recent satisfying and dissatisfying conversations with other African Americans and with Euro-Americans, and to describe strategies for conversational improvement. African Americans talked about the need for persons to be authentic, honest, and real, described the negative impact of feeling powerless, and outlined a need to be expressive in their conduct.

Labels are a category of core symbols. The same label may vary widely in its interpretation. The term *American* is perceived as acceptable and common by many residents of the United States and as ethnocentric and self-centered by residents of Central America and Canada, and is associated with a group that is privileged, wealthy, and powerful by some countries that are not industrialized. *Hispanic* is a general term many social scientists use to describe "persons of Mexican, Puerto Rican, Cuban, Central or South American, or other Spanish culture of origin, regardless of race" (Marin & Marin, 1991, p. 23). Persons may choose to describe their own ethnicity with a much more specific label such as *Mexican American* or *Chicano* or *Chicana*. Chicano and Chicana individuals may have their own ideas about what it means to be a member of that culture. Whether the label was created by members of the group or members of another group provides useful information about what the label means and how it is interpreted.

Cultural groups create and reinforce standards for "performing the culture" appropriately and effectively. **Norms** for conduct are based upon core symbols and *how they are interpreted*. Defining who you are tells you what you should be doing. Norms of appropriate and acceptable behavior, moral standards, and expectations for conduct, and criteria to decide to what degree another is behaving in a competent manner form the prescriptive or evaluative aspect of cultural identity.

An individual is successful at enacting identity when one is accepted as a competent member of the group. Immigrants, for example, are judged to be competent and accepted by members of the U.S. American culture when they speak English, use appropriate greetings, demonstrate respect for the individual rights of their neighbors to privacy, and so forth.

Attention to the property of shared norms gives us the ability to determine what is appropriate from the point of view of the group members. Comparing norms of conduct across groups and identifying norms in intercultural conversations is helpful in figuring out how to improve our own individual effectiveness as a communicator. Finally, identification of norms in this way provides valid information for trainers, teachers, and practitioners as they develop their training programs.

Individual, Relational, and Communal Forms of Identity. Identities have individual, relational, and communal properties. As researchers of culture, we can study culture from the point of view of individuals. Each person has individual interpretations of what it means to be U.S. American or Austrian or Indian, and each person enacts his or her cultural identities slightly differently. If we want to understand why an individual behaves in a particular way, we can ask him or her to talk about that cultural identity and experience as a group member.

When we study culture from a relational point of view we observe the interaction between people, friends, coworkers, or family members, who identify themselves as members of the same or different groups. Then we can identify the themes in their talk such as trust or power.

Collier (1989) found that Mexican American friends emphasized the importance of their relationship by meeting frequently and spending a significant portion of time together. They also described the most important characteristics of friendship as support, trust, intimacy, and commitment to the relationship. In contrast, when Mexican Americans and Anglo-Americans talked about their friendships with one another, they described common activities, goals, and respect for family.

When we study culture in terms of its communal properties, we observe the public communication

contexts and activities in communities and neighborhoods that establish cultural identity. Rituals, rites of passage, and holiday celebrations are other sources of information about how persons use cultural membership to establish community with one another.

Enduring and Changing Property of Identity. Cultural identities are both enduring and changing. As already mentioned, cultures have a history that is transmitted to new members over time. Cultural identities change because of economic, political, social, psychological, and contextual factors, not to mention the influence of other cultural identities. Enacting the cultural identity of being gay or lesbian in the 2000s has certain things in common with being gay in the 1990s and 1980s. Individuals who "come out of the closet" encounter similar stereotypes and ascriptions to those in earlier centuries. However, the political climate in some areas of the country in which ballot initiatives were proposed to limit the rights of gays or link gays with other groups such as sadomasochists, affect the cultural identity of the group. Sometimes context changes how one manifests identity and how intensely one avows an identity. Announcing your affiliation and pride as a member of the Right to Life, anti-abortion coalition, at a rally of pro-abortion supporters is different from attending a Right to Life meeting and avowing your identity in that context.

Affective, Cognitive, and Behavioral Components of Identity. Identities have affective, cognitive, and behavioral components. Persons have emotions and feelings attached to identities. Such emotions change depending upon the situation. Sometimes, a particularly strong or violent avowal of an identity is a signal of the importance of that identity and the degree to which it is perceived to be threatened. Perhaps this knowledge can help us interpret why rioting occurred in South Central Los Angeles after the Rodney King verdict. The cognitive component of identity relates to the beliefs we have about that identity. Persons hold a range of beliefs about each culture group to which they belong, but certain similarities in beliefs become evident when you ask people to talk about what it means to be U.S. American or Thai or a member of Earth First!, an environmentalist group. Members of Earth First! share beliefs in the value of ancient forests, distrust of executives who run the logging companies, politicians who support the lumber industry, and the view that spiking trees and sabotaging logging equipment is sometimes necessary as a form of protest. Such beliefs can be summarized into a core symbol, here the name of the organization, *Earth First!*

The behavioral component of cultural identity focuses on the verbal and nonverbal actions taken by group members. We come to be members of a group through our actions with one another and our reactions to one another. These verbal and nonverbal actions can be studied, and patterns described. The dimensions of cultural variability described by Hofstede (1980) such as collectivism and individualism are patterns of communicative conduct evident when particular cultural identities are enacted. Comparing what groups say and do allows us as researchers to begin to understand why some groups experience frequent misunderstandings or conflict.

Content and Relationship. Identities comprise both content and relationship levels of interpretation. When persons communicate with each other, messages carry information as well as implications for who is in control, how close the conversational partners feel to each other or conversely how hostile they feel toward each other, how much they trust each other, or the degree of inclusion or exclusion they feel.

Sometimes persons use their in-group language to reinforce their in-group status and establish distance from the out-group (Giles, Coupland, & Coupland, 1991). At other times they may use the language of the out-group in order to adapt and align with the out-group. Mexican Americans may speak Spanish when in neighborhood communities to preserve their history and roots and to reinforce their identification and bond as a people. The same persons may speak English at school or at work because the supervisor and executives of the company demand it.

Salience and Intensity Differences. Identities differ in their salience in particular contexts, and identities are enacted with different intensities at different times. The intensities provide markers of strong involvement, and investment in the identity. As a white U.S. American female professor visiting South Africa there were times in which I was most aware of being a white minority among the black majority, times when I was aware of being a U.S. American who was stereotyped somewhat negatively, and times when I was most aware of being a college professor. But, when I learned that female employees in South Africa do not receive maternity leave and receive a lower housing allowance than males, my feminist identity became more salient, causing me to adopt a stronger tone and assert my views about equal pay for equal work in a more direct manner when talking with male executives in corporations.

CULTURAL IDENTITY AND COMMUNICATION COMPETENCE

Using cultural identity as an approach can help us better analyze others' conduct and decide how to do what is mutually competent. Spitzberg and Cupach (1984) point out that communication competence requires motivation and knowledge, as well as skills to demonstrate what behavior is appropriate and effective.

Cultural competence is the demonstrated ability to enact a cultural identity in a mutually appropriate and effective manner. Intercultural competence becomes a bit more complex. **Intercultural competence** is the reinforcement of culturally different identities that are salient in the particular situation. Intercultural competence occurs when the avowed identity matches the identity ascribed. For example, if you avow the identity of an assertive, outspoken U.S. American and your conversational partner avows himself or herself to be a respectful, nonassertive Vietnamese, then each must ascribe the corresponding identity to the conversational partner. You must jointly negotiate what kind of relationship will be mutually satisfying. Some degree of adjustment and accommodation is usually necessary.

A common problem in intercultural communication occurs when persons who describe themselves as the same nationality or ethnicity do not share ideas about how to enact their identity and disagree about the norms for interaction. Chicanos in the United States may differ from second- and third-generation Mexican Americans about the need to speak Spanish or call attention to their heritage. Nonetheless, understanding the identity being avowed and ascribed and noting the intensity with which the identity is avowed, enables us to understand why a particular cultural identity emerges salient in particular situations and therefore what contextual, social, or psychological factors are operating in the situation.

Some benefits of the cultural identity approach in intercultural communication situations include the following: We can acknowledge that all individuals have many potential cultural identities which may emerge in a particular situation. Remembering that identities change from situation to situation can be helpful in overcoming the tendency to treat others as stereotypical representatives of a particular group. Asking for information about what is appropriate for their cultural identity is an effective tool in becoming interculturally competent. Explaining what your own cultural identity norms are and why you behaved in a particular way can also be a useful way to increase the other person's understanding and can help develop relational trust.

Researchers, trainers, and practitioners can utilize the cultural identity approach to identify similarities and differences in behaviors, in interpretations, or in norms. It is possible to begin to explain why group members behave as they do or feel as they do in their conduct with others from the same and different groups. Trainers and teachers can compare group symbols, interpretations, and norms as well as teach others to develop analytical skills to use in their own situations

Cultural identity as an approach to the study of culture and intercultural communication is only one of many approaches. Ongoing research, critique, and application will test the merit of the approach. Hopefully, the approach has sparked the beginning of a dialogue that will continue throughout all of our lifetimes.

References

Banks, J. (1984). *Teaching Strategies for Ethnic Studies* (3d ed.) Boston: Allyn & Bacon.

Braithwaite, D. (1991). "Just how much did that wheelchair cost?": Management of privacy boundaries by persons with disabilities. *Western Journal of Speech Communication,* 55, 254–274.

Carbaugh, D. (1989). *Talking American: Cultural Discourses on Donahue.* Norwood, NJ: Ablex.

Collier, M. J. (1989). Cultural and intercultural communication competence: current approaches and directions for future research. *International Journal of Intercultural Relations,* 13, 287–302.

Collier, M. J., & Thomas, M. (1988). "Cultural Identity: An Interpretive Perspective." In Y. Y. Kim and W. Gudykunst (Eds.), *Theories in Intercultural Communication,* 99–122. Newbury Park, CA: Sage.

Doi, T. (1989). *The Anatomy of Dependence.* Tokyo: Kodansha Publishers.

Geertz, C. (1983). *Local Knowledge.* New York: Basic Books.

Giles, H., Coupland, N., & Coupland, J. (1991). "Accommodation Theory: Communication, Contexts and Consequences." In J. Giles, N. Coupland, & J. Coupland (Eds.), *Contexts of Accommodation: Developments in Applied Sociolinguistics.* Cambridge: Cambridge University Press.

Goldman, A. (1992). The Centrality of "Ningensei" to Japanese Negotiating and Interpersonal Relationships: Implications for U.S.-Japanese Communication. Paper presented at Speech Communication Association Conference, Chicago, Illinois.

Gudykunst, W., & Ting-Toomey, S. (1988). *Culture and Interpersonal Communication.* Newbury Park, CA: Sage.

Hecht, M., Collier, M. J., & Ribeau, S. (1993). *African-American Communication.* Newbury Park, CA: Sage.

Hecht, M., Larkey, L. K., Johnson, J. N., & Reinard, J. C. (1991). A Model of Interethnic Effectiveness. Paper presented at the International Communication Association Conference, Chicago, Illinois.

Hecht, M., Ribeau, S., & Alberts, J. K. (1989). An Afro-American perspective on interethnic communication. *Communication Monographs,* 56, 385–410.

Hofstede, G. (1980). *Culture's Consequences.* Newbury Park, CA: Sage.

Marin, G., & Marin, B. V. (1991). *Research with Hispanic Populations.* Newbury Park, CA: Sage.

Schneider, D. (1976). "Notes Toward a Theory of Culture." In K. Basso & H. Selby (Eds.), *Meaning in Anthropology.* Albuquerque: University of New Mexico Press.

Spitzberg, B. H., & Cupach, W. R. (1984). *Interpersonal Communication Competence.* Newbury Park, CA: Sage.

Concepts and Questions

1. How does viewing intercultural communication from a cultural identity perspective increase your competence as a communicator?
2. In what ways may the adherence to cultural norms vary depending upon one's immediate cultural identity?
3. Collier discusses types of cultures. Using her discussion as a basis for consideration, list the names of various

cultural groups with which you identify. Do you find conflict between any of these identities?

4. How is cultural identity formed?
5. How does ascription contribute to the formation of cultural identity?
6. What are core symbols and how do they contribute to the formation of cultural identity? List several core symbols that relate to your cultural identity.
7. What does Collier mean when she asserts that cultural identities are both enduring and changing?
8. How does cultural identity relate to communication competence?
9. What are some of the benefits of using the cultural identity approach to intercultural communication situations?

An Alternative View of Identity

Guo-Ming Chen

The impact of globalization has led scholars from different disciplines to study the concept of identity from various aspects and encourage people to find, maintain, and negotiate their identity. Unfortunately, abundant research seems to further mystify the concept. Worse, the aggressive advocate of the importance of establishing, authenticating, maintaining, or negotiating one's own or group identity may motivate people to tightly hold their own ego. Like a cocoon, the problem has a tendency to weave a stronghold preventing a person from penetrating the identity of others. Facing this dilemma, this essay attempts to first offer a critical overview of this line of research, and then to propose a different view on the nature of the self and identity from an Asian perspective.

AN OVERVIEW OF IDENTITY RESEARCH

Disciplines of Anthropology, Psychology, and Sociology

Identity has become a significant concept among social science scholars since the 1960s. Identity theory and social identity theory represent the two main perspectives in this line of research. As Hogg, Terry, and White (1995) indicated, identity theory, which was originated in sociology, "deals with the structure and function of people's identity as related to the behavioral roles they play in society"; and social identity theory, which was originated in psychology, "deals

This essay first appeared in the thirteenth edition of this book. All rights reserved. Permission to reprint must be obtained from the author and the publisher. An earlier version of this essay first appeared in *China Media Research*, 5(4), 2009, pp. 109–118. Guo-Ming Chen is Professor in the Department of Communication Studies at the University of Rhode Island, Kingston, Rhode Island.

with the structure and function of identity as related to people's membership in groups" (p. 265).

Identity theory mainly views the social nature of self from the role positions a person occupies, and the role identities vary with respect to their salience (e.g., Stets, 1995; Stryker, 1987). The theory treats society as a differentiated but organized system rather than as an undifferentiated whole, thus the self is a multifaceted and organized social construct emerging from one's roles in society, and the variation in self concepts depends on the diverse role identities. It is the self-defining role identities that provide meaning for self, though meanings acquired by role identities are originated from social interaction.

Social identity theory was rooted in Tajfel's (1963) studies on social and cultural factors in perception, cognition, and beliefs. The theory concentrates on subjects of social self, group processes, and intergroup relations. It stipulates that the social category with which a person identifies defines who the person is (Hogg, 2003). Social identity theory was integrated with self-categorization theory developed in the 1980s (Turner, 1985), which indicates that one's social identity is dictated by how the self and others are categorized into an in-group or an out-group. As a theory of social group, social identity theory does not construct group process from an interpersonal perspective, but is closely intertwined with intergroup relations. It incorporates role identities in group context and opens up studies on a range of group behaviors, such as conformity, discrimination, ethnocentrism, stereotyping, and prejudice (e.g., Hogg, 2006).

Although some scholars believed that it is not possible to reconcile the differences of the two theories, more and more scholars felt the need to establish a general theory that can integrate the two theories to avoid the redundancies of studies on the different aspects of the self and identity. For example, Stets and Burke (2000) argued that the differences between identity theory and social identity theory have more to do with emphasis rather than with kind, thus the two theories can be linked to establish a more complete picture of understanding the self, which in turn will lead to a stronger social psychology.

Stets and Burke further pointed out that an integrated theory needs to consider not only the role and the group, but also the person, as the basis of identity, because the person can provide stability across groups, situations, and roles. According to Stets (1995), personal identities represent a set of meanings that make the self an individual. These meanings may overlap the meanings of role identities, because different identities are from different sources. In addition, some aspects of social identities may be based on personal feelings and values, thus personal identities can become part of social identities characteristics (Deaux, 1992). Hence, role identities and social identities are always closely related to personal identities.

The study of identity in psychology and sociology is even more entangled if we look at it from traditional approaches. As Cote and Levine (2002) pointed out, identity formation and identity maintenance are the two major traditions in the study of self and identity in psychology. The two traditions were founded on Erikson's (1968) works on the three concepts of ego identity, personal identity, and social identity. These concepts represent the three forms of continuity, which include the sense of identification of the self with itself, the relationship between the self and the other, and the integration between the self and the other.

Research on identity formation was further elaborated by Marcia's (1966, 1993) identity status paradigm. Research on identity maintenance or self-psychology, which stemmed from the works of Colley (1902), James (1948), and Mead (1934), was further developed by Gergen (1991) from a postmodern perspective. Gergen identified the romantic, modern, and postmodern as the three periods scholars in the West used to study the self. Unfortunately, the progress of the research on the self and identity from the psychological perspective continues to suffer from [two] problems... being unable to fully appreciate Erikson's classification of the three different identities (i.e., ego, personal, and social) and to adequately theorize the concept of "social" (Cote & Levine, 2002).

Sociological approaches to the study of identity, according to Weigert, Teitge, and Teitge (2007), were also inspired by Erikson's early works on identity. Five distinct sociological traditions were developed: (1) the Chicago School of symbolic interactionism focuses on the emergent and procedural nature of social reality (e.g., Blumer, 1969; Goffman, 1959; Hewitt, 2006;

Strauss, 1959); (2) the Iowa School of symbolic interactionism emphasizes the structural and fixed nature of social reality (e.g., Kuhn & McPartland, 1954; Stryker, 1968; Tajfel, 1981); (3) the sociology of interpretive knowledge emphasizes that the social reality embedded in cultural and historical circumstances directly influences the well-being and survival of human beings (e.g., Berger & Luckmann, 1966); (4) the structural–functionalist perspective stipulates that social order and continuity are maintained by the interdependent subsystems of the society, thus social identity is embedded in the society's institutional structure (e.g., Durkeim, 1964; Parsons, 1968); and (5) the critical theory of identity indicates that identity is grounded in the relationship between individual and social development; the interactive–communicative, the cognitive–affective, and the social–structural represent the three levels of analysis in the study of identity (e.g., Habermas, 1974).

The sociological tradition demonstrates its theoretical richness in the study of identity. However, this theoretical richness also reflects the lack of empirical association in many of its theoretical claims (Cote & Levine, 2002). This lack of empirical evidence inevitably leads to difficulty in reaching a consensus among scholars in the study of identity. In order to better understand the process of identity formation and maintenance, Cote and Levine (2002) also advocated for the convergence between psychological and sociological approaches to the study of the self and identity, especially through the examination of the relevance of "structure" and "agency" and the extent of "inner" versus "outer" origin when conceptualizing identity.

In the discipline of anthropology, identity is embedded in the concept of culture and other dimensions such as boundary, space, place, authenticity, and ethnicity (e.g., Barth, 1969a; Cohen, 1985). According to Cohen (2000), the formation, expression, management, and stability of collective identities are discriminated based on the cultural boundary. Cultural differences usually create a boundary that distinguishes people on both sides not only by degree, but also by kind. Thus, identity within the boundary is construed as being authentic and absolute by people in the group.

The authenticity of the social or cultural identity can be enhanced by the presence of the other.

However, the identity may be contingent and fluid through the cross-boundary interaction. In other words, what seems peripheral to the center of a culture may not be noticed across the boundary line and therefore becomes the center in the peripheral area. Hence, the ascription of a group or cultural identity is possibly subjected to the cross-boundary struggle for control. This indicates the cross-boundary interaction may challenge the collective identity within the group itself.

Identity is therefore encapsulated by the boundary which marks the beginning and the end of a group or community. The cultural experience of the group is a bounded symbolic whole covering with a range of meanings for the development of norms and values that in turn provide a collective sense of identity (Cohen, 1985). The sustainment and maintenance of a coherent collective identity must occur through time, such as a collective memory and lived and shared traditions, and space, such as a mapping of territory and the principle of inclusion and exclusion (Morley, 1995).

Barth (1969b) further pointed out that ethnic boundaries exist despite the interaction of people between two different communities. Geographic and social isolation are not the critical factors in sustaining cultural differences, though the bounded ethnic group and the management of ethnic identity are influenced by the presence of significant others and subject to the on-going negotiations of boundaries between groups of people. Moreover, Barth (2000) argued that boundaries provide a template in which distinct categories of the mind are separated. When dealing and interacting with boundary relations, it is important to understand members' experiences and cognitive categories. Therefore, ethnic identities are interdependent. They are the product of a continuous process of ascribing and self-ascribing and are maintained through a relational process of inclusion and exclusion.

In the study of identity, the emphasis on the concept of culture diverts anthropologists' attention from the aspect of self and individual (Sokefeld, 1999). It is ironic that, given the importance of the concept of culture in anthropology, scholars are unable to give a more focused view on the cultural perception of the self or person and how it affects the emergence of identity. Furthermore, many questions regarding the study of identity from anthropology are still left unanswered. For example, if identity is fluid and changes over time and is reshaped by interactions with members of different ethnic groups, could we say that a group really possesses an identity and this chameleon-like identity can be considered as being authentic (Cohen, 2000)?

The Discipline of Communication Studies

The study of identity in communication is mainly conducted from the intercultural communication perspective, which extends the line of research from the traditions of Tajfel's social identity and Barth's ethnic identity. Intercultural communication scholars agree that identity is socially constructed, interactive, negotiated, relational, multifaceted, and space claimed (e.g., Collier, 1997; Jackson, 2002). They investigate how identity is constructed through and affects interaction, and how it is influenced by dominance and power from the aspects of intergroup approach, cultural approach, critical cultural approach, and postcolonial approach (Shin & Jackson, 2003).

The intergroup approach applies social identity theories to explain the role social identity plays in the process of inter-ethnic communication from the perspectives of uncertainty reduction and ethnolinguistics (e.g., Giles & Johnson, 1987; Gudykunst & Lim, 1986; Kim, 1986). The cultural approach treats communication competence as a culturally and ethnically specific variable. Identity in this approach is considered a cultural product and is formed through culture embedded in group members' interaction. Thus ethnic or cultural identity, as the feeling of belonging to an ethnic culture, is defined by competently using the cultural symbols and affirming the beliefs, norms, and values in that specific cultural context (e.g., Carbaugh, 1996; Philipsen, 1975).

The critical cultural approach is grounded in the sociological perspective of critical theory and expanded on by Hall (1990) through his studies on media presentation of race, identity, culture, and ethnicity. This approach views identity as an ideological construct and representation of a power structure, which mirrors the political inequality and oppression toward class, gender, and race (hooks, 1984, 1992; van Dijk, 1991). Employing the critical cultural approach, intercultural communication scholars have tried to deconstruct the discursive formation of identity and to demystify the structural oppression of marginal groups in the United States (e.g., V. Chen, 1997; Mendoza, 2002). The approach was also extended to study the ethnic identity of Asian–Indian immigrants (Hedge, 1998), gender identity (e.g., Houston, 1992), and the dominance of whiteness (e.g., Nakayama & Martin, 1999). The challenge of Eurocentrism from Afrocentric and Asiacentric paradigms as well is embedded in this approach (e.g., Asante, 1980; Chen, 2006; Chen & Miike, 2006; Dissanayake, 1988; Gunaratne, 1991; Miike, 2003).

Finally, the postcolonial approach can be treated as an extension of the critical cultural approach. As an alternative to the Eurocentric or white-centric perspective, the approach is based on the works of Bhabha (1983) and Spivaak (1986). The basic assumption of the self and identity is that, "the *other* identity is imposed and inscribed by power structures (or colonizers) in a hegemonic way that needs to be *de*-scribed toward reconstruction of a self" (Shin & Jackson, 2003, p. 224). This postcolonial approach argues that the forgotten or erased true self should be recovered through cultural discourse. The cultural differences of class, culture, gender, race, and skin color can be recognized and deconstructed through the process of rejecting the other. The formation of cultural identity is then based on an authentic, unique and indigenous self, where a cultural space is claimed and the collective selfhood can be interplayed with in-group and out-group elements.

The integration of research from various disciplines gives communication scholars an advantage in perceiving the identity from interactive and relational aspects and seeing the tension between the self and the other. However, the cross-cultural advantage did not give communication scholars advantages in conceiving the foundation of identity, i.e., the self, from an angle that is different from traditional social sciences. In other words, the concept of the self or identity is still confined or dominated by . . . Western thinking and practice. In order to remedy this problem, the following section provides an alternative view on the study of the self and identity.

AN ALTERNATIVE VIEW OF THE SELF AND IDENTITY

As Geertz (1979) indicated, individual identity is established in Western culture as a dynamic center of awareness, emotion, and action. As a unique and bound universe, the self has a clear sense of direction, purpose, and volition, and through the realization of the true self, identity is established. The self from the Western perspective is characterized as autonomous and egocentric; it is then important to attend to the self, to assert the self, and to emphasize one's difference from others (Markus & Kitayama, 1991). This Western individualistic self is treated as the center of the universe through which the world is perceived; thus to develop a sense of personal control becomes essential for building and holding the centrality and sovereignty of the self.

The Western conceptualization of the self and identity has been facing challenges from cross-cultural studies, feminism, social constructivism, systems theory, critical theory, and deconstructionism (Sampson, 1989). The cross-cultural research has provided alternative views on self and identity from different cultural traditions. Feminists propose distinct views of person through the reconceptualization of the patriarchal way of perceiving human life. The social constructionists assert that the self and identity are socially and historically constructed rather than occurring naturally. Systems theory sees the self and identity as being relational rather than independent entities. The critical theory argues that self and identity are created for ideological purposes. Lastly, deconstructionists challenge the centrality and sovereignty of the self and its relationship with the society. These views of the study of self and identity open up a venue for exploring the subject from different points of view. This section provides a different view from Asian cultural traditions by focusing on the Taoist perspective.

Buddhism, Confucianism, Hinduism, and Taoism form the foundation of Asian philosophical and religious thoughts, and each of the four traditions provides a specific view on the self and identity. As the dominant paradigm of social life in Far Eastern areas, Confucianism postulates an ethic guideline based on *wu lun* (the Five Codes of Ethics), which governs the five basic human relationships of ruler and subject, father and son, husband and wife, older brother and younger brother, and between friends. The structure of these relationships is particularistic, hierarchical, reciprocal, interrelated, formal, and in-group/out-group distinct (Chen & Chung, 1994).

The self is demonstrated through the role one plays in this relationship network. Ho (1995) indicated that the Confucian self is a relational self, which emerges only in the social presence of others. The Confucian identity is then a relational identity defined by one's social relationships. The self in Confucianism is a subdued self. The ultimate goal of life is to realize the self through self-cultivation in a harmonious relationship. This relation-centered perception of the self dictates that the meaning of a person's life can only be completed in the presence of the other. The absence of another's presence will lead to the loss of one's identity.

Hinduism considers the self an illusion originated from ignorance; thus an individual identity has no way to exist. If there is a true self, it will be identical with the ultimate Brahman. To Hinduism, the realization of the true self, or Atman, means the total loss of individual identity or a surrender of the self to the absolute, ineffable, and ubiquitous Brahman (Ho, 1995).

Similar to Hinduism's deconstruction of the ego, Buddhism holds a view of non-duality on the distinction of the subject and the object and the self-other demarcation must be negated. The Buddhist further claims that the realization of self cannot be sought, because the self does not exist. The non-self view denies the very existence of the self and therefore the individual identity. The universe is in constant flux; there can be no permanent entity. In other words, the Buddhist thought of *anicca* (impermanence) dictates that everything that comes into existence will also cease to exist at a certain point in time. The temporary existence of things is subject to the law of *paticcasamupada* (causes and conditions): when the causes change, so the things will change too. Although these causes come together and dependently originate or conditionally co-produce (*paticcasamupada*) the transient existence, the interrelatedness causes all things. This leads Buddhism to advocate that people should liberate themselves through meditation to reach the state of nirvana, in which there is the total detachment from or no more transmigration of the impermanent self or identity (Watts, 1957).

Taoist View on the Self and Identity

Taoism takes a different route to deal with the self and identity, compared to the views of Confucianism, Hinduism, and Buddhism. Unlike Buddhism and Hinduism, Taoism recognizes the existence of the self and identity, which is different from the Confucian relational self. The Confucian self is an extension of or defined by social relationships. Instead, the self is but a manifestation of the Tao; it is identical with and equally co-produces with the universe. To the Taoist, the duality of subject and object and the demarcation of the self and the other are negated in the oneness of the Tao. This negation of the duality does not imply the undifferentiating between the self and others, but refers to no fixed ideas of the self or to selflessness by giving total freedom to individual identity. It allows the interpenetration and interfusion between the two polarities (Starosta & Chen, 2003). This is different from Hinduism, because after being identical with the Tao, the self or the individual identity will not be lost.

Transcending one's egocentricity results in freedom from partiality and partisanship and achieving equalitarianism among the co-existences. In order to reach this co-existing state within the Tao, the self needs to acquire the ability of great empathy (Chen & Starosta, 2004). Great empathy completely rejects the distinction between subject and object through the process of *wang wo* (forgetting myself), which leads to the transformation of all things, as Chuang Tzu indicated in the chapter of *Qi Wu Lun*:

> Once I, Chuang Chou, dreamt that I was a butterfly and was happy as a butterfly. I was conscious that I was quite pleased with myself, but I did not know that I was Chou. Suddenly I awoke, and there I was, visibly Chou. I do not know whether it was Chou dreaming that he was a butterfly or the butterfly dreaming that it was Chou. Between Chou and the butterfly there must be some distinction. [But one may be the other.] This is called the transformation of things. (Chan, 1963, p. 190)

Through the process of transformation, "The universe and I exist together, and all things and I are one" (p. 186). In other words, things are identical rather than relative, for "this" and "that" produce each other, imply each other, and are identical with each other. As Chuang Tzu further stated:

> There is nothing that is not the "that" and there is nothing that is not the "this.". . . Therefore I say that the "that" is produced by the "this" and the "this" is also caused by the "that." This is the theory of mutual production. . . . The "this" is also the "that." The "that" is also the "this.". . . When "this" and "that" have no opposites, there is the very axis of Tao. (pp. 182–183)

The key to releasing the tension between the self and the other or between two individual identities is being aware of the identification and interpenetration of opposites or polarities. It forms the realm of *da tong* (grand interfusion), mirroring a picture of the wholeness of parts that shows the unity of dualities, the reconciliation of opposites, and a unity in multiplicity. Thus, the Taoist teaching of cultivating egoless selfhood aims to free a person from the four great hindrances of preconceptions, predeterminations, obduracy, and egoism, which were stipulated by Confucius, in order to bring out what is hidden within the self to activate the process of concrescence or unity within multiplicity (Chang, 1963).

According to Chen and Starosta (2004), the state of grand interfusion is achieved through great empathy, which is embedded in two human abilities: creativity and sensitivity. Creativity is the basis of egolessness. It refers to being free from the entanglements of time and space, while at the same time it identifies with all those that are temporal and spatial with common essence. The interaction between the detachment from and identification with the self and the other therefore produces abundant potentialities and possibilities within the realm of Tao. More specifically, creativity is moving from one to many by expanding the unity to diversity, and engenders the manifold diversities of existence.

Sensitivity, on the other hand, contracts the diversity into unity by moving from many to one through the process of differentiation and discrimination. Sensitivity promotes creativity that can produce and reproduce potentiality and possibilities. Through sensitivity an individual is able to obtain "shared communication symbols and project the self into another person's mind by thinking the same thoughts and feeling the same emotions as the person" (p. 13).

Hence, the contraction and expansion between sensitivity and creativity manifests the infinite interfusion and interpenetration of diversities in unity and the potentiality of unity in diversity (Chang, 1963).

It is here that we see the potential contribution of Taoist thinking in presenting an alternative view on the self and identity that is different from the Western practice and other Asian philosophical and religious thoughts. The free movement between subject and object or between the self and the other demonstrates the ability to release the stronghold of the ego, penetrating the cocoon, overcoming the boundary, and diminishing the wall between different identities.

CONCLUSION

The increasing intercultural interaction due to the impact of globalization has impacted the meaning of the self and identity. The dominant Western value of individualism indicates that an individual should strive for independence from others by attending to the self and asserting one's unique personal attributes. The emphasis on differences between the self and the other is likely to deepen the misunderstanding in the dynamic process of intercultural interaction if both parties lack the abilities of empathy or sensitivity. In order to project a distinct identity, a person may be subdued to hold oneself as a castle or cocoon by building a wall or an impenetrable boundary to exclude the other.

In contrast, the Taoist advocates the importance of attending to the self and the other simultaneously by fitting in and being harmoniously interdependent with each other. The authenticity of each other's identity is held and then both identities are integrated into one within the Tao through the process of interpenetration and interfusion with the abilities of creativity and sensitivity. The Taoist method of treating the self and identity avoids the pitfalls of Western's individualism and over-emphasis on the self and individual identity. It is also free from the potential oppression of the self in Confucian teachings and from the annihilation view of the self and identity advocated by Buddhism and Hinduism.

References

Asante, M. K. (1980). Intercultural communication: An inquiry into research directions. In D. Nimmo (Ed.), *Communication Yearbook 4* (pp. 401–411). New Brunswick, NJ: Transaction.

Barth, F. (Ed.). (1969a). *Ethnic groups and boundaries: The social organization of culture difference.* Boston, MA: Little, Brown and Company.

Barth, F. (1969b). Introduction. In F. Barth (Ed.), *Ethnic groups and boundaries: The social organization of culture difference* (pp. 9–38). Boston, MA: Little, Brown and Company.

Barth, F. (2000). Boundaries and connections. In A. P. Cohen (Ed.), *Signifying identities: Anthropological perspectives on boundaries and contested values* (pp. 17–36). New York: Routledge.

Berger, P. L., & Luckmann, T. (1966). *The social construction of reality.* Garden City, NY: Doubleday.

Bhabha, H. (1983). Difference, discrimination, and the discourse of colonialism. In F. Barker, et al. (Eds.), *The politics of theory.* Colchester, UK: University of Essex.

Blumer, H. (1969). *Symbolic interactionism: Perspective and method.* Englewood Cliffs, NJ: Prentice-Hall.

Carbaugh, D. (1996). *Situating selves: The communication of social identities in American scenes.* Albany, NY: State University of New York Press.

Chan, W-t (1963). *A source book in Chinese philosophy.* Princeton, NJ: Princeton University Press.

Chang, C-y (1963). *Creativity and Taoism: A study of Chinese philosophy, art, and poetry.* New York: Harper & Row.

Chen, G. M. (2006). Asian communication studies: What and where to now. *The Review of Communication, 6*(4), 295–311.

Chen, G. M., & Chung, J. (1994). The impact of Confucianism on organizational communication. *Communication Quarterly, 42,* 93–105.

Chen, G. M., & Miike, Y. (2006). The ferment and future of communication studies in Asia: Chinese and Japanese perspectives. *China Media Research, 2*(1), 1–12.

Chen, G. M., & Starosta, W. J. (2004). Communication among cultural diversities: A dialogue. *International and Intercultural Communication Annual, 27,* 3–16.

Chen, V. (1997). (De) hyphenated identity: The double voice in *The Woman Warrior.* In A. Gonzalez, M. Houston, & V. Chen (Eds.), *Our voices: Essays in culture, ethnicity, and communication* (pp. 3–11). Los Angeles, CA: Roxbury.

Cohen, A. P. (1985). *The symbolic construction of community.* New York: Routledge.

Cohen, A. P. (2000). Introduction: Discriminating relations: Identity, boundary and authenticity. In A. P. Cohen (Ed.),

Signifying identities: Anthropological perspectives on boundaries and contested values (pp. 1–13). New York: Routledge.

Colley, C. H. (1902). *Human nature and the social order*. New York: Scribner's.

Collier, M. (1997). Cultural identity and intercultural communication. In L. Samovar & R. Porter (Eds.), *Intercultural communication* (pp. 36–44). Belmont, CA: Wadsworth.

Cote, J. E., & Levine, C. G. (2002). *Identity formation, agency, and culture: A social psychological synthesis*. Mahwah, NJ: Lawrence Erlbaum.

Deaux, K. (1992). Personalizing identity and socializing self. In G. M. Blackwell (Ed.), *Social psychology of identity and the self-concept* (pp. 9–33). London: Surrey University Press.

Dissanayake, W. (Ed.). (1988). *Communication theory: The Asian perspective*. Singapore: Asian Mass Communication Research and Information Center.

Durkeim, E. (1964). *The division of labor in society*. New York: Free Press.

Erikson, E. H. (1968). *Identity: Youth and crisis*. New York: Norton.

Geertz, C. (1979). From the native's point of view: On the nature of anthropological understanding. In P. Rabinow & W. M. Sullivan (Eds.), *Interpretive social science* (pp. 225–241). Berkeley, CA: University of California Press.

Gergen, K. J. (1991). *The saturated self: Dilemmas of identity in contemporary life*. New York: Basic Books.

Giles, H., & Johnson, P. (1987). Ethnolinguistic identity theory: A social psychological approach to language maintenance. *International Journal of the Sociology of Language,* 68, 66–99.

Goffman, E. (1959). *The presentation of self in everyday life*. Garden City, NY: Doubleday.

Gudykunst, W., & Lim, T. S. (1986). A perspective for the study of intergroup communication. In W. Gudykunst (Ed.), *Intergroup communication* (pp. 1–10). London: Edward Arnold.

Gunaratne, S. A. (1991). Asian approaches to communication theory. *Media Development,* 38(1), 53–55.

Habermas, J. (1974). On social identity. *Telos,* 19, 91–103.

Hall, S. (1990). Cultural identity and diaspora. In J. Rutherford (Ed.), *Identity, community, culture, and differences* (pp. 222–237). London: Lawrence & Wiishart.

Hedge, R. S. (1998). Swinging the trapeze: The negotiation of identity among Asian Indian immigrant women in the United States. In D. V. Tanno & A. Gonzalez (Eds.), *Communication and identity across cultures* (International and Intercultural Communication Annual, Vol. 21, pp. 34–55). Thousand Oaks, CA: Sage.

Hewitt, J. P. (2006). *Self and society: A symbolic interactionist social psychology*. Boston: Allyn & Bacon.

Ho, D. Y. F. (1995). Selfhood and identity in Confucianism, Taoism, Buddhism, and Hinduism: Contrasts with the West. *Journal for the Theory of Social Behaviour,* 25(2), 115–139.

Hogg, M. A. (2003). Social identity. In M. R. Leary & J. P. Tangney (Eds.), *Handbook of self and identity* (pp. 462–479). New York: Guilford Press.

Hogg, M. A. (2006). Social identity theory. In P. Burke (Ed.), *Contemporary social psychological theories* (pp. 111–136). Stanford, CA: Stanford Social Sciences.

Hogg, M. A., Terry, D. J., & White, K. M. (1995). A tale of two theories: A critical comparison of identity theory with social identity theory. *Social Psychology Quarterly,* 58(4), 255–269.

hooks, b. (1984). *Feminist theory from margin to center*. Boston, MA: South End.

hooks, b. (1992). *Black looks: race and representation*. Boston, MA: South End.

Houston, M. (1992). The politics of differences: Race, class, and women's communication. In L. Rakow (Ed.), *Women making meaning* (pp. 45–49). New York: Routledge.

Jackson, R. (2002). Cultural contracts theory: Toward an understanding of identity negotiation. *Communication Quarterly,* 50(3/4), 359–367.

James, W. (1948). *Psychology*. Cleveland, OH: World Publishing.

Kim, Y. Y. (Ed.). (1986). *Interethnic communication: Current research* (International and Intercultural Communication Annual, Vol. 10). Beverly Hills, CA: Sage.

Kuhn, M. H., & McPartland, T. S. (1954). An empirical investigation of self-attitude. *American Sociological Review,* 19, 68–76.

Marcia, J. E. (1966). Development and validation of ego identity status. *Journal of Personality and Social Psychology,* 3, 551–558.

Marcia, J. E. (1993). The ego identity status approach to ego identity. In J. E. Marcia, A. S. Waterman, D. R. Matteson, S. L. Archer, & J. L. Orlofsky (Eds.), *Ego identity: A handbook for psychosocial research* (pp. 3–41). New York: Springer-Verlag.

Markus, H. R., & Kitayama, S. (1991). Culture and the self: Implications for cognition, emotion, and motivation. *Psychological Review,* 98(2), 224–253.

Mead, G. (1934). *Mind, self, and society: From the standpoint of a social behaviorist*. Chicago, IL: University of Chicago Press.

Mendoza, S. L. (2002). *Between the homeland and the Diaspora: The politics of theorizing Filipino and Filipino American identities*. New York: Routledge.

Miike, Y. (2003). Beyond Eurocentrism in the intercultural field: Searching for an Asiacentric paradigm. In W. J. Starosta & G. M. Chen (Eds.), *Ferment in the intercultural field: Axiology/value/praxis* (pp. 243–276). Thousand Oaks, CA: Sage.

Morley, D. (1995). *Spaces of identity: Global media, electronic landscape and cultural boundaries*. New York: Routledge.

Nakayama, T., & Martin, J. (1999). Introduction: Whiteness as the communication of social identity. In T. Nakayama & J. Martin (Eds.), *Whiteness: The communication of social identity* (pp. vii–xiv, 177–197). Thousand Oaks, CA: Sage.

Parsons, T. (1968). The position of identity in the general theory of action. In C. Gordon & K. J. Gergen (Eds.), *The self in social interaction* (pp. 11–23). New York: Wiley.

Philipsen, G. (1975). Speaking "like a man" in Teamsterville: Culture patterns of role enactment in an urban neighborhood. *Quarterly Journal of Speech, 61*, 13–22.

Sampson, E. E. (1989). The deconstruction of the self. In J. Shotter & K. J. Gergen (Eds.), *Texts of identity* (pp. 1–19). Newbury Park, CA: Sage.

Shin, C. I., & Jackson, R. L. (2003). A review of identity research in communication theory. In W. J. Starosta & G. M. Chen (Eds.), *Ferment in the intercultural field (International and Intercultural Communication Annual*, Vol. 26, pp. 211–240). Thousand Oaks, CA: Sage.

Sokefeld, M. (1999). Debating self, identity, and culture in anthropology. *Current Anthropology, 40*(4), 417–447.

Spivak, G. C. (1986). Imperialism and sexual difference. *Oxford Literacy Review, 8*, 1–2.

Starosta, W. J., & Chen, G. M. (2003). "Ferment," an ethic of caring, and the corrective power of dialogue. *International and Intercultural Communication Annual, 26*, 3–23.

Stets, J. (1995). Role identities and person identities: Gender identity, mastery identity, and controlling one's partner. *Sociological Perspectives, 38*, 129–150.

Stets, J., & Burke, P. J. (2000). Identity theory and social identity theory. *Social Psychological Quarterly, 63*(3), 224–237.

Strauss, A. L. (1959). *Mirrors and masks: The search for identity*. Glencoe, IL: Free Press.

Stryker, S. (1968). Identity salience and role performance: The importance of symbolic interaction theory for family research. *Journal of Marriage and the Family, 30*, 558–564.

Stryker, S. (1987). Identity theory: Developments and extensions. In K. Yardley & T. Honess (Eds.), *Self and identity* (pp. 89–104). New York: Wiley.

Tajfel, H. (1963). Social identity and intergroup behavior. *Social Science Information, 13*, 65–93.

Tajfel, H. (1981). *Human groups and social categories: Studies in social psychology*. Cambridge: Cambridge University Press.

Turner, J. C. (1985). Social categorization and the self-concept: A social cognitive theory of group behavior. In E. J. Lawler (Ed.), *Advances in group processes: Theory and research* (pp. 77–122). Greenwich, CT: JAI.

van Dijk, T. A. (1991). *Race and press: Critical studies in racism and migration*. New York: Routledge.

Watts, A. W. (1957). *The way of Zen*. New York: Pantheon.

Weigert, A. J., Teitge, J. S., & Teitge, D. W. (2007). *Society and identity: Toward a sociological psychology*. Cambridge: Cambridge University Press.

Concepts and Questions

1. What are Chen's reason and purpose in proposing a new approach to viewing identity?
2. After reading about how anthropology, psychology, and sociology approach the study of identity, which do you find is more closely aligned with your personal concept of what identity is and does?
3. What does "identity" mean to you? How do you manifest your different identities?
4. Explain the cultural approach to studying identity. Do you agree with this perspective? Why or why not?
5. Explain the critical approach to studying identity. Do you agree with this perspective? Why or why not?
6. In your opinion, which of the following is a religion and which is a philosophy? Explain your reasoning.
   a. Confucianism   c. Hinduism
   b. Buddhism   d. Taoism
7. What makes Taoism different from Confucianism, Hinduism, and Buddhism?
8. Can you think of any weaknesses in Chen's Taoist approach to identity? What are they?

American Indian Identity: Communicating Indian-ness

STEVEN B. PRATT

MERRY C. PRATT

LYNDA D. DIXON

An American Indian student, assisting with the administration of a survey on which I was working, asked me a striking question: "Do you want me to administer this questionnaire to only traditional Indians or to 'apples' also?" Asked what he meant by "traditional Indians" or "apples," the Indian student responded, "You know, do you want me to use only real Indians or those who claim to be Indian?" This dialogue between the Indian student and me suggests the significance, recurrence, and unavoidable character of the question for American Indians that occurs in the context of their everyday lives: What exactly constitutes a "real" Indian? A counterpart to that question is: How do real Indians know other real Indians and how do they make themselves known as real Indians to other real Indians? (Pratt, 1985, p. 29.)

AMERICAN INDIAN IDENTITY: COMMUNICATING *INDIAN-NESS*

This essay investigates several areas of what Pratt (1985) identifies as "*Indian-ness*" such as what is an Indian (how is one defined), what is problematic in researching Indians, and what are some contemporary issues of American Indian identity. We attempt to illuminate some pervasive questions for discussion when studying Indians as a cultural group. Although Indians are researched, there are still many misconceptions as to identifying, researching, and understanding Indian identity. Our purpose here is to shed some light on these concerns and to provide you with a better understanding of some issues that are specific to studying the communicative behaviors of the American Indian.

When it comes to American Indians, they are often still misrepresented as to *who* is Indian. In other words, other cultural groups generally do not have the questions associated with being an Indian such as "How much (blood) Indian are you?" or "Are you a real Indian?" Few other groups of people are visible representations of a race, but constantly asked about or assessed as to their degree of cultural authenticity. Because of these inconsistencies, we present this paper as a means to address some of these anomalies and answer some questions about what it means to actually "be Indian." McDaniel, Samovar, and Porter (2009) note that communication and culture are intertwined and "exert a pervasive influence on every aspect of our lives" (p. 13). Thus, in discussing American Indian identity, we emphasize the communicative acts and contexts specific to the American Indian experience.

DEFINING *INDIAN-NESS*

How often are you asked to "prove" who you are in regard to your cultural identity? Most likely, not very often. Let us consider, for example, an Irish American. An Irish American's "Irish-ness" is not often called into question; neither is the Irish person constantly asked if he or she "has been back to the old country" nor proclaimed by the interlocutor that his or her ancestry includes an Irish princess. These statements are routinely encountered by Indians. Although in the case of Indians, one may have a specific blood quantum, this does not necessarily establish this person as a real Indian. Being Indian consists of more than just possessing a certain amount of Indian blood. Simply because a person may *look* Indian, it does not mean that he or she is really Indian, that is, regarded by other Indians as a full-fledged bona fide culturally competent member. Being Indian is comprised of appropriately

This original essay first appeared in the thirteenth edition of this book. All rights reserved. Permission to reprint must be obtained from the lead author and the publisher. Steven B. Pratt is Professor in the Department of Communication at the University of Central Oklahoma. He was born and reared on the Osage Indian reservation. Merry C. Pratt is Associate Professor of Interpersonal Communication at the University of Central Oklahoma. Lynda D. Dixon is Professor in the Department of Interpersonal Communication, School of Communication Studies at Bowling Green State University.

enacting the communicative behaviors that constitute *Indian-ness*. In other words, an Indian must comport himself or herself as an Indian, while enacting appropriate behaviors, i.e., communicating in a way that is truly Indian. However, these "appropriate communicative behaviors" are not often recognizable. Just as culture cannot be taught by using a checklist, one cannot pinpoint a "real" Indian by using the obvious cues such as skin color, facial features, or hair color and texture. Within this paper, we address some of the patterns of communication specific to *Indian-ness*.

Most European Americans have not had the opportunity to spend time socializing with a typical American Indian family in their traditional milieu. They have not been able to observe how the Indian family engages in the maintenance of daily life: to see how Indians love to engage each other in their unique humor, to hear elders tell stories of their past and be able to recognize that in each story lies the lineage and history of their family and tribe, or to be intrinsically involved in "putting on" (i.e., planning and preparing) and participating in a tribal ceremony. The typical European American probably hasn't had the privilege of being a guest on an Indian reservation or a predominantly Indian community to actually observe and be a part of contemporary American Indian life.

Culturally competent Indians, or those Indians who express their identities through communicative patterns can attest to how Indian people tacitly define themselves in their everyday interactions, thus communicating their *Indian-ness*. They notice that whoever is encountered is always greeted as a relative. They recognize how everyone seems to know everyone. They are able to ascertain when it is appropriate to ask questions. They know not only when to interrupt, but also when it is okay just to sit in silence. They understand when it is appropriate to not look at a speaker; they know not to show discomfort when someone orates or prays too long.

The aims of our essay are to focus on American Indian identity: to formulate and articulate the problem of what it means to actually identify and more importantly, to begin the discussion of what constitutes Indian identity. We know that identity is socially constructed (Berger & Luckmann, 1966) and manifested through communication. Therefore, our identity, the very essence of *who we are* is a process bound and defined by our communicative acts. We begin by providing an overview of the problematic nature of identity and being identified.

To begin this journey into Indian life, we focus on American Indian identity in terms of identity negotiation, as well as what it means to be Indian in contemporary American society—with *Indian-ness* as our keystone. Although each American Indian tribe is divergent (e.g., geographically, linguistically), the existence and overlap of communicative commonalities create a unified, indigenous worldview that we refer to as *Indian-ness*.

You're Not a Full Blood, Are You?

Perhaps the most perplexing issue for many people (particularly those in the majority culture) is to understand the nature of tribal or Indian identity. Seldom is one ever asked, "How much white are you?" or "How much white blood do you have?" Like so many things implicit in our lives that do not get our attention until something *makes* us look further, identity is only examined when it is called into question. For example, whites do not often have to explain their whiteness or "verify" how they are part of the European American group. It is absolutely taken for granted. Therefore, for many of those in the majority culture, establishing, expressing, and maintaining identity is not an explicit part of their daily existence, topic of conversation, or object of direct questioning like it is for many American Indians.

This is not true among Indians. A constant for Indians, particularly among each other, is the endless process of establishing, confirming, and attesting to what is termed *Indian-ness* (Pratt, 1995). The question of identity is a question that is literally asked of all Indian people regardless of tribal affiliation. These questions whether posed in a social context by other Indians "What tribe are you?" "Do you sing around the big drum?" "Do you pow-wow?" or by non-Indians "How much Indian are you?" "You're not a full-blood are you?" by federal and tribal agencies "Do you have a CDIB (Certificate of Degree of Indian Blood) or a tribal membership card?" or simply "Are you really an Indian? You don't look like an Indian." are questions of identity that most Indians face on a daily basis. For Indian people, the question of identity is not restricted to identification for tribal and federal social services but also for purposes of determining the cultural competency or *Indian-ness* of one who self-identifies as an American Indian.

Racial, cultural, and gendered identity for most Americans is neither a quantifiable nor a federally documented point of concern. If one chooses to be a member of a racial, cultural, or gendered group all one simply has to do is self-identify, comport one's self in a culturally competent manner, be identified by other group members, or be identified by out-group members as a member of a particular group.

Yet, for the indigenous peoples of this country, the American Indian, this governmental documentation of blood quantum is a requirement for membership and subsequent federal identification. Members of American Indian tribes must provide this documentation in order to enjoy the constitutionally protected rights that are granted to all citizens except the American Indian. Constitutional privileges such as the right to worship in a culturally sanctioned manner, access to health care, voting in tribal elections, management of personal monies, choices of housing, and opportunities for employment hinge upon governmental certification.

DEFINING THE CONTEMPORARY INDIAN EXPERIENCE

The definition of an Indian, or who an Indian is, is a question in flux. For Indian people, there are a variety of ways to identify—e.g., blood quantum or sociolinguistic type. Interestingly, most lay people are unaware of the difference between *Indian-ness* and *tribal-ness* (Pratt, 1998). These two terms are often intertwined and used synonymously, yet they mean very different things. The cultural decline and/or transformation of many American Indian tribes is due to such influencing factors as language loss, intermarriage, death of elders, and relocation. These factors have contributed to tribes moving away from their basic nature of cultural competency. Although many tribes have attempted to preserve their culture, they are working against incredible shifts in thought and time. For centuries, Indians centered their lives around tribal-ness, which eventually gave way to *Indian-ness* as the most recognized mode of social identity.

Therefore, when we refer to the communicative practices and study of Indians, we are generally more focused on their *Indian-ness* as opposed to their tribal-ness.

What is important to note is that although tribal members attempted to hold on to a traditional lifestyle, the tribal way of life began to deteriorate. Change was inevitable. Forced assimilation began to have its effect with many tribal members moving away from the reservation and not returning. Concomitantly, tribes began experiencing the loss of elders and other culturally competent members who had traditionally been responsible for teaching cultural behaviors, and loss of tribal languages. As a result of the relocation of tribal members to urban or non-reservation areas and loss of culturally competent members, the concept of a tribal identity or "tribal-ness" was gradually replaced with a general Indian or *Indian-ness* identity. Thus, *Indian-ness*, replaced "tribal-ness" as a lifestyle or form of social identity.

INDIAN-NESS AND TRIBAL IDENTITY

Pratt's (1996) discussion of the uses of humor as a form of identification among Indians notes that Indian identity is not the same as tribal identity, although belonging to a tribe is a constituent of being an Indian. Tribal identity is derived from an adherence to and acceptance of a unique, rather than a generalized lifestyle. "All tribes have differing languages and customs, but under the rubric of Indian, it is a generalization of a combination of various tribal life ways. Thus, it is this 'generalizability' that creates *Indian-ness*" (Pratt, 1985, p. 239).

There are many ways in which *Indian-ness* can be interpreted. For example, a non-Indian may consider anyone who stereotypically resembles an Indian as having been socialized in a traditional Indian environment and being cognizant of tribal or Indian ways. However, physical appearance is not the sole indicator of cultural competency for "*Indian-ness* to Indian people is a concept that espouses the eclectic life-styles of indigenous people which serves to unify the various tribal groups under one rubric" (Pratt, 1985, p. 239).

Let us consider the role of *Indian-ness* with regard to tribalism. For example, it is possible to be an Indian and an Osage; that is, a person who has been socialized in Osage culture and is accepted as an Osage by other Osages and also maintains an identity with members of other tribes. He or she enacts appropriate communicative behaviors that enable acceptance by other Indians. Moreover, one can be an Indian but not be an Osage. This person has been socialized in an urban or Indian environment, is accepted by other Indians, but has not been socialized into the Osage tribe and is not accepted by other Osages. Finally, it is possible to be an Osage but not be an Indian. This individual has been socialized into the Osage culture, has limited contact with members of other tribes and primarily views his or her world from the cultural template created by Osage life ways.

NEGOTIATING AMERICAN INDIAN IDENTITY

The popularity of films such as *Dances with Wolves*, *Geronimo, Bury My Heart at Wounded Knee, Pocahontas*, and *Last of the Mohicans* has created renewed interest in the indigenous people of this country. As a result of these somewhat historical (albeit romanticized versions) and animated renditions of Indian figures from the 1800s, most people have a preconceived notion of the lifestyle and history of the American Indian. Generally, this notion is based upon information gleaned from sources such as school, personal experience, experiences of others, and primarily, the media. For many, this preconceived image of the contemporary Indian is similar to that of the homogenous picture depicted in chapters and movies of the "Old West"—an image created by Hollywood in which the "Native American (is) devoid of tribal characteristics or regional differences" (Bataille & Silet, 1980, p. xxiii).

This "Old West" image is one in which all Indians possess the same cultural characteristics reflective of the Plains Indian culture and are perceived to be living the cinematic *Dances with Wolves* version of life. In a review of current communication text chapters, which focus upon intercultural communication, we found this overgeneralized, stereotypical image almost always portrayed. Indians are portrayed as living an idyllic, romanticized lifestyle in which they dwell in harmony with nature, are childlike, oblivious to pain, promiscuous, and willingly engage in forms of self-torture.

According to prevalent stereotypes, Indians worship such forces of nature as the wind, water, sun, lightning, thunder, and fire. Indians are often thought to believe in many gods or spirits—typically including a reference to the "Great Spirit." Ganje (2003) contends that Indian stereotypes are propagated through false images of Indians as either spirit guides or noble savages. Another common misconception about Indians concerns tribal religious practices. Although most non-Indians recognize the terms "shaman" and "sweat lodge" as synonymous with Indian religion, few have any idea what they mean or which Indians actually use them (Lustig & Koester, 2006).

Seldom is any evidence provided for their claims nor do they make distinctions among tribal groups. Not all Indians worship inanimate objects such as rocks or thunder; however, most do have a respect for environmental elements stemming from an indigenous worldview. Many Indians are Christians and do not believe in many Gods or spirits and are not able to withstand pain any better than their non-Indian counterparts. Moreover, the medicine wheel and sweat lodge are only utilized by some tribes in the northern plains and are not a part of all Plains Indian culture. Further, not all Indians live in a tipi or hogan; they do not all use dream catchers. That is, these cultural elements are not standard components of all tribal cultures. The few sentences about differing cultural behaviors provide no supporting data and in some cases, cite novels as reference sources.

ISSUES IN RESEARCHING INDIANS

The center of this essay on American Indian identity also poses the most easily identifiable problem for researchers who choose to study American Indian communication. For starters, who is the one that decides who is a real or competent Indian? Is the presence of a Certificate of Degree of Indian Blood (CDIB) proof of *Indian-ness*? If a person simply looks Indian, does that automatically qualify him or her for the study? What if the individual merely self-identifies as an Indian, or claims to be a member of a particular tribe? Should a researcher ask for "proof" of cultural competency (i.e., requesting to see a CDIB card)? In this way you can see that the researcher who studies

American Indians encounters identity issues from the start. Unlike any other cultural group, American Indian identity is called into question even when making themselves available to be studied.

The American Indian, whether as a racial group or tribal group, has been the focus of study for disciplines such as anthropology, sociology, linguistics, semantics, and socio-linguistics. Various aspects of Indian culture—such as how Indians operate on "Indian time" to religious practices—have been studied. However, little research is devoted to identifying or describing Indian communicative behavior such as tribal forms of public oratory, humor, listening, singing, and uses of hedging. Most importantly, for those conducting research among the indigenous people, seldom has the notion of cultural competency or the knowledge and day-to-day enactment of cultural ways been taken into account. When working with minorities, particularly American Indians, researchers are inclined to afford complete cultural competency upon anyone who is identified or self-identifies as an Indian. Many American Indian researchers consider any person who identifies as an Indian as being culturally competent. However, many tribal members are socialized in an urban or non-Indian environment and possess scant knowledge of their tribal background. Think of the implications for this on data collection and research findings.

When conducting research, the question of whether or not one is a culturally competent member and what type of Indian identity they exhibit is not readily addressed. Instead, their cultural expertise is taken for granted, particularly when conducting qualitative research. Social scientists should be concerned with whether or not they are actually testing and identifying Indian or tribal communicative behavior. In addition, they should be concerned with identifying and delineating what Indian or tribal behavior is.

Interestingly, the communicative behavior of the American Indian has primarily been studied from an *a priori* perspective. Rather than attempting to identify specific cultural speech behaviors, (e.g., compliance gaining, listening), contemporary research has glossed or categorized observable cultural communicative acts into European American behavior equivalents.

Contributing further to this problematic nature is the notion that there is neither one common type of Indian identity nor a standard set of behaviors that can be generalized to all Indians. The contemporary Indian may have very little knowledge of tribal background or they may be very well versed in their tribal beliefs and activities; they may have not been socialized in a traditional environment and the behaviors they exhibit are more akin to European Americans; or they have been socialized in a traditional environment and exhibit behaviors reflective of their tribal culture. For Real Indians, a traditional environment is one in which the tribal language is spoken and tribal behaviors are enacted on a daily basis with full understanding of the significance of tribal acts. However, recent ethnographic research has begun identifying and explicating Indian speech acts and communicative behaviors (Carbaugh, 2005; Modaff, 2004; Modaff, Modaff, Pratt, & Buchanan, 2008; Pratt & Buchanan, 2004; Pratt, Pratt, & Miller, in press).

CULTURAL COMPETENCY OR *INDIAN-NESS*

Personal and social identity goes beyond simply checking an appropriate box or self proclamation. Wieder and Pratt (1990) note that being an Indian or culturally competent tribal member "is not something one can simply be, but is something one becomes and/or is, in and as the doing of being and becoming a real Indian" (p. 50). They contend that "doing, being, and becoming" a competent member requires the participation of other culturally competent members for a person must not only know how to "do" being and becoming a culturally competent member, but one must continue to practice what one knows, that is, comport oneself as an Indian.

Current issues in American Indian Identity

Like so many other patterns of human communicative behaviors, identity is not a concern until it is called into question. Writers, scholars, and researchers focus abundant works on African American identity, Asian

American identity, and Hispanic American identity. However, extant research is almost devoid of identity research when it comes to the American Indian experience.

CONCLUSION

So what does it mean to "be Indian?" *Indian-ness* is implicit. *Indian-ness* is identifiable to the informed observer. *Indian-ness* is not skin color. *Indian-ness* is a tacit privilege. True or "real Indians" can identify each other with accuracy, just as they can identify the "wanna-be Indians" or, in current vernacular, "posers." Real Indians can describe what it means to be Indian, although they are not often called to do so—therein lies the paradox of American Indian identity research and identity negotiation. Real Indians are hard pressed to come up with a "list" of what it means to be a real Indian. Real Indians don't make a practice of "doing" Indian, they practice "being" Indian.

This essay emphasizes a communication approach to understanding American Indian identity. This perspective allows us to illustrate how *Indian-ness* is created by the manner in which Indian people speak to others and how others speak to them. Communication is the medium through which identity is expressed. Our focus is to explore not only American Indian identity but also to open discussion on what it means to be a Real Indian. Specifically, we are interested in how Indians communicate their *Indian-ness*. Culture, identity, and in-group membership are interlaced with the threads of interpretation and social discourse.

In particular, American Indian communication research must wrestle free from the culture bound approaches to European American communication research and theories. Kim (2002) calls for a shift from the Anglo-centered forms of human communication research, suggesting that "alternative cultural perspectives will reveal how cultural frameworks powerfully structure both everyday and scientific understandings" (pp. 4–5). We believe that this essay is a first step in exploring the study of American Indian identity as we begin with the questions of what comprises identity, *Indian-ness*, and the intersects with contemporary communication.

References

Bataille, G. M., & Silet, C. L. P. (1980). *The pretend Indians: Images of Native Americans in the movies*. Ames, IA: Iowa State University Press.

Berger, P. L., & Luckmann, T. (1966). *The social construction of reality*. Garden City, NY: Anchor Books.

Carbaugh, D. (2005). *Cultures in conversation*. Mahwah, NJ: Lawrence Erlbaum.

Ganje, L. A. (2003). Native American stereotypes. In P. M. Lester & S. D. Ross (Eds.), *Images that injure: Pictorial stereotypes in the media* (2nd ed.). Westport, CT: Praeger.

Kim, M. S. (2002). *Non-western perspectives on human communication*. Thousand Oaks, CA: Sage.

Lustig, M. W., & Koester, J. (2006). *Intercultural competence: Interpersonal communication across cultures* (5th ed.). Boston: Allyn & Bacon.

McDaniel, E. R., Samovar, L. A., & Porter, R. E. (2009). Understanding intercultural communication: The working principles. In L. A. Samovar, R. E. Porter, & E. R. McDaniel (Eds.), *Intercultural communication: A reader* (12th ed., pp. 6–17). Boston, MA: Wadsworth Cengage Learning.

Modaff, D. P. (2004). Native virtues: Applying traditional Sioux philosophy to the contemporary basic communication course. *Basic Communication Course Annual, 16,* 261–278.

Modaff, D. P., Modaff, J. A. B., Pratt, S. B., & Buchanan, M. C. (2008). UnCONVENTIONal Balance: Marriage, Family, and Research on the Rez. Panel presentation to the 94th annual National Communication Association Convention. San Diego, CA.

Pratt, S. B. (1985). *Being an Indian among Indians*. Unpublished doctoral dissertation, University of Oklahoma.

Pratt, S. B. (1998). Razzing: Ritualized uses of humor as a form of identification among American Indians. In D. V. Tanno & A. Gonzalez (Eds.), *Communication and identity across cultures* (pp. 56–69). Thousand Oaks, CA: Sage.

Pratt, S. B., & Buchanan, M. C. (2004). "I want you to talk for me": An ethnography of communication of the Osage Indian. In M. Fong & R. Chuang (Eds.) *Communicating ethnic and cultural identity* (pp. 261–273). Lanham, MD: Rowman and Littlefield.

Pratt, S. B., Pratt, M. C., & Miller, R. (in press). Osage naming ritual: Communicating cultural identity. In A. Gonzalez, M. Houston, & V. Chen (Eds.), *Our voices: Essays in culture, ethnicity, and communication* (5th ed.). London: Oxford University Press.

Wieder, D. L., & Pratt, S. (1990). On being a recognizable Indian among Indians. In D. Carbaugh (Ed.), *Cultural communication and intercultural contact* (pp. 45–64). Hillsdale, NJ: Lawrence Erlbaum.

Concepts and Questions

1. The essay states that identity is "socially constructed and manifested through communication." Explain this statement and provide an example.
2. What do the authors mean by the term *Indian-ness*?
3. What is the reason behind the Certificate of Degree of Indian Blood (CDIB)? What is the certificate's purpose?
4. What are some of the factors leading to the decline of cultural competency among American Indians?
5. Contrast "tribal identity" and "Indian identity" as discussed in the essay. Why has one become more prevalent than the other?
6. What sources do most non-Indians draw on to construct their image of American Indians? Do these sources present a valid representation? Why?
7. What are some of the difficulties encountered when researching American Indians?
8. How does one become a culturally competent tribal member?
9. What is meant by the phrase "identities are negotiated"?

Understanding Whiteness in the United States

Judith N. Martin

What does it mean to be a white person in the United States? Is there such a thing as a white identity? Is it different from an ethnic identity? Is feeling white different from feeling German American or Italian American? How does being white influence the way we communicate? How is our whiteness expressed in communication?

For many people in the United States, there currently seems to be a degree of confusion and angst about racial and ethnic identity among white people. Some people never think about being white. Some think it seems all right to feel ethnic pride, but not pride in being white. Some feel that they are being forced to think about being white because of issues like affirmative action and "reverse discrimination." This essay attempts to sort out some of these issues and explore the contradictions and tensions in the notion of whiteness as an identity. We also examine how being white in the United States may influence communication, particularly in terms of how this identity develops and is reflected in the labels and words we use to refer to ourselves.

A COMMUNICATION PERSPECTIVE ON IDENTITY

Let's start with a communication perspective on identity. That is, we all have multiple identities (such as gender, religious, ethnicity, race) that make up our self-concept and how we see ourselves. Identities arise from our associations with groups, some voluntary

Courtesy of Judith N. Martin. This article appeared for the first time in the eighth edition of this book. All rights reserved. Permission to reprint must be obtained from the author and the publisher. Judith N. Martin is Professor in the Hugh Downs School of Human Communication, Arizona State University, Tempe, Arizona.

(such as professional and religious affiliations) and some involuntary (such as age and family groups), and then develop through communication with others.

As communication scholars Michael Hecht, Mary Jane Collier, and Sidney Ribeau (1993) have noted, cultural identities are *negotiated, co-created, reinforced, and challenged through communication*. Some identities may be easier to co-create and negotiate than others. For example, does it seem easier to understand and negotiate being female than being white? How is being white negotiated and challenged through communication in today's world?

In addition, as Collier explains earlier in this chapter, our identities are expressed through *norms and labels*—the communicative behaviors and terms that reflect the core symbols or priorities of our group-associated identities. In this book, a number of essays identify the core symbols and norms of various groups like Japanese, African Americans, and Indians. Are there similar norms, labels, and core symbols that are associated with being white in the United States?

One final thing that we need to keep in mind about identities is that they are *dynamic* and *context-related*. I am not just a female, a professor, a white German American. I am all of these, and any one identity may be highlighted or suppressed depending on the situation or context. For example, in some situations, such as when I am the only white person in a conversation or when I am discussing the issue of race, my white identity is highlighted. In other conversations, my professor identity may be emphasized more. We are always in the process of becoming and unbecoming, as we negotiate, develop, and re-form our identities through communication.

Three issues need to be addressed as we apply this communication perspective to understanding white identity: the difference between white racial and ethnic identity, the characteristics of a white identity, and how whites develop a sense of being white.

WHITE RACIAL AND ETHNIC IDENTITY

Race Versus Ethnicity

What is the difference between racial and ethnic identity? Many people believe that race has to do with physical characteristics, whereas ethnicity is more

a sense of a shared culture, belief system, and origin. However, most scholars now reject the biological argument in favor of a more social approach to understanding race. That is, while there may be some physiological basis for racial categories, it is the way in which these categories are constructed and the meaning attached to racial categories that have a profound influence on communication and how identities are negotiated. What are the arguments against physiological definitions?

First, racial categories vary widely in different parts of the world. One contrast is seen in the United States and South America. In the United States, there are two major racial distinctions (black and white), and this distinction is fairly rigid. People seem to have a sense of who is white and who isn't (for example, "you don't look black") and are uneasy when they are unable to categorize someone of mixed racial origin ("But are you white *or* black?"). In contrast, people in Brazil and other South American countries recognize a variety of intermediate racial categories.

A second example of how racial categories are socially constructed is that racial categories have changed throughout U.S. immigration history and some groups have been shifted from one racial category to another at particular points in history. In the eighteenth century, British immigrants struggled to preserve their base of power and even to prevent other Europeans from entering the United States. In the nineteenth century, as more and more southern Europeans immigrated, there was an attempt to classify Irish and Jewish Europeans as nonwhite. Instead, the racial line was drawn around Europe, and those outside (such as the Chinese and Japanese) were then designated as nonwhite (Omi & Winant, 1992). So while the notion of race has some basis in physiology, it probably makes more sense to talk about race *formation* and to think about race as a complex of social meanings that get interpreted through communication, rather than as something fixed, concrete, and objective.

It should also be pointed out that as socially constructed, these categories are relational, exist in relation to each other. Could there be a white without a black category? What does it mean that we tend to see race in the United States in polar categories, white and black? If people do not fit or do not want to fit into these categories, how can they negotiate their identity?

Bounded Versus Dominant/Normative Identities

The relationship between white racial and ethnic identity can be clarified by distinguishing between bounded and dominant identities (Frankenburg, 1993; Trinh, 1986/87). Bounded cultures are those groups we belong to that are specific and not dominant or normative (such as groups defined by religion, gender, ethnicity). For most white people, connections to these groups are clear and easy to talk about. Being Irish American means we celebrate St. Patrick's Day; being Amish means we follow the *"Ordnung"* (the community rules). Growing up German American may mean working hard for the sake of working and not being very verbally expressive. It's easy to recognize and identify these cultural behaviors.

However, what it means to belong to the dominant or *normative* white culture is a much more "slippery" construct, more difficult to define, but just as real. It is not often easy to see what cultural practices or norms link white people together. For example, we usually don't think of Thanksgiving as a white American holiday. Part of the "slipperiness" of this identity is related to the dominant or normative aspect of being white.

Identity and Power

Sometimes the more powerful aspects of identity are the most unrecognized, and power is more strongly linked to aspects of identity that are ascribed, or involuntary. For example, when questioned about identity, males will often not mention gender. They just don't think about it, whereas women are more likely to be aware of how gender is a part of their identity.

The same thing may be true about being white. One reason white people don't think about being white is that they may not need to. Communication scholars Tom Nakayama and Robert Krizek (1995) suggest that this lack of consciousness on the part of whites is possible only because of the power associated with being white. The experiences and communication patterns of whites are taken as the norm from which others are marked or measured. The universal norm then becomes invisible. For example, the news media refer to "black leaders" but never to "white leaders." There is "black on black violence," but European conflicts are not referred to as "white on white violence."

What does it mean that the category "white" is seldom referred to and that whites so rarely talk about the meaning of being white? As Krizek reflects:

> I've gone through life never consciously thinking about labels. I suppose we defined ourselves as one of those people we didn't label, although nobody ever said that. We were just white, not black or brown, and I don't really know what that means. No one ever questioned it (Nakayama & Krizek, 1995, p. 292).

On the other hand, Nakayama (1993) has written about growing up in the South as a fourth-generation Japanese American, with his identity as an American consistently challenged as people frequently asked him where he was *really* from and if he spoke English.

Nakayama and Krizek attempt to show how the "invisibility" of whiteness is related to power by analyzing the "rhetoric of whiteness" or how white people talk about being white when explicitly asked. They found that people often resisted discussing how they felt about being white, which they interpret as reflecting an invisible power in which white is not a category of identity, but black African American, or Chicana is.

A second rhetorical strategy was to say that being white was based on negation, that white is "not something else (not black, brown, yellow, or red)." This seems like a neutral way to talk about being white, but they point out that in this strategy white is again the universal against which other colors are marked. Another strategy confuses whiteness with nationality. Whiteness means white American. As one of their respondents noted, "A lot of times when people think of Americans, I bet you they probably think of white. They probably think it's redundant" (p. 301). What does it mean for all those Americans who are not white?

We can see how difficult it is for people to pin down the meaning of whiteness, but perhaps we'll understand intercultural communication better if we apply the same scrutiny to white identity that we apply to other cultural groups. This lack of awareness on the part of whites may be changing, as we'll discuss later. As issues of race are brought up more and more frequently in the United States (in the O. J. Simpson trial, for example) white people are perhaps thinking more about being white than ever before, and perhaps it will become easier to identify those norms and core symbols of whiteness.

In Chapter 4 Edith Folb argues that there is a relative continuum of power in the United States associated with various identities, ranging from the more powerful groups (whites, males, Protestants, heterosexuals, middle/upper classes, the educated) to less powerful groups (racial minorities, females, religions other than Protestant, gays, the working class, the less educated). And we each may have aspects of our identity that are more or less powerful, depending on which is highlighted in any particular context. Those that are more involuntary or physically marked are more difficult and the most problematic to negotiate.

What happens when our identities are challenged? Growing up as an Amish/Mennonite young woman, I felt marginalized in many social contexts because I was physically marked by a distinctive dress and physical appearance. It was difficult to negotiate anything other than a bounded (Amish) identity. What are the communicative consequences when identities are challenged—when, for example, Asian Americans are asked "Where are you *really* from?" or "Do you speak English?" How does it affect the communication between people when the identities of some are often challenged and others (whites) are rarely challenged?

DIMENSIONS OF WHITE IDENTITY

An interesting question, then, is whether there is a set of cultural norms and symbols shared by most white people. Many scholars feel that there are uniquely white cultural patterns, but that they are often difficult to discern. Sociologist Ruth Frankenburg suggests that one way to understand whiteness is to view it not as simply a racial or ethnic category but rather as a set of three linked dimensions in which power is a key ingredient. These are modified to emphasize the communicative aspect of identity: a location of structural advantage, a standpoint from which to view ourselves and others, and a set of cultural practices (core symbols, labels, and norms).

Whiteness Is a Location of Structural Privilege

Some scholars argue that white identity is linked to the structural advantage of race privilege within the United States but that the two are not synonymous. All whites do not have power and do not have equal access to power. For example, one can point to times in U.S. history when some white cultural groups were not privileged, but rather were viewed as separate or different, as were the Irish in the early part of the twentieth century and the German Americans during World War II.

However, scholars have pointed out that the memory of marginality in these instances has outlasted the marginality. In the latter part of the twentieth century, European immigrant groups are now assimilated and are "just American." Boundaries between Americanness and whiteness have been much more fluid for "white ethnic" groups than for people of color.

How is this dimension of white identity played out in the everyday lives of white people and their communication with others? Peggy McIntosh (1995) has tried to identify the ways in which white privilege affects her daily interactions. See if you can list others:

I can, if I wish, arrange to be in the company of people of my race most of the time.

I can be fairly sure of having my voice heard in a group in which I am the only member of my race.

I can talk with my mouth full and not have people put this down to my color.

I can do well in a challenging situation without being called a credit to my race.

I am never asked to speak for all people of my racial group.

I can worry about racism without it being seen as self-interest or self-seeking.

My culture gives me little [to] fear about ignoring the perspectives and powers of people of other races.

The question then is how does this aspect of white identity influence my communication with others? Perhaps it means that I approach most interactions with a confidence that if I'm nice, most people will be nice back to me. People won't prejudge me as untrustworthy, or "different," or "angry." Or if they see me sitting with other people who are white, they won't think this means I don't want to communicate with people who aren't white. They will judge me and communicate with me as an individual.

Several studies have, in fact, found that whites and African Americans approach interethnic conversations in different ways. Whites rarely talk about issues of power when discussing interethnic communication, whereas it is a more central issue in African American frameworks (Martin, Hecht, & Larkey, 1994). So maybe this is one aspect of being white, the fact that I don't consider power issues in conversations. Perhaps you can think of other ways that privilege may be reflected in whites' communication.

While being white in the United States may mean privilege sometimes, there seems to be an increasing perception that being white does not mean "invisible privilege." Charles A. Gallagher, who interviewed college students in a large innercity campus found that white students thought a lot about being white and saw their whiteness not as a privilege but as a liability. They often felt that minority students were getting more breaks and more privileges. They also felt that they were prejudged by students of color as being racist because they were white.

Some whites feel that being white is not very positive, that whiteness represents blandness (like Wonder Bread), and that it is not very interesting in contrast to the cultural "richness" of other cultural groups. This sometimes leads whites to retrieve their ethnic heritage and identity (Italian American, Irish American, and so on). Ethnicity for white Americans can be almost like a garment that is put on or off at will.

Perhaps this change in identity, this growing awareness of a white identity, is occurring because the changing demographics in the United States means that whites *are beginning to perceive* themselves in the minority. Gallagher (1994) also asked students to estimate the ratio of whites to blacks on campus. Many students reported that they thought the ratio was 30 percent white students, 70 percent black students. The actual ratio was 70 percent white and 30 percent black.

The point here is not the inaccuracy of the perception, or whether whites or minorities are more privileged, but how these perceptions affect intercultural communication. How do we communicate with others if we feel that we are being prejudged as racist? or as privileged? How are these identities negotiated and confirmed or challenged in our intercultural interactions?

Whiteness Is a "Standpoint"

A second dimension of white identity, according to Frankenburg, is a standpoint, a place from which white people look at themselves, at others, and at society. What are some perceptions shared by white people? And how do these perceptions differ from those of other cultural groups?

A dramatic example arose during the trial of the African American celebrity O. J. Simpson, accused of killing his ex-wife, Nicole Brown Simpson, and her friend Ron Goldman. An ABC News poll conducted just before the verdict was handed down showed a profound split between white and black perception: 77 percent of whites thought Simpson was guilty, 72 percent of blacks believed he was innocent (*Arizona Republic*, October 1, 1995, p. A2).

Both whites and blacks saw the same televised trial, the same evidence, heard the same legal arguments, but saw these from two different "standpoints" and arrived at two different conclusions. How could this be? Experts analyzed the two standpoints and tried to understand this dramatic difference in perception in the days immediately following the trial.

Most experts saw the roots of the different perceptions in the different life experiences of African and white Americans. As one columnist explained it:

> Most whites thought Fuhrman [the policeman accused of evidence tampering and racism] was a sick act and an exception. Most blacks, especially those in L.A. thought he was no aberration; they've known others like him. (Wilson, 1995, p. 2)

There are numerous other, perhaps less dramatic examples of how perceptions of whites contrast with those of other U.S. groups. To give just one example, according to a CBS News poll reported in the *Arizona Republic*, 38 percent of whites versus 27 percent of blacks think race relations in the United States are generally good (October 4, 1995). So something about being white influences how we view the world and ultimately how we communicate with others. As one individual reported in Nakayama and Krizek's study:

> "I don't exactly know what it means to be white, but we all know don't we? I mean I never talk about it, but I know that we understand each other at some level. Like when a black guy gets on an elevator or when

you have a choice to sit or stand next to a white person or a black person. You pick the white person and you look at each other, the whites and you just know that you've got it better. You don't say anything but you know. It's in the looks." (p. 298)

Of course, not all whites perceive all situations in the same way. Remember that identity is dynamic, negotiated, and context-dependent. Perhaps it is easier to see shared perceptions in dramatic situations like the Simpson trial or the Rodney King beating and the subsequent trial of white police officers. And even then, it is still difficult to understand how perceptions are related to race.

Again the question comes back to how these varying perceptions, expressions of identity, influence our communication. Are there ways to negotiate these varying perceptions?

Discussions following the O. J. Simpson trial may have presented opportunities for intercultural dialogue and finding some common ground. Blacks saw whites unanimously condemning Mark Fuhrman, and whites heard the same thing from blacks concerning Simpson's pattern of spousal abuse (*Arizona Republic*, October 1, 1995, p. A22).

Whiteness Is a Set of Core Symbols, Norms, and Labels

Core symbols are those values and priorities of a cultural group that are reflected in the norms of behavior and labels used to describe the group (Hecht, Collier, & Ribeau, 1993). Often the *norms* are unmarked; they are not made explicit, and it is hard to identify what norms are uniquely shared by whites. As noted, this difficulty comes partly from the normative and dominant aspect of being white. The dilemma is that white is everything and it is nothing. It is just there, and yet it is difficult to talk about, maybe even embarrassing.

Sometimes, these cultural practices are most clearly visible to those who are not white, to those groups who are excluded. Janet Helms (1990) and others (such as M. Asante, 1973) have attempted to outline values that are shared primarily by white people. For example, they suggest that a strong belief in individualism and an emphasis on linear thinking are two patterns that are most strongly linked to being white and are not universally shared by other cultural groups in the United States.

The *labels* we attach to ourselves and others that characterize ethnicity and/or race may be seen as a category of core symbols and are another way in which identity is expressed. Labels have meaning and are not neutral.

The questions of labels and identity have been of concern to marginalized groups for a long time. One issue revolves around who has the right to name others. Who has the right to use a label? Again power comes into play, for dominant groups can exercise power in naming others. And it is often difficult for the less powerful groups to control their own labels. It is well known that Native Americans have objected to the use of tribal terms as names for sports groups (Redskins), cars (Jeep Cherokee), and other commercial products. Some African Americans object to Aunt Jemima pancake mix and Uncle Ben's rice. It is not widely known that Quakers objected strenuously to the use of the label "Quaker" in Quaker Oats. Would we like a team called "the Fighting Honkeys"? One response of marginalized groups is to take the pejorative label and make it their own, as gay and lesbian groups did in appropriating and using the label "queer."

Dolores Tanno (1994) describes how her multiple identities are reflected in various labels (Spanish, Mexican American, Latina, Chicana). The Spanish label is one she was given by her family and designates an ancestral origin (Spain). The label Mexican American reflects two important cultures that make up her identity. Latina reflects cultural and historical connectedness with others of Spanish descent (such as Puerto Ricans and South Americans) and the Chicana label promotes political and cultural assertiveness in representing her identity. She stresses that she is all these, that each reveals a different facet of her identity: symbolic, historical, cultural, and political.

Similarly, the labels and meanings for African Americans have evolved over the years. Hecht, Collier, and Ribeau (1993) claim that the shift from black to African American as a self-preferred label is founded in issues of self-determination, strength, progress, and control.

What do white people want to be called? When we asked white college students what labels they preferred to use and preferred others to use, they consistently chose the most "normative," the least specific (Martin, Krizek, Nakayama, & Bradford, 1996). They wanted to be called white, or maybe white American, but not white Anglo-Saxon Protestant. What does it mean if whites resist being specifically "located" by geography (Anglo) or history (WASP)? Does it express the right of being the normative group, the one that names and categorizes others but is not itself categorized?

However, this may be changing as our "white" identity is being (re)negotiated and defined in contemporary U.S. society. Perhaps these issues of labels will be discussed more by whites. Perhaps we can explore the meanings for various labels—African Americans, white, European American. Or we can learn to negotiate and call people what they want to be called, as Mary Jane Collier suggests, to affirm the identity that each thinks is important.

WHITE IDENTITY DEVELOPMENT

How do we develop a sense of whiteness? This sense (just like our sense of gender) develops over time and through communication with others. There seem to be several stages of identity development, not with definite beginnings and ends, but stages nonetheless that represent different positions of understanding who we are.

In the United States, minority group members develop a sense of racial and ethnic identity much earlier than majority group members do. As psychologist Rita Hardiman (1994) describes it:

> It has frequently been the case that White students enrolled in my class on racial and cultural issues in counseling expect to be taught all about the cultures of people of color and they are almost always surprised to hear that we will be discussing the White group's experience. Some students remark that they are not White; they are female, or working-class, or Catholic or Jewish, but not White. When challenged, they reluctantly admit that they are White but report that this is the first time they have had to think about what it means for them. (p. 125)

Stage 1: No Social Consciousness

In Hardiman's model, the first stage of identity development is the same for whites and minority groups; in this stage children may be aware of physical differences and some cultural differences but do not feel fearful or hostile and do not feel racially superior. However, eventually they absorb the message from the social environment (family and society) about racial groups.

Stage 2: Acceptance

The second stage, acceptance, represents the internalization of the messages about racial group membership and the acquisition of a belief in the "normalcy" (superiority) of being white. This may be either a passive acceptance or an active acceptance of the dominant socialization. An important point here is that individuals at this stage are not aware that they have been programmed to accept a particular world view about race. It is simply the way things are and is not questioned.

Passive Acceptance. In the passive acceptance stage, there is no conscious identification with being white. Whites at this stage may hold the following subtly racist views but do not see themselves as being racist. Rather, racism is seen as the holding of extreme attitudes, such as those espoused by the Klu Klux Klan.

1. Minority groups are culturally deprived and need help to assimilate.
2. Affirmative action is reverse discrimination because people of color are being given opportunities that whites have never had.
3. White culture, music, art, and literature is "classical"; works of art by people of color are primitive art, or "crafts."
4. People of color are "culturally different" whereas whites are individuals with no group identity, cultures, or shared experience of racial privilege.

People at this stage usually take one of two passive positions with respect to racial issues and interactions with people of color. They either *avoid* or adopt a *patronizing* stance. That is, they may avoid racial issues, avoid being around people of color, or be very polite when they are. Or they may take a patronizing stance, be very solicitous and try to help the less fortunate: "I really feel terrible about the few minority students in my classes. I know it's so hard for them to fit in. I really wish I could figure out some way to make things easier for them."

Active Acceptance. Those whites in the active acceptance stage are very conscious of their whiteness and may express their feelings of superiority collectively (as with a White Student Union). There may be open resentment toward minorities who are perceived to be more advantaged: "Why do all the black students sit together in the Student Union?"

Some whites never move beyond this phase. If they do, it is usually a result of a number of cumulative events. Hardiman describes the transition of one of her students from the active acceptance stage to the next stage:

> [She took] a class in high school on African American authors.... She felt that the authors' experiences had happened long ago and that whatever unfairness existed then had been rectified. Later, after entering college and developing some close relationships with Asian American and African American students, she began to have other experiences that contradicted her assumptions about fairness. An incident in her residence hall involving the indiscriminate rounding up of all Black male students by police, and an ensuing protest over that incident, had a particular effect upon her. She described herself as "waking up to the reality" after this incident. (p. 127)

Stage 3: Resistance

The resistance stage represents a major attitudinal shift, from a position that blames victims for their conditions to one that names and blames a white's own dominant group as the source of racial problems. This resistance may take the form of passive resistance, with little behavioral change, or active resistance—an ownership of racism. Individuals may be embarrassed as they recognize that much of their behavior has been racist. Some may try to distance themselves from other whites or gravitate toward communities of color.

In the active resistance stage, whites believe that changing the white community is the responsibility of whites; they shift from being a good "liberal" helper to being an active agent of change. However, as they make the transition to the next stage, they realize that while they may appreciate communities of color, they are not members of those cultures and they feel a need to redefine whiteness.

Stage 4: Redefinition

In this stage, energy is refocused or redirected to redefining whiteness in nonracist terms. Whites come to see that they do not have to accept the definition of white that is placed on them by society. They can move beyond the connection to racism to see positive aspects of being European American and feel more comfortable being white. However, the difficult challenge here is to identify what white culture is. Sometimes this can be done only by coming into contact with and interacting with people of color, before moving on to redefine one's own white identity. A second task is to identify the ways in which racism is harmful to whites and to move beyond thinking that racism affects only people of color.

Stage 5: Internalization

In this stage, whites are finally able to integrate their whiteness into all other facets of their identity, and this affects other aspects of social and personal identity—sex role, religious role, and so on. At this point, there is less consciousness about identity; all aspects are internalized and manifested in spontaneous behavior.

SUMMARY

This essay attempts to initiate a dialogue about what it means to be white in the United States as we approach the twenty-first century. At this time, it seems that there are competing notions about what is involved in white identity. It is seen as both invisible and real. It is seen as both privilege and liability. It is seen as both positive and negative. And all of these dimensions are played out in our communication with others. Our identities are simultaneously shaping and being shaped by our communication.

It seems appropriate to conclude with some questions for reflection and discussion:

1. When was the first time you were aware of your racial identity? How was it talked about with your friends and family as you were growing up?
2. How did your family talk about ethnicity?
3. If you are white, in what contexts do you think about being white? Do you feel white when you are with only white people?
4. What are the communicative consequences of thinking about race in categories like black and white? What do you feel when you can't easily categorize someone as black or white?

References

Asante, M. K. (aka A. L. Smith), (1973). *Transracial Communication.* Englewood Cliffs, N.J.: Prentice-Hall.

Frankenburg, R. (1993). *White Women, Race Matters: The Social Construction of Whiteness.* Minneapolis: University of Minnesota Press.

Gallagher, C. A. (1994). White construction in the university. *Socialist Review, 1/2,* 167–187.

Hardiman, R. (1994). "White Racial Identity Development in the United States." In E. P Salett and D. R. Koslow (Eds.), *Race, Ethnicity and Self: Identity in Multicultural Perspective,* 117–142. Washington, D.C.: National MultiCultural Institute.

Hecht, M., Collier, M. J., & Ribeau, S. (1993). *African-American Communication.* Newbury Park, Calif.: Sage.

Helms, J. E. (1990). "Toward a Model of White Racial Identity Development." In J. Helms (Ed.), *Black and White Racial Identity: Theory, Research, and Practice,* 49–66, New York: Greenwood Press.

Martin, J. N., Krizek, R. L., Nakayama, T., & Bradford, L. (1996). Labels for white Americans. *Communication Quarterly, 44,* 125–144.

Martin, J. N., Hecht, M. L., and Larkey, L. K. (1994). Conversational improvement strategies for interethnic communication: African American and European American perspectives. *Communication Monographs, 61,* 237–255.

McIntosh, P. (1995). "White Privilege and Male Privilege: A Personal Account of Coming to See Correspondences Through Work in Women's Studies." In M. L. Andersen and P. H. Collins (Eds.), *Race, Class and Gender,* 76–86. Belmont, Calif.: Wadsworth.

Nakayama, T. (1993). "Dis/orienting Identities: Asian Americans, History and Intercultural Communication." In A. Gonzalez, M. Houston, and V. Chen (Eds.), *Our Voices: Essays in Culture, Ethnicity and Communication,* 12–17. Los Angeles: Roxbury.

Nakayama, T., & Krizek, R. L. (1995). Whiteness: A strategic rhetoric. *Quarterly Journal of Speech, 81,* 291–309.

Omi, M., & Winant, H. (1992). "Racial Formations." In P. S. Rothenberg (Ed.), *Race, Class and Gender in the United States,* 26–35. New York: St. Martin's Press.

Tanno, D. (1994). "Names, Narratives, and the Evolution of Ethnic Identity." In A. Gonzalez, M. Houston, & V. Chen (Eds.), *Our Voices: Essays in Culture, Ethnicity and Communication,* 30–33. Los Angeles: Roxbury.

Trinh, T. M. (1986/7). Difference: A special third world women issue. *Discourse,* 8.

Wilson, S. (1995). Black and white perceptions of justice are worlds apart. *Arizona Republic,* October 4, 1995, p. A2.

Concepts and Questions

1. According to Martin, what is the role played by communication in defining one's ethnic identity?
2. How do the dimensions of white ethnic identity differ from the ethnic identity of other co-cultures in U.S. society?
3. What are the development stages of white ethnic identity? Do these stages differ in any significant way from ethnic identity development in other cultures or co-cultures?
4. Explain what Martin is asserting when she writes, "cultural identities are negotiated, co-created, reinforced, and challenged through communication."
5. How did Martin answer the following question: "What is the difference between racial and ethnic identity"?
6. How does Martin define "bounded identities"? How does she define "dominant identities"?
7. Do you believe there is a set of cultural norms and symbols shared by most white people? If yes, what are some of these norms and symbols?
8. What does Martin mean by the word *standpoint*?
9. Can you list some white "core symbols"?
10. How would you answer the following question that was posed by Martin: "How do we develop a sense of whiteness?"

Chicano/a Ethnicity: A Concept in Search of Content

JAMES STEVEN SAUCEDA

POLEMIC INTRODUCTION

As an American citizen of Mexican ancestry who has lived all his life in Los Angeles, as one who first studied Chicano/a ethnicity in the streets, then in a university setting, and who now develops and teaches Chicano/a courses at such institutions as the University of Southern California and the California School of Professional Psychology, I have come to the conclusion that most researchers have completely misunderstood the essential mechanisms of Chicano/a ethnicity.

I state this as a given, irrespective of whether a credentialed citizen lives in the barony of sociology, anthropology, psychology, or ethnic studies. The record of research on the Chicano/a, in fact, must be clearly characterized as misinformed, misguided, and indeed of very little value to anyone seeking knowledge of this group. Historically, various fields of inquiry have produced and marketed scholastically vapid nomenclatures, false and damaging generalities on Chicano/a family structure, unexamined and even ludicrous assumptions of personality and culture. Unfortunately, even as I write, more inaccurate portraits of the Chicano/a are being painted (and under the ironic banner of objective science).

This article is a first formulation of what I see as a corrective exploration into the real working components of Chicano/a ethnicity. It is intended to spur on a new and more detailed investigation into the American congeries of ethnicity in general and the Chicano/a in particular.

I readily admit to the reader that my views often deviate, contradict, and as a rule challenge the status quo regarding the subject. However, I assert that all of my observations find confirmation within the actual experience of the person of Mexican heritage whose ongoing transactional culture is exercised within the territorial boundaries of the United States.

UNDERSTANDING THE TERMS MEXICAN AMERICAN AND CHICANO/A

In 1848, by the signing of the Treaty of Guadalupe Hidalgo, a new phrase was added to the political vocabulary of the United States: the Mexican American. This label was assigned to the highly heterogeneous group formerly known as Mejicanos or Mexicans. Many centuries before this treaty, the Mexican had fully developed a culture fusing two rich heritages: native Indio with European Spanish. Now, officially a third culture, American, was added to the already culturally diverse Mexican people. The formal entrance of American culture into Mexican came as the result of what Abraham Lincoln and Henry Clay considered a calculated and unconstitutional war with Mexico.[1]

Hence it must be understood that the Treaty of Guadalupe Hidalgo initially created the entity of the Mexican American by simply widening the territorial boundaries of America. Many Americans have forgotten, or never realized, that eventually *one half* of Mexican land was acquired by the American invasion of Mexican territory at this time.

Today the term *Mexican American* is more likely to be the identifying label of a second-generation person than of a third-generation person. Peñalosa suggests that those who call themselves Mexican Americans are found near the middle of an ethnicity continuum. He further states that Mexican Americans "are those for whom being of Mexican ancestry is something of which they are constantly conscious and which looms importantly as part of their self-conception. Their Mexican descent may constitute for them a positive value, a negative value, or more generally an ambiguous blend of the two."[2]

The term that is used quite frequently throughout the Southwest, and to my mind most predominantly, is *Chicano/a*. There is much uncertainty as to the origin and present meanings of the term *Chicano/a*. The term can be traced in print to a fictional sketch entitled "El Hoyo" that was published in 1947.[3] At that time the author apparently only meant the term to designate "a short way of saying Mexicano."[4]

But this term, though controversial, remains preferable over the label *Mexican American* when discussing the topic of ethnicity. I assert this preference first because *Chicano/a* is generally thought to be a self-generated term. That is, the group in question created the term to refer to itself. This holds true whether one traces *Chicano/a* to an Indian origin, as in the Nahuatl pronunciation of "Mexicano" as "Me-shi-ca-noh" or to the contraction of "Chicane."[5]

The second reason I use *Chicano/a* over other labels is that it is more self-consciously ethnic. As Meier and Rivera state in *The Chicano: A History of Mexican Americans,* "Chicano" carries "overtones of ethnic nationalism."[6] Peñalosa concurs by placing the term *Chicano* "at the other end of the continuum," that is, at a point of highly invested ethnic identification. He submits further that Chicano/as "are those who are not only acutely aware of their Mexican identity and descent but are committed to work actively for the betterment of their people."[7]

This brief discussion of *Mexican American* vis-à-vis *Chicano/a*, as terms relevant for ethnic investigations, has simply sought to establish *Chicano/a* as the more accurate term to use. It is not a dogmatic position but only a personal attempt to establish a more precise vocabulary for ethnic study of this group.

THE ENTANGLED DEFINITIONS OF ETHNICITY

Isajiw, in a quest to discover an accurate definition of ethnicity, recently examined 65 sociological and anthropological studies.[8] What he found was the startling fact that 52 of these studies provided *no* explicit definition at all.[9] This strongly suggests that researchers generally assume that ethnicity, as a term or concept, requires little to no clarification.

Gleason has given us his frustration regarding the way in which most researchers define ethnicity. "My complaint is not that the reality is complex and elusive; nor is it that terms like melting pot, pluralism, and ethnicity are ambiguous. My complaint rather is that these ambiguous terms are handled as though they had one unequivocal meaning."[10] Casavantes, specifically studying the ethnicity of the Chicano/a, begins his analysis by positing that such discussions are "handicapped because of confusion about what it is that makes a person a member of an ethnic group."[11]

In Isajiw's search for a standardized definition of ethnicity, he was successful in compiling a roster of attributes he believed to be distinctly ethnic. Isajiw's list was created by reducing 27 definitions to the five attributes that recurred most frequently. Thus, according to a general consensus of opinion, ethnic membership requires the following conditions: common culture, common religion, common language, common race, and common ancestral origin.[12]

At first glance it may appear that this roster provides a legitimate, and even easy, way to establish ethnic membership. Ostensibly, all one need do is verify whether any population satisfies these five requirements; and if they do, they may officially be designated as an ethnic group.

Unfortunately, I submit that there are two major problems with this and all similar lists, which truly invalidate their use. First, I maintain that *none* of these five attributes, whether taken singularly or in concert, actually informs us or truly identifies the locus of ethnicity in American subcultures. Second, even if these attributes did establish ethnic membership, I will show that the Chicano/a fails to satisfy *all* five requirements.

Most likely the reader will express surprise at both my assertions. Certainly there is a compelling common-sense type of trust in the ethnic roster presented by Isajiw. Even I do not contest that the roster presents the most "agreed-upon" criteria for ethnicity. My argument is more elemental; I believe the roster actually ignores the *essential* mechanisms of ethnic identification in America. However, I will postpone presenting the crucial features left out of Isajiw's list until *after* I have systematically demonstrated that the Chicano/a experience does not fulfill *any* of Isajiw's list.

The most basic ethnic assumption regarding the Chicano/a is that he or she shares a common culture. It is obvious that the singular term *culture* has pluralistic impact for the Chicano/a. Certainly American culture is shared, but, of course, *all* citizens share in a mainstream or national culture; hence this cannot constitute an ethnic prerequisite.

Typically it is assumed that the Chicano/a shares a traditional Mexican culture (which Peñalosa believes is "initially overriding but subsequently attenuated."[13]) Isajiw's own definition of common culture states that one is "born into a group which shares certain cultural traits and therefore becomes socialized into them."[14]

The fair and logical question to ask at this point is: What are the specific and shared Mexican cultural traits of Chicano/as? Over the years researchers have indeed compiled a fairly consistent list of such traits. These may be summarized from Casavantes' study "Pride and Prejudice: A Mexican American Dilemma": the existence of and reliance upon an extended family; a nonjoiner attitude, that is, refusal to join any volunteer associations; maintenance of traditional values (high resistance to change); staunch anti-intellectualism; behavior dominated by a machismo complex; inability to be future oriented; and a fatalistic attitude (cultural passivity).[15]

These traits do seem to establish specific cultural attributes and therefore appear proper for use as true generalizations of the common cultural background of Chicano/as. Furthermore, most sociological and anthropological literature on Chicano/as subscribes to this list. For instance, Octavio Romano's review essay, "The Anthropology and Sociology of the Mexican-Americans," details how a consensus of opinion may be found among such researchers as William Madsen, Ruth Tuck, Lyle Saunders, Muro S. Edmonson, Florence R. Kluckhohn, Fred Strodbeck, Celia Heller, Julian Samora, and Richard A. Lamanna.[16]

Importantly, however, Casavantes, as well as Romano and others, has convincingly argued that *all* of these so-called cultural traits are in fact only generalized descriptions of *any* people living in poverty.[17] Hence, what researchers have typically done is mistake behaviors determined by economic conditions for specific cultural attributes. The result has been an enduring misconception of Chicano/as as anti-intellectual or as nonjoiners, and so on.

Garcia-Bahne concurs with Casavantes, stating, "Ethnicity and culture become confounded with the realities of living conditions, and the qualities of the family get viewed as if they were static and inherent. Being Chicano, then, automatically and simplistically is taken to be synonymous with having a set of stereotypic values that explain and account for the conditions within which Chicanos find themselves."[18]

It is also important to remember that many studies on Chicano/as are based upon nonrepresentative samples (that is, atypical rural, border-town populations often form the sample). Even in 1973, Alvarez reported that at least 83 percent of the Chicano population was urban.[19] Certainly the 1980 statistic would be significantly higher. It is more than doubtful that the generalizations made by researchers on the rural Chicano are correct, but they certainly cannot be applied to an urban context; and the Chicano is urban.

To summarize, the usual traits ascribed to Chicano/as (as being derived from Mexican culture) are in fact not ethnic at all, but economic. Hence the culture of poverty is being described, not the Chicano/a culture. Now admittedly, traits other than those described above have been submitted as cultural. For instance, Murillo believes, "The cultural differences between the Mexican American and the Anglo (dominant or mainstream population) can be viewed in terms of differences in mental set or orientations, style or 'naturalness' in behavior."[20] This murky differentiation supposedly relates some kind of Latin frame of mind or Latin quality of behavior. Murillo gets even more ambiguous by saying: "To the Mexican American it is much more valuable to experience things directly through intellectual awareness and through emotional experiences rather than indirectly through past accomplishments and accumulation of wealth."[21] Here Murillo is after a Chicano/a "spiritual" trait, but as with his earlier notions, it amounts to nothing more than a vague and visceral assumption. Murillo never provides psychological data or any verification whatever to support his explanation of such Chicano/a cultural traits.

It is safe to say that the reader has now witnessed a thorough undermining of the idea that any clear "common culture" exists among Chicano/as.

The next ethnic prerequisite on Isajiw's roster is that of common religion. The problem with this is that even though statistics show predominant membership in Roman Catholicism, such numbers do not establish common religion. For I take common religion to refer to a highly agreed-upon and practiced religious philosophy. Certainly the impact of any religion upon American ethnicity is most difficult to trace. But what is crucial here is the fact that it is ludicrous to suggest that Chicano/as cannot be Protestants or even atheists without somehow losing their ethnicity.

More directly, Chicano/a participation in Catholicism is fraught with diversity: Witness the Los Angeles example of Católicos por La Raza, a fervent group that asserted in the late 1960s that major changes must be made in the orthodox posture of the church. More recently, Chicano novelists (such as Ron Arias, Thomas Rivera, and Rudolfo Anaya) as well as poets, playwrights, and muralists have reflected a decidedly anti-Catholic sentiment that subverts the idea of a common religion. Casavantes also discounts Catholicism as *not* forming a crucial or essential ethnic requirement.[22]

The third point on Isajiw's ethnic list is common language. This area is easier to dismiss than the first two. For as Alvarez views this matter, in many cases the Chicano/a does *not* speak any Spanish at all.[23] My own experience and years of observation readily confirm this fact. For even in the barrios of East Los Angeles, Chicano teatros often cannot perform their own obras or actos in Spanish. This situation does not, I think, reduce the ethnic portent of teatros, but it does highlight the fact that language cannot be considered an ethnic prerequisite. Certainly if the Spanish language were truly a criterion for Chicano/a ethnicity, I would conservatively estimate that at least one-third of the Chicano/a population would be eliminated.

Common race is yet another stipulation that is pointless when discussing Chicano/a ethnicity. First, the same race, in any strict interpretation, subsumes both the Chicano *and* the dominant Caucasian culture. Second, even if race were reduced to some set of physically distinct or visually observable characteristics, the Chicano/a physiognomy does not comply. As Peñalosa succinctly summarizes the matter, "A large proportion are not physically distinct from the majority American population; hence the group as a whole cannot be characterized in terms of race."[24]

The final criterion of Isajiw's roster is common ancestry. While I agree that most Chicano/as genetically and historically share a similar ancestry, I still maintain that such ancestry is no indication of ethnicity. Stated another way, a person does not have to share a common ancestry to be a bona fide member of Chicano/a ethnicity. To explain my position on common ancestry, I must now submit and elaborate on what I believe actually constitutes Chicano/a ethnic membership.

THE TWO INTERACTING MECHANISMS OF CHICANO/A ETHNICITY

Having rejected all of the status-quo criteria for establishing ethnic membership, I will now present two mechanisms that I assert form a more authentic definition of Chicano/a ethnicity.

I

The most elemental prerequisite for Chicano/a ethnic membership is *one's psychological identification with, and subjective belief of acceptance into, the presumed identity of the group*. In short, the definition of Chicano/a ethnicity rests upon the psychological constructs of identification and acceptance, *not* upon any genetic, socioeconomic, historic, or demographic features (though the latter may encourage identification and acceptance).

This definition is based upon an earlier one of Max Weber's. It was he who correctly postulated that the locus of ethnicity is psychological. I should point out that my reformulation of Weber's definition departs from his own in that he felt "ethnic groups...entertain a subjective belief *in their common descent* because of similarities of physical type or of customs or both; or because of memories of colonialization."[25] While certainly this is generally true of the Chicano/a experience, it is not operationally true of the definition. For one does *not* have to believe that one shares a common descent to be a member of the ethnic group. Although Weber rightly acknowledged that "it does not matter whether or not an objective blood relationship exists,"[26] he still apparently felt that all members of the ethnic group needed to entertain a subjective belief of common descent.

Weber hit upon another key concept that my definition incorporates:

> Ethnic membership...differs from the kinship group precisely by being a *presumed identity*, not a group with concrete social action, like the latter. In our sense ethnic membership does not constitute a group; it only facilitates group formation of any kind, particularly in the political sphere...it is primarily the political community, no matter how artificially organized, that inspires the belief in common ethnicity.[27]

Unfortunately, Weber's decidedly subjective interpretation of ethnicity can be easily misunderstood, I think, as a construct created to dismiss real social groups and their ethno-politico activism. In order to clarify Weber, I must first express my belief that *ethnicity, at its core, is a complex of styles of behavior resulting from existential anxiety and fear of isolation*. In short, ethnicity is essentially a mechanism to reduce individual alienation by creating a sense of community. Most often, common descent provides convenient communal referents, but I maintain these referents *do not establish or propel ethnicity*. The source of ethnicity is existential despair; this condition leads to psychological identification with the ethnic group (which one implicitly presumes, or explicitly is told, he or she inherently belongs within). But the resultant sense of community (which is attributable to social validation the group provides) often is confused with the similar history of one's heritage. That ethnic groups typically provide an authentic buffer to existential anxiety and also provide a focused way to raise self-esteem, I do not deny. I am simply attempting to locate the *actual* mechanism of ethnicity, not diminish at all its importance or potentially positive impact.

What Weber is asserting is that ethnicity is a belief system—not a physical reality (due to traceable objective criteria), but rather a philosophic point of view. It follows, then, that the political community most often establishes the observable contours of an ethnic group. This does not imply, necessarily, that all ethnic consciousness is trumped up by jargonizers wishing only to mobilize a population into political action (though this does occur). It generally means that a group of people with political sensitivity often attempt to discover mutual pride in the cultural contributions (intellectual as well as artistic) of their more or less common ancestry. The result can be a more humane and astute thrust for social action.

To return to the central point, Chicano/a ethnicity is then basically a metaphysical reality, and therefore a physical illusion. Those looking to find a "group" will search in vain; those wishing to quantify Chicano/a traits and behaviors will only discover endless diversity, not a homogeneous personality. It must be remembered that all the alleged ethnic attributes of common culture, religion, and so on are but possible symptoms or badges of ethnicity, not ethnicity itself. Such commonalities may foster a feeling of community (often called ethnic), but without the psychological identification and belief of acceptance into the presumed identity of the group, common culture, religion, and so on are powerless to establish ethnicity. Whereas, if one does have the identification and belief of acceptance into the presumed identity of the group, that person does not need to have a common ancestry or religion and so on to gain ethnic membership.

I draw support for my subjective definition of ethnicity from Luis Valdez's brilliant play *Zoot Suit*. Valdez, from 1965 to the present, has worked to express the range of Chicano/a ethnicity through his unique form of theater. *Zoot Suit*, which was developed and premiered at the Mark Taper Forum in Los Angeles, enjoyed phenomenal success within the Chicano community.

In the play certain assumptions regarding Chicano/a ethnicity are tested; and even though the referents of the play are in the early 1940s, the questions also apply now. One of the pachucos on trial in the Sleepy Lagoon case, as dramatized by Valdez, is unique. Though he shares in all the personality behaviors of his "homeboys" in the barrio of East Los Angeles (that is, style of dress, speech, walk, and so on), he still stands out. The reason is that this pachuco is "Anglo" or "White," and *not* of Mexican ancestry at all.

Valdez has the character first subjected to ridicule, only to make the point that being "Anglo" is irrelevant to his also being Chicano. He is accepted into the group as a "real" Chicano *not* because of similar heritage, but because he has fully identified and felt accepted into the presumed identity of the group.

Another example confirming the idea that Chicano/a ethnicity is psychological was found recently in the *Los Angeles Times*. In an article written by Gerald Haslam, the career of one Amado Muro was explored.

Muro, who died in 1971, was considered by many to be "the funniest, brightest, most moving, accomplished and prolific"[28] of modern Chicano writers. Surprisingly, the point of Haslam's article was that "there was no Muro: there never had been. The semi-educated young Chicano turned out to have been Chester Seltzer, a middle-aged Anglo journalist who had adopted his wife's maiden name (Amada Muro) as a nom de plume."[29] Haslam then dubs Seltzer an "honorary Chicano,"[30] though according to my definition he is a bona fide Chicano like Valdez's characters.

II

Chicano/a ethnic membership is *created by racist intolerance and stereotypic classifications imposed by the mainstream American society.* It seems ironic that the non-Chicano/a population often defines what it is to be Chicano/a, but it does. In fact, so enduring are the racist typifications of the dominant society that if an individual's behaviors resemble those that society labels ethnic, that individual is involuntarily made ethnic.

In the 1940s in Los Angeles, all one had to do to be ethnically identified as Mexican American was to wear a zoot suit. Even today, the government identifies persons eligible for affirmative action by Spanish surname (irrespective of the fact that such a surname does not necessarily imply a minority background).

The result of 132 years of calculated discrimination in America has produced notions of Chicano/a ethnicity that are as inescapable as they are false. For instance, people in Los Angeles typically believe that if you wear starched khaki pants, a long plaid pendleton shirt and a bandanna set low over your eyes that you are not only Mexican, but criminal—not only criminal, but a knife-carrying, dirty gang-member type of criminal, and so on ad nauseum.

Unfortunately, many Chicano/as unwittingly identify with the aggressor and live out the stereotypes of criminality. But their criminal behavior is still the result of the criminal conditions created (and perpetuated against them) by the dominant power structure.

Another repercussion of such racism is the polarization of people of Mexican heritage into an antagonistic form of ethnic identification. Now, the "community" channels its collective anger and alienation through its own racism (peaking further the self-defensiveness of society at large).

In an important book entitled *Ethnopsychoanalysis*, Devereux has articulated well this dysfunctional aspect of ethnicity. I believe that many Chicano/as get caught in such a hypercathected (overemotionally invested) form of ethnicity:

> the contemporary scene abounds in examples of persons stripping *themselves* of all their potentially meaningful class identities, ceasing to be *anything but Xs,* where X denotes a real or spurious ethnos. This process is more impoverishing than ever today, when one's ethnic identity can structure only increasingly limited segments of one's total potential repertoire. Hence, the moment A insists on being *only*—and ostentatiously—an X, twenty-four hours a day, large segments of his behavior, which cannot…be correlated with his ethnic identity, are deprived of any organizing and stabilizing 'skeleton.'[31]

Hence the tantras of "Viva la Raza" or "Yo soy Chicano/a," *if* hypercathected, actually form the signal of an undernourished sense of self, *not* a positive rallying point or a true expression of "el grito" ("the cry" for liberation).

Devereux also points out that many ethnic identity tokens result from a type of "antagonistic acculturation" and "deliberate deviation."[32] I believe that certain Chicano/a behaviors—for example, fashions of clothing, cars, even walking styles—may carry a negative valence or antagonism against mainstream society (as a way to defend or keep more intact one's own ethnic identity). Such antagonism and deviation may result in a healthy sense of self-improvement for the ethnic group (for it goads the group to compete and outdo the dominant society).

Unfortunately, I assert that many trends of Chicano/a ethnicity are primarily dysfunctional because they are motivated by an invidious intent and because they are hypercathected. That there are justifiable reasons for the anger and the urge to permit ethnic identity "to engulf one's other class identities, whose unduplicable accumulation is…the very basis of an authentic identity,"[33] I do not deny. But accepting the above explanation gives one a new tool for better understanding certain facts of Chicano/a contributions to America.

For instance, it explains why it took almost one-and-a-half centuries before a Luis Valdez attempted to commercially utilize a conventional theater, and also why his work *Zoot Suit* failed on Broadway. It failed because of its implicit, invidious statement against all audience members who were not Hispanic or Chicano/a. In short, Chicano/a artists have historically been propelled by an aesthetic impulse that is dissociative, introverted, and *not* integrative. Its overriding disdain for the dominant society has significantly impeded the Chicano/a's ability to creatively borrow and incorporate aspects from the mainstream. Typically, any Chicano/a who attempts to grow through direct transaction with "Anglo" culture is indicted as an ethnic sellout.

But this kind of closed-system approach in Chicano/a ethnicity is not limited to "Anglo" influences. Recently I was with the leader of a band in Los Angeles who dubbed his band's music "Chicano." I asked him why it was "Chicano," and his response was that it was not at all influenced by "foreign" sources (he included jazz as being "black" and rock as being "white"). A similar closed system is Chicano/a Teatro (which generally will not perform before a mainstream audience).

The dream behind such incestuous art is that it retains and refines some "pure" ethnic vision. The reality is that its growth is stunted; such art will remain in a state of malnutrition until it becomes integrated into a fuller context of art proper.

CONCLUSION: OR NOW WE CAN BEGIN

The reader may conceivably be disappointed that I have put forward only two interactive mechanisms as authentically representing Chicano/a ethnicity. But I adhere to Isajiw's own goal when offering a definitional base for discussion: "The aim of an ideally good definition is not to identify as many properties of the phenomenon studied as possible, but to identify the minimum number of properties under which a greater variety of properties could be subsumed, yet which would also clearly indicate which properties should not be included."[34]

I believe that the two mechanisms I presented accurately account for the range of Chicano/a ethnic identity. Furthermore, I have indicated which properties should not be included when defining Chicano/a ethnicity. As I stated at the opening of this paper, I view *all* the ideas presented as a first formulation to help correct and establish a true content to the concept of Chicano/a ethnicity.

I am aware that many may forcefully disagree with my positions (including, if not particularly, other Chicano/as). But I do not view any of my ideas dogmatically; I simply view them as interpretations to be reckoned with.

Notes

1. Glenn W. Price, *Origins of the War with Mexico* (Austin: University of Texas Press, 1970) pp. 89, 91–92.
2. Fernando Peñalosa, "Toward an Operational Definition of the Mexican American," in *Aztlan: Chicano Journal of the Social Sciences,* Spring 1970, Volume I, No. I, p. 4.
3. Edward Simmen, "Chicano: Origin and Meaning" in *Pain and Promise: The Chicano Today,* ed. Edward Simmen (New York: New American Library, 1972), p. 53.
4. Ibid., p. 54.
5. Ibid., p. 54.
6. Matt S. Meier, & Feliciano Rivera, *The Chicanos: A History of Mexican Americans* (New York: Hill and Wang, 1972), p. viii.
7. Peñalosa, p. 4.
8. Wsevolod W. Isajiw, "Definitions of Ethnicity," in *Ethnicity,* 1974, Volume I, No. 2, p. 111.
9. Ibid., p. 111.
10. Philip Gleason, "Confusion Compounded: The Melting Pot in the 1960's and 1970's" in *Ethnicity,* 1979, Volume 6, No. 1, p. 17.
11. Edward Casavantes, "Pride and Prejudice: A Mexican American Dilemma," in *Chicanos: Social and Psychological Perspectives,* ed. Carrol A. Hernandez, Marsha J. Haug, & Nathaniel N. Wagner (Saint Louis, Mo.: The C. V. Mosby Company, 1976), p. 9.
12. Isajiw, p. 117. The list actually registers *twelve* attributes, but only five clearly were most representative.
13. Peñalosa, p. 5.
14. Isajiw, p. 119.
15. Casavantes, p. 11.
16. Octavio Romano, "The Anthropology and Sociology of the Mexican-Americans," in *Voices: Readings From El Grito* (Berkeley: Quinto Sol, 1971), pp. 26–39.
17. Casavantes, pp. 9–14.
18. Betty Garcia-Bahne, "La Chicana and the Chicano Family," in *Essays on La Mujer,* ed. Rosaura Sanchez & Rosa Martinez Cruz (Los Angeles: Chicano Studies Center Publications), p. 30.
19. Rodolfo Alvarez, "The Psycho-Historical and Socioeconomic Development of the Chicano Community in the United States," in *Chicanos: Social and Psychological Perspectives,* p. 47.
20. Nathan Murillo, "The Mexican American Family," in *Chicanos: Social and Psychological Perspectives,* p. 17.

21. Ibid., p. 18.
22. Casavantes, p. 12.
23. Alvarez, pp. 50–54.
24. Peñalosa, p. 3.
25. Weber cited in Isajiw, p. 116.
26. Ibid., p. 116.
27. Ibid., p. 116.
28. Womack cited in "The Strange Case of Chester Seltzer, Honorary Chicano," by Gerald Haslam, *The Los Angeles Times*, April 27, 1980, "West View" section, p. 3.
29. Ibid., p. 3.
30. Ibid., p. 3.
31. George Devereux, *Ethnopsychoanalysis: Psychoanalysis and Anthropology as Complementary Frames of Reference* (Berkeley: University of California Press, 1978), p. 172.
32. Ibid., p. 157.
33. Ibid., p. 172.
34. Isajiw, p. 119.

Concepts and Questions

1. Why does Sauceda believe that the signing of the Treaty of Guadalupe Hidalgo created the phrase "Mexican American"?

2. What distinction does Sauceda make between the phrases "Mexican American" and "Chicano/a"?

3. Why does Sauceda maintain that there is confusion surrounding the word "ethnicity"? How does he believe the word should be defined?

4. Do you agree with Sauceda that "the Chicano/a experience does not fulfill *any* of Isajiw's list"?

5. What does Sauceda believe to be the most elemental prerequisite for Chicano/a membership? Can his prerequisite apply to all ethnic groups? If "yes," why? If "no," why?

6. Do you agree with Sauceda's assertion, made nearly thirty-five years ago, that "Chicano/a ethnic membership is "created by racist intolerance and stereotypic classifications imposed by the mainstream American society"? If the assertion is true, can it be applied to other ethnic groups?

7. Do you believe that the intolerance and stereotyping Sauceda referred to nearly thirty-five years ago is as prevalent today as it was when Sauceda made the assertion?

8. What does Sauceda mean by the phrase "a closed-system" approach to ethnicity?

Straddling Cultural Borders: Exploring Identity in Multiple Reacculturation

CHUKA ONWUMECHILI

PETER O. NWOSU

RONALD L. JACKSON II

INTRODUCTION

The study of multiple reacculturation is very sparse in the intercultural adjustment field. Sussman (2005) suggests that this is so because "the number of Americans or other Westerners re-migrating to their home countries is negligible so no research has examined this phenomenon. But Western return sojourners are plentiful (business executives, students and teachers, missionaries, government and military personnel) and much research has investigated these populations" (p. 30). In essence, because most of intercultural adjustment studies are conducted by Western researchers, most research has focused attention on those incidences common to Westerners. This skewing of research has resulted in the absence of studies on the lives of those who move back and forth across cultures. These rarely studied individuals are better known as cultural transients.

Some scholars such as Onwumechili, Nwosu, Jackson, and James-Hughes (2003); Kim (2001); and

Reprinted courtesy of Chuka Onwumechili, Peter O. Nwosu, and Ronald L. Jackson II. This original essay first appeared in the twelfth edition of this book. All rights reserved. Permission to reprint must be obtained from the authors and the publisher. Chuka Onwumechili is Professor in the Department of Communication at Bowie State University, Bowie, Maryland. Peter O. Nwosu is in the Department of Communications and Associate Vice President for Academic Affairs at Tennessee State University. Ronald L. Jackson II is Professor and Head of the Department of African American Studies at the University of Illinois. He is also Professor of Media & Cinema Studies in the College of Media.

Berry (1999) point out that the lack of accurate global data makes it difficult to track the trend of these transients. The number of transients, however, is likely to be significant because of factors such as large economic gaps between nations and improved and relatively less expensive global transportation. These factors, for instance, have promoted the increase in movement of labor across international borders. For instance, the phenomenon tagged *Taai Hung Yahn*[1] or "astronauts" in Hong Kong describes husbands and single men who shuttle between their new immigrant country in the West where their family now resides and their new businesses in their home country Hong Kong. Other examples include Africans who work in the United States but return frequently to Africa for significant periods in the year, and the frequent border crossings (back and forth) by Mexicans into the United States. Sussman (2005) also points out the rise of another group of transients: "the new Hong Kong immigrant is that of the manager whose work takes him to Shenzhen or Dongguan or Shanghai for a week or month at a time and whose family remains in Hong Kong" (pp. 33–34). Therefore, the incidence of transiency is not only apparent but it is perhaps increasing and driven largely by economics, ease of transportation, and search for respect and status as demonstrated in Onwumechili, Nwosu, Jackson, and James-Hughes (2003).

It is because of the importance of transients and the scarcity of research on their lives that this paper focuses on theorizing about their negotiation of cultural identity as they move from one culture to the other. The essay begins with a review of acculturation research. Then it provides details about the types of intercultural transients. The remainder of the paper applies several cultural identity theories, with particular focus on cultural contracts theory, to the negotiation of transients' identity.

ACCULTURATION RESEARCH

Acculturation studies have been with us for almost a century. Persons (1987) cited Park as one of the earliest researchers in the area. Park carried out a 1914 study of immigrants coming in contact with a host culture and concluded that such immigrants follow a progressive and linear process that began with contact, going through accommodation, and culminating in assimilation. Communication scholars, however, often cite studies in the 1950s as the harbinger of research in acculturation in the field of intercultural communication. One of such early 1950s studies was by Sven Lysgaard (1955) who investigated the cultural adjustment patterns of Norwegian Fulbright scholars to the United States. Lysgaard's study became historical as it provided the field with a model of cultural adjustment pattern of foreigners in a host culture. That model known as the U-curve hypothesized that the adjustment patterns began with a period of euphoria and then advanced to culture shock, recovery, and eventual adjustment.

The U-curve hypothesis was eventually extended to a W-curve by Gullahorn and Gullahorn (1963) who hypothesized that those who had experienced the U-curve pattern are likely to go through a similar pattern upon their return home. Today, both the U-curve and W-curve are no longer considered valid descriptors of cultural adjustment patterns (Onwumechili & Okereke-Arungwa, 2001). The primary reason for this is that several scholars have not found research support for any of the two hypotheses (Sussman, 2001; Berry, 1999; Ward, Kennedy, Okura, & Kojima, 1998; Anderson, 1994; and Brislin, 1981). Berry (1999), for instance, noted that there is more than one possible outcome for individuals who come into contact with a foreign culture. Both the U and W curves failed to acknowledge the possibility of different outcomes for different individuals and instead theorized that all persons are bound to adjust to the host culture. Berry's work, as well as Navas et al. (2007 & 2005) and Bourhis et al. (1997), showed that individuals do not always adjust successfully to a host foreign culture. Instead, they may assimilate, become separated from the host culture or become deviant depending on their response to the culture shock, their choices for coping, and the relationship between their adjustment ideal and reality. Padilla and Perez (2003) also note that there are numerous factors including skin color, accented speech, religious dressing, and gender that may affect choices that persons make on whether to assimilate, adjust, or separate from a host culture. Furthermore, other studies showed that reacculturation for those who return to their home culture after

Figure 1 *The U-curve indicating a process of euphoria upon entry, shock, and depression before recovery and adjustment.*

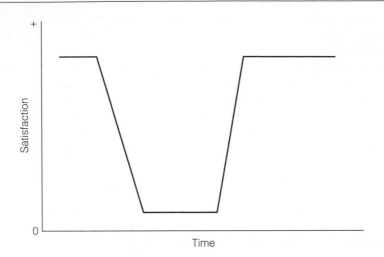

a stay in a foreign culture were not a mere extension of the U curve. Instead, the returning sojourners had significantly different problems which included a fixed perception of the homeland, unawareness of own and other's changes, unexpectedness of reentry problems, among a host of other factors (see Berry, 2005; Cox, 2004; Sussman, 1986; and Uehara, 1986). The U and W curves, however, remain significant at least because of their illustrative value in describing patterns of acculturation for those who eventually adjust to a foreign culture (Onwumechili, Nwosu, Jackson, & James-Hughes, 2003). Figures 1 and 2 provide graphic descriptions of both curves.

Acculturation and reacculturation studies, including those reviewed here, have contributed several important concepts in the first 40 years of the field. These include an understanding of culture shock, patterns of adjustment, and communication competence, among others.

Figure 2 *The W-curve, which extended the U-curve hypothesis to the sojourner's return to the homeland.*

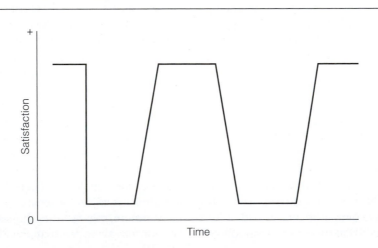

Figure 3 *The cyclical curve, which provides a further extension of the W-curve to depict the process that some transients experience in several encounters with entries and reentries.*

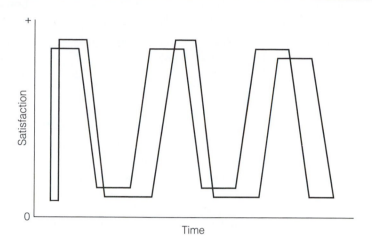

The field, however, has shifted in the last 15 years to a new focus on discovering the effect on cultural identity for individuals who come in contact with foreign cultures (Sussman, 2000; Kim, 2001). This new focus, for example, has included studies in the area of third culture building (Chen & Starosta, 1998; Casmir, 1993) and multiculturalism (Adler, 1982).

It is surprising that in spite of over 50 years of research in the field, the study of a growing group of transients has been largely ignored. Onwumechili, Nwosu, Jackson, and James-Hughes (2003) provide a graphic description, called *cyclical curves*, of the adjustment pattern for transients (see Figure 3). Of course, the figure merely provides an illustrative example of the process for a transient who successfully adjusts across cultures back and forth but the graph does not reflect outcomes for all transients.

TYPOLOGIES OF CULTURAL TRANSIENTS

Onwumechili, Nwosu, Jackson, and James-Hughes (2003) provide a taxonomy of cultural transients using two key variables to describe categories of cultural transients. The variables—length of stay in a culture and function of transient activity—were used to create

(a) short-term socioeconomic/political transients, (b) long-term socioeconomic/political transients, (c) short-term service/employment transients, and (d) long-term service/employment transients.

Socioeconomic/political categorizes those situations where the decision to maintain a link with the transient's country of birth is based on social and/or business reasons. One of the most important differences between the socioeconomic transient and the service/employment transient is that the former is often a citizen of both cultures or at least has permanent residency status. Another important difference between the socioeconomic transient and the service/employment dimension is that for the former, one of the cultural abodes is not used as a place of employment. For the socioeconomic dimension, the place of employment in the home country, if with a large organization, is often with one that does not necessarily seek to hire someone with an international link. Furthermore, the decision to seek a home country employment is socioculturally influenced by the person's affinity with his homeland.

The service/employment category refers to transients whose move is often to seek employment in a foreign continent but whose primary residence is often the country of birth. Transients who are classified under the service/employment category often

Table 1 *Transient Typologies*

Function of Transient Activity	Length of Stay	
	Short-Term (6 months or less in multiple locations)	**Long-Term** (More than 6 months in one location)
Socioeconomic/Political	Brief-staying "astronauts," Nigerian transients	Long-staying "astronauts"
Service-Employment	Agricultural guest workers	Armed Force personnel

enter one of the cultures in order to work on a periodic basis. These transients may often keep work in both cultural locations. Their employment away from home is essentially temporary or seasonal. Their contact with the non-homeland culture has very little to do with social reasons and more to do with employment. We describe each of the categories in detail in the subsequent subsections and Table 1 also shows each typology.

Short-Term Socioeconomic/Political Transients

These transients are those whose reasons for moving repeatedly between two or more cultures are often socioeconomic or political. The short-term identifies these transients as those who spend perhaps six months or less in one culture before moving to the next culture to spend a similar amount of time, back and forth. These types of transients have been in existence as far back as the nineteenth century. Rossler (1995) reported that German craftsmen and artisans denoted such travel patterns in Europe to fill needs for such skills in certain geographical areas.

The length of time is critical in differentiating this group of travelers from the usual vacationers who spend less than a month in visiting a foreign country or place that is culturally different. It is also important to note that because of the short stay of six months or less, transients are often individuals that are self employed or those working in low paying jobs where the turnover is immense. Such a situation allows them to leave the job and easily return to a similar job upon return. Among Nigerians that are involved in this type of intercultural travel are those whose employment is in

the hospitality, transportation (e.g., taxicab business), tax accounting (largely seasonal), or low-paying occupations.

The Hong Kong "astronauts" have been a widely reported group of transients in recent times. Some astronauts can be classified as short-term transients in the socioeconomic category. Chen (1990) reported that one of Hong Kong's "astronauts," Stanley Tam, had flown from Hong Kong to Toronto seven times in 30 months as he shuttled between his job in Hong Kong and his family in Toronto.

Chen points out that sometimes these "astronauts" could earn three times in Hong Kong the income that they could earn in the United States. They felt more secure in the United States and Canada, however, because the social life and schooling were preferred and they had no fear of communist life and policy that could be introduced in Hong Kong by China. Chen added that "Between 30 percent and 60 percent of emigrants are coming back to Hong Kong (after they fled following the handover of Hong Kong to China in 1984) filling important posts left behind by the departure of skilled professionals."

It was a similar situation that drove Nigerians to transiency. Most Nigerians initially traveled to the West before the early 1980s with the plan for a temporary stay after which they would return home to Nigeria for a permanent stay. However, Nigeria's economy collapsed in the early 1980s, a consequence of decades of neglect from military rule, forcing the sojourners to rethink about a permanent return. A large number of those who had a rethink decided to stay permanently in a foreign country, in many cases taking up citizenship. Those who chose to return did not want to take the chance of making a permanent return. Instead, they chose the option of becoming transients (see case in Onwumechili, Nwosu, Jackson, & James-Hughes' report, 2003, pp. 47–48).

Long-Term Socioeconomic/Political Transients

These transients share similar characteristics with their short-term colleagues. We describe them as long-term, however, because they spend a longer period of time in one of the cultures they encounter. In essence, these persons may spend a couple of years in one culture and then sojourn in another country and repeat the process. They do not move from one culture to the other as frequently as do their short-term colleagues.

Some of the Hong Kong "astronauts" also fit into this category. Chen (1990) describes one of such "astronauts" who had returned to Hong Kong after settling in the United States for four years. Chen cited the "astronaut" as stating "I earn about $6,400 a month here (Hong Kong) but couldn't make more than $2,000 if I worked for someone in the United States." Chen also found that in the case of Hong Kong returnees, factors like "language barriers, cultural differences, and the challenge of building a new life" were instrumental in making a decision to become transient. In the same report, Chen described another "astronaut" who immigrated to Australia and stayed two years to satisfy residency requirements before returning to Hong Kong. The transient at the time of Chen's report in 1990 planned to stay in Hong Kong to save money until 1995 before returning once more to Australia. There are other examples such as the case of Andres Bermudez who rose from a foreign farm worker to a large farm contractor in California earning over $300,000 a year (Bakker & Smith, undated; and Mena, 2001). Bermudez later traveled back and forth between the United States and Mexico at least once every three years, staying significant lengths of time, before deciding to run for Mayor of Jerez, Mexico.

Onwumechili, Nwosu, Jackson, and James-Hughes (2003) reported that immigration laws are often critical in determining whether a transient would be short- or long-term. Citizenship provides for travelers to become long-term transients with easy entry and reentry after long absences from a country. The authors also report that several countries, including Ecuador, have recognized the transients' needs by legalizing dual citizenship.

Short-Term Service/Employment Transients

The short-term Service/Employment transient is one who primarily moves across cultural borders because of the demand of work and not because of social considerations. They may choose to work in both cultures and are often in the employ of a large organization that is allowed to hire international labor on temporary or short-term basis. They are short-term because they spend perhaps six months or less in one culture before moving to the next culture to spend a similar amount of time, back and forth.

Seasonal migrant labor groups represent this category of short-term transients. The United States has used these labor groups for years. *The Bracero Program,* for instance, was implemented from 1942 to 1964 and it was used to hire agricultural workers from Mexico to work on farms in the United States (Martin & Martin, 1994). Martin and Martin add that some of these workers "returned year after year" (p. 877). These returnees often had employment in their home country and only worked seasonally in the United States. By the time the program was completed, over four million Mexican farm workers had entered the United States. Several countries including Germany, the United Arab Emirates, Qatar, Kuwait, and Luxembourg also utilize guest workers (Castles, 2006; Jones, 1996; and Rudolph, 1996). The German guest worker system also known as *Gastarbeiter* was initially used after World War II when there was a shortage of industrial workers. The program attracted workers from Turkey, Italy, Greece, and Portugal, among other states. Several of these workers did not return permanently to their home states but began to move transnationally across two countries. The *Gastarbeiter* is still alive today as Turkish citizens stream across the border to Germany to meet shortages in the lower skilled jobs (Castles, 2006; and Rudolph, 1996).

Long-Term Service/Employment Transients

This category of transients shares similar characteristics with their short-term counterparts. They are considered to be long-term transients because they spend a longer period of time in one of the cultures that they encounter. In essence, these persons may spend a couple of years in employment in one culture and then sojourn in another country and then repeat the process. Onwumechili, Nwosu, Jackson, and James-Hughes (2003) identified some sailors and other military personnel who are on overseas tour of military duty as being part of this category of transients. A significant point about military personnel who are on overseas duty is that, unlike their civilian colleagues who frequently encounter foreign culture while overseas, the military personnel are often situated among a network of familiar co-military personnel and friends. They could spend much or all of their time in a foreign land isolated from the host foreign culture by being resident on a military base and surrounding themselves with on-base activities. However, no matter how isolated they may wish to be, they will, at least for brief periods, encounter the host culture when they venture outside the base or come in contact with locals who work on base.

Military personnel on overseas tour are not the only people who can be classified as being members of this category of long-term transients. Foreign employees who are contracted for the long term away from their homeland, for instance, also fit into this category. Several nations, including the United States, Canada, and Germany, have programs that advance the importation of foreign workers to fill shortages of labor in specific employment areas. The United States introduced the H1-B visa which attracts foreigners to the country to fill shortages in several employment areas, but they are not offered citizenship or permanent residency and their stay in the country is dependent on their continued attachment to their employer. These transients may travel back and forth between their homeland and the United States during their period of employment in the United States. In 2000, Germany introduced five-year visas that are designed to attract information technology experts to the country. The German visas have been relatively successful, but like their USA equivalent, they do not offer permanent stay or citizenship. Again, however, like the USA equivalent, it allows those with such visas to become cultural transients straddling the borders of their homeland and Germany.

CULTURAL IDENTITY SHIFTING

Cultural transients are affected by constant challenges to their identities as they move from one culture to the other. There are several theories of cultural identity that allow us to analyze probable cultural effects on the identity of transients. These theories include the *Cultural Identity Model of Cultural Transitions* (CIM), *mindful identity shifting*, *multicultural personhood* (intercultural person), *I-Other dialectic* (e.g., stranger-host), *network theory*, *community builder*, and the *cultural identity model of cultural transitions (CIM)*. Some of these theories are subsumed in Jackson's (1999) cultural contracts theory.

In this section we shall begin our discussion by reviewing the applicability of the Cultural Identity Model which has been used by Sussman (2005) to explain the cultural identity of Hong Kong returnees including "astronauts." We will also review Jackson's cultural contracts theory which is an appropriate theory that is used in explaining the cultural identity struggles of transients.

The typologies of cultural transients, which we discussed earlier, are also salient in the negotiation of a transient's identity. It is difficult, however, to discuss all variables that may affect the transients' negotiation of identity because they are simply too numerous. A transient, for instance, may become demotivated in the process of seeking bi-cultural identity because his or her time in one cultural environment is brief. The opposite will be true for a transient in a long-term cultural environment. Additionally, Padilla's work indicates that a transient's acculturation goal may also be frustrated by local reactions that may include stigmatization, language differentiation, and other types of discriminations. These reactions may force the transient to re-assess his or her cultural identity goal. Furthermore, the transient's cultural value dimension (e.g., collectivism or individualism) may affect how and the type of identity that he or she may prefer to negotiate. In essence, the negotiation of cultural identity is complex and is difficult to categorize precisely because the process of negotiating cultural identity is affected by numerous variables and characteristics. Thus, it is better and more efficient to describe transients' cultural identity effects independent of transient typologies. We will, therefore, discuss briefly some of those cultural identity effects in the subsequent sections.

The Cultural Identity Model (CIM)

Sussman (2005) introduced the CIM in order to understand the consequences of the sojourner's return home, but she has also used it to investigate remigration in Hong Kong. Sussman (2005) notes that an individual's cultural identity may change during an intercultural encounter, but it remains latent and only becomes "salient upon commencement of repatriation" (p. 5). The cultural encounter after repatriation leads to optional cultural identity shifts. These shifts are labeled as subtractive, additive, affirmative or intercultural. Those who experience subtractive cultural identity outcome (discomfort with home culture upon return) are those who had left home with low cultural identity with their homeland but with the capability for moderate cultural flexibility. They also had high adaptation with the foreign culture. Those who experience additive cultural identity outcome (discomfort with home culture upon return) are those who had left home with moderate cultural identity with their homeland and had high cultural flexibility which led to high adaptation with the foreign culture. Those who experience affirmative cultural identity outcome (comfort with home culture upon return) are those who had left home with high cultural identity with their homeland but had low cultural flexibility and, thus, they had low adaptation with the foreign culture. Those who experience intercultural identity outcome (comfort with home culture upon return) are those who had left home with low cultural identity with their homeland but had high cultural flexibility and, thus, had high adaptation with the foreign culture. It is this later group, intercultural identity, that appear to describe individuals who are more likely to be comfortable with the life of a transient as they have very high

cultural flexibility that allows them to adapt to several cultures in their back and forth movement. Sussman's (2005) research, however, found that only few of the Hong Kong remigrants fell into that category.

Other Effects of Identity Shifting

Several other theories of cultural identity shifting require discussion at this point. For instance, Langer's (1989) discussion of *Mindfulness and Identity Shifting* which is based on three explicit criteria that include creation of new categories, openness to new information, and the awareness of more than one cultural perspective. Langer posits that individuals are active, or mindful, in seeking to negotiate a cultural identity when they come into contact with a new cultural environment. The opposite is an individual who engages in mindless communication where the person is oblivious of cultural events around him or herself and instead is largely "intransigent." Langer's discussion of the creation of a new cultural identity category is consistent with the discussions of *Third Culture Building* (TCB) by Chen and Starosta (1998) and Casmir (1993, 1999). Here, Casmir argues that a person builds a third cultural identity by using interpersonal, mass media, and the desire to acculturate. This person then develops a beneficial and cooperative culture with the host environment.

Additionally, Langer's first criterion of creation of new cultural category is also largely consistent with Sussman's CIM and the conceptions of *Multicultural Personhood* by several scholars (see Kim, 2001; Milhouse, Asante, & Nwosu, 2001; Kim & Ruben, 1988; and Adler, 1982). Multicultural personhood, however, is somewhat different from TCB in subtle ways. TCB argues that the individual interacts with a host to build a third culture that melds some aspects of the individual's culture with aspects of the host culture. Whereas, multicultural personhood, which has also been referred to as both "intercultural" (Sussman, 2001 & 2005; and Kim, 2001) and "transcultural" (Milhouse, Asante, & Nwosu, 2001), is more than merely building a third culture from the contact between two or more cultures. Instead, Sussman (2005) describes it as an identity that allows the individual to "hold multiple cultural identities simultaneously and draw on each as the need requires. . . .

This identity shift paradigm is neither the integration of home and host culture values (hybridization) nor the bicultural strategy which results from the acculturation experience but rather an identity in which the repatriates define themselves as world citizens and are able to interact appropriately or effectively in many countries or regions switching cultural frames as needed" (p. 9). Milhouse, Asante, and Nwosu suggest further that being transcultural requires one to free oneself from the obsessions of one's culture—to free oneself from one's cultural prison, and to be able to see things from varying and multiple perspectives, and to act out in such ways.

Networks Upon Reentry

Network analysis is critical to the understanding of the transient's relationships with others. Network analysis, however, has been rarely used in the discussion of cultural identity among intercultural communication scholars. Network is best understood as a set of relationships. It contains a set of objects and a description of relationships between or among the objects (Kadushin, undated; Weimann, 1989; and Boissevain, 1974). Network analysis is important in understanding the transient's negotiation of cultural identity because identity is not created in isolation but it is only understood, developed, changed or modified in the process of interacting and relating with others.

Two key network principles help explain problems that transients encounter and, thus, those principles are important in predicting how a transient's cultural identity might shift over time. One of those principles is that of propinquity. Propinquity proposes that network relationships are strengthened by geographical proximity. The other principle is that of homophily which predicts that the more the members of a network share in common, the stronger the relationships. Abdelhady (2006), McCarthy (2005), and Jenkins (2005) have all cited networks as assisting cultural travelers, in the long term, with alleviating feelings of dislocation in the economic, cultural, religious, and political spheres. For the transient, however, his or her relationship with a network may develop a pathology over time because the transient often severs geographical proximity and fails to share events and acts with his friends for a significant amount of time

because of his or her travels to the "other" culture. The travels end up disrupting the network which repairs itself by developing a modified network of relationship that excludes the "absentee" transient. In essence, the transient will struggle to reenter the network upon reentry. This type of network pathology is significant in determining how the transient creates his or her cultural identity. More detailed discussion can be found in Weimann's (1989) discussion of networks and strengths of friendship ties and Boissevain's (1974) analysis of the relationship between personal networks and the social environment.

Transients and Cultural Contracts

Jackson's (1999, 2002) conception of cultural contracts explains an implied but mindful agreement between cultural interactors to coordinate a relationship. Onwumechili, Nwosu, Jackson, and James-Hughes (2003) note that the theory stands out because "it recognizes the possibility of intracultural contract negotiations among friends, acquaintances, family, and strangers" (p. 55). While they agree that most of the theories discussed earlier are useful in understanding several aspects of negotiating cultural identity, they stress that cultural contracts theory appears to be the appropriate theory for predicting how transients might shift their cultural identity.

Jackson (1999 & 2002) argues that cultural contracts theory is particularly important and essential in answering the question "What is it that is negotiated?" The answer to this significant question is muted in theories of identity negotiation but the use of the metaphor "contracts" brings to the fore the answer to the question. Invariably, not only does Jackson's theory provide an illuminating answer, it also for the first time brings together the concepts of identity and intercultural negotiation in simple to understand terms.

The theory points out that everyone has negotiated at least one cultural contract over their lifetime and that each contract has an impact on the person's identity. It denies the existence of a "non-cultural" or culturally generic contract. Thus, all contracts are "cultural." This point has implications for our understanding of identity negotiation of transients. In essence, it raises the question as to whether a transient can be "intercultural" as defined by Sussman's CIM theory. Can a transient who has traveled to a few European and East African countries and has achieved cultural competence in each of those claim to have developed an intercultural/global identity (as conceived by Sussman) when he or she comes into contact with Senegal for the very first time? The cultural contracts theory would say "No." She or he cannot claim that such contracts are "generic" and, thus, applicable to Senegal even though the individual signed several cultural contracts in those various visits. If that someone were to use that supposedly "generic" culture, then the cultural contracts theory would describe it as intent to use a prenegotiated contract.

This brings us to a discussion of the types of cultural contracts that can be negotiated and how they apply to transients. They are *ready-to-sign, quasi-completed*, and *co-created* contracts (see Table 2). Each type of contract demonstrates the following salient premises—that identities require affirmation, they are in flux, they are only understood interactively, and they are indubitably contractual.

Ready-to-sign contracts describe situations where the transient has already made a determination on his/her cultural identity and feels little need to adjust that decision. This fits the example of Senegal that we had previously discussed. In essence, the transient has negotiated with the self and shows little or no interest in constantly adjusting to the culture that

he/she enters and reenters repeatedly. Onwumechili, Nwosu, Jackson, and James-Hughes (2003) point out that "over time, it is fairly common for a reacculturating transient to take routine trips to the same location and become less and less mindful of subtle differences among the hosts upon reentry. They have changed very little of themselves in the process" (p. 56). They go on to cite the works of Kim (2001) and Sussman (2001) by noting that "naturally, the stress of multiple reacculturation can be exhausting and one means of lessening such stress is to avoid major adjustments to behaviors, attitudes and perspectives" (p. 56). On the face of it, a ready-to-sign contract may seem the appropriate option for a transient to use in developing a cultural identity. The acculturation literature, however, is steeped in warnings against the development of a cultural identity that is based on a ready-to-sign contract. Cross (1995) warns of possible shock and stress because culture is always in flux (never static) and, thus, identities should not be static. Moreover, no one is an island to himself or herself. Thus, in order to ensure ongoing cultural competence it seems that transients must remain open, to a certain degree, as advised by Ting-Toomey (1999).

The *quasi-completed contract* is preferred by a transient who is neither fixed in his/her ways nor fully committed to co-creating a cultural system.

Table 2 *Cultural Identity Contracts and Transients*

	Ready-To-Sign	Quasi-Completed	Co-Created
Description	Cultural identity is predetermined. There is no room for negotiations during multiple reentry interaction.	Cultural identity is a mixture of predetermined identity and result of some openness to negotiation during multiple reentry interaction.	Cultural identity is fully open to negotiation during multiple reentry interaction.
Purpose	To avoid stress that may be caused by multiple adjustments.	Careful choice of when to adjust in order to achieve predetermined goals.	Seeks full acceptance by hosts. Transient works towards full competence.
Drawbacks	Culture shock. There could also be lack of ongoing competence in at least one cultural location.	There is possible cultural marginalization in each cultural system.	Stressful. Transients must be socially active during each reentry. Each host feels unfulfilled by relationship with transient because each host seeks the transient's assimilation to the local culture and not a co-created cultural outcome.

Instead, the transient is in a "cultural limbo" or middle ground where full reacculturation is not an acceptable option. In a sense, this type of cultural contract is somewhat prenegotiated and, at the same time, partially open for negotiation. Transients who choose this cultural contract option may do so based on their reentry purpose as predicted by Onwumechili, Nwosu, Jackson, and James-Hughes (2003). For instance, a Nigerian transient who initially migrated to the United States and has assumed a new cultural identity that is largely influenced by his stay in the United States may decide to apply a quasi-completed cultural contract upon reentries to Nigeria. The transient realizes that he or she has changed and that some cultural distance now exists between what he or she used to be and what he or she is now. To bridge this gap, the transient may consciously seek situations where he/she demonstrates competence with the local Nigerian culture. The transient, in this example, is not fully committed to opening himself or herself to changing a cultural identity that had been largely influenced by multiple stays in the United States. Instead, the transient shows some willingness to negotiate an "accommodation" of the Nigerian culture; it is never an openness to co-create nor is it ever an intention to entirely reject the Nigerian culture to which he or she reenters repeatedly in travels.

The third type of cultural contract is the *co-created contract*. Here, cultural identity is fully open to negotiation. Little is held back. The co-created contract is one in which the transient is fully committed to jointly negotiating a third culture with members of the host culture. Several scholars point to this type of cultural contract as desirable (Ting-Toomey, 1999; and Langer, 1989). The transient's choice of this contract, however, is not always met with acceptance by family and friends (Onwumechili, Nwosu, Jackson, & James-Hughes, 2003), and one's own local culture or community. The family and friends of a transient who reenters his initial home culture always expect the returnee transient to be unchanged. Thus, they are more likely than not to frown at the transient's attempt to co-create a different culture, a different identity from what the family and friends, and the local culture or community are familiar with.

A cultural contract is a metaphorical theory that helps us to better understand how transients negotiate cultural identity. It does not, however, inform us on how this group of international travelers copes with the obvious stress that is associated with straddling cultures and negotiating identity. To learn about what transients do for coping we have to refer to the work of Cross and Strauss (1998). Both authors point to the use of buffering, bonding, bridging, and code switching to ameliorate the stress of negotiating identity. The first strategy—buffering—is a defensive strategy used to soften or block out the stress. In essence, the transient may rationalize his or her resistance to cultural influence or seek other persons with similar identity. The latter three strategies are strategies that reach out to the host culture to seek ways to assist in adjusting to a new identity. For instance, the transient may seek to renew membership in a social network (bonding), verbal demonstration of an understanding of a cultural ritual (bridging), or switching to host cultural behavior in certain contexts (code switching).

CONCLUSION

In this essay we have attempted to re-capture several issues that we previously raised in a 2003 published article (see Onwumechili, Nwosu, Jackson, & James-Hughes). We have also added germane literature from more recent sources in an attempt to better understand multiple reacculturation which generates the cyclical curve experienced by some transients. We have also focused much of our writing on an important aspect of the lives of transients, which is the process of negotiating cultural contracts in order to develop cultural identities during their travels.

It is important to understand that while we advance the cultural contracts theory as an appropriate framework for understanding how transients negotiate their identity, we do not deny the importance of the other theoretical frameworks. In fact, we have shown how other theoretical frameworks might provide us with insights on the lives of transients, particularly as they seek to define their cultural identity. The task ahead is still enormous as scholars attempt to understand this group of sojourners.

Note

1. While the Chinese words refer to "astronauts," they also can loosely mean "man without a wife."

References

Abdelhady, D. (2006). Beyond home/host networks: Forms of solidarity among Lebanese immigrants in a global era. *Identities: Global Studies in Culture and Power,* 13, 427–453.

Adler, P. (1982). Beyond cultural identity: Reflections on cultural and multicultural man. In L. Samovar & R. Porter (Eds.), *Intercultural communication: A reader.* Belmont, CA: Wadsworth.

Anderson, L. (1994). A new look at an old construct: Cross-cultural adaptation. *International Journal of Intercultural Relations,* 18, 293–328.

Bakker, M., & M. Smith (undated). El Rey del Tomate: Migrant political transnationalism in Mexico. (Available online). http://www.Hcd.ucdavis.edu/faculty smith/

Berry, J. (2005). Acculturation: Living successfully in two cultures. *International Journal of Intercultural Relations,* 29(6), 697–712.

Berry, J. (1999). Intercultural relations in plural societies. *Canadian Psychology,* 40, 12–21.

Boissevain, J. (1974). *Friends of friends: Networks, manipulators, and coalitions.* New York: St. Martin's Press.

Bourhis, R., L. Moise, S. Perreaut, & S. Senecal (1997). Towards an interactive acculturation model: A social psychological approach. *International Journal of Psychology,* 32(6), 369–386.

Brislin, R. (1981). *Cross-cultural encounters.* New York: Pergamon Press.

Casmir, F. (1999). Foundations for the study of intercultural communication based on a third culture building model. *International Journal of Intercultural Relations,* 23, 91–116.

Casmir, F. (1993). Third culture building: A paradigm shift for international and intercultural communication. *Communication Yearbook,* 16, 407–428.

Castles, S. (2006). Guest workers in Europe: A resurrection? *International Migration Review,* XL(4), 741–766.

Chen, K. (1990, January 6). Hong Kong's frequent-flyer "Astronauts." *San Francisco Examiner.*

Chen, G., & W. Starosta (1998). *Foundations of intercultural communication.* Needham Heights, MA: Allyn & Bacon.

Cox, B. (2004). The role of communication, technology, and cultural identity in repatriation adjustment. *International Journal of Intercultural Relations,* 28(3/4), 201–219.

Cross, S. (1995). Self-construals, coping and stress in cross-cultural adaptation. *Journal of Cross-Cultural Psychology,* 26(6), 673–697.

Cross, W., & L. Strauss (1998). The everyday functions of African American identity. In J. Swim & C. Stangor (Eds.), *Prejudice: The target's perspective.* New York: Academic Press.

Gullahorn, J. T., & J. E. Gullahorn (1963). An extension of the U-curve hypothesis. *Journal of Social Issues,* 19(3), 33–47.

Jackson, R. L. (2002). Exploring African American identity negotiation in the academy: Toward a transformative vision of African American communication scholarship. *Howard Journal of Communication,* 12(4), 43–57.

Jackson, R. L. (1999). *The negotiation of cultural identity.* Westport, CT: Praeger Press.

Jenkins, W. (2005). Deconstructing diasporas: Networks and identities among the Irish in Buffalo and Toronto. *Immigrants and Minorities,* 23(2/3), 1870–1910.

Jones, P. (1996). Immigrants, Germans and national identity in the new Germany: Some policy issues. *International Journal of Popular Geography,* 2(2), 119–131.

Kadushin, C. (undated). Introduction to social network theory. (Available online). http://www.home.eathlink.net/~ckadushin/

Kim, Y. (2001). *Becoming intercultural: An integrative theory of communication and cross-cultural adaptation.* Newbury Park, CA: Sage Publications.

Kim, Y., & B. Ruben (1988). Intercultural transformation: A systems theory. In Y. Kim & W. Gudykunst (Eds.), *Theories in intercultural communication* (pp. 299–321). Newbury Park, CA: Sage Publications.

Langer, E. (1989). *Mindfulness.* Reading, MA: Addison-Wesley.

Lysgaard, S. (1955). Adjustment in a foreign society: Norwegian Fulbright grantees visiting the United States. *International Social Science Bulletin,* VII, 145–151.

Martin, P. & Martin, D. (1994). *The endless quest: Helping America's farm workers.* Boulder, CO: Westview Press.

McCarthy, A. (2005). 'Bands of fellowship': The role of personal relationships and social networks among Irish migrants in New Zealand, 1861–1911. *Immigrants and Minorities,* 23(2/3), 339–358.

Mena, J. (2001, June 30). Three men, two nations, one dream. *Los Angeles Times,* p. A1.

Milhouse, V., M. Asante, & P. Nwosu (2001). Introduction. In V. Milhouse, M. Asante, & P. Nwosu (Eds.), *Transcultural realities: Interdisciplinary perspectives on cross-cultural relations.* Newbury Park, CA: Sage Publications.

Mora, M. (2006). Self-employed Mexican immigrants residing along the United States-Mexico border: The earnings effect of working in the United States versus Mexico. *International Migration Review,* XL(4), 885–898.

Navas, M., A. Rojas, M. Garcia, & P. Pumares (2007). Acculturation strategies and attitudes according to the relative acculturation extended model (RAEM): The perspectives of natives versus immigrants. *International Journal of Intercultural Relations,* 31(1), 67–86.

Navas, M., M. Garcia, J. Sanchez, A. Rojas, P. Pumares, & J. Fernandez (2005). Relative acculturation extended model (RAEM): New contributions with regard to the study of acculturation. *International Journal of Intercultural Relations,* 29(1), 21–37.

Onwumechili, C., P. Nwosu, R. Jackson II, & J. James-Hughes (2003). In the deep valley with mountains to climb: Exploring identity and multiple reacculturation. *International Journal of Intercultural Relations,* 27, 41–62.

Onwumechili, C., & J. Okereke-Arungwa (2001). Research and training in cross-cultural readjustment: Recommendations for advancements. In V. Milhouse, M. K. Asante, & P. Nwosu (Eds.), *Transcultural realities: Interdisciplinary perspectives on cross-cultural relations* (pp. 267–279). Thousand Oaks, CA: Sage Publications.

Padilla, A., & W. Perez (2003). Acculturation, social identity, and social cognition: A new perspective. *Hispanic Journal of Behavioral Sciences,* 25(1), 35–55.

Persons, S. (1987). *Ethnic studies at Chicago: 1905–45.* Urbana: University of Illinois Press.

Rossler, H. (1995). Traveling workers and the German labor movement. In D. Hoerder & J. Nagler (Eds.), *People in transit: German migrations in comparative perspective, 1820–1930* (pp. 127–146). Washington, DC: German Historical Institute.

Rudolph, H. (1996). The new gastarbeiter system in Germany. *New Community,* 22(2), 287–300.

Sussman, N. (2005). People on the move: The transnational flow of Chinese human capital. Paper presented at the Hong Kong University of Science and Technology, October 20–22.

Sussman, N. (2001). Repatriation transitions: Psychological preparedness, cultural identity, and attributions among American managers. *International Journal of Intercultural Relations,* 25(2), 109–123.

Sussman, N. (2000). The dynamic nature of cultural identity throughout cultural transitions: Why home is not so sweet. *Personality and Social Psychological Review,* 4, 355–373.

Sussman, N. (1986). Reentry research and training: Methods and implications. *International Journal of Intercultural Relations,* 10(2), 235–253.

Ting-Toomey, S. (1999). *Communicating across cultures.* New York: Guilford Publications.

Uehara, A. (1986). The nature of American student reentry adjustment and perception of the sojourn adjustment. *International Journal of Intercultural Relations,* 10(4), 415–438.

Ward, C., Y. Okura, A. Kennedy, & T. Kojima (1998). The U-curve on trial: A longitudinal study of psychological and sociocultural adjustment during cross-cultural transition. *International Journal of Intercultural Relations,* 22(3), 277–291.

Weimann, G. (1989). Social networks and communication. In M. Asante & W. Gudykunst (Eds.), *Handbook of international and intercultural communication* (pp. 186–203). Newbury Park, CA: Sage Publications.

Concepts and Questions

1. What are some reasons people are moving across borders?
2. What is the U-curve hypothesis? What are its stages? Why do Onwumechili, Nwosu, and Jackson believe it is no longer an accurate tool for analyzing culture shock?
3. What are some factors that can influence the reentry process?
4. How does cultural identity influence the reentry process?
5. What are the key variables that can mediate transient activity?
6. What are the three types of cultural contracts that can be negotiated? How do they apply to transients?
7. Which of these three contracts do you believe would be most useful if you were in the role of a cultural transient?

International Cultures: Understanding Diversity

All persons are puzzles until at last we find in some word or act the key to the man, to the woman; straightway all their past words and actions lie in light before us.

EMERSON

It is not the language but the speaker that we need to understand.

INDIAN ADAGE FROM THE VEDAS

There never were in the world two opinions alike, no more than two hairs or two grains; the most universal quality is diversity.

MICHEL DE MONTAIGNE

One of the most self-evident truisms about human communication is that your past experiences affect your behavior in both subtle and manifest ways. This axiom is so transparent that people often overlook its impact on social perception and interaction. Reflect for a moment on some of those situations when you and a friend shared what you believed to be the *same experience*, yet when you discussed the event later, you discovered there were differences in your perceptions of that "shared experience." We offer a simple example to make the point. If you and an acquaintance were hiking on a mountain trail and a large dog came bounding up to you, that event could be perceived quite differently, depending upon each person's *prior experience* with dogs. You might have had a dog as a child, therefore, you perceived the dog as friendly. You may even have knelt in order to pet the dog. However, your hiking companion may have been bitten by a dog as a child, therefore, had a very different perception and reacted to the dog by moving away and showing signs of fear. Although this example may seem rather mundane, nevertheless, it focuses attention on the fundamental idea that the stimuli you received from the environment were the same as your friend, but because you each had a unique personal history, you experienced a specialized set of feelings, sensations, and responses. In short, we all have our private histories that shape the way we see the world.

The previous example was not only uncomplicated, it also kept cultural comparisons out of the scenario. However, when the element of culture is added to any discussion of perception, interpretations take on added significance. You are not only a product of your personal experiences but also are influenced by your cultural experiences. As indicated in Chapter 1, *culture* refers to those accumulations of knowledge, beliefs, views, values, and behaviors that are acquired and shared by a large group of people and passed from one generation to the next. In this sense, culture affects you both consciously and unconsciously; it not only teaches you how and what to think but also assists you in defining values such as what is good and what is evil, what is appropriate and what is not, what is worth striving for and what should be avoided. In short, your culture helps you to develop unique patterns of social perception and tells you how to see and interpret your world. Furthermore, culture teaches you such things as how close to stand to strangers, how to greet friends, when to speak and when to remain silent, and even how to display your anger in a culturally accepted manner. When you are interacting with others and become disturbed by their actions, you can, for instance, cry, become physically violent, shout, or remain silent. The behaviors you display are a manifestation of what you have learned, and they are strongly influenced by your culture.

The cultural influences we have been talking about affect your ways of perceiving and acting; they contain the societal experiences and values that are embedded in your culture. Because these behaviors are so much a part of your persona, there is a danger that you might fail to remember that these behaviors are culturally engendered and usually vary from culture to culture. For example, someone from Japan might remain silent if disturbed by another's actions, whereas an Israeli or an Italian would more likely vigorously verbalize their displeasure. As you might predict, cultural understanding comes more easily when your cultural experiences are similar to those of the people with whom you are interacting. Conversely, when disparate backgrounds are brought to a communication encounter, it is often more difficult to share internal states and feelings. In this chapter we focus on some of these difficulties by examining various experiences, values, and perceptual backgrounds found among a sampling of international cultures.

The need for intercultural understanding should be obvious. We live in a world where people of diverse cultures are in constant interaction with one another. The nightly news makes it abundantly clear that all cultures are linked in a kind of global community. Even if you don't want to be a member of the "community"—you are. Events that happen in one part of the world can and do influence events all over the world. Whether it be concerns about the global economy; concerns about food, water, or energy; global warming; disagreements among religious traditions; or major differences in sociopolitical philosophies, no culture can remain isolated from or unaffected by the rest of the world.

Two principles are crucial if you are to relate effectively to people from varied international cultures: (1) you must have knowledge about the diversity of people from other cultures, and (2) you must respect their differences. This chapter presents a series of essays that will assist you with both of those assignments. Through these essays you will explore the rich variety found in several international cultures. Although these cultures represent only a small portion of the countless cultures found throughout the world, they are somewhat representative and should enable you to discover how people in other cultures develop their view of the world. To a great extent, a culture's worldview determines how its members perceive themselves, each other, and their place in the universe; it serves as an underlying pattern for interaction within a culture. Because of the importance of a culture's worldview, we begin with a glimpse of the variations found in three such views—Confucianism, Hinduism, and Islam. Our purpose is to demonstrate how these points of reference can influence the way people see the world and behave in that world.

An African adage states: "There is no distinction between religion and the rest of life. All life is religion." Although this might be a slight overstatement, it is true that religion, in whatever form it takes, is an important part of life for billions of people. And today, more than ever, with religion serving as the motivation and false justification for violence, a culture's religion has consequences beyond its boundaries. We are not only referring to the religious clashes that plague so much of the world, but also to the sway religious traditions exercise on the communication styles and perceptions of the members of those traditions.

A vivid example of how communication and religion are linked can be found in Confucianism, the topic of our first selection by June Ock Yum. In her essay, "The Impact of Confucianism on Interpersonal Relationships and Communication Patterns in East Asia," Yum sketches an intriguing picture of the ways Confucianism can influence how people view and interact with other people. Since this article first appeared more than twenty-five years ago, the contact between East and West has increased in both frequency and intensity. You can now observe, and even be part of, the interactions between Asia and the United States in a variety of arenas. Hence, it is fitting that we include Yum's selection in this current edition.

Yum traces the various components of Confucian philosophy and explains how these ideas guide many Asian patterns of interaction. For example, within the teaching of Confucius there is a major emphasis on empathy; status and role relationships; ritual and protocol; and the use of indirect instead of direct language. As a counterpoint to these characteristics, Yum makes frequent comparisons to North American interaction patterns so that you can understand the differences between these two cultures, and how people of these cultures might react when engaging in face-to-face communication.

We next turn to a country with a population of more than 1 billion—India. At its current rate of growth, it is predicted that India will pass China as the world's most populous nation within fifteen years. We began to include readings about India in our book long before it became a world power. Our decision over thirty years ago was a wise one because India is now a major force in the new era of globalization. As the American business community outsources manufacturing and service elements to India, international negotiations have become commonplace. A most significant aspect of what businessmen have learned is that communication with Indians—as was the case for East Asians in the preceding essay—must include an exploration of the religious tradition of that country.

In "Some Basic Cultural Patterns of Hindus in India," Nemi C. Jain demonstrates how this thousand-year-old Hindu tradition is still part of Indian culture. Specifically, Jain examines how Hindu beliefs in reincarnation, concepts of karma and dharma, aims of life, paths to salvation, residuals of the caste system, and a spirit of tolerance are acted out in everyday life. This provides a basis for understanding the frame of reference common to much of India and a feeling for what it is to be Hindu.

Not only has Egypt been in the news recently, but in a very real sense it has been in the news for centuries. Egypt is one of the world's oldest civilizations, with a history that dates to at least 3000 BCE. Although relatively small in land mass (193 square miles), the importance of Egypt's population, estimated to be in excess of 83 million cannot be overlooked. Throughout Egypt's long history its intellectual and cultural impact on the world, combined with its geographic location, have given Egypt a critical role, not only in the Middle East but throughout the world. Egypt's neighbors and countries as far away as the United States continue to watch the impact of the "Arab Spring" with both interest and concern.

Polly Begley isolates a number of cultural elements that must be considered if you are to understand the perceptions and cultural patterns of the Egyptian people. First, Begley discusses Egyptian worldview and religion. The Egyptian worldview comprises a combination of various African civilizations and beliefs. Parts of this worldview are classified as ancient, dating back thousands of years. Other beliefs about God, the universe, social relationships, and hierarchical structures are derived from Islam. Second, Begley explains how hierarchies according to age, gender, and experience are crucial for the Egyptian. The Arabic language is also an important cultural element. As is the case with most other Arabic cultures, Egyptians see Arabic as the one language selected by Allah to transmit his message to the Arab people. Language also helps establish and reaffirm national identity. Using these three elements of culture—religion, hierarchical structure, and language—as a backdrop, Begley offers numerous examples of how these elements direct interaction between Egyptians and non-Egyptians on an interpersonal level.

With a population of nearly 150 million people, and as one of the world's major superpowers, it is fitting that we include in this special edition an essay on Russian culture. Mira Bergelson helps you understand this multinational culture in an essay titled "Russian Cultural Values and Workplace Communication Patterns." Like so many of the essays in this book, Bergelson begins her contribution with a reminder of the importance of intercultural communication in today's world. She notes: "Cross-cultural communication issues, and their potential for creating obstacles to effective, successful, and professional interactions, have become a critical aspect of the movement toward a globalized society." To keep many of these damaging and destructive issues from impeding communication between Russians and Americans, Bergelson presents a number of insights into Russian culture. She opens her essay by looking at four key Russian values that reflect the Russian worldview. These values are emotionality (expressing the way one feels), judgmental attitudes (passing moral judgments on other people), fatalism (the Russian belief that they "have no control over the world"), and irrationality (the belief that the world is an irrational place).

Bergelson also discusses how discrepancies and variances that exist between "Russian traditional and Soviet era cultures" can be misunderstood. These differences often create inconsistencies in how people holding either orientation view the world.

In addition to the discussion on the differences in these two historical perspectives, Bergelson offers a detailed evaluation of the communication patterns that exist in both Russia and the United States. According to Bergelson, these differences can "bring about misunderstandings or create conflict." She is primarily concerned with differences in politeness patterns as they relate to Russians and Americans. After examining six of these differences, she concludes that, "taken collectively, Russians are more insistent on expressing and reviving solidarity politeness." This is a style, Bergelson believes, that at least for Americans seems to lack expressions of deferential politeness. Bergelson concludes her analysis by presenting a grid that compares ten communication and cultural variables found in Western culture, the former Soviet style culture, and traditional Russian culture: the I/We orientation, human relationships, activity orientation, time orientation, relation to nature, form and substance, progress, history, freedom and discipline, and age.

In the final essay in this chapter, Lisa Skow and Larry Samovar examine a very distinctive culture found on the continent of Africa. Nearly thirty years ago in their article "Cultural Patterns of the Maasai," Skow and Samovar presented an examination of this culture—a culture that has for centuries sought to preserve its special way of life and its unique set of communication patterns. Although tourists visit Maasai villages in great numbers, the Maasai have shunned Western influences and managed to reject Western forms of government, values, dress, language, music, and religion. Skow and Samovar help you to understand this culture by explaining the communication patterns of the Maasai as they apply to that culture's history, values, worldview, and verbal and nonverbal processes. The authors also suggest that these five communication components can be applied to any culture as a way of determining how their members might interact with members of a different culture.

The Impact of Confucianism on Interpersonal Relationships and Communication Patterns in East Asia

JUNE OCK YUM

INTRODUCTION

New communication technology has removed many of the physical barriers against communication between the East and the West, but there remain philosophical and cultural barriers, which are not well understood. The increased opportunity for interaction between different cultural groups, however, has sensitized some scholars to the need to study Eastern perspectives on communication.

Most cross-cultural studies of communication simply describe foreign communication patterns and then compare them to those of North America, rarely going beneath the surface to explore the source of such differences. This paper goes beyond these limitations and explores the philosophical roots of the communication patterns in East Asian countries, before comparing them to those of North America. The assumption here is that communication is a basic social process and that, as such, it is influenced by the philosophical foundations and value systems of the society in which it is found.

There is always a danger in generalizing certain cultural patterns to large geographical areas. Even though we often refer to "Eastern" or "Asian" perspectives, there are many patterns, sometimes contradictory,

within the region. For instance, the popular notion that Asians are more spiritual than Westerners might apply to India but not to China, Korea, or Japan. Nakamura (1964) has maintained that the Chinese and the Japanese are much more nonmetaphysical than Westerners. For this reason, this paper is limited to the East Asian countries of China, Korea, and Japan, those that have been most influenced by Confucian philosophical principles. Other countries that have been influenced by Confucianism are expected to have similar characteristics. For instance, Vietnam, the only country in Southeast Asia to have been influenced more by China than India, also exhibits the strong emphasis on social relationships and devotion to the hierarchical family relations that are the essence of Confucian doctrines (Luce & Summer, 1969).

SOCIAL RELATIONSHIPS VERSUS INDIVIDUALISM

If one has to select the main difference between East Asian and North American perspectives on communication, it would be the East Asian emphasis on social relationships as opposed to the North American emphasis on individualism. According to Hofstede (1980), individualism–collectivism is one of the main dimensions that differentiate cultures. He defined individualism as the emotional independence of individual persons from groups, organizations, or other collectivities. Parsons, Shils, and Olds (1951) have suggested that self-orientation versus collectivity orientation is one of the five basic pattern variables that determine human action. Self-orientation occurs when a person gives "priority in a given situation to his own private interests, independently of their bearings on the interests or values of a given collectivity" (Parsons, Shils, & Olds, 1951, p. 81), as opposed to taking directly into account the values and interests of the collectivity before acting.

The individualism–collectivism dichotomy, however, is not identical to the difference between the East Asian emphasis on social relationships and North American emphasis on individualism. In East Asia, the emphasis is on proper social relationships and their maintenance rather than any abstract concern for a general collective body. In a sense, it is a collectivism only among those bound by social networks. For example, a recent study on the Chinese value system found that the Confucian value of reciprocity and proper relationships was not correlated with Hofstede's individualism–collectivism dimension (Chinese Culture Connection, 1987). Hui and Triandis (1986) have recommended that collectivism be treated in two different ways: (1) as a concern for a certain subset of people and (2) as a concern for a generalized collectivity of people.

In the 1830s, the French social philosopher Alexis de Tocqueville coined the term *individualism* to describe the most notable characteristic of American people. Bellah, Madsen, Sullivan, Swidler, and Tipton (1985, pp. vii, 142) agree that individualism lies at the very core of American culture, contending that "individualism...has marched inexorably through our history" and that "we believe in the dignity, indeed the sacredness, of the individual. Anything that would violate our right to think for ourselves, judge for ourselves, make our own decision, live our lives as we see fit, is not only morally wrong, it is sacrilegious." According to Varenne (1977), there is but one system of principles regulating interpersonal relationships in America and that is individualism.

Even though many Americans feel they must get involved, they are also committed to individualism, including the desire to cut free from the past and define one's own self. Thus, the primary mode of American involvement is choosing organizations that one can voluntarily join or voluntarily withdraw from. Varenne (1977, p. 53) said that Americans perceive social structure "not as a system made up of different groups considered to be in a symbiotic relationship, but rather of different individuals who come together to do something."

Considering this cultural orientation, it is not surprising that the dominant paradigm of communication is an individualistic one. Each communicator is perceived to be a separate individual engaging in diverse communicative activities to maximize his or her own self-interest.

In contrast, the most notable characteristic in East Asia is the emphasis on social relationships. Hall and Beardsley (1965) have maintained that, compared to East Asian countries, North America is in the Stone Age when it comes to social relationships. This East Asian preoccupation with social relationships stems from the doctrines of Confucianism.

CONFUCIANISM

In the philosophical and cultural history of East Asia, Confucianism has endured as the basic social and political value system for over 1,000 years. One reason (and indication) that Confucianism has had such a profound impact is that it was adopted as the official philosophy of the Yi dynasty for 500 years in Korea, of the Tokugawa shogunate in Japan for 250 years, and of many dynasties in China.

Confucianism was institutionalized and propagated both through the formal curricula of the educational system and through the selection process of government officials. Confucian classics were required textbooks in the school systems throughout the history of China, Korea, and Japan before modern educational curricula were implemented. Government officials used to be selected through national exams that mostly examined the knowledge and the level of understanding of Confucian philosophy.

Another reason Confucianism has exerted a much stronger impact than the other religious, philosophical systems of East Asia (such as Buddhism and Taoism) is that it is a pragmatic and present-oriented philosophy. When a student named Tzu-lu asked Confucius about serving spirits, Confucius said, "If one cannot yet serve men, how can he serve the spirits?" Asked about death, Confucius replied, "If you do not understand life, how can you understand death?" (McNaughton, 1974, p. 145). Max Weber commented, "Confucianism is extremely rationalistic since it is bereft of any form of metaphysics and in the sense that it lacks traces of nearly any religious basis....At the same time, it is more realistic than any other system in the sense that it lacks and excludes all measures which are not utilitarian" (quoted by Nakamura, 1964, p. 16).

Confucianism is a philosophy of human nature that considers proper human relationships as the basis of society. In studying human nature and motivation, Confucianism sets forth four principles from which right conduct arises: *jen* (humanism), *i* (faithfulness), *li* (propriety), and *chih* (wisdom or a liberal education).

The cardinal principle, *jen* (humanism), almost defies translation since it sums up the core of Confucianism. Fundamentally it means warm human feelings between people. *Jen* is like a seed from which spring all the qualities that make up the ideal man. In addition, *jen* refers to the possession of all these qualities to a high degree. The actual practice or embodiment of *jen* in our daily lives is closely related to the concept of reciprocity. Confucius said that practicing *jen* is not to do to another man what you yourself don't want. In his own words: "If there's something that you don't like in the person to your right, don't pass it on to the person on your left. If there's something you don't like in the person to your left, don't pass it on to the person on your right" (McNaughton, 1974, p. 29).

It is suggested that Confucius himself once picked out reciprocity (*shu*) as the core of his thought. Confucius said, "There has never been a case where a man who did not understand reciprocity was able to communicate to others whatever treasures he might have had stored in himself" (McNaughton, 1974, p. 28). Therefore, practicing *jen* implies the practice of *shu*, which in turn means to know how it would feel to be the other person, to become like-hearted, and to be able to empathize with others.

The second principle of Confucianism is *i*, meaning faithfulness, loyalty, or justice. As the definition suggests, this principle also has strong implications for social relationships. Like *jen, i* is a difficult concept to translate. It may be easier to understand *i* through its opposite concept, which is personal or individual interest and profit. *I* is thus that part of

human nature that allows us to look beyond personal, immediate profit and to elevate ourselves to the original goodness of human nature that bridges ourselves to other people (Yum, 1987). According to the principle of *i*, human relationships are not based on individual profit but rather on the betterment of the common good.

If *jen* and *i* are the contents of the Confucian ethical system, *li* (propriety, rite, respect for social forms) is its outward form. As an objective criterion of social decorum, *li* was perceived as the fundamental regulatory etiquette of human behavior. Mencius suggested that *li* originated from deference to others and reservation of oneself. Confucius said that *li* follows from *jen,* that is, from being considerate to others. Only when people overcome themselves and so return to propriety can they reach humanness. On the other hand, propriety without humanness was perceived to be empty and useless.

The Impact of Confucianism on Interpersonal Relationship Patterns

At least three of the four principles of Confucianism deal directly with social relationships. Under such a strong influence, East Asian countries have developed interpersonal relationship patterns that are quite different from the individualistic pattern of North America. Table 1 illustrates these five differences.

Table 1 *Comparison Between the North American and the East Asian Orientations to Interpersonal Relationship Patterns*

East Asian Orientations	North American Orientations
1. Particularistic	Universalistic
Particular rules and interaction patterns are applied depending upon the relationship and context	General and objective rules are applied across diverse relationships and context
2. Long-term and asymmetrical reciprocity	Short-term and symmetrical reciprocity or contractual reciprocity
3. Sharp distinction between in-group and out-group members	In-group and out-group distinction is not as sharp
4. Informal intermediaries. Personally known intermediaries	Contractual intermediaries Professional intermediaries
Frequently utilized for diverse relationships	Utilized only for specific purposes
5. Personal and public relationships often overlap	Personal and public relationships are often separate

Particularistic versus Universalistic Relationships

Human relationships under Confucianism are not universalistic but particularistic. As we described earlier, the warm human feelings of *jen* are exercised according to one's relationship with another person. Ethics in Confucian thought, therefore, are based on relationships and situations rather than on some absolute and abstract good. Instead of applying the same rule to everybody with whom they interact, East Asians differentially grade and regulate relationships according to the level of intimacy, the status of the persons involved, and the particular context. The East Asian countries have developed elaborate social interaction patterns for those whose social position and relationship to oneself is known, but there are few universal patterns that can be applied to someone who is not known.

From a North American point of view, applying different rules to different people and situations may seem to violate the sacred code of fairness and equality that accompanies the individualistic values. In North America, human relationships are not particularized. Rather, one is supposed to treat each person as an integral individual and apply general and objective rules. For instance, it is quite common in America for people to say "Hi" or "Good morning" to anybody they encounter during their morning walk, or to strike up a conversation with another person waiting in line. If you said "Hello" or "Good morning" to a stranger in Korea, you would be looked upon as a rather odd person.

The East Asian approach suggests that it is more humanitarian to consider the particular context and the persons involved in understanding the action and behavior rather than evaluate them according to generalized rules which to a certain extent are impersonal.

Long-Term Asymmetrical Reciprocity versus Short-Term Symmetrical or Contractual Reciprocity

Reciprocity as an embodiment of *jen* is the core concept in Confucianism, just as individualism is the core concept of the North American culture. While people may voluntarily join together for specific purposes in North America, each individual remains equal and independent; thus people join or drop out of clubs without any serious group sanctions. Commitments and obligations are often perceived as threats to one's autonomy or freedom of action. Relations are symmetrical–obligatory—that is, as nearly "paid off" as possible at any given moment—or else contractual—the obligation is to an institution or to a professional with whom one has established some contractual base (Condon & Yousef, 1975).

In contrast, Confucian philosophy views relationships as complementary or asymmetrical and reciprocally obligatory. In a sense, a person is forever indebted to others, who in turn are constrained by other debts. Dependence is not looked down upon. Rather, dependency is accepted as a necessary part of human relationships. Under this system of reciprocity, the individual does not calculate what he or she gives and receives. To calculate would be to think about immediate personal profits, which is the opposite of the principle of mutual faithfulness, *i*. It is somewhat unusual in Korea, for example, for a group of friends, colleagues, or superior and subordinates to go "Dutch" and split the bill for dinner or drinks. Rather, each person takes turns and pays for the whole group. In North America, people generally insist on "paying their own way." The practice of basing relationships on complementary obligations creates warm, lasting human relationships but also the necessity to accept the obligations accompanying such relationships.

In-group/Out-group Distinction

North American culture does not distinguish as strongly between in-group members and out-group members as East Asian countries do. Allegiance to a group and mobility among groups are purely voluntary, so that the longevity of membership in and loyalty to a particular group are both limited.

Mutual dependence as prescribed by the Confucian principle of *i*, however, requires that one be affiliated and identify with relatively small and tightly knit groups of people over long periods of time. These long-term relationships work because each group member expects the others to reciprocate and also because group members believe that sooner or later they will have to depend on the others.

People enmeshed in this kind of network make clear distinctions between in-group and out-group members. For example, linguistic codes for in-group members are often different from those for out-group members. What is inside the group and what is outside it have drastically different meanings.

Informal Intermediaries versus Contractual Intermediaries

Because the distinctions between in-group and out-group members are so strict, it is imperative to have an intermediary to help one initiate a new relationship in East Asia. Confucian emphasis on propriety (*li*) also dictates that one has to follow proper rituals in establishing a new relationship, and an intermediary is part of such rituals. The intermediary has an in-group relationship with both parties and so can connect them. One strategy is for the intermediary to bring up an existing relationship that links the two parties, for example, explaining that "you are both graduates of so-and-so college" or "you are both from province A." Alternatively, the intermediary can use his or her own connections with them to create an indirect sense of in-groupness, for example, explaining that one is "my junior from high school" and the other "works in the same department as I do."

Intermediaries in the United States, however, are mostly professional or contractual in nature: lawyers, negotiators, marriage counselors, and the like. The intermediary is an objective third person who does not have any knowledge of the parties' characteristics other than those directly related to the issue at hand. Also, the intermediary deals with each party as a separate, independent individual. Using personal connections to attain a desired goal does occur in the United States, but such a practice may be frowned on as nepotism and may also be perceived as giving up one's own individual freedom.

Overlap of Personal and Public Relationships

The Confucian concept of *i* leads to a strong distaste for a purely business transaction, carried out on a calculated and contractual basis. Therefore, in East Asian countries there is a tendency to mix personal with public relationships. Even though the obvious purpose of a meeting is for business, both parties feel more comfortable if the transaction occurs on a more personal, human level. According to the principles of social reciprocity, there are several steps to follow if you want to develop an effective business relationship in Korea (Lee, 1983): (1) have frequent contacts over a relatively lengthy period of time, (2) establish a personal and human relationship, (3) if possible, create some common experiences such as sports, drinking, or travel, (4) foster mutual understanding in terms of personality, personal situations, and the like, and (5) develop a certain level of trust and a favorable attitude. The goal is to diminish the clear distinction between a personal relationship and a public relationship. It is implied that if one develops a warm personal relationship, a good public relationship will follow, because it is based on trust and mutual reciprocity. Such qualities are expected to endure rather than be limited to the business deal of the moment.

In the United States, there is a rather sharp dichotomy between private and public life. Since the primary task of the individual is to achieve a high level of autonomous self-reliance, there is an effort to separate the two lives as much as possible. Since the notion of "organizational man" is contradictory to the self-reliant individual, there is a certain level of anxiety about becoming an organizational man (Bellah et al., 1985). Some also perceive private life as a haven from the pressure of individualistic, competitive public life, and as such it must be protected.

THE IMPACT OF CONFUCIANISM ON COMMUNICATION PATTERNS

Confucianism's primary concern with social relationships has strongly influenced communication patterns in East Asia. In general, it has strengthened patterns that help to build and maintain proper human relationships. Table 2 compares East Asia and North America in terms of communication patterns.

Table 2 *Comparison between the North American and the East Asian Orientations to Communication Patterns*

East Asian Orientations	North American Orientations
1. Process orientation	Outcome orientation
Communication is perceived as a process of infinite interpretation	Communication is perceived as the transference of messages
2. Differentiated linguistic codes	Less differentiated linguistic codes
Different linguistics codes are used depending upon persons involved and situations	Linguistic codes are not as extensively differentiated as in East Asia
3. Indirect communication emphasis	Direct communication emphasis
The use of indirect communication is prevalent and accepted as normative	Direct communication is a norm despite the extensive use of indirect communication
4. Receiver centered	Sender centered
Meaning is in the interpretation	Meaning is in the messages created by the sender
Emphasis is on listening, sensitivity, and removal of preconception	Emphasis is on how to formulate the best messages, how to improve source credibility, and how to improve delivery skills

Process- versus Outcome-Oriented Communication

Since the main function of communication under Confucian philosophy is to initiate, develop, and maintain social relationships, there is a strong emphasis on the kind of communication that promotes such relationships. For instance, it is very important in East Asia to engage in small talk before initiating business and to communicate personalized information, especially information that would help place each person in the proper context. Communication is perceived to be an infinite interpretive process (Cheng, 1987), which cannot be compartmentalized into sender, message, channel, and receiver. It presumes that each partner is engaged in an ongoing process and that the relationship is in flux.

In contrast, when the main function of communication is to actualize autonomy and self-fulfillment, as in North America, the outcome of the communication is more important than the process. With short-term, discontinuous relationships, communication is perceived to be an action that is terminated after a certain duration and then replaced by a new communication. Tangible outcomes in terms of friends gained, opponents defeated, and self-fulfillment achieved become the primary function of communication.

Differentiated versus Less Differentiated Linguistic Codes

East Asian languages are very complex and are differentiated according to social status, the degree of intimacy, age, sex, and the level of formality. There are also extensive and elaborate honorific linguistic systems in East Asian languages (Brown & Levinson, 1978; Ogino, Misono, & Fukushima, 1985).

These differentiations are manifested not only in referential terms but also in verbs, pronouns, and nouns. They result from Confucian ethical rules that place the highest value on proper human relationships (*i*) and on propriety (*li*). McBrian (1978) has argued that language forms an integral component of social stratification systems, and the hierarchical Confucian society is well represented by the highly stratified linguistic codes in Korea.

Martin (1964) has proposed that one of the main differences between English, Japanese, and Korean is the levels of speech. In both Korean and Japanese, there are two axes of distinction: the axis of address and the axis of reference. The axis of address is divided into plain, polite, and honorific while the axis of reference is divided into humble and neutral (Martin, 1964). An honorific form is used to refer to the receiver's action, while a humble form is used to refer to the sender's action; the reverse would not be appropriate. The most deferential form of speech combines the honorific address form for receiver and the humble form of self-reference.

The English language also employs different codes depending upon intimacy and status difference between the speaker and listener. In general, however, English forms of address are reasonably well described by a single binary contrast: first name (FN) versus title plus last name (TLN) (Brown & Ford, 1964). Certain European languages also contrast the familiar and formal forms, such as *tu* and *vous* in French. The use of FN or TLN can either be reciprocal (both sides use the same form of address) or nonreciprocal (one side uses FN and the other side uses TLN). Status and intimacy also play a role in greetings. For example, "Hi" is more common to intimates and to subordinates while "Good morning" is for distant acquaintances and superiors (Brown & Ford, 1964). In contrast, Ogino, Misono, and Fukushima (1985), working in Japan, found 210 different word forms, through 8 address situations, which can be put into 20 different categories. Moreover, in modern American English practice, the distance between the mutual FN and mutual TLN represents only a very small increment of intimacy, sometimes as small as five minutes of conversation. In East Asian communication situations, the distance between very honorific languages and very informal ones is quite large and more often than not cannot be altered even after a long acquaintance.

In English, the speech level is defined mainly by address forms, while in Korean or Japanese, pronouns, verbs, and nouns all have different levels. Thus, in English "to eat" is "to eat" regardless of the person addressed. In the Korean language, however, there are three different ways of saying "to eat": *muk-da* (plain), *du-shin-da* (polite), and *chap-soo-shin-da* (honorific). Different levels of a verb are often accompanied by different levels of a noun: Rice may be *bap* (plain), *shik-sa* (polite), or *jin-ji* (honorific).

In English, the pronoun "you" is used to refer alike to the old and young, to the president of the country, and to the child next door. In East Asian languages, there are different words for "you" depending upon the level of politeness and upon the relationship. There is also the compulsory or preferential use of a term

of address instead of the pronoun, as when one says: *Jeh sh Wang. Shin.shen.de shu .ma?* (Literally, "Is this Mr. Wang's book?") instead of "Is this your book?" (Chao, 1956, p. 218). Actual role terms, such as professor, aunt, student, and so forth, are used in place of the pronoun "you" even in two-partner communication because they clarify and accentuate the relationships between the two communicators better than the simple second person reference. Since Confucianism dictates that one should observe the proprieties prescribed by a social relationship, the generalized "you" does not seem to be appropriate in most communication situations in East Asian countries.

This differentiation of linguistic codes in East Asian cultures bears out the familiar psycholinguistic principle that for language communities the degree of lexical differentiation of a referent field increases with the importance of that field to the community (Brown & Ford, 1964). The importance of social relationships in Confucian societies has therefore promoted the differentiation of linguistic codes to accommodate highly differentiated relationships.

Emphasis on Indirect Communication versus Emphasis on Direct Communication

Most cultures have both direct and indirect modes of communication. Metaphor, insinuations, innuendos, hints, and irony are only a few examples of the kinds of indirect communication that can be found in most linguistic communities. According to Searle (1969), indirect speech acts occur when the speaker communicates to the hearer more than he or she actually says by referring to some mutually shared background information and by relying on the hearer's powers of rationality and inference. Brown and Levinson (1978) have suggested that indirect speech acts are universal because they perform a basic service in strategies of politeness.

Even though the indirect mode of communication seems to be universal, however, the degree to which it is elaborated varies from culture to culture. For instance, the Malagasy speech community values an indirect style (Keenan, 1974), while Sabra culture prefers a straight-talking (*dugri*) style (Katriel, 1986). Rosaldo (1973) maintained that the Euro-American association of direct talk with a scientific and democratic attitude may not hold true in different cultural contexts. In Ilongot society, for example, direct talk is perceived as authoritarian and exclusionary while indirect language is perceived as accommodating and sensitive to individual wishes.

Brown and Levinson (1978) have suggested that politeness phenomena in language (indirectness is just one of them) derive from the notion of "face," the public self-image that every member wants to claim for himself or herself. According to Katriel (1986), indirect speech acts are the result of predominant concern for the other person's face. The Confucian legacy of consideration for others and concern for proper human relationships has led to the development of communication patterns that preserve one another's face. Indirect communication helps to prevent the embarrassment of rejection by the other person or disagreement among partners, leaving the relationship and each other's face intact. Lebra (1976) suggested that "defending face" is one of the main factors influencing Japanese behavior. She listed a number of concrete mechanisms for defending face, such as mediated communication (asking someone else to transmit the message), refracted communication (talking to a third person in the presence of the hearer), and acting as a delegate (conveying one's message as being from someone else), which are all indirect forms of communication.

The use of the indirect mode of communication in East Asia is pervasive and often deliberate. In comparing Japanese and American organizations, it has been noted that American employees strive to communicate with each other in a clear, precise, and explicit manner, while Japanese often deliberately communicate in a vague and indirect manner (Hirokawa, 1987; Pascale & Athos, 1981). The extensive nature of indirect communication is exemplified by the fact that there are sixteen evasive "maneuvers" that can be employed by the Japanese to avoid saying no (Imai, 1981).

It has also been suggested that there is a significant difference in the level of indirectness between North American and East Asian communication patterns. An American might say "The door is open" as an indirect way of asking the hearer to shut the door, while in Japan, instead of saying "The door is open," one often says "It is somewhat cold today." This is even more indirect, because no words refer to the door (Okabe, 1987). Operating at a still higher level of indirection, one Japanese wife communicated to her husband her discord with her mother-in-law by slight irregularities in her flower arrangements (Lebra, 1976).

One of Grice's maxims for cooperative conversation is "manner," which suggests that the speaker should avoid obscurity of expression and ambiguity (Grice, 1975). This direct communication is a norm in North America, despite the extensive use of indirect communication. Grice's principle would not be accepted as a norm, however, in East Asia. Okabe (1987) has shown that in Japan, the traditional rule of communication, which prescribes not to demand, reject, assert yourself, or criticize the listener straightforwardly, is a much more dominant principle than Grice's maxim of manner.

Reischauer (1977, p. 136) concluded that "the Japanese have a genuine mistrust of verbal skills, thinking that these tend to show superficiality in contrast to inner, less articulate feelings that are communicated by innuendo or by nonverbal means." Thus, even though both North American and East Asian communication communities employ indirect communication, its use is much more prevalent and accepted as normative in the former than the latter.

Receiver versus Sender Centeredness

North American communication very often centers on the sender, and until recently the linear, one-way model from sender to receiver was the prevailing model of communication. Much emphasis has been placed on how senders can formulate better messages, improve source credibility, polish their delivery skills, and so forth. In contrast, the emphasis in East Asia has always been on listening and interpretation.

Cheng (1987) has identified infinite interpretation as one of the main principles of Chinese communication. The process presumes that the emphasis is on the receiver and listening rather than the sender or speech making. According to Lebra (1976, p. 123), "anticipatory communication" is common in Japan, in which, instead of the speaker's having to tell or ask for what he or she wants specifically, others guess and accommodate his or her needs, sparing him or her embarrassment in case the verbally expressed request cannot be met. In such cases, the burden of communication falls not on the message sender but on the message receiver. A person who "hears one and understands ten" is regarded as an intelligent communicator. To catch on quickly and to adjust oneself to another's position before his or her position is clearly revealed is regarded as an important communication skill. One of the common puzzles expressed by foreign students from East Asia is why they are constantly being asked what they want when they are visiting in American homes. In their own countries, the host or hostess is supposed to know what is needed and serve accordingly. The difference occurs because in North America it is important to provide individual freedom of choice; in East Asia, it is important to practice anticipatory communication and to accommodate accordingly.

With the emphasis on indirect communication, the receiver's sensitivity and ability to capture the under-the-surface meaning and to understand implicit meaning becomes critical. In North America, an effort has been made to improve the effectiveness of senders through such formal training as debate and public speech, whereas in East Asia, the effort has been on improving the receiver's sensitivity. The highest sensitivity is reached when one empties the mind of one's preconceptions and makes it as clear as a mirror (Yuji, 1984).

Recently, there has been increased interest in listening in the United States as well. Both communication scholars and practitioners recognize that listening is not only necessary from the instrumental aspect of communication (comprehension) but, more importantly, for the affective aspect (satisfaction of being listened to).

DISCUSSION

This paper compared the East Asian emphasis on social relationships with the North American emphasis on individualism. These two emphases produce very different patterns of interpersonal relationships and communication. The conclusions drawn in this paper are not absolute, however. Each culture contains both orientations to some degree. It is simply more probable that East Asians would exhibit certain patterns of communication, such as indirect communication, more often than North Americans, and vice versa.

The North American preoccupation with individualism and related concepts, such as equality, fairness, and justice, and its far-reaching influences on the whole fiber of society are well documented. On the other hand, the importance of social relationships as a key to the East Asian countries has been recognized only recently. For instance, investigations of Japanese management styles have found that one of the fundamental differences between Japanese and American management is the personalized, interdependent relationships among employees and between managers and employees in Japan. These human relationships are related to loyalty and high productivity. It is not uncommon to explain such relationships away as merely a result of other organizational practices, such as lifelong employment. If one looks under the surface, however, one realizes that it is derived from a thousand-year-old Confucian legacy, and that similar human relationship patterns are found outside of large organizations. Consequently, attempts to transplant such a management style to North America with its philosophical and cultural orientation of individualism cannot be entirely satisfactory. The culture itself would have to be modified first.

There has been increasing concern in North America about the pursuit of individualism at the expense of commitment to larger entities such as the community, civic groups, and other organizations. It has been suggested that modern individualism has progressed to such an extent that most Americans are trapped by the language of individualism itself and have lost the ability to articulate their own need to get involved (Bellah et al., 1985). Although individualism has its own strength as a value, individualism that is not accompanied by commitments to large entities eventually forces people into a state of isolation, where life itself becomes meaningless.

If human beings are fundamentally social animals, it is necessary to balance the cultural belief system of individualism with the need to get involved with others. Americans have joined voluntary associations and civic organizations more than any other citizens of the industrialized world. However, such recent phenomena as the "me" generation and young stockbrokers who pursue only personal gain at the expense of their own organizations or the society as a whole can be perceived as pathological symptoms of individualism driven to its extreme. Bellah et al. (1985, p. 284) have maintained that "social ecology is damaged not only by war, genocide, and political repression. It is also damaged by the destruction of the subtle ties that bind human beings to one another, leaving them frightened and alone." They strongly argue that we need to restore social ecology by making people aware of our intricate connectedness and interdependence.

The emphasis of Confucianism on social relationships is conducive to cooperation, warm relaxed human relations, consideration of others, and group harmony, but it has costs as well. Under such social constraints, individual initiative and innovation are slow to appear, and some individuals feel that their individuality is being suffocated. Because of the sharp distinction between in-groups and out-groups, factionalism may be inevitable. Within such well-defined sets of social relationships, people have a well-developed sense of obligation but a weak sense of duty to impersonal social entities.

Ironically, the solution for both the North American problems of excessive individualism and the excessive adherence to in-groupness in East Asia is the same: to be receptive to others. For the North Americans, this means accepting the limitations of self-reliance, becoming committed to a group, and putting the common good ahead of personal wants. For the East Asians, this means making their group boundaries more flexible and accepting outsiders with humanness and commitment to the common good.

There have been substantial changes in the East Asian societies since World War II. There has been an irrepressible influx of Western values; imported films and television programs are ubiquitous. However, it is not easy to change several hundred years of Confucian legacy. In Japan, for example, a greater proportion of young people than old expressed a preference for a boss endowed with the virtues of humanness and sympathy over a more efficient boss who would not ask for extra devotion (Dore, 1973). A similar finding was reported in Korea. When Korean workers, mostly in manufacturing plants, were asked their reasons for changing jobs, those who answered "a better human relationship and more humane treatment" still outnumbered those who answered "better payment" (Kim, 1984).

It seems inevitable, however, that the East Asian countries will see an increasing number of people who do not have traditional, binding relationships as the society moves further toward industrialization and higher mobility. The task will be to find a way for such people to cope with life without the protection of close in-group memberships and to learn to find satisfaction in expressing individual freedom and self-reliance.

References

Bellah, R., Madsen, R., Sullivan, W., Swidler, A., & Tipton, S. (1985). *Habits of the Heart: Individualism and Commitment in American Life*. New York: Harper & Row.

Brown, R. W., & Ford, M. (1964). "Address in American English." In D. Hymes (Ed.), *Language in Culture and Society*. New York: Harper & Row.

Brown, R., & Levinson, S. (1978). "Universals in Language Usage: Politeness Phenomena." In E. Goody (Ed.), *Questions and Politeness*. Cambridge: Cambridge University Press.

Chao, Y. R. (1956). Chinese terms of address. *Language*, 32, 217–241.

Cheng, C. Y. (1987). "Chinese Philosophy and Contemporary Communication Theory." In D. L. Kincaid (Ed.), *Communication Theory: Eastern and Western Perspectives*. New York: Academic Press.

Chinese Culture Connection. (1987). Chinese values and the search for culture-free dimensions of culture. *Journal of Cross-Cultural Psychology,* 18, 143–164.

Condon, J., & Yousef, F. (1975). *An Introduction to Intercultural Communication*. New York: Bobbs-Merrill.

Dore, R. (1973). *British Factory, Japanese Factory: The Origins of National Diversity in Industrial Relations*. Berkeley and Los Angeles: University of California Press.

Grice, P. H. (1975). "Logic and Conversation." In P. Cole and J. L. Morgan (Eds.), *Studies in Syntax*. Vol. 3. New York: Academic Press.

Hall, J., & Beardsley, R. (1965). *Twelve Doors to Japan*. New York: McGraw-Hill.

Hirokawa, R. (1987). "Communication Within the Japanese Business Organization." In D. L. Kincaid (Ed.), *Communication Theory: Eastern and Western Perspectives*. New York Academic Press.

Hofstede, G. (1980). *Culture's Consequences*. Newbury Park, Calif.: Sage.

Hui, C. H., & Triandis, H. C. (1986). Individualism-collectivism: A study of cross-cultural research. *Journal of Cross-Cultural Psychology,* 17, 225–248.

Imai, M. (1981). *Sixteen Ways to Avoid Saying No*. Tokyo: Nihon Keizai Shimbun.

Katriel, T. (1986). *Talking Straight: Dugri Speech in Israeli Sabra Culture*. Cambridge: Cambridge University Press.

Keenan, E. (1974). "Norm Makers, Norm Breakers: Uses of Speech by Men and Women in a Malagasy Community." In R. Bauman and J. Sherzer (Eds.), *Explorations in the Ethnography of Speaking*. Cambridge: Cambridge University Press.

Kim, S. U. (1984). *"Kong-jang no-dong-ja-ye ee-jik iyu"* ("Reasons for Changing Jobs Among Factory Workers"). *Hankook Daily Newspaper*, May 2 (in Korean).

Lebra, T. S. (1976). *Japanese Patterns of Behavior*. Honolulu: The University Press of Hawaii.

Lee, K. T. (1983). *Hankook-in ye u-shik koo-jo* (Cognitive Patterns of Korean People). Seoul: Shin-Won Moon-Wha Sa (in Korean).

Luce, D., & Sommer, J. (1969). *Viet Nam—The Unheard Voices*. Ithaca, N.Y.: Cornell University Press.

McBrian, C. (1978). Language and social stratification: The case of a Confucian society." *Anthropological Linguistics,* 2, 320–326.

McNaughton, W. (1974). *The Confucian Vision*. Ann Arbor: University of Michigan Press.

Martin, S. E. (1964). "Speech Levels in Japan and Korea." In D. Hymes (Ed.), *Language in Culture and* Society. New York: Harper & Row.

Nakamura, H. (1964). *Ways of Thinking of Eastern Peoples*. Honolulu: East-West Center Press.

Ogino, T., Misono, Y. & Fukushima, C. (1985). Diversity of honorific usage in Tokyo: A socio-linguistic approach based on a field survey. *International Journal of Sociology of Language,* 55, 23–39.

Okabe, K. (1987). "Indirect Speech Acts of the Japanese." In D. L. Kincaid (Ed.), *Communication Theory: Eastern and Western Perspectives*. New York: Academic Press.

Parsons, T., Shils, E., & Olds, J. (1951). "Categories of the Orientation and Organization of Action." In T. Parsons and E. A Shils (Eds.), *Toward a General Theory of Action*. Cambridge, Mass.: Harvard University Press.

Pascale, R., & Athos, A. (1981). *The Art of Japanese Management: Application for American Executives*. New York: Warner Communications.

Reischauer, E. (1977). *The Japanese*. Cambridge: Harvard University Press.

Rosaldo, M. (1973). I have nothing to hide: The language of Ilongot oratory. *Language in Society,* 11, 193–223.

Searle, J. R. (1969). *Speech Acts*. Cambridge: Cambridge University Press.

Varenne, H. (1977). *Americans Together: Structured Diversity in a Midwestern Town*. New York and London: Teacher College Press.

Yuji, A. (Trans. N. Chung). (1984). *Ilbon-in ye usik koo-jo* (Japanese Thought Patterns). Seoul: Baik Yang Publishing Co. (in Korean).

Yum, J. O. (1987). "Korean Philosophy and Communication." In D. L. Kincaid (Ed.), *Communication Theory: Eastern and Western Perspectives*. New York: Academic Press.

Concepts and Questions

1. According to Yum, what is one reason Confucianism has endured?

2. In terms of communication behavior, compare an orientation toward social relationships with an orientation toward individualism.

3. What are the four Confucian principles of right conduct? How do they contribute to communication behavior?

4. How do East Asian concepts of in-group and out-group differ from those of North Americans? How might these differences affect intercultural communication?

5. How does Confucianism affect linguistic codes?

6. What are the major differences in the ways interpersonal bonding takes place in Eastern and Western cultures?

7. How do Eastern values concerning equality differ from Western values?

8. How does the rate of self-disclosure differ in Eastern and Western cultures?

9. What does Yum mean when she says that Confucianism is a philosophy of human nature?

10. Do you agree with Yum's observation that it is not easy to change cultural values that have been in place for several hundred years?

Some Basic Cultural Patterns of India

NEMI C. JAIN

Why study basic cultural patterns of India? To many Americans, the word *India* brings to mind a wonderland peopled with snake charmers, bearded and turbaned giants, Ganges bathers, *dhoti*-clad peasants, and lumbering elephants—all parading past, with the Taj Mahal serving as the backdrop.[1] But if this is all that India is about, then why has the United States given more than $10 billion in loans, grants, and agricultural products since India's independence from British rule in 1947? Why is there so much concern in the halls of Congress, in the mass media, and in the corridors of the United Nations over the question of whether India will "make it"? In short, why the persistent anxiety, concern, and interest about a country and people who reside far away from American shores, not just in miles but in culture, language, habits of thought and life?[2]

The desire to find answers to these questions—and the very existence of the questions themselves—is one of the characteristics that distinguishes this generation from all others that have gone before. No major country lies farther away in miles from the United States than does India. It is becoming increasingly obvious, however, that "no man is an island" and that actions in one part of the globe cause reactions in many other countries of the world. India is a most suitable culture for study because her preeminence (along with Communist China) in Asia and her leadership role among nations of the Third World point toward her importance in international affairs. More importantly, India's cultural tradition provides an instructive contrast to American cultural patterns.[3]

Courtesy of Nemi C. Jain. This original essay first appeared in the third edition of this book. All rights reserved. Permission to reprint must be obtained from the author and the publisher. Nemi C. Jain is Professor Emeritus, Hugh Downs School of Human Communication, Arizona State University.

Indian culture has a long continuous history that extends over 5,000 years. Very early, India evolved a distinctive culture and religion, Hinduism, which was modified and adjusted as it came into contact with outside elements. In spirit, however, India has maintained the essential unity of the indigenous doctrines and ideas of Hinduism. It is this characteristic of Indian culture that has enabled it to withstand many vicissitudes and to continue to mold the lives of millions of people in India and abroad.[4]

Like any other culture, the Indian culture is complex and consists of many interrelated beliefs, values, norms, social systems, and material cultural elements. In spite of the multiethnic, multilingual, and highly stratified nature of contemporary Indian society, India is united by a set of basic cultural patterns that are widely shared among the Hindus who comprise about 80 percent of India's population of over 650 million. The major aim of this article is to outline some of these basic cultural patterns that have persisted over the thousands of years of Indian history, patterns that continue to influence many aspects of Indian social institutions and that affect communication and thought patterns of millions of Hindus in India and abroad. More specifically, this article will describe briefly the following interrelated categories of basic cultural patterns of India: (1) worldview, (2) reincarnation, (3) *Dhamm,* (4) caste system, and (5) spirit of tolerance.

Each of these categories includes several specific cultural beliefs, values, and norms that are closely interrelated. Each cultural pattern represents a continuum, and within the same culture, variations of the pattern normally occur. Contradictions among cultural patterns are probably universal throughout societies. Despite internal variations and contradictions, there is an overall integration to the patterns of Hindu Indian culture. It is possible to simplify its description by isolating the various cultural patterns and considering them one at a time.

WORLDVIEW

One of the unique characteristics of Indian culture is its worldview involving the Hindu concepts of *Brahman* and *Atman*. In Hinduism, the Supreme Being is the impersonal *Brahman,* a philosophical Absolute, serenely blissful, beyond all limitations either ethical or metaphysical. *Brahman* is the supreme reality. The basic Hindu view of God involves infinite being, infinite consciousness, and infinite bliss. The chief attributes to be linked with *Brahman* are *sat, chit,* and *ananda;* God is being, awareness, and bliss. Even these words cannot claim to describe him literally, however, for the meanings they carry for people are radically unlike the senses in which they apply to God.[5]

The Hindu conception of the universe is essentially cyclic. Hinduism does not believe in an absolute beginning or end of the universe but maintains that creation, existence, and destruction are endless processes ever repeating. This does not preclude a belief in the creation or end of a particular universe. This present world, for example, had a beginning and will have an end; but it is a mere link in the endless chain of universes that preceded it and are yet to succeed it. This world was created by *Brahman* and after a definite period will be destroyed and replaced by another world that will suffer a similar fate.[6]

According to Hinduism, the *Brahman* is in a sense the very world itself, including both living and nonliving aspects of the universe. Hinduism recognizes the relationship between living and nonliving parts of the universe. It emphasizes the need for understanding the nature of relationships among human beings, other living organisms, and nonliving creations of God, including mountains, rivers, and other aspects of the physical universe. Hinduism lays considerable emphasis on the value of all created life, including animals, birds, and trees. It is indeed interesting to note that the gods of the Hindu pantheon are associated with animals. *Shiva,* who has *Nandi* or the Bull as his mount (*vahana*), is regarded as the Lord of animals, *Pasupathi.* Likewise, *Vishnu* has the Serpent and *Garuda; Brahma,* the Swan; *Indra,* the Elephant; *Surya* (Sun God), the Horse; *Durga,* the Lion; *Ganesha,* the Rat; and *Muruga,* the Peacock. Among the ten principal incarnations (*avataras*) of Lord *Vishnu,* three—*Matsya* (the Fish), *Kurma* (the Tortoise), and *Varaha* (the Boar)—are in animal forms, while the fourth, *Narasimha,* is in a form that is half man and half lion. According to Hindu beliefs, the Buddha's former births were also in animal forms. The Hindus have naturally invested the animals with an element of divinity. This association of gods with the animal world is indicative of a healthy attitude toward nature. The same association is true of mountains, rivers, and

trees, which have more than an ordinary significance in Indian life—many are considered sacred and holy. In short, Indian culture takes into its fold all nature. Hinduism emphasizes the importance of harmony among human beings, other living organisms, and the physical creations of the universe.[7]

In Hinduism, *Brahman* is also conceived of as the Supreme Soul of the universe. Every living soul is a part of the *Brahman,* a particular manifestation of the *Brahman.* These particular manifestations, individual souls, seem to change from generation to generation, but actually only the unimportant, outer details change—a body, a face, a name, a different condition or status in life. The *Brahman,* however, veiled behind these deceptive "realities," is continuous and indestructible. This hidden self or *Atman* is a reservoir of being that never dies, is never exhausted, and is without limit in awareness and bliss. *Atman* is the infinite center of every life. Body, personality, and *Atman* together comprise a human being.[8]

A Hindu cannot believe in the *Brahman* without believing also in a firm bond among all people, since they are all manifestations of the *Brahman.* Furthermore, a Hindu cannot really believe in any individual as a distinct and separate person, because Hinduism contends that each individual is only a tiny part of the whole universe, which is the *Brahman.*[9]

The eternal *Atman* is usually buried under the almost impenetrable mass of distractions, false ideas, and self-regarding impulses that compose one's surface being. The aim of human life is to cleanse the dross from one's being to the point where its infinite center, the eternal *Atman,* will be fully manifest.[10]

What kind of world do we have? Hinduism answers: (1) a multiple world that includes innumerable galaxies horizontally, innumerable tiers vertically, and innumerable cycles temporally; (2) a moral world in which the law of *Karma* never wavers; (3) a middle world that will never in itself replace the supreme as destination for the human spirit; (4) a world that is *maya,* deceptively tricky in that its multiplicity, materiality, and welter of dualities appear ultimate whereas these are in fact provisional only; (5) a training ground that can advance human beings toward the Highest; (6) a world that is *lila,* the play of the divine in its cosmic dance, untiring, unending, resistless, but ultimately gentle, with a grace born of infinite vitality.[11]

REINCARNATION

The Hindu belief in reincarnation affirms that individual souls enter the world, by God's power, and pass through a sequence of bodies or life cycles. On the subhuman level, the passage is through a series of increasingly complex bodies until at last a human one is attained. Up to this point, the soul's growth is virtually automatic. With the soul's graduation into a human body, this automatic, escalator mode of ascent comes to an end. The soul's assignment to this exalted habitation is evidence that it has reached self-consciousness, and with this estate come freedom, responsibility, and effort. Now the individual soul, as a human being, is fully responsible for its behavior through the doctrine of *Karma*—the moral law of cause and effect. The present condition of each individual life is a product of what one did in the previous life; and one's present acts, thoughts, and decisions are determining one's future states.[12]

This concept of *Karma* and the completely moral universe it implies carries two important psychological corollaries. First, it commits the Hindu who understands it to complete personal responsibility. Each individual is wholly responsible for his or her present condition and will have exactly the future he or she is now creating. Conversely, the idea of a moral universe closes the door to all appeals to chance or accident. In this world there is no chance or accident. *Karma* decrees that every decision must have its determinate consequences, but the decisions themselves are, in the last analysis, freely arrived at. Or, to approach the matter from the other direction, the consequences of a person's past decisions condition his or her present lot, as a card player is dealt a particular hand but is left free to play that hand in a number of ways. This means that the carrier of a soul, a human being, as it threads its course through innumerable human bodies, is guided by its choice, these in turn being decided by what the soul wants at each particular stage of its pilgrimage.[13]

Never during its pilgrimage is the individual soul completely adrift and alone. From start to finish its nucleus is the *Atman*. Underlying its whirlpool of transient feelings, emotions, and delusions is the self-luminous, abiding point of God himself. Although he is buried too deep in the soul to be noticeable, he is the sole ground of a person's being and awareness. God alone energizes the surface self in all that it does; in the end it is his radiance that melts the soul's thick cap that at first hides his glory almost completely but becomes at last a pure capacity for God. After reaching this level of purity, the individual soul passes into complete identification with God.[14] This state for an individual soul is called *Moksha* or *Nirvana*—when the soul is free from the process of reincarnation or transmigration and has merged with the *Brahman*, from whence it originated in the first place.

According to Hinduism, the aim of life is the gradual revelation in one's human existence of the eternal within oneself. The general progress is governed by the law of *Karma* or moral causation. The Hindu religion does not believe in a God who from his judgment seat weighs each case separately and decides on its merits. He does not administer justice from without, enhancing or remitting punishment according to his will. God is *in* each individual, and so the law of *Karma* is organic to human nature. Every moment each person is on trial, and every honest effort will do him or her good in this eternal endeavor. The character that each individual builds will continue into the future until he or she realizes oneness with God.[15]

DHARMA

The concept *of Dharma* is another unique feature of Hinduism and Indian culture. *Dharma* refers to a code of conduct that guides the life of a person both as an individual and as a member of society. It includes ideals and purposes, influences and institutions that shape the character of a person. It is the law of right living, the observance of which secures the double object of happiness on earth and salvation. The life of a Hindu is regulated in a very detailed manner by the laws of *Dharma*. Personal habits, social and family ties, fasts and feasts, and actions are all conditioned by it.[16]

Dharma is the binding law that accounts for the cohesion in the social system throughout the history of Indian society. Since *Dharma* is trans-individual, no social contract proves necessary; harmony is achieved when everyone "follows" his or her own *Dharma*. *Dharma* is a code of conduct supported by the general conscience of the people. It is not subjective in the sense that the conscience of the individual imposes it, nor external in the sense that the law enforces it. It is the system of conduct that the general opinion or spirit of the people supports. *Dharma* does not force people into virtue but trains them for it. It is not a fixed code of mechanical rules but a living spirit that grows and moves in response to the development of the society.[17]

Dharma has two sides that are interdependent: the individual and the social. The conscience of the individual requires a guide, and one must be taught the way to realize one's purpose and to live according to spirit and not sense. The interests of society require equal attention. *Dharma,* on the social level, is that which holds together all living beings in a harmonious order. Virtue is conduct contributing to social welfare, and vice is its opposite. It is frequently insisted that the highest virtue consists in doing to others as you would be done by. Both the individual and the social virtues are included in what are called *nitya karmas,* or obligatory duties, which are cleanliness or *saucam,* good behavior and manners or *acharam,* social service or *panchamahyajnas,* and prayer and worship or *sandhyavandanam.* The *varnashrama dharma,* which deals with the caste system and the stages of the individual life, develops the detail about *Dharma* at the individual and social level.[18]

The concept of *Dharma* at the individual level recognizes four stages in each person's life. In the first stage of *Brabmacharya* (student phase), the obligations of temperance, sobriety, chastity, and social service are firmly established in the minds of the young. All have to pass through this discipline, irrespective of caste, class, wealth, or poverty. In the second stage of *Grahastha* or householder, the individual undertakes the obligations of family life, becoming a member of a social body and accepting its rights and obligations. Self-support, thrift, and hospitality are enjoined in this stage. Caste rules are relevant only to this stage. At this stage, the individual's energies and interests turn naturally outward. There are three fronts for satisfying human wants at this stage: one's family, one's vocation, and the community to which one belongs. Normally the person will be interested in all three. This is the time for satisfying the first three human wants: pleasure through the family primarily, success through the vocation, and duty through one's responsibilities as a citizen.[19]

In the third stage of *Vanaprastha* (retirement) the individual is required to check his or her attachment to worldly possessions, suppress all the conceits bred in through the accidents of the second stage (such as pride of birth or property, individual genius, or good luck), and cultivate a spirit of renunciation. It is the time for working out a philosophy into oneself, the time of transcending the senses to find and dwell at one with the timeless reality that underlies the dream of life in this natural world. Beyond retirement the final stage in which the goal is actually reached is the state of the *sannyas,* a disinterested servant of humanity who finds peace in the strength of spirit. A state of perfect harmony with the Eternal is reached, and the education of the human spirit terminates.[20]

CASTE SYSTEM

The caste system is a unique feature of Indian culture. The caste rules relate to the social functions of individuals. According to Hinduism, a person's nature can be developed only by a concentration of one's personality at a particular point in the social order. Since human beings show one or the other of the three aspects of mental life (thought, feelings, and action) in a greater degree, the *dvijas* or the twice-born are distinguished into the three classes of men of thought, men of feeling, and men of action. Those in whom no one quality is particularly developed are the *Sudras.* The four castes correspond to the intellectual, militant, industrial, and unskilled workers, who are all members of one organic whole.[21]

Accordingly, Indian society has been divided into the fourfold classification of castes, hierarchically from higher to lower castes: (1) *Brahmins*—priests or seers who have such duties as that of teaching, preaching, assisting in the sacrificial processes, giving alms, and receiving gifts; (2) *Kashtriyas*—protectors of life and treasure, identified with the administrative or the ruling classes; (3) *Vaisyas*—cultivators, traders, businesspeople, and herders; and (4) *Sudras*—artisan specialists such as carpenters, blacksmiths, and laborers. In the course of time, there developed a fifth group, ranked so low as to be considered outside and beneath the caste system itself. The members of this fifth "caste-less" group are variously referred to as "Untouchables," "outcastes," "Scheduled Castes," or (by Gandhi) *Hari-jans,* "children of God." People in this group inherit the kinds of work that in India are considered least desirable, such as scavenging, slaughtering animals, leather tanning, and sweeping the streets and footpaths.[22]

Although the caste system began as a straightforward, functional division of Indian society, it was later misinterpreted by priests as permanent and immutable as the word of God. Accordingly, the caste system was justified in terms of the "immutable and inborn" qualities of individuals, the unchangeable result of "actions in previous incarnations" and the unalterable basis of Hindu religion.[23]

The particular caste a person belongs to is determined by birth. Each caste has its appropriate status, rights, and duties. There are detailed rules about communication and contact among people of different castes. A caste has considerable influence on the way of life of its members. Most important relations of life, above all marriage, take place within the caste. Castes have great power over their members. To break caste is to cut oneself off from one's group, which means from family, from friends, and from all of those who live in the same way. One who cuts oneself off has no hope of being adopted by another group—not only is ostracized by one's own group but will not be accepted even by a lower caste.[24] Thus, the caste is a major "significant other" influence in the Indian culture and continues to affect the day-to-day lives of millions of Hindus, especially in villages and small towns.

SPIRIT OF TOLERANCE

An outstanding feature of Indian culture is its tradition of tolerance. Indian culture, because of the influence of Hinduism, believes in universal toleration and accepts all religions as true. Indian culture is comprehensive and suits the needs of everyone, irrespective of caste, creed, color, or sex. It has universal appeal and makes room for all. It has the modesty to admit the propriety of other points of view. This idea has been beautifully developed in the Jaina theory *of Syadvada* or the theory of *may be.* According to this theory no absolute affirmation or denial is possible. As all knowledge is

probable and relative, the other person's point of view is as true as one's own. In other words, it suggests that one must show restraint in making judgments—a very healthy principle. One must know that one's judgments are true only partially and can by no means be regarded as true in absolute terms. This understanding and spirit of tolerance has been largely responsible for the advancement of Indian culture. This attitude has helped to bring together the divergent races with different languages and religious persuasions under a common culture.[25]

This brief exposition of Indian culture has shown its highly pluralistic and dynamic qualities. Through the examination of worldview, reincarnation, *Dharma,* the caste system, and the spirit of tolerance, Indian culture has been seen to embody such basic values as synthesis (*samanvaya*), desire to know the truth (*satyajijnasa*), nonviolence (*abimsa*), and above all the attitude of toleration. This view of Indian culture has further explained the role and influence of Hindu thought as it is manifest in Indian culture and has shown that the two are inseparable. What India needs is to realize herself, to broaden her spiritual heritage, not to rest upon the foundation already nobly erected by her own saints and scholars, but to continue along the same inspiring lines.[26]

Notes

1. Fersh, Seymour. *India and South Asia.* (New York: Macmillan, 1965), p. 1.
2. Fersh, pp. 1–3.
3. Fersh, p. 3.
4. Sreenivasa Murthy, H. V., & S. U. Kamath. *Studies in Indian Culture.* (Bombay: Asia Publishing House, 1973), pp. 4–5.
5. Smith, Huston. *The Religions of Man.* (New York: Harper & Row, 1958), p. 72.
6. Thomas, P. *Hindu Religion, Customs and Manners,* 3rd ed. (Bombay: D. B. Taraporevala Sons & Co., 1956), p. 1.
7. Murthy & Kamath, pp. 7–8.
8. Smith, pp. 27–28.
9. Katz, Elizabeth. *India in Pictures.* (New York: Sterling Publishing, 1969), pp. 36–37.
10. Smith, pp. 27–28.
11. Smith, p. 85.
12. Smith, p. 76.
13. Smith, p. 77.
14. Smith, p. 79.

15. Radhakrishnan, S. *Indian Religions*. (New Delhi: Vision Books Private Ltd., 1979), pp. 52–53.
16. Radhakrishnan, pp. 70–71.
17. Radhakrishnan, p. 61.
18. Radhakrishnan, p. 62.
19. Smith, p. 62.
20. Smith, pp. 62–63.
21. Radhakrishnan, pp. 63–64.
22. Chopra, S. N. *India: An Area Study*. (New Delhi: Vikas Publishing House Private Ltd., 1977), pp. 26–27.
23. Chopra, pp. 27–28.
24. Fersh, pp. 17–21.
25. Murthy and Kamath, p. 5.
26. Murthy and Kamath, p. 8.

Concepts and Questions

1. What does Jain mean when he writes that "Hinduism is an amorphous body of beliefs, philosophies, worship practices, and codes of conduct"?

2. Why is knowing something about a culture's worldview important for effective communication with people of that culture?

3. How would you describe Jain's explanation of a reality that is "undivided" and "unconditional"? How does that reality differ from the Western view of reality?

4. What is meant by the phrase, "At the deepest level, existence is boundless"?

5. At the heart of the Hindu view of the world is the following: "Hindus believe that ordinary means of acquiring knowledge—human senses, human reason, and empirical methods—cannot penetrate the profound and undivided ultimate level of reality." How would this notion influence perception and the "defining" of reality?

6. What do you see as the link between *dharma* and ethics? Does your culture's worldview have a concept similar to *dharma*? What is it?

7. What is meant by "The Spirit of Tolerance" in the Hindu tradition?

8. Jain asserts that "An understanding of Indian worldview, and the influence of these cultural patterns on communication behavior, will improve the quality of intercultural communication between people of India and other cultures." Do you agree? If so, why?

Communication with Egyptians

POLLY A. BEGLEY

Cairo made my eyeballs ache. It is a city of coloured splendour, alive and moving, with a hundred gay pigments astir in the sunshine, and every thoroughfare stuffed full, as it seems, of processioning and pageantry.

ARTHUR EDWARD COPPING, 1910

As the sun rises above the ancient land of Pharaohs, the *Muezzin* calls faithful Muslims to prayer over the city's loudspeakers. Egypt, claiming more than 4,000 years of history, is a country of extremes: An ancient center of learning and mystery, overwhelming poverty next to grand architectural wonders, sandstorms and sunshine mingling with smog, and the fertile Nile Valley surrounded by desert. The 6,671 kilometers of the Nile River is lifeblood for Egyptian civilization. The Nile is known as a "precious gift yet a perilous master" (Crawford, 1996, p. 39). The unpredictable river gives life through its waters while periodically destroying canals, houses, or entire towns.

People have long been intrigued by Egyptian culture—mysterious pyramids, sacred temples hewn from rocky cliffs, enigmatic hieroglyphs, and centuries-old traditions. The Greek historian Herodotus, born around 484 BCE, was one of the first scholar–tourists to extol the wonders of Egypt to the rest of the world. Modern architecture, philosophy, mathematics, literature, and science have all been influenced by Egyptian wisdom. Specifically, Socrates, Aristotle, and Pythagoras all learned from the Egyptians. Even our alphabet may have evolved from ancient hieroglyphs (Crawford, 1996). Modern Egyptologists still wonder at the near-perfect preservation of writings on 3,000- to 4,000-year-old stones and temples.

In villages along the Nile today, the *Fellahin,* or peasants, employ the same tools and agricultural methods from Pharaonic periods. Government experts sent to these communities are told that modern irrigation ideas are unnecessary because "we have done it this way for thousands of years." Clearly, one must know a great deal about Egypt's history, customs, and traditions before she or he is prepared to appreciate the rich tapestry of its culture.

We cannot presume that this brief essay can comprehensively cover thousands of years of history and tradition. Scholars who focus on cultural studies know that learning is a continual process. Even a lifetime of study and experience, however, would not be enough to unravel the secrets of Egyptian civilization. The purpose of this review, then, is to seek an understanding of interactions among Egyptians and non-Egyptians by examining relevant cultural characteristics. Specifically, the primary emphasis will be on aspects of culture that influence intercultural communication. To this end, we will discuss the three important aspects of culture: (1) worldview and religion, (2) values, and (3) language.

EGYPTIAN WORLDVIEW AND RELIGION

Worldview represents common perceptions among the members of a cultural group. Samovar and Porter (2000) define *worldview* as "a culture's orientation toward such things as God, nature, life, death, the universe, and other philosophical issues that are concerned with the meaning of life and with 'being'" (p. 11). A religion or philosophy essentially attempts to explain the unexplainable for the people of a particular community.

The Egyptian worldview began as a culmination of various African civilizations and beliefs. The name *Egypt* came from the Greek name *Aegyptos,* but before that it was *Kemet,* Blackland, to the native peoples (Crawford, 1996). When the Sahara dried up and became a desert, several African groups migrated to the Nile Valley. The harsh famine and flood cycles of life near the Nile forced the people to become organized and ever vigilant. Religion was an important part of this orderly existence, and as many as 2,000 deities were part of Kemetic beliefs. The lack of distinction between science, art, and religious philosophy is reflected

in the belief that each action in everyday life was the earthly symbol of a divine activity.

Kemet developed into a great civilization because of divine leadership and geography. The Pharaohs were incarnations of the Universal God, Horus, and they ruled with absolute and divine power in early Kemet. The first monarch, Menes, established his dynasty around 3150 BCE when he united upper and lower Kemet. The nation had an advantage geographically during the early dynastic period because vast scorching deserts protected the population from invaders on most sides (Brega, 1998). Herodotus wrote of a mighty army of 50,000 soldiers that was literally swallowed by the sands about 2,500 years ago. Archaeologists recently discovered remains deep in the desert that may prove the tale of this lost army (Stowe, 2000). Essentially, ancient Kemet people could focus on nation building, art, science, and philosophy because they were spared from the threat of external attack.

Today, Pharaonic-era beliefs are confined to museums and tourist sites, but traces of Kemet could never be completely erased from the Nile, sands, and people of this ancient land. In 619 CE, nomadic Arabs invaded Egypt, and eventually Islam replaced other religious beliefs to become the prevailing worldview in modern Egypt. Ancient Egyptian history is considered to be anti-Islamic and has been replaced with Islamic history in Egyptian schools (Gershoni & Jankowski, 1995). Christianity is the only other religious minority and has dwindled to less than 13 percent of the population. A small enclave of Christians lives in central Egypt, but violence plagues their relations with their Muslim neighbors. Egyptian Muslims find solace in the religious beliefs of Islam and answer questions of existence through the sacred words of the Islamic holy book (Koran). An examination of Islamic history, principles, contemporary practices, and the role of religious beliefs within politics can provide insight into the behavioral and communicative patterns of its adherents.

Islamic History

The historical roots of Islamic beliefs are important to intercultural communication because religion influences every part of everyday life in Egyptian Muslim communities. Islam began with Mohammed, who was the last of God's prophets. God spoke to Mohammed through the angel Gabriel about 610 CE, and the messages were recorded in the Koran. The Koran, the book of Islam, is the only miracle claimed by Mohammed and considered to be the exact words of God. This holy book contains 114 chapters (or *suras*) and outlines the will of God for the loyal followers of Islam (Waines, 1995).

Although descriptions of Mohammed range from praising to condemning, no one can argue that he did not have a vast influence on all of Arabia, including Egypt. Historically, the Middle East was turbulent. Vast areas, harsh deserts, warring tribes, and a precarious value placed on human life contributed to turmoil in the region. Although numerous leaders had previously attempted to create a consolidated empire, Mohammed and his followers were able to unite all of Arabia under their control. When Islam was first introduced to Egyptians, an established set of ancient beliefs dated back thousands of years. These beliefs included countless deities and complicated rituals for Egyptians. In contrast, Islamic beliefs were easy to understand and to follow for the common people.

Islamic beliefs dominate every moment from birth to death and beyond. Almost 85 percent to 90 percent of Egypt's population, and more than 1 billion people worldwide, are followers of Islam. Muslims seek Islam to find "the peace that comes when one's life is surrendered to God" (Smith, 1991, p. 222). This worldview reflects one of the youngest and fastest growing major religions in the world. Some of the reasons this religion is appealing to a large number of people can be understood by examining the principles of Islam such as tenets, pillars, and universal allure.

Islamic Principles

Four tenets are central to understanding Islam: (1) it is a monotheistic religion; (2) God created the world; (3) humans are fundamentally good from birth because they are God's creations and without "original sin." Muslims believe in the innate goodness of humanity, but contemporary societies "forget" their divine origins; and (4) for each Muslim there will be a day of judgment when God decides whether each person will go to heaven or be condemned to hell (Smith, 1991). Islam outlines five pillars for Muslims. First, *shahada* (creed) is the confession of faith: *"La ilaha illa 'llah"* and is translated as "There is no God but God, and Muhammad

is his prophet" (Smith, 1991, p. 244). Second, *salat* (prayer) is an important part of everyday life. Muslims are required to stop for prayer five times a day facing in the direction of the holy city of Mecca. Murphy (1993) described the call to prayer in Cairo, Egypt: "'God is great', the muezzins proclaim, their words furiously amplified to rock concert proportions through the city's narrow and winding streets, a celebration of holiness at 70 decibels" (p. 1). Third, *zakat* (giving alms) to the poor is expected of each person. Fourth, *sawm* (fasting) during the month of Ramadan is required. This fast prompts Muslims to be disciplined and reminds them to be more charitable to the hungry and the poor within their societies. Finally, the *hajj* (pilgrimage) to Mecca is a requisite trip for those who are able to make the journey (Nigosian, 1987). Islam possesses a universal allure, which appeals to Egyptians. This allure comes about, first, because Islam is a religion of action, not of contemplation. Second, Muslims from all cultural and ethnic groups are recognized as equal members within the religion. Believers are thus united in an international fraternity of Islam. Mohammed's words are clear on this issue: "A Muslim is the brother of a Muslim; he neither oppresses him nor does he fail him, he neither lies to him nor does he hold him in contempt" (Lippman, 1995, p. 185). Third, Islam does not require complicated rituals or sacrifices. If one repeats the shahada creed, then he or she is a Muslim. Good Muslims follow the five pillars. The accepting simplicity of Islam unites and strengthens the people of Egypt.

Islam and Politics

Egyptian government has long recognized the power of Islam within the general populace. Each political group publicly supports the *Shari-a* (religious laws), advocates that religious principles should be taught in schools, and allows family concerns to be decided by Islamic ideologies. The constitution also declares Islam the state religion. Government support of Shari-a, however, has not prevented a rising number of secular laws. An ongoing Egyptian dilemma stems from trying to balance Islamic religious laws with attempts to bring modernization to industry and business. The introduction of new technology and Western influences have promoted lenient secular laws that are often contrary to traditional religious standards.

An increasing number of secular laws, technological advances, outside influence, a population explosion, and rising unemployment have created factions of religious fundamentalism. Some Egyptians believe that problems in their country are the result of society, especially the government, ignoring the principles of Islam. Religious beliefs offer the hope of stability and orderliness during times of agitation and change. This Islamic fundamentalism has caused increased demands for a return to Shari-a (Sisk, 1992), which has resulted in increasing numbers of Egyptians following the Islamic pillars and practicing segregation by gender; more women in recent years have adopted full or partial veils in public places, and sporadic protests of foreign intrusion have occurred in Egyptian cities.

Sojourners should be aware of Islamic religious beliefs while conducting business or traveling in Egypt. The Koran exhorts everyone, especially women, to cover themselves modestly. Egyptians wear less revealing clothing and feel more comfortable communicating with others who adopt conservative attire. Egyptians also feel that it is their responsibility to help others in need. There is a long tradition of Egyptians taking anyone into their tent for sustenance or shelter from the harsh desert. Sojourners who receive help while in Egypt are told that "God wills it," as explanation for Egyptian hospitality. Travelers or business executives who display knowledge of and respect for Islamic beliefs are more likely to establish friendships and profitable business relations in Egypt. Although religious beliefs are an important part of Egyptian culture, they are only one part of understanding communication with Egyptians. In the next section, we will consider Egyptian cultural values that are relevant to intercultural communication.

Egyptian Values

Cultural values are vital areas of study for intercultural communication scholars. Samovar and Porter (2000) state that:

> Cultural values define what is worth dying for, what is worth protecting, what frightens people, what are proper subjects for study and for ridicule, and what types of events create group solidarity. Most important, cultural values guide both perception and behavior. (p. 11)

If we can discover why people act a certain way, their fears, and their passions, then we can begin to understand how to improve communication among people of diverse cultures. Three fundamental values in Egyptian culture are tradition, relationships, and hierarchical devotion.

Tradition

World histories reveal that the groups of people who have had the richest traditions have also had long-lived societies. Weick (1995) points out that cultures characterized by a "tradition of conduct" or that have a "well-developed folklore of action should survive longer than those that do not" (p. 126). These traditions of conduct serve to pass expertise and experience to the next generations. An Egyptian proverb points out the worth of past knowledge: *Lost is the person who forgets his or her past*. Because Egyptian culture is 4,000 to 5,000 years old, it is not surprising that tradition is an important value.

This importance within the Egyptian population is reflected in several different ways. Egypt has a tradition of being a rural nation. The peasant farmers along the Nile are proud of their farming heritage and are often resistant to change. Ancient paintings depict types of donkey-powered water wheels that are still in use today. Egyptians have survived countless epidemics, floods, droughts, and conquerors. The population has "a centuries-old capacity for letting life flow by, a little like the Nile, . . . and it is as though the present generations had inherited a seen-it-all-before attitude from their forbears" (Wayne & Simonis, 1994, p. 33). Their unity in pleasure and suffering, while holding onto their traditions, contributes to the endurance of Egyptian culture for thousands of years.

Religious traditions, as previously mentioned, are an important part of life in Egypt. Ancient Egyptians thought that "every action, no matter how mundane, was in some sense a religious act: plowing, sowing, reaping, brewing, building ships, waging wars, playing games—all were viewed as earthly symbols for divine activities" (West, 1995, p. 46). Contemporary Egyptians also maintain that their religious beliefs play a pivotal role in family, politics, business, and education.

Egyptians may express polite interest in the traditions and ancestors of guests in their country. Higher regard is attributed to the person who can recite details about his or her family members from the past four to five hundred years. This strong value placed on tradition serves to pass on knowledge, but can also inhibit rapid changes. Visitors to Egypt should never underestimate the amount of time that it will take to establish relationships, new contacts, or introduce technological innovations.

Relationships

Egyptians have the capability to endure, but there is still something that frightens them. The people of Egypt fear loneliness, and they wish to always be surrounded by a network of relatives and friends (Hopwood, 1982). They combat loneliness by placing great value on relationships. The importance of relational harmony developed from the time Menes united upper and lower Kemet in 3150 BCE. Nile Valley inhabitants found that collectivism was the most effective way for a diverse group of people with limited resources to live in peace.

In Egyptian collectivism, family, social, and business are all relationships that are taken seriously and give Egyptians great pleasure. The crucial events of a person's lifetime are birth, marriage, and death. These principal daily concerns of everyday life emphasize the interconnectedness of the individual with the family. Each person represents a social collective and sacrifices his or her needs for the greater good of that group.

Reassurance and warmth from familial relations are feelings replicated in other relationships. Kinship terms are used in various situations to reinforce positive connections among people. For example, "Egyptian politicians, from the President on down, emphasize their position as 'father figures' to the masses" (Inhorn, 1996, p. 159). The family is the basic building block of society and is a model for interactions throughout society.

The first questions that Egyptians ask guests in a conversation concern group affiliations. "Where is your family?" "Where is your father?" "Where are your classmates or co-workers?" Egyptians assume that people prefer group travel or activities. Tourists commonly report that locals never give oral directions, but always insist on accompanying them directly to their destination—no matter how far away.

A relational focus is also reflected in the blurred boundary lines between social and business interactions. Officials constantly maintain open-door policies and engage in friendly discussions with several people at one time. Building and maintaining good relations take priority over other activities in society. Egyptians often conduct lengthy business meetings without ever touching on business matters. A sojourner in Egypt realizes the power of relations after waiting at an Egyptian Embassy for five hours to get a visa. Even then, there is no guarantee the paperwork will be processed before closing time. On the other hand, if good relations have been established with the family who runs the hotel, then its members may realize that one of their son's classmates works in the embassy. The visa would be delivered within half an hour to the door of the hotel after a single phone call. Relationships are a source of pleasure and are also a way to get things done in a rigidly structured society.

Hierarchical Structure

Hierarchies according to age, gender, and experience are crucial in Egyptian society. Ancient traditions outline the proper place and behavior of each person in society. Interpersonal relationships are characterized by "a worldview professing the existence of a cosmic hierarchical order: The sound order of things is a descending scale of superiors and subordinates" (Yadlin, 1995, p. 157). The cosmic order begins with the major religions of Egypt. Pharaohs were considered to be god-rulers who were divine mediators for the people. The Nile civilization may have been one of the first matriarchal civilizations because ancient Pharaohs inherited the throne through the female bloodline (Crawford, 1996). In this agrarian society, male and female deities ruled from the heavens, and both men and women were responsible for the collective security of the family.

In Islam as well, humans submit to God's will in all matters. God is the ultimate creator, authority, and judge for all people. The first words that sojourners will learn upon arrival in Egypt are *Insha'allah*. The translation of this word is, "If God wills it." Explanations such as, "God decides," or "It's when God wants it," reflect the accepted order of life. Muslims do not question their fate because God alone knows their destiny.

A part of that destiny for Egyptians is fulfilling their roles in the overall social structure of society.

In Muslim families, the oldest male in the family wields authority and power. This patriarch is responsible for the safety and well-being of his family members. Sons and daughters consider carefully how their public behavior influences their family. The oldest son may conduct business or interactions with international contacts, but the father makes final decisions. Muslims regard these roles and practices as a natural part of life, and women and men are staunch advocates and devotees of the traditional hierarchical order. Hierarchies are produced and reinforced through the language of family and societal communication.

Egyptian Language and Culture

Language is a powerful tool. Our manner of speech can have a significant influence on another's behavior. The words that we choose can reflect the way that we look at the world and perceive others. For centuries, Arabs have recognized the power of language and have used Arabic to convey unity, worldview, and artistic impressions. Arabic is one of the oldest living languages in the world. It is the beautiful and flamboyant language spoken by Egyptians and other people of the Middle East.

If you venture into an Egyptian city, you will hear the rhythmic Arabic verses of the Koran chanted aloud during daily prayers. Walls of Egyptian mosques are not painted with pictures or scenes—they are covered with decorative Arabic calligraphy. A sojourner who learns a few words of Arabic will quickly gain friends in this region. Egyptians are also willing to share their knowledge of Arabic with others. On many occasions, a well-timed response of *Mish muskmlla* (no problem) or *Insha'allah* (if God wills it) will elicit approval and improve relations with Egyptians.

Arabic and Unity

What we say, how we say it, and why we say it are all related to our culture. Egyptians use their language to construct appropriate national identities and unity within the population. For example, Egyptians did not consider themselves Arabs until the 7th century when Arabic became the predominant way to communicate

in the region (Lippman, 1995). Today, Egyptian children learn only in Arabic and are taught to memorize and proudly recite lengthy verses of the Koran. The Middle East consists of various countries, cultural, and ethnic groups, but Egyptians will readily proclaim, "But we are all Arabs!"

Arabic helps promote unity within a region just as different linguistic styles can cause disunity. For example, bargaining in Egypt is considered to be an enjoyable way to pass time and build relationships. Historically, Egyptians expect and love haggling, but for Israelis, "trading was not a pleasurable pastime, but part of a struggle for survival in a hostile environment. Thus, where bargaining has positive connotations for the Arab, for the Israeli it is reminiscent of a rejected and despised way of life" (Cohen, 1990, p. 139). Negotiations between Israel and Egypt have been taking place since 1948, and their different linguistic styles have caused more than one impasse during talks.

Arabic and Worldview

Arabic is used to convey the Islamic worldview. "Classical Arabic (which is also the written language) is sacred" because it is the dialect of the Koran (Hall, 1977, p. 31). The importance of the Koran within Islamic societies actually preserved the integrity of the classical tongue. Other major languages branched out into various dialects, or became obsolete, but classical Arabic is still widely spoken among Muslims of every region. Public prayers and ceremonies worldwide are conducted in Arabic even if the Muslim adherents are not Middle Eastern Arabs.

Second, *jihad* is an Arabic word from the Koran that has often been incorrectly translated as "holy war." The mere mention of an Islamic *jihad* has been depicted within Western literature as religious fanatics on a killing rampage, and terrorist attacks are automatically attributed to Islamic fundamentalists (Hopfe, 1976). "Literally the word [*jihad*] means 'utmost effort' in promotion and defense of Islam, which might or might not include armed conflict with unbelievers" (Lippman, 1995, p. 113). Although there are some violent fundamentalist groups, these factions cannot realistically represent the whole of Islamic followers.

Finally, Western readers of Koranic translations have reported that the holy book is repetitive, confusing, and lacks compelling features (Nigosian, 1987). Muslims maintain that these translations do not reflect the astounding beauty and rhythmic qualities of the original Arabic verses. The linguistic style of Koranic writings serves as a model for literature and speech throughout Islamic societies.

Writing as Art

Ancient hieroglyphs used the same word to signify both writing and art. Ancient Kemetic texts focused on "medicine, science, religion, social and cosmic organization, and the life cycle" (Crawford, 1996, p. 9). Arabic is now used as an art form in Egypt. One of the foremost sights in every Egyptian city is the Mosque decorated inside from top to bottom with Arabic calligraphy. Egyptian homes commonly have a scroll depicting the 99 names of God in exquisite script. The mastery of spoken and written classical Arabic is indicative of education and rank in Egypt. Arabic is a language that pleases the eyes, ears, and spirits of the people. Sojourners who learn Arabic or adopt a descriptive and elegant style of speaking in another language will attain a higher level of credibility while in Egypt.

CONCLUSION

This article reviews aspects of the Islamic worldview, cultural values, and language that influence communication with Egyptians. Visitors to Egypt find that travel or business ventures are more rewarding experiences if they take the time to learn about specific cultural characteristics. If its 5,000 years of history and tradition can provide a rich cultural heritage and wisdom for Egyptians, then other cultures can also learn from one of the oldest civilizations in the world.

References

Brega, I. (1998). *Egypt: Past and present.* New York: Barnes & Noble.

Cohen, R. (1990). Deadlock: Israel and Egypt negotiate. In F. Korzenny & S. Ting-Toomey (Eds.), *Communicating for peace: Diplomacy and negotiation,* 14 (pp. 136–153). Newbury Park, CA: Sage Publications.

Crawford, C. (1996). *Recasting ancient Egypt in the African context: Toward a model curriculum using art and language.* Trenton, NJ: Africa World.

Gershoni, I., & Jankowski, J. P. (1995). *Redefining the Egyptian nation, 1930–1945.* New York: Cambridge University.

Hall, E. T. (1977). *Beyond culture.* Garden City, NY: Anchor Books.

Hopfe, L. M. (1976). *Religions of the world.* Beverly Hills, CA: Glencoe.

Hopwood, D. (1982). *Egypt: Politics and society 1945–1981.* London: Allen and Unwin.

Inhorn, M. C. (1996). *Infertility and patriarchy: The cultural politics of gender and family life in Egypt.* Philadelphia: University of Pennsylvania.

Lippman, T. W. (1995). *Understanding Islam: An introduction to the Muslim world* (2nd ed.). New York: Meridian.

Murphy, K. (1993, April 6). World report special edition: A new vision for Mohammed's faith. *Los Angeles Times,* p. 1.

Nigosian, S. (1987). *Islam: The way of submission.* Great Britain: Crucible.

Samovar, L. A., & Porter, R. E. (2000). Understanding intercultural communication: An introduction and overview. In L. A. Samovar & R. E. Porter (Eds.), *Intercultural communication: A reader,* 9th ed., pp. 5–16. Belmont, CA: Wadsworth.

Sisk, T. D. (1992). *Islam and democracy: Religion, politics, and power in the Middle East.* Washington, DC: United States Institute of Peace Press.

Smith, H. (1991). *The world's religions: Our great wisdom traditions.* San Francisco, CA: Harper Collins.

Stowe, M. A. (2000, August 28). Swallowed by the sands: Archaeologists hope to solve the mystery of Persia's lost army of Egypt. *Discovering Archaeology: Scientific American.* [Internet] www.discoveringarchaeology.com/articles.082800-sands.shtml

Waines, D. (1995). *An introduction to Islam.* Great Britain: Cambridge University.

Wayne, S., & Simonis, D. (1994). *Egypt and the Sudan,* 3rd ed. Hawthorn, Australia: Lonely Planet.

Weick, K. (1995). *Sensemaking in organizations.* Thousand Oaks, CA: Sage Publications.

West, J. A. (1995). *The traveler's key to ancient Egypt: A guide to the sacred places of ancient Egypt.* Wheaton, IL: Quest Books.

Yadlin, R. (1995). The seeming duality: Patterns of interpersonal relations in a changing environment. In S. Shamir (Ed.), *Egypt from monarchy to republic: A reassessment of revolution and change,* p. 151. Boulder, CO: Westview Press.

Concepts and Questions

1. Why does Begley say it is hard to "think like an Egyptian"?
2. What aspects of Islamic history offer insights into Egyptian culture? What aspects of your own culture would offer valuable insights for someone wanting to study your culture?
3. Why does Begley assert that "Islamic beliefs dominate every moment from birth to death and beyond"?
4. Begley offers four tenets central to understanding Islam. What are they? Does your worldview have similar or dissimilar tenets?
5. What does Begley mean when she writes, "Islam is a religion of action, not contemplation"? Is your religion one of action or contemplation?
6. Why is the Arabic language so very important to Egyptians? What aspects of their language make it unique?
7. What does Begley imply when she talks about Arabic as art?
8. What communication patterns within your culture might present problems when communicating with someone of Egyptian culture?

Russian Cultural Values and Workplace Communication Patterns

Mira Bergelson

CULTURAL SENSITIVITY AND CULTURAL KNOWLEDGE

Cross-cultural communication issues, and their potential for creating obstacles to effective, successful organizational and professional interactions, have become a critical aspect of the movement toward a globalized society. Competent communication, a central instrument for an organization to create a sustainable competitive advantage, is further complicated when cultural differences must be managed (Persikova, 2002). To overcome these communication difficulties and lessen misunderstandings, individuals and professional organizations have instituted cross-cultural training programs, one of which is discussed in the final section of this essay.

In addition to general intercultural sensitivity training, corporate managers need to acquire culture-specific knowledge before embarking on an overseas assignment. This requirement is made difficult by the amount of available cultural information and the need to determine what is beneficial and what is useless. For instance, noting that characters in Russian films always seem to be quarreling (while, in fact, they are not) can be confusing. Just observing this activity as a behavioral display will only produce negative opinions (a reason Soviet—and now Russian—films never enjoyed commercial success in the United States). But spending time and effort to analyze what the

This original essay first appeared in the thirteenth edition of this book. All rights reserved. Permission to reprint must be obtained from the author and the publisher. Mira Bergelson is Professor in the Department of Linguistics and Information Technology of Foreign Languages and Regional Studies at the Lomonosov Moscow State University.

behavior may denote, and how it relates to other facets of Russian culture, can often provide insight into problems of cross-cultural organizational communication and group dynamics.

In this paper, I examine some of the seemingly unrelated and isolated pieces of Russian cultural information in a systematic way. Specifically, I look at *surface representations* of certain *basic cultural values*, which will enable you to draw correct *cultural inferences*. For instance, in the example from the Russian movie, we have a surface (behavioral) representation—loud and intense pronunciation. This activity may be considered as "too loud, too emotional" and evaluated negatively by an outsider who unconsciously compares it to similar situations in his or her own culture ("people speak loudly and emotionally when they quarrel"). However, the communicative behavior displayed in the movie can be used to gain knowledge of the basic, invisible cultural values underpinning the activity (e.g., *demonstrating attitudes* and *directness of communication* is acceptable and normative).

This illustration demonstrates the limitations of relying on surface representations of behavioral traits to understand a culture. The enlightened outsider will be able to assign a cultural value to the observable behaviors, and use that knowledge to effectively manage cultural differences. Culturally mindful communications will arise from the process of making cultural inferences only after surface representations have been attributed to basic cultural values. Therefore, in order to fully understand Russian communicative behaviors one must have an appreciation of the basic cultural values which form the Russian worldview.

RUSSIAN CULTURAL VALUES REFLECTING BASIC WORLDVIEW

Linguistic research of cross-culture communication and related cultural anthropology topics generally agree that basic cultural values, which indicate a culture's worldview, are often reflected in certain "key words" or "key concepts" (Shmeliov, 2002). Wierzbicka's (1992) influential book on cross-cultural pragmatics provides generalizations about the basic values and features of Russian culture.

Emotionality

For Russians, expressing the way you feel (both good and bad) and attention to what other people say about their feelings is favorably considered in a wide variety of contexts. From this, it is clear that for Russians relationships are more important than the contextual reality.

This cultural feature can be observed in language strategies such as heavy use of "culturally loaded words" like *dusha*—"soul," which signals the importance of the inner world, and in the abundance and great variety of active emotional verbs (as if emotions emerge on their own and are not just experienced)—*volnovat'sja, pechalit'sja, udivljat'sja, radovat'sja*—as compared to names for emotional states *be glad, be sad, be angry, be happy*. In the realm of proper names, Russia is famous for having lots of nicknames (expressive derivation), not only toward children as in English (e.g., *Teddy, Tommy*) but toward adults without distinction of age or gender. These are used in a variety of contexts to express the extremely important role of closeness and intimacy and to communicate the minute aspects of feelings between individuals and the subtle shades of their relations—in other words, the ability to express *solidarity politeness* by minimizing social distance.

Judgmental Attitudes

Russians have an inclination toward judgmental attitudes, with a tendency for ethical evaluation. Among Russians, one can expect to be morally judged and it is considered appropriate to treat others the same way. Russians are eager to voice their opinions, and people expect, and sometimes require from others, moral evaluations of mutual loyalty, respect, and sincerity. This cultural value is reflected in the Russian language by the abundance (as compared to English) of nouns—both positive and negative—expressing absolute moral judgment. This is quite different from using adjectives, which describe only a feature of a person, because nouns classify a person as a certain type.

Fatalism

Many Russians possess an attitude of "having no control over the world." The realm of the uncontrollable, and thus unconceivable, is quite broad. This is directly opposite of American pragmatism when assessing and dealing with difficulties.

Irrationality

The world is considered an irrational place, and a Russian may behave and think as if unable to always rely on objective methods of analysis and logic. This is in opposition to American positivism.

These Russian cultural values give rise to the following behavioral attitudes, which can create difficulties when interacting with Westerners in an organizational context:

- Relationships are more important than results.
- Intrapersonal reality can often become external.
- The realm of the uncontrollable and, thus, unconceivable is broader than in the West.
- Things can go wrong or get worse at any moment.[1]
- One cannot completely rely on objective methods of analysis and causality.
- Ethical evaluations are important and there is a tendency toward them.

There are, of course, many more cultural obstacles than those mentioned above. For example, problems can arise due to the variation between Russian traditional and Soviet era cultures. Modern Russia is a huge conglomerate of significantly contradictory cultural patterns. What makes it different from, say, the multiculturalism of the United States is the lack of a legacy: Neither historically, nor *de jure* was multiculturalism acclaimed in the national context. Still, recently there are some positive trends in public opinion about the real values of multiculturalism, a position often advocated by top Russian authorities, and it is proclaimed as one of the pillars of the modern Russian state. Yet, Russia in all its ethnic and regional variations is one nation with one rather diverse culture. And the main divisions in that culture are along slightly different lines: between traditional (T), inherited from the Soviet system (S), and westernized (W) cultural models. Therefore, one of the main cross-cultural communication problems for an outsider is deciding which cultural pattern (T, S, or W) one is dealing with at any given moment with any given individual. Some of the more easily detectable cultural patterns of the Traditional and Soviet co-cultures include:

- A deep mistrust between the authorities and the people
- General pessimism
- Lack of critical thinking, and negotiation skills
- No, or little, respect for laws and rules
- A deep-rooted practice of deceiving higher authorities, to color the truth, and to use roundabout ways
- Mistrust of commercial activities (Jacobs, 1992)

From a Western perspective, these patterns of behavior may seem contradictory, but Russians consider them to be the focus, the central line, of their history. Thus, Russians often feel sensitive, vulnerable, and angry towards what they consider to be "Western cultural imperialism." Partially, this attitude is a result of what Westerners consider "The End of the Cold War," but what Russians consider as "Transformations"—changes on a scale that no country has ever experienced before (Holden, Cooper, & Carr, 1998). These transformations embraced all aspects of public and private life—transformation of the political system, transition from a command to a market economy, new federal relations, new foreign policies, etc.

None of these changes went well, and most Russians believe that things should have been done differently and cannot agree on what exactly went wrong. They do agree, however, that the world paid insufficient attention to the enormity of what was done and to the suffering people experienced in transitioning from the Soviet era. As a result, the very idea of *changes* can be a problem in Russian organizations when Western managers attempt to introduce and implement new management techniques of constant change. Changes are generally viewed in Russian culture, especially in its more traditional layers, as a threat, and people want to avoid them.

CULTURALLY INFLUENCED COMMUNICATION PATTERNS

It is one thing to recognize that values vary between cultures, but it is of perhaps greater importance to understand how those values influence culture-specific behavioral patterns, especially communication patterns.

These communication patterns have been described in Hymes' (1974) model of SPEAKING. Gumperz (2001) posits that certain linguistic structures serve as clues to interpretation of meaning and inferences based on cultural assumptions of the participants.

I will now discuss the variant communication patterns that can bring about misunderstandings or create conflict during Russian-U.S. communicative interactions. My observations are informed by Kasper's (1996) discussion of Politeness Theory. The focus is on those Russian communication patterns that can lead to communicative failures both during the interaction and subsequent to the interaction by eroding a participant's perception of the other.

Western (Anglo-American) and Russian Politeness Strategies and Communication Patterns

It is clear that culturally different communication practices can lead to failures in a cross-cultural organizational context—be it in the workplace, at the negotiation table, or choosing management strategies. A situation can be aggravated by the fact that language capabilities—even more so, fluency—does not necessarily help mitigate these failures. This is because that while "pure" language mistakes (e.g., grammar, wrong lexical choices, pronunciation, etc.) are easily recognized as such, clumsly handling of politeness strategies or speech acts usage can be taken as personality traits (Kniffka, 1995). Thus, a person acting out his culture's politeness and other discourse strategies may seem to a representative of another culture as rude and imposing, or insecure and indirect, leading to a perception of the person as an unreliable partner or a pushy employee (Thomas, 1984).

Politeness Related Problems

Research conducted by Ratmayr (1998) and Wierzbicka (1992), as well as others, has demonstrated that the following oppositions are generally valid for interpersonal communication between Russians and Americans.

Russians	Americans
Value solidarity politeness more than deferential politeness	Pay more attention to negative politeness
Express more emotive data	More conventionally indirect in requests
Invest more effort into supporting requests by using justifications	Preface corrections with positive remarks more than Russians
Directness with familiars is associated with sincerity	Directness with familiars is associated with imposition on their freedom
There is a vast selection of Russian words and expressions used to show warmth and inoffensive closeness with familiars and intimates, thus amplifying positive politeness	When translated into English, these Russian words and expressions are typically rendered into expressions of patronizing attitudes, thus becoming offensive
Friends normally considered intimates	Friends normally considered familiars
Express more politeness to friends	Express more politeness to strangers

Taken collectively, Russians are more insistent on expressing and reviving solidarity politeness. It normally means a smaller distance between equals. But, from a Western point-of-view, this style lacks expression of deferential politeness, which can create problems for teamwork. Leontovich (2002) provides an extensive treatment of cross-cultural communication between Russians and Americans.

Information-processing Related Problems

In a cross-cultural communication setting, an extremely important factor is how one's messages and behaviors are interpreted by the other person. Specifically, as relates to this case, how a U.S. business representative processes the Russian representative's communicative acts will influence the assigned meaning. Without an understanding of the Russian culturally influenced communication practices, a U.S. businessperson may well assign negative or incorrect meaning.

The following are examples of normative Russian communicative behaviors that can become pitfalls in a cross-cultural environment.

- *Communication style is not targeted at reaching a consensus*—At least that is how it may be judged by Western participants at a business meeting with Russians. In normal conversational turntaking, Russians will often start with "no!" (*njet!*)
- *Offering wrong or no answers to your questions, or "knowing better what you need."* This means that judgments, or "good advice," are a common Russian response to information-seeking behaviors. For example, asking a Russian colleague for a name of a potential partner (X) for an activity (Y) in town (Z) may lead to the answer "Person (M) in town (N) will better suit your activity (Y). This does not imply rudeness or an unwillingness to cooperate, but just the opposite—friendliness and a desire to cooperate and help. This type of exchange is especially common between equals in an informal context—e.g., "Why do you use this chair? It is bad for your back!"
- *Addressee's responsibility for information.* In Russia, a person interested in getting information has to ask for it, and those who possess the information—especially institutions—do not feel compelled to provide it without additional urging (i.e., you need this train schedule—you find a way to get it). And even when provided, the information can be inexplicit and incomplete. This Russian communication characteristic is extremely different from the U.S. style, where providing full, explicit, comprehensive information to the public is a primary duty of an organization. An example of how a U.S. businessperson could become frustrated by this Russian practice can be from a simple request for a phone number. When using the provided number, the U.S. representative may find it does not work as given but requires an additional code. The American may well ask the Russian provider, "Why didn't you tell me this before?" The Russian would reply, "You did not ask!" This communicative trait is drastically opposite to the demands of the modern communications age and has been changing rapidly—at least in the "new economy" spheres like Internet commerce.

- *Potential mistrust of "objective truths."* This culturally based feature can be especially disconcerting to U.S. partners when dealing with organizational issues. Imagine introducing new software to Russian colleagues and getting surprised looks and annoyed objections—"Why should we change anything? The old one works pretty well?" In a cross-cultural exchange, this communicative trait may be perceived as irrational or argumentative. The U.S. member may feel mystified by the need to discuss things that seem self-evident.
- *Parallel processing of information.* This is what Hall (1959) calls polychronous, as opposed to monochronous, culture. The Russian multifocus time orientation can easily lead to misinterpretations of behaviors by single-focus U.S. businesspersons.

Culture and Business: Applied Communication Patterns

The West has historically considered Russia to be enigmatic (e.g., "a riddle, wrapped in a mystery, inside an enigma" was coined by Winston Churchill). However, the Western perception of Russia being difficult to understand has been heightened by the societal changes the country has experienced over the past two decades. For Russian business, the problems arising from the globalization process have been exacerbated by the dramatic changes wrought by the collapse of the former Soviet Union. Basically, Russians must now confront the issues associated with the emergence of a new culture, a new national identity, and an absolutely new business culture. The enormous, dramatic changes, plus the embedded basic values of the traditional Russian culture, are coalescing to shape the business culture of modern Russia.

Research, anecdotal evidence, and personal impressions confirm that in organizational settings expectation gaps between Westerners and Russians (e.g., managers, entrepreneurs, professionals, staff, etc.) form one of the main obstacles to conducting business, creating successful partnerships, and organizing efficient work teams. Below are some of the widely supported statements from "both parties" that can strain relations between Russians and Westerners (Holden, Cooper, & Carr, 1998).

Western Attitude	Russian Attitude
Russians don't know how to work hard	Westerners have no appreciation of recent societal changes
Business problems are simple in Russia	Westerners don't know how to teach and how to transfer skills to Russians
Change is impossible in Russia	The West has failed to manage effective relationships with Russian partners
Russians lack experience and know how	Westerners have no interest in "Russian mentality"
Russians must follow the Western consultant's advice	Relationship management must be based on equivalence
Russians rely too much on an intuitive approach	Russian staff feels undervalued, underutilized, and discriminated against

APPLICATION

From the preceding paragraphs, it is evident that Russian–U.S. cross-cultural communication in a business setting can be laden with challenging difficulties arising from culturally varied communicative styles and behaviors. The question then becomes how does one successfully navigate around these potential problem areas? Knowledge is, of course, the answer. Each party, both Russian and U.S., has an obligation to be generally aware that culture shapes one's worldview in the form of beliefs and values which, in turn, influence communication styles, and all of this becomes manifest in the workplace. But when people of different cultures interact in the workplace, a broad appreciation of cultural influences will likely prove insufficient in preventing misunderstandings and miscommunications. Indeed,

when working toward a common goal, such as in a cross-cultural business endeavor, more specific cultural knowledge relating to the other business partner is required.

In the field of cross-cultural communication, role-playing games have proven to be an effective means of instilling culture specific information, developing cultural sensitivity, and internalizing cross-cultural business skills. One example of such a game was created by the author and titled "Let's get to know each other." Modeled after "The Emperor's Pot," by Batchelder (1996), the game stresses the important issues of Russian–Western professional communication, bringing out such concerns as the unpredictability of a cross-culture partner and multiple factors that may influence that partner's behavior. The role-play has varying levels of complexity and can be used in different formats depending on the types of expertise needed or available. Appendix I provides examples

Appendix I
Russian Culture Models

Cultural Model	W-culture (Western-oriented)	S-culture (Soviet style)	TR-culture (Traditional Russian)
I/We Orientation	Individual	Group	Group
Human Relationships	Individual	Ranked	Mutual
Activity Orientation	Doing	Pretending to be doing	Being
Time Orientation	Future	Future/Past	Present/Past
Relation to Nature	Control	Control/Abuse	Yielding, conformity
Form and Substance	Style is important	Outward form is of major importance	Inner substance is important, outward appearance is deceiving; one needs to look into one's soul

Progress	Progress is good	Technical progress is good; social changes are bad	Technical progress is dangerous because it leads to social changes that are bad
History	History is a linear progression, a development for good	Ideology shapes history	History is a cyclical and controversial phenomenon
Freedom/Discipline, Authority	Rules/laws must be obeyed even if you don't like it. The less authority interference with people the better	Caution and formal obedience to official authority. No consideration for individual rights. Vertically organized hierarchy regarded as most orderly and effective	Strong suspicion of authority
Age	Age means higher position in the official ranks; youth cannot be trusted for they have no experience	It is not fashionable and convenient to be old, for old people still live in the Soviet past	There is a big gap between generations; old people must be supported for what they have done for each of us and because they suffered through all the Soviet times
Money	Brings you everything you want; Money is easy to earn today, but one needs a lot of it to have a decent lifestyle; spending a lot is good; price is regarded as an index of quality	People got spoiled by easy money-making, and those who worked all their life don't have enough to support their families; those who have money are all criminals	Too bad there is such a dire need for money; the pursuit of money usually spoils
Work	Workaholics are not very popular in Russia. Still, they report a very high level of work-related stress in the new economy	Work is not even considered a means to an end	A means to an end rather than an end in itself; has no value in itself
Education	Education is very important, but it must be oriented at getting a well-paying profession, not just knowledge. It is also important that the degree be from a prestigious university	Enjoys respect as a source of discipline and a means to an end, especially to attain skill, money status; affects family prestige	Has even greater spiritual value of one's true activity. Being educated means being cultured
Moral Superiority	There is nothing special about Russians except that they had to survive under hard conditions —both physically, politically and economically, so they now try to catch up with the West	A moral smugness stemming from a conviction that Russian people possess a set of cultural values and conditions that have made them unique	

of some of the information that participants in the role game may use (see also, Batchelder, 1996, p. 99).

It must be noted, however, that role-playing games represent only one means of acquiring culture-specific information. There is, of course, a growing body of literature on how to do business in specific cultures. There are also many books and journal articles devoted to the role of culture in international business, and there is a growing number of websites that provide both culture general and culture-specific information. Regardless of the source, the first step is to recognize the important role that culture plays when representatives of different nations interact.

References

Batchelder, D. (1996). The Emperor's Pot. Experiential Activities for Intercultural Learning. In H. N. Seelye, (Ed.), *Experiential Activities for Intercultural Learning* (pp. 85–99). Yarmouth, ME: Intercultural Press, Inc.

Gumperz, J. J. (2001). Interactional sociolinguistics: A personal perspective. In D. Schiffrin, D. Tannen, & H. E. Hamilton (Eds.), *Handbook of Discourse Analysis*. Malden, MA: Blackwell.

Hall, E. T. (1959). *The Silent Language*. New York, Doubleday.

Holden, N., Cary Cooper, & Jennifer Carr (1998). *Management Cultures in Collision: Dealing with New Russia*. New York: Wiley.

Hymes, D. (1974). *Foundations in Sociolinguistics: An Ethnographic Approach*. Philadelphia: University of Pennsylvania Press.

Jacobs, J. (1992). *Systems of Survival*. Random House, Inc. http://en.wikipedia.org/wiki/Systems_of_Survival

Kasper, G. (1996). *Politeness. Handbook of Pragmatics*. Amsterdam, Verschueren.

Kniffka, H. (1995). *Elemente einer kulturkontrastiven Linguistik*. Frankfurt am Main; Berlin; Bern; New York; Paris; Wien: Lang.

Leontovich, O. (2002). *Russkie i amerikantsy: Paradoksy mezhkul'turnogo obschenija*. Volgograd: Peremena.

Persikova, T. (2002). *Mezhkul'turnaja kommunikatsija i korporativnaja kul'tura*. Moskva, Russia: Logos.

Ratmayr, R. (1998). *Hoeflichkeit als kulturspezifisches Konzept: Russisch im Vergleich*. 174–182.

Shmeliov, A. (2002). *Russkaja jazykovaja model' mira: Materialy k slovarju*. Moskva, Russia: jazyki slavjanskoj kul'tury.

Thomas, J. (1984). "Cross-cultural discourse as 'Unequal encounter': Towards a pragmatic analysis." *Applied Linguistics* 5(3): 227–235.

Wierzbicka, A. (1992). *Semantics, culture, and cognition: universal human concepts in culture-specific configurations*. New York: Oxford University Press.

Concepts and Questions

1. What idea is Bergelson trying to convey when she discusses Russian films?
2. What does Bergelson mean when she speaks of *surface representations*?
3. How would you explain the Russian values of emotionality, judgmental attitudes, fatalism, and irrationality? Do you see the same four values being reflected in the United States?
4. How would you explain Bergelson's observation that "Modern Russia is a huge conglomerate of significantly contradictory cultural patterns"? Does the same generalization apply to the United States?
5. Why do Russians "feel sensitive, vulnerable, and angry toward what they consider to be Western cultural imperialism"? Should they feel this way?
6. What are some differences between politeness patterns in Russia and the United States?
7. What are some examples of normative Russian communicative behaviors that "become pitfalls in a cross-cultural environment"?
8. Bergelson asserts that "It is evident that Russian–U.S. cross-cultural communication in a business setting can be laden with challenging difficulties arising from culturally varied communicative styles and behaviors." What do you believe to be some of the difficulties?
9. Using Appendix I as a guide, compare and contrast the Western orientations with those of traditional Russians on some of the following dimensions: (1) I/We Orientation, (2) Human Relationships, (3) Activity Orientation, (3) Time Orientation, (4) Relation to Nature, (5) Progress, (6) History, and (6) Age.

Cultural Patterns of the Maasai

LISA SKOW

LARRY A. SAMOVAR

For many years critics of intercultural communication have charged that the field focuses on a handful of cultures while seriously neglecting others. For example, the literature abounds with material concerning Japan and Mexico, but there is very little to be found if one seeks to understand the cultures of India or black Africa. As economics and politics force a global interdependence, it behooves us to examine cultures that were previously excluded from our scrutiny.

The motivation for such analysis can take a variety of forms. Our desire for more information might be altruistic, as we learn that 40,000 babies die of starvation each day in developing countries. Or we may decide that we need to know about other cultures for more practical reasons. Strong ties with African countries can lead to economic, educational, and technological exchanges beneficial to individuals on both sides of the globe. Regardless of our motives, the 1990s and beyond will offer countless examples that demand that we look at cultures that we have ignored in the past. This article is an attempt to explore one of those cultures, specifically, that of the Maasai of East Africa.

If we accept the view of culture held by most anthropologists, it becomes nearly impossible to discover all there is to know about any one group of people. That is to say, how does one decide what is important about a culture if Hall (1976) is correct when he writes, "there is not one aspect of human life that is not touched and altered by culture" (p. 14)?

Courtesy of Lisa Skow and Larry A. Samovar. This original essay first appeared in the sixth edition of this book. All rights reserved. Permission to reprint must be obtained from the authors and the publisher. Lisa Skow is Clinical Professor in the Department of Health Services, School of Public Health at the University of Washington. Larry A. Samovar is Professor Emeritus, School of Communication, San Diego State University.

The decision as to what to include and exclude in any analysis of a culture is usually based on the background of the researcher. Someone interested in the music of a culture would obviously look at the portion of the culture relating to that specific topic and, in a sense, abstract only part of the total phenomenon called culture.

A researcher interested in intercultural communication is also faced with the problem of what to select from the total experiences of a people. What, in short, do we need to know if our goal is to understand the behavior of another culture? One answer to this question is found in the work of Samovar and Porter (1997). They have proposed a model of intercultural communication that can be used as a guide in selecting what aspects of culture need to be incorporated into any discussion of intercultural communication. This article will address the three major components of that model: perception, verbal processes, and nonverbal processes.

BACKGROUND

The East African countries of Kenya and Tanzania know firsthand about Western culture. They have lived through Western government, language, culture, and, unfortunately, oppression. Even today, more than two decades after each country received its independence, Western culture still has a profound influence on the people of Kenya and Tanzania. However, because there are so many different ethnic groups in these countries, it has not had the same impact and influence on each group. The Kikuyu of Kenya have adopted Western culture with such enthusiasm that one wonders what are "proper" Kikuyu traditions and customs and what are Western influences. On the other end of the Western continuum are the Maasai of southern Kenya and northern Tanzania, who have, for a number of reasons, rejected much of the culture presented by the West. They have largely shunned Western forms of government, dress, language, music, religion, and frequently even assistance. The Maasai are often referred to as "true Africans" because of their "purity"—a purity of which they are very proud.

Africa may be changing at an extraordinarily fast pace, but the Maasai are one group of people who seem content to continue their own way of life. This article hopes to offer some insight into that way of life.

PERCEPTION

One of the basic axioms of intercultural communication, and one that is part of the Samovar and Porter (1997) intercultural model, is that culture and perception work in tandem. That is to say, our cultural experiences determine, to a large extent, our view of the world. Those experiences that are most important are transmitted from generation to generation as a means of assuring that the culture will survive beyond the lifetime of its current members. Therefore, to understand any culture it is necessary to examine those experiences that are deemed meaningful enough to be carried to each generation. One way to study those experiences is through the history of a culture. The history of any culture can offer insight into the behaviors of the culture as well as explain some of the causes behind those behaviors. Let us therefore begin our analysis of the Maasai people by looking at those aspects of their history that link current perceptions to the past.

History

While the history of any culture is made up of thousands of experiences, there are often a few significant ones that serve to explain how that culture might view the world. In the case of the Maasai, there are three historical episodes that have greatly influenced their perception of themselves, other people, and events. These historical occurrences center on their creation, fierceness, and reaction to modernization.

The history of the Maasai is the history of a people with an oral tradition. Like all cultures who practice the oral tradition, the content and customs that are transmitted are largely found within the stories, poetry, and songs of the people. To the outsider they appear vague and only loosely based on facts. Some historians, along with the aid of Maasai elders, have attempted to link the stories and folklore with the available information about the Maasai's past, a past that helps explain many of the perceptions and values held by the Maasai.

Most accounts of the origin of the Maasai as a unique culture begin with the belief that they were part of a larger group that was migrating south during a severe drought (Kipury, 1983). The group found themselves trapped in a deep valley so they constructed a bridge that was to transport them out of the valley. Folk tales and history go on to tell the story of how the bridge collapsed before all the people escaped. Those who were left behind are now thought to be the Somali, Borana, and Rendile peoples. Those who managed to escape the dryness of the valley went on to be the true Maa-speaking people.

While the above rendition of early Maasai history is uncertain in answering questions regarding the origins of the Maasai, it does reveal one very important aspect of how history and perception are linked. This story helps explain how the Maasai perceive themselves compared to other tribes. It also helps an outsider understand the strong feelings of pride that are associated with the Maasai culture. For the Maasai, the story of their origin, even if it is speculation, tells them they are better than other tribes of East Africa who did not come from the north nor escape across the bridge—regardless of how long ago that arrival might have been.

The Maasai's history of warfare and conflict is yet another source of knowledge about the perception of themselves and non-Maasai. Before the advent of colonialism in the latter part of the nineteenth century, other tribes in Kenya such as the Kikuyu, Akamba, and Kalenjin were often attacked by the Maasai. The attacks were fierce and usually resulted in their enemies being forced from their lands. Some Maasai, particularly the elders, still see themselves as the conquerors of other tribes, and even today, the Maasai still have the reputation of being warlike. Non-Maasai Kenyans may warn visitors of the "terrible" Maasai and their propensity for violence. A former colleague of one of the authors often expressed her distrust of the Maasai, believing that they would harm her simply because she was from the Kikuyu tribe. She had heard about the Maasai's fierceness and their dislike of other tribes who dressed in Western clothes. Whether entirely accurate or not, this perception of them as warlike influences both the behavior of the Maasai and the behavior of those who come in contact with them.

A third historical period that has shaped the perceptions of the Maasai is the preindependence period of Kenya. Because the Maasai occupied vast areas of land in Kenya, the British colonialists turned an eye toward acquiring this valuable property. Through numerous agreements, great parcels of land were turned over to the colonialists. The Maasai were settled on new tracts of land that were much less desirable than the ones they were leaving, and they soon began to realize that not only were they giving up their prime land but they were also seeing a number of promises made by the colonialists being broken. In response to these two conclusions, the Maasai adopted an attitude of passive resistance to all Western innovations and temptations to become "modern." While most other parts of Kenya were altering their culture through education and technology, the Maasai had become disillusioned with those who were seeking to alter their way of life, and hence they refused to change (Sankan, 1971).

The rejection of cultural conversion by the Maasai has had immense consequences on them and the people around them. On one hand it has caused the government and other tribes to perceive them as stubbornly traditional, backward, uneducated, and isolated. However, for the Maasai, resistance to change is yet another indication of their strength and long history of power. Other more Westernized tribes, such as the Kikuyu, feel the Maasai are backward and not in tune with changing Kenya. Ironically, the Kikuyu seem to have a love–hate relationship with the Maasai: scorn for their refusal to be more modern yet respect for their retaining their traditional customs.

Values

What a culture values, or doesn't value, also helps determine how that culture perceives the world. Therefore, understanding what the Maasai regard as good or bad, valuable or worthless, right or wrong, just or unjust, and appropriate or inappropriate can help explain the communication behavior of their culture.

Children. For a Maasai man or woman to be without children is a great misfortune. The Maasai strongly believe that children continue the race, and more important, they will preserve the family—hence, children are highly valued. The Maasai embrace the idea that a man can "live" even after death if he has a son who can carry on his name, enjoy his wealth, and spread his reputation. In addition, they value children because they offer the senior Maasai a continuous supply of workers. The Maasai have a saying that illustrates

this point: "More hands make light the work." Children supply those hands. Unfortunately, this value is in direct conflict with the Kenyan government's family planning program to curb Kenya's dangerously high population growth. While the central government tries to emphasize the need to control the population, for the Maasai the man with the most children, no matter how poor he is, is the wealthiest and happiest of all men.

Cattle. The Maasai culture revolves around the cow, on which they greatly depend for their food, clothing, housing, fuel, trade, medicine, and ceremonies. Cattle have given the Maasai their traditionally nomadic lifestyle. The more cattle a man has the more respected he is. Cattle are usually killed only on designated occasions such as for marriage and circumcision ceremonies or when special guests visit. The Maasai believe that all cattle were originally given to them by God. There is even a folk tale that tells of the Maasai descending to earth with cattle by their sides. This belief justifies their taking cattle from other tribes, even if it is in violation of the law.

Groups. Families and life-stage groups are at the core of the Maasai community. Because children are so highly valued, the family must be strong and central in their lives. An overwhelming portion of a Maasai child's education is still carried out in the home, with the grandparents, not the schools, providing the content of the culture.

Life-stage groups are specifically defined periods in the lives of all Maasai, particularly males. Traditionally, all men must go through four stages of life: childhood, adolescence (circumcision), moranship (warriorhood—junior and senior), and elder-hood (junior and senior). Women must pass through childhood, circumcision, and then marriage. Each of these stages places a strong emphasis on the group. Attempts to get Maasai students to raise their hands and participate in formal classrooms are often futile. Drawing attention to oneself in a group setting is unacceptable because the tribe and the life-stage group are far more valuable than the individual (Johnstone, 1988).

Elders: Male and Female. Maasai children must give respect to any person older than themselves, whether a sibling, grandmother, or older member of the community. They must bow their heads in greeting as a sign of humility and inferiority. Even young circumcised men and women (aged fifteen to twenty-five years) must bow their heads to male elders, particularly if the elders are highly respected in the community.

The Maasai believe the older you become the wiser you become and that a wise individual deserves a great deal of deference and respect. Part of the strong emphasis placed on elders is that the Maasai hold their history in such high regard, and it is the oldest members of the tribe who know most of the history. Young people cannot know the "truth" until they progress through each of the life-stage groups.

For Maasai youths getting older indicates a change in social status. When male Maasai students return from a school holiday with their heads shaved, this indicates that they have just gone through circumcision and initiation into another life-stage. They have become men and are instantly perceived by other students and themselves as different, even older, and deserving of more respect.

Pride. Pride for the Maasai means having the virtues of obedience, honesty, wisdom, and fairness. A man may be an elder in name only, for if he does not exhibit these characteristics, he is not a respected man in the community. A woman's pride is often defined by how well she keeps her home, by whether she is an obedient wife, and by the number of children she has.

Outsiders, whether black or white, perceive the Maasai loftiness and pride as a kind of arrogance. The Maasai themselves, because they are traditionally pastoralists, still look down on strictly agricultural tribes such as the Kikuyu.

Their strong sense of pride is also fueled by their view of themselves as warriors. As noted earlier, they have always been feared by other tribes and the colonialists. Their folklore is replete with tales of their fighting with incredible fearlessness, even when their primitive weapons faced their enemies' modern bullets. For them the battles were to preserve the "true African" way of life and to protect their cattle.

Beauty. Beauty is yet another value that is important to the Maasai. Both men and women adorn themselves with elaborate beads, body paint, and other jewelry.

Maasai children, especially girls, begin wearing jewelry almost from the moment of birth. One of the primary duties a woman has is to make necklaces, bracelets, bangles, belts, and earrings for their husband, children, friends, and herself. Adornment is also a way for a woman to attract a husband, and Maasai women are very meticulous in selecting jewelry for special celebrations. Maasai warriors still spend much of their day painting themselves with red ochre, and they also plait and braid their hair, which is grown long as a sign of warriorhood.

Beauty and bodily adornment are so valued in the Maasai culture that they have distinctive jewelry and dress to wear during certain periods of each life-stage. For example, one can tell if a boy has just recently been circumcised because he wears a crown of bird carcasses. Thus, we can conclude that beauty is more than superficial for the Maasai; it is a reflection of a very important value that often steers perception in one direction or another.

WORLDVIEW

The worldview of a culture is yet another factor that greatly modifies perception. In the Samovar and Porter (1988) model, worldview deals with a culture's orientation toward such things as God, humanity, the universe, death, nature, and other philosophical issues that are concerned with the concept of being. In short, it is that perception of the world that helps the individual locate his or her place and rank in the universe. It influences nearly every action in which an individual engages. Our research would tend to agree with this observation. The Maasai's worldview has three components that greatly control their life and hence their perception of the universe: coexistence with nature, religion, and death.

Nature. For the Maasai, nature must always be held in the highest regard. They believe that their very existence depends solely on nature's benevolence, Their lifestyle is one that sees them interacting with the elements: Without rain their cattle will die, and in a sense so will they, for as we pointed out earlier, cattle supply most of the basic needs of the Maasai.

The Maasai also embrace the view that nature cannot be changed; it is too powerful. But they do acknowledge that nature itself changes without their intervening, and what they must do is change as nature fluctuates. Adapting to nature is most evident in the Maasai's seminomadic lifestyle. They carry coexistence to the point where they will not kill or eat wild animals unless they pose a threat or there is a severe drought. For the Maasai cultivating and hunting are seen as destructive to nature: Cultivation forces humans to deal directly with nature, changing and altering it to their specifications and needs; hunting for food is seen as something even worse, for then nature is not only being changed but it is being destroyed (Rigby, 1985).

Religion. The second aspect of worldview, religion, is closely tied to the Maasai perception of nature. The Maasai have one god called "Engai," but this god has two very distinct personalities and therefore serves two purposes: "Engai Narok," the black god, is benevolent and generous and shows himself through rain and thunder; "Engai Nanyokie," the red god, is manifested in lightning. To the Maasai, God encompasses everything in nature, friendly or destructive (Saitoti & Beckwith, 1980). In fact, the word "Engai" actually means "sky." Cattle accompanied the Maasai people to earth from the sky and thus cattle are seen as mediators between humans and God as well as between humans and nature. Therefore, herding is traditionally the only acceptable livelihood, since it is God's will. Not to herd would be disrespectful to Engai and demeaning to a Maasai (Salvadon & Fedders, 1973),

There is a Maasai proverb that states, "The one chosen by God is not the one chosen by people" (Rigby, 1985, p. 92). Thus, not surprisingly, the Maasai have no priests or ministers; there is no one who represents God or purports to speak for God. There are "laiboni" who are considered the wisest of the elders and often cast curses and give blessings, but they do not represent God or preach. The Maasai have no religious writings, only oral legends, therefore the elders are important in the religious life of the people.

What is most significant is that God (Engai) is found in nature. Some Maasai households rise at dawn to pray to the sun, which is seen as a manifestation of Engai. God is found in many other forms in nature for the Maasai: rain, grass, and even a particularly beautiful stone. God is nature and cannot be artificially symbolized in a cross or a building. Since nature is God, people must live in harmony with God and the Maasai must work together. This is a different view of God than the one offered by Christianity, in which God is separate from humans and is even from a different world.

Death. The third aspect of the Maasai worldview is how they perceive death. As with most cultures, death brings sorrow to those left behind by the deceased; however, cultures differ in how they respond to death. The response of the Maasai directly coincides with their belief in the coexistence of nature and human beings; therefore, except for the "laiboni" (wise men), all corpses are left out in the open to be devoured by hyenas and other scavengers. The assumption behind this action is clear, at least to the Maasai, who believe that after they have had a full life and enjoyed the benefits of nature, it is only fitting that their bones go back to the earth so they can be used to prepare the land for future life. For the Maasai there is a circular, mutually beneficial relationship between nature and humanity.

VERBAL PROCESSES

In the most basic sense, language is an organized, generally agreed upon, learned symbol system used to represent human experiences within a geographic or cultural community. Each culture places its individual imprint on words—how they are used and what they mean.

Language is the primary vehicle by which a culture transmits its beliefs, values, and norms. Language gives people a means of interacting with other members of their culture and a means of thinking, serving both as a mechanism for communication and as a guide to social reality. Anyone interested in studying another culture must therefore look at the way a culture uses language and also the experiences in their environment they have selected to name. Research on the Maasai culture reveals two language variables that offer a clue into the workings of this particular group of people: their use of metaphors and their reliance on proverbs.

Metaphors

Wisdom in the Maasai culture is marked not just by age and prudence but also by language use. Elders make decisions at tribal meetings based on speeches offered by various members of the group. The most successful speakers are those whose eloquence is embellished and ornate. The metaphor offers the gifted speaker a tool to demonstrate his mastery of words. Heine and Claudi (1986) explain the importance of metaphor to the Maasai when they write:

> Maa people frequently claim that their language is particularly rich in figurative speech forms. Nonliteral language, especially the use of metaphors, is in fact encouraged from earliest childhood on, and the success of a political leader depends to quite a large extent on the creative use of it. (p. 17)

Because of the value placed on the metaphors, Johnstone (1988) writes, "Whenever there were big meetings to decide important matters, the men always spoke in proverbs, metaphors, and other figurative language." Messages are full of elaborate symbolism—blunt and simple words are rarely used.

The information in Table 1, developed by Heine and Claudi (1986), helps clarify some of the types of metaphors employed by the Maasai. These few examples demonstrate how most of the metaphors in the Maa language reflect what is important in their culture. For example, the use of the umbilical cord to refer to a very close friend is indicative of the value placed on childbirth and of the strong bonds between members of the same age-set. In addition, an age-set generation is formally established when a select group of elders kindles the fire on the day that a new generation of boys will be circumcised (Heine & Claudi, 1986). These age-sets form both a unique governing body and a social hierarchy in all Maasai communities.

Proverbs

Like metaphors, proverbs are an integral part of the Maasai language. Massek and Sidai (1974) noted that "a Maasai hardly speaks ten sentences without using at least one proverb" (p. 6). These proverbs have common elements and themes that are directly related to the Maasai value system.

Proverbs convey important messages to the members of a culture because they often deal with subjects that are of significance. Therefore, the assumption behind examining the proverbs is a simple one—discover the meaning of the proverb and you will understand something of what is important to its user. This axiom is exceptionally true for the Maasai, for here one encounters proverbs focusing on respect, parents, children, wisdom, and proper conduct. Let us look at some of these proverbs as a way of furthering an understanding of the Maasai culture.

1. "Meeta enkerai olopeny." (The child has no owner.) Maasai children are expected to respect all elders, not just those in the immediate family. It is very common for children to refer to older men as "Father" and to older women as "Mother."
2. "Memorata olayoni oataa menye." (One is never a man while his father is still alive.) Even as junior elders, Maasai men do not always leave their father's homestead. It is not until a man attains the full status of senior elder that he usually establishes his own home with his wife (wives) and children. In addition, the very name of male children is indicated with the word "ole," which means "son of," placed between the first and last names.

Table 1

Category	Maasai Word	Basic Meaning	Metaphorical Meaning
Object + Animal	Olmotonyi	Large bird	Eagle shoulder cape
Person + Animal	Enker	Sheep	Careless, stupid person
Person + Object	Sotua	Umbilical cord	Close friend
Quality + Object	Olpiron	Firestick	Age-set generation

A Maasai male is very often characterized by his father's name and reputation.

3. "Eder olayioni o menye, neder entito o notanye." (A boy converses with his father while a girl converses with her mother.) This proverb is representative of both the restricted relationships between the opposite sexes in a family and the strict divisions of labor found in the Maasai culture. Young girls learn to do household chores at an early age, and by age seven their brothers are responsible for tending the family herd.

4. "Menye marrmali, menye maata." (Father of troubles, father without.) In the Maasai culture there is a conviction that a man with no children has more problems than a man with many children. They believe that even a man with a fine herd of cattle can never be rich unless he also has many children. This proverb simply serves to underscore those facts.

5. "Ideenya taa anaa osurai oota oikati." (You are as proud as lean meat with soot on it.) Being proud is a well-known characteristic of the Maasai. So strong is this value that the Maasai are often criticized by other African tribes. To sustain the reality and the perception of pride, a Maasai must always add to his accomplishments, and courageous acts and large families are two common behaviors that present an image of a proud person. It should be noted, however, that foolish pride is looked down upon as a sign of arrogance.

6. "Medany olkimojino obo elashei." (One finger does not kill a louse.) The need to cooperate is crucial to the Maasai culture, and this proverb reinforces that belief. As noted earlier, the Maasai community is a highly communal one, one that is well-structured and based on group harmony and decision making. The family unit is particularly dependent on cooperation and accord. On most occasions wives care for each other's children. Cattle are kept together and shared, with ownership only a secondary consideration.

In this section on proverbs we see the connection between what a culture talks about and what it embraces and acknowledges to be true. This link between words and behavior only serves to buttress the belief that verbal symbols represent a device by which a culture maintains and perpetuates itself.

NONVERBAL PROCESSES

Nonverbal systems represent yet another coding system that individuals and cultures use as a means of sharing their realities. Like verbal symbols, nonverbal codes are learned as part of the socialization process—that is, each culture teaches its members the symbol and the meaning for the symbol. In the case of the Maasai, there are a number of nonverbal messages that, when understood, offer the outsider some clues as to the workings of this foreign culture.

Movement and Posture

The Maasai show their pride and self-regard by the way they carry themselves. They are tall and slender and have a posture that reflects an appearance of strength and vigor. There is, at first glance, a regal air about them and at times they appear to be floating. "The morans [warriors], especially, walk very erect and relatively slowly. It's like they are in so much command of their environment that they are absolutely at ease" (Johnstone, personal correspondence, 1988).

The posture and movement of Maasai women also mirrors an attitude of pride and self-assurance. They are also tall and slender and have a gait that is slow and self-confident. Their heads are held high as a way of emphasizing their confidence and superiority over other tribes.

Paralanguage

The Maasai people utilize a number of sounds that have special meanings. The most common is the "eh" sound, which is used extensively, even though the Maasai language is ornate and metaphorical. When uttered, the sound is drawn out and can have a host of different interpretations; it can mean "yes," "I understand," or "continue." Although similar to the English regulators "uh huh" and "hmmm," "eh" is used more frequently and appears to dominate short, casual conversations among the Maasai.

Touching

While public touching between the sexes among the Maasai is usually limited to a light handshake, same-sex touching is common. Simple greetings between the sexes consist of a very light brush of the palms; in fact, so light is the touch, the hands appear barely to touch. If two women are good friends, however, they may greet each other with a light kiss on the lips. If they have not seen each other recently, they may embrace and clutch each other's upper arms. Men will frequently drape their arms around each other while conversing. When children greet an elder, they bow their heads so that the elder may place his or her hand on the young person's head, which is a sign of both respect and fondness. There is a great deal of affection to be found among the Maasai, and touching is one way of displaying that affection.

Time

The meaning cultures attach to time also reveals something of their view toward life and other people. The Maasai are unique in their treatment of time. Unlike the Westerner, for the Maasai there is always enough time: Their life is not governed by the clock; they are never in a hurry. This casual attitude produces a people who are self-possessed, calm, and most of all, *patient.*

Children are taught very early that there is never a need to rush. The vital chore of tending the family cattle requires that children stay alert and attentive to the herd's needs and safety, but such a chore also requires eight to ten hours of patient solitude.

This endless display of patience by the Maasai people is in direct contrast to time-conscious Americans. For example, public transportation in Kenya is not run on a firm schedule; buses and "matatus" (covered pick-up trucks) leave for their destinations when they are full. As do most Kenyans, the Maasai understand this. Inquiries from Americans as to when a vehicle will be departing are often answered with "just now." "Just now," however, can mean anywhere from five minutes to an hour.

Even though the present is fully enjoyed, the Maasai culture is very past-oriented. This strong tie to the past stems from the view that wisdom is found not in the present or the future, but rather in the past. The future is governed by the knowledge of the elderly, not by the discoveries of the young. The insignificance

of the future is apparent in how the Maasai perceive death: There is nothing after death unless one is a "laibon" (wise man).

Space

Space, as it relates to land and grazing, is truly communal. Traditionally nomadic pastoralists, the Maasai did not regard any land as theirs to own but rather perceived all land as theirs to use. Rigby (1985) explains that the pastoral Maasai "do not conceive of land as 'owned' by any group, category, community or individual" (p. 124). He explains, however, that today most Maasai practice a subtle marking of territory. Each clan now has its own area and for the most part, clan boundaries are observed. Yet concepts of "land rights" and "trespassing" are still viewed as Western notions.

The Maasai's perception of private space is very different from Western perceptions. Maasai do not need or ask for much private space while in public settings. Lining up in a systematic order, and taking one's turn, is not part of the Maasai experience—public facilities, therefore, at least to the outsider, often appear disorderly. It is not uncommon to see a vehicle designed to hold fifteen packed with thirty occupants, and none of them complaining. For the Maasai, space is like time—there is always enough of it.

CONCLUSION

It has been the intent of this article to offer some observations about the Maasai culture. It is our contention that by knowing something about the perceptions and language systems of a culture, one can better understand that culture. This increased understanding provides us with a fund of knowledge that can be helpful in formulating messages directed to a group of people different from ourselves. It can also aid in interpreting the meanings behind the messages we receive from people who appear quite different from us. As Emerson wrote, "All persons are puzzled until at last we find some word or act, the key to the man, to the woman; straightaway all their past words and actions lie in light before us."

References

Hall, E. (1976). *Beyond Culture*. Garden City, N.Y.: Anchor.

Heine, B., & Claudi, U. (1986). *On the Rise of Grammatical Categories*. Berlin: Deitrich Reimer Verlag.

Johnstone, J. (1988, March 30). Personal correspondence.

Kipury, N. (1983). *Oral Literature of the Maasai*. Nairobi: Heinemann Educational Books.

Massek, A. O., & Sidai, J. O. (1974). *Eneno oo Lmaasai—Wisdom of the Maasai*. Nairobi: Transafrica Publishers.

Rigby, P. (1985). *Persistent Pastoralists: Nomadic Societies in Transition*. London: Zed Books.

Saitoti, T. O., & Beckwith, C. (1980). *Maasai*. London: Elm Tree Books.

Salvadon, C., & Fedders, A. (1973). *Maasai*. London: Collins.

Samovar, L. A., & Porter, R. E. (1997). "Approaching Intercultural Communication." In L. A. Samovar & R. E. Porter (Eds.), *Intercultural Communication: A Reader*, 8th ed. Belmont, Calif.: Wadsworth.

Sankan, S. S. O. (1971). *The Maasai*. Nairobi: Kenya Literature Bureau.

Concepts and Questions

1. What historical antecedents of Maasai culture contribute to their current worldview?

2. How does the Maasai's orientation to children affect their worldview?

3. In what ways might the Maasai worldview affect intercultural communication?

4. How does the Maasai use of metaphor differ from the North American use? How could this difference affect intercultural communication?

5. Skow and Samovar offer the following quotation by Edward T. Hall: "There is not one aspect of human life that is not touched and altered by culture." Do you agree with Hall? If so, why?

6. Why is it important to learn about the history of a culture? What aspects of the history of your culture do you deem important? Why?

7. How would you compare the values of the Maasai culture with the values of your own culture? Would a clash of these values present problems when you were communicating with a Maasai?

8. Compare three of the Maasai proverbs with three proverbs from your own culture.

9. Compare some of the Maasai's nonverbal behaviors with some of the actions found in your culture.

4

Co-Cultures: Living in a Multicultural World

*We need every human gift and cannot afford
to neglect any gift because of artificial barriers
of sex or race or class or national origin.*

MARGARET MEAD

*Whenever you find yourself on the side of the
majority, it's time to pause and reflect.*

MARK TWAIN

*Human beings draw close to one another by
their common nature, but habits and customs
keep them apart.*

CONFUCIAN SAYING

In the late 1960s people began to realize that while international cultures were important to the study of intercultural communication, the large number of co-cultures dispersed throughout the United States were also important to this study. These were the millions of people who held a type of "membership" in their particular co-culture while also being part of the dominant mainstream culture. In this chapter we turn to some of those co-cultures and examine their values, beliefs, and communication patterns. Our rationale for such an investigation is as valid today as it was when the first edition of this work appeared more than forty years ago. Simply put, in the United States, and throughout the world, multiculturalism is recognized as an essential constituent that influences both current history and the future direction of every country. In this chapter we examine the dynamics of domestic multiculturalism by investigating a series of co-cultures composed of people who reside in the United States.

Co-cultures often have many of the defining characteristics found in any culture—a specialized language system, shared values, a collective worldview, recognizable communication patterns, and a common history. Members of a co-culture usually share a number of other similar characteristics, such as religion, economic status, ethnic background, age, gender, or sexual preference. As noted, with increasing frequency many people living in the United States hold dual or even multiple co-cultural memberships. A gay African American man would be considered a member of two co-cultures. A Russian woman who emigrated to the United States and married a man who had emigrated from India would be a member of multiple co-cultural groups.

These diverse co-cultures bring their experiences and ways of interacting to an intercultural encounter. Their distinctive communicative behaviors may be baffling to outsiders. This diversity can become prominent when, for instance, members of a collectivistic co-culture, such as Asian Americans, interact with someone from the highly individualistic Euro-American dominant culture. For example, a Vietnamese American, with strong extended family ties, might feel it important to ask to be excused from work to help celebrate his uncle's birthday. But a Euro-American, more focused on the nuclear family, may view such a request as an inappropriate excuse for a day off.

What we have been suggesting is that the United States is a pluralistic, multicultural society, with minority groups representing over a third of the total population ("Census," 2010). This creates a vital need for competent communication between the dominant culture and the numerous co-cultures, as well as between the co-cultures themselves. Insufficient information about these co-cultures can produce stereotypes and prejudice. This often leads to incorrect and damaging assumptions about people from co-cultures. An appreciation for the unique experiences of these co-culture members will help overcome many communication problems.

The rich cultural diversity and complexity of U.S. society flows from an extensive number of co-cultures. However, we are only able to examine a limited number of co-cultures in this chapter. Our selections are based on three considerations: (1) we faced serious space constraints; (2) we wanted to include some social groups that are often at odds with the dominant culture; and (3) we wanted to emphasize the range of different co-cultures. To this end we selected representations from both the major co-cultures and from those less often encountered. You will also learn about additional co-cultures as you read about specific groups in subsequent chapters.

Our first essay in this chapter, "Who's Got the Room at the Top?" was written by Edith A. Folb. She was one of the first scholars to write about many of the problems that can occur when members of the dominant culture interact with co-cultures. Folb called this form of communication intracultural communication. She used the prefix "intra" to highlight the notion that although these two groups shared many of the same values and beliefs, they had a host of specialized characteristics that influenced communication when the two groups came together. Folb's analysis is as pertinent today as it was when she introduced it more than forty years ago.

Folb believes that the crucial characteristic in *intracultural communication*—communication between members of the same dominant culture who hold slightly different values—is the interrelationship of power, dominance, and nondominance. She examines these three variables as they apply to "blacks, Native Americans, Chicanos, women, the aged, the physically challenged" and other groups that have been "caste marked." Folb contends that caste marking often means the co-cultures we just mentioned are negatively identified. Singling out these groups affects issues of "power, dominance, and social control." As you might imagine, these three components greatly impede communication between the two groups.

Our second selection investigates one of the groups mentioned by Folb—people with disabilities. By some estimates, 20 percent of the population in the United States can be classified as disabled, suffering from sensory, physical, or mental disabilities. This group has grown in recent years as war veterans from Afghanistan and Iraq have returned home with serious disabilities. These veterans can suffer not only from physical wounds that may have resulted in lost limbs, paralysis, blindness, or dementia, but also from posttraumatic stress disorder (PTSD), a disabling, dysfunctional, emotional state. People with a disability often find themselves misunderstood, marginalized, or even cut off from the dominant nondisabled culture. The problem is that for many people, the disabled are not recognized as a distinct co-culture. However, as Dawn O. Braithwaite and Charles A. Braithwaite point out, people with disabilities, like members of all co-cultures, belong to two very distinct groups, and therefore, are very much a co-culture. In their essay "'Which Is My Good Leg?': Cultural Communication of Persons with Disabilities," the authors examine how people with disabilities view their communicative relationships with nondisabled persons. Reviewing research consisting of more than one hundred in-depth interviews with adults with physical disabilities, the Braithwaites discovered that in this co-culture people go through a process of redefinition involving three steps: (1) redefining the self as a part of the "new" culture, (2) redefining disability, and (3) redefining disability for the dominant culture. We believe, as we did over twenty-five years ago when this article was first introduced, that being familiar with these steps will help you improve your ability to interact and communicate effectively with members of the disabled co-culture.

It is obvious that during the last four decades, and continuing today, much attention has been paid to a co-culture once taken for granted—women. In addition, because women were so much a part of American culture, they were seldom perceived as having a series of experiences that, in many ways, made them different from the males who composed the dominant culture. As feminist research became a viable area of investigation, people began to study what it meant to be female while also holding membership in the male-dominated mainstream culture. One of the major differences that became evident through these studies dealt with how each group communicated. These differences, and many of the reasons behind them, were of major concern to Judy C. Pearson in an essay she wrote more than twenty-five years ago. In "Gender and Communication: Sex Is More Than a Three-Letter Word," Pearson begins with a discussion of how gender differences are formed very early in life. She examines both verbal and nonverbal variations found among young children. Pearson also investigates many of the problems created by gender-driven variations in person perception and communication. Stereotyping and male bias are examples of some of the problems Pearson maintains often impede gender interaction. Although many attitudes, perceptions, and even statutes have changed in recent decades, this essay retains much of its relevance regarding gender differences in communication.

Our next piece is as pertinent today as when we initially presented it more than twenty years ago. In "An African American Communication Perspective," Sidney A. Ribeau, John R. Baldwin, and Michael L. Hecht study the communication style of the African American co-culture. The essay focuses on satisfying and dissatisfying conversational themes, conversational strategies, and communication effectiveness from an intercultural perspective. Specifically, they identify seven variables that often have an impact on intercultural communication: negative stereotypes, acceptance, personal expressiveness, authenticity, understanding, goal attainment, and power dynamics. It is the authors' belief, and ours, that understanding these six communication variables and how they are manifested during cross-cultural interaction can enrich intercultural interaction.

As early as 1976, in the second edition of this reader, we included an essay on the gay and lesbian experience. From that time until the present we have included contributions dealing with various components of how this co-culture interacts with the dominant culture. The final essay of this chapter continues this tradition by introducing you to the communicative behaviors and dynamics associated with the gay and lesbian co-culture. In his article "In Plain Sight: Gay and Lesbian Communication and Culture," William F. Eadie acknowledges that there is a disparity of views, ranging from hostility to acceptance, regarding the gay and lesbian community. As a means of diminishing this antagonism, he challenges you to become acquainted with the cultural characteristics and communication style of gay and lesbian members in our society.

Eadie presents three general statements about lesbian and gay culture: (1) being open about sexual orientation is a political statement; (2) lesbian and gay culture must deal with tensions relating to how open one should be about their sexuality; and (3) although lesbian and gay culture is generally characterized as being about sexual attraction and desire, being lesbian or gay is about much, much more than just sex. The essay also provides insight into lesbian and gay communication behaviors and how sexual attraction and intimacy are negotiated. Eadie's essay offers firsthand insight into the lesbian and gay community and provides an opportunity for you to increase your understanding of this co-culture.

Who's Got the Room at the Top? Issues of Dominance and Nondominance in Intercultural Communication

Edith A. Folb

"If a phenomenon is important, it is perceived, and, being perceived, it is labeled." So notes Nathan Kantrowitz, sociologist and student of language behavior. Nowhere is Kantrowitz's observation more apparent than in that realm of communication studies concerned with the correlates and connections between culture and communication—what the editors of this text have termed "intercultural communication." Our contemporary technology has brought us into both literal and voyeuristic contact with diverse cultures and customs, from the Stone Age Tasaday to the computer age Japanese. Our domestic liberation movements, moreover, have forced upon our consciousness the existence and needs of a multiplicity of groups within our own nation. So, the phenomenon of culture-linked communication is pervasively before us. And, as scholars concerned with culture and communication, we have tried to identify and characterize what we see. This attempt to "label the goods," as it were, has generated a profusion of semantic labels and categories—international communication, cross-cultural communication, intercultural communication, intracultural communication, trans-racial communication, interracial communication, interethnic communication. What we perceive to be important, we label.

Some may chide us for our penchant for classification—an example of Aristotelian excessiveness, they may say. However, I see it as a genuine attempt to understand what we do individually and collectively, what we focus on within the field of communication studies. I believe this effort to characterize what we do serves a useful function: It continually prods us to examine and expand our vision of what culture-linked communication is, and, at the same time, it helps us bring into sharper focus the dimensions and differences within this area of study. As Samovar and Porter (1982) remind us, "There is still a great need to specify the nature of intercultural communication and to recognize various viewpoints that see the phenomenon somewhat differently" (p. 2). It is my intention in this essay to attempt what the editors of this text suggest, to look at the correlates and connections between culture and communication from a different point of view, one that examines the properties and issues of dominance and nondominance in communicative exchange. The essay is speculative and sometimes polemical. And the focus of my interest and discussion is the realm of intracultural communication.

THE CONCEPT OF INTRACULTURAL COMMUNICATION

The label "intracultural communication" is not unknown within the field of communication studies, although it is one that has not been widely used. Sitaram and Cogdell (1976) have identified intracultural communication as "the type of communication that takes place between members of the same dominant culture, but with slightly differing values" (p. 28). They go on to explain that there are groups ("subcultures") within the dominant culture who hold a minimal number of values that differ from the mainstream, as well as from other subgroups. These differences are not sufficient to identify them as separate cultures, but diverse enough to set them apart from each other and the culture at large. "Communication between members of such subcultures is *intracultural communication*" (Sitaram & Cogdell, 1976, p. 28).

In another vein, Sarbaugh (1979) sees intracultural communication as an indicator of the degree of cultural experience shared (or not shared) by two people—the more culturally homogeneous the participants, the greater the level of "intraculturalness" surrounding the communicative act. For Sitaram and Cogdell, then, intracultural communication is a phenomenon that operates within a given culture among its members; for Sarbaugh, it is a measure of homogeneity that well may transcend country or culture.

Like Sitaram and Cogdell, I see intracultural communication as a phenomenon that functions within a single, designated culture. However, like Sarbaugh, I am concerned with the particular variables within that context that importantly influence the degree and kind of cultural homogeneity or heterogeneity that can and do exist among members of the culture. Furthermore, the variables of particular interest to me are those that illuminate and underscore the interrelationship of power, dominance, and nondominance in a particular culture.[1] Finally, I believe that the concept of hierarchy, as it functions within a culture, has a deep impact on matters of power, dominance, and nondominance and, therefore, on both the form and content of intracultural communication.

As a backdrop for the discussion of dominance and nondominance in an intracultural context, I would like to formulate a frame of reference within which to view the discussion.

A FRAME OF REFERENCE FOR INTRACULTURAL COMMUNICATION

Society and Culture

Thomas Hobbes, the seventeenth-century political philosopher, left us an intriguing legacy in his work, *Leviathan*. He posited a hypothetical starting point for humankind's march to political and social organization. He called it "the state of nature." In this presocietal state, the biggest club ruled. Kill or be killed was the prevailing modus operandi. Somewhere along the evolutionary road, our ancestors began to recognize a need to change their ways—if any of them were to survive for very long. The principle of enlightened self-interest became the name of the game. Our forebears, however grudgingly, began to curb their inclination to kill, maim, steal, or otherwise aggress upon others and joined together for mutual survival and benefit.

The move was one of expediency, not altruism. "Do unto others as you would have them do unto you," whatever its religious import, is a reiteration of the principle of enlightened self-interest.

So, this aggregate of beings came together in order to survive, and, in coming together, gave up certain base instincts, drives, and predilections. "Society" was formed. Those who may scoff at this postulated state of nature need only remember back to the United States' final pullout from Vietnam. The media showed us, in all too brutal detail, the rapidity with which a society disintegrates and we return to the force of the club.

But let us continue with the telling of humankind's tale. It was not sufficient merely to form society; it must be maintained. Controls must be established to ensure its stability. Thus, the social contract was enacted. It was, indeed, the social contract that ensured mutual support, protection, welfare, and survival for the society's members.

However, social maintenance and control did not ensure the perpetuation of the society as an intact entity, carrying along its cumulative and collective experiences, knowledge, beliefs, attitudes, the emergent relationship of self to other, to the group, to the universe, to matters of time and space. That is, it did not ensure the perpetuation of society's accoutrements—its culture. Institutions and structures were needed to house, as it were, the trappings of culture. So, culture was not only embodied in the precepts passed on from one generation to another, but also in the artifacts created by society to safeguard its culture. Looked at in a different light, culture is both a blueprint for continued societal survival as well as the pervasive cement that holds the social mosaic together. Culture daily tells us and shows us how to be in the universe, and it informs future generations how to be.[2]

From the moment we begin life in this world, we are instructed in the cultural ways that govern and hold together our society, ways that ensure its perpetuation. Indeed, the social contract that binds us to our society and our culture from the moment of birth is neither of our own choice nor of our own design. For example, we are labeled by others almost immediately—John, Sandra, Pearl, David. Our genders are determined at once and we are, accordingly, swaddled in appropriate colors and treated in appropriate ways.[3]

As we grow from infancy to childhood, the socialization process is stepped up and we rapidly internalize the rules of appropriate and inappropriate societal behavior. Religion, education, recreation, health care, and many other cultural institutions reinforce our learning, shape and regulate our behavior and thought so they are orderly and comprehensible to other members of our society. Through the socialization process the human animal is transformed into the social animal. Thus, society is maintained through instruction and indoctrination in the ways of the culture.

But the question that pricks and puzzles the mind is: Whose culture is passed on? Whose social order is maintained? Whose beliefs and values are deemed appropriate? Whose norms, mores, and folkways are invoked?

Hierarchy, Power, and Dominance

In most societies, as we know them, there is a hierarchy of status and power. By its very nature, hierarchy implies an ordering process, a sense of the evaluative marketing of those being ordered. Our own vernacular vocabulary abounds with references to hierarchy and concomitant status and power: "top dog," "top banana," "king pin," "king of the mountain."

High status and attendant power may be accorded to those among us who are seen or believed to be great warriors or hunters, those invested with magical, divine, or special powers, those who are deemed wise, or those who are in possession of important, valued and/or vital societal resources and goods. Of course, power and high status are not necessarily—or even usually—accorded to these specially designated members of the society in some automatic fashion. Power, control, and subsequent high status are often forcibly wrested from others and forcibly maintained. Not everyone abides by the social contract, and strong-arm rule often prevails, as conquered, colonized, and enslaved people know too well.

Whatever the basis for determining the hierarchy, the fact of its existence in a society assures the evolution and continued presence of a power elite—those at the top of the social hierarchy who accrue and possess what the society deems valuable or vital. And, in turn, the presence of a power elite ensures an asymmetrical relationship among the members of the society. In fact, power is often defined as the ability to get others to do what you want and the resources to force them to do your bidding if they resist—the asymmetrical relationship in its extreme form.

But the perpetuation of the power elite through force is not the most effective or efficient way of ensuring one's position at the top of the hierarchy. It is considerably more effective to institute, encourage, and/or perpetuate those aspects of culture—knowledge, experiences, beliefs, values, patterns of social organization, artifacts—that subtly and manifestly reinforce and ensure the continuation of the power elite and its asymmetrical relationship within the society. Though we may dismiss Nazism as a malignant ideology, we should attend to the fact that Hitler well understood the maintenance of the power elite through the manipulation and control of culture—culture as propaganda.

Though I would not imply that all power elites maintain themselves in such an overtly manipulative way, I would at least suggest that the powerful in many societies—our own included—go to great lengths to maintain their positions of power and what those positions bring them. And to that end, they support, reinforce, and, indeed, create those particular cultural precepts and artifacts that are likely to guarantee their continued power. To the extent that the culture reflects implicitly or expressly the needs and desires of the power elite to sustain itself, it becomes a vehicle for propaganda. Thus, cultural precepts and artifacts that govern such matters as social organization and behavior, values, beliefs, and the like can often be seen as rules and institutions that sustain the few at the expense of the many.

So, we come back to the question of whose rules, whose culture? I would suggest that when we in communication studies refer to the "dominant culture" we are, in fact, not talking about numbers. That is why the label "minorities" is misleading when we refer to cultural groups within the larger society. Blacks in South Africa and women in the United States are not numerical minorities—but they are not members of the power elite either. In fact, when we talk about the concept of dominant culture, we are really talking about power—those who *dominate* culture, those who historically or traditionally have had the most persistent and far-reaching impact on culture, on what we think and say, on what we believe and do in our society.

We are talking about the culture of the minority and, by extension, the structures and institutions (social, political, economic, legal, religious, and so on) that maintain the power of this minority. Finally, we are talking about rules of appropriate and inappropriate behavior, thought, speech, and action for the many that preserve power for the few. Dominant culture, therefore, significantly reflects the precepts and artifacts of those who dominate culture and is not necessarily, or even usually, a reference to numbers, but to power.

So, coming full circle, I would suggest that our socialization process, our social introduction to this aggregate of people who form society, is an introduction to a rule-governed milieu of asymmetrical societal organization and relationship, and the communicative behaviors and practices found there are likewise asymmetrical in nature. As the witticism goes, "All men (perhaps even women) are created equal—some are just more equal than others."

Given this frame of reference, I would now like to explore some definitions and concepts that, I believe, emerge from this perspective. It is my hope that the discussion will provide the reader with another way to look at intracultural communication.

A NOMENCLATURE FOR INTRACULTURAL COMMUNICATION

The Concept of Nondominance

As already indicated, I view intracultural communication as a phenomenon that operates within a given cultural context. However, my particular focus, as suggested, is not a focus on numbers but an attention to dominance, nondominance, and power in the cultural setting. That is, how do nondominant groups intersect and interact with the dominant culture membership (with those who enact the precepts and support the institutions and systems of the power elite)? For purposes of discussion and analysis, I will take most of my examples from the geopolitical configuration called the United States.

By "nondominant groups" I mean those constellations of people who have not historically or traditionally had continued access to or influence upon or within the dominant culture's (that is, those who dominate culture) social, political, legal, economic,

and/or religious structures and institutions. Nondominant groups include people of color, women, gays, the physically challenged,[4] and the aged, to name some of the most prominent. I use the expression "nondominant" to characterize these people because, as suggested, I am referring to power and dominance, not numbers and dominance. Within the United States, those most likely to hold and control positions of real—not token—power and those who have the greatest potential ease of access to power and high status are still generally white, male, able-bodied, heterosexual, and youthful in appearance if not in age.[5]

Nondominant people are also those who, in varying degrees and various ways, have been "invisible" within the society of which they are a part and at the same time bear a visible caste mark. Furthermore, it is this mark of caste identity that is often consciously or habitually assigned low or negative status by members of the dominant culture.

The dimensions of invisibility and marked visibility are keen indicators of the status hierarchy in a given society. In his book, *The Invisible Man*, Ralph Ellison instructs us in the lesson that nondominant people—in this instance, black people—are figuratively "invisible." They are seen by the dominant culture as no one, nobody and therefore go unacknowledged and importantly unperceived.[6] Furthermore, nondominant peoples are often relegated to object status rather than human status. They are viewed as persons of "no consequence," literally and metaphorically. Expressions such as, "If you've seen one, you've seen them all"; "They all look alike to me"; "If you put a bag over their heads, it doesn't matter who you screw" attest to this level of invisibility and dehumanization of nondominant peoples, such as people of color or women. Indeed, one need only look at the dominant culture's slang repertory for a single nondominant group, women, to see the extent of this object status: "tail," "piece of ass," "side of beef," "hole," "gash," "slit," and so on.

At the same time that nondominant peoples are socially invisible, they are often visibly caste marked. Though we tend to think of caste in terms, say, of East Indian culture, we can clearly apply the concept to our own culture. One of the important dimensions of a caste system is that it is hereditary—you are born into a given caste and are usually marked for life as a member. In fact, we are all born into a caste, we are all caste marked. Indeed, some of us are doubly or multiply caste marked. In the United States, the most visible marks of caste relate to gender, race, age, and the degree to which one is able-bodied.

As East Indians do, we too assign low to high status and privilege to our people. The fact that this assignment of status and privilege may be active or passive, conscious or unconscious, malicious or unthinking does not detract from the reality of the act. And one of the major determinants of status, position, and caste marking relates back to who has historically or traditionally had access to or influence upon or within the power elite and its concomitant structures and institutions. So, historically blacks, native Americans, Chicanos, women, the old, the physically challenged have at best been neutrally caste marked and more often negatively identified when it comes to issues of power, dominance, and social control.[7]

Low status has been assigned to those people whom society views as somehow "stigmatized." Indeed, we have labels to identify such stigmatization: "deviant," "handicapped," "abnormal," "substandard," "different"—that is, different from those who dominate. As already suggested, it is the white, male, heterosexual, able-bodied, youthful person who both sets the standards for caste marking and is the human yardstick by which people within the United States are importantly measured and accordingly treated. As Porter and Samovar (1976) remind us, "We [in the United States] have generally viewed racial minorities as less than equal; they have been viewed as second class members of society—not quite as good as the white majority—and treated as such. . . . Blacks, Mexican Americans, Indians, and Orientals are still subject to prejudice and discrimination and treated in many respects as colonized subjects" (p. 11). I would add to this list of colonized, low-status subjects women, the physically challenged, and the aged. Again, our language is a telling repository for illuminating status as it relates to subordination in the social hierarchy: "Stay in your place," "Don't get out of line," "Know your place," "A woman's place is chained to the bed and the stove," "Know your station in life" are just a few sample phrases.

It is inevitable that nondominant peoples will experience, indeed be subjected to and suffer from, varying degrees of fear, denial, and self-hatred of their caste

marking. Frantz Fanon's (1963) characterization of the "colonized native"—the oppressed native who has so internalized the power elite's perception of the norm that he or she not only serves and speaks for the colonial elite but is often more critical and oppressive of her or his caste than is the colonial—reveals this depth of self-hatred and denial.

In a parallel vein, the concept of "passing," which relates to a person of color attempting to "pass for" white, is a statement of self-denial. Implicit in the art of passing is the acceptance, if not the belief, that "white is right" in this society, and the closer one can come to the likeness of the privileged caste, the more desirable and comfortable one's station in life will be. So, people of color have passed for white—just as Jews have passed for Gentile or gay males and females have passed for straight, always with the fear of being discovered "for what they are." Physical impairment, too, has been a mark of shame in this country for those so challenged. Even so powerful a figure as F.D.R. refused to be photographed in any way that would picture him to be a "cripple."

If the act of passing is a denial of one's caste, the process of "coming out of the closet" is a conscious acceptance of one's caste. It is an important political and personal statement of power, a vivid metaphor that literally marks a rite of passage. Perhaps the most striking acknowledgement of one's caste marking in our society relates to sexual preference. For a gay male or lesbian to admit their respective sexual preferences is for them to consciously take on an identity that our society has deemed abnormal and deviant—when measured against the society's standard of what is appropriate. They become, quite literally, marked people. In an important way, most of our domestic liberation movements are devoted to having their membership come out of the closet. That is, these movements seek not only to have their people heard and empowered by the power elite, but to have them reclaim and assert their identity and honor their caste. Liberation movement slogans tell the story of positive identification with one's caste: "Black is beautiful," "brown power," "Sisterhood is powerful," "gay pride," "I am an Indian and proud of it."

The nature and disposition of the social hierarchy in a given society, such as the United States, is reflected not only in the caste structure, but also in the class structure and the role prescriptions and expectations surrounding caste and class. Although the power structure in the United States is a complex and multileveled phenomenon, its predominant, generating force is economic. That is, the power elite is an elite that controls the material resources and goods in this country as well as the means and manner of production and distribution. Though one of our national fictions is that the United States is a classless society, we have, in fact, a well-established class structure based largely on economic power and control. When we talk of lower, middle, and upper classes in this country, we are not usually talking about birth or origins, but about power and control over material resources, and the attendant wealth, privilege, and high status.

There is even a kind of status distinction made within the upper-class society in this country that again relates to wealth and power, but in a temporal rather than a quantitative way—how long one has had wealth, power, and high-class status. So, distinctions are made between the old rich (the Harrimans, the Gores, the Pews) and the new rich (the Hunt family, Norton Simon, and their like).

Class, then, is intimately bound up with matters of caste. Not all, or even most, members of our society have the opportunity—let alone the caste credentials—to get a "piece of the action." It is no accident of nature that many of the nondominant peoples in this country are also poor peoples. Nor is it surprising that nondominant groups have been historically the unpaid, low-paid, and/or enslaved work force for the economic power elite.

Finally, role prescriptions are linked to both matters of status and expectations in terms of one's perceived status, class, and caste. A role can be defined simply as a set of behaviors. The set of behaviors we ascribe to a given role is culture-bound and indicative of what has been designated as appropriate within the culture vis-a-vis that role. They are prescriptive, not descriptive, behaviors. We hold certain behavioral expectations for certain roles. It is a mark of just how culture-bound and prescriptive these roles are when someone is perceived to behave inappropriately—for example, the mother who gives up custody of her children in order to pursue her career; she has "stepped out of line."

Furthermore, we see certain roles as appropriate or inappropriate to a given caste. Though another of our national myths—the Horatio Alger myth—tells us that there is room at the top for the industrious, bright go-getter, the truth of the matter is that there is room at the top if you are appropriately caste marked (that is, are white, male, able-bodied, and so on). The resistance, even outright hostility, nondominant peoples have encountered when they aspire to or claim certain occupational roles, for example, is a mark of the power elite's reluctance to relinquish those positions that have been traditionally associated with privileged status and high caste and class ranking. Though, in recent years, there has been much talk about a woman Vice-President of the United States, it has remained just talk. For that matter, there has not been a black Vice-President or a Hispanic or a Jew. The thought of the Presidency being held by most nondominant peoples is still "unspeakable."

The cultural prescription to keep nondominant peoples "in their place" is reinforced by and reinforces what I refer to as the "subterranean self"—the culture-bound collection of prejudices, stereotypes, values, and beliefs that each of us embraces and employs to justify our worldview and the place of people in that world. It is, after all, our subterranean selves that provide fuel to fire the normative in our lives—what roles people ought and ought not to perform, what and why certain individuals are ill- or well-equipped to carry out certain roles, and our righteously stated rationalizations for keeping people in their places as we see them. Again, it should be remembered that those who dominate the culture reinforce and tacitly or openly encourage the perpetuation of those cultural prejudices, stereotypes, values, and beliefs that maintain the status quo, that is, the asymmetrical nature of the social hierarchy. Those who doubt the fervent desire of the power elite to maintain things as they are need only ponder the intense and prolonged resistance to the Equal Rights Amendment. If women are already "equal," why not make their equality a matter of record?

The foregoing discussion has been an attempt to illuminate the meaning of nondominance and the position of the nondominant person within our society. By relating status in the social hierarchy to matters of caste, class, and role, it has been my intention to highlight what it means to be a nondominant person within a culture that is dominated by the cultural precepts and artifacts of a power elite. It has also been my intention to suggest that the concept of "dominant culture" is something of a fiction, as we in communication studies traditionally use it. Given my perspective, it is more accurate to talk about those who dominate a culture rather than a dominant culture per se. Finally, I have attempted to point out that cultural dominance is not necessarily, or even usually, a matter of the numbers of people in a given society, but of those who have real power in a society.

Geopolitics

The viewpoint being developed in this essay highlights still another facet of dominance and nondominance as it relates to society and the culture it generates and sustains—namely, the geopolitical facet. The United States is not merely a territory with certain designated boundaries—a geographical entity—it is a geopolitical configuration. It is a country whose history reflects the clear-cut interrelationship of geography, politics, economics, and the domination and control of people. For example, the westward movement and the subsequent takeover of the Indian nations and chunks of Mexico were justified by our doctrine of Manifest Destiny, not unlike the way Hitler's expansionism was justified by the Nazi doctrine of "geopolitik." It is no accident that the doctrine of Manifest Destiny coincides with the rapid growth and development of U.S. industrialization. The U.S. power elite wanted more land in which to expand and grow economically, so it created a rationalization to secure it.

Perhaps nowhere is a dominant culture's (those who dominate culture) ethnocentrism more apparent than in the missionary-like work carried on by its members—whether it be to "civilize" the natives (that is, to impose the conquerors' cultural baggage on them), to "educate them in the ways of the white man," or to "Americanize" them. Indeed, the very term *America* is a geopolitical label as we use it. It presumes that those who inhabit the United States are the center of the Western hemisphere, indeed its only residents.[8] Identifying ourselves as "Americans" and our geopolitical entity as "America," in light of the peoples who live to the north and south of our borders, speaks to both our economic dominance in this hemisphere and our ethnocentrism.

Identifying the United States in geopolitical terms is to identify it as a conqueror and controller of other peoples, and suggests both the probability of nondominant groups of people within that territory and a polarized, even hostile relationship between these groups and those who dominate culture. What Rich and Ogawa (1982) have pointed out in their model of interracial communication is applicable to most nondominant peoples: "As long as a power relationship exists between cultures where one has subdued and dominated the other...hostility, tension and strain are introduced into the communicative situation" (p. 46). Not only were the Indian nations[9] and parts of Mexico conquered and brought under the colonial rule of the United States, but in its industrial expansionism, the United States physically enslaved black Africans to work on the farms and plantations of the South. It also economically enslaved large numbers of East European immigrants, Chinese, Irish, Hispanics (and more recently, Southeast Asians) in its factories, on its railroads, in its mines and fields through low wages and long work hours. It coopted the cottage industries of the home and brought women and children into the factories under abysmal conditions and the lowest of wages.

Indeed, many of the nondominant peoples in this country today are the very same ones whom the powerful have historically colonized, enslaved, disenfranchised, dispossessed, discounted, and relegated to poverty and low caste and class status. So, the asymmetrical relationship between the conquerer and the conquered continues uninterrupted. Although the form of oppression may change through time, the fact of oppression—and coexistent nondominance—remains.

It has been my desire throughout this essay to speculate about the complex ways in which society, culture, position, and place in the societal hierarchy affect and are affected by the matters of dominance, power, and social control. To this end, I have chosen to identify and characterize configurations of people within a society not only along a cultural axis but along a socioeconomic and a geopolitical axis as well. I have tried to reexamine some of the concepts and definitions employed in discussions of culture-linked communication in a different light. And I have chosen the issues and conditions surrounding dominance and nondominance as points of departure and return. As I said at the beginning of this essay, the content is speculative, exploratory, and, hopefully, provocative.

Above all, it is intended to encourage dialogue and exchange about the conditions and constraints surrounding intracultural communication.

Notes

1. See Folb (1980) for another perspective on the intersection of power, dominance, and nondominance as they operate within a discrete microcultural group, the world of the black ghetto teenager.
2. For a fascinating account of how and what kind of culture is transmitted from person to person, see Margaret Mead's *Culture and Commitment* (1970).
3. Mary Ritchie Key's book, *Male/Female Language* (1975), provides an informative discussion of the ways in which females and males are catalogued, characterized, and compartmentalized by our language. She illuminates its effects on how we perceive ourselves, as well as discussing how others perceive us through the prism of language.
4. The semantic marker "physically challenged" is used in lieu of other, more traditional labels such as "handicapped," "physically disabled," or "physically impaired," because it is a designation preferred by many so challenged. It is seen as a positive, rather than a negative, mark of identification.
5. In a country as youth conscious as our own, advanced age is seen as a liability, not as a mark of honor and wisdom as it is in other cultures. Whatever other reservations people had about Ronald Reagan's political aspirations in 1980, the one most discussed was his age. His political handlers went to great lengths—as did Reagan himself—to "prove" he was young in spirit and energy if not in years. It was important that he align himself as closely as possible with the positive mark of youth we champion and admire in this country.
6. It is no mere coincidence that a common thread binds together the domestic liberation movements in this country. It is the demand to be seen, heard, and empowered.
7. See Nancy Henley's *Body Politics* (1977) for a provocative look at the interplay of the variables power, dominance, and sex as they affect nonverbal communication.
8. The current bumper sticker, "Get the United States Out of North America," is a pointed reference to our hemispheric self-centeredness.
9. Neither the label "Indian" nor the label "native American" adequately identifies those people who inhabited the North American continent before the European conquest of this territory. Both reflect the point of view of the labeler, not those so labeled. That is why many who fought for the label "native American" now discount it as not significantly different from "Indian."

References

Fanon, Frantz (1963). *Wretched of the Earth*. New York; Grove Press.

Folb, Edith A. (1980). *Runnin' Down Some Lines: The Language and Culture of Black Teenagers*. Cambridge, Mass.: Harvard University Press.

Porter, Richard E., & Larry A. Samovar (1976). "Communicating Interculturally." In Larry A. Samovar and Richard E. Porter (Eds.), *Intercultural Communication: A Reader* (2nd ed.) Belmont, Calif.: Wadsworth.

Rich, Andrea L., & Dennis M. Ogawa (1982). "Intercultural and Interracial Communication: An Analytical Approach." In Larry A. Samovar and Richard E. Porter (Eds.), *Intercultural Communication: A Reader* (3rd ed.) Belmont, Calif.: Wadsworth.

Samovar, Larry A., & Richard E. Porter (Eds.). (1982). *Intercultural Communication: A Reader* (3rd ed.) Belmont, Calif.: Wadsworth.

Sarbaugh, L. E. (1979). *Intercultural Communication*. Rochelle Park, N.J.: Hayden Book Co.

Sitaram, K. S., & Roy T. Cogdell (1976). *Foundations of Intercultural Communication*. Columbus, Ohio: Merrill.

Concepts and Questions

1. What is Folb referring to when she notes, "If a phenomenon is important, it is perceived, and, being perceived, it is labeled"? Tie your response to the major thesis of Folb's essay.
2. How do you define the term "intracultural communication"?
3. Why does Folb believe that the concepts of hierarchy and dominance are directly linked to matters of intracultural communication?
4. Do you believe that issues of hierarchy are as prevalent today as they were more than forty years ago when Folb wrote her essay?
5. What are some of the most important "teachings" of your culture that helped shape your norms, values, and methods of communication?
6. How is Folb using the term "power elites"? Are there "elites" in your culture? Who are they?
7. Using Folb's definition, what are some nondominant groups in your culture? How does one become a member of such a group?
8. What does Folb mean when she asserts that nondominant people are often "caste marked"? Do you agree with her claim?
9. How is Folb using the phrase "geopolitical"?

"Which Is My Good Leg?": Cultural Communication of Persons with Disabilities

Dawn O. Braithwaite

Charles A. Braithwaite

UNDERSTANDING COMMUNICATION OF PERSONS WITH DISABILITIES AS CULTURAL COMMUNICATION

Jonathan is an articulate, intelligent, 35-year-old professional man who has used a wheelchair since he became paraplegic when he was 20 years old. He recalls inviting a nondisabled woman out to dinner at a nice restaurant. When the waitperson came to take their order, she looked only at his date and asked, in a condescending tone, "And what would *he* like to eat for dinner?" At the end of the meal the waitperson presented Jonathan's date with the check and thanked her for her patronage.[1]

Kim describes her recent experience at the airport: "A lot of people always come up and ask can they push my wheelchair. And, I can do it myself. They were invading my space, concentration, doing what I wanted to do, which I enjoy doing; doing what I was doing *on my own*....And each time I said, 'No, I'm doing fine!' People looked at me like I was strange, you know, crazy or something. One person started pushing my chair anyway. I said [in an angry tone],

'Don't touch the wheelchair.' And then she just looked at me like I'd slapped her in the face."

Jeff, a nondisabled student, was working on a group project for class that included Helen, who uses a wheelchair. He related an incident that really embarrassed him. "I wasn't thinking and I said to the group, 'Let's run over to the student union and get some coffee.' I was mortified when I looked over at Helen and remembered that she can't walk. I felt like a real jerk." Helen later described the incident with Jeff, recalling,

> At yesterday's meeting, Jeff said, "Let's run over to the union" and then he looked over at me and I thought he would die. It didn't bother me at all; in fact, I use that phrase myself. I felt bad that Jeff was so embarrassed, but I didn't know what to say. Later in the group meeting I made it a point to say, "I've got to be running along now." I hope that Jeff noticed and felt OK about what he said.

Although it may seem hard for some of us to believe, these scenarios represent common experiences for many people with physical disabilities and are indicative of what often happens when people with disabilities and nondisabled others communicate.

The passage of the Americans with Disabilities Act of 1990 (ADA), a "bill of rights" for persons with disabilities, highlighted the fact that they are now a large, vocal, and dynamic group within the United States (Braithwaite & Labrecque, 1994; Braithwaite & Thompson, 2000). People with disabilities constitute a large segment of the American population that has increased over the years; estimates of how many people in the United States have disabilities run as high as one in five (Cunningham & Coombs, 1997; Pardeck, 1998).

There are two reasons for increases in the numbers of persons with disabilities. First, as the American population ages and has a longer life expectancy, more people will live long enough to develop disabilities, some of them related to age. Second, advances in medical technologies now allow persons with disabilities to survive life-threatening illnesses and injuries where survival was not possible in earlier times. For example, when actor Christopher Reeve became quadriplegic after a horse-riding accident in May 1995, advances in medical technology allowed him to survive his injuries and to live with a severe disability.

In the past, most people with disabilities were sheltered, and many spent their lives at home or living in institutions; today, they are very much a part of the American mainstream. Each of us will have contact with people who have disabilities within our families, among our friends, or in the workplace. Some of us will develop disabilities ourselves. Marie, a college student who was paralyzed after diving into a swimming pool, remarked:

> I knew there were disabled people around, but I never thought this would happen to me. I never even *knew* a disabled person before *I* became one. If before this happened, I saw a person in a wheelchair, I would have been uncomfortable and not known what to say.

Marie's comment highlights the fact that many nondisabled people feel uncomfortable, some extremely so, interacting with people who are disabled. As people with disabilities continue to live, work, and study in American culture, there is a need for people with and without disabilities to know how to communicate effectively.

DISABILITY AND CULTURAL COMMUNICATION

Our goal in this essay is to focus on communication between nondisabled persons and persons with disabilities as *intercultural communication* (Carbaugh, 1990). People with disabilities use a distinctive speech code that implies specific models of personhood, society, and strategic action that differ from those of nondisabled people. People with disabilities develop distinctive meanings, rules, and ways of speaking that act as a powerful resource for creating and reinforcing perceptions of cultural differences between people with and without disabilities. The distinctive verbal and nonverbal communication used by people with disabilities creates a sense of cultural identity that constitutes a unique social reality.

Several researchers have described the communication of disabled and nondisabled persons as intercultural communication (Braithwaite, 1990, 1996; Emry & Wiseman, 1987; Fox, Giles, Orbe, & Bourhis, 2000; Padden & Humphries, 1988). That is, we recognize that people with disabilities develop certain unique communicative characteristics that are not shared by the majority of nondisabled individuals. In fact, except for individuals who are born with disabilities, becoming disabled is similar to assimilating from being a member of the nondisabled majority to being a member of a minority culture (Braithwaite, 1990, 1996). The onset of a physical disability requires learning new ways of thinking and talking about oneself, and developing new ways of communicating with others.

Adopting a cultural view of disability in this chapter, we start by introducing communication problems that can arise between persons in the nondisabled culture and those in the disabled culture. Second, we discuss some of the weaknesses of the earlier approaches researchers used to understand communication between nondisabled and disabled persons. Third, we discuss research findings from interviews with people who have physical disabilities that show them engaged in a process of redefinition; that is, they critique the prevailing stereotypes about disability, and they communicate in order to redefine what it means to be part of the disabled culture. Last, we talk about important contributions both scholars and students of intercultural communication can make to improve relations between people with and without disabilities.

Challenges for Communicators Who Are Disabled

As we adopt a cultural view and attempt to understand the communicative challenges faced by people with disabilities, it is useful to understand what a disability is. We start by distinguishing between "disability" and "handicap." Even though people often use these two terms interchangeably in everyday conversation, their meanings are quite different. The two terms imply different relationships between persons with disabilities and the larger society. The term *disability* describes those limitations that a person can overcome or compensate for by some means. Crewe and Athelstan (1985) identify five "key life functions" that may be affected by disability: (a) mobility, (b) employment, (c) self-care, (d) social relationships, and (e) communication. Many individuals are able to compensate for physical challenges associated with the first three key life functions through assistive devices (e.g., using a wheelchair or cane or using hand controls to drive a car), through training (e.g., physical therapy or training on how to take care of one's personal needs), through assistance (e.g., hiring a personal care assistant), or through occupational therapy to find suitable employment.

A disability becomes a *handicap* when the physical or social environment interacts with it to impede a person in some aspect of his or her life (Crewe & Athelstan, 1985). For example, a disabled individual with paraplegia can function well in the physical environment using a wheelchair, ramps, and curb cuts, but he or she is handicapped when buildings and/or public transportation are not accessible to wheelchair users. When a society is willing and/or able to create adaptations, people with disabilities are able to lead increasingly independent lives, which is very important to their self-esteem and health (Braithwaite & Harter, 2000; DeLoach & Greer, 1981). For people with disabilities, personal control and independence are vitally important, and "maintenance of identity and self-worth are tied to the perceived ability to control the illness, minimize its intrusiveness, and be independent" (Lyons, Sullivan, Ritvo, & Coyne, 1995, p. 134). This does not mean that people with disabilities deny their physical condition, but rather that they find ways to manage it, to obtain whatever help they need, and to lead their lives (Braithwaite & Eckstein, 2003).

It is important to realize that the practical and technological accommodations that are made to adapt the physical environment for people with disabilities are useful for nondisabled people as well. Most of us are unaware of just how handicapped we would be without these physical adaptations. For example, the authors' offices are located on the upper floors of our respective office buildings, and we often get to our office via elevator. We know that stairs take up a significant amount of space in a building. Space used for the stairwell on each level takes the place of at least one office per floor. The most space-efficient way to get people to the second floor would be a climbing rope, which would necessitate only a relatively small opening on each floor. However, how many of us could climb a rope to reach our offices? Clearly, we would be handicapped without stairs or elevators. When a student is walking with a heavy load of library books, automatic door openers, ramps, curb cuts, elevators, and larger doorways become important environmental adaptations that everyone can use and appreciate.

Physical limitations become handicaps for all of us when the physical environment cannot be adapted to meet our shortcomings.

Challenges to Relationships of People with Disabilities

Although it is possible to identify and find accommodations for physical challenges associated with mobility, self-care, and employment, the two key life functions of social relationships and communication often present much more formidable challenges. It is often less difficult to detect and correct physical barriers than it is to deal with the insidious social barriers facing people with disabilities. Coleman and DePaulo (1991) label these social barriers as "psychological disabling," which is common in Western culture where "much value is placed on physical bodies and physical attractiveness" (p. 64).

When people with disabilities begin relationships with nondisabled people, the challenges associated with forming any new relationship are often greater. For nondisabled people, this may be due to lack of experience interacting with people who are disabled, which leads to high uncertainty about how to interact with a person who is disabled (Braithwaite & Labrecque, 1994). Nondisabled persons may be uncertain about what to say or how to act. They are afraid of saying or doing the wrong thing or of hurting the feelings of the person with the disability, much as Jeff was with his group member, Helen, in the example at the beginning of this essay. As a result, nondisabled persons may feel overly self-conscious, and their actions may be constrained, self-controlled, and rigid because they feel uncomfortable and uncertain (Belgrave & Mills, 1981; Braithwaite 1990; Dahnke, 1983; Higgins, 1992). Their behaviors, in turn, will appear uninterested or unaccepting to the person who is disabled. The nondisabled person will need to figure out how to communicate appropriately. Higgins (1992) pointed out that sometimes these communication attempts are not successful: "Wishing to act in a way acceptable to those with disabilities, they may unknowingly act offensively, patronizing disabled people with unwanted sympathy" (Higgins, 1992, p. 105).

High levels of uncertainty can negatively affect interaction and relationship development between people. It becomes easier to avoid that person rather than deal with not knowing what to do or say. Interestingly, researchers have found that the type of disability a person possesses does not change the way nondisabled persons react to them (Fichten, Robillard, Tagalakis, & Amsel, 1991). Although uncertainty reduction theory can be overly simplistic, especially when applied to ongoing relationships, this theory is useful in understanding some of the initial discomfort nondisabled people may feel when interacting with a stranger or early acquaintance who is disabled. Understanding the effects of uncertainty, people with disabilities work to devise ways to help nondisabled others reduce their discomfort (Braithwaite, 1990, 1996; Braithwaite & Labrecque, 1994).

Even when a nondisabled person tries to "say the right thing" and wants to communicate acceptance to the person with the disability, his or her nonverbal behavior may communicate rejection and avoidance instead (Thompson, 1982). For example, people with disabilities have observed that many nondisabled persons may keep a greater physical distance, avoid eye contact, avoid mentioning the disability, or cut the conversation short (Braithwaite, 1990, 1991, 1996). These nondisabled persons may be doing their best not to show their discomfort or not crowd the person with the disability. However, the outcome may be that the person with the disability perceives they do not want to interact. In this case, a person's disability becomes a handicap in the social environment as it can block the development of a relationship with a nondisabled person, who finds the interaction too uncomfortable.

Complicating matters, many nondisabled people hold stereotypes of people from the disabled culture. Coleman and DePaulo (1991) discuss some of these stereotypes concerning disabled people:

> For example, they often perceive them as dependent, socially introverted, emotionally unstable, depressed, hypersensitive, and easily offended, especially with regard to their disability. In addition, disabled people are often presumed to differ from nondisabled people in moral character, social skills, and political orientation. (p. 69)

Stereotypes like these do nothing but raise the level of uncertainty and discomfort the nondisabled person is experiencing.

When nondisabled persons make the effort to overcome discomfort and stereotypes to interact with people from the disabled culture, they often find themselves with conflicting expectations. On the one hand, Americans are taught to "help the handicapped." At the same time, Americans conceptualize persons as "individuals" who "have rights" and "make their own choices" (Carbaugh, 1988) and thus are taught to treat all people equally. However, when nondisabled persons encounter a person with a disability, this model of personhood creates a real dilemma. How can you both help a person and treat that person equally? For example, should you help a person with a disability open a door or try to help him up if he falls? If you are working with a blind person, should you help her find a doorway or get her lunch at the cafeteria? These dilemmas often result in high uncertainty for nondisabled people, who often end up trying to give more help than people with disabilities want or need (Braithwaite & Eckstein, 2003). In the end, it may simply seem easier to avoid situations in which you might have to interact with a disabled person rather than face feelings of discomfort and uncertainty (this is how many people react to communicating with people from other cultures). However, avoidance is not a very good solution in the end, especially if this person is to be a member of your work group or family, for example.

It should not be surprising to learn that most people with disabilities are well aware of the feelings and fears many nondisabled persons have. In fact, in research interviews, people with disabilities tell us they believe they "can just tell" who is uncomfortable around them or not. They are able to provide a great amount of detail on both the verbal and nonverbal signals of discomfort and avoidance of nondisabled persons (Braithwaite, 1990, 1996; Braithwaite & Eckstein, 2003), and they develop communication strategies to help them interact in these situations. For example, people with disabilities tell us that when they meet nondisabled persons, they will communicate in ways designed to get the discomfort "out of the way." They want the nondisabled person to treat them as a "person like anyone else," rather than focus solely on their disability (Braithwaite, 1991, 1996). For example, they may talk about topics they believe they have in common with the nondisabled person, such as cooking, sports, or music.

People with disabilities develop strategies to help them handle situations in which they may need help from nondisabled others in order to help reduce the uncertainty and discomfort of the nondisabled person (Braithwaite & Eckstein, 2003). For example, two men who are wheelchair users who need help getting out of their van in parking lots described how they plan ahead to get the help they need:

> Well, I have a mobile phone....I will call into the store and let the store manager or whoever know, "Hey, we're in a White minivan and if you look out your window, you can see us! We're two guys in wheelchairs; can you come out and help us get out of the van?"

These men plan ahead in order to avoid having to ask others for help which may place nondisabled strangers in potentially uncomfortable communication situations. Other people described situations in which they might accept help that they did not need because they understood that refusing help might increase the discomfort and uncertainty of the nondisabled person.

CHANGING THE FOCUS OF RESEARCHERS

When we first began looking at the research on communication between nondisabled and disabled persons, three problems came clearly to the forefront (for a recent summary, see Thompson, 2000). First, very little was known about the communication behavior of disabled people. Although a few researchers have studied disabled persons' communication, most of them have studied nondisabled persons' *reactions* to disabled others. These studies on "attitudes toward disabled persons" are analogous to the many studies that look at majority members' attitudes toward other "minority groups." A look at the intercultural communication literature as a whole reveals few studies from the perspective of persons representing minority groups. Although there has been some improvement over the years, there is still relatively little information on communication from the perspective of people with disabilities.

A second, related problem is that many researchers talk *about* people with disabilities, not *with* them.

People with disabilities have rarely been represented in survey data. Most often these studies consist of nondisabled people reporting their impressions of disabled people. In experimental studies, the disabled person is most often "played" by a nondisabled person using a wheelchair (and not surprisingly, most people can tell that this is not a disabled person!). There are still too few studies that give us a sense of how people with and without disabilities communicate in actual conversations.

Third, and most significant, the research has most often taken the perspective of the nondisabled person; that is, researchers tend to focus on what people with disabilities should do to make nondisabled others feel more comfortable. Coming from this perspective, researchers do not consider the effects of communication on the person with the disability. For example, several studies have found that nondisabled persons are more comfortable when people with disabilities disclose about their disability, so the researchers suggest that disabled people should self-disclose to make nondisabled others more comfortable. Braithwaite (1991) points out that these researchers have forgotten to look at how self-disclosing might affect people who are disabled. Therefore, what we see coming from much of the nondisabled-oriented research is an *ethnocentric bias* that ignores the perspective of people from the disabled culture. Although there has been more research from the perspective of disabled interactants in recent years, there are still too few empirical studies, and we are left with a very incomplete picture of the communication of people who are disabled.

In the remainder of this essay, we will present selected findings from ongoing studies conducted from the perspective of people with disabilities that help us understand the communication of people with and without disabilities from a cultural perspective. These research findings come from more than 100 in-depth interviews completed by the first author with adults who are physically disabled. All of these people have disabilities that are visible to an observer, and none of them has significant communication-related disabilities (e.g., blindness, deafness, speech impairments). The goal of the research has been to describe communication with nondisabled people from the frame of reference of people who are disabled. Doing research by talking *with* people who are disabled helps to bring out information important to them and allows people with disabilities to describe experiences from their own cultural framework.

PROCESS OF REDEFINITION

A central theme emerging from the interviews is what we call *redefinition*; that is, people who are disabled critique the prevailing stereotypes about being disabled, they create new ways of perceiving themselves and their disability, and they develop ways of communicating as a result. We were able to see three types of redefinition: (a) redefining the self as part of a "new" culture, (b) redefining the concept of disability, and (c) redefining disability for the dominant culture.

Redefining the Self as Part of the Disabled Culture

In research interviews, many people with disabilities talk about themselves as part of a minority group or a culture. For some of the interviewees, this definition crosses disability lines; that is, their definition of "disabled" includes all those who have disabilities. For others, the definition is not as broad; when they think of disability, they are thinking about others with the same type of disability they have. For example, some of the people with mobility-related disabilities also included blind and deaf people with the discussed disability, and others talked only about other wheelchair users. However narrowly or broadly they define it, many do see themselves as part of a minority culture. For example, one of the interviewees said that being disabled "is like *West Side Story*. Tony and Maria; White and Puerto Rican. They were afraid of each other; ignorant of each other's cultures. People are people." Another man explained his view:

> First of all, I belong to a subculture [of disability] because of the way I have to deal with things, being in the medical system, welfare. There is the subculture. . . . I keep one foot in the nondisabled culture and one foot in my own culture. One of the reasons I do that is so that I don't go nuts.

This man's description of the "balancing act" between cultures demonstrates that membership in the disabled culture has several similarities to the experiences of other American cultural groups. Many of the interviewees have likened their own experiences to those of other cultural groups, particularly to the experiences of American people of color. Interviewees describe the loss of status and power that comes from being disabled, and they perceive that many people are uncomfortable with them simply because they are different.

When taking a cultural view, it is important to recognize that not everyone comes to the culture the same way. Some people are born with disabilities, and others acquire them later. For those people who are not born with a disability, membership in the culture is a process that emerges over time. For some, the process is an incremental one, as in the case of a person with a degenerative disease such as multiple sclerosis that develops over many years. For a person who has a sudden-onset disability, such as breaking one's neck in an accident and "waking up a quadriplegic," moving from the majority (a "normal" person) to the minority (a person who is disabled) may happen in a matter of seconds. This sudden transition into the disabled culture presents many significant challenges of redefinition and readjustment in all facets of an individual's life (Braithwaite, 1990, 1996; Goffman, 1963).

If disability is a culture, when does one become part of that culture? Even though a person is physically disabled, how one redefines oneself, from "normal" or nondisabled to disabled, is a process that develops over time. It is important to understand that becoming physically disabled does not mean one immediately has an awareness of being part of the disabled culture (Braithwaite, 1990, 1996). In fact, for most people, adjusting to disability happens in a series of stages or phases (Braithwaite, 1990; DeLoach & Greer, 1981; Padden & Humphries, 1988). DeLoach and Greer (1981) describe three phases of an individual's adjustment to disability: (1) stigma isolation, (2) stigma recognition, and (3) stigma incorporation. Their model helps us understand what is occurring in the process of adjustment to disability as acculturation. During this process, persons with disabilities progress from the onset of their disability to membership in the disabled culture.

Imagine the experience of Mark, a college student majoring in physical education who has a car accident and wakes up to find he is paralyzed. Mark enters the first phase, *stigma isolation*, upon becoming disabled.

At this point, he is focusing on rehabilitation and all of the physical changes and challenges he is experiencing. It is likely that Mark has not yet noticed the changes in his social relationships and communication with nondisabled others.

The second phase, *stigma recognition,* begins when Mark realizes that his life and relationships have changed dramatically and he will need to find ways to minimize the effects of his disability as much as possible. Mark may try to return to normal routines and old relationships; for example, he may return to college. This can be a frustrating phase, because often things have changed more than the person at first realizes. Mark may try to reestablish his old relationships, only to find that his friends are no longer comfortable with him or that they can no longer share activities they had in common. For example, Mark may find it hard to maintain relationships with his friends from his softball team. Mark's friends, who were visiting him around the clock in the hospital, may not know what to do or say around him and may even start to avoid him. It is at this point that individuals who are disabled start to become aware that they are now interacting as members of a different culture than they were before, and they begin to assimilate the new culture into their identity and behavior (Braithwaite, 1990, 1996). Mark may notice how his friends are treating him, and he may not enjoy their company much at this point either.

This begins the third phase, what DeLoach and Greer (1981) call *stigma incorporation.* At this point, persons with a disability begin to integrate being disabled into their identity, their definition of self. The person begins to understand both the positive and negative aspects of being disabled and begins to develop ways to overcome and cope with the negative aspects of disability (DeLoach & Greer, 1981). In this stage of adjustment, people with disabilities develop ways of behaving and communicating so that they are able to function successfully in the nondisabled culture (Braithwaite, 1990, 1996). For example, after all he has experienced, Mark may find he now has an interest in psychology and sees more career opportunities there. When he switches his major, he finds he has a knack for statistics that he never knew he had, organizes a study group for his statistics class, and starts to make new friends.

Braithwaite (1996) argues that stigma incorporation represents what Morse and Johnson (1991) have labeled "regaining wellness," which occurs when individuals begin to take back control of their own lives and relationships, live as independently as possible, and adapt to new ways of doing things in their lives. Individuals develop ways of communicating with nondisabled others that help them live successfully as part of the disabled and nondisabled cultures simultaneously (Braithwaite, 1990, 1991, 1996; Braithwaite & Labrecque, 1994; Emry & Wiseman, 1987). This is what researchers call interability, intergroup communication (see Fox et al., 2000).

In this third phase, then, the person incorporates the role of disability into his or her identity and into his or her life. One man said, "You're the same person you were. You just don't do the same things you did before." Another put it this way: "If anyone refers to me as an amputee, that is guaranteed to get me madder than hell! I don't deny the leg amputation, but I am *me.* I am a whole person. *One.*" It is during this phase that people can come to terms with both the negative and positive changes in their lives. One woman expressed it this way:

> I find myself telling people that this has been the worst thing that has happened to me. It has also been one of the best things. It forced me to examine what I felt about myself...my confidence is grounded in me, not in other people. As a woman, I am not as dependent on clothes, measurements, but what's inside me.

The late actor Christopher Reeve demonstrated the concept of stigma incorporation in an interview with Barbara Walters, four months after his devastating accident:

> You also gradually discover, as I'm discovering, that your body is not you. The mind and the spirit must take over. And that's the challenge as you move from obsessing about "Why me?" and "It's not fair" and move into "Well, what is the potential?" And, now, four months down the line I see opportunities and potential I wasn't capable of seeing back in Virginia in June...genuine joy and being alive means more. Every moment is more intense than it ever was.

One implication of this example is that stigma incorporation, becoming part of the disabled culture, is a process that develops over time.

Redefining Disability

A second type of redefinition discussed by interviewees is redefining the concept of disability. For example, one interviewee explained, "People will say, 'Thank God I'm not handicapped.' And I'll say, 'Let's see, how tall are you? Tell me how you get something off that shelf up there!'" His goal in this interchange is to force others to see disability as one of many *characteristics* of a person. From this perspective, everyone is handicapped in one way or another by our height, weight, sex, ethnicity, or physical attributes, and people must work to overcome those characteristics that are handicapping. Short people may need a stool to reach something on a high shelf, and people who are very tall may be stared at and certainly will not be able to drive small, economy-size cars. Most middle-aged professors cannot climb a rope to their office and need the accommodation of stairs. Similarly, people with disabilities must adapt to the physical and social challenges presented to them. One interviewee, who conducts workshops on disability awareness, talked about how he helps nondisabled people redefine disability:

> I will say to people, "How many of you made the clothes that you're wearing?" "How many of you grew the food that you ate yesterday?" "How many of you built the house that you live in?" Nobody raises their hand. Then after maybe five of those, I'll say, "And I bet you think you're independent." And I'll say, "I'll bet you, if we could measure how independent you feel in your life versus how independent I feel in mine, then I would rate just as high as you do. And yet here I am 'depending' on people to get me dressed, undressed, on and off the john, etc. It's all in our heads, folks. Nobody is really independent." I can see them kind of go "Yeah, I never thought of it that way." And they begin to understand how it is that somebody living with this situation can feel independent. That independence really is a feeling and an attitude. It's not a physical reality.

It is also important to remember that, like any characteristic that we have, disability is context-specific. For example, a blind person will function better in a dark room than sighted persons, who will find themselves handicapped in that environment. The first author of this chapter spent several days at Gallaudet University in Washington, DC. At Gallaudet, where most students are deaf, it was the *author* who was disabled, as she needed interpreters to talk with the students there. At Gallaudet, people talk about being part of Deaf culture, but not about being disabled.

Redefining disability can also be reflected through changing the language we use to talk about disability. One interviewee objected to the label "handicapped person," preferring the label "persons with a handicapping condition." He explained why: "You emphasize that person's identity and then you do something about the condition." The goal is to speak in ways that emphasize the *person,* rather than the disability. One interviewee, who had polio as a child, rejected the term "polio victim" and preferred to label herself as "a person whose arms and legs do not function very well." Talking with disability activists around the nation, we find many different approaches to language and labels about disability. One way we have found to accentuate the person is to talk about *people* with disabilities" rather than "disabled people." The goal is to emphasize the person first, before introducing the disability, much like using the label "people of color." These are all forms of strategic action that help to create and maintain a sense of unique cultural identity among persons with disabilities (Braithwaite, 1996; Braithwaite & Thompson, 2000).

Redefining disability is also reflected in sensitizing oneself to commonly used labels for being disabled, such as being a "polio victim" or an "arthritis sufferer," or being "confined to a wheelchair" or "wheelchair bound." When trying to redefine disability as a characteristic of the person, one can change these phrases to a "person with polio," a "person who has arthritis," or a "wheelchair user." Some researchers suggest that we avoid talking about the communication of disabled and nondisabled people and instead use the phrase "interability communication" (see Fox et al., 2000). At first glance, it may be tempting to think this is no more than an attempt at political correctness, but those who understand language and culture know how strongly the words we use influence our perception of others, and theirs of us. The way people with disabilities are labeled will affect how they are seen by others and how they perceive themselves.

One of the more humorous and, at the same time, powerful examples of language regarding disability is the use of "TABs" to refer to nondisabled people. "TAB" is short for "temporarily able-bodied." One interviewee joked, "Everyone is a TAB... I just got mine earlier than you!" Being called a TAB serves to remind nondisabled persons that no one is immune from disability. From this perspective, everyone is becoming disabled! It certainly does challenge our perspective to think about that. To end our discussion of disability and language, whatever labels we choose to use, it is clear that the language both creates and reflects the view of people with disabilities and disabled culture.

In addition to redefining disability, the interviewees also redefined "assisting devices" such as wheelchairs or canes. For example, one man told the following story about redefining his prosthetic leg:

Now there were two girls about eight playing and I was in my shorts. And I'll play games with them and say "Which is my good leg?" And that gets them to thinking. Well, this one [he pats his artificial leg] is not nearly as old as the other one!

Another interviewee redefined assisting devices this way: "Do you know what a cane is? It's a portable railing! The essence of a wheelchair is a seat and wheels. Now, I don't know that a tricycle is not doing the exact same thing." Redefining assisting devices helps us see how they might mean different things to disabled and nondisabled persons. For example, several interviewees expressed frustration with people who played with their wheelchairs. One interviewee exclaimed, "This chair is not a toy, it is *part of me*. When you touch my chair, you are touching *me*." Another woman, a business executive, expanded on this by saying, "I don't know why people who push my chair feel compelled to make car sounds as they do it." In these examples, then, the problem is not the disability or the assisting device, but how one perceives the person using them.

Redefining Disability within Nondisabled Culture

Last, as people with disabilities redefine themselves as members of a culture, they also define what it means to have a disabling condition. Our experience is that people with disabilities are concerned with changing the view of disability within the larger culture (Braithwaite, 1990, 1996). Most people with disabilities we have encountered view themselves as public educators on disability issues. People told stories about taking the time to educate children and adults on what it means to be disabled. They are actively working to change the view of themselves as helpless, as victims, or as ill, and the ensuing treatment such a view brings. One wheelchair user said:

People do not consider you, they consider the chair first. I was in a store with my purchases on my lap and money on my lap. The clerk looked at my companion and not at me and said, "Cash or charge?"

This incident with the clerk represents a story we heard from *every* person in some form or another, just as it happened to Jonathan and his date at the beginning of this chapter. One woman, who has multiple sclerosis and uses a wheelchair, told of shopping for lingerie with her husband accompanying her. When they were in front of the lingerie counter, the clerk repeatedly talked only to her husband, saying, "And what size does she want?" The woman told her the size, and the clerk looked at the husband and said, "And what color does she want?"

Persons with disabilities recognize that nondisabled persons often see them as disabled first and as a person second (if at all). The most common theme expressed by people with disabilities in all of the interviews is that they want to be *seen and treated as a person first*. One man explained what he thought was important to remember: "A lot of people think that handicapped people are 'less than' and I find that it's not true at all....Abling people, giving them their power back, empowering them." The interviewees rejected those situations or behaviors that would not lead them to be seen. A man with muscular dystrophy talked about the popular Labor Day telethon:

I do not believe in those goddamned telethons... they're horrible, absolutely horrible. They get into the self-pity, you know, and disabled folk do not need that. Hit people in terms of their attitudes then try to deal with and process their feelings. And the telethons just go for the heart and leave it there.

One man suggested what he thought was a more useful approach:

> What I am concerned with is anything that can do away with the "us" versus "them" distinction. Well, you and I are anatomically different, but we're two human beings! And at the point, we can sit down and communicate eyeball to eyeball; the quicker you do that, the better!

Individually and collectively, people with disabilities do identify themselves as part of a culture. They are involved in a process of redefinition of themselves, and of disability. They desire to help nondisabled people understand and internalize a redefinition of people of the disabled culture as "persons first."

CONCLUSION

The research we have discussed highlights the usefulness of viewing disability from a cultural perspective. People with disabilities do recognize themselves as part of a culture, and understanding communication and relationships from this perspective sheds new light on the communication challenges that exist. Some time ago, Emry and Wiseman (1987) first argued for the usefulness of intercultural training about disability issues. They called for unfreezing old attitudes about disability and refreezing new ones. Our experience indicates that people with disabilities would agree with this goal.

We have asked people with disabilities whether they had training in communication during or after their rehabilitation. We anticipated that they would have received information and training to prepare them for changes in their communication and relationships after becoming disabled. We speculated that this education would be especially critical for those who experience sudden-onset disabilities because their self-concepts and all of their relationships would undergo such radical changes. Surprisingly, we found that less than 30 percent of the interviewees received disability-related communication training.

We believe intercultural communication scholars can help design research and training that could help make the transition from majority to minority an easier one (Braithwaite, 1990; Emry & Wiseman, 1987). We are encouraged by some advances that are taking place in educational and organizational settings (e.g., Colvert & Smith, 2000; Herold, 2000; Worley, 2000). We also see the need for research that expands to different types of disabilities—for example, for those with invisible disabilities (e.g., emphysema, diabetes) and socially stigmatized disabilities such as HIV. Overall, we see important contributions for communication scholars to make. When Braithwaite and Thompson (2000) published their *Handbook of Communication and People with Disabilities,* they were struck by how many researchers in communication studies are now studying disability communication and how many of these scholars are disabled. Clearly, the future does look brighter than when we began our work in disability and communication some years back. However, we still have a long way to go.

We do believe that students of intercultural communication should have an advantage in being able to better understand the perspective of people with disabilities, as presented in this essay. We hope that you will be able to adapt and apply intercultural communication concepts and skills to interactions with persons in the disabled culture. We believe that people with disabilities themselves will better understand their own experience if they study intercultural communication and come to understand the cultural aspects of disability.

In closing, taking an intercultural perspective on communication and disability culture leads us to suggest the following practical proscriptions and prescriptions.

DON'T:

- *Avoid* communication with people who are disabled simply because you are uncomfortable or unsure.
- *Assume* that people with disabilities cannot speak for themselves or do things for themselves.
- *Force* your help on people with disabilities.
- *Use terms* such as "handicapped," "physically challenged," "crippled," "victim," and the like, unless requested to do so by people with disabilities.
- *Assume* that a disability defines who a person is.

DO:
- *Remember* that people with disabilities have experienced others' discomfort before and likely understand how you might be feeling.
- *Assume* that people with disabilities can do something unless they communicate otherwise.
- *Let people with disabilities tell you* if they want something, what they want, and when they want it. If a person with a disability refuses your help, don't go ahead and help anyway.
- *Use terms* such as "*people* with disabilities" rather than "disabled people." The goal is to stress the *person first,* before the disability.
- *Treat* people with disabilities as *persons first,* recognizing that you are not dealing with a disabled person but with a *person* who *has* a disability. This means actively seeking the humanity of the person with whom you are speaking, and focusing on individual characteristics instead of superficial physical appearance. Without diminishing the significance of a person's physical disability, make a real effort to focus on all the many other aspects of that person as you communicate.

Note

1. The quotes and anecdotes in this chapter come from in-depth interviews with people who have visible physical disabilities. The names of the participants in these interviews have been changed to protect their privacy.

References

Belgrave, F. Z., & Mills, J. (1981). Effect upon desire for social interaction with a physically disabled person of mentioning the disability in different contexts. *Journal of Applied Social Psychology, 11,* 44–57.

Braithwaite, D. O. (1990). From majority to minority: An analysis of cultural change from nondisabled to disabled. *International Journal of Intercultural Relations, 14,* 465–483.

Braithwaite, D. O. (1991). "Just how much did that wheelchair cost?": Management of privacy boundaries by persons with disabilities. *Western Journal of Speech Communication, 55,* 254–274.

Braithwaite, D. O. (1996). "Persons first": Expanding communicative choices by persons with disabilities. In E. B. Ray (Ed.), *Communication and disenfranchisement: Social health issues and implications* (pp. 449–464). Mahwah, NJ: Erlbaum.

Braithwaite, D. O., & Eckstein, N. (2003). Reconceptualizing supportive interactions: How persons with disabilities communicatively manage assistance. *Journal of Applied Communication Research, 31,* 1–26.

Braithwaite, D. O., & Harter, L. (2000). Communication and the management of dialectical tensions in the personal relationships of people with disabilities. In D. O. Braithwaite & T. L. Thompson (Eds.), *Handbook of communication and people with disabilities: Research and application* (pp. 17–36). Mahwah, NJ: Erlbaum.

Braithwaite, D. O., & Labrecque, D. (1994). Responding to the Americans with Disabilities Act: Contributions of interpersonal communication research and training. *Journal of Applied Communication Research, 22,* 287–294.

Braithwaite, D. O., & Thompson, T. L. (Eds.). (2000). *Handbook of communication and people with disabilities: Research and application.* Mahwah, NJ: Erlbaum.

Carbaugh, D. (1988). *Talking American.* Norwood, NJ: Ablex.

Carbaugh, D. (Ed.). (1990). *Cultural communication and intercultural contact.* Hillsdale, NJ: Erlbaum.

Coleman, L. M., & DePaulo, B. M. (1991). Uncovering the human spirit: Moving beyond disability and "missed" communications. In N. Coupland, H. Giles, & J. M. Wiemann (Eds.), *Miscommunication and problematic talk* (pp. 61–84). Newbury Park, CA: Sage.

Colvert, A. L., & Smith, J. W. (2000). What is reasonable: Workplace communication and people who are disabled. In D. O. Braithwaite & T. L. Thompson (Eds.), *Handbook of communication and people with disabilities: Research and application* (pp. 141–158). Mahwah, NJ: Erlbaum.

Crewe, N., & Athelstan, G. (1985). *Social and psychological aspects of physical disability.* Minneapolis: University of Minnesota, Department of Independent Study and University Resources.

Cunningham, C., & Coombs, N. (1997). *Information access and adaptive technology.* Phoenix, AZ: Oryx Press.

Dahnke, G. L. (1983). Communication and handicapped and nonhandicapped persons: Toward a deductive theory. In M. Burgoon (Ed.), *Communication yearbook* 6 (pp. 92–135). Beverly Hills, CA: Sage.

DeLoach, C., & Greer, B. G. (1981). *Adjustment to severe physical disability: A metamorphosis.* New York: McGraw-Hill.

Emry, R., & Wiseman, R. L. (1987). An intercultural understanding of nondisabled and disabled persons' communication. *International Journal of Intercultural Relations, 11,* 7–27.

Fichten, C. S., Robillard, K., Tagalakis, V., & Amsel, R. (1991). Casual interaction between college students with various disabilities and their nondisabled peers: The internal dialogue. *Rehabilitation Psychology, 36,* 3–20.

Fox, S. A., Giles, H., Orbe, M., & Bourhis, R. (2000). Inter-ability communication: Theoretical perspectives. In D. O. Braithwaite & T. L. Thompson (Eds.), *Handbook of communication and people with disabilities: Research and application* (pp. 193–222). Mahwah, NJ: Erlbaum.

Goffman, E. (1963). *Stigma: Notes on the management of spoiled identity*. New York: Simon & Schuster.

Herold, K.P. (2000). Communication strategies in employment interviews for applicants with disabilities. In D. O. Braithwaite & T. L. Thompson (Eds.), *Handbook of communication and people with disabilities: Research and application* (pp. 159–175). Mahwah, NJ: Erlbaum.

Higgins, P. C. (1992). *Making disability: Exploring the social transformation of human variation*. Springfield, IL: Charles C. Thomas.

Lyons, R. F., Sullivan, M. J. L., Ritvo, P. G., & Coyne, J. C. (1995). *Relationships in chronic illness and disability*. Thousand Oaks, CA: Sage.

Morse, J. M., & Johnson, J. L. (1991). *The illness experience: Dimensions of suffering*. Newbury Park, CA: Sage.

Padden, C., & Humphries, T. (1988). *Deaf in America: Voices from a culture*. Cambridge, MA: Harvard University Press.

Pardeck, J. T. (1998). *Social work after the Americans with Disabilities Act: New challenges and opportunities for social service professionals*. Westport, CT: Auburn House.

Thompson, T. L. (1982). Disclosure as a disability management strategy: A review and conclusions. *Communication Quarterly, 30,* 196–202.

Thompson, T. L. (2000). A history of communication and disability research: The way we were. In D. O. Braithwaite & T. L. Thompson (Eds.), *Handbook of communication and people with disabilities: Research and application* (pp. 1–14). Mahwah, NJ: Erlbaum.

Worley, D. W. (2000). Communication and students with disabilities on college campuses. In D. O. Braithwaite & T. L. Thompson (Eds.), *Handbook of communication and people with disabilities: Research and application* (pp. 125–139). Mahwah, NJ: Erlbaum.

Concepts and Questions

1. How does becoming disabled lead to changes in a person's communication patterns?
2. What are some of the cultural problems inherent in communication between nondisabled people and people with disabilities?
3. Why do Braithwaite and Braithwaite believe you should learn about the communication patterns of people with disabilities? What purpose will be served by your knowing this information?
4. Give examples of what the Braithwaites mean when they say that "the distinctive verbal and nonverbal communication used by persons with disabilities creates a sense of cultural identity that constitutes a unique social reality"?
5. How would you distinguish between *disability* and *handicap*?
6. Why is nonverbal communication a factor when non-disabled people and people with disabilities engage in communication?
7. Enumerate the problems Braithwaite and Braithwaite describe relating to the current research being conducted on communication of persons with disabilities.
8. What is meant by the term *redefinition*?
9. How would you answer the following question: If disability is a culture, then when does one become part of that culture?

Gender and Communication: Sex Is More Than a Three-Letter Word

JUDY C. PEARSON

Are men or women more likely to use the words *puce, aquamarine, ecru,* and *mauve*? If a speaker discussed carburetors, pistons, overhead cams, and cylinders, would you guess that the speaker was male or female? Is the chief executive officer of a Fortune 500 company more likely to be a man or a woman? In almost any organization, are men or women more likely to have jobs as secretaries? Every day we make observations and predictions about people's sex on the basis of their communicative behaviors and the roles they have in our culture. Sex and communication is not a topic with which you are unfamiliar, although you may not realize that a great deal of theorizing and research has gone into this topic.

While an interest in the relationship between sex and communication may be traced to the beginning of this century (Stopes, 1908), the past 15 years have produced the bulk of the research on *gender* and communication. The relationships among women, men, and communication are complex and bear careful scrutiny. This essay is concerned with some of the issues that allow us to conclude that "sex is more than a three-letter word" in the field of communication.

HOW ARE SEX, GENDER, AND COMMUNICATION RELATED?

To understand how sex, gender, and communication are related, we must understand the history of the research in this area. The term *sex* is used to refer to biological differences between people. Before the mid-1970s, studies in communication that considered sex differences simply categorized people on the basis of their biological differences and observed differences in communicative behavior. For example, we observed that women smile more frequently than do men (Argyle, 1975), that men speak more loudly than do women (Markel, Prebor, & Brandt, 1972), that women are more likely to be observed or watched than are men (Argyle & Williams, 1969), and that men are more likely to interrupt others than are women (Zimmerman & West, 1975). Our use of the word *gender* is deliberate and important for our discussion.

In 1974, Sandra Bem created a new conceptualization of sex, as far as roles are concerned. Before this time, people were categorized on masculinity and femininity measures as being more or less of each of these measures. In other words, masculinity was placed at one end of the continuum and femininity was placed at the other end, as illustrated in Figure 1. An individual, through a series of questions, is categorized as masculine or feminine or somewhere in between. We should note that the more masculine one indicated that he or she was, the less feminine he or she was. An individual could not be high in both masculinity and femininity or low in both categories.

In private conversations, Bem explained that she felt limited by this conceptualization of masculinity and femininity. She perceived of herself as possessing a number of masculine traits *and* a number of feminine traits. In other words, she felt that she should score high in both masculinity and femininity. Instead, when she was categorized, her score indicated that she was somewhere between masculine and feminine and was thus viewed as neither feminine nor masculine.

Bem (1974) created a new way to conceive of and measure sex roles in the Bem Sex Role Inventory. She suggested that masculinity and femininity are separate dimensions and that one might be high in

Courtesy of Judy C. Pearson. This original essay first appeared in the fifth edition of this book. All rights reserved. Permission to reprint must be obtained from the author and the publisher. Judy C. Pearson is Professor of Communication at North Dakota State University.

Figure 1

Masculinity	Feminity

Figure 2

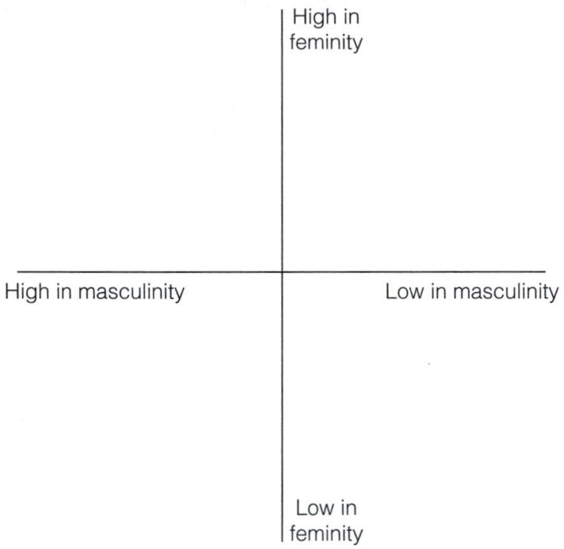

masculinity and low in femininity (masculine), low in masculinity and high in femininity (feminine), high in masculinity and high in femininity (androgynous), or low in masculinity and low in femininity (undifferentiated). This view is depicted in Figure 2.

Although Bem's change may appear to be a fairly simplistic one, it radically altered the way women's and men's roles were categorized. At first, women and men were viewed as different because of biological traits alone. Then they could be categorized as masculine, feminine, or in between. Finally, Bem suggested that people should be categorized on the extent to which they internalize society's standards for masculine and feminine behaviors. Thus a biological male may be highly feminine or a biological female may be very masculine. When sex roles became a psychological, rather than a physical, variable, we began to talk about gender rather than sex. Sex still refers to biological differences between people; gender refers to internalized predispositions to masculine and feminine roles. As you will see, understanding the difference between sex and gender is critical for our understanding of gender and communication.

Communication Creates Gender

Communication is related to gender in two ways. First, to a large extent, *communication creates gender.* How does communication create gender? Our communicative exchanges tell us what our roles are, and they encourage or discourage us from internalizing predispositions relating to masculinity or femininity.

Early theorists like William James, Charles Cooley, John Dewey, and I. A. Thomas all contributed to a theory that George Herbert Mead (1934) originated. That theory—symbolic interactionism—has important implications for us. Mead felt that people were actors, not reactors. He suggested that people develop through three stages.

The preparatory stage includes the stage in which infants imitate others by mirroring. The toddler may wash a surface, put on mommy's or daddy's shoes, or pat the dog. The child does not necessarily understand the imitated acts.

In the *play stage,* the child actually plays the roles of others. She may pretend to be mommy, daddy, the postal carrier, a fire fighter, a nurse, or a doctor. Each role is played *independently*; the behaviors are not integrated into a single set of role behaviors. In other words, the child does not play a super-woman who is a mother, a wife, a runner, an airplane pilot, a writer, and a teacher.

In the *game stage,* the child responds simultaneously in a generalized way to several others. The child generalizes a composite role by considering all others' definitions of self. The person thus develops a unified role from which he or she sees the self. This perception is the overall way that other people see the individual. People unify their self-concepts by internalizing this composite view. This self-picture emerges from years of symbolically interacting, or communicating, with others.

Your integrated self will tend toward the behaviors others encourage you to perform and will tend away from behaviors that others discourage you from performing. From birth, men and women are treated differently because of their genitalia. We dress male and female babies in different kinds and colors of clothing. Parents respond differently to male and female infants (Bell & Carver, 1980). We describe male and female babies with different adjectives: boys are strong, solid, and independent, whereas girls are loving, cute, and sweet. People describe identical behavior on the part of infants differently if they are told the infant is a boy or a girl (Condry & Condry, 1976). Preschool children observe commercials and cartoons on television, listen to stories, and play with toys that depict "appropriate" sex roles. In many ways, people are treated differently because of their sex.

Communicative Behavior Is Related to Gender

A second way that communication and gender are related is that our specific use of verbal and nonverbal codes is highly related to gender. You know that different roles invite different languages. For example, terms like *bits, RAM, ROM, motherboard, modem, memory, monitor, hard disk, CPT, CRT,* and *CPU,* are common in the language about computers. Similarly, words like *coma, carcinoma, cardiovascular, chemotherapy, colostomy,* and *capillary* are common in the language of medicine.

Masculine and feminine individuals use different languages, and they put their words together differently. Maybe you never thought about the fact that sex roles place people in different subcultures. Psychological gender roles also place people in separate subcultures just as sex, race, and age do. All subcultures create special languages. Adolescents, for instance, purposefully talk in ways that their parents do not understand. ("Cool" and "neat" are replaced by "tubular," "grody to the max," "I'm so sure," and "mega-hard," which in turn are supplanted by "rad" and "wick.")

Masculine and feminine people similarly establish their own ways of talking as a result of being members of separate subcultures. Why do subcultures establish separate languages? We can offer at least two reasons: (1) A special language is developed to conduct the subculture's function or business and (2) a special language allows a subculture to symbolize its identity as a subculture. Feminine people may be more likely to know color terms such as *ecru* and *mauve* because they use these terms in their work, just as masculine people may use terms related to motors and engines in their work. Furthermore, feminine individuals may over-use adjectives to demonstrate that they are part of a feminine subgroup; masculine individuals may rely upon four-letter swear words to demonstrate their subculture.

A caveat is in order. Even when subcultures develop separate languages, their members often understand the language of the other subculture. They may even use the alternative language in their own subculture. For example, we may associate traditional four-letter swear words with masculine individuals, but feminine individuals understand these terms and sometimes use them as well—but in the exclusive company of other feminine persons. Masculine individuals may not touch each other in a caring way in mixed company, but they certainly rely on hugging, stroking, and touching on the football field.

Similarly, people may feel free to engage in out-of-role behavior when they are within the safety of an established relationship, but they will not engage in out-of-role behavior in the company of mere acquaintances and strangers. Dindia, Fitzpatrick, and Williamson (1986), for instance, showed that wives are likely to behave in a submissive manner with males other than their husbands whereas they behave in a dominant way with their spouses.

What are a few of the differences between the two subcultures? Bonaguro and Pearson (1986) determined that feminine individuals are more animated than masculine individuals and those with undifferentiated identities, and that feminine types are more relaxed than are androgynous and masculine types. Feminine individuals are less argumentative than are masculine individuals (Rancer & Dierks-Stewart, 1985). Feminine types are likely to be relational, while masculine types are apt to be goal-oriented (Serafini & Pearson, 1984). The feminine individual is generally higher than her masculine counterpart in empathy, caring, and nurturing (McMillan, Clifton, McGrath, & Gale, 1977). Finally, feminine females report that they disclose personal information about themselves less frequently than do androgynous females, whereas masculine men have lower disclosure scores than do androgynous men (Greenblatt, Hasenauer, & Freimuth, 1980). (For a comprehensive review of gender and sex differences in communication behaviors, see Pearson, 1985.)

WHAT PROBLEMS EXIST?

As you might guess, the subject of gender and communication is in upheaval. There are at least three problems that account for our difficulty in coming to grips with effective and appropriate communication across these subcultures. First, most people still assume that sex and gender are synonyms. Second, we often confuse our *perceptions* of behavior with actual behavior. Third, both communication and U.S. culture have a masculine bias.

Sex and Gender Are Presumed to Be Synonymous

The first problem is that while sex and gender are highly related (men are more likely to be masculine than are women, and women are more likely to be feminine than are men), they are not identical. Furthermore, a great number of people are androgynous (possess both male and female qualities) or undifferentiated (possess neither male nor female qualities). The concepts of sex and gender were never identical, and the two have become increasingly disparate in recent times. Let us consider the impact that recent changes have made on the concepts of sex and gender.

Our world and the roles of women and men in it are undergoing rapid change, but our interactions do not acknowledge these changes. To a great extent, we tend to live in the past. We behave on the basis of the naturalistic fallacy: What is (or has been) is what should be. For example, if you ask someone in Iowa how farming should be done, he or she will tell you that it should be done on relatively small plots of land owned by individual families. If you ask someone in New York who should control the major networks, he or she will tell you it should be persons trained in telecommunications and broadcast journalism. But family farms are nearly a thing of the past, and NBC and ABC are owned, operated, and controlled by large multinational corporations.

Our world has changed, and this change makes it impossible for us to know everyone we must deal with. More and more often we communicate with people on some basis other than an interpersonal one, such as on the basis of cultural and sociological information, and we categorize people simplistically on the basis of surface or demographic cues (biological sex) rather than on the basis of unique and idiosyncratic personal characteristics, including their gender role (knowing them interpersonally).

In days gone by, people often communicated only with members of their own communities and families. People knew a great deal about those with whom they interacted. They would know that one should not talk about sex with one's aunt, that one should hug one's grandparents, and that one should treat one's teachers with respect. People seldom traveled to other cities, states, and nations. Today such travel is commonplace. People are called upon to interact quickly with strangers and acquaintances in a wide variety of new settings.

We make errors in our assessments of other people in brief encounters for a variety of reasons. For instance, we may rely upon implicit personality theory, which suggests that our own experiences and assumptions about human nature are shared by others. For example, one may assume that everyone has a high achievement motivation and competes to win, not understanding that many people develop a fear of success. We may make the fundamental attribution error, which is underestimating situational influences on behavior and attributing behavior to internal personal characteristics alone. As an example, one may assume that a bartender is cold and closed-mouthed, not recognizing that her job description and her negative past experiences with others in bars dictate such behavior.

In our interactions with women and men, we are most likely to err, however, on the basis of four other errors in person perception. First, when we stereotype, we assume, for example, that all men are cold and unfeeling. Second, when we rely upon social roles, we assume, for example, that all mothers are nurturing. Third, when we make logical errors (assume that because a person has one characteristic, he or she will have other characteristics that "go together"), we assume, for example, that women who dress like "ladies" will also talk like them. Fourth, when we engage in wishful thinking (seeing others as we would like them to be rather than as they are), we assume, for example, that our husbands will be like our fathers.

Perceptions of Behavior Are Confused with Actual Behavior

The second problem is that we often confuse our perceptions of behavior with actual behavior. In other words, we may view a given behavior of a woman as negative, but we may judge the same behavior to be positive when a man exhibits it. For instance, a businesswoman may be labeled "aggressive, pushy, and argumentative," whereas her male counterpart who exhibits the same behavior may be viewed as "ambitious, assertive, and independent." Countless studies have demonstrated that when women and men engage in identical behavior, the behavior is devalued for the woman. For example, Goldberg (1968), in a classic study, demonstrated that when an essay was attributed to either a woman or a man, the same essay was given a higher grade when respondents believed it was written by a man and a lower grade when respondents believed it was written by a woman. Furthermore, both women and men demonstrated their prejudice toward women.

One reason that we confuse perceptions of behaviors with actual behaviors comes from the literature on gender and communication itself. In all areas of inquiry, we must ask the question that Whitney Houston made famous in her song, "How will I know?" In the area of social science, and especially in the area of gender and communication, this question is particularly critical. Social science research can rely on self-perceptions, perceptions of others, or on actual observed behavior. In some cases, researchers have relied upon the perceptions of others to determine how women and men communicate. For instance, people may be asked if they believe that women or men speak more often. Although relatively recent behavioral research suggests that men talk more than women (Swacker, 1975), most people, when asked, guess that women talk more than men. Similarly, in research on whether masculine or feminine managers are viewed as more successful, researchers oftentimes asked subordinates and others in the work environment for their opinions. Although these perceptions may be valuable, they may also be value-laden, relying more on stereotypes than on actual observations.

Some research on gender and communication has relied upon individual's self-reports or self-perceptions. People have reported on their own communicative behaviors, but as we have learned recently, our self-reports may be based more on our notions of the ideal, or on a perfect example, than on our actual behaviors (Hample, 1984; Pavitt & Haight, 1986). Or, we may be responding on the basis of social desirability. In addition, we may forget how we actually behaved because of the passage of time (Sulloway & Christensen, 1983).

Recently, some research has turned to indices of actual behavior. In other words, we have begun to measure people's actual communicative behaviors to determine the extent to which women and men communicate differently or similarly. Although these research reports are fewer in number than are the studies that have relied upon self-perceptions or self-report data, they suggest that the differences between women and men may be fewer than we once believed, that they may be based on factors other than sex as we have suggested, and that the rationale offered for the differences may be different from what we originally posited.

For example, if one asks most people if women or men exhibit more hostility and use more profanity and expletives, they would probably guess men. However Staley (1978) tested that commonsense view. She asked students between the ages of 18 and 47 to complete a questionnaire that listed a series of emotional situations. In each case, she asked the respondents to report the expletive they would use, to report the expletive they predicted a member of the opposite sex would use, and to define each expletive they provided. Surprisingly, she found that men and women averaged about the same number of expletives per questionnaire. She did find a great difference in predicted responses, however. Men predicted the use of far fewer expletives for women, and women predicted the use of far more expletives for men. Both women and men judged the use of expletives by women as weaker than males' use, even when the terms were identical. Staley thus demonstrated that women and men may be more alike than different on the usage of expletives; nonetheless, people still perceive of women's and men's behavior as being different.

None of these methods of learning about gender and communication is inherently superior to the others, but we should note that each one provides us with different answers. Sometimes we want to know how an individual perceives of himself or herself.

In some cases, we may find others' perceptions of people important. Often we want to determine actual behavior. We always want to make sure that our means of making assessments is consistent with our research goal. Perhaps more importantly we want to ensure that people do not confuse their perceptions of behaviors with actual behaviors.

Our Culture and Our Communication Evidence a Masculine Bias

The third problem that is relevant to gender and communication is that both communication and our culture have a male bias. Our culture and our communication exhibit masculinity. An increasing amount of research demonstrates that the symbols we use to communicate are man-made. The language that we use was created primarily by men, for men. The words we have available reflect male experiences and they encourage male domination.

Kramarae (1981) proposed that female/male communication can be best understood in terms of the muted group theory. This theory suggests that women are a muted (or silenced) group because of their exclusion from the creation of human symbols. Basically, she explains that males perceive the world and then create symbols to represent their experiences. Because women's experiences are different, and because women are not allowed to create an alternative set of symbols, women are muted. Eventually, women learn to use the male symbols, but the symbols are useful only insofar as women are willing to see the world through "male eyes."

What are some obvious examples of man-made words? We might consider the language of business. Although the business world may be viewed as an area that is open to both women and men, when you listen carefully you find that it is primarily a "male club." Many business cliches, for example, come straight from sports—a decidedly male activity. If you want to be successful, you have to "keep your eye on the ball," be a "boy wonder," "keep your head down," be a "team player," be a "pinch hitter," and "tackle the job." What do you avoid? You don't want to be "in the penalty box," "under fire," "under the gun," "in the cellar," be a "disqualified player," have a "jock mentality," or be "caught with your pants down."

We can also build the argument that language is male-dominated when we deal with so-called generic pronouns. When we talk about people in general, which pronoun do we choose? Most people use the male form to refer to both men and women. We use "he," "his," and "him" to refer to men *and* to refer to both men and women. We use "she" and "her" to refer to women, but we do not use these words to refer to both women and men. Why is it that the latter terms are not equally appropriate?

Language does not serve all of its users equally well. Women are left out far more often than men, but both men and women find that language limits the expression of their experiences. Students of gender and communication have created *sexlets,* which are "sniglets" about male and female experiences for which our language has no single words. The following examples are made-up "words" that are not currently in everyday use. First, suggestions from the women: "Sexpectations": when a man takes a woman out for a nice dinner, maybe a movie, and then expects sex at the end of the evening; and "PMS'ed off": the frustration a woman feels with male friends who always claim that when a woman is angry, she must be expecting her period. The men suggested: "Chronoloneliness": how one male felt when he had not seen his girlfriend for a long time; and "condomnesia": when you finally get your girlfriend ready for the big moment, she asks if you have protection, and you must admit that you forgot.

Our research has been similarly flawed in that it has encouraged a masculine bias. The U.S. culture, as we have observed, is one that exhibits masculinity. In other words, male values, attitudes, and perspectives dominate. Our government, our industry, and most of our public organizations are headed by men. Even our private associations, including friendships and family life, are dominated by men. As a result the investigations of women in male-dominated cultures have been, at the very least, biased. Wood, McMahan, and Stacks (1984) observe:

the contexts for the bulk of study on women's communication are invariably male contexts: task groups, businesses, organizations. The tendency to study masculine activities and environments, then, achieves two outcomes. First, it constitutes an implicit argument for the importance of masculine issues, enterprises, and settings and a corresponding argument for the unimportance of feminine concerns, activities, and contexts. Second, it distorts descriptions, assessment, and understanding of women's communication by consistently observing it in alien environments. (p. 41)

The social settings of our inquiries, then, have encouraged the continuation of a male-dominated social order. Deaux (1984) observes, "Some tasks may not be neutral arenas in which to test possible differences" (p. 107). We should be wise to heed the words of Kramarae (1981), who observed "Social scientific research is not impersonal, apolitical, and factual, but interpretive" (p. vi).

HOW CAN WE SOLVE THE PROBLEMS OF COMMUNICATION AND GENDER?

Can we solve the problems we face in the area of communication and gender? We can if we are willing to engage in three practices. First, we must separate our perceptions of ourselves and of other people from the behaviors that we, or they, exhibit. Second, we need to view sex and gender as distinctly different constructs. Third, we need to understand the role of the masculine culture and the way it shapes both our perceptions and our behaviors.

Separate Perceptions of Behaviors from Actual Behaviors

We must recognize that people's perceptions of another person's behavior may vary dramatically. At the very minimum, we must understand how our own attitudes, values, and perceptions intervene when we observe, predict, and evaluate the behavior of others.

The area of organizational communication provides an example. Within the past decade, researchers have begun to examine the role of women as leaders and managers. In general, in organizational research, we tend to use outcome variables such as productivity to determine the influence of independent variables such as information availability, upward and downward communication, and openness. However, when we investigate the influence of sex roles in the organization, we use people's *perceptions* of women in their positions. For instance, we do not study whether productivity increases or decreases when women serve as managers; instead we ask employees whether they prefer to work for a man or a woman. Given the current state of affairs, it is not difficult to guess which sex they prefer.

Research on communication and sex is no better. Too often we assume that masculine communication is standard. In other words, we begin with a masculine model of communication and then we look at women's communication to see how it differs from that model. Or, we study women's communication in clearly masculine contexts such as the masculine workplace. We also assume that women's behaviors determine their effectiveness. In other words, we don't take into account that women are often devalued simply because they are women. The most competent woman may be viewed negatively simply because she is a woman.

View Sex and Gender as Distinctive Constructs

Second, we need to view sex and gender as distinctly different constructs. We are in the midst of a paradigmatic shift concerning sex and gender. Intercultural communication students are familiar with the notion of "passing," in which members of lower status groups sometimes attempt to pass as members of higher status groups. For instance, light-skinned blacks sometimes attempt to pass as white. In the same way, many women in contemporary society have attempted to pass as men. A number of successful female managers have done so by adopting masculine characteristics. Similarly, female graduate students often try to outperform their male counterparts. In the professional ranks, too, including medicine and law, women are regularly more masculine in their behavior than are the men with whom they work.

There are now more dual-career couples in our society than there are single-career couples. While some of us applaud the fact that women now have opportunities to work outside the home as well as within it, we should recognize what is occurring. To a large extent, dual-career marriages are made up of two masculine individuals. Biologically, the marriages include a man and a woman, but behaviorally, the marriages include two masculine types.

Changes in our social groupings encourage us to consider sex and gender as separate constructs. We cannot assume that women are feminine or that men are masculine. In some instances, just the opposite is the case.

Understand the Role of the Masculine Culture

Third, we need to understand the role of the masculine culture and how it shapes both our perceptions and our behaviors. Men are in charge of our culture, and masculine values and traits are generally viewed as superior to feminine values and traits. When women pass as men, they gain momentary success in the workplace at low-level positions, but they may never become CEOs of Fortune 500 companies. Furthermore, they may lose far more by discarding their feminine side than they gain in the workplace. Masculine behaviors have been shown to lead to physical destruction and disabilities. For example, heart attacks, strokes, and many forms of cancer are more prevalent in men than in women. As women have gained opportunities to compete with men, their rates of death from these diseases have increased. We must understand the inherent sexism that defines the U.S. culture and the values that are associated with the masculine perspective. Furthermore, we must consider whether we wish to continue the status quo.

SUMMARY

This essay has discussed some of the theorizing and research that has gone on in the area of communication and gender. You have seen how gender and communication are related, the problems that occur in considering sex, gender, and communication, and how we might solve some of those problems in our everyday interactions as well as in our research. At this point, we hope you agree that, in communication, sex is more than a three-letter word.

BIBLIOGRAPHY

Argyle, M. *Bodily Communication.* New York: International Universities Press (1975).

Argyle, M., & M. Williams. "Observer or Observed? A Reversible Perspective in Person Perception." *Sociometry* 32 (1969), 396–412.

Bell, N. J., & W. Carver. "A Reevaluation of Gender Label Effects: Expectant Mothers' Responses to Infants." *Child Development* 51 (1980), 925–927.

Bem, S. "The Measurement of Psychological Androgyny." *Journal of Consulting and Clinical Psychology* 42 (1974), 155–162.

Bonaguro, E. W., & J. C. Pearson. *The Relationship between Communicator Style, Argumentativeness, and Gender.* Paper presented to the Speech Communication Association, Chicago, IL (November 1986).

Condry, J., & S. Condry. "Sex Differences: A Study of the Eye of the Beholder." *Child Development* 47 (1976), 812–819.

Deaux, K. "From Individual Differences to Social Categories." *American Psychologist* (1984), 105–116.

Dindia, K., M. A. Fitzpatrick, & R. Williamson. *Communication and Control in Spouse Versus Stranger Interaction.* Paper presented to the Speech Communication Association, Chicago, IL (November 1986).

Goldberg, P. "Are Women Prejudiced against Women?" *Transaction* 6 (1968), 28.

Greenblatt, L., J. Hasenauer, & V. Freimuth. "Psychological Sex Type and Androgyny in a Study of Communication Variables." *Human Communication Research* 6 (1980), 117–129.

Hample, D. "On the Use of Self-Reports." *Journal of the American Forensic Association* 20 (1984), 140–153.

Kramarae, C. *Women and Men Speaking.* Rowley, MA: Newbury House Publishers (1981).

Markel, N., L. Prebor, & J. Brandt. "Biosocial Factors in Dyadic Communication: Sex and Speaking Intensity." *Journal of Personality and Social Responsibility* 23 (1972), 686–690.

McMillan, J., A. K. Clifton, D. McGrath, & W. S. Gale. "Women's Language: Uncertainty or Interpersonal Sensitivity and Emotionality?" *Sex Roles* 3 (1977), 545–559.

Mead, G. H. *Mind, Self, and Society.* Chicago: University of Chicago Press (1934).

Pavitt, C., & L. Haight. "Implicit Theories of Communicative Competence: Situational and Competence Level Differences in Judgments of Prototype and Target." *Communication Monographs* 53 (1986), 221–235.

Pearson, J. C. *Gender and Communication.* Dubuque, IA: William C. Brown Company (1985).

Rancer, A., & K. Dierks-Stewart. "The Influence of Sex and Sex-Role Orientation on Trait Argumentativeness." *The Journal of Personality Assessment* 49 (1985), 61–70.

Serafini, D., & J. Pearson. "Leadership Behavior and Sex Role Socialization: Two Sides of the Same Coin." *The Southern Speech Communication Journal* 49 (1984), 396–405.

Staley, C. "Male-Female Use of Expletives: A Heck of a Difference in Expectations." *Anthropological Literature* 20 (1978), 367–380.

Stopes, C. C. *The Sphere of "Man": In relation to That of "Woman" in the Constitution.* London: T. Fisher Unwin (1908).

Sulloway, M., & A. Christensen. "Couples and Families As Participant Observers of Their Interaction." *Advances in Family Intervention, Assessment, and Theory* 3 (1983), 119–160.

Swacker, M. "The Sex of the Speaker As a Socio-linguistic Variable." In *Language and Sex: Difference and Dominance,* ed. B. Thorne and N. Henley. (Rowley, MA: Newbury House Publishers, 1975) 76–83.

Wood, J. T., E. M. McMahan, & D. W. Stacks. "Research on Women's Communication: Critical Assessment and Recommendations." In *Feminist Visions: Toward a Transformation of the Liberal Arts Curriculum,* ed. D. L. Fowlkes and C. S. McClure. (University, AL: The University of Alabama Press, 1984) 31–41.

Zimmerman, D., & C. West. "Sex Roles, Interruptions and Silences in Conversation." In *Language and Sex: Difference and Dominance,* ed. B. Thorne and N. Henley (Rowley, MA: Newbury House Publishers, 1975) 105–129.

Concepts and Questions

1. How are the terms "sex" and "gender" used differently by Pearson? Why is an understanding of the terms important to an analysis of gender communication?

2. According to Pearson, in what ways are a person's use of verbal and nonverbal communication linked to gender?

3. Why, according to Pearson, do subcultures (co-cultures) establish separate languages?

4. More than thirty years ago Pearson wrote, "Our world and the roles of women and men in it are undergoing rapid change, but our interactions do not acknowledge these changes." Do you believe her assertion is still valid today?

5. According to Pearson, what are the four errors women and men make during interaction? Do you agree with her conclusions?

6. Do you agree or disagree with Pearson that language reflects a male-dominated bias? If you agree, can you think of some contemporary examples?

7. What does Pearson mean when she writes that we need to view sex and gender as distinctly different constructs?

8. Why do you believe Pearson used the phrase, "sex is more than a three-letter word"?

An African American Communication Perspective

SIDNEY A. RIBEAU,
JOHN R. BALDWIN,
MICHAEL L. HECHT

African American communication is as complex as the culture from which it emerges. Taken from the shores of Africa, the enslaved captives were forced to create a means of expression consistent with an African cultural tradition, yet responsive to life in the new world. The fusion of past traditions with slavery, and post-slavery experiences in the rural South and North, created a unique ethnic culture for the group known as African Americans.

The communicative style of African American ethnic culture is captured in a number of studies that investigate linguistic characteristics, social relationships, and verbal and nonverbal messages. This early research, which is primarily descriptive, provides an introduction to a rich and promising line of inquiry. Our work expands the discussion of African American discourse to include empirical investigations of the interpersonal dimensions that characterize this unique ethnic communication system. We are particularly interested in (1) the identification of satisfying and dissatisfying conversational themes, (2) conversational improvement strategies, and (3) communication effectiveness. A few important assumptions support our work and provide a context for this research.

Courtesy of Sidney A. Ribeau, John R. Baldwin, and Michael L. Hecht. This original essay first appeared in the seventh edition of this book. All rights reserved. Permission to reprint must be obtained from the authors and the publisher. Sidney A. Ribeau is President of Howard University. John R. Baldwin is Professor of Communication and Coordinator of the Communication Studies Unit at Illinois State University. Michael L. Hecht is Distinguished Professor of Communication Arts and Sciences at Pennsylvania State University.

UNDERLYING ASSUMPTIONS

We consider communication to be problematic—an interactive event during which persons assign meanings to messages and jointly create identities and social reality. This process is multi-dimensional and extremely complex. Attribution of meaning to symbols requires the interpretation of messages and negotiation of social worlds. The process is replete with the potential for failure which is magnified when ethno-cultural factors are introduced. Ethnic cultures consist of cognitive (for example, values, beliefs, norms) and material (for example, food, dress, symbols) characteristics that distinguish them from mainstream American culture. For successful communication to occur, these potential problems must be anticipated and managed.

Here we use an interpretive approach that utilizes the perceptions of cultural actors to explain their communicative behavior. The descriptions and narrative accounts provided by interactions enable one to glimpse a world normally reserved for members of the shared community. It is this world that we seek to unfold.

Culture and ethnicity are the concepts that govern our exploration of African American communication. **Culture** consists of the shared cognitive and material items that forge a group's identity and ensure its survival. Culture is created, shared, and transmitted through communication. **Ethnicity** pertains to the traditions, heritage, and ancestry that define a people. It is particularly apparent in a group's expressive forms. (We take as axiomatic the existence of ethnic cultures in America, and recognize African American culture as a fundamental element of life in America.)

Our early work is governed by the conceptual assumptions listed, and a practical concern: *research on African American communication should assist the practitioner in improving relationships between African Americans and European Americans.* It is our belief that the communication discipline has much to offer the area of human relations. This line of research is intended to make a contribution to that effort. To that end we began with studies of (1) intragroup communication issues, (2) interethnic communication issues,

and (3) conversational improvement strategies. The remainder of this paper will report our findings and discuss their implications. First, however, we frame these studies within an understanding of communication effectiveness.

COMMUNICATION EFFECTIVENESS

Many scholars have provided valuable information about what behaviors and communication people believe to be effective (Martin, 1989, 1993; Martin & Hammer, 1989; Pavitt & Haight, 1985; Ruben, 1977, 1989). "Competent" or "effective" communication has been defined in many ways (Spitzberg & Cupach, 1984; Spitzberg & Hecht, 1984; Wiemann & Bradac, 1989). One way to define **effective** behavior is that which is productive and satisfying for both partners. Communication is appropriate if it follows the rules and expectations the partners have; these expectations vary depending on the context the speakers are in or the relationship between them. The positive feelings the communicators have when their expectations are met make up the "satisfying" part of our definition (Hecht, 1978, 1984). The expectations may be met because a relationship is satisfying (McLaughlin & Cody, 1982), or because the communicators were able to function effectively in a new situation (Vause & Wiemann, 1981).

In view of effective communication, we see *communication issues* as "the agenda for effective communication held in common by members of the group" (Hecht, Collier, & Ribeau, in press, p. 127). That is, they are aspects of communication, which, if missing, pose problems for the communication; they are expectations about communication. Since different ethnic groups have different shared histories and ways of seeing the world, we believe that the unspoken, often subconscious, rules that one co-culture has for effective or satisfying communication may differ from those imposed by another. Further, given the impact of historical race and power relationships in the United States, it seems likely that African Americans (and other American cultures) would apply differing rules for measuring effective communications with in-group and out-group members.

INTRAGROUP COMMUNICATION ISSUES

We started by trying to understand how African Americans communicate among themselves. We asked African Americans, Mexican Americans, and European Americans to describe satisfying or dissatisfying conversations they had experienced with a member of their own ethnic group (Hecht & Ribeau, 1984). We found that the expectations of the groups were in some ways different, in others similar. Mexican Americans differed the most, with African Americans and European Americans responding more similarly.

Mexican Americans, for example, tended to seek closely bonded relationships, seeing the relationship itself as rewarding. Within this ethnic group, satisfying communication involved nonverbal communication and acceptance of self. In comparison, African Americans, and to a greater extent, European Americans, were self-oriented—that is, they saw the reward in something the other partner might provide for them, instead of in the existence of the relationship.

In keeping with this idea of potential reward, European Americans tended to look more to the future of the relationship. This echoes a previous study in which European Americans found communication with friends more satisfying when there were signs of intimacy that confirmed the future of the relationship (Hecht, 1984). At the same time, European Americans demonstrated less concern and interest for the partner in the conversation (other orientation) than did African Americans.

African Americans, on the other hand, found greater satisfaction in conversations where both partners were more involved in the topic. Intimacy was therapeutic and foundational to the relationship, and trust was highly important. While conversation was goal-oriented, at the same time it was important that ideas and feelings be exchanged. Where the Mexican Americans found bonding a priority for relationships, the African Americans surveyed found bonding conditional—to be established only if that exchange of ideas took place. In light of this, genuineness ("being real") and expressiveness were important, and were communicated through expressive style, passion, and

deep involvement with the topic. Helping one another was an integral part of satisfying interaction, supporting goal-oriented relationships. Because both parties may be trying to meet the same goals, it is necessary that those goals be clearly understood; thus, understanding is also important. African Americans found satisfaction when they knew where the conversation was going.

INTERGROUP COMMUNICATION ISSUES

We next sought to understand the agenda for effective interethnic communication—specifically, communication between blacks and whites (Hecht, Collier, & Ribeau, in press; Hecht, Larkey, & Johnson, 1992; Hecht & Ribeau, 1987; Hecht, Ribeau, & Alberts, 1989; Hecht, Ribeau, & Sedano, 1990). In this research, we identified seven primary issues important to those African Americans studied: (1) negative stereotyping, (2) acceptance, (3) personal expressiveness, (4) authenticity, (5) understanding, (6) goal attainment, and (7) power dynamics. In describing these issues, we provide quotes from African American responses to interviews and surveys to illuminate the findings.

Negative Stereotyping

Negative stereotyping is "the use of rigid racial categories that distort an African American's individuality. This violates the concept of uniqueness, something research has shown to be very important to African Americans" (Hecht, Collier, & Ribeau, in press). Negative stereotyping occurred in two ways. The first, and more obvious, was when European Americans in the study racially categorized African Americans—that is, when they treated them as a member of a group, or ascribed to them characteristics of the group, instead of treating them like individuals.

Indirect stereotyping occurred when European Americans talked to African Americans about what were seen to be "African American topics," such as sports or music. Some African Americans reported that this type of behavior made them want to withdraw, or caused them to see their conversational partner with disdain. One male African American, while seeing the introduction of such topics as an attempt to find common interests, saw those who brought them up as "patronizing or unaware," and felt that other African Americans felt the same way. Another type of indirect stereotyping is when European Americans ask or expect African Americans to speak on behalf of all African Americans. One participant *did feel satisfied* about her conversation because she "didn't feel put on the spot to speak for the whole of the black race." Another female was satisfied when the other person spoke to her "as another person and didn't let my color interfere with the conversation."

Acceptance

The second issue is *acceptance*, "the feeling that another accepts, confirms, and respects one's opinions" (Hecht, Collier, & Ribeau, in press, p. 131). Frequently, African Americans did not feel accepted by European Americans. For example, some persons interviewed said African Americans sometimes try to make up for "cultural deprivation" and "talk rather than listen in order to cover up." They act "cool," flippant, or talkative, sometimes using stylized speech. Some of the participants saw these behaviors as responses to stereotypes, either in the sense that the African Americans were trying to control the conversation to preempt the stereotypes, or that they were trying to avoid recognizing them. One person strongly volunteered that African Americans are no longer concerned about what European Americans feel or accept. At the same time, many of those interviewed felt that acceptance was a characteristic of satisfying conversations. This acceptance might be shown by positive nonverbal behaviors, similar dress, feeling comfortable with the conversation, "mutual respect for each other's beliefs" and even, at times, acting "cool" or removed.

Personal Expressiveness

Personal expressiveness refers to the verbal and nonverbal expression of thoughts, ideas, or feelings. While many African Americans mentioned some aspect of expressiveness, how that expressiveness is played out varies from person to person. Some saw honesty, integrity, and the open sharing of ideas

as valuable; others felt it important to keep their feelings hidden in intercultural communications. For example, one African American woman expressed dissatisfaction with a conversation because "I maintained control and did not curse her out." Opinions are important, but the emphasis is on expressing feelings—"talking from the heart, not the head." In contrast, non-expressive European Americans might be seen as racist or standoffish. Interestingly, many participants—more females than males—expressed the need to portray a tough exterior. African Americans need to "be cool," and not let European Americans know what they are thinking or feeling. History had an impact here with some of the women participants, pointing out that African American women have had to be strong both in response to prejudice and often as the head of the household. A possible explanation for the contrasting answers is that some African Americans value toughness and "coolness" until barriers of fear and mistrust are broken down; then, it becomes important to express who one really is.

Authenticity

Authenticity is tied directly to the concept of being oneself, of being genuine. Both African and European Americans perceived authenticity on the part of their conversational partner when the other was seen as revealing personal information—being honest, "being real," "being themselves," or expressing personal feelings freely. One African American male complained about "so many phony conversations—white people trying to impress African Americans with their liberalness." Straightforwardness, or "telling it like it is," is one aspect of authenticity; the opposite of this is avoidance of the truth through double talking or fancy language.

At the same time, many African American males engage in self-presentation; they try to create an acceptable image of themselves through "high talk" and "stylin'." "You dress as if you had money even if you don't." Creating an acceptable self-image becomes critical when a demeaning image has been externally imposed by European American society. In this light, stylized behavior to African Americans emerges as a sign of strength, not a lack of authenticity.

Understanding

Understanding is the feeling that messages are successfully conveyed. This theme was expressed when people felt that information was adequately exchanged or learning took place. One person noted that "there was a genuine exchange of thinking, feeling, and caring." Unfortunately, understanding can be hampered by cultural differences or differences in upbringing. One female commented that "if people don't share the same life experiences, they can't be expected to truly understand each other. If whites haven't been exposed to blacks, there will be a 'fear of the unknown.'"

Goal Attainment

Goal attainment, or achieving desired ends from a conversation, was mentioned more in satisfying than in dissatisfying conversations. It is closely linked to understanding in that without some mutual understanding no goals will be met. Goals might include finding the solution to some problem, exchanging information, or finishing some project. But cultural misunderstandings can get in the way of goals. As one male responded: "Blacks and whites may come away with different meanings from a conversation because concepts aren't defined in the same way. The members of the ethnic groups tend to think in a different manner." Because of this, African Americans often find conversations with European Americans unrewarding, but those rewarding conversations are "like gates opening,"

Power Dynamics

Power dynamics, the last category, contains two main themes; powerlessness and assertiveness. *Powerlessness,* a feeling of being controlled, manipulated, or trapped, resulted from behaviors that rob African American conversational partners of the right to express their ideas freely. One participant objected to the term "powerlessness" as "putting things in white terms"; the label is not as important to us as the behaviors it describes. European Americans were seen as manipulating when they tried to control the topic, tried to persuade through subtlety, or would not let the African Americans finish their thoughts.

One European American communicator "tried to carry on the conversation all by himself...he would keep talking and interrupted me whenever I tried to say something."

Extreme assertiveness and confrontation used by African Americans, called "Mau Mauing" by one participant, is the other half of power dynamics. African Americans, it was commented, often talk with one another in a way that "whites would consider antagonistic or brutal." For this reason, many African Americans *code switch,* or change their communication style and language, when they interact with European Americans. Assertive speaking among some African Americans is exemplified by "the dozens," a put-down game in which one person puts down or makes fun of another person. It should be emphasized, however, that this type of assertiveness is by no means universal to all African Americans.

COMMUNICATION IMPROVEMENT STRATEGIES

While interethnic communication issues are characteristics or behaviors that can help or hurt these communications, the African American participants believed *improvement strategies* can enhance conversation. These are things communicators can do to help make the interaction more satisfying. While our initial research found six strategies (Hecht & Ribeau, 1987; Hecht, Ribeau, & Alberts, 1989; Martin, Larkey, & Hecht, 1991), later research has expanded the list to twelve: (1) asserting one's point of view, (2) positive self-presentation, (3) be open and friendly, (4) avoidance, (5) interaction management, (6) other-orientation, (7) inform/educate, (8) express genuineness, (9) confront, (10) internal management, (11) treat others as individuals, and (12) language management. We describe these again with quotes from African Americans to expound.

Asserting One's Point of View

Assertiveness, in both style and substance, includes using such expressions as "stress," "assert," or "emphasize my point." This strategy grew out of dissatisfying conversations and was recommended for aiding

African Americans' persuasion or argumentation efforts. The purpose is not simply to inform, but to gain agreement. Examples of this point of view are expressed in these comments: "Just simply be more vocal in the conversation. This in itself will give you a sense of control or power." "I continue to put across what I believe."

Positive Self-Presentation

Two methods of positive self-presentation attempt to reverse the other person's impressions. One method of self-presentation is to deliberately contradict stereotypes: "I just make sure my actions and conversation don't fit the negative stereotype." The other method is to point out positive attributes or accomplishments: "I try to make others see what I know, that is, when I'm being talked down to I try to show my intelligence."

Be Open and Friendly

This strategy, used most often to improve dissatisfying conversations, is similar to positive self-presentation, but without the deliberate desire to impress. Again, the participants varied in their views on openness, or open-mindedness. Some respondents felt European Americans should "be more patient, not assume anything, find out first." However, some African Americans rejected openness as a European American, middle-class female attribute, preferring to present themselves as strong, more closed. Friendliness includes being considerate of the other, polite, and courteous.

Avoidance

In a dissatisfying conversation, one might avoid either the conversation itself (by leaving), or the topics that are sensitive or demeaning. The first strategy is indicated by those who "terminate the conversation," or "remove myself from the conversation." The second is used when an African American perceives that some topics just cannot be discussed with certain individuals. Possible methods of avoidance include "not bringing up the subject," or changing the subject. ("I don't think it's beneficial to try to change the other person.")

Interaction Management

Either the African or the European American can attempt to manage the flow of the interaction. This might be done to reduce problems or just to improve a conversation. Possible strategies within this category include managing immediate interaction ("take turns," "work toward a compromise"), postponing the problem ("request a time to talk it over"), or finding different means of communication ("write a note"). Sometimes the conversation can be better managed by "just talking a little more" or spending "more time" together.

Other-Orientation

A concern for or interest in the other person was a sign of satisfying relationships, and might be created in different ways. Involving the other person in the conversation or finding common ground was one method suggested: "Think or talk about something that both can identify with." Others emphasized listening to the other person's thoughts and opinions: "learn by listening," "placing them in our shoes," and "try to look at it from both sides." Either party can improve the conversation with this strategy.

Inform/Educate

Information was often shared to educate or inform the conversational partner, in contrast to "asserting one's point of view." One should "tactfully educate by giving more information," and "if the conversation is that important, try and explain whatever you feel is being misunderstood." More facts should be given, sometimes specifically citing African American history to help others understand. At the same time, African Americans sometimes mentioned the need to ask European Americans more questions. This strategy attempts to resolve the issues raised by stereotyping and lack of understanding.

Express Genuineness

This strategy, genuineness, addresses the issue of authenticity, of "being yourself." Comments in this category valued honesty and expressing feelings.

Some participants opened up in hopes that their conversation partner would follow. Others saw it in terms of a need to "share your feelings of a lack of accomplishment," in attempting to have a satisfying conversation or to "ask the person to be for real." While these suggestions seem confrontational, they are geared toward moving the other into more honest expression.

Confront

Confrontation implies "either a direct confrontation of the issue or using questions to place the burden back on the other person" (Hecht, Collier, & Ribeau, in press). Strategies in this category include "Correct misconceptions in a shrewd, effective manner," or opposing "I believe you must always confront stereotyping by saying, 'It sounds as if you are making generalizations that may not be applicable to me.'" Examples of direct questions are "Just say, 'but how do *you* feel about it?' If they don't answer, it's obvious that it at least makes them feel uncomfortable," or "Ask why and how they got that stereotype."

Internal Management

Rather than focusing on specific behaviors to improve interaction, these comments described ways for African Americans to think about or deal with the situation. Some of these suggestions included acceptance, objectivity, and nondefensiveness: "I do my best to control my thoughts," "Think first of who you are, how you feel about yourself," and "Put the situation in proper perspective, that is, lose a battle to win the war."

Treat Others as Individuals and Equals

Leave race, color, or stereotypical beliefs entirely out of the conversation some suggested: "Talk to each other without having the sense of color in the conversation." Treat people based on who they are, and nothing else: "Decisions should be made based on each individual" or "Get to know me then judge me." This strategy, voiced most often to fight the stereotyping issue, primarily advocates desired behavior by the European American conversation partner.

Language Management

A few strategies that did not fit in the other categories are grouped here including: avoid slang or jargon and use clear articulation. "Refrain from using unfamiliar jargon" and "talk the same language" are examples of comments in this area. This strategy was used to resolve problems of a lack of understanding.

Note that the African American participants recommended some of these strategies primarily as things they should do (for example, assertiveness, positive self-presentation, avoidance, internal management, inform/educate, confront, language management); some as things European Americans should do (treat others as individuals); and some as things both should do (be more open and friendly, interaction management, express genuineness, other-orientation). Second, it should be noted that within each category (for example, be more open and friendly) there is a diversity of thought among African Americans as to how or if that strategy should be used.

The African Americans we interviewed felt that these strategies might be successful for improving a conversation, but not always. When stereotyping or lack of acceptance takes place, for example, no strategies are seen as effective—it is like "bouncing off a brick wall." If African Americans "see signs of racism, patronizing behavior, or other put downs, they turn off quickly." The first few minutes of a conversation can make or break the conversation—and the relationship.

CONCLUSION

It is often tempting to state communication effectiveness theories (or others) as if they applied to the way all people behave. However, the studies described here demonstrate that rules for effective or satisfying communication behavior vary, depending on the ethnicity of the group, as well as the situation. Further, the research shows a diversity and complexity among African Americans (Hecht & Ribeau, 1991). Finally, African Americans' own descriptions reveal clear suggestions, both for African Americans and European Americans, for how to make interethnic communication more rewarding for all concerned.

References

Hecht, M. L (1978). "Toward a Conceptualization of Inter-personal Communication Satisfaction." *Quarterly Journal of Speech*, 64, 47–62.

Hecht, M. L. (1984). "Satisfying Communication and Relationship Labels: Intimacy and Length of Relationship as Perceptual Frames of Naturalistic Conversation." *Western Journal of Speech Communications*, 48, 201–216.

Hecht, M. L., Collier, M. J., & Ribeau, S. (in press). *African American Communication: Identity and Cultural Interpretations.* Newbury Park, CA: Sage.

Hecht, M. L., Larkey, L. K., & Johnson, J. N. (1992). "African American and European American Perceptions of Problematic Issues in Interethnic Communication Effectiveness." *Human Communication Research*, 19, 209–236.

Hecht, M. L., & Ribeau, S. (1984). "Ethnic Communication: A Comparative Analysis of Satisfying Communication." *International Journal of Intercultural Relations*, 8, 135–151.

Hecht, M. L., & Ribeau, S. (1987). "Afro-American Identity Labels and Communicative Effectiveness." *Journal of Language and Social Psychology*, 6, 319–326.

Hecht, M. L., & Ribeau, S. (1991). "Sociocultural Roots of Ethnic Identity: A Look at Black America." *Journal of Black Studies*, 21, 501–513.

Hecht, M. L., Ribeau, S., & Alberts, J. K. (1989). "An Afro-American Perspective on Interethnic Communication." *Communication Monographs*, 56, 385–410.

Hecht, M. L., Ribeau, S., & Sedano, M. V. (1990). "A Mexican American Perspective on Interethnic Communication." *International Journal of Intercultural Relations*, 14, 31–55.

Martin, J. N. (1989). "Behavioral Categories of Intercultural Communication Competence: Everyday Communicators' Perceptions." *International Journal of Intercultural Relations*, 13, 303–332.

Martin, J. N. (1993). "Intercultural Communication Competence." In R. Wiseman and J. Koester (Eds.), *International and Intercultural Communication Annual*, 17.

Martin, J. N., Larkey, L. K., & Hecht, M. L. (February, 1991). *"An African American Perspective on Conversational Improvement Strategies for Interethnic Communication."* Paper presented to the Intercultural and International Communication Conference, Miami, Florida.

Martin, J. N., & Hammer, M. R. (1989). "Behavioral Categories of Intercultural Communication Competence: Everyday Communicators' Perceptions." *International Journal of Intercultural Relations*, 13, 303–332.

McLaughlin, M., & Cody, M. J. (1982). "Awkward Silences: Behavioral Antecedents and Consequences of the Conversational Lapse." *Human Communication Research*, 8, 229–316.

Pavitt, C., & Haight, L. (1985). "The 'Competent Communicator' as a Cognitive Prototype." *Human Communication Research*, 12, 225–242.

Ruben, B. D. (1977). "Guidelines for Cross-cultural Communication Effectiveness." *Group and Organizational Studies*, 12, 225–242.

Ruben, B. D. (1989). "The Study of Cross-cultural Competence: Traditions and Contemporary Issues." *International Journal of Intercultural Relations*, 13, 229–239.

Spitzberg, B. H., & Cupach, W. R. (1984). *Interpersonal Communication Competence.* Beverly Hills, CA: Sage.

Spitzberg, B. H., & Hecht, M. L. (1984). "A Component Model of Relational Competence." *Human Communication Research*, 10, 575–600.

Vause, C. J., & Wiemann, J. M. (1981). "Communication Strategies for Role Invention." *Western Journal of Speech Communication*, 45, 241–251.

Wiemann, J. M., & Bradac, J. J. (1989). "Meta-theoretical Issues in the Study of Communication Competence: Structural and Functional Approaches." In B. Dervin and M. J. Voight (Eds.), *Progress in Communication Sciences*, Vol. 9, 261–284. Norwood, NJ: Ablex.

Concepts and Questions

1. How do Ribeau, Baldwin, and Hecht differentiate between *culture* and *ethnicity*?

2. How would you define "*effective behavior*"?

3. What do Ribeau, Baldwin, and Hecht mean when they suggest that Mexican Americans, European Americans, and African Americans differ in the rewards they receive from their relationships?

4. Can you think of some examples of "indirect stereotyping"?

5. What are Ribeau, Baldwin, and Hecht referring to when they write about "personal expressiveness"?

6. Have you ever experienced "power dynamics" when communicating with someone of a culture different from your own?

7. What does the phrase "code switching" mean?

8. From your own personal experiences, can you add any "communication improvement strategies" to those advanced by Ribeau, Baldwin, and Hecht?

In Plain Sight: Gay and Lesbian Communication and Culture

William F. Eadie

Just the idea of unique gay and lesbian communication patterns that create culture is a controversial one. Some may dismiss it as part of a "gay agenda" to promote acceptance where there can be none. An extreme case of this position could be found in the African country of Uganda, where at the time this essay was written a law was pending that could have mandated execution for anyone showing same-sex affection.

If there is a gay agenda in the United States, however, it is diverse enough to consist of many different viewpoints. In this essay, I'll present some of those viewpoints on communication and culture in the lesbian and gay community. I use the term "viewpoints" because there is no precise way to define, measure, and track developments in lesbian and gay culture, so we have to rely on observers to analyze and present what they see. Many of those viewpoints will be backed by data collected through systematic research, but some will reflect general observations of societal trends.

My experience as a gay man has helped me to see that a major issue facing lesbians and gays in contemporary U.S. society is that it is easy to hide. Defying societal pressures and choosing to live openly as a lesbian or gay man is thus a political act, one that has ramifications, both positive and negative, for many of our everyday interactions. And, it is from those everyday interactions that cultural differences are created.

Courtesy William F. Eadie. This original essay appeared for the first time in the eleventh edition. All rights reserved. Permission to reprint must be obtained from the author and the publisher. Earlier versions of this essay have appeared in previous editions. William F. Eadie is Professor of Journalism and Media Studies at San Diego State University, San Diego, California.

Below, I'll elaborate how this personal information becomes political. I'll include material on the "outsider" status that lesbians and gay men feel in society, the media's role in creating and perpetuating stereotypes, and the processes by which those stereotypes have been changing. I'll discuss the coming-out process, the role of communication in that process, and how gay men and lesbians eventually are able to achieve intimacy and find themselves a community. I'll provide examples of how people manage the tensions of displaying their sexuality to others, how public spaces are made safe for communication, how same-sex partners negotiate sexual attraction, and the problems entailed in achieving and maintaining intimacy in same-sex relationships.

WHEN THE PERSONAL IS POLITICAL

The Not-So Hidden Outsiders

More than other non-majority groups, lesbians and gay men have a better chance of living undetected by individuals within mainstream society. While ethnicity and national origin are relatively easy to discern merely by looking at an individual, sexual orientation is not readily apparent.

Of course, there are plenty of people who think that they can tell otherwise. When I was in high school, students called Thursday "Queersday" and passed around the story that those who wore green on Thursday would be saying to all that they were queer (a term that had a negative meaning in those days).

Why would students focus on clothing as an indicator that a classmate was gay? Perhaps it is because children from an early age are made very aware of differences between them and others, and by adolescence there is tremendous pressure to conform. A person who dresses differently enough to be beyond the boundaries of conformity communicates "outsider" status.

And, lesbian, gay, bisexual, transgendered, and questioning youth feel their outsider status intensely. One of the most eloquently written descriptions of these feelings comes from Paul Monette's (1992) award-winning memoir, *Becoming a Man*:

Everyone else had a childhood, for one thing—where they were coaxed and coached and taught all the short-hand....And every year they leaped further ahead, leaving me in the dust with all my doors closed.... Until I was twenty-five, I was the only man I knew who had no story at all....That's how the closet feels, once you've made your nest in it and learned to call it home. Self-pity becomes your oxygen. (p. 1)

Of course, what is in fashion changes rapidly and probably isn't a good indicator of sexuality over time. In urban areas, one can easily find straight and gay men and women who dress alike.

If clothing is becoming less and less of a give-away, then what clues do people use to judge sexuality? Rieger, Linsenmeier, Gygax, Garcia, and Bailey (2010) attempted to answer that question by having homosexual and heterosexual men and women guess the sexuality of similar aged men and women who had been recorded answering informal questions about their interests. Rieger et al. asked their raters to base their judgments on appearance (by viewing a photo only), reading a transcript of the person's description of their interests, listening to an audio recording of the response, watching a video that revealed the person's movement pattern only, or watching and listening to a video of the individual giving the response. Results indicated that the raters were over 80 percent accurate in guessing the sexuality of the people they rated, regardless of whether the rater was heterosexual or homosexual. Raters were most accurate when viewing the video with all of the potential cues available and the least accurate when viewing the movement only.

A second study by the same research team asked a different set of raters to indicate the degree to which the people being rated seemed to be masculine or feminine. Raters attributed more feminine qualities to the gay men and more masculine qualities to the lesbian women, while reversing the pattern for the heterosexual men and women they saw.

This study debunks to some degree the idea that lesbians and gay men have a special ability to recognize each other (a phenomenon called "gaydar"). The raters who were lesbian or gay had no overall ability to recognize other lesbian and gay individuals, and both groups were quite accurate in identifying sexuality from six to ten second video clips. Contrast this finding with research on deception that indicates that raters seeing similar length clips have no better than a 50/50 chance of guessing whether someone is lying or telling the truth (Levine, 2009), and an over 80 percent accuracy rate is quite impressive.

The second study by Rieger et al. (2010) confirmed that if men seem to act "feminine" or women act "masculine" they are likely to be assumed to be gay. But, the results could also be confirming stereotypes. If young people can accurately judge the sexuality of 80 percent of their peers in less than ten seconds, they might have done so and then assumed that the men acted more feminine and the women more masculine and rated accordingly.

And, what about the 20 percent whose sexuality was not judged accurately? Accuracy might be improved with time. For example, Kitzinger (2005) found that if individuals do not talk about their heterosexual relationships, or if they are vague in the pronouns or labels used to describe the relationships they do have, they may be assumed to be gay. And, vocal tone that sounds stereotypically gay will evoke negative judgments, even if individuals are told that the speaker is heterosexual (Gowen & Britt, 2006). Gay men and lesbians may, through experience, become better at sorting out these more subtle clues, but their first impressions of sexuality are likely to be no more accurate than those of heterosexuals.

Indeed, some gay men and lesbians may incorporate aspects of opposite-gender behavior in order to be noticed by other gay men and lesbians. But, the adoption of these behaviors doesn't necessarily mean that the individual would rather *be* the opposite gender. Most lesbians and gay men are happy being women or men; they are simply emotionally and sexually attracted to members of the same gender.

Media and Stereotypes

Media portrayals of lesbians and gays have helped both to perpetuate stereotypes and, more recently, to promote tolerance and acceptance. According to Fejes and Petrich (1993), who reviewed a large number of studies on how lesbians and gays had been portrayed in films, on television, and in the news, gay characters in entertainment were often cast as farcical, weak, or menacing.

Smyth (2004) identified four classic stereotypes of gay men: (1) gay males are effeminate, (2) gay males are "sick" or mentally ill, (3) gay males are sexual predators, and (4) gay males are "violent, libido-driven monsters." Smyth studied stories that appeared in *Time* and *Newsweek* between 1946 and 2002, and he found that there were three distinct periods reflecting differences in how these periodicals covered gays. From 1946 to 1969, the newsmagazines portrayed gay men almost exclusively from a dark point of view, as sexually deviant, predatory, and sick. From 1969, following the Stonewall Riots, to 1980, coverage focused mostly on the emerging Gay Liberation movement, and reactions to that movement, mostly from religious or quasi-religious groups. While the articles themselves often focused on an emerging gay male identity and political agenda, there were still mentions of the old stereotypes in many of the articles. It was also during this period that the American Psychiatric Association removed homosexuality from its list of mental illnesses. From 1980 to 2002, the number of articles about gays surged dramatically. Portrayals of gay men as effeminate dropped sharply, though the news magazines still were interested in gay serial killers and unusual sexual practices. The prevalence of HIV and AIDS among gay men helped to perpetuate the "sick" stereotype, and coverage of the spread of AIDS perpetuated the stereotype of the sexual predator.

Similarly, Branchik (2007) analyzed representations of gay men in print advertising from 1917 to 2004 and found that these representations passed through four stages that were roughly equivalent to changes in societal views of gay men. These stages were (a) recognizing the men as being homosexual, (b) ridiculing them, (c) accepting them as "cutting edge," and (d) portraying them with respect.

Streitmatter (2009) also traced mainstream media portrayals of gay men. He believed that these portrayals moved away from ridicule in 1977, with the debut of *Soap*, the first television series to feature a recurring openly gay character. He thought that Branchik's (2007) "respect" stage began in 1993 with the debut of the film, *Philadelphia*, which starred Tom Hanks as a gay attorney who had AIDS (it would be years before an openly gay actor would portray a gay character in film or television—or that an openly gay

actor such as Neil Patrick Harris would prove to be popular playing heterosexual roles).

Streitmatter (2009) believed that the next stage of acceptance would be showing male–male or female-female love-making on network television. Indeed, in December 2009, the ABC soap opera, *One Life to Live*, broke this new ground by featuring the show's recurring gay character making love with another man.

Even though stereotypes have been dissipating in media coverage, they persist in many people's thinking. And, like all stereotypes, they have some basis in fact. Some scholars would characterize these stereotypes as being products of *heterosexism*. That is, they arise from an assumption that behavior of heterosexual individuals is "normal" and behavior of homosexual individuals is "deviant," as opposed to merely "different." In fact, there are probably more heterosexual men who are effeminate, sick, predatory, or prone to sex-related criminal acts than there are gay men, because same-sex orientation is statistically still very much the exception (independent estimates range anywhere from 2–10 percent of the population).

Of course, I have been discussing twenty-first-century ideas about same-sex orientation. It has not always been thus, and in fact there is considerable historical evidence that sexuality with others of the same gender has in the past been honored instead of looked on with suspicion (see, for example, Boswell, 1994; Crompton, 2003; Greenberg, 1988).

Overcoming Stereotypes

One way that many people seem to have of letting go of their stereotypes is to meet someone who doesn't fit them. A 2009 Gallup Poll (Morales, 2009) indicated that knowing even one gay person affected the degree to which one felt positively about same-sex relationships. Those who knew at least one lesbian or gay person also reported less discomfort about interacting with lesbian or gay individuals generally. Those with liberal political and social views were more likely to say that they knew someone who was gay than were those who held moderate or conservative views.

Media viewing can also affect individuals, even if they do not know anyone who is gay. A study of viewers of the television show *Will and Grace*, which featured gay characters in leading roles, found that they held more positive attitudes toward lesbians and gays than did people who did not watch the show (Schiappa, Gregg, & Hewes, 2006). While one might expect that people seek out television programming that fits with their attitudes, positive attitudes toward lesbians and gays persisted even among those viewers who did not claim to have lesbian or gay friends.

Though these numbers indicate that attitudes are changing, there is still danger associated with being openly lesbian or gay. In particular, this danger seems to affect people under 21 to the greatest degree. For example, Huebner, Rebchook, and Kegeles (2004) reported on a survey of 1248 gay and bisexual men aged 18–27. Overall five percent of those surveyed reported that they had been the victims of anti-gay violence, while eleven percent indicated that they had been discriminated against because they were gay. But, of those under 21, the numbers jumped to ten percent as having experienced anti-gay violence, while half reported that they had been discriminated against because they were gay. Horn (2006) found that adolescents aged 14–16 are most likely to exhibit hostility toward lesbian and gay peers and open displays of hostility decline as adolescents age into young adulthood. Nevertheless, the possibility of being reviled for being open about one's sexuality remains throughout one's life.

These data bring us back to the point that being openly lesbian or gay is a political statement. When the odds are not strong that others will have a favorable attitude toward you as a lesbian or gay man and when the odds are even greater that your openness at a young age may result in negative, even violent, consequences, no wonder many non-heterosexual individuals keep that information to themselves. They may date members of the opposite sex and may also marry and have families. Men in this situation may seek anonymous same-sex encounters outside of marriage, because the means for having such encounters are often readily (though, not always legally) available. These men may also deny that they have any same-sex attraction. Public health workers call these individuals MSMs, or "Men who have Sex with Men." People in the African-American and Latino communities call this practice being "on the down low" (Wolitski et al., 2006).

The Process of Coming Out

Despite the potential for negative consequences, it is healthier for people to be open about their same-sex attraction. But, getting to that point is not always easy. D'Augelli (1994) theorized what he called "six interactive stages that non-heterosexual" individuals pass through as they develop an identity. The stages are:

1. Recognizing that one's attractions and feelings are not heterosexual, as well as telling others that one is not heterosexual.
2. Summarizing self-concepts, emotions, and desires into a personal identity as gay/lesbian/bisexual.
3. Developing a non-heterosexual social identity.
4. Disclosing one's identity to parents and redefining familial relationships afterward.
5. Developing capabilities to have intimate gay/lesbian/bisexual relationships.
6. Becoming a member of a gay/lesbian/bisexual community.

It is possible that these stages can be passed through quickly, but it is equally as likely that these stages will progress slowly if at all (and, individuals may work on multiple stages at once or may double-back to previous stages). Each stage requires some degree of change to how one talks and each stage requires the ability to share with others what heretofore one considered to be private information. As people search for new ways of talking and for what they might consider to be the "right words" to say, they look to the examples of others. This process of learning to communicate differently helps lesbian and gay individuals to assimilate into the lesbian/gay/bisexual community.

The fact that disclosure of information about one's sexuality may evoke responses ranging from delight to spews of hateful words makes such disclosure a political one. "Political" communication, in this case, is constituted by messages that have the potential for promoting controversy. "Political" also means that such a disclosure tends to carry with it an assumption that the speaker holds a set of attitudes and beliefs that may be at odds with those of the listener. Such assumptions may not be correct ones.

Communication and Identity Formation

D'Augelli's (1994) stages of identity formation are called "interactive" because they rely on communication with others to occur. As same-sex attraction is controversial information, lesbians and gays beginning on D'Augelli's stages need to find strategies for disclosing this information. These initial disclosures will usually be tentative and told to a confidant, often a trusted friend or an adult who is not a parent. The initial messages may not be in the form of "I am lesbian," but may be more general statements such as, "I'm having trouble with starting to date. My friends are dating, but I'm not," or even a statement such as, "I'm not sure that people like me; I don't fit in very well." The realization that one is attracted to members of the same sex may be present, but the individual may be choosing to hide that information behind what is often legitimate confusion. Depending on the response, the individual may finally say that they think they are more attracted to members of the same sex than to members of the opposite sex, or they may label themselves lesbian, gay, or bisexual. In many cases, the first formulation of sexual identity might be "I'm bisexual," because the speaker may believe that this statement is more socially-acceptable than "I'm gay" (Rust, 2002).

Once some form of admission that "I am different" is made the gay or lesbian person will begin to look for information that will help her to figure out what is going on. Sometimes this information search is confined to books, magazines, or informational web sites. Other times the information may come from pornography or erotica or from seeking out places where gays or lesbians gather, including online (Gray, 2009).

Sometimes, these places will be ones where anonymous sex might be had. Males in particular may try to experiment with gay sex to see if they find it to be exciting. The fact that sex in public places is usually against the law may add to the thrill of the experience.

As the lesbian or gay individual has contact with other lesbians and gays and compares themselves favorably to those other individuals, the idea that "I am different" should eventually become, "I am lesbian," or "I am gay." At that point, the dilemma becomes whether and if so how to let others know of one's sexual identity.

Coming Out as Event

The process of "coming out of the closet" is actually described by all of D'Augelli's (1994) stages, taken collectively. The moments when the lesbian or gay individual actually tells the people closest to them of their sexual identity should ideally be (1) when that individual is ready and prepared to make the disclosure, and (2) when the other members are ready to hear what this individual has to say. In many cases, however, these scenes are not nearly so clean and well planned. Parents may learn about their child's sexuality, for example, by catching them with same-sex pornography, by reading their diaries, or by discovering them with a same-sex partner. Or, initial sexual experimentation may lead to trouble with the law or with delinquency. Or, the individual may burst out with the information at an emotional, but unplanned, moment.

Reactions to this information will be varied. The ideal reaction, from the lesbian or gay person's point of view, is described in advice available on the website of the support organization, Parents and Friends of Lesbians and Gays (PFLAG) (Human Rights Watch & Parents and Friends of Lesbians and Gays, n.d.):

- Ask respectful questions to show you are interested.
- Be honest. If you feel awkward, say so. Ask the "dumb" questions.
- Laugh a little, but do it gently and respectfully. Don't use slang terms that could be considered to be derogatory.
- Send gentle signals that it's all right to continue to talk with you about being lesbian or gay.[1]

Still, there are many families where parents and siblings do not process this news in nearly as supportive a manner. Some family members may immediately cut off contact with the lesbian or gay member. Some families may try to persuade the lesbian or gay person that "this is a phase" or that "you can change."

No wonder that individuals who are questioning their sexuality are reluctant to talk to others about it until they are sure of a lesbian or gay identity. And no wonder that some people stay in the closet for years. Many lesbian and gay individuals feel tensions in their relationships with family, work, and social and religious institutions (e.g., Calzo & Ward, 2009; Gortmaker & Brown, 2006; McDermott, 2006). Lesbians and gays may resolve these tensions in a variety of ways. They may decide to create alternative support institutions, such as "families of choice," as opposed to "families of origin." They may strive to achieve at work or in an arena where they can gain recognition. They may become part of alternative social and religious structures. They may also become politically active, seeking to root out and eliminate discrimination wherever they find it. If they join political groups, these groups may employ tactics ranging from traditional lobbying to attention-grabbing demonstrations where same-sex couples deliberately engage in public displays of affection. (For an analysis of the political dimensions of two men kissing in public, see Morris & Sloop, 2006.)

Achieving Intimacy

It is usually difficult for a lesbian or gay person to progress to D'Augelli's (1994) fifth stage, learning how to develop intimate same-sex relationships, without having completed at least some of the fourth stage, allowing the people who matter to them to know them as sexual beings. Intimacy, by its very nature, demands a degree of honesty that is usually suppressed by the need to hide a major portion of one's self. In addition, fear of being discovered, fear of what others will think, or fear of losing one's job can keep people in hiding and afraid of their own sexuality. But, sometimes finding another person to trust and love can help an individual to be more open about same-sex attraction. Of course, intimate relationships can and do happen between people who can't be open with others. Sometimes, these relationships are described to others as "roommates" or "friends," which is how a neighbor of mine described his living arrangement with his partner of seventeen years when I first met him. As soon as he realized that I was sympathetic, however, he began talking to me in much more open terms. The ability to be openly a part of an intimate relationship in the community at large is a test of not only how accepting people have become of their own

sexuality but how interactions with the community can create a climate where the couple are accepted and included by those around them.

Building Community

D'Augelli's (1994) final stage entails becoming a part of a lesbian/gay/bisexual community. This stage, too, does not necessarily wait for the other stages to finish, but can occur even while completing the earliest stages of the process. High school gay-straight alliance clubs can provide a supportive place to be different in an environment that puts a high premium on conformity. Universities may provide both a means for "out" lesbians and gays to gather but also often provide private groups, typically run by a professional staff member, where questioning students can explore their sexuality. Lesbian and gay community centers also provide "coming out" workshops and other social services designed to assist people to find a community and to feel as though they belong there.

Being in community typically involves having a concentration of like-minded people with whom to interact on a daily basis. The 2000 U.S. Census was the first to allow individuals to identify themselves as same-sex couples, and Gates and Ost (2004) compiled the Census data to learn about lesbian and gay living patterns. They found that gay male and lesbian women couples tend to live on the East or West Coasts of the U.S., though not necessarily in the same locales. The ten most popular spots for gay male couples to live were San Francisco, CA, Fort Lauderdale, FL, Santa Rosa, CA, Seattle-Bellevue-Everett, WA, New York, NY, Jersey City, NJ, Los Angeles-Long Beach, CA, Santa Fe, NM, Oakland, CA, and Miami, FL. Gay male couples tended to live in places that had higher concentrations of other gay couples, and they tended to live in more urban areas. For lesbian couples, the most popular places were often in college towns: Santa Rosa, CA, Santa Cruz-Watsonville, CA, Santa Fe, NM, San Francisco, CA, Oakland, CA, Burlington, VT, Portland, ME, Springfield, MA, Corvallis, OR, and Madison, WI. Gates and Ost also reported that 99 percent of U.S. counties had at least one same-sex couple living there.[2]

In an update based on 2008 data, Gates (2009) refined his results to distinguish between same-sex spouses (people who specifically designated themselves in that manner) and same-sex unmarried partners. In terms of places of residence, the patterns were similar to those reported earlier; in particular, same-sex spouses tended to live in states where their partnership could be recognized legally. Gates' analysis also revealed some demographic characteristics of same-sex spouses: they were more likely to be women who were raising children, and they tended to have lower incomes and higher levels of unemployment than did unmarried partners. Despite the lower incomes, they were more likely to be homeowners, however.

Gates (2009) also found that same-sex spouses and opposite-sex spouses were more alike than different. They were similar in average age, income, rate of home ownership, education levels, and degree to which both partners were of the same or different ethnicities. The only differences Gates found were that same-sex spouses were less likely to be raising children and less likely for both partners to be employed than were different-sex spouses.

Once in a community, gays and lesbians will often become involved in social organizations, such as square dancing or choral singing, business and networking groups such as a lesbian and gay Chamber of Commerce, and causes that benefit the community as a whole. There have even begun to be retirement communities created for lesbians and gays (Neville, 2007).

Over time, gay men have been involved in prevention of HIV/AIDS transmission and in raising funds for research on this disease, which began in the gay community but now affects far more heterosexual people worldwide. Lesbians have actively been involved in raising awareness about breast cancer and in funding breast cancer research. Both groups have campaigned against laws that allow discrimination in hiring and housing or which criminalize private and consensual sexual practices commonly engaged in by lesbian and gay couples. These campaigns culminated in the U.S. Supreme Court's 2003 decision in *Lawrence v. Texas*, where Justice Anthony Kennedy, writing for the Court majority, declared that two gay men could engage in consensual sexual activity in the privacy of one's home and "still retain their dignity as free persons."

Most recently, the lesbian and gay community has been galvanized by a drive to legalize marriage for same-sex couples. This drive created a great amount of national debate, as well as spawning both decisions to allow same-sex marriages as well as legal attempts to restrict the term, "marriage," to recognizing relationships among opposite-sex couples. But, the *New York Times'* decision to print announcements of the unions of same-sex couples in its wedding announcements pages did much for increasing the social acceptability of those relationships.

COMMUNICATION AND THE TENSIONS OF BEING GAY

In U.S. culture, gays and lesbians needed to remain hidden yet visible for so long that they developed ways of signaling their sexual orientation to like-minded people that would remain oblique to society as a whole. Or, they chose to be so flamboyant that their sexuality could not be ignored.

The author and playwright Oscar Wilde proved to be a masterful practitioner of hiding a gay subtext in his stories and plays, work that was acclaimed by mainstream critics and audiences alike. For example, in his novella, *The Picture of Dorian Gray*, Wilde concocted a tale about a man who finds the secret to staying eternally beautiful and youthful. The secret is a portrait of himself that he has hidden in his attic. The portrait, not the man, is the one that ages. Ultimately, the story ends in horror, and the man receives his comeuppance, but its central fantasy appealed to the soul of every gay man who read it. Wilde himself was married to a woman but had many dalliances with young men, including with at least one long-term lover. Tried in court for being a homosexual, a crime in Victorian England, Wilde defended himself by claiming that he merely enjoyed the company and energy of younger men. Wilde was convicted and jailed, however, and the experience left him sick and defeated, unable to produce the kind of tales that had once made him the toast of London.

Camp as Gay Sensibility

Wilde has been credited not only as being the person around which our modern ideas about same-sex love were conceived but also as being the first practitioner of "camp." Camp has evolved into a central concept in understanding gay culture. In her famous 1964 essay,

"Notes on 'Camp'," critic Susan Sontag defined camp as a "sensibility," as opposed to an idea or a thing. Sensibilities, according to Sontag, are difficult to describe, but she argued that camp is a sensibility that requires aesthetic appreciation, because it is a style or taste. Since styles and tastes change frequently, however, one must be nimble and not given to set ways of seeing the world. Indeed, camp often turns the world on its ear, relying on exaggeration and a tendency to see double meaning in words and acts. Camp is theatrical, an attempt to be and do extraordinary things. Camp is "fabulous" (Sontag, 1964).

In a later essay, Meyer (1994) extended Sontag's analysis to argue that camp encompasses how lesbians and gays perform their lives in front of others. Camp is the embodiment of how gay individuals manage the tensions of being open about their sexuality in a society that brands them as deviant. Rather than hide one's difference, camp helps the gay or lesbian person to find an alternative way of being in the world, a "queer" reality that doesn't have to rely on the norms of mainstream society, a reality that, in fact, often mocks those norms.

A good example of this alternate reality is the concept of drag. Drag not only bends the idea of gender by allowing men to dress up as women and women as men, but it requires that the "drag queen" or "drag king" play with the character in some way.

Perhaps a good way of explaining drag would be to compare it to female impersonation. Let's say that both a drag queen and a female impersonator are portraying actress and pop star Madonna. The female impersonator will attempt to look and sound as much like Madonna as possible, to create the illusion of Madonna as a tribute to her talent. The drag queen, on the other hand, will portray an exaggerated version of Madonna, playing with her persona to distort it in humorous or ironic ways.

Drag also allows an individual to be "someone else," at least for a while. One acquaintance of mine confided to me, "When I go to a bar in drag, all of the cute boys want to talk to me. I have a quick mouth, and they love my comebacks. But, out of drag I'm a large, older man, and if I went into the same bar as that person those boys wouldn't have anything to do with me. In drag, I'm fun and safe, but out of drag I'm someone to be avoided."

While camp originated as an integral part of gay life, Whitney (2006) has argued that it has been co-opted by the heterosexual world and as such may become a subtle means of oppressing the gay community while disguising itself as a liberating experience for all. Time and experience will tell whether this argument, while provocative, turns out to be valid.

It's About Sex, but Not Only About Sex

Of course, the point of same-sex attraction is that gays and lesbians want to find someone of the same gender with whom to be physically, emotionally, and spiritually intimate. Recall, however, that while D'Augelli's (1994) stages of developing a non-heterosexual identity included the capacity to form and maintain intimate same-sex relationships, D'Augelli placed this capacity down his list, after coming out to family and friends. Clearly, a lot of developing a lesbian and gay identity involves exploring one's same-sex attraction and learning to flirt with and meet people who might be candidates for intimate relationships. And, many, if not most, lesbians and gays do not wait until they have found their "soul mate" before having sex. Gay men often talk about finding Mr. Right, as opposed to finding Mr. Right-Now. But, as you might imagine, the latter is much easier to locate.

Making Public Communication Safe

Meeting other lesbian and gay people face to face and in public is not an easy task, however. If one is in a "safe" space, where everyone there is gay or accepting of same-sex attraction, then conversing openly is not a problem. Bars have traditionally filled this role, though to a greater extent for men than for women. Coffee houses and some community-based restaurants have also emerged as bar alternatives, especially for gay and lesbian youth who are not of legal drinking age, and for those who may want a less pressured atmosphere. Social and volunteer organizations also serve as safe spaces for lesbians and gays to meet.

Meeting someone outside of these spaces can be tricky, especially if one isn't sure that the other person shares one's same-sex attraction. In public places, contact is usually established by exchanging gazes, typically more than once. Holding another's gaze is generally interpreted as a sign that the other person might be interested. A conversation will often ensue, and an early task in that conversation will be to say something socially acceptable but that the other person can identify as a gay reference. Leap (1996), who has studied how gay men talk, both in the U.S. and internationally, provided an example of a conversation between a clothing sales clerk and a customer:

C: What are you asking for these? *[Points to one set of gray sweatshirts]*

S: Oh, I'm afraid they're not on sale today. But that colored shirt would look nice on you. *[Points to a pile of lavender sweatshirts, which are on sale]*

C: Yeah, I know. I own a few of them already. *[Grins]*

S: *[Grins back, no verbal comment]* (1996, p. 13)

Undoubtedly, these men walked away from this conversation with the knowledge that they were both gay. They understood that fact by (a) the reference to "lavender" a color generally associated with being gay, (b) the exaggerated response to the suggestion that the lavender shirt would look good on the customer, and (c) the fact that both men had exchanged mutual glances prior to beginning the conversation and they both grinned at the end of it. The conversational space was thus "safe," though still public, and if the two had been interested in pursuing each other's company further they could have exchanged contact information.

Online environments have burgeoned as purportedly safe places for gay men and lesbians to interact and meet others. Various dating sites have sprung up and offered services to people seeking same-sex dates, as well as to those seeking opposite-sex dates, though one of the most popular, eHarmony, did so only under court order (Colker, 2009). In fact, eHarmony created a separate site for same-sex clients, called "Compatible Partners" but placed a disclaimer on the site's front page that the company's compatibility questionnaire was developed using married heterosexual couples, implying that it might not work for same-sex relationships.

Negotiating Sexual Attraction

The above example involved two men who might have been interested in each other as potential friends or potential dates. When gay men are looking for sex partners, however, they will tend to use mostly nonverbal signals to do so. What gay men call "cruising," typically starts with making eye contact with someone as the two pass each other. If one is interested, that person will typically slow down and look back. If the other person also looks back, one person may begin to follow the other person. The two might stop and begin a conversation, or they might silently look for a place to have sex (there is a classic set of photographs that illustrates this sequence online at http://phillips-depury.liveauctioneers.com/lot2509621.html).

Generally, when men engage in an anonymous sexual encounter, the less they know about the other person the better. And, many choose to avoid the danger of sex in public by going to any of several Internet sites that feature ads from gays or lesbians looking for a "hook-up" in a particular geographical area (Ashford, 2006). Of course, cruising isn't limited to gay men, and using the Internet to find partners for dating or sex is a pervasive activity for people of all sexualities. And, like a lot of relational communication activity, interaction patterns on the Internet don't seem to be terribly different whether one is straight or gay.

One common feature of gay Internet sex sites is postings by men who say that they are bisexual. Gay men often scoff at the notion of bisexuality, saying that men who claim to be bisexual are really gay and in denial. Empirical support for this claim comes from research (Rieger, Chivers, & Bailey, 2005) on arousal patterns of men who claimed to be straight, gay, and bisexual. Gay men were aroused more by erotic pictures of men, while straight men were aroused by erotic pictures of women, as might be expected. Men who claimed to be bisexual, however, tended to show arousal patterns that resembled those of gay men. When questioned, however, those men claimed that they were aroused about equally by the erotic images of both men and women.

This study reminds us that people define their own sexuality and choose the label that they believe fits them best, including being "asexual" (for details of this emerging movement, see http://www.asexuality.org). There is no definitive test that demonstrates one's sexual orientation, and sexual orientation is probably determined by a number of factors, including both biological and social influences. Many people experience sexual orientation as something about which they had no choice, however (American Psychological Association, 2008), and most claim that their sexual orientation is something they cannot change. In fact, the American Psychological Association has reported that there is no scientific evidence that therapy designed to change one's sexual orientation is either safe or effective.

Nevertheless, it is clear that a number of individuals exhibit attraction to both men and women, and Rust (2002, 2009), in reviewing the scholarly literature on bisexuality, has argued that we may be more upset by not being able to put a person into either the heterosexual or homosexual camp than anything else. Bisexuality seems to be more acceptable in women than in men, and, in fact, some scholars are currently investigating whether women demonstrate a more fluid sexuality than do men (Bergner, 2009; Wade, 2007).

Negotiating Intimacy

Most lesbians and gay men put a high premium on dating and forming intimate relationships. Their courtship communication patterns in many ways resemble those of their heterosexual counterparts in similar age groups. Only a couple of differences have been found so far. One is that both lesbians and gay men are more likely to remain in touch with their former partners after the relationship ends (Peplau & Fingerhut, 2007). A second is that lesbian couples are quite adept at managing conflict in their relationships (Roisman et al., 2008).

Lesbian and gay couples do have unique issues to negotiate on their way to achieving intimacy at all of the physical, emotional, and spiritual (Tan, 2005) levels, however. For one thing, the issue of "who does what" in the relationship has to be worked out bit by bit. In heterosexual relationships, societal expectations for the roles that men and women play can either be followed or they can be reversed by the couple's decision. In lesbian and gay relationships, couples generally reject the notion that one of them plays the "man" and the other plays the "woman." So, each physical or emotional task has to be worked out, either consciously, or by one person taking on that task and having it become part of who that person is in the relationship. Many lesbians and gay men also reject

that their relationships should have to conform to the normative expectations of the heterosexual community (Slagle, 2006). These issues often revolve around setting rules for how much physical, emotional, or spiritual attraction is allowed to each member of the couple outside of the relationship: lesbian and gay couples may not conform to heterosexual definitions of "cheating" in their relationships.

Studies of gay male couples in San Francisco (Hoff & Beougher, 2010; Hoff, Beougher, Chakravarty, Darbes, & Neilands, 2010; Hoff, Chakravarty, Beougher, Darbes, Dadasovich, & Neilands, 2009) have provided details on negotiation processes regarding sexual practices. These studies were based on surveys and interviews regarding whether couples had agreements regarding sex outside of the relationship, how those agreements functioned, whether they had been broken, and how the breaks had been handled.

Couples often reported that they had agreements about sexual matters, particularly the degree to which monogamy was expected, but that those agreements were not always explicit (and, in a few cases, the researchers found that each of the pair had a different understanding of the agreement). The agreements were generally unique to the relationship but could be classified as varying by how exclusive the relationship was expected to be, sexually, and if sex with others was allowed with whom (e.g., no ex-boyfriends) and under what circumstances (e.g., only with one's partner present). Breaks were handled depending on how long the agreement was in place. Breaks early on prompted being more specific or renegotiating the conditions, but a break after the agreement had been in place and stable for a while might call for a re-examination of the relationship itself. While couples with all sorts of agreements reported being satisfied with this aspect of their relationships, monogamous couples as a group tended to report that they felt more invested in their agreements, more satisfied with their relationships, and greater intimacy, trust, and equality in the relationship.

And, there are certainly differences in the sexual area. Storkey (2001) contended that men typically have difficulty achieving emotional closeness and that sex is often seen as the route to shedding inhibitions and achieving intimacy. For women, however, emotional warmth is typically an end in itself and those feelings need to be present before women commit to the relationship in a sexual manner. According to this analysis, it would not be surprising to find that most gay men look for sexual attraction and compatibility before working on emotional commitment, while most lesbian couples work on emotional connection first before committing to sex.

This negotiation work is hard, and if it becomes too hard or leads to major conflict before the couple has committed to each other there will be a tendency to break off the relationship, rather than to work through the conflicts.

The fact that same-sex couples have no legal standing in many parts of the United States also means that couples either have to keep their finances and other matters separate. Or, they may have legal documents drafted spelling out their agreements, all the while knowing that the validity of those documents might be challenged successfully, perhaps by members of one individual's family, at some future date.

SOME CLOSING THOUGHTS

In writing this essay, the readers I was keeping in mind were traditionally aged university sophomores and juniors. So, I tried to select and emphasize material that I thought might be most relevant to both the intellectual and emotional journeys of 19- or 20-year-olds. Clearly, not every second or third year college student is 19 or 20 years old, and if you fall into that category my examples may not fit where you are in your life so well.

I also tried to emphasize material that might be common to both lesbians and gay men. Because there has been much more research on the communication and relationship patterns of gay men than on lesbians, and because I am a gay man, this choice probably means that readers interested in lesbians as a group may feel disappointed in what they learned from this chapter. For example, research indicating that lesbians are less likely to be "out" at work (McDermott, 2006) is interesting but beyond the scope of what I wanted to cover. If you'd like to understand more about the psychology of lesbians and gay men, I'd refer you to book-length works such as Coyle and Kitzinger (2002).

I have also ignored the "T," or transgender, part of the "LGBT" formulation. Earlier in this chapter,

I wrote that exhibiting the behavior of the other gender doesn't necessarily identify one as a lesbian woman or gay man, and I commented that many, if not most, of us were quite happy being men or women. Transgendered individuals, on the other hand, do sense that they ought to be the opposite gender from what they are, physically. Much of the research on transgendered individuals is still quite new (see Papoulias, 2006, for a summary) and is related to a burgeoning body of scholarship on gender identity (see, for example, Factor & Rothblum, 2008). Some transgendered individuals identify as being lesbian or gay, while others do not. The American Psychological Association has a good publication with answers to questions about gender identity available online at http://www.apa.org/topics/sexuality/transgender.aspx

Finally, I have not written about many of the issues about which many lesbians and gay men care deeply, as well as about several of the tensions that exist within the lesbian and gay community. These tensions include poverty and homelessness among lesbians and gays, particularly youth; racism and sexism; concerns about how to foster healthy communication among lesbians and gay men of different ages (Hajek & Giles, 2002) or between gays and straights (Hajek & Giles, 2005); and worries that lesbian and gay culture is becoming too mainstream, resulting in the possible loss of the community's identity (Hattersley, 2004; McNamara, 2004).

Despite these shortcomings, I hope that I have provided you with some insight about communication among gay men and lesbians and how that communication manifests itself in the U.S. as a "culture." It used to be said that the members of the lesbian and gay community were "hiding in plain sight." Now that so many are no longer hiding, I hope that this information will help you to understand the ways in which members of this community may be different from others and the ways we are the same.

Notes

1. Brault, M. (2008). *Disability Status and the Characteristics of People in Group Quarters*. U.S. Census Bureau: Disability. Retrieved 15 April 2010 from http:/www.census.gov/hhes/www/disability/GQdisability.pdf

2. Census Bureau Estimates Nearly Half of Children Under Age 5 are Minorities. (2009). U.S. Census Bureau News: Department of Commerce. Retrieved 15 April 2010 from http://www.census.gov/Press-Release/www/releases/archives/population/013733.html

References

American Psychological Association. (2008). Answers to your questions: For a better understanding of sexual orientation and homosexuality. Washington, DC: Author. Retrieved from www.apa.org/topics/sorientation.pdf

Ashford, C. (2006). The only gay in the village: Sexuality and the net. *Information & Communications Technology Law,* 15, 275–289.

Bergner, D. (2009, January 25). What do women want? *New York Times Magazine,* 26–33, 46, 51–52.

Boswell, J. (1994). *Same-sex unions in premodern Europe.* New York: Villard.

Branchik, B. J. (2007). Pansies to parents: Gay male images in American print advertising. *Journal of Macromarketing,* 27, 38–50.

Calzo, J. P., & Ward, L. M. (2009). Contributions of parents, peers, and media to attitudes toward homosexuality: Investigating sex and ethnic differences. *Journal of Homosexuality,* 56, 1101–1116.

Colker, D. (2009, March 31). EHarmony launches gay matchmaking service. *Los Angeles Times.* Retrieved from http://articles.latimes.com/2009/mar/31/business/fi-eharmony31

Coyle, A., & Kitzinger, C., Eds. (2002). *Lesbian and gay psychology: New perspectives.* Oxford: Blackwell.

Crompton, L. (2003). *Homosexuality and civilization.* Cambridge: Harvard University Press.

D'Augelli, A. R. (1994). Identity development and sexual orientation: Toward a model of lesbian, gay, and bisexual development. In E. J. Trickett, R. J. Watts, & D. Birmans (Eds.), *Human diversity: Perspectives on people in context* (pp. 312–333). New York: Oxford University Press.

Factor, R., & Rothblum, E. (2008). Exploring gender identity and community among three groups of transgender individuals in the United States: MTFs, FTMs, and gender queers. *Health Sociology Review,* 17, 235–253.

Fejes, F. & Petrich, K. (1993). Invisibility. homophobia and heterosexism: Lesbians, gays and the media. *Critical Studies in Mass Communication,* 10, 395-442.

Gates, G. J. (2009). *Same-sex spouses and unmarried partners in the American community survey,* 2008. Los Angeles: The Williams Institute, UCLA. Retrieved from http://www.law.ucla.edu/WilliamsInstitute/pdf/ACS2008_Final(2).pdf

Gates, G. J., & Ost, J. (2004). *The gay and lesbian atlas.* Washington, DC: The Urban Institute Press.

Gortmaker, V. J., & Brown, R. D. (2006). Out of the college closet: Differences in perceptions and experiences among out and closeted lesbian and gay students. *College Student Journal,* 40, 606–619.

Gowen, C. W., & Britt, T. W. (2006). The interactive effects of homosexual speech and sexual orientation on the stigmatization of men. *Journal of Language & Social Psychology,* 25, 437–456.

Gray, M. L. (2009). Negotiating identities/queering desires: Coming out online and the remediation of the coming-out story. *Journal of Computer-Mediated Communication* 14, 1162–1189.

Greenberg, D. (1988). *The construction of homosexuality.* Chicago: University of Chicago Press.

Hajek, C. & Giles, H. (2002). The old man out: An intergroup analysis of intergenerational communication among gay men. *Journal of Communication,* 30, 698–714.

Hajek, C., & Giles, H. (2005). Intergroup communication schemas: Cognitive representations of talk with gay men. *Language & Communication* 25, 161–181.

Hattersley, M. (2004, January–February). Will success spoil gay culture? *Gay and Lesbian Review Worldwide,* 11, 33–34.

Herek, G. M. (2002). Heterosexuals' attitudes toward bisexual men and women in the United States. *Journal of Sex Research,* 39, 264–274.

Hoff, C. C., & Beougher, S. C. (2010). Sexual agreements among gay male couples. *Archives of Sexual Behavior,* 39 (3), 774–778.

Hoff, C. C., Beougher, S. C., Chakravarty, D., Darbes, L. A., & Neilands, T. B. (2010). Relationship characteristics and motivations behind agreements among gay male couples: Differences by agreement type and couple serostatus. *AIDS Care,* 22 (7), 827–835.

Hoff, C. C., Chakravarty, D., Beougher, S. C., Darbes, L. A., Dadasovich, R., & Neilands, T. B. (2009). Serostatus differences and agreements about sex with outside partners among gay male couples. *AIDS Education and Prevention,* 21, 25–38.

Horn, S. S. (2006). Heterosexual adolescents' and young adults' beliefs and attitudes about homosexuality and gay and lesbian peers. *Cognitive Development,* 21, 420–440.

Huebner, D. M., Rebchook, G. M., & Kegeles, S. M. (2004). Experiences of harassment, discrimination, and physical violence among young gay and bisexual men. *American Journal of Public Health,* 94, 1200–1203.

Human Rights Watch & Parents and Friends of Lesbians and Gays (n.d.). A straight guide to GLBT Americans. Retrieved from http://www.pflag.org/fileadmin/user_upload/Support/straightguideWEB.pdf

Kitzinger, C. (2005). "Speaking as a heterosexual": (How) does sexuality matter for talk-in-interaction? *Research on Language and Social Interaction, 38,* 221–265.

Leap, W. L. (1996). *Word's out: Gay men's English.* Minneapolis: University of Minnesota Press.

Levine, T. R. (2009). Deception. In Eadie, W. F. (Ed.), *21st century communication: A reference handbook* (pp. 471–478). Thousand Oaks, CA: Sage Publications.

McDermott, E. (2006). Surviving in dangerous places: Lesbian identity performances in the workplace, social class and psychological health. *Feminism & Psychology, 16,* 193–211.

McNamara, M. (2004, April 25). When gay lost its outré. *Los Angeles Times.* Retrieved from http://www.latimes.com/features/lifestyle/la-ca-mcnamara25apr25,1,6298374.story

Meyer, M., Ed. (1994). *The politics and poetics of camp.* London: Routledge.

Monette, P. (1992). *Becoming a man: Half a life story.* New York: Harcourt Brace Jovanovich.

Morales, L. (2009, May 29). Knowing someone gay/lesbian affects views of gay issues. Retrieved from http://www.gallup.com/poll/118931/knowing-someone-gay-lesbian-affects-views-gay-issues.aspx

Morris, C. E., & Sloop, J. M. (2006). "What lips these lips have kissed": Refiguring the politics of queer public kissing. *Communication & Critical/Cultural Studies, 3,* 1–26.

Neville, T. (2007, April 6). Birds of a feather. *New York Times,* Retrieved from http://www.nytimes.com/2007/04/06/travel/escapes/06retire.html?ex=1334116800&en=5c1bf7a5b0bf7bbb&ei=5124&partner=permalink&exprod=permalink

Papoulias, C. (2006). Transgender. *Theory Culture & Society, 23,* 231–233.

Peplau, L. A., & Fingerhut, A.W. (2007). The close relationships of lesbians and gay men. *Annual Review of Psychology, 58,* 405–424.

Rieger, G., Chivers, M., & Bailey, J. (2005). Sexual arousal patterns of bisexual men. *Psychological Science, 16,* 579–584. doi:10.1111/j.1467-9280.2005.01578.x.

Rieger, G., Linsenmeier, J. A. W., Gygax, L., Garcia, S., & Bailey, J. M. (2010). Dissecting "gaydar": Accuracy and the role of masculinity–femininity. *Archives of Sexual Behavior, 39,* 124–140. doi: 10.1007/s10508-008-9405-2.

Roisman, G., Clausell, E., Holland, A., Fortuna, K., & Elieff, C. (2008). Adult romantic relationships as contexts of human development: A multimethod comparison of same-sex couples with opposite-sex dating, engaged, and married dyads. *Developmental Psychology, 44,* 91–101. doi:10.1037/0012-1649.44.1.91.

Rust, P. (2002). Bisexuality: The state of the union. *Annual Review of Sex Research, 13,* 180–240.

Rust, P. C. R. (2009). Bisexuality in a house of mirrors: Multiple reflections, multiple identities. In P. L.Hammack & B. J. Cohler (Eds.), *The story of sexual identity: Narrative perspectives on the gay and lesbian life course* (pp. 107–130). New York: Oxford University Press.

Schiappa, E., Gregg, P., & Hewes, D. (2006). Can one TV show make a difference? *Will & Grace* and the parasocial contact hypothesis. *Journal of Homosexuality, 51,* 15–38.

Slagle, R. (2006). Ferment in LGBT studies and queer theory: Personal ruminations on contested terrain. *Journal of Homosexuality, 52,* 309–328.

Smyth, M. (2004, May). (Mis-)Shaping gay, lesbian, and bisexual representations in popular discourse: historical analyses. Paper presented at the International Communication Association, New Orleans.

Sontag, S. (1964, Autumn). On '"Camp." *The Partisan Review, 30.*

Storkey, E. (2001). *Origins of difference: The gender debate revisited.* Grand Rapids, MI: Baker Academic.

Streitmatter, R. (2009). *From 'perverts' to 'fab five': The media's changing depiction of gay men and lesbians.* New York: Routledge.

Tan, P. P. (2005). The importance of spirituality among gay and lesbian individuals. *Journal of Homosexuality, 49,* 135–144.

Wade, N. (2007, April 10). Pas de deux of sexuality is written in the genes. *New York Times.* Retrieved from http://www.nytimes.com/2007/04/10/health/10gene.html?ex=1333857600&en=87d00a870b9db178&ei=5124&partner=permalink&exprod=permalink

Whitney, E. (2006). Capitalizing on camp: Greed and the queer marketplace. *Text & Performance Quarterly, 26,* 36–46.

Wolitski, R. J., Jones, K. T., Wasserman, J. L., & Smith, J. C. (2006). Self-identification as "Down Low" among men who have sex with men (MSM) from 12 US cities. *AIDS Behavior, 10,* 519–529.

Concepts and Questions

1. Why would some readers be eager to read Eadie's article but others would prefer to avoid it?

2. Does Eadie's personal history affect your attitudes toward the lesbian and gay culture? How?

3. How does revealing one's lesbian or gay sexuality become a political statement? What specific behaviors might be interpreted as a political statement?

4. How do media portrayals of lesbians and gays perpetuate stereotypes? And how do the media foster positive images toward gays and lesbians?

5. What are the six interactive stages through which non-heterosexual individuals pass as they develop their identity?

6. How does Eadie describe the process by which gays and lesbians deal with the tensions associated with being open about sexuality?

7. What is the role of "camp" in the lesbian and gay culture? How would you explain "camp"?

8. What does Eadie mean when he refers to being in a "safe" space when meeting other lesbian and gay people?

9. What are some of the unique gay communication patterns Eadie describes? How do these forms of communication serve the gay culture?

10. What are some of the "societal expectations" that men and women are expected to adhere to in the "straight" community?

5

Intercultural Messages: Verbal and Nonverbal Interaction

You are as many a person as languages you know.

ARMENIAN PROVERB

If we spoke a different language, we would perceive a different world.

LUDWIG WITTGENSTEIN

Great things can be said in silence.

POLISH PROVERB

Since the first edition of this book more than forty years ago we have stressed the notion that one of our most distinguishing features as a species is our ability to create symbols to represent reality. This rare gift has enabled humans to evolve and develop a highly complex and elaborate language system that permits each person, regardless of culture, to receive, store, retrieve, manipulate, and generate symbols that stand for something else. By simply making certain sounds, producing marks on paper, striking the keys on a keyboard, or initiating movements of their bodies, people can relate to and interact with others. This marriage of nature and nurture means each of us can "tell" others how we are feeling, what we are thinking, and what we want to know. At first glance, verbal and nonverbal language appear effortless: you create an action (saying "hello" or smiling), and other people respond to what you have done. Yet, as you may know from personal experience, accurately sharing your ideas and feelings is not a trouble-free affair. Communication is a multifaceted activity that is subject to a host of variables. The series of readings in this chapter seeks to explain some of those complexities—especially as they apply to the symbols you exchange in the intercultural setting. More specifically, this chapter contends that a culture's use of verbal and nonverbal language involves not only words but also forms of reasoning, how discourse is performed, specialized linguistic devices such as analogies and idioms, the use of time and space, unique ways of moving, and behaviors that display emotions. Hence, understanding the verbal and nonverbal language of any culture implies viewing symbol sharing from this larger perspective. This eclectic outlook toward verbal and nonverbal language will help you recognize and appreciate the interaction patterns of cultures and co-cultures that are different from your own.

We begin by pointing out three important precepts regarding language. First, language (be it verbal or nonverbal) is a set of symbols (vocabulary) that evoke more or less uniform meanings among a particular population and set of rules (grammar and syntax) for using the symbols. In the broadest sense, language is the symbolic representation of a people, and it includes their historical and cultural background as well as their approach to life and ways of living and thinking. Second, verbal and nonverbal meanings are learned as part of a person's cultural affiliation. Third, the meanings people give to symbols reside within each individual. In each culture people learn to attach meaning to an elaborate set of verbal and nonverbal symbols. Although we consider verbal and nonverbal forms of symbolic interaction separately for convenience, it should be remembered that they are interrelated. Both involve elaborate symbol systems in which writing, speaking, or some other action represents an idea or feeling contained inside the person. Nonverbal behavior usually accompanies verbal behavior, and people may rely on nonverbal cues to aid in decoding the verbal symbols. Although verbal and nonverbal messages often work together, the two symbol systems have some important differences. These differences can help explain some of the confusion that arises when people from dissimilar cultures attempt to interact.

When you communicate verbally with members of your own culture, you use words with seeming ease because there is a learned form of agreement among all parities about the meanings the words evoke. Your experiential backgrounds are similar enough that you share *basically* the same meanings for most of the word symbols used in everyday communication. However, as mentioned earlier, even within your own culture, you may disagree about the meanings of some word symbols. As words move further from the reality of sense data, they become more abstract, and then there is far less agreement about appropriate meanings. Most people would understand what is being implied if someone uttered the words, "Please come here." However, when highly abstract words are used, agreement on what is being said might be harder to achieve. For example, highly abstract words such as *worship, spirituality, freedom, free choice, mental illness, "The Tea Party," equal opportunity, social equality, terrorism,* and *civil liberties* seldom have the same meaning for everyone. If you doubt this, ask some friends what they think of when they hear those words. You will find that people have different notions of these concepts, and consequently, different meanings for these words. Because their experiences have been different, they most likely have different beliefs, attitudes, values, concepts, and expectations. Yet all, or perhaps most, of these people are from the same culture. Their backgrounds, experiences, and concepts of the universe are relatively uniform. When cultural diversity is added to the process of decoding words, a much larger range in meanings and usage is found.

As just noted, what comes to be symbolized and what the symbols represent are very much functions of culture. Similarly, how symbols are used is also imbedded in culture; how you speak or think about things follows rules you have learned as a member of a specific culture. This relation between language and culture is not unidirectional—each influences the other. But what you think about and how you express your thoughts is rooted in your culture.

The aim of the preceding discussion was to demonstrate that language and culture are inseparable. In fact, it would be difficult to determine which is the voice and which is the echo. How you learn, employ, and respond to symbols is rooted in your culture. Hence, this part of the book highlights these symbols to help you understand a number of the complexities, subtleties, and nuances of language.

Some of the problems we have discussed regarding verbal communication can be applied to nonverbal communication. In fact, in many ways nonverbal communication is even more intricate than verbal interaction. Nonverbal communication can be problematic in two ways. First, nonverbal communication is often unconscious and ambiguous. In most instances you employ nonverbal symbols without thinking about what postures, what gestures, or even what personal distance is appropriate for each situation. In short, much of nonverbal communication is automatic. Second, interpreting nonverbal communication is characterized by some ambiguity. You notice two people talking and one has a clenched fist. You must decide if they are agreeing, are about to get into a fight, or are expressing exhilaration over what has just transpired. Even perceiving someone in tears can produce a variety of responses. Are these tears of joy or sorrow? Think for a moment of all the different interpretations that can be attached to touch, gaze, attire, movement, space, and the like when you send and receive messages. Successful intercultural communication requires that you recognize and understand culture's influence on both verbal and nonverbal interaction. It is the purpose of this chapter to assist you in that understanding. Whether it be the possible confusion generated by all the potential meanings for a particular word (*Jihad* may symbolize a holy war or a war within oneself) or a random touch, uncertainty is built into intercultural exchanges.

In our first essay, "The Nexus of Language, Communication, and Culture," Mary Fong introduces some fundamental ideas about the relationship between language and culture. Professor Fong's work has appeared in numerous editions of this book. She was one of the first communication scholars to explain how perception, culture, and language are connected. In the essay we selected for this anniversary edition, Fong begins with a review of the Sapir-Whorf hypothesis. This hypothesis, which proposed the notion of linguistic relativity, was one of the first modern observations of the relationship between language and culture. After her description of the hypothesis, she then traces later developments in this area that have led to ethnographic research approaches to the study of language and culture. To demonstrate the workability of the hypothesis, Fong applies the methodology of ethnography to a series of studies focusing on Chinese language to highlight the ways ethnographic approaches can be used to learn about another culture. She also maintains that you can learn about Chinese culture by examining some of the linguistic practices. For example, she explains that notions of face saving are reflected in the way Chinese language deals with compliments, indirectness, and modesty.

One of the major reasons we have included the next essay in this anniversary edition is that the Middle East is, and has been, a part of the world where clashes, both verbal and physical, have a lengthy, sad, and bloody history. In fact, the antecedents of today's conflict between Israeli-Jews and Palestinian-Arabs reach back thousands of years. Traditional discord notwithstanding, there might be ways the negative stereotypes, mutual distrust, and severe miscommunication, which highlight even today's relationships, could be managed through an understanding of what Donald G. Ellis and Ifat Maoz call "transformative dialogues." In "Dialogue and Cultural Communication Codes between Israeli-Jews and Palestinians," the authors posit that the Israeli-Jewish and Arab cultures have developed unique speech codes that reflect their nearly polar-opposite cultural differences. Ellis and Maoz suggest that the Arabic language employs speech codes that seek to "accommodate" or "go along with," which orients speakers toward harmonious relationships, whereas the Israeli-Jewish speech codes are direct, pragmatic, assertive, explicit, and clear. These speech code differences are essentially the opposite of one another and, according to Ellis and Maoz, are partially responsible for the failure of dialogue to resolve the conflict between the two cultures. The authors believe that by studying these speech codes you can gain some insight into the linguistic bases of cultural conflict and be better prepared to help mediate that conflict.

In every edition of this reader we have stressed that there are as many communication styles as there are cultures. Combined with that assertion is the reminder that if you have knowledge of the way other people communicate—that is, how they use language—you can improve the quality of your communication with them. As we have already noted, the study of language is important because language is a model of culture—it is a reflection of the experiences of that culture. We now turn to yet another culture's special use of language as a way of underscoring the integrated nature of language, culture, and intercultural communication. This time the focus is on Mexican culture. Both internationally and domestically, contact between the dominant American culture and Mexicans is more prevalent than ever. Mexico and the United States share a long and often contentious border. Within the United States, the Hispanic co-culture is the fastest growing and currently accounts for approximately 16 percent of the total population. To better communicate with people of this co-culture, we turn to an essay that uses language as a tool for increased understanding. The premise is a simple one: The words people use often reflect their culture. For example, because the dominant culture of the United States is highly individualistic, the "I" punctuates nearly every sentence. For Mexican culture, proverbs and sayings (called *dichos*) provide valuable information regarding the values, attitudes, and beliefs upon which the culture operates. In "Mexican *Dichos*: Lessons through Language" Carolyn Roy explores how Mexican values are expressed through *dichos,* popular sayings that convey values through proverbs, adages, and refrains. Roy discusses how the values of cheerful acceptance of the "will of God," the need to place trust in others with great care, the significance of appearances, the necessity to guard one's privacy and not breach the privacy of others, prescribed gender roles, a communal spirit, and the importance of family are expressed and reinforced through Mexican *dichos.*

We have already mentioned that verbal and nonverbal communication work in tandem. Verbal communication uses sounds to symbolize a person's feelings and ideas, whereas nonverbal communication employs diverse behaviors (movements, posture, facial expressions, gestures, eye contact, physical appearance, space, time, and vocal nuances) to represent a person's reality. In addition to working together, verbal and nonverbal symbols are deeply rooted in culture. Thus, what might be a positive sign in one culture (the thumbs up in the United States) may have a very different meaning in another culture (the equivalent of the middle finger in Iraq). Our point is simple, an awareness of the role nonverbal behaviors play during interaction is crucial if you are to appreciate all aspects of intercultural communication.

For this reason we have included readings on nonverbal communication since the first edition of this book.

We turn to nonverbal communication with an essay that offers a detailed summary of how culture and nonverbal communication are inseparable. In the selection "In Different Dimensions: Nonverbal Communication and Culture," Peter Andersen offers a synopsis of the topic of nonverbal communication rather than an examination of a single culture. Rooted in Andersen's article is the idea that nonverbal codes, like verbal languages, shift from culture to culture. To help us appreciate and understand these codes, Andersen begins by briefly summarizing the basic codes of nonverbal communication: physical appearance (attire), proxemics (space and distance), chronemics (time), kinesics (facial expressions, movements, gestures), haptics (touch), oculesics (eye contact and gaze), vocalics (paralanguage), and olfactics (smell). After his discussion of these basic codes, Andersen moves to an analysis of how these codes can differ from one culture to another. He explores these differences as they apply to high and low contexts, individualism and collectivism, power distance, uncertainty, immediacy, expressiveness, and gender.

Our next essay moves us from a discussion of cultures in general to an analysis of how the nonverbal variables highlighted by Andersen are acted out in a particular culture. This specialized investigation is offered by Edwin R. McDaniel in "Japanese Nonverbal Communication: A Reflection of Cultural Themes." As a means of demonstrating the link between culture and communication, McDaniel examines the communication behaviors of Japanese culture and traces the reasons for these behaviors. By presenting what he refers to as "cultural themes," McDaniel explains how Japan's social organizations, historical experiences, and religious orientations are directly connected to Japanese nonverbal behavior. In a propositional survey, McDaniel presents a series of eleven propositions that tie various cultural themes to how the Japanese perceive and use kinesics (movement), oculesics (eye contact), facial expressions, proxemics, touch, personal appearance, space, time, vocalics or paralanguage, silence, and olfactics (smell).

We conclude this chapter with an essay by Aaron Castelan Cargile titled "Language Matters." Cargile's central thesis is that cultural misunderstandings can occur even when people speak the same language. The reason, of course, should be obvious at this stage of the book. Language includes much more than the definitions of words. Although Cargile draws his examples from verbal communication, much of his analysis can be applied to nonverbal communication because both involve abstracting meaning from the symbols people produce.

Cargile begins by reiterating one of the basic premises of this chapter: the symbols we employ are a reflection of our experiences, and as those experiences vary, so does the manner in which we employ language. Cargile's analysis is concerned both with symbols and with the way people employ those symbols. He examines how differences in accents, vocabularies, and rates of speech might have an impact on interaction between people from different cultures or co-cultures. Cargile's concern is that these variations in language use can promote inaccurate and negative perceptions and stereotypes. He concludes with some advice on how to avoid engaging in the destructive behaviors created by misunderstanding another person's accent, vocabulary, or rate of speech.

The Nexus of Language, Communication, and Culture

Mary Fong

Throughout the centuries, scholars around the world have been interested in both oral and written languages and the role they serve in contributing to cultural societies. Confucius observed that proper human conduct maintains a civil society, and cautions: "If language not be in accordance with the truth of things, affairs cannot be carried on to success." Saint-Exupery's comment that "to grasp the meaning of the world of today we use a language created to express the world of yesterday" and the Biblical injunction "may the words of my mouth and the meditation of my heart be acceptable in thy sight, oh Lord" also reflect this concern. In the current era, anthropologists, linguists, psychologists, philosophers, and communication scholars continue to try to fathom the role of language and communication in human activity and its nexus to culture.

In this essay I first define language, communication, and culture. Then, I examine briefly some basic perspectives about the relationship between language, communication, and culture. In the course of this analysis I begin with a description of the Sapir–Whorf hypothesis and then review the more current directions of language, communication, and culture research. Finally, in order to demonstrate some of the relationships between language, communication, and culture using qualitative methodologies, I draw from research on the Chinese culture to demonstrate the nexus of language, communication, and culture in examples from both cultural and intercultural interactions.

Courtesy of Mary Fong. This original essay first appeared in the 10th edition. All rights reserved. Permission to reprint must be obtained from the publisher and the author. Mary Fong teaches in the Department of Communication Studies at California State University, San Bernardino.

INTERRELATIONSHIP OF LANGUAGE, COMMUNICATION, AND CULTURE

Language, communication, and culture are intricately intertwined with one another. Language is a symbolic system in which meaning is shared among people who identify with one another. Both verbal and nonverbal aspects of language exist. In the study of language and culture, the verbal aspect of both written and spoken communications has been the predominant focus of research.

Spoken language is a vehicle for people to communicate in social interaction by expressing their experience and creating experience. Words reflect the sender's attitude, beliefs, and points of view. Language expresses, symbolizes, and embodies cultural reality (Kramsch, 1998). Communication cannot exist without language, and language needs the process of communication to engage people in social interaction.

Both language and communication reflect culture. For Sherzer (1987), culture is the organization of individuals who share rules for production and interpretation of behavior. Language and communication represent an individual's symbolic organization of the world. Language is a medium that reflects and expresses an individual's group membership and relationships with others. Both written and oral languages are shaped by culture, and in turn, these languages shape culture. As Kramsch points out: Culture both liberates and constrains. It liberates by investing the randomness of nature with meaning, order, and rationality and by providing safeguards against chaos; it constrains by imposing a structure on nature and by limiting the range of possible meanings created by the individual (1998, p. 10).

With this same tenor, language and communication both liberate and constrain. Language and communication enable people to express themselves, while simultaneously constraining them to conform to shared cultural standards. Culture is a social system in which members share common standards of communication, behaving, and evaluating in everyday life.

PERSPECTIVES ON LANGUAGE AND CULTURE

A major proponent of linguistic relativity and one of the first modern observations of the relationship between language and culture is the Sapir-Whorf hypothesis. This notion proposes a deterministic view that language structure is necessary in order to produce thought. In other words, language and its categories—grammar, syntax, and vocabulary—are the only categories by which we can experience the world. Simply stated, language influences and shapes how people perceive their world, their culture. This vision dominated scholarly thinking as a point of discussion, research, and controversy for more than five decades.

The Sapir–Whorf hypothesis also holds that language and thought co-vary. That is, diversity in language categories and structure lead to cultural differences in thought and perceptions of the world. This position is known as linguistic relativity. Sapir (1951) believes that the "real world" is largely built on the unconscious language habits of the group. Benjamin Whorf was a student of Edward Sapir at Yale University from about 1931 (Carroll, 1992). Initial publications of Whorf's (1956) views about language and culture were printed in a series of articles in 1940–1941. He writes:

> We cut nature up, organize it into concepts, and ascribe significances as we do, largely because we are parties to an agreement to organize it in this way—an agreement that holds throughout our speech community and is codified in the patterns of our language. (p. 213)

Sapir and Whorf's ideas have been understood to mean that people who speak different languages segment their world differently. Thus, any language, such as Russian, Chinese, or German, structures a "Russian," "Chinese," or "German" reality by framing and screening what these cultural members pay attention to. If there is a word for "it" in their language, then cultural members know that "it" exists, and if not, "it" is nonexistent to them.

For instance, when I was five years old, I remember my mother asked me to stick out my tongue so that she could look at it. She looked at it briefly and said in Chinese Cantonese, "Ni yao yi hay," meaning, "you have heat." My mother observed the texture, color, and coating of my tongue and lips. In the Chinese culture, it is common knowledge than an aspect of our physical health is viewed in terms of yi hay (heat) or leung (cool), which are extreme conditions that may be balanced through various types of foods and herbs. It is not the actual temperature of the food, but rather the nature of the food that produces a cool or warm effect on your body. If a person eats too many fried and baked foods and not enough cool foods such as particular fruits, vegetables, and liquids, then the person will eventually have a condition of too much heat in the body. If a person has a cool condition, one way to increase the heat in one's body is to lessen the consumption of cool foods and to increase one's diet to warm nature foods. This is one way that the Chinese strive to maintain a healthy physical balance.

This is an example of a "Chinese" reality of framing and screening what these cultural members pay attention to. On the other hand, the "American" reality promotes eating a well-balanced diet from the four main food groups: fruits and vegetables, meat and poultry, breads and grains, and dairy products. The American reality does not typically categorize food as warm or cold in nature in understanding and maintaining a balanced diet to increase one's health.

The system of labeling food, drink, medicines, herbs, illnesses, and medical procedures as either cold or hot is based on a system originating with the ancient Greeks and spreading to Central Asia (Dresser, 1996). For instance, as perceived in many Asian cultures, after a major surgery or childbirth, the body loses blood, energy, and heat. Therefore, the heat must be replenished, and avoidance of drinking cold water, eating cool foods, or taking showers is recommended. Middle Eastern and Latin American peoples also have a system of classifying foods, medicines, and procedures, but all cultural groups may differ in varying degrees depending on their principles (Dresser, 1996).

The situation of my mother observing my physical condition and the examples of foods, medicines, and procedures provide instances of how various cultural people segment their world and reality in varying ways. Furthermore, this natural cultural process of thinking and perceiving influences how members may communicate by accepting or rejecting particular foods, medicines, and procedures in certain circumstances. A person who is not familiar with another person's cultural ways will be likely to misinterpret the person's actions.

Another scholar, Brown (1958), in part disagreed with the Sapir–Whorf hypothesis and argued that a cultural member's worldview is not determined by language. He held, rather, that people categorize their world by attaching labels to what is out there. People use language to do what they need it to do. According to Brown, people will label an object, an idea, a process, and so forth based on the importance and utilization it has for them. For example, CDs, DVDs, cell phones, and the Internet are relatively new inventions that need labeling through language so that people can communicate their ideas about them. Because antiquated technology such as a record player, a rotary phone, and a slide rule is no longer important or used by people, the once common labels for these objects are now archived in museums and hardly referred to in conversation. Brown's position, however, supports the idea of linguistic relativity because the perceptual categories that are frequently used receive labels, whereas, unused or insignificant categories may not be labeled.

Several research studies on color terms and color perception tested the Sapir–Whorf hypothesis (Berlin & Kay, 1967; Bruner, Oliver, & Greenfield, 1966; Greenfield & Bruner, 1966; Kay & Kempton, 1984). Eastman (1990) reviewed these studies that supported the idea of linguistic relativity and stated that: "[I]t appears to be the case that world view is a matter more of linguistic relativity than linguistic determinism" (p. 109).

Other researchers have found it difficult to test how strongly the structure of a language influences the worldview of people because reliable methods in assessing the worldview of a cultural people independently of the language they speak are needed (Brown, 1976; Carroll, 1967; Kay & Kempton, 1984). The deterministic view of the Sapir–Whorf hypothesis is not taken seriously (Kramsch, 1998). Carroll (1992) believes that researchers and theorists generally regard the Sapir–Whorf as either uncomfirmable or incorrect because the evidence offered in its support is viewed as being flawed. He further contends that if the hypothesis can be sustained, it would only suggest a weak influence of language structure on thought.

The linguistic-relativity view of the Sapir–Whorf hypothesis is its strength and contribution in understanding an aspect of the differences in language and culture. It is not so much if languages can be translated into one another, which they can, for the most part, if two speakers are of different languages; but rather, the two speakers coming from different cultures are operating under different language and communication systems that are designed differently, which influences their perceptions and interpretation of an event. As Kramsch (1998) suggests, speakers from different cultures define reality or categorize experience in different ways. Achieving understanding across languages is dependent on common conceptual systems rather than on structural equivalences. They may differ in terms of the meaning and value of a concept.

CURRENT RESEARCH TRENDS AND DIRECTIONS

In 1974 Hymes described the development of linguistic research in the first half of the twentieth century, which was distinguished by a drive for the autonomy of language as an object of study and a focus on description of [grammatical] structure, and in the second half of the century, which was distinguished by a concern for the integration of language in sociocultural context and a focus on the analysis of function (p. 208).

Hymes' description was accurate because the second half of the twentieth century has marked several research methods, such as discourse analysis, pragmatics, ethnography of communication, rhetorical analysis, and quantitative analysis, as ways to investigate the linkages of language, communication, and culture. Examples of themes of interest to researchers are the relationship between language and context, the relationship between language and identities (i.e., personal identity, social role identity, and cultural/ ethnolinguistic identity), and multiple functions and meanings of language and communication in relationship to culture (Ting-Toomey, 1989).

Current approaches to the study of language, communication, and culture are developmental, interactional, and social psychological. The developmental approach focuses on language acquisition and cultural communication practices simultaneously in the language development stages of a child. Developmental theorists are interested in understanding the connection between the cognitive processing in a culture (Ting-Toomey, 1989). The interactional approach investigates what people are doing with speech as they interact face-to-face in a particular interactional context. Interactional theorists are interested in identifying appropriate communication styles and norms in various cultures (Ting-Toomey, 1989). The social psychological approach explores the underlying factors that influence language choices in multilingual communication contexts. For example, group comparison factors, identity salience factors, and attitudinal and motivational factors have significant association to the language accommodations process in intergroup communication situations. Social psychological theorists are interested in delineating specific social psychological conditions that account for first-language or second-language usage in majority and minority groups in cultural communities globally (Ting-Toomey, 1989).

For some researchers, the controversy over whether language determines or reflects thought or thought determines or reflects language is not the primary concern. According to Sherzer (1987), what is at issue is the analysis of discourse as the "embodiment of the essence of culture and as constitutive of what language and culture relationship is all about." Sherzer (1987) also views discourse as the intersection where language and culture interrelate. He states: "It is discourse that creates, recreates, focuses, modifies, and transmits both culture and language and their intersection" (p. 295).

For Sherzer (1987), culture is the organization of individuals who share rules for production and interpretation of behavior. Language represents an individual's symbolic organization of the world. Language is a medium that reflects and expresses an individual's group membership and relationships with others. Discourse analysis derives from pragmatics and speech act theory (Saville-Troike, 1989). Pragmatics or speech act theory refers to the study of the connotative (inner) and denotative (outer) meanings of "expressions when used in a conversation or a written work" (Paul, 1987, p. 101). According to Silverstein (1976), pragmatics is "the study of the meaning of linguistic signs relative to their communicative functions" (p. 20). Pragmatics also entails cultural members applying their knowledge of the world to the interpretation of what is said and done in interaction (Fromkin & Rodman, 1983; Gumperz, 1982).

The ethnography of communication provides the researcher with a framework of observation and interviewing techniques to facilitate capturing the interlocutors' meanings in various communicative acts both culturally and interculturally. The ethnographer endeavors to describe the communicative choices that interlocutors make. This involves describing and accounting for the interpretive systems and practices through which members construct actions and deal with behaviors.

Hymes (1962), the originator of the ethnography of communication, states that the "study of speech as a factor in cognitive and expressive behavior leads to concern with the ethnographic patterning of the uses of speech in a community" (p. 102). Investigating language, communication, and culture is discovering not only linguistic structural regularities, but also regularities of usage that have motives, emotions, desires, knowledge, attitudes, and values attached to them. An essential aim of studies on language, communication, and culture using the ethnography of communication approach is to make implicit cultural beliefs, attitudes, values, norms of interpretation, rules of speaking, norms of interaction, and so forth explicit in order to understand and to practice communication competence within a particular culture, and eventually in intercultural interactions.

LANGUAGE STUDIES

Some of the sample findings in the cultural and intercultural studies that follow are illustrations of language and culture analysis. The qualitative methods—discourse analysis, pragmatics, and ethnography of communication—jointly provide tools and perspectives to make possible an in-depth examination of the communicative phenomena.

A Cultural Study

An ethnographic study of the Chinese New Year celebration in Hong Kong (Fong, 2000) provides one instance of the manner in which the Chinese employ language to reverse bad luck. By examining a speaking pattern that is used when someone makes a negative comment during the Chinese New Year, it is possible to understand how Chinese people are prepared to avoid arguments and negative talk during the Chinese New Year. It is possible to understand how Chinese are prepared to handle a rule violation committed. Chinese people engage in positive talk and try to avoid arguments and negative talk during the Chinese New Year. Spoken words are carefully watched to avoid saying words that signify death, sickness, poverty, or anything else unlucky. All of the participants in this cultural study agreed with the same ideas as the following participant, who explains why negative comments during the New Year celebrations are avoided:

> Of course you don't say unlucky things. Always be positive. Chinese New Year is supposed to be a happy occasion. Try not to say something unlucky, like mentioning death or misfortune. Say it after the New Year. Perhaps some people may even think that saying those things during Chinese New Year will bring bad luck in the coming year. Those things may happen.

If someone accidentally talks about something unfortunate or utters a negative comment during this holiday, the rule of positive speaking is violated in this context. The hearer of the message may say[1]:

/tsɔi^1/or/tsɔi^1,dai^6 gæt^7 lei^6 si^6/
("lucky" or "very lucky, auspicious")

Another expression that participants in the study reported is:

/tou^3 hæu^2 sæy^2 dzɔi^3 gɔŋ^2 gwɔ^3/*
("Spit out your saliva; speak once more.")

These expressions are said in order to reverse the bad luck that has been invited into good luck.

To understand what linguistic devices the Chinese employ, it is necessary to understand a few rules of behavior and speaking. Shimanoff (1980) proposes an "If...then..." method of concisely stating a rule of behavior. To develop Shimanoff's method of stating behavioral rules, I will add a "because...meaning..." sequence in order to add a meaning component to a formulation of a communication rule.

In this situation, the sequential rule statement begins with the initial linguistic "If..." slot that provides information on the particular context, condition, or situation, like a speech event, speech act, or genre. It is followed by the "then..." slot, which refers to the speaking and/or behavioral interaction pattern discovered from the researcher's ethnographic data analysis.

The third linguistic device, the "because..." slot, provides a concise rationale for why people of a particular culture behave the way they do. Here, an underlying belief or value system or cultural principle may be revealed to provide an explanation for a people's way of communicating. The final linguistic device, the "meaning..." slot, serves the same function as Hymes' component norm of interpretation of a symbol, the speaking and/or behavioral interaction pattern, a particular speech act, speech event, scene, and so forth.

These sequential rules statement provides the following formula:

If...(context, condition, or situation like a speech event, speech act, or genre)...

then...(speaking and/or interaction pattern)...

because...(belief or value system or cultural principle)...

meaning...(norm of interpretation of a symbol, speaking pattern, interaction pattern, a particular speech act, speech event, scene, etc.)

Applying these sequential rules to the Chinese custom of reversing the negative comments can be expressed in a concise rule statement using the following formula:

If a person makes a negative comment on Chinese New Year Day, *then* a Hong Kong Chinese person who hears it should say:

/tsɔi^1/or/tsɔu^1, dai^6 gæt^7 lei^6 si^6/
("lucky" or "very lucky, auspicious")

/tou^3 hæu^2 sæy^2 dzɔi^3 gɔŋ^2 gwɔ^3/*
("Spit out your saliva; speak once more.")

because this is believed to counteract the bad luck and create good luck, *meaning* that the negative comments will not come true in the coming new year.

An Intercultural Study

An intercultural study on compliment interactions between Chinese immigrants and European Americans from the perspective of Chinese immigrants (Fong, 1998) found that both cultural groups have differing ways of speaking in compliment interactions (Chen, 1993; Chiang & Pochtrager, 1993; Fong, 1998). European Americans on the West Coast and in the Midwest generally accept a compliment (Chen, 1993; Chiang & Pochtrager, 1993; Fong, 1998).

On the other hand, the literature reports that Chinese have the tendency to deny compliments in order to give an impression of modesty (Chen, 1993; Chiang & Pochtrager, 1993; Gao, 1984; Zhang, 1988). In one study (Fong, 1998), an informant from Mainland China explained the primary difference and the internal similarity between the two cultural groups:

> On the surface I say "no, no, no."…But inside I accept it. I feel really excited. In western culture, they say "yes" means accept the compliment. But in China, people say "no," but really, really accept the compliment. Different [speaking] way, but the feeling is the same. (p. 257)

Four adaptations by Chinese immigrant participants (CIPs) to European-American compliments were found. An orientation is a state or condition that is changeable from one interaction to another depending on the CIP's adaptation to intercultural communication differences. Four orientations in which the CIP can be located are (1) intercultural shock state, (2) intercultural resistance state, (3) intercultural accommodation state, and (4) bi-cultural competence state. For the purpose of this essay, we will capture a glimpse of one of the orientations, the intercultural shock state, in order to have a sense of Chinese immigrants' thinking and speaking patterns.

Affectively, CIPs reported feeling uncomfortable, unnatural, uneasy, nervous, stressed, embarrassed, surprised, shocked, or afraid when a European American complimented them. The situational outcome of the intercultural compliment interaction for CIPs, however, was an appreciation in receiving praise because they felt accepted, liked, and welcomed by European Americans. CIPs reported that compliments helped them reduce some of their stress as a newcomer to the United States.

Cognitively, CIPs in the intercultural shock state have minimum knowledge of the intercultural communication differences in compliment interactions with European Americans. Before coming to the United States, CIPs reported that they were not familiar with the European Americans' generosity in giving (1) compliments, (2) compliments containing strong positive adjectives, (3) compliments intended to encourage a person after an unsatisfactory performance, and (4) compliments on a wide variety of topics; and they were unfamiliar with (5) accepting compliments and (6) face-to-face compliments in all types of relationships.

Behaviorally, five speaking patterns were found; two examples are provided here. One type of a compliment response that Chinese immigrants used was the Direct Denial + Verbal Corrective/Prescriptive response. Following is a reported intercultural compliment interaction:

(AMERICAN) BOYFRIEND: You're the most beautiful person that I've seen.

(HONG KONG) GIRLFRIEND: Oh gaaa. Oohh. Please don't say that.

Because Chinese immigrants value indirectness and modesty, the compliment was interpreted as being direct (e.g., face-to-face, expressing openly with positive adjectives on the complimentee's appearance), which is contrary to the reported Chinese way of compliment interactions. The response was made to avoid self-praise and to suggest to the complimenter not to make such a direct compliment.

CIPs who were in the intercultural shock state were also found to use the Silence response. The following intercultural compliment interaction is reported to have occurred at work:

(AMERICAN FEMALE) BOSS: I want to thank you for doing a wonderful job. You're very, very nice.

(CHINESE FEMALE) WORKER: [silence]

Chinese immigrant interlocutors value modesty highly, but they are also aware of one of the American values of directly accepting and appreciating compliments. The compliment was interpreted as direct (i.e., face-to-face, expressing openly their positive thoughts with positive adjectives), which is contrary to the reported Chinese way of compliment interactions. The response was made because Chinese immigrant recipients reported that they felt ambivalent about which cultural response to use, thus the Chinese immigrant recipient remained silent.

CONCLUSION

The excerpt from the cultural study (Fong, 2000) illustrates the Chinese way of thinking and speaking. When a negative comment is made during the Chinese New Year holiday, the Chinese way of thinking is interpreting the incident as forthcoming bad luck in the coming new year. Through speech, however, the perceived bad luck is reversed to good luck.

The intercultural compliment interaction study (Fong, 1994) sheds light on the way Chinese immigrants in the intercultural shock state reveal patterns of thinking and speaking. The denial response is a pattern of speaking that is commonly used in the intercultural shock state. CIPs in this orientation essentially perceive European Americans as being generous in giving compliments with relatively strong positive adjectives, and in accepting compliments.

Current ethnographic methods hold that the best way to capture a view of language, communication, and culture is to observe the communicative phenomenon in a naturalistic setting and to have cultural members identify and classify the interaction or event as being culturally significant. The crossroads of language, communication, and culture is found in the culturally shared meaning of ideas and behaviors that are voiced as symbolic utterances, expressions, dialogue, and conversations in such various contexts as interpersonal and group interactions, research interviews, and public speaking forums.

In the two qualitative studies described in this essay, the ways of speaking and thinking were the two primary interrelated foci that reveal and reflect the outer and inner shared substances of communications that primarily make up a speech community. To examine a speech community's patterns of speaking without also discovering the norms of interpretation or the shared sociocultural knowledge of cultural members is to silence their cultural humanness as a speech community. To study only the shared sociocultural knowledge of cultural members and not attend

to how it is relevant to their way of speaking is to lose an opportunity to understand more about different cultural communication styles. In accomplishing this goal, potential sources at borderlines and intersections of cultural differences are able to richly understand and resolve intercultural conflicts.

Both examples of findings from the mentioned qualitative studies illuminate, in part, what Hymes (1974) has suggested:

> It has often been said that language is an index to or reflection of culture. But language is not simply passive or automatic in its relation to culture.... Speaking is itself a form of cultural behavior, and language, like any other part of culture, partly shapes the whole; and its expression of the rest of culture is partial, selective. That selective relation, indeed, is what should be interesting to us. Why do some features of a community's life come to be named—overtly expressible in discourse—while others are not? (p. 127)

Note

1. The International Phonetic System was used in transcribing this and other Chinese dialogue.

References

Berlin, B., & Kay, P. (1967). *Universality and evolution of basic color terms.* Working Paper #1, Laboratory for Language Behavior Research, University of California, Berkeley.

Bruner, J., Oliver, R. R., & Greenfield, P. M. (1966). *Studies in cognitive growth.* New York: John Wiley & Sons.

Brown, R. (1958). *Words and things.* New York: The Free Press.

Brown, R. (1976). In Memorial Tribute to Eric Lennenberg. *Cognition, 4,* 125–153.

Carroll, J. B. (1967). Bibliography of the Southwest Project in Comparative Psycholinguistics. In D. Hymes (Ed.), *Studies in southwestern ethnolinguistics* (pp. 452–454). The Hague: Mouton.

Carroll, J. B. (1992). Anthropological linguistics: An overview. In W. Bright (Ed.), *International encyclopedia of linguistics.* New York: Oxford University Press.

Chen, R. (1993). Responding to compliments: A contrastive study of politeness strategies between American English and Chinese speakers. *Journal of Pragmatics, 20,* 49–75.

Chiang, F., & Pochtrager, B. (1993). A pilot study of compliment responses of American-born English speakers and

Chinese-born English speakers. (Available in Microfiche only, ED 356649).

Dresser, N. (1996). *Multicultural manners*. New York: John Wiley & Sons.

Eastman, C. M. (1990). *Aspects of language and culture* (2nd ed.). Novato, CA: Chandler & Sharp Publishers.

Fong, M. (1994). Patterns of occurrence of compliment response types. In a doctoral dissertation, *Chinese immigrants' interpretations of their intercultural compliment interactions with European-Americans*. Seattle: University of Washington.

Fong, M. (1998). Chinese immigrants' perceptions of semantic dimensions of direct/indirect communication in intercultural compliment interactions with North Americans. *The Howard Journal of Communications*, 9, 3.

Fong, M. (2000). 'Luck talk' in celebrating the Chinese New Year. *Journal of Pragmatics*, 32, 219–237.

Fromkin, V., & Rodman, R. (1983). *An introduction to language* (3rd ed.). New York: CBS Publishing and Holt, Rinehart, & Winston.

Gao, W. (1984). *Compliment and its reaction in Chinese and English cultures*. Working papers in discourse in English and Chinese. Canberra: Canberra College of Advanced Education, 32–37.

Greenfield, P. M., & Bruner, J. S. (1966). Culture and cognitive growth. *International Journal of Psychology*, 1, 89–107.

Gumperz, J. J. (1982). *Discourse strategies*. New York: Cambridge University Press.

Hymes, D. (1962). The ethnography of speaking. In T. Gladwin & W. Sturtevant (Eds.), *Anthropology and human behavior* (pp. 99–137). Washington, DC: Anthropological Society of Washington.

Hymes, D. (1964). Toward ethnographies of communication: The analysis of communicative events. *American Anthropologist*, 66, 21–41.

Hymes, D. (1974). *Foundations in sociolinguistics: An ethnographic approach*. Philadelphia: University of Pennsylvania Press.

Kay, P., & Kempton, W. (1984). What is the Sapir–Whorf Hypothesis? *American Anthropologist*, 86, 65–79.

Kramsch, C. (1998). *Language and culture*. London, England: Oxford University Press.

Paul, A. (1987). Review of Joseph H. Greenberg, *Language in the Americas*. In "In Brief Books," *The Chronicle of Higher Education*, July 15, 6.

Sapir, E. (1951). The status of linguistics as a science. In D. Mandelbaum (Ed.), *Selected writings*. Berkeley: University of California Press.

Saville-Troike, M. (1989). *The ethnography of communication* (2nd ed.). New York: Basil Blackwell.

Sherzer, J. (1987). A discourse-centered approach to language and culture. *American Anthropologist*, 89, 295–309.

Shimanoff, S. B. (1980). *Communication rules: Theory and research*. Beverly Hills: Sage.

Silverstein, M. (1976). Shifters, linguistics categories, and cultural description. In K. H. Basso & H. A. Selby (Eds.), *Meaning in anthropology* (pp. 11–56). Albuquerque: University of New Mexico Press.

Ting-Toomey, S. (1989). Language, communication, and culture. In S. Ting-Toomey & F. Korzenny (Eds.), *Language, communication, and culture* (pp. 9–15). Newbury Park: Sage.

Whorf, B. L. (1940/1956). *Language, thought, and reality: Selected writings of Benjamin Lee Whorf* (J. B. Carroll, Ed.). Cambridge, MA: MIT Press.

Zhang, Z. (1988). A discussion of communicative culture. *Journal of Chinese Language Teacher Association*, 23, 107–112.

Concepts and Questions

1. What does Fong mean when she writes: "Language and thought vary with one another"? Do you agree?
2. Can you think of specific examples that illustrate the link between culture and language?
3. Can you explain what Fong means when she states that language influences and shapes how people perceive their world and their culture?
4. What is meant by the following phrase: "People who speak different languages segment their world differently"?
5. How do Chinese immigrants and Americans differ in their compliment interactions?
6. When referring to Sherzer, what does Fong means when she writes: "Culture is the organization of individuals who share rules for production and interpretation of behavior"?
7. How do the Chinese use language to reverse bad luck?
8. In what ways do the Chinese and the Americans express themselves differently?

Dialogue and Cultural Communication Codes between Israeli-Jews and Palestinians

DONALD G. ELLIS

IFAT MAOZ

Even a casual observer of contemporary political events knows that Israeli-Jews and Palestinian-Arabs are locked in severe conflict that often becomes violent. The origins of the conflict between Israeli-Jews and Palestinian-Arabs can be traced to the end of the nineteenth century with the appearance of political Zionism and the resulting waves of Jewish immigration to Palestine. Zionism sought to establish a Jewish State in Palestine. On the same land, however, lived Arabs, with a Palestinian national identity. This resulted in a clash between the Jewish and Palestinian communities over the ownership of the land, the right for self-determination, and statehood. Violence between the two communities first erupted in the 1920s and has pervaded the relationship in various forms, and with varying degrees of intensity, since that time (Kelman, 1997; Rouhana & Bar-Tal, 1998).

The communal clash that characterized the first decades of the twentieth century escalated into a war that involved the neighboring Arab states. This war erupted after the United Nations (UN) declared, in November 1947, the partition of Palestine into two states—one Arab and one Jewish. The Palestinians rejected the UN partition plan, and an independent Jewish state was established in 1948. Israel won the

war, and most Palestinians who lived in the portion of Palestine on which Israel was now established were dispersed to the neighboring Arab countries, partly having fled war zones and partly having been expelled by Israeli forces (Maoz, 1999).

Other historical turning points in the relationship between Israelis and Palestinians include the 1967 war between Israel on one side, and Egypt, Jordan, and Syria on the other, which brought the remainder of Palestine under Israeli control. The first *intifada*, or uprising, was an uprising of the Palestinians in the West Bank and Gaza strip territories, expressing resistance to the Israeli occupation of these territories. It began in 1987 and lasted until 1993 (Rouhana & Bar-Tal, 1998).

In 1993 peace accords were signed in Oslo, Norway, which signaled a breakthrough in the relations between Israelis and Palestinians. This dramatic agreement included an exchange of letters of mutual recognition between representatives of the two peoples, which was followed by a declaration of principles that stipulated the establishment of a Palestinian authority in Gaza and Jericho as a first step in Palestinian self-rule (Kelman, 1997). At this point, which was indeed historic, prospects for the success of the peace process seemed exceptionally good. There was hope that the peace accords would end violence and lead to reconciliation; however, a few years after signing the accords, it became clear that this optimism was premature.

A chain of violent incidents began in November 1995 with the assassination of the then Israeli Prime Minister and continued with several terrorist attacks in the first half of 1996. These events signaled a slowdown in the Israeli-Palestinian peace process. Increasingly, the adversaries presented obstacles and impediments to the peace process, posed problems for the implementation of the different stages of the agreements, and violated the agreements. In October 2000, the Al Aqsa *intifada* broke out, and the relationship between the Israelis and the Palestinians again took a violent turn.

Yet, political leaders from both sides continue to try and return to peace making and peace building. Although the conflict centers on the issue of land, and who has legitimate rights to the land—an issue that has strong historical, religious, and emotional significance—it is also a cultural conflict, a conflict over identities and recognition. The political and cultural differences between Israeli-Jews and Palestinians involve negative stereotypes, mutual delegitimization, and severe miscommunication. Dialogue and group encounters are one way to cope with these difficult problems. Dialogue sessions between Israeli-Jews and Palestinians involve a process of transformative communication aimed at improving the relations between the sides (Maoz, 2000a).

TRANSFORMATIVE COMMUNICATION BETWEEN GROUPS IN CONFLICT

Intergroup dialogues are useful venues for growth, change, and conflict management. Transformative dialogue between cultural groups in conflict helps reduce prejudice and hostility and foster mutual understanding (Gergen, 1999). Such dialogue experiences have been successful at helping groups cope with conflict in Northern Ireland, South Africa, and the Middle East.

The notion of transformative contact or dialogue, when used in the context of intergroup conflict, draws heavily from the contact hypothesis in social psychology. This theory was first presented by Allport (1954) and since has been the subject of numerous studies (Amir, 1976; Pettigrew, 1998). The contact hypothesis states that under certain conditions, contact between groups in conflict reduces prejudice and changes negative intergroup attitudes. The contact hypothesis is optimal under certain conditions:

1. The two groups should be of equal status, at least within the contact situation. Contact of unequal status, where the traditional status imbalance is maintained, can act to perpetuate existing negative stereotypes.
2. Successful contact should involve personal and sustained communication between individuals from the two groups.
3. Effective contact requires cooperative interdependence, where members of the two groups engage in cooperative activities and depend on one another in order to achieve mutual goals.
4. Social norms favoring equality must be the consensus among the relevant authorities.

TRANSFORMATIVE DIALOGUES BETWEEN ISRAELIS AND PALESTINIANS

The first attempts to address the dispute between Israelis and Palestinians by means of structured communication events were in interactive problem-solving workshops developed by Herbert Kelman from Harvard University in the early 1970s and have been conducted since then by him and his colleagues (Kelman, 1997). These workshops brought together politically active and influential Israelis and Palestinians for private, direct communication facilitated by unofficial third-party mediators (Kelman, 1995, 1997). Since the Oslo peace agreements in 1993, numerous Israeli-Palestinian dialogue events are conducted each year that are targeted at grassroots populations from both sides (Adwan & Bar-On, 2000). These dialogue events typically last two to three days and are aimed at building peace and reconciliation through processes of constructive communication (Maoz, 2000b). Both Israelis and Palestinians facilitate the dialogues. In some sessions all of the participants meet, and in others they are divided into smaller groups. There are also several uni-national meetings where participants meet only with members of their own group. Dialogues are conducted either in English, or Hebrew and Arabic that is translated.

The concept of "dialogue" as discussed by scholars such as Martin Buber, Carl Rogers, and Mikhail Bakhtin is the general guiding principle of these groups. That is, the goal of the communication is to avoid "monologue," or the pressure of a single authoritative voice, and to strive for "dialogue," which emphasizes the interplay of different perspectives where something new and unique emerges. At its best, dialogue is a search for deep differences and shared concerns. It asks participants to inquire genuinely about the other person and avoid premature judgment, debate, and questions designed to expose flaws.

The process of change and transformation during dialogue is difficult, complex, and slow. Many issues enter the mix of politics, psychology, culture, and communication. In our work we have found that the communication process remains central. There is simply no possibility for reconciliation and peace without sustained interaction. Therefore, we direct our attention to the issues in culture and communication that characterize these groups. The remainder of this article is devoted to explaining the cultural communication codes that typify interactions between Israeli-Jews and Palestinians and how these speech codes are expressed in actual dialogues when Israeli-Jews and Palestinians are arguing.

SPEECH CODES

Whenever groups of people live in a culture, they have certain characteristics and behaviors in common. We know, for example, that people in cultures dress similarly, share tastes in food preparation, and have many common attitudes, but they also share orientations toward communication. Members of cultural communities share principles of language use and interpretation. This simply means that your use of language (word choice, slang, accents, syntax) and your tendencies to interpret and understand this language in a certain way depend on your cultural membership. For example, assume you overheard the following conversation (Ellis, 1992):

JESSE: Yea, I'm thinkin' 'bout getting some new ink.

GENE: Really, where you gonna put it?

JESSE: Oh, I don' know. I've still got some clean spots.

For the moment, this conversation is probably pretty confusing and odd. What does it mean to "get new ink"? Why is Gene concerned about where to put it? What do "clean spots" refer to? Who are these people, and what cultural functions is this conversation serving? Is Jesse thinking about buying a new bottle of ink for his fountain pen and Gene does not think there will be room for it on his messy desk?

This is a conversation between two tattoo enthusiasts who live and work among others in a tattoo culture that has developed norms of speaking. If you were a member of the culture and understood the "speech code," then you could participate in this conversation easily and competently. You would know that "new ink" refers to a "new tattoo" and that "clean spots" were places on the body that had no tattoos. You would understand the personal identity satisfaction that members of this culture gain from their unique code of communication.

Jesse and Gene are speaking in a cultural code, and you can only understand and participate in the conversation if you understand the code. The concept of speech codes has been studied by Bernstein (1971), Ellis (1992, 1994), and Philipsen (1997). Philipsen's treatment is most thorough in communication, and it is the perspective we rely on here. But first we describe two cultural communication codes termed *dugri* and *musayra* known to characterize Israeli-Jews and Arabs, respectively. This discussion will be followed by an elaboration of the concept of speech codes and an explanation of their role in intercultural communication dialogues for peace.

Israeli-Jewish and Arab cultures have emerged from the special circumstances of their history, and different norms of communication emerge from this history. These contrasting speech codes can make for difficult and uncoordinated communication. Several researchers have described an Arab communication code called *musayra* (e.g., Feghali, 1997; Katriel, 1986). *Musayra* means "to accommodate" or "go along with." It is a way of communicating that orients the speaker toward a harmonious relationship with the other person. *Musayra* emerges from the core values of Arab culture that has to do with honor, hospitality, and collectivism. An Arab speaker who is engaging in the code of *musayra* is being polite, indirect, courteous, and nonconfrontive to the other member of a conversation.

More specifically, *musayra* is composed of four communication features. The first is *repetition* in which the communication is characterized by repetitive statements that are formulaic in nature. Repetition is used primarily for complimenting and praising others, which is an important communication activity when you are trying to be gracious and accommodating. Repetition is also used as an argumentative style where repeated phrases are used to influence beliefs rather than Western-style logic. *Indirectness* is a second feature of the *musayra* code. This communication strategy reflects the cultural tendency to be interpersonally cautious and responsive to context. By being indirect, one can shift positions easier to accommodate the other person. Indirectness also facilitates politeness and face saving. *Elaboration* is a third feature, which pertains to an expressive and encompassing style. It leads to a deeper connection between speakers and affirms relationships. The final characteristic is *affectiveness* or an intuitive and emotional style. Again, this allows for identification with the other person and the maintenance of an engaged relationship.

The speech code of Israeli-Jews is a sharp contrast to *musayra*. Israeli-Jews employ a direct, pragmatic, and assertive style. This style has been termed *dugri* by Katriel (1986). *Dugri* means "straight talk" and is a well-documented code used by Israeli-Jews. *Dugri* is the opposite of *musayra*. *Dugri* speech is "to the point," with the communication of understanding and information as the most important communicative goals. Emotional appeals and personal niceties are of secondary importance. In *musayra* it is important to maintain the face or positive image of the other speaker. In *dugri* speech the speaker is more concerned with maintaining his or her own image of clarity and directness. *Dugri* and *musayra* are excellent examples of speech codes. Philipsen (1997) describes five main ideas that characterize cultural speech codes. We can see how these ideas are powerfully ingrained in the communication of cultural members and are often responsible for misunderstanding and problems in intercultural communication. We further elaborate on *dugri* and *musayra* by explaining them within the context of the five principles of speech codes.

Speech Codes Are Culturally Distinctive

Speech codes are identified with a specific people in a specific place. When you first listen to someone speak, you often ask or wonder, "Where are they from?" Language is always identified with locations such as countries (e.g., American English, British English, or Australian English), regions (e.g., the South, East), or neighborhoods. Israeli *dugri* speech is associated with native-born Israelis of Jewish heritage in the land of Israel. The code is unique to Jews primarily of European heritage, and the code became crystallized in the pre-state period of the 1930s and 1940s (Katriel, 1986). *Musayra* is culturally distinct for speakers of Arabic and members of Arabic cultures; however, its geographic location is more complex than *dugri* because Arabic cultures are more geographically diverse. In both cases, however, when speakers of a code change geographic locations, they modify their code use.

Speech Codes Result from a Psychology and Sociology Unique to the Culture

Speech codes are intimately connected to the psychological qualities of a culture. They are related to how people see themselves. In other words, certain attitudes, values, and states of mind are more descriptive of one culture than another. For example, an Arab using a *musayra* code is maintaining consistency with his culture's expectations of honor. Honor is a controlling psychological value that legitimates a modesty code and the hospitality that one bestows. To use a *musayra* code—to be indirect, affective, and polite—is to maintain honor and express a distinct psychology of Arabs. Israeli-Jews, on the other hand, use *dugri* to express their strong native identity. This identity is rooted in the pride and strength they feel with respect to the state of Israel. Historically, Jews were a dislocated and oppressed people, but the establishment of the state of Israel altered this historical condition. *Dugri* speech is a communicative expression of this pride.

The Meaning and Significance of Messages Fundamentally Depend on Codes

You may be familiar with the maxim that "meanings are in people, not words." This means that true understanding of a communication depends on the people speaking and the code they use. When people communicate, they are performing some type of action, and others interpret that action. The interpretation relies on the speech code. When an Arab speaker deploys a *musayra* code and is polite, indirect, and courteous, a non-code user might interpret this speech as being weak, obsequious, or manipulative. This interpretation can lead to communication problems. Israeli-Jews have a reputation for being rude and aggressive. The *dugri* code contains a directness of style that includes bluntness and forthrightness. It is not uncommon to hear Israeli-Jews in a meeting say things like "you are wrong" or "not true." This kind of directness is considered rude by many people, but not if you understand the code. A listener who "speaks" the *dugri* code will not come to any hasty conclusions about the dispositions of the other speaker because the same code is used to define the communicative act. In other words, bold utterances such as "you are wrong" are understood as normal ways of speaking rather than a rude way of speaking.

Speech Codes Are Located in the Language and Communication of Native Speakers

This simply means that speech codes are on display in the language of others. These codes are not inside the heads of others or contained in the generalities about culture. They are empirically observable in the communication of cultural members. Thus, when a native Israeli speaks directly and bluntly, the *dugri* code is very apparent. Speech codes are also found in the ritualized functions of communication. These are the known and repeated ways of organizing interaction, and they have code-specific symbolic forms. A greeting ritual is an example. An African American will greet another African American differently than he would a white person. These people might use certain vocabulary and body movements to signal a bond or friendship. The same is true for *dugri* and *musayra*. Both have symbolic forms that project and affirm an identity. By studying these symbolic forms and communication patterns, we can discover how the cultural world is orderly rather than chaotic.

Speech Codes Can Be Used to Understand, Predict, and Control Communication

The artful understanding and use of speech codes can be used to improve communication. People do not communicate like machines. Even if they are steeped in cultural codes, they often think reflectively about the code and alter typical patterns. This means there is potential for change and opportunities to avoid the more troublesome aspects of codes. An Israeli who is being very *dugri* can learn to recognize how others perceive him or her and perhaps alter certain patterns of communication. Moreover, situations can alter speech codes. In the next section of this essay, we explain how codes are influenced by particular communication situations.

ARGUMENT BETWEEN ISRAELI-JEWS AND PALESTINIANS

Argument is a persistent characteristic of the relationship between Israeli-Jews and Palestinians. In fact, argument is important to these groups because at least it is an acceptable mechanism of conflict resolution. We would rather these two groups argue than shoot at each other. We might expect from the previous discussion that *dugri* speech would be characteristic of Israeli-Jews and the mode of speech preferred by them during argument since Israeli-Jews have a speech code that includes an argumentative style. *Musayra*, on the other hand, is not argument oriented at all. Interestingly, the little research that exists on Arab argument patterns is consistent with *musayra*. Hatim (1991), in a study devoted to this issue, found that argumentation in modern Arabic is related to politeness and saving face.

Group status is one of the problems for groups in dialogue situations. When cultural groups are different in status, the arguments produced by the high-status groups can carry more weight. Israeli-Jews, given their military and economic advantages, carry considerably more status into dialogues. Moreover, their speech codes are more conducive to argument. But dialogue groups that work to promote open discussion and equal relations can help lessen status differences. They become a context that levels differences. Even though Arabs come from a cultural background where argument is considered disrespectful, there are situations where this difference can be diminished.

In our studies (Maoz & Ellis, in press; Ellis & Maoz, 2001), we found that the arguments during political dialogues between Israeli-Jews and Palestinians were not necessarily consistent with expectations from cultural speech codes. In other words, the Israeli-Jews do not necessarily use more assertive arguments, and the Arabs are not necessarily less overtly aggressive. It appears that the dialogue context of communication does alter speech codes and provides an environment for more equal status discussion. Palestinians are more assertive during these dialogues than speech code theory would suggest. They speak more and engage in more reasoning and elaboration. This means that they state propositions and then support them with evidence in the classic tradition of argument.

The Israeli-Jews are somewhat consistent with the *dugri* code because they are quick to object to allegations and challenge assertions made by the Palestinians. Their experience with the *dugri* code makes it easy for them to sharply deny charges and demand justifications. But these dialogues do provide an environment for transformative communication because they afford the Palestinians an opportunity to accuse the Israeli-Jews of historical injustices. This is why the Israeli-Jews are typically on the defensive with objections and challenges to various statements. But, interestingly, the Israeli-Jews are also more hesitant and submissive in these dialogues. They qualify their arguments, backtrack, and provide context. Again, they are being challenged and responding in an accommodating and yielding manner rather than in a style associated with *dugri*. The dialogue context, and its transformative qualities, is probably responsible for these changes because typical roles are altered.

This dialogue context may also strengthen the sense of unity for groups with minority status, and the communication patterns reflect this fact. The Palestinians argue in such a way that they elaborate and provide evidence for arguments in a manner much more akin to *dugri* than their own *musayra*. They clearly use the context to transform themselves into a power coalition. The Palestinians engage in a form of "tag-team" argument (Brashers & Meyers, 1989). This is where one's own group engages in a repetitive elaboration of a point to produce the perception of unity. Following is an example of a tag-team argument. The Palestinians are expressing their anger about being prevented from entering Jerusalem. The Israelis say it is because of security, but the Palestinians "gang up" on the Israelis saying that the security measures—which are check points that the Palestinians must pass and are monitored by the Israeli military—do not work and it is just harassment.

PAL: If we go into Jerusalem not through the *Machsom* (Hebrew word for "checkpoint"), I can go in. They see me, and they don't care. It is that they want to make it difficult for me.

PAL: There are three ways to go from Bethlehem to Jerusalem.

PAL: If I want to go to Jerusalem, I am there in five minutes.

PAL: Sixty thousand Palestinians every day go to Israel without permission, every day; forty thousand with permission. So it's not security, it's politics. This is the information. I am not saying this to support.

The Palestinians are emboldened. The dialogue context helps transform the indigenous code of each group. This is an important matter with respect to the power relationship between each group. It suggests that the speech codes are pliant and that situations and activities can be found that reduce the cultural strength of these codes and make change and growth more possible. Moreover, these communication experiences balance the relationship between hostile and unequal groups in order to promote egalitarianism and make future interactions more productive.

CONCLUSION

In this article we have explained and illustrated cultural communication patterns between Israeli-Jews and Palestinians. These two groups are in bitter conflict and experiencing tremendous pressures and tensions for reconciliation and change. Clearly, national leaders and negotiators for peace need to solve the legal and legislative issues with respect to land, sovereignty, and other legal obligations. But true peace and prosperity "on the ground" will come only when these two groups learn to work together and improve communication. We have shown in this essay that each national group has evolved a different code and orientation to communication. These codes can be bridges or barriers to communication. Although communication codes are relatively firm, they are not unyielding. We have shown that there are contexts and situations in which codes do not predict communication behavior. But more important, a thorough understanding of codes is necessary for dialogue and negotiation. Even words that are translated the same from different languages carry additional cultural baggage that is lost in the translation. Words are not neutral. They acquire their meaning from a culturally charged set of symbols that make up a speech code. The task for the future is to continually explore the nature of speech codes and their role in dialogue and conflict management.

References

Adwan, S., & Bar-On, D. (2000). *The Role of non-governmental organizations in peace building between Palestinians and Israelis*. Jerusalem: PRIME (Peace Research Institute in the Middle East), with the support of the World Bank.

Allport, G. (1954). *The nature of prejudice*. Reading, MA: Addison-Wesley.

Amir, Y. (1976). *The role of intergroup contact in change of prejudice and ethnic relations*. In P. Katz (Ed.), *Towards the elimination of racism* (pp. 245–308). New York: Pergamon.

Bernstein, B. (1971). *Class, codes and control*. Volume 1. London: Routledge & Kegan Paul.

Brashers, D. E., & Meyers, R. A. (1989). Tag-team argument and group decision making: A preliminary investigation. In B. E. Gronbeck (Ed.), *Spheres of argument: Proceedings of the sixth SCA/AFA conference on argumentation* (pp. 542–550). Annandale, VA: Speech Communication Association.

Ellis, D. G. (1992). Syntactic and pragmatic codes in communication. *Communication Theory*, 2, 1–23.

Ellis, D. G. (1994). Codes and pragmatic comprehension. In S. A. Deetz (Ed.), *Communication yearbook* 17 (pp. 333–343). Thousand Oaks, CA: Sage Publications.

Ellis, D. G., & Maoz, I. (2001). *Cross-cultural argument interactions in dialogues between Israeli-Jews and Palestinians*. Unpublished manuscript.

Feghali, E. (1997). Arab cultural communication patterns. *International Journal of Intercultural Relations*, 21, 345–378.

Gergen, K. (1999). *Toward transformative dialogue*. A paper presented to the 49th Annual Conference of the International Communication Association, San Francisco, CA, May 27–31 1999.

Hatim, B. (1991). The pragmatics of argumentation in Arabic: The rise and fall of a text type. *Text*, 11, 189–199.

Katriel, T. (1986). *Talking straight: Dugri speech in Israeli sabra culture*. London, England: Cambridge University Press.

Kelman, H. (1995). Contributions of an unofficial conflict resolution effort to the Israeli-Palestinian breakthrough. *Negotiation Journal*, 11, 19–27.

Kelman, H. (1997). Group processes in the resolution of international conflicts: Experiences from the Israeli-Palestinian case. *American Psychologist*, 52, 212–220.

Maoz, I. (2000a). Multiple conflicts and competing agendas: A framework for conceptualizing structured encounters between groups in conflict—The case of a coexistence project between Jews and Palestinians in Israel. *Journal of Peace Psychology*, 6, 135–156.

Maoz, I. (2000b). An experiment in peace: Processes and effects in reconciliation aimed workshops of Israeli and Palestinian youth. *Journal of Peace Research*, 37, 721–736.

Maoz, M. (1999). From conflict to peace? Israel's relations with Syria and the Palestinians. *Middle East Journal*, 53, 393–416.

Maoz, I., & Ellis, D. G. (in press). Going to ground: Argument in Israeli-Jewish and Palestinian encounter groups. *Research on Language and Social Interaction*.

Philipsen, G. (1997). A theory of speech codes. In G. Philipsen & T. L. Albrecht (Eds.), *Developing communication theories* (pp. 119–156). Albany: State University of New York Press.

Pettigrew, T. (1998). Intergroup contact theory. *Annual Review of Psychology*, 49, 65–85.

Rouhana, N., & Bar-Tal, D. (1998). Psychological dynamics of intractable ethnonational conflicts: The Israeli-Palestinian case. *American Psychologist*, 53, 761–770.

Concepts and Questions

1. What roles do land rights, religion, and cultural conflict play in defining the communicative dynamics of Israeli-Jews and Palestinian-Arabs?

2. What do Ellis and Maoz mean when they refer to "transformative communication"?

3. How does transformative communication help improve the communication between groups in conflict?

4. What conditions must be met between two groups in conflict before the contact hypothesis will help reduce prejudice and negative intergroup attitudes?

5. How does the concept of "dialogue," as discussed by Martin Buber, Carl Rogers, and Mikhail Bakhtin, provide guiding principles for transformative dialogue?

6. How do cultural differences in speech codes affect communication between Israeli-Jews and Palestinian-Arabs? Provide some examples of differences in speech codes for each of these groups.

7. What have been the major circumstances that have led to the development of the unique speech codes among Israeli-Jews and Palestinian-Arabs?

8. *Musayra*, which means "to accommodate" or "to go along with," plays a major role in the speech codes of Palestinian-Arabs. What are the four communicative features of *musayra*?

9. How do the speech codes of Israeli-Jews differ from those of the Palestinian-Arabs?

10. What do Ellis and Maoz mean when they assert that the meaning and significance of messages fundamentally depend on speech codes?

Mexican *Dichos*: Lessons through Language

Carolyn Roy

MEXICAN CULTURE AND ITS REFLECTED IMAGES

The late Octavio Paz, one of Mexico's most renowned writers, asserts in his classic *The Labyrinth of Solitude: Life and Thought in Mexico* that the Mexican's "face is a mask" (Paz, 1961, p. 29). Paz thereby implies that knowing the Mexican national character might be impossible. Carlos Fuentes, another of Mexico's most esteemed men of letters, employs the imagery of dark, ancient Aztec polished hematite mirrors reflecting the soul of Mexico when he writes: "Is not the mirror both a reflection of reality and a projection of the imagination?" (Fuentes, 1992, p. 11). Despite the self-confessed inscrutable nature of Mexican national character, *dichos*—popular sayings including, but not limited to, *proverbios*/proverbs, *adagios*/adages, and *refranes*/refrains—open an avenue for exploring the attributes most esteemed and salient in Mexican popular culture. Using Fuentes' metaphor, however, our understanding of Mexican culture remains but a darkly reflected image. Our understanding is further obscured by the difficulty of precise idiomatic translation of the complex Mexican language that hybridizes the Spanish brought from Europe with the intricately nuanced indigenous languages, predominantly Nahuatl, of Mexico's native peoples. Nevertheless, popular sayings heard from the northern reaches of the Chihuahuan desert to the highlands of southern Chiapas do provide insight into some commonly held values in Mexican culture.

Such popular sayings transmit "what a culture deems significant" (Samovar & Porter, 2001, p. 36).

Examination of these orally transmitted traditional values offers an excellent means of learning about another culture because these oft-repeated sayings fuse past, present, and future. These sayings focus our attention on basic principles accepted within the culture. The premise of this present exercise is that we can learn much about Mexican values through scrutiny of these distilled lessons of life transmitted through their language.

While some of these popular sayings are uniquely Mexican, many more of them were brought to Mexico by Spaniards after 1519; therefore, they reflect the fusion of cultures, especially Castillian and Muslim, found in recently "reconquered" and unified early sixteenth-century Spain. Because many values are universally human, similar sayings may be found just as often in cultures around the globe. For example, most cultures attribute some responsibility for a child's character or nature to the parents; hence, in the United States one might hear, "like father, like son," or "a chip off the old block," while in Mexico the close approximation is *de tal palo, tal astilla* (from such a stick, such a splinter). But the proverb *Al nopal nomás lo van a ver cuando tiene tunas* (One only goes to see the cactus when it has prickly pear fruit) derives specifically from the Mexican milieu. However, one might readily overhear a parent in the United States complaining to an adult child: "You only come to see me when you want something." So the principle of the saying is universal, while the expression relates uniquely to its culture. Although some sayings are culturally unique and others universal, our purpose here is to focus on specific Mexican sayings that reflect some of the values of that culture.

MEXICAN DICHOS

Popular sayings—*dichos*—reflect many of the basic values of contemporary Mexican society, although the roots of these expressions of popular culture extend far back into both European and pre-Columbian Native American civilizations. Although many of these expressions demonstrate the universality of proverbs generally, many uniquely mirror Mexican reality. Yolanda Nava writes about Latin American culture in general, but her observation applies equally well

Courtesy of Carolyn Roy. This original essay appeared for the first time in the tenth edition. Carolyn Roy is a faculty member in the Department of History at San Diego State University, San Diego, California.

to Mexican sayings in particular. She notes: "*Dichos* feel good on the tongue...they are, after all, a verbal shorthand which...elders used countless times to remind [one]...to behave wisely" (Nava, p. 35). *Dichos* may be pithy condensations of wisdom gained through centuries of experience. They are one form of transmitting folk wisdom. The sayings selected here might be heard in any Mexican household.

Many of the proverbs in the following sections may be readily consulted in Sellers (1994), but caution must be exercised in reviewing Sellers' interpretations of these *dichos*. One must always maintain cognizance of the cultural context. While a Mexican might playfully jest, saying, *No hagas hoy lo que puedas hacer mañana* (Don't do today what you can put off until tomorrow), such should not be taken literally (as Sellers apparently does, p. 26). This inverted *dicho* merely jocularly reminds the listener that one should *No dejar para mañana lo que se puede hacer hoy* (Not put off until tomorrow what can be done today), a well-known adage in many cultures.

The Mexican tradition of playfulness with words, as in the previous example, or the use of double meaning [*doble sentido*] (often with obscured sexual undertones—most frequently heard with such apparently innocuous words as *huevos*/eggs, *aguacates*/avocados, and so on, used as anatomical designations), or in using a word for its exact opposite, has ancient roots in pre-Columbian Mexican linguistic practices. Among the Aztecs, it was proper practice to refer to an older person as "my dear young one," much as a Mexican mother today may call her toddler "my dear father" [*mi papito*]. Those expressions chosen for discussion here reflect some of the values central to Mexican popular culture. These values include cheerful acceptance of the "will of God," the need to place trust with great care, the significance of appearances, the necessity to guard one's privacy and not breach that of others, prescribed gender roles, a communal spirit, and the importance of family.

Acceptance of "God's Will"

No hay mal que por bien no venga. (There is no bad that good does not accompany.) Mexicans have often been characterized as fatalistic, but their nature seems more than merely accepting of the inevitable. Much of Mexican folk wisdom relates to acceptance of poverty and even laughing at it. Mexican folk seem to relish the challenge of finding happiness in the face of adversity. Some of the most frequently heard proverbs reflect that optimism. This proverb might be equated to: "It's an ill wind that brings nobody good," but that does not carry the same positive outlook that the Spanish phrase indicates. Closer to the Mexican concept might be: "Every cloud has a silver lining."

Mejor reír que llorar. (Better to laugh than to cry.) If one laughs at adversity, whether that is a simple upset of plans or that which is most inevitable—death—then there is nothing that can disturb one's happiness. Much of Mexican art reflects the duality of life and death, as can be seen in art from pre-Columbian times to the present. The very popular woodcuts of José Guadalupe Posada depicting skeletons in scenes that range from the mundane to the hilariously outrageous clearly demonstrate the Mexican's friendly attitude toward death. If one can laugh, then there is no need for lament.

El hombre propone y Dios dispone. (Man proposes and God disposes.) Few Mexican women would dare to make plans, whether it be meeting for lunch tomorrow or making plans for a child's future, without adding before concluding those plans, *Si Dios quiere* (If God wills). It would be presuming much to think that one could control the future; that is viewed as in God's hands alone. In the South of the United States, one hears a similar expression made popular by Southern folklorists: "If the Lord's willing and the creek don't rise," but this seems less an attitude of fatalistic acceptance than an almost humorous excuse in the event of inclement weather in the backwoods. Whereas, *Si Dios quiere* is an expression used almost exclusively by Mexican women, "If the Lord's willing" may be used by males or females.

No por mucho madrugar amanece más temprano. (No matter how early one rises, the sun will not come up any sooner.) One must simply accept what one cannot change. Nothing is accomplished by unnecessary effort. Only the foolish will attempt to defy the forces of nature.

Cuando el pobre tiene para carne sea vigilia. (When the poor have [money] to buy meat, it must be Lent.) The poor must accept that when they have the good fortune to have money, then it will be a time of fasting [not eating meat]. The poor must accept that they will not have good luck. This is an instance of making fun of—of laughing at—adversity. If I am poor, I should expect to eat beans and tortillas, not meat.

Quien canta su mal espanta. (He who sings frightens away his grief.) By singing, the individual can dispel sadness and drive away gloom. Singing and other forms of music accompany most private Mexican gatherings, but can also be heard in the Metro stations and on street corners of metropolitan centers.

Sparing Bestowal of Trust

En confianza está el peligro. (There is danger in trust.) For the Mexican to place trust in another, particularly anyone who is not a blood relative, is very high esteem. But when one does bestow trust, then the greatest harm possible would be to betray that trust. It is a great risk to have faith in another; therefore, trust must never be granted lightly.

La confianza tambien mata. (Trust also kills.) Betrayal of trust kills the spirit as surely as a bullet might kill the body. And the betrayal of trust would be the gravest ill that one friend could commit against another. Another *dicho* conveys the gravity of betrayal of trust: ¡*Ni te fíes de amigo reconciliado, ni de manjar dos veces guisado*¡ (Do not trust a reconciled friend nor a dish twice cooked!) If a trust has been betrayed, the lost trust can never be recovered.

Del dicho al hecho hay mucho trecho. (From said to done, there is a great gap.) One should not trust that promises will be fulfilled. Even with the best of intentions, circumstances intervene, thus one should always be prepared to accept less than is promised, thereby avoiding disappointment.

Músico pagado toca mal son. (The musician who has been paid plays bad music.) The most foolish act that an employer could commit would be to pay the worker before the task is completed. Such an employer would not be viewed as kind or generous, merely foolish. If a worker is paid in advance, then the foolish employer deserves to be treated with contempt. One of the first lessons to be learned when interacting within Mexican culture is that easy trust is not valued. Trust/*confianza* must be given sparingly and only after being earned.

Reserving payment until the work is completed is viewed as prudent. The lesson of the saying is that paying for a job before it is completed produces bad results.

The Importance of Appearances

Díme con quien andas y te diré quien eres. (Tell me with whom you associate [walk, travel], and I will tell you who you are.) Whom you choose as your companions and associates reflects your quality. If you associate with "common people," then you will be judged common. It follows that one always seeks to associate with people of higher status in order to improve on one's station in life. In English one hears, "Birds of a feather flock together," but that does not fully convey the idea that one can rise in status by associating with a better class of people.

Quien anda con lobos a aullar se aprenda. (One who goes around with wolves learns to howl.) In this same vein is the Biblical principle in English: "Evil companions corrupt good morals." If you run with the wolves, you will learn their wild ways; therefore, one should avoid such savages and associate with cultured society. One must choose associates with great care. They not only reflect one's position, but they also influence one's character.

El que es buen gallo dondequiera canta. (A good rooster can crow anywhere.) Despite the previous admonitions, quality is quality no matter the circumstance. A person of true character will show that character in all circumstances, but a person of poor character will not be able to measure up in difficult circumstances.

Respect for Privacy

Agua que no has de beber, déjala correr. (Water that you do not have to drink, leave it to flow.) Aranda translates this as: "Don't meddle in others' affairs; don't start trouble." If you stir up the water, then it will be undrinkable for anyone. So let everyone tend to their own problems and thus avoid spreading them to others.

Bueno aconsejar, mejor remediar. (It is good to give advice, but it is better to solve the problem.) When there is a problem, it is good to give advice when it is sought, but it would be better to solve the problem. If you cannot solve the problem, then refrain from giving advice. And there are even times when the truth is better left unsaid, as attested by the proverb: *Si dices la verdad no pecas, pero no sabes los males que suscitas* (If you tell the truth you do not sin, but you don't know the troubles you cause. [So keep your own counsel]).

En boca cerrada no entran moscas. (Flies do not enter a closed mouth.) If you keep your mouth shut, then you will not have to worry about "putting your foot in it." Be careful of what you say, because *Un resbalón de lengua es peor que el de los pies*¡ (A slip of the tongue is worse than a slip of the foot.) The foot will heal, but damage done by words will not. Also, *Rezarle sólo a su santo*¡ (Pray only to your saint); that is, only someone who can help you should know of your problems.

Gender Roles

Mejor quedarse para vestir los santos que tener que desvestir un borracho. (It is better to remain to dress the saints than to have to undress a drunk.) Women who do not marry are often referred to as "those who stay to dress the saints"; that is, they spend their lives caring for the images of the saints, which often involves making new garments for the images or painting and refurbishing them. Thus, single women often justify their unmarried state by suggesting that they prefer dressing the saints' images to having to undress a drunken husband.

Más vale solo que mal acompañado. (It is better to remain single than to be disagreeably accompanied.) In a society in which women are viewed as weak and vulnerable, single women must justify their unmarried state, so that women most often cite the refrain that it is better to be single than to have an unbearable spouse.

A la mujer ni todo el amor ni todo el dinero. (To a woman neither all your love nor all your money.) A "real" Mexican male must maintain control of himself and his money. Men make a practice of allocating a certain portion of their income to women for maintaining the household, but the rest of their earnings belong to them. One of the great enigmas of Mexican culture is the dichotomy of *machismo* [strong, dominant males] versus *marianismo* [long-suffering, submissive females]. This concept is most readily seen in the fact that cantinas/bars are exclusively for males (and women of ill-repute).

Triste está la casa donde la gallina canta y el gallo calla. (Sad is the house where the chicken crows and the rooster is quiet.) The proper role for a man is as the master of his house, and the woman should be silent. It is a reversal of proper roles for the Mexican woman to make the decisions and the man to allow her to do so. In English a similar refrain is: "A whistling girl and a crowing hen always come to some bad end." Women are assigned their proper roles and men theirs. A sad state results when these roles are reversed.

Communalism

Mucha ayuda, poco trabajo. (Much help, little work.) When many work together, it is little work for any of them. When work is shared, it goes quickly and is not much effort for anyone. The tradition of communal work precedes European contact with the New World. Among the Aztecs, taking turns at doing community service was widely practiced.

Vida sin amigos, muerte sin testigos. (Life without friends, death without witnesses.) [Life without friends, no mourners when it ends.] If one does not live so as to have many friends, then death will come with no one there to mourn that death. In Mexican culture it is extremely important that there be mourners to accompany the deceased. It has long been common practice to pay mourners so that the dead will be accompanied to the cemetery. Again, this reflects the importance of one's public persona, one's appearance to the rest of the world, even in death.

Family

¿A dónde vas que valgas más? (Where are you going that you are worth more?) Where would you be valued more than at home? The Mexican family is extended, but still very close. When an individual needs help, the family is expected to supply it. The understanding is that you are always better off at home.

Amor de padre o madre, lo demás es aire. (The love of mother or father, everything else is air.) Compared to a mother or father's love, there is nothing else of importance. Father and mother will love and support their children when everyone and everything else fails. It is not unusual to encounter adult children living in the home of their parents and even rearing their own children in that same home. At times this is done out of economic necessity, but just as often it is because of the bond of the extended family. Grandparents become the caregivers for the offspring and take a hand in their upbringing.

SUMMARY

Popular sayings reflect basic cultural values. They do not even require literacy because they transmit the values orally to all who hear them. They metaphorically condense timeless lessons into readily recalled phrases. Through *dichos* we are reminded that our experiences are not unique; others have experienced the same things in other times and other places and left us messages to guide us. By reviewing a selection of Mexican *dichos*, one readily perceives some of that culture's more significant values: cheerful acceptance of one's lot in life, the need to exercise caution when placing trust, the importance of appearances, the sanctity of privacy, proper gender roles, communalism, and family.

References

Aranda, C. (1977). *Dichos: Proverbs and sayings from the Spanish*. Santa Fe: Swanstone Press.

Ballesteros, O. (1979). *Mexican proverbs: The philosophy, wisdom, and humor of a people*. Burnet, TX: Eakin Press.

Burciaga, J. (1997). *In few words/en pocas palabras: A compendium of Latino folk wit and wisdom*. San Francisco: Mercury House.

Fuentes, C. (1992). *The buried mirror: Reflections on Spain and the New World*. New York: Houghton Mifflin.

Nava, Y. (2000). *It's all in the frijoles: 100 famous Latinos share real-life stories, time-tested dichos, favorite folktales, and inspiring words of wisdom*. New York: Fireside.

Paz, O. (1961). *The labyrinth of solitude: Life and thought in Mexico*. New York: Grove Press.

Samovar, L. A., & Porter, R. E. (2001). *Communication between cultures* (4th ed.). Belmont, CA: Wadsworth.

Sellers, J. M. (1994). *Folk wisdom of Mexico*. San Francisco: Chronicle Books.

Concepts and Questions

1. How does the study of familiar sayings help us understand some of the important values of a particular culture?
2. Which Mexican sayings discussed by Roy are heard in other cultures?
3. Can you think of some sayings from your own culture and relate the specific values they represent?
4. What are your favorite familiar sayings? Why have you selected these?
5. What sayings in the United States stress the value of individualism?
6. What Mexican sayings reflect the underlying religious philosophy of the culture?

In Different Dimensions: Nonverbal Communication and Culture

PETER A. ANDERSEN

L ong ago, before the Internet, before the global economy, before even the television and the airplane, most people spent their lives within their own cultures. Only rarely across the generations did sojourners, traders, or warriors encounter people from other cultures. Not so today. Cultures are colliding and communicating at an ever-accelerating rate. For several decades international travel has been increasing, and international trade is at an all-time high (Brown, Kane, & Roodman, 1994). Countries throughout the world encounter new immigrants from dramatically different cultural backgrounds. Moreover, the technological revolution and especially the Internet "will blur national boundaries and it will transform the nation state in a way humans have not witnessed for a millennium" (Andersen, 1999b, p. 540). The probability of communicating with people from other cultures in our daily interactions is greater than ever before.

On the streets of London, Los Angeles, Sydney, or Singapore dozens of languages are being spoken. Although language differences are highly apparent, they are only the tip of a very large cultural iceberg. Culture is primarily an implicit nonverbal phenomenon because most aspects of one's culture are learned through observation and imitation rather than by explicit verbal instruction or expression. The primary level of culture is communicated implicitly, without awareness, chiefly by nonverbal means (Andersen, 1999a; Hall, 1984; Sapir, 1928). In most situations, intercultural interactants do not share the same language. But languages can be learned, and

larger communication problems occur in the nonverbal realm. Nonverbal communication is a subtle, nonlinguistic, multidimensional, and spontaneous process (Andersen, 1999a). Indeed, individuals are little aware of their own nonverbal behavior, which is enacted mindlessly, spontaneously, and unconsciously (Andersen, 1999a; Burgoon, 1985; Samovar & Porter, 1985).

Because we are not usually aware of even our own nonverbal behavior, it becomes extremely difficult to identify and master the nonverbal behavior of another culture. At times we feel uncomfortable in other cultures because we intuitively know something isn't right. "Because perceptions of nonverbal behaviors are rarely conscious phenomena, it may be difficult for us to know exactly why we are feeling uncomfortable" (Gudykunst & Kim, 1992, p. 172). Sapir was among the first to note that "we respond to gestures with an extreme alertness and, one might almost say, in accordance with an elaborate and secret code that is written nowhere, known by none, and understood by all (Sapir, 1928, p. 137).

This article first will briefly explore eight codes of nonverbal communication: physical appearance, proxemics, chronemics, kinesics, haptics, oculesics, vocalics, and olfactics; briefly define and situate culture; and finally discuss six primary dimensions of cultural variation, including immediacy, individualism, gender, power distance, uncertainty-avoidance, and cultural contextualization, that help explain the thousands of cross-cultural differences in nonverbal behavior.

NONVERBAL CODES

Most discussions of nonverbal intercultural communication have been anecdotal, descriptive, and atheoretical, where numerous examples of intercultural differences for each nonverbal code are discussed in detail. Recapitulation of the various nonverbal codes of intercultural communication is not a primary purpose here. Thus, the basic codes of nonverbal communication will be discussed only briefly, along with references that provide detailed and excellent analyses of how each nonverbal code differs interculturally.

The most externally obvious code of nonverbal behavior is physical appearance—the most important code used during initial encounters. Cultural attire is obvious and leads to ethnic stereotypes. During a field study of touch conducted at an international airport, I witnessed Tongans in multicultural ceremonial gowns, Sikhs in white turbans, Hasidic Jews in blue yarmulkes, and Africans in white dashikis—all alongside Californians in running shorts and halter tops. Little formal research has been conducted on the impact of physical appearance on intercultural communication. Discussions of intercultural differences in appearance are provided by Scheflen (1974) and Samovar, Porter, and Stefani (1998). Although blue jeans and business suits have become increasingly accepted attire internationally, local attire still abounds. Preoccupation with physical appearance is hardly a new phenomenon. Since the dawn of culture, humans from the upper Paleolithic period (40,000 years ago) to the present have adorned their bodies in a great variety of ways (Samovar et al., 1998).

Perhaps the most fundamental code of nonverbal behavior is proxemics, communication via interpersonal space and distance. Research has documented that cultures differ substantially in their use of personal space, their regard for territory and the meanings they assign to proxemic behavior (Gudykunst & Kim, 1992; Hall, 1959, 1976; Scheflen, 1974). For example, people from Mediterranean and Latin cultures maintain close distance, whereas people from Northern European and Northeast Asian cultures maintain greater distances. But this behavior also is highly contextual. At rush hour in Tokyo the normally respectful, distant Japanese are literally jammed into subways and trains.

Chronemics—or the study of meanings, usage, and communication of time—is probably the most discussed and well-researched nonverbal code in the intercultural literature (Bruneau, 1979; Gudykunst & Kim, 1992; Hall, 1959, 1976, 1984). These analyses suggest that cultural time frames differ so dramatically that if only chronemic differences existed, then intercultural misunderstandings would still be considerable. In the United States, time is viewed as a commodity that can be wasted, spent, saved, and used wisely (Andersen, 1999a). Of course, many cultures have radically different concepts of time. In most less

developed countries, life moves to the rhythms of nature, the day, the seasons, the year. Such human inventions as seconds, minutes, hours, and weeks have no real meaning. Things are experienced polychronically and simultaneously, whereas, in Western culture time is modularized and events are scheduled sequentially, not simultaneously.

People's kinesic behavior differs from culture to culture, including some aspects of their facial expressions, body movements, gestures, and conversational regulators (Gudykunst & Kim, 1992; Hall, 1976; Samovar et al., 1998; Scheflen, 1974). Gestures differ dramatically in meaning, extensiveness, and intensity. Stories abound in the intercultural literature of gestures that signal endearment or warmth in one culture but may be obscene or insulting in another.

Tactile communication, called haptics, also shows considerable intercultural variation (Andersen & Leibowitz, 1978; Ford & Graves, 1977; McDaniel & Andersen, 1998; Samovar et al., 1998). Recent research has shown vast differences in international and intercultural touch in amount, location, type, and public or private manifestation (Jones, 1994; McDaniel & Andersen, 1998).

One important code of nonverbal communication that has attracted considerably less intercultural research attention is oculesics, the study of messages sent by the eyes—including eye contact, blinks, eye movements, and pupil dilation (Gudykunst & Kim, 1992; Samovar et al., 1998). Because eye contact has been called an "invitation to communicate," its variation cross-culturally is an important communication topic.

Vocalics, or paralanguage, the nonverbal elements of the voice, also has received comparatively little attention from intercultural researchers (Gudykunst & Kim, 1992; LaBarre, 1985; Samovar et al., 1998; Scheflen, 1974). Music and singing, universal forms of aesthetic communication, have been almost completely overlooked in intercultural research, except for an excellent series of studies (Lomax, 1968) that identified several groups of worldwide cultures through differences and similarities in their folk songs.

Finally, olfactics, the study of interpersonal communication via smell, has been virtually ignored in intercultural research despite its importance (Samovar et al., 1998). Americans are the most smell-aversive culture in the world (Andersen, 1998). While most of the world's people emit natural body smells, the cultures in the most developed parts of the world use an array of cosmetics to eliminate body odor or to replace it with natural smells.

SITUATING AND DEFINING CULTURE

Along with traits, situations, and states, culture is one of the four primary sources of interpersonal behavior (Andersen, 1987). Culture is the enduring influence of the social environment on our behavior, including our interpersonal communication behavior. Culture is a learned set of shared perceptions about beliefs, values, and needs that affect the behaviors of relatively large groups of people (Lustig & Koester, 1999). Culture exerts a considerable force on individual behavior through what Geertz (1973) called "control mechanisms—plans, recipes, rules, instructions (what computer engineers call 'programs')—for the governing of behavior" (p. 44). Culture has similar and powerful, though not identical, effects on all residents of a cultural system. As another group of researchers explains: "Culture can be behaviorally observed by contrasting intragroup homogeneity with intergroup heterogeneity" (Andersen, Lustig, & Andersen, 1986, p. 11).

Personal traits and culture are sometimes confused because both are enduring phenomena (Andersen, 1987). Traits have multiple causes (Andersen, 1987), only some of which are the result of culture. Culture has also been confused with situation because both are part of one's social environment; however, culture is an enduring phenomenon, whereas, situation is a transient one with an observable beginning and end. Culture, along with genetics, is the most enduring, powerful, and invisible shaper of our communication behavior.

Dimensions of Cultural Variation

Thousands of anecdotes regarding nonverbal misunderstandings between persons from different cultures have been reported. Although it may be useful to know that Arabs stand closer during communication than Americans, the Swiss are more time conscious than Italians, and Asians value silence more than Westerners, we need more than this basic approach.

Because the number of potential pairs of cultures are huge and the number of possible nonverbal misunderstandings between each pair of cultures is similarly large, millions of potential intercultural anecdotes are possible (Andersen, 1999a). What is needed is some way to organize, explain, and understand this plethora of potential problems in intercultural communication. Some initial research has shown that cultures can be located along dimensions that help explain these intercultural differences. Most cultural differences in nonverbal behavior are a result of variations along the dimensions discussed as follows.

High and Low Context. The first cultural dimension of communication proposed decades ago is context— the degree to which communication is explicit and verbal or implicit and nonverbal. Hall (1976, 1984) has described high-context cultures in considerable detail: "A high context (HC) communication or message is one in which most of the information is either in the physical context or internalized in the person, while very little is in the coded, explicit, transmitted parts of the message" (Hall, 1976, p. 91). Another group of researchers explains: "In a high-context culture such as that of Japan, meanings are internalized and there is a large emphasis on nonverbal codes" (Lustig & Koester, 1999, p. 108). Married couples or old friends skillfully use HC or implicit messages that are nearly impossible for an outsider to understand. The situation, a smile, or a glance provides implicit meaning that does not need to be articulated. In HC situations or cultures, information is integrated from the environment, the context, the situation, and nonverbal cues that give the message meaning that is unavailable in the explicit verbal utterance.

Low-context (LC) messages are the opposite of HC messages; most are communicated via explicit code usually via verbal communication (Andersen, 1999a; Hall, 1976). LC messages must be detailed, unmistakably communicated, and highly specific. Unlike personal relationships, which are high-context message systems, institutions such as courts of law and formal systems such as mathematics and computer languages require explicit LC systems because nothing can be taken for granted (Hall, 1984).

There is vast cultural variation in the degree of context used in communication. Research suggests that the lowest-context cultures are Swiss, German, North American, and Scandinavian (Gudykunst & Kim, 1992; Hall, 1976, 1984). In these cultures, literal meaning, specific details, and precise time schedules are valued at the expense of context. Low-context cultures employ cognitive and behavioral systems based on Aristotelian logic and linear thinking (Hall, 1984) and may be pathologically verbal. Cultures that have some characteristics of both HC and LC systems would include the French, English, and Italian (Gudykunst & Kim, 1992), which are less explicit than Northern European cultures.

The highest HC cultures are found in Asia, especially China, Japan, and Korea (Elliott Scott, Jensen, & McDonough, 1982; Hall, 1976, 1984; Lustig & Koester, 1999). Although most languages are explicit, LC communication systems, in China even the language is an implicit, high-context system. To use a Chinese dictionary, one must understand thousands of characters that change meaning in combination with other characters. Zen Buddhism, a major influence in Asia, places a high value on silence, lack of emotional expression, and the unspoken, nonverbal parts of communication (McDaniel & Andersen, 1998). Americans often complain that the Japanese never "get to the point," but they fail to recognize that HC culture must provide a context and setting and let the point evolve (Hall, 1984). In a recent study of airport farewell episodes, McDaniel and Andersen (1998) found Asians to be the least tactile of any cultural group on earth. The influence of Buddhism and the value placed on context rather than emotional expression probably explains this finding. American Indian cultures with ancestral migratory roots in East Asia are remarkably like contemporary Asian culture in several ways, especially in their need for high context (Hall, 1984). Latin American cultures—a fusion of Iberian (Portuguese-Spanish) and Indian traditions—are also high-context cultures. Likewise, southern and eastern Mediterranean people and people from the Persian Gulf, including Persians, Arabs, Greeks, and Turks, are HC cultures as well.

Communication is used very differently in HC and LC cultures. Andersen, Hecht, Hoobler, and Smallwood (2002) suggest that these differences between HC and LC communication can be explained by four principles.

1. Verbal communication and other explicit codes are more prevalent in low-context cultures such as the United States and Northern Europe. People from LC cultures are often perceived as excessively talkative, belaboring of the obvious, and redundant. People from HC cultures may be perceived as nondisclosive, sneaky, and mysterious.

2. HC cultures do not value verbal communication the same way that LC cultures do. Elliot et al. (1982) found that more verbal people were perceived as more attractive in the United States, but less verbal people were perceived as more attractive in Korea, which is an HC culture.

3. HC cultures are more reliant on and tuned in to nonverbal communication. In LC cultures, most people, particularly men, fail to perceive as much nonverbal communication as do members of HC cultures. Nonverbal communication provides the context for all communication (Watzlawick, Beavin, & Jackson, 1967), but people from HC cultures are particularly affected by these contextual cues. Thus, facial expressions, tensions, movements, speed of interaction, location of the interaction, and other subtle forms of nonverbal communication are likely to be more easily perceived by and have more meaning for people from HC cultures.

4. In HC cultures, interactants expect more than in LC cultures (Hall, 1976). People in HC cultures anticipate that communicators will understand unspoken feelings, implicit gestures, and environmental clues that people from LC cultures do not process. Given that both cultural extremes fail to recognize these basic communication differences, intercultural attributions about behavior are often incorrect.

In conclusion, HC cultures rely more on nonverbal communication and less on verbal communication. Generally, HC cultures are also somewhat more collectivistic and less individualistic than LC cultures (Gudykunst Matsumoto, Ting-Toomey, Nishida, Kim, & Heyman, 1996; Andersen et al., 2002). Given this fact, it is appropriate that the next dimension of culture to be examined is individualism/collectivism.

Individualism/Collectivism. A culture's degree of individualism versus collectivism is one of the most extensively researched dimensions of culture.

Individualism/collectivism determines how people live together: alone, in families, or tribes (Hofstede, 1980), their values, and how they communicate. Americans are extreme individualists for better or worse. Americans take individualism for granted and are blind to its impact until travel brings us into contact with less individualistic, more collectivistic cultures.

Individualism has been applauded as a blessing and has been elevated to the status of a national religion in the United States. Indeed, the best and worst in our culture can be attributed to individualism. Proponents of individualism have argued that it is the basis of liberty, democracy, freedom, and economic incentive and serves as protection against tyranny. Conversely, individualism has been blamed for our alienation from one another, loneliness, selfishness, and narcissism. Indeed, Hall (1976) has claimed that as an extreme individualist, "Western man has created chaos by denying that part of his self that integrates while enshrining the part that fragments experience" (p. 9). There can be little doubt that individualism is one of the fundamental dimensions that distinguishes cultures. Western culture is individualistic, so people rely on personal judgments to a greater degree than group decisions. Eastern cultures emphasize harmony among people, between people and nature, and value collective judgments (Andersen et al., 2002). Tomkins (1984) demonstrated that an individual's psychological makeup is the result of this cultural dimension. Western civilization has tended toward self-celebration, positive or negative. In Asian culture, another alternative is represented, that of harmony among people and between people and nature.

In a landmark intercultural study of individualism in 40 noncommunist countries, Hofstede (1980) reported that the 10 most individualistic nations (starting with the most) were the United States, Australia, Great Britain, Canada, the Netherlands, New Zealand, Italy, Belgium, Denmark, and Sweden, all of which primarily derive from European cultures. The least individualistic nations (starting with the least) were Venezuela, Colombia, Pakistan, Perú, Taiwan, Thailand, Singapore, Chile, and Hong Kong, all of which are Asian or South American cultures. Likewise, Sitaram and Codgell (1976) reported that individuality is a primary value in Western cultures, of secondary importance in African cultures, and of little importance in Eastern and Muslim cultures. Even though the United States is the most individualistic country on earth (Andersen, 1999a; Hofstede, 1982), some of its regions and ethnic groups diverge in their degree of individualism. Elazar (1972) found that the central Midwest and the Mid-Atlantic states have the most individualistic political culture, whereas, the Southeast is the most traditional and least individualistic; however, this relationship is all relative and, by world standards, even Alabama is an individualistic culture. As Bellah and colleagues (1985) stated: "Individualism lies at the very core of American culture.... Anything that would violate our right to think for ourselves, judge for ourselves, make our own decisions, live our lives as we see fit, is not only morally wrong, it is sacrilegious" (p. 142). Likewise, different ethnic groups may vary within a culture. African Americans, for example, greatly emphasize individualism (Hecht, Collier, & Ribeau, 1993), whereas, Mexican Americans emphasize group and relational solidarity more (Andersen et al., in press). Indeed, our extreme individualism makes it difficult for Americans to interact with and understand people from other cultures. We are unique; all other cultures are less individualistic. As Condon and Yousef (1983) stated: "The fusion of individualism and equality is so valued and so basic that many Americans find it most difficult to relate to contrasting values in other cultures where interdependence greatly determines a person's sense of self" (p. 65).

The degree to which a culture is individualistic or collectivistic affects the nonverbal behavior of that culture in every way. First, people from individualistic cultures are more remote and distant proximally. Collectivistic cultures are interdependent; as a result, the members work, play, live, and sleep in proximity to one another. One recent study reports that people in individualistic cultures are more distant proximally than collectivists (Gudykunst et al., 1996). Hofstede (1980) cites research suggesting that, as hunters and gatherers, people lived apart in individualistic, nuclear families. When humans became agricultural, the interdependent extended family began living in proximity in large families or tribal units. Urban–industrial societies returned to a norm of individualism, nuclear families, and a lack of proximity to one's neighbors, friends, and co-workers.

Kinesic behavior tends to be more coordinated in collectivistic cultures, where people match one another's facial expressions, and body movements are in sync with each other. Where families work collectively, movements, schedules, and actions need to be highly coordinated (Argyle, 1975). In urban cultures, family members often do their "own thing," coming and going, working and playing, eating and sleeping on different schedules. People in individualistic cultures also smile more than do people in normatively oriented cultures (Tomkins, 1984). Individualists are responsible for their relationships and their own happiness, whereas, normatively or collectively oriented people regard compliance with norms as a primary value and personal or interpersonal happiness as a secondary value (Andersen, 1999a). Matsumoto (1991) reports that "collective cultures will foster emotional displays of their members that maintain and facilitate group cohesion, harmony, or cooperation, to a greater degree than individualistic cultures" (p. 132). Porter and Samovar (1998) report that people in individualistic cultures display a wider range of emotions particularly to out-groups than are displayed by collectivists, who are discouraged from showing a range of positive and/or negative emotions outside of the immediate in-group.

In a similar vein, Lustig and Koester (1999) maintain that "people from individualistic cultures are more likely than those from collectivistic cultures to use confrontational strategies when dealing with interpersonal problems; those with a collectivist orientation are likely to use avoidance, third-party intermediaries, or other face-saving techniques" (p. 123). In collectivistic cultures, people suppress both positive and negative emotional displays that are contrary to the mood of the group, because maintaining the group is a primary value (Andersen, 1999a). Bond (1993) found the Chinese culture to be lower in frequency, intensity, and duration of emotional expression than other cultures. Bond asserts that "the expression of emotion is carefully regulated out of a concern for its capacity to disrupt group harmony and status hierarchies" (p. 245).

People in individualistic cultures are encouraged to express emotions because individual freedom is a paramount value. Research suggests that people in individualistic cultures are more nonverbally affiliative.

Intuitively, the reason for this is not obvious because individualism does not require affiliation; however, Hofstede (1982) explained:

> In less individualistic countries where traditional social ties, like those with extended family members, continue to exist, people have less of a need to make specific friendships. One's friends are predetermined by the social relationships into which one is born. In the more individualistic countries, however, affective relationships are not socially predetermined but must be acquired by each individual personally. (p. 163)

In individualistic countries such as the United States, affiliativeness, dating, flirting, small talk, smiling, and initial acquaintance are more important than in collectivistic countries where the social network is more fixed and less reliant on individual initiative. Bellah et al. (1985) maintain that for centuries in the individualistic and mobile North American society, people could meet more easily and their communication was more open; however, their relationships were usually more casual and transient than those found in more collectivistic cultures.

In an impressive study of dozens of cultures, Lomax (1968) found that a country's song and dance styles were related to its level of social cohesion and collectivism. Collectivistic cultures are higher in "groupiness" and show both more cohesiveness in singing and more synchrony in their dance style (Lomax, 1968). It isn't surprising that rock dancing, which emphasizes separateness and "doing your own thing," evolved in individualistic cultures such as England and the United States. These dances may serve as a metaphor for the whole U.S. culture, where individuality is more prevalent than in any other place (Andersen, 1998).

Power Distance. Another basic dimension of intercultural communication is power distance—the degree to which power, prestige, and wealth are unequally distributed in a culture. Power distance has been measured in many cultures using Hofstede's (1980) Power Distance Index (PDI). Like individualism, power distance varies greatly among cultures. Cultures with high PDI scores have power and influence concentrated in the hands of a few rather than more equally distributed throughout the population. Condon and Yousef (1983) distinguish among three cultural patterns:

democratic, authority-centered, and authoritarian. The PDI is highly correlated (.80) with authoritarianism, as measured by the F scale (Hofstede, 1980).

High PDI countries, from highest to lowest, are the Philippines, Mexico, Venezuela, India, Singapore, Brazil, Hong Kong, France, and Colombia (Hofstede, 1982), all of which, except for France, are southern countries located near the equator. Likewise, Gudykunst and Kim (1992) report that both African and Asian cultures generally maintain hierarchical role relationships characteristic of high power distance. Asian students are expected to be modest and deferent nonverbally in the presence of their instructors. Likewise, Vietnamese people consider employers to be their mentors and will not question orders.

The lowest PDI countries are, respectively, Austria, Israel, Denmark, New Zealand, Ireland, Sweden, Norway, Finland, Switzerland, and Great Britain (Hofstede, 1980), all of which are European or of European origin, middle-class, democratic, and located at high latitudes. The United States is slightly lower than the median in power distance, indicating smaller status differentials than in many other countries. Cultures differ in terms of how status is acquired. In many countries, such as India, class or caste determines one's status. In the United States, power and status is typically determined by money and conspicuous material displays (Andersen & Bowman, 1999).

As suggested previously, the latitude of a country is an important force in the determiner of power distance. Hofstede (1980) claims that latitude and climate are one of the major forces shaping a culture. He maintains that the key intervening variable is that technology is needed for survival in a colder climate, which produces a chain of events in which children are less dependent on authority and learn from people other than authority figures. Hofstede (1982) reports a high, .65 correlation between PDI and latitude. In a study conducted at 40 universities throughout the United States, Andersen, Lustig, and Andersen (1990) report a −.47 correlation between latitude and intolerance for ambiguity, and a −.45 correlation between latitude and authoritarianism. This suggests that residents of the northern United States are less authoritarian and more tolerant of ambiguity. Northern cultures may have to be more tolerant and less autocratic to ensure cooperation and survival in harsher climates.

It is obvious that power distance would affect a culture's nonverbal behavior. In high PDI cultures, such as India, a rigid caste system may severely limit interaction, as in the case of India's "untouchables." More than 20% of India's population are untouchables who lie at the bottom of India's five-caste system (Chinoy, 1967). Any contact with untouchables by members of other castes is strictly forbidden and considered "polluting." Certainly, tactile communication among people of different castes is greatly curtailed in Indian culture. High PDI countries with less rigid stratification than India may still prohibit free interclass dating, marriage, and contact, all of which are taken for granted in low PDI countries.

Social systems with large power discrepancies also produce unique kinesic behavior. Cultures with high power distance encourage emotions and nonverbal displays that reveal status differences. For instance, in high-power-distance cultures, people are expected to show only positive emotions to high-status others and only negative emotions to low-status others (Matsumoto, 1991). According to Andersen and Bowman (1999), subordinates' bodily tension is more obvious in power-discrepant relationships. Similarly, Andersen and Bowman (1999) also report that in power-discrepant circumstances, subordinates smile more in an effort to appease superiors and appear polite. The continuous smiles of many Asians are a culturally inculcated effort to appease superiors and smooth social relations—behaviors that are appropriate to a high PDI culture.

The power distance of a culture also affects vocalic and paralinguistic cues. Citizens of low PDI cultures are generally less aware that vocal loudness may be offensive to others. American vocal tones are often perceived as noisy, exaggerated, and childlike (Condon & Yousef, 1983). Lomax (1968) has shown that in countries where political authority is highly centralized, singing voices are tighter and the voice box is more closed, whereas, more permissive societies produce more relaxed, open, and clear sounds.

Uncertainty. Some cultures value change and ambiguity, whereas, others value stability and certainty. Uncertainty is a cultural predisposition to value risk and ambiguity (Andersen et al., 2002; Hofstede, 1980). At the individual level, this quality is called tolerance for ambiguity (Martin & Westie, 1959). People with intolerance of ambiguity have high levels of uncertainty avoidance and seek clear, black-and-white answers. People with tolerance of ambiguity have low levels of uncertainty avoidance and tend to be more tolerant, to accept ambiguous answers, and to see many shades of gray. Similarly, Hofstede (1980) reports that a country's neuroticism or anxiety scores are strongly correlated with uncertainty avoidance. High uncertainty avoidance is negatively correlated with risk taking and positively correlated with fear of failure.

Countries vary greatly in their tolerance for uncertainty. In some cultures, freedom leads to uncertainty, which leads to stress and anxiety. Hofstede (1980) maintained that intolerance of ambiguity and dogmatism are primarily a function of the uncertainty-avoidance dimension rather than the power-distance dimension. The 10 countries with the highest levels of uncertainty avoidance are Greece, Portugal, Belgium, Japan, Perú, France, Chile, Spain, Argentina, and Turkey (Hofstede, 1980). Countries whose culture originated in the Mediterranean region, especially southern European and South American countries, dominate the list. The 10 countries lowest in uncertainty avoidance and highest in tolerance are Singapore, Denmark, Sweden, Hong Kong, Ireland, Great Britain, India, the Philippines, the United States, Canada, and New Zealand. This list is dominated by Northern European and South Asian cultures, many of which were countries that were originally part of the British Empire. Not surprisingly, these low-uncertainty-avoidant countries have a long history of democratic rule that is likely to be the cause and an effect of uncertainty avoidance. Catholic countries are higher in uncertainty avoidance, whereas, Protestant, Hindu, and Buddhist countries tend to be more accepting of uncertainty (Hofstede, 1980). Eastern religions and Protestantism tend to be less "absolute," whereas, Catholicism is a more "absolute" and certain religion. Andersen, Lustig, and Andersen (1990) report that intolerance for ambiguity is much higher in the American South than in the Northern states, tending to reflect the international pattern of latitude and tolerance.

Few studies have examined nonverbal behavior associated with uncertainty. Hofstede (1980) maintains that countries high in uncertainty avoidance tend to display emotions more than do countries that are low in uncertainty avoidance. Furthermore, he reports that the emotional displays of young people are tolerated less in countries with high uncertainty avoidance. Certainly, disagreement and nonconformity are not appreciated if uncertainty avoidance is high. Nonverbal behavior is more likely to be codified and rule-governed in countries with high uncertainty avoidance. This seems to fit a country such as Japan, but the hypothesis remains to be tested and is somewhat speculative. Hofstede (1980) found that nations high in uncertainty avoidance report more stylized and ritual behavior, so we should expect that nonverbal behavior is more prescribed in these cultures. When people from the United States communicate with people from a country such as Japan or France (both high in uncertainty avoidance), the Americans may seem unruly, nonconforming, and unconventional, whereas, their Japanese or French counterparts might seem too controlled and rigid to the Americans (Lustig & Koester, 1999).

During the past decade, research on uncertainty reduction and avoidance has been extended from interpersonal communication to the study of intercultural communication (Berger & Gudykunst, 1991; Gao & Gudykunst, 1990; Gudykunst, 1993, 1995; Gudykunst & Hammer, 1988), resulting in Gudykunst's Anxiety/Uncertainty Management Theory. The theory seeks to explain attitudes and behaviors toward strangers and members of other cultures (Gudykunst, 1995). Interacting with people outside of our group induces physiological arousal that is experienced as anxiety. This is consistent with the work of Hofstede (1980), who has shown that people in uncertainty-avoidant countries experience and show more anxiety than in other countries. The theory suggests that more secure, uncertainty-tolerant groups are more positive and accepting toward people from another group or culture. Of course, much of this takes place at subtle nonverbal levels. People from cultures that embrace uncertainty are much more likely to treat strangers with positive nonverbal behaviors such as smiles and other indications of immediacy and warmth.

Immediacy. Immediacy behaviors and interpersonal warmth are actions that signal closeness, intimacy, and availability for communication rather than avoidance and greater psychological distance

(Andersen, 1985, 1998). Examples of immediacy behaviors are smiling, touching, eye contact, closer distances, and more vocal animation. Some scholars have labeled these behaviors as "expressive" (Patterson, 1983). Cultures that display considerable interpersonal closeness or immediacy have been labeled "contact cultures" because people in these countries stand closer together and touch more (Hall, 1966). People in low-contact cultures tend to stand apart and touch less. According to Patterson (1983):

> These habitual patterns of relating to the world permeate all aspects of everyday life, but their effects on social behavior define the manner in which people relate to one another. In the case of contact cultures, this general tendency is manifested in closer approaches so that tactile and olfactory information may be gained easily. (p. 145)

Interestingly, contact cultures are generally located in warmer countries nearer the equator and low-contact cultures are found in cooler climates farther from the equator. Explanations for these latitudinal variations have included energy level, climate, and metabolism (Hofstede, 1980; Andersen, Lustig, & Andersen, 1990). Evidently, cultures in cooler climates tend to be more task-oriented and interpersonally "cool," whereas cultures in warmer climates tend to be more interpersonally oriented and interpersonally "warm." Even within the United States, the warmer latitudes tend to be higher-contact cultures. Andersen, Lustig, and Andersen (1990) report a .31 correlation between latitude of students' university and touch avoidance. These data indicate that students at universities located in the so-called Sunbelt are more touch-oriented. Pennebaker, Rimé, and Sproul (1994) found a correlation between latitude and expressiveness within dozens of countries. Northerners are more expressive than southerners, according to their data, in Belgium, Croatia, France, Germany, Italy, Japan, Serbia, Spain, Switzerland, and the United States, with an overall difference within the entire Northern Hemisphere. Pennebaker et al. (1994) conclude:

> Logically, climate must profoundly affect social processes. People living in cold climates devote more time to dressing, to providing warmth, to planning ahead for food provisions during the winter months....

In warm climates, people are more likely to see, hear, and interact with neighbors year around. Emotional expressiveness then would be more of a requirement. (pp. 15–16)

Similarly, Andersen, Lustig, and Andersen (1990) conclude:

> In Northern latitudes societies must be more structured, more ordered, more constrained, and more organized if the individuals are to survive harsh weather forces....In contrast, Southern latitudes may attract or produce a culture characterized by social extravagance and flamboyance that has no strong inclination to constrain or order their world. (p. 307)

Traditionally, research has shown that high-contact cultures comprise most Arab countries, including North Africa; the Mediterranean region, including France, Greece, Italy, Portugal, and Spain; Jews from both Europe and the Middle East; Eastern Europeans and Russians; and virtually all of Latin America (Condon & Yousef, 1983; Jones, 1994; Jones & Remland, 1982; Mehrabian, 1971; Patterson, 1983; Samovar, Porter, & Jain, 1981; Scheflen, 1972). Australians are moderate in their cultural contact level, as are North Americans (Patterson, 1983). Research generally found that low-contact cultures comprise most of Northern Europe, including Scandinavia, Germany, and England; British Americans; white Anglo-Saxons (the primary culture of the United States); and virtually every Asian country, including Burma, China, Indonesia, Japan, Korea, the Philippines, Thailand, and Vietnam (Andersen, Andersen, & Lustig, 1987; Heslin & Alper, 1983; Jones, 1994; Jones & Remland, 1982; McDaniel & Andersen, 1998; Mehrabian, 1971; Patterson, 1983; Remland, 2000; Samovar, Porter, & Jain, 1981; Scheflen, 1972). Recent research reported by Remland (2000) suggests that people do touch significantly more in southern Europe than in northern Europe.

Other recent research suggests that the biggest differences in immediacy are not between North America and Europe, both of which are probably moderate to high contact cultures. Compared to the rest of the world, Asia is an extreme noncontact culture (McDaniel & Andersen, 1998; Remland, Jones, & Brinkman, 1991). These two studies question whether Hall's (1966) original designation of some cultures as "low contact" is an oversimplification. Whether a generational shift or internationalization may have produced this change is unclear, but much of the Western world, including the United States, appears to be a contact culture. Indeed, McDaniel and Andersen's (1998) study of public touch suggests that the biggest difference is between Asians, who rarely touch in public, and virtually every other culture, which all manifest higher degrees of public touching. These findings are consistent with other research suggesting that China and Japan are distinctly nontactile cultures (Barnland, 1978; Jones, 1994).

Without a doubt, cultures differ in their immediacy. In general, people living in northern countries, northern parts of individual countries, and traditional cultures, as well as Asians, are the least immediate and expressive. Conversely, people living in the south, modern countries, and non-Asian cultures are the most expressive and immediate. Obviously, these findings are painted with a fairly broad brush and will await a more detailed cultural portrait.

Gender. Perhaps the most researched issue in social science during recent decades is gender. While humans can be viewed as masculine or feminine, so can nations and cultures. The gender orientation of culture has an impact on many aspects of nonverbal behavior. This includes the nonverbal expressions permitted by each sex, occupational status, nonverbal aspects of power, the ability to interact with strangers or acquaintances of the opposite sex, and all aspects of interpersonal relationships between men and women. According to one research group: "Numerous studies have examined gender as an individual characteristic, but gender has been neglected as a cultural dimension" (Andersen et al., 2002). Gender, as discussed in this article, refers to the rigidity of gender rules. In masculine cultures, gender rules are more rigid and traits such as strength, assertiveness, competitiveness, and ambitiousness are valued. In more feminine or androgynous cultures, attributes such as affection, compassion, nurturance, and emotionality are valued (Bem, 1974; Hofstede, 1980). In less rigid cultures, both men and women can express more diverse, less stereotyped sex-role behaviors.

Cross-cultural research shows that girls are expected to be more nurturant than boys, although there is considerable variation from country to country

(Hall, 1984). Hofstede (1980) has measured the degree to which people of both sexes in a culture endorse masculine or feminine goals. Masculine cultures regard competition and assertiveness as important, whereas feminine cultures place more importance on nurturance and compassion. Not surprisingly, the masculinity of a culture is negatively correlated with the percentage of women in technical and professional jobs and positively correlated with segregation of the sexes in higher education (Hofstede, 1980).

Countries with the 10 highest masculinity index scores, according to Hofstede (1980), are Japan, Austria, Venezuela, Italy, Switzerland, Mexico, Ireland, Great Britain, Germany, and the Philippines. The 10 countries with the lowest masculinity scores are Sweden, Norway, the Netherlands, Denmark, Finland, Chile, Portugal, Thailand, and Perú. Not surprisingly, high-masculinity countries have fewer women in the labor force, have only recently afforded voting privileges to women, and are less likely to consider wife rape a crime than are low-masculinity countries (Seager & Olson, 1986).

Not surprisingly, the Scandinavian countries, with their long history of equal rights for women, are at the top of the list of feminine countries. But why would South American cultures be less masculine and not manifest the Latin pattern of machismo? Iberian countries like Spain and Portugal have relatively feminine cultures, as do their South American cultural descendants like Chile and Perú. Hofstede (1980) suggests that machismo is more present in the Caribbean region than in the remainder of South America. In fact, South America, as compared to Central America, has a much higher percentage of working women, much higher school attendance by girls, and more women in higher education (Seager & Olson, 1986).

Considerable research suggests that androgynous patterns of behavior (that is, both feminine and masculine) result in more self-esteem, social competence, success, and intellectual development for both males and females (Andersen, 1999). Nonverbal styles where both men and women are free to express both masculine traits (such as dominance and anger) and feminine traits (such as warmth and emotionality) are likely to be both healthier and more effective. Buck (1984) has demonstrated that males may harm their health by internalizing emotions rather than externalizing them as women usually do. Internalized emotions that are not expressed result in more stress and higher blood pressure. Not surprisingly, more masculine countries show higher levels of stress (Hofstede, 1980).

Considerable research has demonstrated significant vocal differences between egalitarian and nonegalitarian countries. Countries in which women are economically important and where sexual standards for women are permissive show more relaxed vocal patterns than do other countries (Lomax, 1968). Moreover, those egalitarian countries show less tension between the sexes, more vocal solidarity and coordination in their songs, and more synchrony in their movement (Lomax, 1968).

The United States tends to be a masculine country, according to Hofstede (1982), although it is not among the most masculine. Intercultural communicators should keep in mind that other countries may be either more or less sexually egalitarian than the United States. Because most countries are more feminine (that is, nurturant and compassionate), Americans of both sexes often seem loud, aggressive, and competitive by world standards. Likewise, Americans' attitude toward women may seem sexist in extremely feminine locations such as Scandinavia.

Most important, in relatively more feminine countries, both men and women can engage in either masculine or feminine nonverbal behaviors. In masculine countries, the nonverbal behavior of men and women is carefully proscribed and must adhere to a narrower sexual script. So, for example, in feminine countries like Sweden and Norway, women can engage in more powerful speaking styles, wear masculine clothing, and be more vocally assertive. Similarly, men in feminine countries can show emotions such as sadness or fear and engage in more nurturant and less dominant behaviors.

CONCLUSIONS

Studying these six cultural dimensions cannot ensure competence in intercultural communication. The beauty of international travel and even travel within the United States is that it provides a unique perspective on one's own and others' behavior. Combining cognitive knowledge from intercultural readings and courses

with actual encounters with people from other cultures is the best way to gain intercultural competence.

A full, practical understanding of the dimensions along which cultures differ—along with knowledge of how specific communication acts differ cross-culturally—has several practical benefits.

1. Such knowledge will highlight and challenge assumptions about our own behavior. The structure of our own behavior is invisible and taken for granted until it is exposed and challenged through study of cultures and actual intercultural encounters. Indeed, Hall (1976) stated that ethnic diversity in interethnic communication can be a source of strength and an asset from which one's self can be discovered.

2. This discussion should make it clear that attributions about the nonverbal communication of people from other cultures are bound to be wrong. No dictionary or code of intercultural behavior is available. You cannot read people like books, not even people from your own culture. Understanding that someone is from a masculine, collectivistic, or high-context culture, however, will make his or her behavior less confusing and more interpretable.

3. Despite the Internet and global media, intercultural diversity is likely to persist for centuries. Indeed, some countries are still discovering or rediscovering their ethnic identity. Global migrations and a global economy mean that diverse intercultural interactions will be increasingly common. If you enjoy living in a diverse world, you have come to the right planet in the right century. Let us hope that we celebrate this great, diverse, intertwined tapestry of diversity we call the human race.

References

Andersen, J. F., Andersen, P. A., & Lustig, M. W. (1987). Opposite-sex touch avoidance: A national replication and extension. *Journal of Nonverbal Behavior*, *II*, 89–109.

Andersen, P. A. (1985). Nonverbal immediacy in interpersonal communication. In A. W. Siegman & S. Feldstein (Eds.), *Multichannel integrations of nonverbal behavior* (pp. 1–36). Hillsdale, NJ: Lawrence Erlbaum.

Andersen, P. A. (1987). The trait debate: A critical examination of the individual differences paradigm in intercultural communication. In B. Dervin & M. J. Voigt (Eds.),

Progress in communication sciences, Vol. VIII (pp. 47–82). Norwood, NJ: Ablex.

Andersen, P. A. (1998). The cognitive valence theory of intimate communication. In M. T. Palmer & G. A. Barnett (Eds.), *Progress in communication sciences, Volume XIV: Mutual influence in interpersonal communication: Theory and research in cognition, affect, and behavior* (pp. 39–72). Stamford, CT: Ablex.

Andersen, P. A. (1999a). *Nonverbal communication: Forms and functions.* Mountain View, CA: Mayfield.

Andersen, P. A. (1999b). 1999 WSCA Presidential address. *Western Journal of Communication*, 63, 339–543.

Andersen, P. A., & Bowman, L. (1999). Positions of power: Nonverbal influence in organizational communication. In L. K. Guerrero, J. A. DeVito, & M. L. Hecht (Eds.), *The nonverbal reader* (pp. 317–334). Prospect Heights, IL: Waveland Press.

Andersen, P. A., Hecht, M. L., Hoobler, G. D., & Smallwood, M. (2002). Nonverbal communication across culture. In B. Gudykunst & B. Mody (Eds.), *Handbook of international and intercultural communication.* Thousand Oaks, CA: Sage.

Andersen, P. A., & Leibowitz, K. (1978). The development and nature of the construct touch avoidance. *Environmental Psychology and Nonverbal Behavior*, 3, 89–106.

Andersen, P. A., Lustig, M. W., & Andersen, J. F. (1986). *Communication patterns among cultural regions of the United States: A theoretical perspective.* Paper presented at the annual convention of the International Communication Association, Chicago.

Andersen, P. A., Lustig, R., & Andersen, J. F. (1990). Changes in latitude, changes in attitude: The relationship between climate and interpersonal communication predispositions. *Communication Quarterly*, 38, 291–311.

Argyle, M. (1975). *Bodily communication.* New York: International Universities Press.

Barnland, D. C. (1978). Communication styles in two cultures: Japan and the United States. In A. Kendon, R. M. Harris, & M. R. Key (Eds.), *Organization of behavior in face to face interaction* (pp. 427–456). The Hague: Mouton.

Bellah, R. N., Madsen, R., Sullivan, W. M., Swidler, A., & Tipton, S. (1985). *Habits of the heart: Individualism and commitment in American life.* New York: Harper & Row.

Bem, S. L. (1974). The measurement of psychological androgyny. *Journal of Consulting and Clinical Psychology*, 42, 155–162.

Berger, C. R., & Gudykunst, W. B. (1991). Uncertainty and communication. In B. Dervin & M. Voigt (Eds.), *Progress in communication sciences* (vol. 10, pp. 21–66). Norwood, NJ: Ablex.

Bond, M. H. (1993). Emotions and their expression in Chinese culture. *Journal of Nonverbal Behavior*, 17, 245–262.

Brown, L. R., Kane, H., & Roodman, D. M. (1994). *Vital signs 1994: The trends that are shaping our future.* New York: W. W. Norton.

Bruneau, T. (1979). The time dimension in intercultural communication. In D. Nimmo (Ed.), *Communication yearbook* 3 (pp. 423–433). New Brunswick, NJ: Transaction Books.

Buck, R. (1984). *The communication of emotion.* New York: Guilford Press.

Burgoon, J. K. (1985). Nonverbal signals. In M. L. Knapp & G. R. Miller (Eds.), *Handbook of interpersonal communication* (pp. 344–390). Beverly Hills, CA: Sage.

Chinoy, E. (1967). *Society.* New York: Random House.

Condon, J. C., & Yousef, F. (1983). *An introduction to intercultural communication.* Indianapolis, IN: Bobbs-Merrill.

Elazar, D. J. (1972). *American federalism: A view from the states.* New York: Thomas P. Crowell.

Elliot, S., Scott, M. D., Jensen, A. D., & McDonough, M. (1982). Perceptions of reticence: A cross-cultural investigation. In M. Burgoon (Ed.), *Communication yearbook* 5 (pp. 591–602). New Brunswick, NJ: Transaction Books.

Ford, J. G., & Graves, J. R. (1977). Differences between Mexican-American and white children in interpersonal distance and social touching. *Perceptual and Motor Skills*, 45, 779–785.

Gao, G., & Gudykunst, W. B. (1990). Uncertainty, anxiety, and adaptation. *International Journal of Intercultural Relations*, 14, 301–317.

Geertz, C. (1973). *The interpretation of cultures.* New York: Basic Books.

Gudykunst, W. B. (1993). Toward a theory of effective interpersonal and intergroup communication: An anxiety/uncertainty management (AUM) perspective. In R. L. Wiseman & J. Koester (Eds.), *Intercultural communication competence* (pp. 33–71). Newbury Park, CA: Sage.

Gudykunst, W. B. (1995). Anxiety/Uncertainty Management (AUM) Theory: Current status. In R. L. Wiseman (Ed.), *Intercultural communication theory* (pp. 8–58). Thousand Oaks, CA: Sage.

Gudykunst, W. B., & Hammer, M. R. (1988). Strangers and hosts. In Y. Kim & W. Gudykunst (Eds.), *Cross-cultural adaptation* (pp. 106–139). Newbury Park, CA: Sage.

Gudykunst, W. B., & Kim, Y. Y. (1992). *Communicating with strangers: An approach to intercultural communication.* New York: Random House.

Gudykunst, W. B., Matsumoto, Y., Ting-Toomey, S., Nishida, T., Kim, K., & Heyman, S. (1996). Influence of cultural individualism-collectivism, self-construals, and individual values on communication styles across cultures. *Human Communication Research*, 22, 510–543.

Hall, E. T. (1959). *The silent language*. New York: Doubleday.

Hall, E. T. (1966). A system of the notation of proxemic behavior. *American Anthropologist*, 65, 1003–1026.

Hall, E. T. (1976). *Beyond culture*. Garden City, NY: Anchor.

Hall, E. T. (1984). *The dance of life: The other dimension of time*. Garden City, NY: Anchor.

Hecht, M. L., Collier, M. J., & Ribeau, S. A. (1993). *African-American communication: Ethnic identity and cultural interpretation*. Newbury Park, CA. Sage.

Heslin, R., & Alper, T. (1983). Touch: A bonding gesture. In J. M. Wiemann & R. Harrison (Eds.), *Non-verbal interaction* (pp. 47–75). Beverly Hills, CA: Sage.

Hofstede, G. (1980/1982). *Culture's consequences* (abridged ed.). Beverly Hills, CA: Sage.

Jones, S. E. (1994). *The right touch: Understanding and using the language of physical contact*. Cresshill, NJ: Hampton Press.

Jones, T. S., & Remland, M. S. (1982, May). *Cross-cultural differences in self-reported touch avoidance*. Paper presented at the annual convention of the Eastern Communication Association, Hartford, CT.

LaBarre, W. (1985). Paralinguistics, kinesics, and cultural anthropology. In L. A. Samovar & R. E. Porter (Eds.), *Intercultural communication: A reader* (pp. 272–279). Belmont, CA: Wadsworth.

Lomax, A. (1968). *Folk song style and culture*. New Brunswick, NJ: Transaction Books.

Lustig, M. L., & Koester, J. (1999). *Intercultural competence: Interpersonal communication across culture*. New York: HarperCollins.

Martin, J. G., & Westie, F. R. (1959). The intolerant personality. *American Sociological Review*, 24, 521–528.

Matsumoto, D. (1991). Cultural influences on facial expressions of emotion. *Southern Communication Journal*, 56, 128–137.

McDaniel, E. R., & Andersen, P. A. (1998). Intercultural variations in tactile communication. *Journal of Nonverbal Communication*, 22, 59–75.

Mehrabian, A. (1971). *Silent messages*. Belmont, CA: Wadsworth.

Patterson, M. L. (1983). *Nonverbal behavior: A functional perspective*. New York: Springer-Verlag.

Pennebaker, J. W., Rimé, B., & Sproul, G. (1994). *Stereotype of emotional expressiveness of Northerners and Southerners: A cross-cultural test of Montesquieu's hypotheses*. Unpublished paper, Southern Methodist University, Dallas, TX.

Porter, R. E., & Samovar, L. A. (1998). Cultural influences on emotional expression: Implications for intercultural communication. In P. A. Andersen & L. K. Guerrero (Eds.), *Handbook of communication and emotion: Research theory, applications and contexts* (pp. 451–472). San Diego, CA: Academic Press.

Remland, M. S., Jones, T. S., & Brinkman, H. (1991). Proxemic and haptic behavior in three European countries. *Journal of Nonverbal Behavior*, 15, 215–232.

Remland, M. S. (2000). *Nonverbal communication in everyday life*. Boston, MA: Houghton Mifflin.

Samovar, L. A., & Porter, R. E. (1985). Nonverbal interaction. In L. A. Samovar & R. E. Porter (Eds.), *Intercultural communication: A reader*. Belmont, CA: Wadsworth.

Samovar, L. A., Porter, R. E., & Jain, N. C. (1981). *Understanding intercultural communication*. Belmont, CA: Wadsworth.

Samovar, P. A., Porter, R. E., & Stefani, L. A. (1998). *Communication between cultures*. Belmont, CA: Wadsworth.

Sapir, E. (1928). The unconscious patterning of behavior in society. In E. S. Drummer (Ed.), *The unconscious* (pp. 114–142). New York: Knopf.

Scheflen, A. E. (1972). *Body language and the social order*. Englewood Cliffs, NJ: Prentice-Hall.

Scheflen, A. E. (1974). *How behavior means*. Garden City, NY: Anchor.

Seager, J., & Olson, A. (1986). *Women in the world atlas*. New York: Simon & Schuster.

Sitaram, K. S., & Codgell, R. T. (1976). *Foundations of intercultural communication*. Columbus, OH: Charles E. Merrill.

Tomkins, S. S. (1984). Affect theory. In K. R. Scherer & P. Ekman (Eds.), *Approaches to emotion* (pp. 163–195). Hillsdale, NJ: Lawrence Erlbaum.

Watzlawick, P., Beavin, J. H., & Jackson, D. D. (1967). *Pragmatics of human communication*. New York: W. W. Norton.

Concepts and Questions

1. What does Andersen mean when he writes that "the primary level of culture is communicated implicitly, without awareness, by primarily nonverbal means"?

2. Do you agree with Andersen that two of the most fundamental nonverbal differences in intercultural communication involve space and time? From your experiences, what two nonverbal areas have you found most troublesome when interacting with people from different cultures?

3. From your personal experiences, can you think of different ways people in various cultures greet, show emotion, and beckon?

4. Do you believe that intercultural communication problems are more serious when they involve nonverbal communication or verbal communication?

5. What is kinesic behavior? How does it vary from one culture to another? What types of communication problems can be caused by cultural differences in kinesic behavior?

6. The term haptics refers to patterns of tactile communication. How does tactile communication differ among cultures? Can you think of examples of how tactile communication differs among members of co-cultures? What type of communication problems might arise when people with different touching orientations interact?

7. How does physical appearance affect first impressions during interaction? How are expectations of physical appearance related to the informal-formal dimension of culture?

8. How does immediacy affect interpersonal interaction? What differences in behaviors would you expect from high- and low-contact cultures? In what way would violations of immediacy expectations affect intercultural communication?

9. How is the degree of individualism within cultures manifest in nonverbal behavior?

10. What is the relationship between power distance and kinesic behavior? How is high-power distance displayed? How is low-power distance displayed?

Japanese Nonverbal Communication: A Reflection of Cultural Themes

Edwin R. McDaniel

Modern technological advances have made the world a much smaller place, promoting increased interactions between peoples of different nations and cultures. Growing international economic interdependencies and expanding multinational security alliances have significantly increased the importance of effective intercultural encounters. Individuals from diverse cultures are interacting with each other more and more frequently—in professional, diplomatic, and social venues.

The most critical aspect of this burgeoning transnational intercourse is, of course, communication. The ability to understand and be understood is central to successful cross-cultural activities. Comprehension, however, must go beyond a topical awareness of another culture's communicative practices and behaviors. An appreciation of the cultural antecedents and motivations shaping an individual's communication conventions is necessary for understanding how and why a particular practice is used.

An established method of explaining the cultural motivations of human behavior is to identify and isolate consistent themes among a social grouping. Anthropological writings have posited that each culture manifests a "limited number of dynamic affirmations" (Opler, 1945, p. 198), referred to as themes. According to Opler (1945), these cultural themes promote and regulate human behavioral activities that are

Courtesy of Edwin R. McDaniel. This original essay appeared for the first time in the eighth edition of this book. All rights reserved. Permission to reprint must be obtained from the author and the publisher. Edwin R. McDaniel is a retired Professor of Intercultural Communication from Aichi Shukutoku University, Nagoya, Japan.

societally encouraged and condoned. To illustrate this approach, Opler (1945) used an examination of the social relations of the Lipan Apaches to demonstrate how thematic study could provide insight into cultural beliefs and behaviors.

In communication studies, the concept of thematic commonality has been used by Burgoon and Hale (1984, 1987) to help explicate relational communications. They conceptualized a series of "interrelated message themes" (Burgoon & Hale, 1987, p. 19), which have been purported to have application to both verbal and nonverbal exchanges. These proposed themes, or *topi,* have become a supposition cited in studies of interpersonal relations communication (e.g., Buller & Burgoon, 1986; Coker & Burgoon, 1987; Spitzberg, 1989).

Burgoon and Hale's (1984) concept of identifying consistent themes to assist in the explanation of a communication process possesses significant utility for additional, more comprehensive employment. The innovation has clear application to the study of culture-specific communication predispositions.

Using the Japanese as a cultural model, this essay makes practical application of the thematic consistency concept advanced by Opler (1945, 1946) and Burgoon and Hale (1984, 1987). The objective is to illustrate how nonverbal communication practices function as a reflection, or representation, of societal cultural themes. Employing a standard taxonomy of nonverbal communication codes and addressing each individually, cultural themes influencing and manifested by the code are discussed in a propositional format. Additionally, the essay strives to demonstrate how cultural influences can subtly shape a society's communication conventions.

JAPANESE CULTURAL THEMES

Japan's predominantly homogeneous population embodies a particularly rich array of cultural themes. The more prevalent themes include group affiliation (collectivism), hierarchy, social balance or harmony (*wa*), empathy, mutual-dependency, perseverance and sacrifice (*gaman*), humility, and formality (ritual, tradition, and protocol) (Caudill, 1973; Lebra, 1976; Reischauer, 1988).

Confucian-based collectivism exerts a significant influence on Japanese communication patterns. The nation's racial and cultural homogeneity creates a strong identity bond and facilitates intragroup and interpersonal familiarity. This societal closeness promotes an instinctive, nonverbal understanding among Japanese people. Their cultural similitude abets an intuitive, nonverbal comprehension by diminishing the requirement to orally specify numerous details (Barnlund, 1989; Ishii, 1984; Kinosita, 1988; Kitao & Kitao, 1985; Morsbach, 1988a; Nakane, 1970; Westwood & Vargo, 1985; Yum, 1988).

The Japanese concept of collectivism is epitomized by their usage of the term *nihonjinron* to express self-perceived uniqueness as both a nation and a people. This idea of distinctive originality provides the Japanese with a focus for social cohesiveness. Their propensity for group affiliation has created a social context referred to as *uchi-soto,* or inside–outside. This context can also be viewed as in-group (possessing membership) and out-group (no involvement). Within the security of their respective in-group (*uchi*), the Japanese can be quite expressive and display considerable nonverbal affiliation with other members. Much less interaction will occur in an out-group (*soto*) situation (Gudykunst & Nishida, 1984; Gudykunst, Nishida, & Schmidt, 1989; Gudykunst, Yoon, & Nishida, 1987; Lebra, 1976, 1993).

The hierarchical nature of Japanese society and an inexorable compulsion for social balance or harmony (*wa*) increases the reliance on nonverbal behaviors and concomitantly discourages verbal exchanges. A hierarchy exists in every instance of group or interpersonal interaction. In this superior–subordinate environment, the junior is socially compelled to assume a passive role, awaiting and hopefully anticipating the senior's desires or actions. The senior, desiring to exemplify humility and avoid any social or personal discord, will endeavor to nonverbally ascertain the junior's expectations.

The cultural pressure for social balance dictates the course of all Japanese activities and creates a pervasive acceptance of ambiguity and vagueness during any communication endeavor. Reluctant to arbitrarily advance personal opinions or attitudes, the Japanese will draw on the situational context and attempt to instinctively discern what the other person is thinking

(Hall & Hall, 1990; Ishii, 1984; Ishii & Bruneau, 1991; Kitao & Kitao, 1985; Lebra, 1976; Morsbach, 1988a; Munakata, 1986; Reischauer, 1988).

The cultural trait of empathy (*omoiyari*) also lessens the Japanese reliance on verbal exchanges. In Japan, considerable value is placed on an individual's ability to empathetically determine the needs of another person. During interpersonal encounters, the Japanese often use indirect or vague statements and depend on the other person's sensitivity to ascertain the desired meaning of the interaction (Doi, 1988; Ishii, 1984; Lebra, 1976).

PROPOSITIONAL SURVEY

Considered in isolation, a nonverbal code normally provides only partial interpretation of the intended message. This study, however, is not concerned with the code's proposed message, but instead attempts to demonstrate how the code is culturally based and motivated. To this end, in each of the following propositions (denoted as P1, P2, etc.), specific nonverbal communication codes are shown to reflect one or more cultural themes common to Japanese society.

P1: *Japanese kinesics reflect the cultural themes of (1) group orientation, (2) hierarchy, (3) social balance, (4) formality, and (5) humility.*

The Japanese enjoy a wide array of kinesic activities, especially gestures (Caudill & Weinstein, 1969; March, 1990; Seward, 1983). Usage, however, is situational and often limited to males (Richie, 1987). A Japanese manager, for instance, might rely on gestures to communicate with work subordinates (Sethi, 1974), thereby demonstrating the cohesive familiarity common among in-group (*uchi*) members.

The Japanese are more relaxed and expressive within their in-group. Away from the in-group, however, the use of body language is usually remarkably restrained (Cohen, 1991; Ishii, 1975). In public, it is common to see both Japanese men and women sitting quietly and unobtrusively, with hands folded (March, 1990). This self-restraint of body movement in out-group (*soto*) environments is designed to avoid attention and maintain situational harmony or balance.

As another example of concern for social balance, Japanese hand gestures are never used in reference to a person who is present at the time. Instead, they are employed when referring to some absent party (Richie, 1987). This behavior, quite naturally, reduces the opportunity for offending anyone present and helps sustain contextual harmony.

The most common activity associated with Japanese kinesics is the bow, which is an integral and repetitive part of daily social interaction. The Japanese bow is used when meeting someone, when asking for something, while apologizing, when offering congratulations, when acknowledging someone else, and when departing, to mention just a few instances. Historically a sign of submission, the bow is a contemporary ritual that continues to convey respect and denote hierarchical status. The junior person bows first, lowest, and longest. An improperly executed bow can be interpreted as a significant insult (Hendry, 1989; Ishii, 1975; Kitao & Kitao, 1987, 1989; Morsbach, 1988b; Ramsey, 1979; Richie, 1987; Ruch, 1984).

Traditional Japanese women exhibit a distinct kinesic activity by obscuring facial areas with their hands or some object[1] (Ishii, 1975; Ramsey, 1981). Ramsey's (1981) investigation of this phenomenon concluded that women utilized these adaptors for impression management. An explicit intent of these actions is to evoke a perception of humility when in the presence of a social superior.

P2: *Japanese oculesics reflect the cultural themes of (1) hierarchy, (2) social balance, and (3) humility.*

In Japan, prolonged eye contact is considered rude, threatening, and disrespectful.[1] The Japanese are taught, from childhood, to avert their gaze or look at a person's throat. When one is part of an audience, looking away or simply sitting silently with eyes closed indicates attention to, and possibly agreement with, the speaker. Direct, sustained eye contact is normally avoided, unless a superior wants to admonish a subordinate (Hall & Hall, 1990; Ishii, 1975; Kasahara, 1986; Kitao & Kitao, 1987, 1989; March, 1990; Morsbach, 1973; Richie, 1987; Ruch, 1984; Watson, 1970).

By avoiding eye contact, the participants in communication simultaneously evince an air of humility and sustain situational *wa*. The employment of direct eye contact by a superior is a clear exercise of hierarchical prerogative (March, 1990).

P3: *Japanese facial expressions reflect the cultural themes of (1) social balance and (2) gaman.*

As is common to all aspects of their social behavior, the Japanese do not normally evince any significant emotion through public facial displays. The most commonly observed expressions are either a placid, unrevealing countenance or a nondescript smile, whose actual meaning or intent may be totally indecipherable. A smile can indicate happiness or serve as a friendly acknowledgement. Alternatively, it may be worn to mask negative emotions, especially displeasure, anger, or grief (Gudykunst & Nishida, 1993; Kitao & Kitao, 1987, 1989; Matsumoto, 1996; Morsbach, 1973).

For the Japanese, the smile is simply a part of social etiquette, designed to help sustain harmony. In a social environment, the Japanese would consider it unpardonable to burden someone else with an outward show of elation, irritation, or anguish. Eschewing any external display of negative emotion is an example of perseverance or self-sacrifice (*gaman*) to avoid disrupting the social balance (*wa*). The smile is also used to avoid conflict; a Japanese person might simply smile in order to avoid answering an awkward question or giving a negative answer (Ishii, 1975; Kitao & Kitao, 1987, 1989; Nakane, 1970; Ruch, 1984; Seward, 1972).

P4: *Japanese proxemic behaviors reflect the cultural themes of (1) in-group affinity, (2) hierarchy, and (3) balance.*

The Japanese attitude toward personal space is, on the surface, complex and often seemingly contradictory. In uncrowded situations, they assiduously strive to maintain personal space intervals that are even greater than those maintained by Americans. Conversely, when on a train or bus they offer no resistance to frequent or even prolonged body contact with total strangers. Personal space is also close among friends or family members (Hall, 1990; Richie, 1987).

This apparent dichotomy is the result of their societal group orientation, vertical structure, and constant concern for social balance. In an uncrowded out-group environment, the Japanese maintain their personal space, which also provides a psychological barrier

against the unknown, such as the hierarchical status and group affiliation of others (Ishii, 1975; Morsbach, 1973; Watson, 1970). If forced into proximity with an out-group member, the Japanese will assume a façade of unperturbable passivity in an effort to maintain situational harmony. I have often observed the Japanese projecting an air of composed detachment while being subjected to suffocating conditions in a crowded Tokyo subway car.

Among in-group members, where strong social ties exist, personal space is dramatically reduced. Traditionally, family members commonly slept in the same room, within easy touching distance of each other (Caudill & Plath, 1966). Male white-collar co-workers (*salarimen*) sitting close together and patting each other on the back during after-work drinking excursions are a common sight in Japanese bars.

Japanese proxemic behavior has been the subject of several investigations. In a study involving status manipulation, Japanese subjects exhibited signs of anxiety in reaction to an interviewer's forward lean (Bond & Shiraishi, 1974). Iwata's (1979) study of Japanese female students disclosed that individuals with high self-esteem evinced a negative reaction to crowding. This behavior is consistent with the Japanese concept of hierarchy. Self-esteem would be proportional with social status, which would predicate greater interpersonal distance in out-group situations.

P5: *Japanese tactile conventions reflect the cultural themes of (1) in-group affinity and (2) social balance.*

Studies of Japanese maternal care have disclosed that children experience considerable touch from their mothers (Caudill & Plath, 1966; Caudill & Weinstein, 1969). Even today, parents and their young children often share the same bed. The amount of public tactile interaction drops dramatically, however, after childhood, and the individual is expected to conform to societal nontouch standards (Barnlund, 1975; McDaniel & Andersen, 1998; Montague, 1978). Indeed, adult Japanese actively avoid public displays of interpersonal physical expressiveness[1] (Barnlund, 1989; Malandro & Barker, 1983) unless in a close-knit in-group setting.

For adults, in-group (*uchi*) touching is acceptable (Lebra, 1976). This is especially evident when male co-workers are drinking (Miyamoto, 1994). In an out-group (*soto*) situation, touch is uncommon unless it results inadvertently from crowding, and then it is simply ignored (Ishii, 1975; Morsbach, 1973; Ramsey, 1985). These conventions again indicate the value placed on group affiliation and harmony.

P6: *Japanese personal appearance reflects the cultural themes of (1) collectivism, (2) group affiliation, (3) social balance, and (4) hierarchy.*

The central theme of Japanese external appearance is, quite simply, group identity and status. The ubiquitous dark suit dominates the business world, and everyone, men and women alike, normally opts for conservative styles. Small lapel pins or badges identifying the individual's company are frequently worn.[2] Blue-collar workers normally wear a uniform (such as coveralls or smocks) distinctive to their corporation (Condon & Yousef, 1983; Hall, 1981; Harris & Moran, 1979; March, 1990; Morsbach, 1973; Ruch, 1984).

The general proclivity for conservative dress styles and colors emphasizes the nation's collectivism and, concomitantly, lessens the potential for social disharmony arising from nonconformist attire. Lapel pins and uniforms signal a particular group affiliation, which in turn helps determine a person's social position.

Although not specifically nonverbal, the Japanese business card, or *meshi*, must be discussed. It exerts considerable influence on Japanese nonverbal behavior and communication in general. The initial impression of an individual is derived from his or her *meshi*. The card must be of the appropriate size and color and, in addition to the individual's name, list the person's company and position. This facilitates rapid determination of the individual's group affiliation and personal station, which dictates the correct deportment and appropriate speech levels for participants engaging in interpersonal dialogue (Craft, 1986; Morsbach, 1973; Ruch, 1984).

P7: *Japanese use of space reflects the cultural themes of (1) hierarchy and (2) group orientation.*

The Japanese hierarchical contextualization of space is best exemplified by the standard spatial array of governmental and corporate offices. Numerous desks, occupied by lower-level employees, are lined, facing each other, hierarchically in rows in a large, common room, absent of walls or partitions.

The supervisors and managers are positioned at the head of each row. This organization encourages the exchange of information, facilitates multitask accomplishment, promotes group cooperation and solidarity, and facilitates rapid discernment of the work-center rank structure. Seating arrangements at any formal or semi-formal function are also based on hierarchy (Hamabata, 1990; Ramsey, 1979; Ramsey & Birk, 1983; Ruch, 1984; Takamizawa, 1988).

In explaining the Japanese perception of space as a hierarchical concept, Hall (1990) offers an insightful illustration. Neighborhood houses in Japan are numbered in the order they are constructed, regardless of actual location along the street.

P8: *Japanese use of time reflects the cultural themes of (1) hierarchy, (2) group orientation, and (3) social balance.*

Hall and Hall (1990) have indicated that the Japanese use time polychronically among themselves and monochronically when conducting business with foreigners. The rigid adherence to schedules when dealing with foreigners is in contrast with the temporal flexibility exhibited during interactions with other Japanese. This demonstrates an ability to adjust to dynamic situations. For example, schedules may have to be altered in order to accommodate the desires of a senior, which reflects hierarchical sensitivities.

The Japanese decision-making process characterizes the influence of group orientation and social balance on the usage of time. In almost every interpersonal context, it is necessary to build a consensus before announcing a decision. This process, concerned with maintaining social balance among group members, can take days, weeks, or even months (Hall, 1988; Nakane, 1970; Stewart, 1993).

P9: *Japanese vocalics reflect the cultural themes of (1) hierarchy, (2) social balance, and (3) empathy.*

The Japanese make ample use of paralanguage in their conversations. During interpersonal discussions, the Japanese will constantly use small, culturally unique, gestures (*aizuchi*) and utterances (e.g., *hai, soo, un,* or *ee*) to demonstrate their attentiveness (Harris & Moran, 1979; Nishida, 1996). These vocalics possess a cultural motivation. Hierarchy is demonstrated by the adjustment of voice tone and pitch to fit the speaker's position of junior or senior (Morsbach, 1973). Additionally, the feedback stream indicates that the listener is paying attention to the speaker, which helps maintain positive social relations (*wa*) between the two individuals.

For the Japanese, laughter can possess a variety of meanings. Laughter can signal joy, of course, but it is also used to disguise embarrassment, sadness, or even anger (Seward, 1972). Use of laughter in the latter modes is designed to maintain situational harmony and avoid any potential for interpersonal discord.

In a 1989 study, White analyzed tape-recorded English-language conversations of Americans and native Japanese. The Japanese participants employed significantly more feedback responses than did the Americans. Unable to ascertain a linguistic reason for this greater use of vocalics, White (1989) concluded it was a cultural influence. The listener was believed to be exhibiting a sensitivity to the speaker's viewpoint and feelings (in other words, was expressing empathy).

P10: *Japanese use of silence reflects the cultural themes of (1) hierarchy, (2) social balance, and (3) empathy.*

The salient role of silence in the Japanese communication process is attributed to a general mistrust of spoken words and an emphasis on emotionally discerning the other person's intentions (empathy). Silence is considered a virtue as well as a sign of respectability and trustworthiness (Buruma, 1985; Cohen, 1991; Hall & Hall, 1990; Ishii, 1975, 1984; Lebra, 1976, 1993; Morsbach, 1988a).

A pronounced feature of Japanese conversations is the many short pauses or breaks, referred to as *ma*. According to Matsumoto (1988), the Japanese closely attend to these brief conversational breaks. The pauses may convey meaning, demonstrate respect, or be an attempt to assess the other person or the situation (Di Mare, 1990; Doi, 1973, 1988).

Instances of *ma* in Japanese discourse can impart a variety of messages, with the context supplying the actual meaning. Silence is employed to tactfully signal disagreement, nonacceptance, or an uncomfortable dilemma. A period of silence can be used to consider an appropriate response or formulate an opinion. Also, a junior may remain silent in deference to a senior (Graham & Herberger, 1983; Morsbach, 1973; Ramsey & Birk, 1983; Ueda, 1974).

P11: *The Japanese use of olfactics reflects the cultural theme of social balance.*

Little information is available concerning the Japanese attitude toward odors. Kasahara (1986) asserted that the Japanese propensity for cleanliness creates a preference for an environment totally absent of odors. Although there is no supporting evidence, the near-ritualistic tradition of taking frequent baths and the desire to refrain from personal offense lends credence to this supposition.

CONCLUSIONS

The preceding propositions suggest that the use of and reliance on nonverbal communication is actually a part of Japanese behavioral psychology motivated by cultural imperatives. If this concept is accepted, the benefits of employing cultural motivations to investigate a society's nonverbal communication habits, or other communication patterns, becomes self-evident. Application of cultural themes to communicative dispositions could provide a salient methodology for examining and better understanding both cultural-specific and intercultural communication phenomena.

Potential benefits derived from practical application of this approach are especially promising. Greater appreciation of the cultural imperatives behind communicative behaviors would directly enhance intercultural communication competence. An individual engaged in an intercultural communication exchange would better understand both *what* the other person was doing and *why* he or she was doing it.

The suggested design is not, however, free of limitations. Several perceived impediments exist that require additional investigation and clarification before implementation of wider theoretical application.

A particularly important aspect that demands greater inquiry relates to the identification of cultural themes. As discussed earlier, Japan presents an unusually homogeneous culture when compared with other nations. This societal similitude facilitates discernment of both cultural themes and their motivations. Moreover, the cultural themes can then be reliably applied across almost all dimensions of Japanese society.[3]

Other societies, such as the United States, do not have the degree of cultural congruency extant in Japan. For these cases, identification and application of consistent cultural themes to the composite ethnicities is fraught with considerable difficulty and potential peril. Any motivation to stereotype themes across an entire heterogeneous populace must be tempered by a resolve to treat ethnic divisions as both separate entities and as integral parts of the greater societal whole.

Another dilemma requiring meditation concerns units of measurement. The nonverbal communication patterns of a culture are largely observable and measurable. Culture, as an entity itself and as a motivator of communication behaviors, is not, however, readily quantifiable. Most studies dealing with cultural influences have relied on recounts of personal experiences and observations (anecdotal documentation).

Many studies incorporate "culture" as a somewhat ethereal, abstract manifestation of humankind's imagination. Others have approached "culture" empirically and attempted to employ scientific measurements. Hofstede, for instance, used survey questionnaires and statistical analysis in an effort to determine the role of culture in the formation of value systems that affect "human thinking, organizations, and institutions in predictable ways" (1980, p. 11). Similarly, Osgood, May, and Miron have made noteworthy progress in statistically quantifying intangible attributes, what they term "subjective culture" (1975, p. 4).

The progress of Hofstede (1980) and Osgood, May, and Miron (1975) suggests that culture is not entirely beyond the scope of objective quantification. Their achievements provide benchmarks for empirical examination of the influence of cultural themes on communication behaviors.

Thematic universality is also an area of potential peril for theoretical application of cultural themes to communicative practices. Specifically, the investigator must not axiomatically assume that similar themes beget similar behaviors when moving among cultures. A theme prompting a specific behavioral action in one culture may generate an entirely different pattern in another cultural environment. To obviate this possible pitfall, each culture must be examined as a unique entity. The identification of common cultural themes and communication practices across a substantial number of societies is needed before theoretical application can be made on unexamined cultures.

Further investigation is also needed to determine if any of the cultural themes are codependent. For example, if hierarchy is manifested by a culture, will formality or another theme also be present?

The preceding constraints should not be interpreted as a repudiation of the proposed approach to explaining communicative practices. Rather, they are simply areas of concern that must be investigated and clarified before cultural themes can be reliably employed to help discern and understand societal communication predispositions. Resolution of these concerns will instill the concept with increased application, additional rigor, and greater parsimony.

Notes

1. Although sometimes moving at a seemingly glacial pace, culture is actually a dynamic process, as individuals avail themselves of modern technologies they are exposed to and often adopt different social practices. This diffusion of cultural behaviors can and does exert change. With this in mind, we must recognize that the nonverbal communicative behaviors of the Japanese, as discussed in this article, are undergoing change. For example, except in rural areas, one seldom sees young Japanese women place their hand over their mouth. Direct eye contact is becoming increasingly common, especially in interactions with Westerners. Public touch is becoming more acceptable, and young Japanese couples can be seen cuddling in Tokyo's parks.
2. Even this established tradition is undergoing change. A recent article in a Japanese business newspaper bemoaned the fact that many of the younger employees were eschewing the company's lapel pins.
3. This is not to suggest that the Japanese are a wholly homogenous group uninfluenced by other cultures. For example, Japan has three large minority groups—Koreans, Ainu, and Burakumin—which possess distinct cultural characteristics. In recent years, the urban areas of Japan have also experienced a growing influx of foreign workers, coming from all parts of the globe. These immigrants bring their own values, beliefs, and behaviors, some of which are diffused, in varying degrees, into the Japanese culture.

References

Barnlund, D. (1975). *Public and private self in Japan and the United States: Communicative styles of two cultures.* Tokyo: Simul.

Barnlund, D. (1989). *Communicative styles of Japanese and Americans: Images and Realities.* Belmont, CA: Wadsworth.

Bond, M. H., & Shiraishi, D. (1974). The effect of body lean and status of an interviewer on the nonverbal behavior of Japanese interviewees. *International Journal of Psychology,* 9 (2), 117–128.

Buller, D. B., & Burgoon, J. K. (1986). The effects of vocalics and nonverbal sensitivity on compliance. *Human Communication Research,* 13, 126–144.

Burgoon, J. K., & Hale, J. L. (1984). The fundamental topic of relational communication. *Communication Monographs,* 51, 193–214.

Burgoon, J. K., & Hale, J. L. (1987). Validation and measurement of the fundamental themes of relational communication. *Communication Monographs,* 54, 19–62.

Buruma, I. (1985). *A Japanese mirror.* New York: Penguin Books.

Caudill, W. (1973). General culture: The influence of social structure and culture on human behavior in modern Japan. *The Journal of Nervous and Mental Disease,* 157, 240–257.

Caudill, W., & Plath, D. (1966). Who sleeps with whom? Parent–child involvement in urban Japanese families. *Psychiatry,* 29, 344–366.

Caudill, W., & Weinstein, H. (1969). Maternal care and infant behavior in Japan and America. *Psychiatry,* 32, 12–43.

Cohen, R. (1991). *Negotiating across cultures.* Washington, DC: U.S. Institute of Peace.

Coker, D. A., & Burgoon, J. K. (1987). The nature of conversational involvement and nonverbal encoding patterns. *Human Communication Research,* 13, 463–494.

Condon, J. C., & Yousef, F. (1983). *An introduction to intercultural communication.* Indianapolis, IN: Bobbs-Merrill.

Craft, L. (1986). All in the cards: The mighty *meishi. TOKYO Business Today, May,* 61–64.

Di Mare, L. (1990). *Ma* and Japan. *Southern Communication Journal,* 55, 319–328.

Doi, T. (1973). The Japanese patterns of communication and the concept of *amae. The Quarterly Journal of Speech,* 59, 180–185.

Doi, T. (1988). Dependency in human relationships. In D. I. Okimoto & T. P. Rohlen (Eds.), *Inside the Japanese system: Readings on contemporary society and political economy* (pp. 20–25). Stanford, CA: Stanford University Press.

Graham, J. L., & Herberger, R. A. (1983). Negotiations abroad: Don't shoot from the hip. *Harvard Business Review,* 83, 160–168.

Gudykunst, W. B., & Nishida, T. (1984). Individual and cultural influences on uncertainty reduction. *Communication Monographs,* 51, 23–36.

Gudykunst, W. B., & Nishida, T. (1993). Interpersonal and intergroup communication in Japan and the United States. In W. B. Gudykunst (Ed.), *Communication in Japan and the United States* (pp. 149–214). Albany: State University of New York Press.

Gudykunst, W. B., Nishida, T., & Schmidt, K. (1989). The influence of culture, relational, and personality factors on uncertainty reduction processes. *Western Journal of Speech Communication,* 53, 13–29.

Gudykunst, W. B., Yoon, Y. C., & Nishida, T. (1987). The influence of individualism–collectivism on perceptions of communication in ingroup and outgroup relationships. *Communication Monographs,* 54, 295–306.

Hall, E. T. (1981/1976). *Beyond culture.* New York: Anchor Books, Doubleday.

Hall, E. T. (1988). The hidden dimensions of time and space in today's world. In F. Poyatos (Ed.), *Cross-cultural perspectives in nonverbal communication* (pp. 145–152). Lewiston, NY: C. J. Hogrefe.

Hall, E. T. (1990/1966). *The hidden dimension.* New York: Anchor Books, Doubleday.

Hall, E. T., & Hall, M. R. (1990/1987). *Hidden differences: Doing business with the Japanese.* New York: Anchor Books, Doubleday.

Hamabata, M. M. (1990). *Crested kimono: Power and love in the Japanese business family.* Ithaca, NY: Cornell University Press.

Harris, P. R., & Moran, R. T. (1979). *Managing cultural differences.* Houston, TX: Gulf Publishing.

Hendry, J. (1989/1986). *Becoming Japanese: The world of the pre-school child.* Honolulu: University of Hawaii Press.

Hofstede, G. (1980). *Culture's consequence: International differences in work-related values.* Newbury Park, CA: Sage.

Ishii, S. (1975). Characteristics of Japanese nonverbal communicative behavior. *Occasional Papers in Speech.* Honolulu: Department of Speech, University of Hawaii.

Ishii, S. (1984). *Enryo-Sasshi* communication: A key to understanding Japanese interpersonal relations. *Cross Currents,* 11, 49–58.

Ishii, S., & Bruneau, T. (1991). Silence and silences in cross-cultural perspective: Japan and the United States. In L. A. Samovar & R. E. Porter (Eds.), *Intercultural communication: A reader* (6th ed.) (pp. 314–319). Belmont, CA: Wadsworth.

Iwata, O. (1979). Selected personality traits as determinants of the perception of crowding. *Japanese Psychological Research, 21,* 1–9.

Kasahara, Y. (1986). Fear of eye-to-eye confrontation among neurotic patients in Japan. In T. S. Lebra & W. P. Lebra (Eds.), *Japanese culture and behavior: Selected readings* (Rev. ed.) (pp. 379–387). Honolulu: University of Hawaii Press.

Kinosita, K. (1988). Language habits of the Japanese. *Bulletin of the Association for Business Communication, 51,* 35–40.

Kitao, K., & Kitao, S. K. (1985). *Effects of social environment on Japanese and American communication.* (ERIC Document Reproduction Service, No. ED 260 579).

Kitao, K., & Kitao, S. K. (1987). *Differences in the kinesic codes of Americans and Japanese.* East Lansing, MI: Department of Communication, Michigan State University. (ERIC Document Reproduction Service, No. ED 282 400).

Kitao, K., & Kitao, S. K. (1989). *Intercultural communication between Japan and the United States.* Tokyo: Eicho-sha Shinsha Co. (ERIC Document Reproduction Service, No. ED 321 303).

Lebra, T. S. (1976). *Japanese patterns of behavior.* Honolulu: University of Hawaii Press.

Lebra, T. S. (1993). Culture, self, and communication in Japan and the United States. In W. B. Gudykunst (Ed.), Communication in Japan and the United States (pp. 51–87). Albany: State University of New York Press.

Malandro, L. A., & Barker, L. L. (1983). *Nonverbal communication.* Menlo Park, CA: Addison-Wesley.

March, R. M. (1990/1989). *The Japanese negotiator: Subtlety and strategy beyond Western logic.* New York: Kondansha.

Matsumoto, D. (1996). *Unmasking Japan: Myths and realities about the emotions of the Japanese.* Stanford, CA: Stanford University Press.

Matsumoto, M. (1988). *The unspoken way: "Haragei": Silence in Japanese business and society.* New York: Kondansha. (Original work published in 1984 in Japanese under the title *Haragei.*)

McDaniel, E. R., & Andersen, P. A. (1998). International patterns of tactile communication: A field study. *Journal of Nonverbal Behavior, 22,* 59–75.

Miyamoto, M. (1994). *Straitjacket society: An insider's irreverent view of bureaucratic Japan.* New York: Kodansha International.

Montague, A. (1978). *Touching: The human significance of the skin* (2nd ed.). New York: Harper & Row.

Morsbach, H. (1973). Aspects of nonverbal communication in Japan. *Journal of Nervous and Mental Disease, 157,* 26277.

Morsbach, H. (1988a). The importance of silence and stillness in Japanese nonverbal communication: A cross-cultural approach. In F. Poyatos (Ed.), *Cross-cultural*

perspectives in nonverbal communication (pp. 201–215). Lewiston, NY: C. J. Hogrefe.

Morsbach, H. (1988b). Nonverbal communication and hierarchical relationships: The case of bowing in Japan. In F. Poyatos (Ed.), *Cross-cultural perspectives in nonverbal communication* (pp. 189–199). Lewiston, NY: C. J. Hogrefe.

Munakata, T. (1986). Japanese attitudes toward mental illness and mental health care. In T. S. Lebra & W. P. Lebra (Ed.), *Japanese culture and behavior: Selected readings* (Rev. ed.) (pp. 369–378). Honolulu: University of Hawaii Press.

Nakane, C. (1970). *Japanese society.* Berkeley: University of California Press.

Nishida, T. (1996). Communications in personal relationships in Japan. In W. B. Gudykunst, S. Ting-Toomey, & T. Nishida (Eds.), *Communication in personal relationships across cultures* (pp. 102–117). Thousand Oaks, CA: Sage.

Opler, M. E. (1945). Themes as dynamic forces in culture. *American Journal of Sociology, 51,* 198–206.

Opler, M. E. (1946). An application of the theory of themes in culture. *Journal of the Washington Academy of Sciences, 36,* 137–166.

Osgood, C. E., May, W. H., & Miron, M. S. (1975). *Cross-cultural universals of affective meaning.* Urbana: University of Illinois Press.

Ramsey, S. J. (1979). Nonverbal behavior: An intercultural perspective. In M. K. Asante, E. Newmark, & C. A. Blake (Eds.), *Handbook of intercultural communication* (pp. 105–143). Beverly Hills, CA: Sage.

Ramsey, S. J. (1981). The kinesics of femininity in Japanese women. *Language Sciences, 3,* 104–123.

Ramsey, S. J. (1985). To hear one and understand ten: Nonverbal behavior in Japan. In L. A. Samovar & R. E. Porter (Eds.), Intercultural communication: A reader (4th ed.) (pp. 307–321). Belmont, CA: Wadsworth.

Ramsey, S. J., & Birk, J. (1983). Training North Americans for interaction with Japanese: Considerations of language and communication style. In D. Landis & R. W. Brislin (Eds.), *The handbook of intercultural training, Vol. III: Area studies in intercultural training* (pp. 227–259). New York: Pergamon Press.

Reischauer, E. O. (1988). *The Japanese today: Change and continuity.* Cambridge, MA: Belknap Press of Harvard University.

Richie, D. (1987). *A lateral view: Essays on contemporary Japan.* Tokyo: The Japan Times.

Ruch, W. (1984). *Corporate communication: A comparison of Japanese and American practices.* Westport, CT: Quorum Books.

Sethi, S. P. (1974). Japanese management practices: Part I. *Columbia Journal of World Business, 9,* 94–104.

Seward, J. (1972). *The Japanese.* New York: William Morrow.

Seward, J. (1983). *Japanese in action* (Rev. ed.). New York: Weatherhill.

Spitzberg, B. H. (1989). Issues in the development of a theory of interpersonal competence in the intercultural context. *International Journal of Intercultural Relations, 13,* 241–268.

Stewart, L. P. (1993). Organizational communication in Japan and the United States. In W. B. Gudykunst (Ed.), *Communication in Japan and the United States* (pp. 215–248). Albany: State University of New York Press.

Takamizawa, H. (1988). *Business Japanese: A guide to improved communication.* New York: Kondansha International.

Ueda, T. (1974). Sixteen ways to avoid saying "no" in Japan. In J. C. Condon & M. Saito (Eds.), *Intercultural encounters with Japan* (pp. 185–192). Tokyo: Simul Press.

White, S. (1989). Backchannels across cultures: A study of Americans and Japanese. *Language in Society, 18,* 59–76.

Watson, M. O. (1970). *Proxemic behavior: A cross-cultural study.* The Hague: Mouton.

Westwood, M. J., & Vargo, J. W. (1985). Counselling double-minority status clients. In R. J. Samuda (Ed.), *Intercultural counselling and assessment: Global perspectives* (pp. 303–313). Lewiston, NY: C. J. Hogrefe.

Yum, Y. (1988). The impact of Confucianism on interpersonal relationship and communication patterns in East Asia. *Communication Monographs, 55,* 374–388.

Concepts and Questions

1. What are "cultural themes," and how may we benefit from their study?
2. What are the major Japanese cultural themes that influence intercultural communication?
3. Can you think of any North American cultural themes that could influence how Americans use nonverbal communication?
4. How does Confucian-based collectivism help control Japanese nonverbal communication?
5. What cultural themes are seen as the basis for Japanese kinesic behavior? Are the same or different themes active in U.S. American nonverbal behavior?
6. What are the most obvious activities associated with Japanese kinesic behavior? What would be a U.S. American counterpart?
7. How does culture influence personal appearance in Japanese and U.S. American culture?
8. What are the cultural underpinnings of silence in Japan? How does the Japanese manipulation of silence affect intercultural communication?
9. Describe differences in the use of *vocalics* or paralanguage in Japan and the United States. How might these differences lead to misunderstandings during intercultural communication?

Language Matters

Aaron Castelan Cargile

One of the many challenges we face as participants in intercultural encounters is coping with language differences. In some cases, we may not speak the same language as our conversational partner. When not a single word in an exchange can be understood, the challenge of successful communication is quite obvious. In other cases, however, our partner may be at least competent (if not fluent) in our language, or vice versa. On these occasions, it may seem that the challenge of coping with language differences is minimal or nonexistent. Yet it must be realized that even when interacting people speak the same language, such as English, they don't always speak the same "language."

Consider, for example, a New York businessman interviewing a West Virginian job candidate who answers questions with an Appalachian drawl. Or imagine a teacher correcting her African American pupils' use of the word *hood,* or a hurried store manager addressing a complaint from a customer speaking in a slow and measured pace. In these situations, the participants may both be speaking English and their words may indeed be mutually intelligible, but these interactions can often leave them feeling misunderstood and without a sense of connection. This is because the language used in these examples, while seemingly the same, is really different: The speakers employed different accents, vocabularies, and different rates of speech than the listeners. And it is these seemingly minor language differences that usually present one of the biggest challenges to successful intercultural communication.

Courtesy of Aaron Castelan Cargile. This original essay first appeared in the ninth edition of this book. All rights reserved. Permission to reprint must be obtained from the author and the publisher. Aaron Castelan Cargile teaches in the Department of Communication Studies, California State University, Long Beach.

THE DIFFICULTIES OF LANGUAGE DIFFERENCES

In most instances, it is human nature to prefer similarity to difference. Research demonstrates that people tend to like others who possess attitudes and traits similar to their own, and to dislike others with dissimilar attitudes and traits (e.g., Byrne, 1971; Byrne & Clore, 1970; Clore & Byrne, 1974). Consequently, friendships are formed more readily with people perceived to be similar (Kim, 1991; Lea & Duck, 1982), and people from similar groups (e.g., culture groups, religious groups, sport team groups, etc.) are typically treated better than people from other different groups (Hinkle & Schopler, 1986; Mullen, Brown, & Smith, 1992; Turner, Brown, & Tajfel, 1979).

This preference for similarity is part of the interculturally relevant phenomenon of *ethnocentrism.* According to Sumner (1940), ethnocentrism occurs when members of a culture view themselves as the center of everything, and judge other cultures according to the standards and practices of their own culture. Of course, when others are judged relative to one's own culture, those who are most similar appear to be better. Ethnocentrism occurs naturally in people across all cultures. Unfortunately, this can be compounded when language differences are encountered.

When most people read the term *language differences,* they often think of situations in which communicators must express themselves in two different linguistic systems—for example, Japanese and French. As mentioned earlier, this situation presents an obvious challenge. To communicate without the help of a translator, participants are usually forced to use a series of grunts, gestures, or some limited vocabulary, in a struggle to convey even the most basic idea. (Try using just your body to ask a classmate, "Where is the airport?") Situations such as these may result in frustration and miscommunication, but at least participants are aware of their difficulties. In an effort to work around them, people are likely to accept, and even invite, messages or modes of expression that they would not consider "normal" otherwise (e.g., making airplane noises in an attempt to refer to the airport). These are situations in which people generally tolerate other, comparably minor,

differences between their own and another's use of language because without such tolerance, no communication could take place.

In addition to the language differences that occur when two different systems of symbolic code are used, language differences also may be present even when the same symbolic code is used—for example, when both participants speak fluent English. As described earlier, people can speak with different accents, different vocabularies, and different rates of speech, to name only a few of the many behaviors referred to by the term *language* (see Bradac, 1990). These kinds of language differences present participants with other sorts of difficulties. When the New York businessman interviews the West Virginian job applicant, he comprehends with little difficulty what is being said. Chances are, however, that he probably will not feel completely at ease during the interaction or afterward when he decides the other person's fate of employment. Sadly, these feelings may come regardless of what the applicant has said. The applicant may be thoroughly qualified for the job, and he may answer all interview questions satisfactorily, but the words running through the businessman's mind may be the same as those heard by June Tyler during a closed door meeting with a senior partner in a law firm, "Be careful about hiring anyone with a mountain accent" (Pasternak, 1994, p. A16). The discomfort felt by the businessman when faced with this fully qualified job applicant is an example of a second class of difficulties that can be brought about by language differences. These are not difficulties of comprehension; they are difficulties of fair evaluation and equal treatment, and they present a larger challenge to intercultural communication because people tend to be less aware of them.

In the above example, it could be the case that the New York businessman is consciously aware of his decision to discriminate against the job applicant based on his Appalachian accent. Though such discrimination is illegal, many people freely admit that a Southern accent is oftentimes inappropriate and will suggest that it should be abandoned in favor of other accents. For example, soon after Atlanta was awarded the 1996 summer Olympics, a column appeared in the *Atlanta Business Chronicle* encouraging citizens to "get the South out of our mouth" in order to impress the expected visitors (reported in Pearl, 1991). Unlike the open prejudice in this example, however, it is also possible that the businessman would not be aware of his discriminatory motives. Instead, he might experience only some general sense that the applicant was not quite as "sharp" as the others, and that he or she somehow did not "seem right" for the job, even though these impressions could unknowingly be fostered by the speaker's accent. Whether or not he is aware of it, the businessman's naturally developed ethnocentrism can lead him to evaluate and treat people who speak with different accents less favorably than similar sounding others.

In the case of accented speech, it is difficult to predict whether or not a listener will be consciously aware of the language difference. Depending on the person, the situation, and the specific accents involved, someone else's accent may seem as if it stands out, or it may blend in imperceptibly. When it comes to other, less complex language differences, such as those in vocabulary or speech rate, it is even less likely that the listener will hold conscious awareness of those differences. You may not often realize when someone speaks more slowly than you do, but you may still have the vague impression that they are not quite "with it." As this example suggests, awareness is not necessary for language differences to affect our judgment and treatment of other people. Sadly, this is what makes seemingly "minor" language differences particularly problematic. Unlike the earlier example in which the obviousness of the language differences held the promise of making people more tolerant of one another's behaviors, the less perceptible differences are more difficult to account for and cope with because of their relative subtlety. As a consequence, it becomes easier for us to put down and discriminate on the basis of language against someone who speaks our language differently than someone who does not speak it at all.

Although language can be studied from a variety of behavioral perspectives, our attitudes toward language differences and their influence on intercultural communication can be traced to three major characteristics: accents, speech styles, and speech rates.

ACCENTS

Of the language behaviors that have been investigated, accent is one of the most revealing. Research has shown that listeners have clear attitudes toward those who speak "differently." American listeners who themselves speak with a standard American accent, consistently prejudge others with "Appalachian," "Spanish," "German," and "African American" vernacular-accented speech as less intelligent, poorer, less educated, and less status-possessing than standard accented speakers (Bradac & Wisegarver, 1984; Johnson & Buttny, 1982; Ryan & Carranza, 1975; Tucker & Lambert, 1969). For example, Bishop (1979) found that white female respondents evaluated African American confederates as less responsible and less desirable co-workers when they spoke "black" as opposed to "white" English. Similarly, Giles, Williams, Mackie, and Rosselli (1995) discovered that Anglo respondents rated the same bi-dialectical speaker *as* less literate and more lower class when he spoke English with a "Hispanic" accent, compared to an "Anglo" accent.

Surprisingly, though, standard accented listeners are not the only ones who look down on many nonstandard accented speakers. Even listeners who themselves speak with a nonstandard accent often judge that others who sound like themselves have low social standing. For example, a study by Doss and Gross (1992) revealed that African American respondents perceive same-race standard English speakers as more competent than those who spoke African American vernacular English. As this last example suggests, the complex reality of intercultural communication is not that we think badly of everyone who speaks differently. Indeed, research indicates that some "foreign" accented speakers are not perceived by Americans to be less competent or inferior—for example, British-accented English speakers (Stewart, Ryan, & Giles, 1985). Similarly, listeners who speak with a standard accent sometimes judge nonstandard-accented speakers to be equal to standard-accented speakers along some dimensions—for example, being "friendly" and "good natured" (Ryan, Hewstone, & Giles, 1984). In terms of intercultural communication, this accent attitude research makes it abundantly clear that we often prejudge others in unflattering and potentially harmful ways based on accent alone.

SPEECH STYLES

In addition to accent, a speaker's choice of words or grammatical phrase may also lead others to some potentially harmful and erroneous prejudgments. As creatures dependent on and skilled at communicating, we know that a message can be expressed in one of any number of ways. For example, one shopper may say to another, "Hey! Please hand that package of undershirts over here. Thanks." Alternatively, that same shopper might say, "[cough]. Ummm. Excuse me. You wouldn't mind passing that bag of T-shirts to me, would you? Thank you." In both instances, the same idea (or message content) is expressed. However, the speech styles are quite different. In the first message, listeners may gain the impression that the speaker is strong and confident, whereas the second message might suggest that the speaker is weak, uncertain, and, consequently, socially unattractive. Such impressions may or may not be deserved. Regardless, listeners (usually subconsciously) treat the speech styles that our messages take as accurate information about our character and abilities.

Powerful and Powerless Styles

Speech that includes features such as hesitations (e.g., "hmm"), hedges (e.g., "I sort of think so"), tag questions (e.g., "It's cold in here, isn't it?"), and polite forms (e.g., "Excuse me") are called powerless. On the other hand, speech styles that exhibit a relative absence of these features are called powerful. Powerful and powerless speech styles refer to particular forms of language usage rather than to the notion that all truly powerful and powerless people employ one style or the other. In actuality, research has shown that a significant overlap is found between a so-called powerless style and speech styles typically used by women (Crosby & Nyquist, 1977; Lakoff, 1975; Mulac & Lundell, 1986). This does not indicate, however, that all women are powerless. It simply suggests that the speech style often used by women usually leads others to perceive them as less powerful than men. Indeed, several studies have documented that whoever uses the language features included in this powerless speech style (whether a woman or a man) is thought

by listeners to be both less socially attractive (e.g., less trustworthy and less likable) and less competent (e.g., less educated and less intelligent) than others not using this style (Bradac, Hemphill, & Tardy, 1981; Bradac & Mulac, 1984; Erickson, Johnson, Lind, & O'Barr, 1978). Thus, an unintentional choice of words or phrase may unknowingly, both to the speaker and the listener, lead to some unfavorable and potentially inaccurate judgments that can make any type of communication more difficult.

SPEECH RATES

Alongside accent and speech style, speech rate is another important language behavior. Speakers naturally vary in the number of words or syllables they utter per minute. This can be a function of their personality, their age, the situation, or their fluency in a normative language. Regardless of the actual source of the speech rate variability (e.g., is someone speaking slowly because he or she is scared, shy, old, or has just learned the language?), listeners consistently think that people who speak faster are more competent and more socially attractive than people with a relatively slow rate of speech (Brown, 1980; Street & Brady, 1982).

There is also some evidence that this relationship between speech rate and listener evaluations is affected by the rate at which the listener him- or herself speaks. As we might expect by realizing that people are ethnocentric, fast-speaking listeners especially prefer others who speak fast, and slow-speaking listeners especially prefer others who speak slowly (Giles & Smith, 1979; Street, Brady, & Putman, 1983). Both instances demonstrate yet again that we do not evaluate favorably those who sound different from ourselves.

LANGUAGE-BASED DISCRIMINATION

Up to this point, we have considered evidence that points to the many ways in which language differences can lead to prejudging another's character and ability based on language use alone. These same language differences also can lead to discrimination. Oftentimes, when others sound different from ourselves, we not only think unfavorably of them, but also in many cases treat them unfairly. This fact has been most clearly demonstrated in the case of people who speak with "different" accents.

There are perhaps few contexts in which someone else's behavior is more important for our own well-being than in the employment interview or in the courtroom. In both instances, the fate of people's livelihood—or even their lives—can hang in the balance of decisions made by a selection interviewer or a jury. Because of this, it would seem especially critical to treat people equitably in these situations. Yet even here evidence points to the fact that unfair treatment can be provoked by a speaker's use of language. For example, Seggie (1983) presented standard-accented or nonstandard-accented voices to listeners and told them that the speaker stood accused of one of several crimes. On the audiotapes, the speakers were heard protesting their innocence regarding the crime of which they had been accused. Listeners were then asked to make a decision regarding the probable guilt or innocence of the speaker. The results showed that standard-accented speakers were more often seen as guilty when the crime was embezzlement, whereas nonstandard-accented speakers were more often judged guilty when the crime was physical assault. Listeners thus more often associated white-collar crimes with standard-sounding defendants and crimes of violence with nonstandard-sounding defendants. Although these listeners were not actual jury members, the results plainly suggest that people can be treated differently based on their accent alone—treatment that is particularly unfair in the case of a nonstandard-accented speaker accused of a violent crime.

In the case of a job interview, in an important study by Henry and Ginzberg (1985), individuals with different ethnic or racial accents made telephone inquires about jobs advertised in a newspaper. Job applicants who spoke with a nonstandard accent were most often told that jobs had been filled. Applicants with a standard accent, however, were most often invited to appear for a personal interview, even after the nonstandard speakers were informed that applications for the position were no longer being accepted. In a similar study, de la Zerda and Hopper (1979) asked employers from San Antonio, Texas, to predict the likelihood of a speaker being hired for each of three positions: supervisor, skilled technician, and semi-skilled laborer. A comparison of standard American- and (Mexican American) Spanish-accented speakers revealed that standard speakers were favored for the supervisor position, whereas Spanish-accented speakers were more likely to be hired for the semiskilled position. It would thus be doubly hard for a Spanish-accented speaker to be hired as a supervisor because he or she would be seen not only as less appropriate for this position, but also as more appropriate for the lower-skilled (and lower-waged) job. Sadly, these and other results (e.g., Giles, Wilson, & Conway, 1981; Kalin & Rayko, 1978) clearly illustrate that people can both be prejudiced against others who sound different and discriminate against these speakers in ways that may jeopardize both their livelihood and their lives.

IMPLICATIONS FOR INTERCULTURAL COMMUNICATORS

This article has shown that humans often develop unfavorable language attitudes about others who speak with accents, use different speech styles, or employ different speaking rates. In addition, we have seen that these same unfavorable attitudes occasionally develop toward similar sounding others. We have also seen how these speech-based attitudes can lead to stereotyping and prejudicial behavior. The connection between this and intercultural communication should be obvious, yet it bears further examination.

The term *intercultural communication* typically invokes visions of people from two (or more) different countries interacting with one another, as for example, an American customs officer talking with a French tourist. In addition, the term can be applied to interactions between people from the same nation, but from different co-cultures, as in the case of exchanges between Asian Americans and African Americans. Regardless of which type of intercultural communication is being considered, language attitudes are relevant because language use typically varies between intercultural communication participants. As we have learned, language refers to more than the formalized linguistic code used for expression (e.g., English or French); it refers also to speech styles, speech rate, and accent (among other language behaviors).

Thus, even intercultural communication participants from the same nation, who grew up speaking the same language, can have systematically different ways of speaking. For example, an Asian American speaker will often have a different accent and speech style than an African American listener. Even in the rare case when language use does not vary (e.g., an African American speaking standard American English with an Anglo-American), the expectation that it will vary ensures the relevancy of language attitudes. Consequently, attitudes about language use remain important features that affect all types of intercultural communication.

When international participants do not share the same native tongue, the language differences are often striking and numerous. This situation provides many opportunities for language attitudes to influence intercultural communication. In these instances, participants not only will speak with different accents, but also may have internalized different ideas about appropriate styles of talk and different abilities to govern their language use. The American customs agent, for example, may form a steadfast and distinctly unfavorable impression of the French tourist who speaks grammatically correct English but with a French accent. To his ear, the tourist's natural accent may make her sound uneducated, her (learned) polite speech style may make her sound powerless, and her unavoidably slow speech rate (which comes when any of us first learn a second language) may make her sound unintelligent. All of these (and other) language differences can combine to create a powerfully negative impression, because attitudes about one language behavior (e.g., accent) can serve to reinforce attitudes about another (e.g., speech rate). Even if the tourist were to perform a favorably appraised language behavior (e.g., to use impressively "big" words), selective perception could cause the customs agent to ignore it. Of course, as we have seen, not all attitudes about foreign-sounding speech are negative. But because a large majority of these attitudes are, language attitudes become a critical impression-formation tool that must be managed carefully in intercultural interactions among international participants.

When participants come from the same nation but different co-cultures, the language differences may not be as striking. Even so, the ability of language attitudes to influence interaction does not diminish; in fact, they may intensify. Co-cultures can still socialize differences in all forms of language behavior. For example, Asian Americans may use polite forms of talk more than Anglo-Americans, and speakers from the South may engage in slower speech than those from the North. Because these differences appear, or because we expect them to appear, language attitudes still play an important role in intercultural communication between co-cultural group members. Consequently, responsible communicators should seek both to understand and to manage their language attitudes.

HOW DO WE MANAGE LANGUAGE ATTITUDES?

As discussed earlier, language attitudes, like many other attitudes and stereotypes, are both a natural and sometimes useful feature of social life. Language not only is a tool for expression, but also can provide valuable information about others in certain situations. For example, slow speech may actually indicate that a speaker is having difficulty organizing his or her thoughts. In other situations, however, slow speech may not indicate anything about a speaker's mental processing or capacity. Thus, language attitudes can provide critical, readily available, and yet usually unreliable information about our conversational partners. Given this, how should responsible intercultural communicators manage language attitudes?

The first and most important thing to do is to recognize when your responses to others are based on language attitudes alone, and when they are based on other, more objective, and more reliable information. For example, in universities across the United States, students often respond unfavorably to foreign-born teaching assistants and professors. In fact, on some campuses more than two out of five students withdraw or switch from a class when they find out their teacher is a nonnative speaker of English (Rubin & Smith, 1988). In addition, many other students make complaints of the variety that forced Illinois to pass a fluency law for college instructors (Setter, 1987). Who is responsible for such student dissatisfaction? In some cases, there really are instructors with verifiably poor language skills. In many other cases, though, it may in fact be the stereotypical and prejudicial language attitudes developed by the students themselves that is responsible.

On first hearing an instructor's accent, students often will unknowingly make assumptions about the instructor's personality and (language) skills based solely on their own attitudes toward foreign-accented speakers (e.g., "this teacher isn't too friendly, too smart, and he doesn't speak good English"). The instructor may, in fact, be or do none of the things that the student assumes. Even so, because language attitudes have the power to initiate selective perceptions, the students may create, in their own minds, evidence to support their views. In particular, they may "hear" the instructor make grammatical mistakes that he has not really made (Cargile & Giles, 1996). Students can then, in turn, point to these "mistakes" as justification for their attitudes and a reason for responding unfavorably to the instructor. Thus, a class may end up with an instructor who is in fact friendly, smart, and who speaks grammatically correct and comprehensible English, but because students have unknowingly based their responses on their attitudes toward foreign-accented speech alone, they may feel dissatisfied with their instruction.

As the above scenario illustrates, in the end, the evaluations that we make of other speakers may be more a product of our own attitudes than the speakers' behaviors. The trouble is that we rarely realize this, and as a result we believe the other is entirely responsible for our reactions. Consequently, the first step we should take in dealing with language attitudes is to learn to recognize their role in the evaluation process. Ask yourself, "Am I thinking this about the person only because of the way that he or she speaks?" You may answer "no" to this question; thus indicating that the role that language attitudes are playing is minimal and perhaps justified. You may, however, answer "yes," suggesting that your attitudes about language use are exerting an undue and likely problematic influence on your behavior. Once you learn to recognize the role language attitudes play in your responses, a second step should be to seek out and integrate additional information into the evaluation process—especially when the answer to the above question is "yes." Your attitudes may lead you to believe one thing about a speaker, but your job as a responsible intercultural communicator is to test, to the best of your abilities, whether your evaluation is accurate and appropriate. For example, in the case of a normative English speaking instructor, find out about his or her educational background, prior teaching experience, and real English competency through patient listening (and perhaps some careful questioning) before passing the easy, ready-made judgment that this person lacks the intelligence and ability to be a successful teacher. Of course, this kind of "fact checking" and follow-up is effortful and never easy. It is, however, critical to managing our language attitudes well. Calling on language attitudes in intercultural interaction is nearly unavoidable. Thus, the secret is to tap their potential as a source of information without being poisoned by their power to lead listeners down a road of prejudice and discrimination.

References

Bishop, G. D. (1979). Perceived similarity in interracial attitudes and behaviors The effects of belief and dialect style. *Journal of Applied Social Psychology, 9*, 446–465.

Bradac, J. J. (1990). Language attitudes and impression formation. In H. Giles & W. P. Robinson (Eds.), *Handbook of language and social psychology* (pp. 387–412). Chichester, UK: Wiley.

_____, Hemphill, M. R., & Tardy, C. H. (1981). Language style of trial: Effects of "powerful and powerless" speech upon judgments of victims and villains. *Western Journal of Speech Communication, 45*, 327–341.

_____, & Mulac, A. (1984). Attributional consequences of powerful and powerless speech styles in a crisis intervention context. *Journal of Language and Social Psychology, 3*, 1–20.

_____, & Wisegarver, R. (1984). Ascribed status, lexical diversity, and accent: Determinants of perceived status, solidarity, and control of speech style. *Journal of Language and Social Psychology, 3*, 239–255.

Brown, B. L. (1980). Effects of speech rate on personality attributions and competency evaluations. In H. Giles, W. P. Robinson, & P. Smith (Eds.), *Language: Social psychological perspectives* (pp. 294–300). Oxford, UK: Pergamon.

Byrne, D. E. (1971). *The attraction paradigm.* San Diego, CA: Academic Press.

_____, & Clore, G. L. (1970). A reinforcement model of evaluative responses. *Personality: An International Journal, 1*, 103–128.

Cargile, A., & Giles, H. (1996, November). *Language attitudes toward varieties of English: An American Japanese context.*

Paper presented at the Speech Communication Association annual conference, San Diego, CA.

Clore, G. L., & Byrne, D. E. (1974). A reinforcement affect model of attraction. In T. L. Huston (Ed.), *Foundations of interpersonal attraction* (pp. 143–170). San Diego, CA: Academic Press.

Crosby, F., & Nyquist, L. (1977). The female register: An empirical study of Lakoff's hypotheses. *Language in Society, 6,* 519–535.

de la Zerda, N., & Hopper, R. (1979). Employment interviewers' reactions to Mexican American speech. *Communication Monographs, 46,* 126–134.

Doss, R. C., & Gross, A. M. (1992). The effects of black English on stereotyping in interracial perceptions. *The Journal of Black Psychology, 18,* 47–58.

Erickson, B., Johnson, B. C., Lind, E. A., & O'Barr, W. (1978). Speech style and impression formation in a court setting: The effects of "powerful" and "powerless" speech. *Journal of Experimental Social Psychology, 14,* 266–279.

Giles, H., & Smith, P. (1979). Accommodation theory: Optimal levels of convergence. In H. Giles & R. N. S. Clair (Eds.), *Language and social psychology* (pp. 45–65). Baltimore, MD: University Park Press.

Giles, H., Williams, A., Mackie, D. M., & Rosselli, F. (1995). Reactions to Anglo and Hispanic American accented speakers: Affect, identity, persuasion, and the English only controversy. *Language and Communication, 14,* 102–121.

Giles, H., Wilson, R., & Conway, A. (1981). Accent and lexical diversity as determinates of impression formation and employment selection. *Language Sciences, 3,* 92–103.

Henry, F., & Ginzberg, E. (1985). *Who gets the* work: A *test of racial discrimination in employment.* Toronto: Urban Alliance on Race Relations and Social Planning Council of Metropolitan Toronto.

Hinkle, S., & Schopler, J. (1986). Bias in the evaluation of in-group and out-group performance. In S. Worchel & W. G. Austin (Eds.), *Psychology of intergroup relations* (pp. 196–212). Chicago: Nelson Hall.

Johnson, F. L., & Buttny, R. (1982). White listeners' responses to "sounding black" and "sounding white": The effects of message content on judgments about language. *Communication Monographs, 49,* 33–49.

Kalin, R., & Rayko, D. (1978). Discrimination in evaluative judgments against foreign accented job candidates. *Psychological Reports, 43,* 1203–1209.

Kim, H. J. (1991). Influence of language and similarity of initial intercultural attraction. In S. Ting Toomey & F. Korzenny (Eds.), *Cross cultural interpersonal communication* (pp. 213–229). Newbury Park, CA: Sage.

Lakoff, R. (1975). *Language and woman's place.* New York: Harper & Row.

Lea, M., & Duck, S. (1982). A model for the role of clarity of values in friendship development. *British Journal of Social Psychology, 21,* 301–310.

Mulac, A., & Lundell, T. L. (1986). Linguistic contributions to the gender-linked language effect. *Journal of Language and Social Psychology, 5,* 81–101.

Mullen, B., Brown, R., & Smith, C. (1992). In-group bias as a function of salience, relevance, and status integration. *European Journal of Social Psychology, 22,* 103–122.

Pasternak, J. (1994, March 29). Bias blights life outside Appalachia. *Los Angeles Times,* pp. A1–A16.

Pearl, D. (1991, December 13). Hush mah mouth! Some in South try to lose the drawl. *Wall Street Journal,* p. A 1.

Rubin, D. L., & Smith, K. A. (1988). Effects of accent, ethnicity, and lecture topic on undergraduates' perceptions of nonnative English speaking teaching assistants. *International Journal of Intercultural Relations, 14,* 337–353.

Ryan, E. B., & Carranza, M. A. (1975). Evaluative reactions of adolescents toward speakers of standard English and Mexican American accented English. *Journal of Personality and Social Psychology, 31,* 855–863.

Ryan, E. B., Hewstone, M., & Giles, H. (1984). Language and intergroup attitudes. In J. Eiser (Ed.), *Attitudinal judgment* (pp. 135–160). New York: Springer.

Secter, B. (1987, September 27). Foreign teachers create language gap in colleges. *Los Angeles Times,* pp. A1, A26–27.

Seggie, I. (1983). Attribution of guilt as a function of ethnic accent and type of crime. *Journal of Multilingual and Multicultural Development, 4,* 197–206.

Stewart, M. A., Ryan, E. B., & Giles, H. (1985). Accent and social class effects on status and solidarity evaluations. *Personality and Social Psychology Bulletin, 11,* 98–105.

Street, R. L., & Brady, R. M. (1982). Speech rate acceptance ranges as a function of evaluative domain, listener speech rate, and communication context. *Communication Monographs, 49,* 290–308.

Street, R. L., Brady, R. M., & Putman, W. B. (1983). The influence of speech rate stereotypes and rate similarity on listeners' evaluations of speakers. *Journal of Language and Social Psychology, 2,* 37–56.

Sumner, W. G. (1940). *Folkways.* Boston: Ginn & Co.

Tucker, G. R., & Lambert, W. E. (1969). White and Negro listeners' reactions to various American English dialects. *Social Forces, 47,* 463–468.

Turner, J. C., Brown, R. J., & Tajfel, H. (1979). Social comparison and group interest in in-group favoritism. *European Journal of Social Psychology, 9,* 187.

Concepts and Questions

1. Do you believe Cargile is correct when he notes that "research demonstrates that people tend to like others who possess attitudes and traits similar to their own and to dislike others with dissimilar attitudes and traits"?
2. How do language differences compound the problems associated with ethnocentrism?
3. Can you think of examples that illustrate Cargile's point that "language differences also may be present even when the same symbolic code is used"?
4. According to Cargile, what are examples of situations in which accents influenced someone's perception of another person? Has accent ever influenced your perception of another person? How?
5. Can you think of examples in your own life when a speaker's choice of words or grammatical phrases may have contributed to some harmful and erroneous prejudgments?
6. Why is speaking rate a variable in intercultural communication? What cultures have you interacted with that speak at a rate different from your own? Did that influence your encounter with the person?
7. In what settings do we most often see discrimination based on speech differences?
8. Do you agree with Cargile when he asserts that "when participants come from the same nation, but different co-cultures, the language differences may not be as striking"?
9. According to Cargile, how should responsible intercultural communicators manage language attitudes?

6 Cultural Contexts: The Influence of the Setting

Live together like brothers and do business like strangers.

ARAB PROVERB

Human history is increasingly a race between intercultural education and disaster. . . . If education is not intercultural, it is probably not education, but rather the inculcation of nationalist or religious fundamentalism.

DAVID COULBY

If you are not in tune with the universe, there is sickness in the heart and mind.

NAVAJO SAYING

The ability to communicate effectively with people from diverse cultures and co-cultures necessitates that you not only have knowledge of the principles of communication and their relationship to the dynamics of culture but that you also understand how intercultural communication functions in various social settings. We have thus far presented you with essays that (1) introduced the foundations of intercultural communication, (2) discussed the importance of cultural identity, (3) revealed the diversity between international cultures and domestic co-cultures, and (4) discussed how the cultural diversity in both verbal and nonverbal behavior has an impact on the communication process. We now introduce you to another principle of communication you must understand if you are to be proficient in the practice of intercultural communication—the cultural context.

All human interaction takes place within specific social and physical environments. We call this environment the *social context*. Your consideration of the social context is important because the setting is never neutral; it always exerts influence on how communication participants ought to behave. Therefore, when you communicate with someone, you must be aware of the specific social context and adapt your communicative behavior so that it is appropriate to the particular situation. Think for a moment about the following social contexts: football stadium, night club, university cafeteria, physician's office, classroom, business meeting, or place of worship. These social environments contain many physical and social elements that influence how you will produce and respond to messages. What you wear, what you talk about, to whom you talk, and even the volume of your voice is governed by the social context. You have learned appropriate patterns of communicative behavior for a variety of social contexts within your own culture. But, as with other aspects of intercultural communication, the appropriate patterns of behavior for various social contexts are culturally diverse. When you find yourself in an unfamiliar social context without an internalized set of rules to act as a guide, you may encounter communication problems you do not recognize or understand.

The impact and influence of the social context on communication lies rooted in three interrelated assumptions:

1. *Communication is rule governed* (i.e., each encounter has implicit and explicit rules that regulate conduct). These rules apply to everything from what is appropriate attire to what topics may be discussed.
2. *The setting helps define which "regulations" are in operation.* Reflect for a moment on your own communication behavior as you move to and from the following settings: classroom, courtroom, church, hospital, basketball game, and movie theater. Visualize how your behavior changes as you move from one place to another.
3. *Most communication rules have been learned as part of one's cultural experiences.* Although cultures might share the same general settings, their specific notions of appropriate behavior for each context reflect the values and attitudes of that culture. For instance, turn-taking; the use of time, space, and language; appropriate manners; displays of nonverbal behavior; the appropriateness of silence; and the control of the communication flow are primarily extensions of culture.

In this chapter we offer essays that discuss the interrelationships among context, culture, and communication. Although intercultural communication occurs in a wide variety of contexts, we have selected three social environments where you are most likely to find yourself interacting with people from diverse cultures: *business, education,* and *health care.*

In some of our early editions international business was seldom mentioned because most trade took place within each culture's geographical borders. However, in the past thirty years there has been a rapid expansion of international business, and its impact on the global economy is now common. Many former national companies have transformed themselves into global, transnational entities with offices, employees, production, and service facilities located throughout the world. Even within the United States the impact of culture on business is evident. The United States now relies on a multicultural workforce. Most companies, whether local, regional, national, or international, have workers from diverse cultural backgrounds. One's associates, clients, subordinates, and even supervisors are often from different cultures and even from different countries. Many aspects of business life, such as negotiation, decision making, policy formulation, socializing, gender relationships, marketing techniques, management structure, human resource management, gift giving, and patterns of communication, are now affected by cultural diversity.

What is true of the importance of intercultural business communication also applies to the education setting. The forces of globalization, immigration, and population growth have caused classrooms in the United States and elsewhere to become multicultural/multinational communities. In the United States nearly one in three students now self-identifies as African American, Latino, Asian, Pacific Islander, Arab, or American Indian. According to the Pew Research Center, in 2007, nationwide 59 percent of students were white, 20 percent Hispanic, 15 percent African American, and 6 percent Asian. Approximately 10 million U.S. students come from homes where English is not the primary language, and more than 49 million students are classified as having limited English proficiency (LEP). In addition, as reported in the August 10, 2012, edition of *The Week*, during the 2010–11 academic year there were more than 1 million foreign students enrolled in U.S. universities. In short, the makeup of classrooms has experienced a major transformation in the last thirty years. Schools now must accommodate widely diverse learning styles, interaction patterns, preferences for competition or cooperation, differences in the use and meaning of silence, as well as the status and role of the teacher.

The presence of global and multicultural populations also affects health care providers and clients. The cultural context is important for a number of reasons. First, the promotion of health and the prevention of disease is an urgent priority for any civilized culture. Second, some diseases are highly contagious and can be easily transmitted into a host culture. Third, and from a cultural perspective most important, is cultural diversity in perceptions about the causes, treatment, and prevention of illness. And finally, members of dissimilar cultures may utilize different communication patterns and styles when they interact in the health care setting. Members of one culture, for instance, may talk openly and freely to a health care provider about their medical situation, whereas members of another culture may be reluctant to talk or to reveal personal information.

As we have just highlighted, understanding how communication operates in the multicultural business setting, the educational environment, and the health care setting becomes more important as cultural diversity increases. Therefore, this special volume includes six of the best essays from past editions that are concerned with these settings.

We begin with decision making in the business organization setting. Business executives frequently make decisions about whether to hire additional employees or to make changes in product design or production practices or whether the company should merge with or acquire a competitor. The process by which decisions are made is a dynamic of the culture of the business organization. But this business culture is strongly influenced by the deep structure of the culture of the society in which the business operates. Thus, you will find that the processes by which decisions are reached and accepted vary culturally and may be quite different from those of your culture. An excellent example of this diversity can be seen in how decisions are made in Eastern cultures as compared to Western cultures. To give you a glimpse of these differences, we have selected an essay by Kazuo Nishiyama titled "Japanese Style of Decision Making in Business Organizations." Professor Nishiyama's essay provides an extremely clear and succinct analysis of how Eastern collectivistic cultures engage in decision making. From this essay you will (1) understand how collectivism plays a large part in Japanese decision making; (2) become familiar with the concept of *ringi,* which is the Japanese decision-making protocol; (3) gain an understanding of the vital role informal face-to-face discussions play in reaching consensus on a decision; and (4) receive advice on how Western business people should proceed when engaged in business negotiations or discussions with Japanese counterparts.

Professor Nishiyama begins with a background discussion about corporate culture in Japan and how it fosters strong group orientation. He then discusses how Japanese decision making follows a *ringi,* or group decision-making protocol. This style of decision making is rooted in the Japanese traditions of interpersonal harmony, cooperation, and consensus.

Kaigi, or a face-to-face conference, is the key to decision making. This conference proceeds quite differently from a typical business meeting in most Western organizations. Nishiyama points out that in most Western business meetings, proposals will be debated until a decision is reached. In the Japanese system, "the Japanese business meeting is an occasion to formally confirm what has been already decided informally through intensive *nemawashi* [informal discussions]."

Nishiyama concludes his essay with detailed advice for Western business people who are involved in negotiations or decision making with Japanese counterparts. He suggests that Westerners maintain close personal contacts, that they do not rush their Japanese counterparts, and that they do not consider *ringi* as a negative, slow process. In addition, he suggests that Westerners bring gifts for their Japanese counterparts, that they acquire a good understanding of Japanese culture and social customs, that they do not talk too much, that they be patient, and finally, that they try to provide visual aids in Japanese.

Although the diversity found between Eastern and Western cultures is often troublesome, there are also important differences between U.S. American and European business cultures. Michael Hinner's analysis of German and American business cultures describes how to prevent some of the misunderstanding that often occurs when members of these cultures interact. From his analysis you will (1) gain insight into the similarities between the German and American business cultures, (2) recognize how European geography plays a role in the development of German cultural values, (3) see how the German tendency toward uncertainty avoidance influences their cultural behaviors, (4) gain some insight into the German legal system and its influence on the conduct of business, (5) learn about the differences between German and American corporate organizations, and (6) see some of the major differences between German and American methods of doing business.

Hinner first relates how the German and American economies are similar because they are capitalistic and market driven. He then shows how Germany's position in the heart of Europe, which placed it in the center of wars and conflicts going back to antiquity, has influenced the development of many German cultural values. High uncertainty avoidance is a major characteristic of German culture. Hinner suggests that this has led the Germans to create many rules and regulations that help minimize risks in advance and promote the successful accomplishment of any task at hand.

As background for further understanding German culture, Hinner shows how the German legal system differs from that of the United States. German law is code-based, whereas American law is case-based. German law seeks to anticipate illegal actions and to list them expressly in the legal code as illegal. Law in the United States applies the principle of analogy and may be extended to cover new circumstances.

Hinner continues by describing the differences between German and American corporate organization. German companies are controlled by two different boards: a management board and a supervisory board. The management board operates the company, and the supervisory board determines that management policies and operations are always in the best interest of shareholders. By describing the organization of American corporations and the role of their boards and CEOs, Hinner demonstrates how business organizations in Germany differ from those in the United States.

Hinner concludes his essay with a discussion of communication problems that can arise during business negotiations between Americans and their German counterparts. He explains how diversity in some cultural values influences the interactions. For instance, while both Americans and Germans tend to be monochronic in their work routines, Germans are more rigid and believe small talk to be a waste of time; meetings should commence immediately with the business at hand. Also, the German need for order and organization requires that in any business meeting the Germans will want to have an initial and comprehensive understanding of all aspects of a problem before attempting to solve it.

We next consider the educational context in a multicultural society. Classrooms represent a setting where the sway of culture must be considered as the children of immigrants are being educated in their new homelands worldwide. The faces of students and the languages they speak are as diverse as those found in the business setting. Cultural diversity affects thinking habits, learning strategies, communication patterns and styles, prejudice and stereotyping, educational expectations, and classroom behavior. Educational practices affected by cultural diversity can be observed in nearly every classroom from the lower levels to the university setting. Students not only reflect the influences of the host society but also the diversity of the many cultures participating in international education programs.

In their essay "Intercultural Communication in the University Classroom," Lisa M. Skow and Laurie Stephan show us the role culture plays in the learning and teaching processes at the university level. After establishing the increasing growth rate of international students in U.S. institutions of higher learning, they examine how cultural values influence intercultural classroom communication and discuss how culture leads to different learning and teaching styles. Finally, they indicate how culture-specific verbal and nonverbal behavior influence communication between students and teachers.

In "Culture and Communication in the Classroom," an essay that has appeared in numerous previous editions, Geneva Gay introduces the semiotic relationship that exists among communication, culture, teaching, and learning. From this essay you will (1) learn to recognize some of the critical features and pedagogical potentials for different ethnic groups of color, (2) develop an awareness of some key assertions about culture and communication in teaching and learning in general, (3) understand some of the major characteristics of the communicative modes of African Americans, Native Americans, Asian Americans, and European Americans, (4) learn how culture influences classroom participation in communication, (5) become aware of the conditions under which students of the various cultures will participate, and (6) see how participation patterns are governed by culture.

We then examine the ramifications of culture on the health care setting. Cultural beliefs about health, disease, and treatment are critical because they often differ significantly. For example, a simple question such as "How do you catch a cold?" can elicit a variety of answers. Depending on the person's culture, answers can range from standing in a draft to being the victim of a supernatural spirit or spell. Health care providers face numerous communication problems when interacting with clients from diverse cultural backgrounds. For example, in male-dominated cultures men speak for their women, and the interview or discussion of illness must pass through the male to the woman client. Conflict can also arise due to U.S. laws regarding the disclosure of health information. In numerous societies cultural beliefs prohibit the disclosure of "bad news" to the patient. This information must be passed to the family who will then decide what and how much to reveal to the patient.

Patricia Geist-Martin has been a pioneer in exploring the cultural dimensions of health care communication in multicultural societies. Her essay, "Negotiating Cultural Understanding in Health Care Communication," examines the complex and dynamic features of communication in the health care context. She begins by linking culture, health, and communication. She then provides a cultural sensitivity model of health care communication for educating health care providers, for clinical practice, and for patient empowerment. Next, Geist-Martin examines specific case examples that demonstrate the problems encountered by both providers and patients when culturally specific beliefs and practices of patients are ignored during diagnosis and treatment. She concludes by proposing avenues for overcoming the obstacles revealed in programs for expanding our notions of culture and culturally sensitive health care.

A multicultural society strongly affects the health care setting because cultural beliefs about health, disease, and caregiver–patient communication can differ significantly. In the last essay of this chapter, Nagesh Rao reports the initial findings of an ongoing investigation into physician–patient communication across cultures. Through interviews conducted worldwide, Rao seeks to develop a base of information that will ultimately lead to a model of intercultural health care communication.

In "'Half-truths' in Argentina, Brazil, and India: An Intercultural Analysis of Physician–Patient Communication," Rao provides an insightful view of how physicians from these cultures view the diversity within their countries. In addition, Rao shows how physicians operating within a collectivist cultural environment would choose to reveal news of serious or terminal illness to patients.

Japanese Style of Decision Making in Business Organizations

KAZUO NISHIYAMA

Western scholars and businesspeople are still very critical of Japanese decision-making processes as being intuitive and irrational. They are often frustrated and even dismayed that seemingly ultra-modern Japanese business organizations have not adopted more objective and rational approaches to decision making as expected. The Japanese organizations may all claim that they have modernized decision-making processes with extensive use of Web sites for dissemination and e-mails for exchanges of in-house information. Except for nontraditional IT-related companies, however, almost all other companies still continue to use the traditional *ringi-seido* (group decision making) and *kaigi* (face-to-face conference). The obvious reason for this continuation is that these traditional methods of communication are not only acceptable but also feasible in the context of Japanese corporate culture. Therefore, it is important to examine specific aspects of Japanese culture that instill and perpetuate the particular type of interpersonal relationships and decision-making practices in Japanese business organizations.

EMPLOYMENT SYSTEM IN JAPAN

Japanese companies are still group-oriented organizations despite the fact that the younger Japanese generation is becoming more individualistic. The major reason for perpetuation of group orientation among Japanese salaried workers is how they are recruited and how they are trained and indoctrinated into their workplace (Nishiyama, 1995). The following are the most common personnel recruitment practices used in Japan today:

1. Japanese companies usually recruit new employees from among new graduates of high schools and universities during the month of April. The new recruits go through induction training together at the company's training center. This training will last two or more weeks. They all live together and engage in group-oriented activities in addition to listening to lectures by senior members of the company. This "bonding" among the new recruits is considered a very important aspect of their entire career with the company. When talking about comradeship, they often say, *onaji kama no meshi wo tabeta nakama* (comrades who eat rice from the same rice cooker).

2. Japanese companies are still reluctant to hire workers who have had previous work experience with other companies. They fear that the experienced workers, called *"chuuto saiyoo sha"* (mid-career recruits), may disrupt interpersonal harmony among those who have been hired directly into the company upon completion of their education. There are, however, many exceptions today in recruitment policies. For example, IT-related companies need experienced workers who can bring with them specific, advanced skills and technical knowledge. These companies even recruit computer programmers from China, Singapore, and India because they have no time to train programmers from among new Japanese recruits, and the foreign programmers are comparatively cheaper to hire.

3. All Japanese companies use different classifications of employees in order to retain good and loyal workers and to differentiate them from other less desirable workers. There are *honyatoi* (regular employment), *rinjiyatoi* (temporary employment), *paato* (part-time employment), *keiyaku shain* (contract employee), *haken shain* (dispatched employee), etc. Those workers who are employed as regular employees usually have good educational backgrounds and personal qualifications. They comprise a group of "elite workers" who can look forward to becoming members of management and receiving lifetime employment, plus annual advancement. Temporary employees (*rinjiyatoi*) are hired when the company

needs to augment its workforce for a specific period of time. They will never be given lifetime employment, no matter how long and how hard they work for the organization. They may receive only a few basic fringe benefits, and are the first ones to be fired whenever the workload is reduced. Part-time workers (*paato*) are given hourly wages without fringe benefits. Contract employees are hired for a certain period of months or years. Computer programmers from China, for example, are contract employees hired for one or two years. Dispatched employees (*haken shain*) are recruited by a *jinji haken kaisha* (personnel dispatch company) and assigned to client companies. Many English teachers working for multinational Japanese corporations are dispatched employees. They receive their wages and fringe benefits from their personnel dispatch company, not from the corporations they work for as English teachers. Still another classification is called *friitaa* or *frii arubaitaa* (casual workers). They are young Japanese men or women who do not have any career plans or ambitions to succeed in their professions. They work whenever or wherever they decide to work as temporary workers.

Among these groups of workers, only the regular employees are bona fide employees of the company they work for. There is a distinct separation between and among these differently classified employees. These groups of employees do not interact with each other on the same level of comradeship and interpersonal trust. In fact, the regular employees sometimes discriminate against other groups and cooperate with them only with a certain amount of suspicion.

BUILDING UP INTERPERSONAL RELATIONSHIPS

The above discussion clearly shows that establishing close relationships and a group-oriented mentality is reserved for regular employees. And this process begins with the induction training when they are first hired and the elaborate *nyushashiki* (entering company ceremony). During the induction training, all new employees are required to learn the "President's Teachings" (corporate missions and mottos), the "Company Song," the

corporate history and philosophy, etc. All learning takes place through group activities. Those who attend the same induction training sessions become *doohai* (the same-year comrades) and they will continue to associate with each other as such (Nishiyama, 2000).

This entering company ceremony is a major annual event just like a commencement ceremony. The president, top executives, managers, senior employees, and some parents attend the ceremony. The president welcomes the new recruits and also challenges them to work hard for the corporate goals in his inspirational speech. In response, a representative of the new recruits answers his challenge. In fact, every recruit becomes a new member of the corporate family and pledges his alliance and loyalty to the company (Rohlen, 1974). New generations of Japanese workers do not particularly like this type of induction, but they are often forced to accept these traditional practices.

Even though a Japanese company tries to establish one unified work group, it is also true that there are *habatsu*, or factions, within the company. The factions are often based on *gakubatsu*, or school cliques, *senpaikoohai kankei* (senior–junior relationship), and city or state of birth. The managers who graduated from a certain university will give personal favors to the new recruits from the same university in exchange for the latter's loyalty. If, for example, University A's graduates hold powerful executive positions in a company, the graduates of the same university will be treated better than University B's graduates. Naturally, the senior members who took good care of the new recruits will make the latter feel obligated to them, creating a mutual-dependency relationship. Obviously, relationships among these factions can become troublesome at times because of intense inter-faction rivalries and conflict.

RINGI OR GROUP DECISION MAKING

The *ringi* style of decision making is deeply rooted in Japanese culture, which emphasizes interpersonal harmony, cooperation, and consensus. Today, it is often said that modern Japanese organizations have been streamlining or rationalizing this outdated process due to wide use of in-house Web sites and e-mail networks (McDaniel, 2003). It is still true, however, that the *ringi* system, even in its modified form, is being used to satisfy a number of important sociocultural demands among the members of most Japanese business organizations. It is almost impossible for the Japanese to abandon this process and adopt a Western decision-making style where individuals at the top management level make decisions.

Unlike their counterparts in Western business organizations, Japanese executives and managers are not real independent decision makers. A Japanese company president, for example, cannot make a quick and independent decision on his own, unless he is the founder and the majority owner of the company. And if he does so too frequently, he will be accused of being a *wanman shahoo* (dictator president). Japanese companies may use the title "Chief Executive Officer," but this Japanese C.E.O. does not have the same decision-making authority as his counterpart in Western business organizations. The position of president is oftentimes honorary and given to one before his retirement or promotion to the position of a chairman. He will never, therefore, risk making any unpopular decisions on his own. His decisions are usually based on group consensus. Actually, the person in charge of decision making is *senmu torishimari yaku* (managing director) who actually runs the daily affairs of his company. But he still needs the president's seal of approval on any decisions that he may make. In addition, he still needs other executives and managers' concurrence and support.

Process of *Ringi* Decision Making

The *ringi* process begins with a *kiansha* (plan initiator), usually a lower- or middle-ranking manager (supervisor or section chief), who is in charge of drafting a *ringisho* (proposal). Before drafting this document, he discusses the general idea informally with key executives, managers, and supervisors. Only after getting fairly positive initial reactions from them will he draft the proposal document. This document includes the request for a decision, supporting data and information, detailed explanations, and justifications. This informal discussion is called *nemawashi*, which literally means "twisting the tree roots around." In practice, *nemawashi* refers to holding many face-to-face, informal, behind-the-scene discussions about a proposal

among all the people who would be involved in implementing any decision to be made later.

The act of *nemawashi* is analogous to twisting a planted tree around to cut off bothersome roots or "objections" so that it can be uprooted easily. The *nemawashi* process is a sounding board for unofficially testing the responses to a proposed idea without any risk of unnecessarily causing loss of face for any one individual or group. In this process, no one individual or group can claim all the credit if it is successful, and at the same time, no one will be blamed should it fail.

Once a *ringi* proposal is completed, the initiator circulates it to every executive and manager who will be asked to approve it after careful review. The circulation is executed in reverse order of each individual's hierarchical position, beginning with the lowest-ranked supervisor, to middle management, top management, and finally to the president. The cover sheet of the proposal has many small boxes for *han* (seal of approval) to be affixed by all those who will review and approve it. The proper order of circulation is strictly adhered to because skipping any person on the hierarchical ladder will cause serious procedural and interpersonal problems. If any of the managers or executives have questions or objections, the initiator will have to answer them in person. The decision can be delayed indefinitely until the person who is objecting receives convincing justification based on new data and information. When all the seals of approval have been obtained, the document will be hand delivered to the president for his approval. This final approval from the president, called *kessai* (final approval), is the last step in the *ringi* decision-making process.

Suppose, for example, that a Japanese faculty member wants to invite an American professor to a Japanese private university as a visiting professor. The Japanese professor will begin *nemawashi* (informal consultation) among his colleagues. He needs to find out whether or not any professor in his department objects to inviting this particular U.S. professor. If he is a junior assistant professor, he will have to gain the approvals of senior professors, who may have more power. Only then can he ask his department chairperson to request that the personnel department begin the necessary paperwork for employing this foreign professor. Unlike an American university, this Japanese university chairperson needs to obtain the approval of his dean and the university president. Naturally, he has to prepare a lengthy *ringi* document and go through the process as explained above.

If one of the professors objects for any reason, the assistant professor needs to tactfully persuade this objecting professor. His reason for objection could be that he feels threatened by the visiting professor, maybe because the visitor is very famous in the same field of study. Or perhaps he received a rather negative review of his conference paper from the visitor in the past. In this case, the junior professor is required to mediate the situation. If the objecting professor grudgingly agrees to go along, he will make sure that he will receive *kashi* (credit) from the junior professor. This means that the latter owes a favor to the former, and he will have to repay this *kari* (debt) later on. During the process of *nemawashi, kashi-kari kankei* (obligatory relationship) is established quite frequently within any Japanese organization (Nishiyama, 2000).

Kaigi, or Face-to-Face Conference

Kaigi in Japanese business organizations outwardly appears to be similar to a business meeting or conference in Western business organizations. However, it is quite different from a typical Western-style meeting in its purpose, procedure, content of discussion, and participation of attendees. Generally speaking, the purpose of a Western-style business meeting is to facilitate decision making in face-to-face situations. In contrast, the Japanese business meeting is an occasion to formally confirm what has been already decided informally through intensive *nemawashi*. In many instances, Japanese participants go through the ritual of asking questions and debating certain points. But in fact, they are merely saying what has been discussed and agreed upon beforehand. And they do not want surprise questions or strong objections from any one of the participants during the actual meeting.

In the Western cultural context, it is acceptable to change one's mind about what has been informally agreed upon prior to the meeting, if a much better idea or new compelling evidence is presented. In the Japanese cultural context, however, such changing of one's mind is a serious social infraction and betrayal of interpersonal trust. Any agreement that has been reached during informal consultations is considered a firm commitment. It is different from a tentative commitment or personal opinion that Western businesspeople usually try to obtain when going through the process of "touching the bases."

The role of each Japanese participant is different from that of his Western counterpart. The Japanese chairperson's main role is not to aggressively take direct control over the decision-making process, but to mediate the consensus-building process among all participants. In fact, the second-ranking person (usually *buchoo*, or department head) will do most of the talking and direct other participants to contribute to the ongoing discussion in a predetermined order. Each of the junior-ranking participants presents a brief report prepared in advance and seeks everyone's approval. The participants seldom disagree with others during face-to-face meetings because they have probably talked about his report informally and obtained everyone's concurrence beforehand. There may be a few questions for clarifications, but open arguments or heated discussions will not be permitted. In some instances when important decisions are being made, the president or the top executive may show up at the conference just for a few minutes to give the participants moral support. However, they would never stay long and participate in the actual decision-making process. *Kao wo dasu* (showing one's face) has a significant meaning in this context.

If a junior participant wishes to voice his opinion, he will preface his remarks by saying, "I may be making this comment based on my limited experience and I may be wrong, but..." or he may also say, "Please tell me if you think I am wrong, but...." He needs to take a tentative approach and also show humility in order not to cause loss of face among any of the participants. Other participants will also hesitate to voice frank opinions or disagreement, because they fear even their constructive criticisms could be taken as personal attacks or insults. They all tend to look for subtle verbal or nonverbal cues and try to understand how the other participants feel about what is being discussed.

The above discussion seems to indicate that Japanese businesspeople would never exchange their frank, honest opinions or comments. They do so, however, by intentionally creating informal opportunities outside the conference rooms. They frequently go out together for drinking and dining where they exchange their true feelings. An unhappy participant may even complain bitterly, pretending that he has had too much to drink, but he is allowed to do so because this is one of the ways to appease the dissatisfied member. The Japanese call this method of communicating while drinking alcohol *"nomini-cation"* (drink and communicate). Even in this *nomini-cation* context, it is important for all the participants to remember their position in the organizational hierarchy. A so-called "drunk person" is expected to apologize to his senior members on the following morning for his misbehavior. He might say, "I am sorry I was so drunk last night. I don't remember what I said," even if he remembers clearly what he complained about.

Unlike the Japanese counterpart, an American chairperson controls the discussion of a conference and encourages active participation from the participants. He might even challenge every participant to openly voice his or her own opinions and comments. And the participants feel free to exchange constructive criticisms and objections based on their knowledge and experience without fear of being ostracized or alienated.

Westerners, particularly Americans, are often frustrated when they attend a so-called "decision-making conference" in Japan. They are often dismayed because they expect that the Japanese participants across the conference table would act the same way as they do. They usually find it difficult to read subtle verbal and nonverbal cues offered by the Japanese participants. For example, the Japanese would say "yes, yes" and nod their head in agreement, this is called *aizuchi* (nodding in agreement), but these verbal and nonverbal cues do not mean they are agreeing at all in most instances. They may mean "I hear what you are saying," "Please explain more," or "I will pretend I agree with you for now, but I still have objections." Another problem is that in the Japanese language, they can say, "Yes, I don't agree with you, which literally means, "Yes, you are right. I don't agree with you" (Nishiyama, 2000).

In order to accurately assess what the Japanese counterparts mean by what they say, it is often necessary for the Americans to go out drinking and dining with a few of their Japanese counterparts. Perhaps one of the Japanese participants may help them "interpret" what has transpired during the conference. He may divulge certain important information *ofureko* (off-the-record) during after-hours *nomini-cation*.

ADVICE ON OVERCOMING COMMUNICATION DIFFICULTIES

1. *Maintain close personal contacts.*
   It is extremely important to cultivate and maintain close interpersonal relationships with those who are in charge, because decisions are often made on personal preference, not merely on objective facts and data. For example, an American who makes a good impression on the initiator of a *ringi* proposal can win the latter's friendship. The Japanese representative will keep the American informed as to the progress of the decision making by the involved top executives. Sending direct e-mail reminders will not work in this context.

2. *Do not rush Japanese counterparts.*
   Western businesspeople are always working by setting deadlines for actions, because "Time is of the essence" in their culture. They must understand that Japanese deadlines are more flexible, especially when the Japanese side is the buyer in a business deal. In Japan, "A customer is king," and they expect that a seller, who has a lower status, will abide by his customer's deadline.

3. *Do not consider ringi negative because it is slow and cumbersome.*
   The *ringi* process is indeed slow and cumbersome, but implementation of the decision is swift once it is made. For example, the visiting professor in the above example does not have to worry about acquainting himself with his new Japanese colleagues because everyone in the department will already know who he is and what he has written. They may even know about his wife, children, and other personal matters. Indeed, the "Welcome Mat" will be laid out upon his arrival.

4. *Bring gifts for Japanese counterparts.*
   Gift-giving is still an important custom in establishing amicable interpersonal relationships. A gift does not have to be an expensive one, but it should be a token of friendship. For example, an American businessperson may give a bottle of Johnny Walker whiskey or a carton of American cigarettes when visiting a Japanese counterpart for the first time. This small gift is not considered as a bribe in Japan, as it is a common practice among Japanese businesspeople. And the Japanese side

will usually give back to the American an *okaeshi* (return gift) when he is leaving Japan.

5. *Good understanding of Japanese culture and social customs is necessary for successful participation in the decision-making conference.*

   Seating should be arranged strictly according to each participant's status, not by work group or area of specialization. The order of speaking and of asking questions should also be based on the relative status of the Japanese participants. Seniority and ranking are important. For example, a junior manager cannot speak up before his senior manager speaks. And, he must wait for a subtle signal, verbal or nonverbal, from the senior before he can speak.

6. *Do not talk too much and do not dominate discussions.* Western businesspeople have a tendency to dominate verbal exchanges when participating in a business conference with the Japanese. They believe that winning arguments or using logical persuasion will bring about good results. On the contrary, Japanese participants may be offended by an aggressive and argumentative presentation from the Western counterparts. They may win the argument, but they will lose the deal. When English is used as a medium of communication, the Japanese participants feel handicapped. They may need more time to think in Japanese first and translate their thoughts into English. During meetings and official functions, U.S. business representatives should never help a Japanese counterpart with English by trying to put words into their mouths.

7. *Be patient and disregard the "Western time orientation."* Westerners are generally "clock-oriented" whereas the Japanese are "people-oriented." This means that Japanese people are more inclined to adjust the handling of time based on who is speaking. For example, each participant could be asked to make his or her comment within five minutes, but a senior Japanese participant might take more than ten minutes and ramble along in broken English. But it would be extremely rude to stop him before he finishes what he wants to say. In this situation, who is speaking is more important than what the time restraint is.

8. *It is a good strategy to prepare visual aids in Japanese.* In order to facilitate accurate communication, visual aids such as charts, graphs, figures, or slides should be used. The Japanese usually want to have written documents that cover important data and information. This strategy will help them better understand what is being explained in English.

CONCLUSION

Despite the fact many Japanese companies claim that they are revamping the traditional decision-making practices, it seems that they are not able to make drastic changes. Clearly, they must change their personnel recruitment and training system first if they wish to create a new corporate culture amenable to more efficient digital communication. To remove the fear among managers of not knowing what is going on, the Japanese companies still continue to provide information to every level of management by the use of the *ringi* decision-making system. And in order to have amicable interpersonal relationships, Japanese managers still want to hold face-to-face conferences, even though they sometimes find it unnecessary to participate in time-consuming meetings.

During the economic boom years, prior to the burst of Japan's "Bubble Economy" in the early 1990s, there were some innovative measures to change the traditional personnel management system by doing away with permanent employment and seniority-based compensation. The subsequent recession, however, forced many Japanese companies to restructure or scale down their operations. This situation, in turn, created the fear of losing jobs among all levels of managers and they again went back to the more comfortable and nonthreatening methods of decision making that they had been used to. Those companies that claim that they streamlined decision-making practices still use *ringi* and *kaigi* in making important decisions. These traditional, culturally based methods of decision making, however modified, will continue to be used as long as Japan's corporate culture requires them.

Index of Japanese Terms

aizuchi	nodding in agreement
buchoo	department head
chuuto saiyoo sha	mid-career recruit
doohai	the same-year comrade

gakubatsu	school clique
friitaa, frii arubaitaa	casual worker
habatsu	faction
haken shain	dispatched employee
han	seal
honyatoi	regular employee
jinji haken kaisha	employee dispatch company
kaigi	face-to-face conference
kao wo dasu	showing one's face
kari	debt
kashi	credit
kashi-kari kankei	obligatory relationship
keiyaku shain	contract employee
kessai	final approval
kiansha	initiator
nemawashi	informal consultation
nyushashiki	company entering ceremony
nomini-cation	drink and communicate
ofureko	off-the-record
okaeshi	return gift
onaji kama no meshi	comrades who ate rice
wo tabeta nakama	from the same cooker
paato	part-time worker
ringi	group decision making
ringisho	proposal for decision
rinjiyatoi	temporary worker
senmu torishimari yaku	managing director
senpai-koohai kankei	senior–junior relationship
wanman shahoo	dictator president

References

McDaniel, E. R. (2004). *Changing Japanese Organizational Communication Patterns: The Impact of Information Technology*. San Diego State University Center for International Business Education and Research (CIBER). Working Paper Services C04-015.

Nishiyama, K. (1995). *Japan-U.S. Business Communication*. Dubuque, Iowa: Kendall/Hunt.

Nishiyama, K. (2000). *Doing Business with Japan: Successful Strategies for Intercultural Communication*. Honolulu: University of Hawaii.

Rohlen, T. (1974). *For Harmony and Strength: Japanese White-Collar Organization in Anthropological Perspective*. Berkeley, CA: University of California.

Suggested Readings

Castells, M. (2000). *End of millennium* (2nd ed.). Malden, MA: Blackwell.

Gudykunst, W.B., & Nishida, T. (1994). *Bridging Japanese/North America differences*. Thousand Oaks, CA: Sage.

Hall, I. (1998). *Cartels of the mind: Japan's Intellectual closed shop*. New York: Norton.

Japan External Trade Organization. (1992). *Japanese corporate decision-making*. Tokyo: Author.

March, R. M. (1980). *The Japanese negotiator: Subtlety and strategy beyond Western logic*. Tokyo: Kodansha International.

Quasha, S., & McDaniel, E. R. (2003). Reinterpreting Japanese business communication in the information age. In L. Samovar & R. Porter (Eds.), *Intercultural communication: A reader* (10th ed., pp. 283–292). Belmont, CA: Wadsworth.

Yoshida, S. (2002). Globalization and issues of intercultural communications: Doing successful business in Asia. *Vital Speeches of the Day*, 68(22), 708–771.

Yoshimura, N., & Anderson, P. (1997). *Inside the Kaisha: Demystifying Japanese business behavior*. Boston: Harvard Business School Press.

Concepts and Questions

1. Why is the group-oriented mentality important in Japanese business organizations?
2. How does the Japanese employment system foster group orientation?
3. Why are Japanese employers reluctant to hire employees who have worked for other companies?
4. Nishiyama has indicated that although companies try to establish one unified work group, there may be factions within the company. What are the bases for these factions? How do these factions fit with the idea of a group-oriented workforce?
5. What are the cultural significances of the Japanese *ringi* decision-making process?
6. How does the *ringi* process differ from decision-making processes in Western organizations?
7. Why is it important for a Western businessperson to understand the *kaigi* process?
8. In what ways do face-to-face conferences in Japanese business organizations differ from those in Western business organizations?
9. In group-oriented Japanese business organizations where harmonious relationships are important, do Japanese business people have a means to exchange and express frank and honest opinions? Explain.

Comparing and Contrasting German and American Business Cultures

Michael B. Hinner

At first glance, German and American business cultures seem very similar. After all, both economies are capital based and market driven. Shares of large German and American corporations are traded in both countries. In fact, numerous German corporations have been active on the American market for many decades now, e.g., Bayer, BMW, Braun, T Mobile, Volkswagen, as have been many American corporations on the German market, e.g., Coca Cola, Ford, IBM, McDonald's, Microsoft. The list of such companies could easily be extended. But a closer look at German and American business cultures also reveals differences—differences that emerge slowly and only after a longer period of contact, cooperation, or interaction. If and when such differences do emerge, their root cause, i.e., cultural differences, is often not identified as a reason for these differences; instead, other readily perceivable factors are used to provide an explanation for these differences and difficulties, e.g. differences in the distribution network, personality characteristics, financial resources, etc. (Harris & Moran, 1996; Hofstede & Hofstede, 2005; Trompenaars & Hampden-Turner, 1998). One need only recall the failed Daimler Chrysler merger to realize the scope of the potential difficulties (Edmunds Auto Observer, 2007, May 17). While some cultural problems might arise prior to establishing close business relationships, most

tend to surface later during the day-to-day business routine after a relationship is in place (Harris & Moran, 1996; Hofstede & Hofstede, 2005; Trompenaars & Hampden-Turner, 1998). If one is not sensitized to culture, then one will not consider it as a factor in the analysis of business phenomena and instead consider other explanations (Hinner, 2005).

CULTURE

Most people do not consider culture to be an issue if the participants appear to be fairly similar to one another (Chen & Starosta, 1998; Gudykunst & Kim, 1997; Samovar et al., 1998). It seems that people need to associate culture with something tangible and visible to realize that differences do exist between the interactors. It is usually only when someone speaks a different language, wears different clothes, and works in an entirely different work environment that most people perceive a difference (Gudykunst & Kim, 1997; Klopf, 1998; Samovar et al., 1998). But in today's global economy, many international business partners are fluent in English, wear similar business clothes, and often work in similar office environments so that "surface" differences tend to blend into a similar appearance (Harris & Moran, 1996; Hofstede & Hofstede, 2005; Samovar et al., 1998; Trompenaars & Hampden-Turner, 1998). But culture is more than external appearance, i.e. artifacts. Culture also includes social organization and interaction, i.e., sociofacts, and cognitive patterns, i.e. mentifacts that are not always readily apparent to the observer but are expressed by the actions and behavior of people as well as in the thinking and decision making process (Chen & Starosta, 1998; Gudykunst & Kim, 1997; Klopf, 1998; Martin & Nakayama, 1997; Samovar et al., 1998). These "hidden" differences, though, often emerge and cause problems in the day-to-day routine of human interaction (Hofstede & Hofstede, 2005; Klopf, 1998; Samovar et al., 1998).

If, however, the external differences are striking, then the participants of an intercultural encounter will probably expect to encounter difficulties since these differences are perceivable as such (Chen & Starosta, 1998; Gudykunst & Kim, 1997; Klopf, 1998; Martin & Nakayama, 1997; Samovar et al., 1998). But one does not expect to encounter difficulties if there are

---

few external differences and/or the actors appear to exhibit similar behavior.[1] All the more surprising then if differences are encountered when least expected. Because these differences are not anticipated, they become all the more surprising due to their *unexpectness*. And this is the crux of culture: People tend to associate cultural differences with exotic differences, and few expect culture to play any role in modern international business relationships (De Mooij, 2007; Harris & Moran, 1996; Hofstede & Hofstede, 2005; Trompenaars & Hampden-Turner, 1998); especially if two Western cultures are involved in an international business transaction as is, for example, the case with Germans and Americans who share a long tradition of contact and interaction.

German and American Similarities

In fact, German and American cultures have many similarities because they share, to some extent, a common European heritage. In fact, many Americans trace their family roots back to German immigrants (German American, 2007). Conversely, the majority of Germans have been exposed to and influenced by American culture since the end of World War II (*Facts about Germany,* 1998; Jankuhn et al., 1983; Zentner, 1980). This close relationship of both cultures is also illustrated by the many German loanwords in American English and the many English loanwords in German. For example, *kindergarten, kaffeeklatsch,* or *sauerkraut* in American English,[2] and *Designerbaby, Evergreen,* or *Preshave* in German.[3] Likewise, many German products have become icons in the United States, e.g., the Volkswagen Beetle and Bayer aspirin as have U.S. products in Germany, e.g., Levi's jeans and Coke. The list of similarities and parallels could be extended easily.

German and American Differences

But the transfer and exchange of products and cultural artifacts between Germany and the United States is not always identical because adjustments also must be made to local tastes. While in Germany the *Frankfürter Würstchen* can be served with mustard and possibly a roll or even a serving of *sauerkraut,* in the United States franks are served on a bun with a topping of sauerkraut, mustard, and/or ketchup and called "hot dogs." Or McDonald's, for example, includes beer in its program of beverages in Germany; something it is just starting to offer to its customers in the United States. And Coca Cola adapted the taste of its soft drinks to German taste buds; in particular, Fanta and Cherry Coke (Hinner, 1998). The average Bayer aspirin tablet sold in Germany has a higher dosage than in the United States which explains why aspirin is usually only sold in pharmacies in Germany (Hinner & Rülke, 2002). And while the Volkswagen Jetta is a very popular car among young drivers in the United States, many young Germans consider it to be a car for senior citizens because the Jetta has a trunk, a symbol of stodginess, and not a hatchback, a sign of being hip.[4]

Culture and Consumers

The Volkswagen Jetta example illustrates how the same product can have different associations among consumers in different cultures. It, thus, becomes quickly apparent that classic market segmentation is insufficient in an intercultural context (De Mooij, 2007; Sandhusen, 1997). This may be illustrated by the following example. Single, female secretaries aged twenty to twenty-five years who live in the suburbs and commute to work in the city, listen to the same music, pursue the same hobbies, and have a similar disposable income might be classified as one and the same market segment (Homburg & Krohmer, 2003; Meffert, 2000) even though they live and work in Germany and the United States. Marketing considers these perceivable factors to be helpful in developing marketing campaigns directed at this consumer group. Yet despite all these surface similarities, differences do exist which can translate into missed business opportunities. These differences, though, are not found in classic segmentation categories because these differences rest in cultural differences (De Mooij, 1007; Hinner, 1998; Hinner, 2004; Hinner & Rülke, 2002). If culture is not a criterion in the segmentation, it will not be considered by marketers. So if a German shoe manufacturer were to target this particular market segment, the company would probably assume that American secretaries wear footwear similar to German secretaries. Company representatives might actually have encountered American secretaries while visiting the United State on a business trip and noticed that American secretaries also wear high heels in the office. But the Germans might not have noticed that many American secretaries also wear sneakers during the commute to work and only change to high heels in the office. German secretaries, in contrast, tend to wear the same shoes during the commute and in the office. Without any knowledge of this slight but relevant difference in behavior, the German shoe manufacturer would miss out on an important bit of information that could also have consequences for the business. But probably no one would deliberately point out these differences because everyone would assume that all secretaries exhibit similar behavior in a similar context regardless of whether it is Germany or the United States. From this example, though, it should be apparent that direct comparisons based on classic market segmentation can miss out on important consumer behavior if cultural differences are not considered (De Mooij, 2007). This case also illustrates how people perceive, interpret, and evaluate the behavior of others on the basis of their own past experiences in similar situations instead of attempting to discover the real reason for the observed behavior (Adler & Rodman, 2003).

Characteristics of Culture

That is why this essay looks at how a country's culture influences and, to some degree, determines the business culture of that country. After all, business people are also members of a society at large and its culture and, thus, affected by the same cultural factors that influence all other members of that society. Germany shall serve as an example for comparison with American culture to demonstrate how two relatively closely related cultures are actually quite different from one another in how their businesses are organized, how their business people interact with one another, and how they solve problems. The examination of German culture will reveal many particulars of German culture and, thus, help explain the artifacts, sociofacts, and mentifacts of German business culture and why they are in some instances similar to and in other instances quite different from American business culture.[5]

"The how and why behind a culture's collective action can be traced to its (1) worldview (religion),

(2) family structure, and (3) history and government. Working together, these three social forces create, transmit, maintain, and reinforce the basic elements found in all cultures" (Samovar et al., p. 88). The worldview is essential in explaining how the universe functions and the role people play in it. From this core belief system, a society develops its values. Values are standards of behavior and, thus, essential for human interaction and in forming personal attitudes which reflect what one thinks of these standards. These core beliefs and values are transmitted by society at large and the family. After all, culture is learned and passed down from one generation to the next (Samovar et al., 1998). So in many ways, the recounting of the past and the lessons learned (or not) play an important role in the instruction of the subsequent generation(s). History, whether it is family or national history, helps create identity in that it tells people who they are and where they come from (Lustig & Koester, 2006; Oetzel, 2009; Samovar et al., 1998).

> when we refer to history as one of the deep structures of a culture, we are also talking about a culture's formal and informal government, its sense of community, its political system, its key historical "heroes," and even its geography. All of these, working in combination, provide the members of every culture with their identity, values, goals, and expectations. (Samovar et al., 1998, p. 111)

And finally, the environment needs to be added as a fourth element because the environment can determine, for example, what food people eat and what houses are built with what materials. Sometimes a similar environment can produce a similar solution. For example, houses built in regions with a lot of snow have steep roofs to allow the snow to slide off easily; thus, reducing the likelihood of the roof collapsing due to the weight of the accumulated snow. In contrast, houses in hot and dry regions tend to have flat roofs since they do not have to worry about too much precipitation accumulating on the roof. The same applies to the business environment. If the environmental factors are similar, then similar artifacts may be produced and/or used. That is why a factory equipped with similar assembly technology will look fairly similar in many parts of the world. But how it is organized, how people interact and communicate with one another, and how they reach decisions will vary from one culture to another (Hofstede, 2005). In other words, artifacts can be similar if the environment is similar, but the sociofacts and mentifacts can be quite different.

General Disposition and Individual Diversity

It should, though, be kept in mind that the discussion of "typical" behavioral norms refers to generalities and that individual behavior can and will vary, even deviate considerably, from these cultural "standards." Often, a specific microculture will exhibit sometimes radically different behavior from other microcultures within the same macroculture (Chen & Starosta, 1998; Klopf, 1998; Lustig & Koester, 2006; Oetzel, 2009; Samovar et al., 1998), e.g., teenagers vs. senior citizens, bankers vs. construction workers, atheists vs. fundamentalists. Nonetheless, active members of a particular culture will have learned when and where what behavioral standards and norms are expected. Otherwise, a person will not be able to interact successfully in a particular cultural environment (Chen & Starosta, 1998; Klopf, 1998; Lustig & Koester, 2006; Oetzel, 2009; Samovar et al., 1998). This demonstrates that certain standards and norms can be identified and that people can learn these standards and norms if they wish to.

GERMAN CULTURE

As Samovar et al. (1998) point out, culture is rooted in and influenced by history and geography. Germany's location in the heart of Europe has placed it in the center of conflict for a very long time (Herrmann, 1988; Jankuhn et al., 1983; Zentner, 1980). The conflicts go back to classical antiquity and only stopped recently with the fall of the Berlin Wall in 1989 (*Facts about Germany,* 1998). These ceaseless wars and the resultant chaos are often cited as a reason for the great desire to avoid uncertainty, provide a degree of predictability, establish order, and maintain stability (Lord, 1998). Consequently, many rules and regulations were created in Germany in order to reduce uncertainty as much as possible (Hofstede & Hofstede, 2005).

It is generally assumed in Germany that these rules and regulations have proven their worth because they help minimize risks in advance which, in turn, results in the successful accomplishment of the task at hand and the creation of future stability (Schroll-Machl, 2002).

A History of Political Disunion

Germany has also a long history of regional autonomy (*Facts about Germany,* 1998; Herrmann, 1988; Jankuhn et al., 1983; Zentner, 1980). In fact, a unified country did not exist until 1871 which was divided again into two separate states for slightly more than 40 years after World War II (*Facts about Germany*, 1998; Herrmann, 1988). In other words, Germany has only been unified politically as a country for less than a century. With such political disunion, Germany has a very different tradition than neighboring countries like France or Denmark, for example (Zentner, 1980). Over time, this strong regional diversity led to many regions being associated with specific characteristics. For example, Swabians, who live in Southwestern Germany, are said to be frugal, Bavarians, who live in Southeastern Germany, are said to be jovial, and Northern Germans are said to be taciturn. This regional division is also reflected in the German constitution which guarantees the federal states a number of privileges and rights which sets Germany apart from many neighboring countries like France, Italy, or Denmark (*Facts about Germany*, 1998). The long history of political disunion also helps explain why to this day German companies have fairly autonomous departments and business units with little or no communication between the various organizational compartments of a company (Opitz, 2003).

Linguistic Diversity

The traditional division of Germany is also expressed in linguistic differences. The German language has three principal dialect groups, namely Low German in the north, Middle German in the center, and High German in the south (König, 1989; Waterman, 1976). The primary difference between the principal dialects is expressed by the consonant shift of *p, t, k* to *f, s, ch* so that Low German *peper, water, maken* become

High German *Pfeffer, Wasser, machen* (König, 1989; Waterman, 1976). The dialect difference is actually more complex and includes many regionally unique words and phrases and grammatical differences which make mutual understanding very difficult (König, 1989; Waterman, 1976). For example, the word *butcher* can be *Fleischer, Fleischhacker, Metzger,* or *Schlachter* depending on where one lives and works in Germany (König, 1989). And the grammatical gender of the noun *Cola* can be feminine, i.e., *die Cola*, or neuter, i.e., *das Cola* (*Duden*, 2006). In fact, it is often easier for a person from Northern Germany to understand a native of the Netherlands than a fellow German from Southern Germany. Since language is a symbolic expression of culture and classified as a cultural artifact (Klopf, 1998; Samovar et al., 1998), this linguistic variety of Germany clearly expresses the degree of regional cultural diversity in Germany.

Companies seeking to enter the German market need to take this linguistic diversity into consideration especially when the product names could result in misunderstandings, confusion, or even rejection. For example, the *potato* is called *Kartoffel* in Standard German as well as some parts of Northern Germany, but it is called *Grumbeere* in some parts of Western Germany, *Erdäpfel* in Southeastern Germany, *Nudel* in parts of Northeastern Germany to name only some variations because there are many others (König, 1989). One can well imagine what the consequences would be for a distributor of potatoes in Germany because the regional names are often unknown outside the respective regions. In fact, *Nudel* will result in a misunderstanding because in Standard German *Nudel* is a *noodle* and not a potato.

Religious Division

In addition to linguistic variety, German regional differences are also expressed by traditional religious differences. Germany has been divided roughly into a Protestant north and a Catholic south and west since the Reformation in the 16th century (Herrmann, 1988; Jankuhn et al., 1983; Zentner, 1980). And with German reunification, an atheistic east must be added—legacy of 40 years of communism (*Facts about Germany,* 1998). While most children in West Germany celebrate either communion or confirmation,

i.e., Christian ceremonies, most East German children celebrate the *Jugendweihe,* i.e., a secularized ceremony to admit adolescents into adult society. This regional difference in religion results in different public holidays throughout Germany because the majority of legal holidays in Germany are religious holidays. Consequently, a predominately Protestant state will be closed for business on different days throughout the year than a Catholic state in Germany. In the predominately Catholic Rhineland, for example, virtually all businesses shut down during the *Karneval,* i.e., Mardi gras, season which lasts for about a week. And the dichotomy of the German work ethic, i.e., working very hard on the job but also having six weeks of paid vacation per year and strictly separating work from pleasure, may also be explained by the broad mix of the Protestant work ethic and the Catholic *joie de vivre* found within Germany.

East and West Germany

East Germany looks back on 40 years of communism preceded by 12 years of Nazi dictatorship; this means that three generations of East Germans lived under totalitarianism. In West Germany, the 12 years of Hitler and the Holocaust were followed by 60 years of democracy and early integration into Western alliances such as NATO and the European Community (*Facts about Germany,* 1998). It is, therefore, not surprising that new regional differences evolved after World War II as well. While East Germans also point to differences among Saxons and Brandenburgers, there is also a transcending issue of East vs. West Germans, i.e., *Ossis* and *Wessis.*[6] This difference between East and West is reflected in a number of opinion polls and election results. The former communist party of East Germany, now called *Die Linke,* i.e., The Left, still racks up around a quarter to a third of all the votes in East Germany while in West Germany the same party gets only one vote in ten. During the last federal elections in 2009, for example, the Left party got 26.4 percent of the votes in East Germany and only 8.3 percent of the votes in West Germany which translates into 11.9 percent for all of Germany (ARD.de, 2009) since the population in West Germany is more than three times larger than in East Germany. While in West Germany the Left party only reached fifth place in among the five major

German political parties, they gained second place in East Germany—only three percent behind Chancellor Merkel's Christian Democrats[7] (CDU) and well ahead of the other three major political parties. The Left party actually ended up winning the most votes in two East German states, namely Brandenburg and Saxony Anhalt, and reached second place in the remaining three East German states, i.e., Mecklenburg Western Pomerania, Saxony, and Thuringia (ARD.de, 2009). These figures clearly speak volumes of the political division in East and West Germany. An interesting twist of the East–West division has recently emerged in the Left party where there was talk of an inner party divide between members from West and East Germany (Welt Online, 2010, January, 19).[8] Twenty years after German reunification, the majority of East Germans still do not identify themselves with the Federal Republic of Germany while the majority of West Germans do according to a recent survey (Siemon, 2007, March 22).

This political division has also created a different approach to work and what role the government should assume. While most West Germans would not work on Sundays or public, i.e., religious, holidays, East Germans typically do work on those days without such reservations. Compared to East Germans, most West Germans would be willing to take more risks which explains the greater proportion of entrepreneurship in West Germany. On the other hand, the many years of scarcity in East Germany resulted in more improvisation among East Germans than West Germans (Facts about Germany, 1998). But forty years of communism still seem to have left their legacy. A 2008 poll taken before the economic crisis, showed that 61 percent of East Germans felt the government did not provide enough guarantees to protect their jobs, 69 percent thought the government should do more about medical care, and 79 percent believed that the government needed to augment the state retirement program. In contrast to East Germans, West Germans did not expect the government to assume such a significant role in these matters believing that some private initiative is also needed (Sächsische Zeitung, 2008, March 26). In fact, most East Germans feel that social and welfare programs are more important than individual freedom; an opinion that is not shared by West Germans (Schuler, 2010, February 19).

Consensus and Parity

These strong regional differences probably also contributed to the use of so many rules and regulations in Germany because otherwise it would not have been possible to reach any consensus. In fact, Standard German can be considered an artificial dialect that combines a number of aspects from the principal dialects to achieve some degree of mutual comprehension (König, 1989; Waterman, 1976). But it also helps explain why consensus is so important to German culture because it helped establish a unified national identity. The concept of consensus and parity is even anchored in the German constitution, the *Grundgesetz*, i.e., the Basic Law (*Facts about Germany*, 1998). After World War II, when the Basic Law was written in West Germany, the notion of shared fiscal revenues was applied to the principle of state parity, i.e., the so-called *Länderausgleich*. This constitutional provision specifies that the rich federal states have to allocate a certain portion of their revenues to poorer states in order to assist the poorer states. This redistribution of wealth was designed to create economic parity among all the federal states so that no inhabitant would be forced to live in a state that offers fewer amenities than the other states (*Facts about Germany*, 1998).[9]

Not surprisingly, East Germany under communism went a step further and implemented a rigorous program of identical services and products throughout the entire country. Hence, regardless of regional traditions, a centralized system of uniformity was introduced and enforced in East Germany, and the social class system officially abolished (*Facts about Germany*, 1998; Herrmann, 1988). After German reunification, the principle of parity was extended to the new federals states in East Germany with the introduction of the Solidarity Pact which includes a special tax to help finance the enormous costs of German reunification so that the East German infrastructure is raised to West German standards in addition to the usual *Länderausgleich* (*Facts about Germany*, 1998). Consensus and parity are so ensconced in German thinking that it is also present in many aspects of German business culture including corporate policy and governance as will be shown below.

Government System

Germany is a federal republic, and regional differences play an important role in the German governmental system. The nationally elected parliament is called the *Bundestag*, and the party or parties having a parliamentary majority head the federal government under the leadership of the Federal Chancellor (*Facts about Germany*, 1998). The Chancellor, thus, automatically has a parliamentary majority in the *Bundestag*. All federal bills must be passed by a majority vote in the *Bundestag* (*Facts about Germany*, 1998). All legislation affecting the interests of the states must additionally be approved by the *Bundesrat*, the other legislative body which represents the interests of the states (*Facts about Germany*, 1998). Unlike the United States Senate, the German *Bundesrat* "does not consist of elected representatives of the people but of members of the state governments or their representatives" (*Facts about Germany*, 1998, p. 174). After a bill has passed the appropriate legislative chamber(s), it must be signed by the Federal President to become a law (*Facts about Germany*, 1998). The Federal President heads the German nation but not the federal government which is headed by the Federal Chancellor as noted above (*Facts about Germany*, 1998). Germany has, thus, two separate and distinct executive offices, i.e., one for matters of state and another for matters of government. The United States, in contrast, unites both executive positions in the office of the President. This division of the executive office into two separate offices with distinct duties and responsibilities is a feature that is repeated in many other German administrative organizations such as schools and universities as well as corporations while this is not the case in the United States.

Legal System

Not surprisingly, German and American laws are based on different legal principles. Traditionally, German law is code based while American law is case based (*Facts about Germany*, 1998; Howard, 1965).[10] German law seeks to anticipate illegal actions which have to be listed expressly in the legal code to be deemed illegal. If an action has not been anticipated and, thus, is not included in the legal code, it is not considered to be illegal.[11] The German legal code, therefore, has to be constantly amended in order to keep abreast of changes in society or technology. This is different from law in the United States which applies the principle of analogy (Howard, 1965). Thus, for example, legal provisions regulating horse-drawn carriages were interpreted in the United States to also include automobiles when cars first appeared on America's roads since horse-drawn carriages and horseless carriages are both road vehicles designed to transport people. In Germany, the traffic law had to be amended expressly to also include automobiles. Something similar occurred with copyright regulations and the introduction of new technologies such as photocopiers, computers, and MP3 players. In each instance, the German legal code had to be amended; in some cases the amendments got amended. German law, therefore, seeks to establish great precision which usually results in very comprehensive (and cumbersome) legal codes. Hence, the German legal principle conforms to the general concept prevalent in Germany of attempting to break everything down to the most precise subcategory possible which is designed to reduce uncertainty. By breaking everything down to the smallest possible category, it is assumed that the size of the problem is also reduced and, thus, making the problem more manageable.

Educational System

Education is important in shaping and transmitting culture (Chen & Starosta, 1998, Gudykunst & Kim, 1997; Klopf, 1998, Samovar et al., 1998). Not surprisingly, the German educational system reflects the regional differences of Germany as well because education is a matter of the individual states as specified by the Basic Law (*Facts about Germany*, 1998).[12] At the same time, there are also a number of similarities for all German states that are, to some degree, quite unique to Germany. Most German states decide during the fourth grade, i.e., when children are nine or ten years old, which type of secondary school a child is to attend. There are typically three types of secondary school in Germany: The *Hauptschule,* which is to prepare students for vocational careers, the *Realschule*, which is to prepare students for clerical positions, and the *Gymnasium*, which is to prepare students for university studies (*Facts about Germany,* 1998). Theoretically, it is possible for students of both the *Hauptschule* and *Realschule* to also attend universities (*Facts about Germany,* 1998), but in practice it does not happen very often. Thus, effectively barring the majority of students from university studies which is one reason why the United Nations criticized the German secondary education system a few years ago (*Sächsische Zeitung,* 2007, March 22). This educational segmentation is also continued in the apprenticeship and trainee programs in which adolescents are trained for a very specific, albeit highly qualified vocation (*Facts about Germany,* 1998). Even the university education is typically based on narrowly focused degrees which revolve around curricula that only contain courses of the subject in question. So if someone majors in mathematics, that person will typically only need to take math courses. As a consequence, the German educational system—at the primary, secondary, vocational, and college level—produces highly specialized professionals while essentially shunning a general, broader, interdisciplinary education.[13]

Labor Market

Because German employees have typically been trained in very narrowly defined vocations and professions, it is often difficult to switch job fields since the employees do not have comparable skills and training in another occupation. In fact, German employers look for job candidates who fit precisely the job description contained in the wanted ads because these descriptions had been created based on the standardized occupational qualification. This is very different from the United States where it is generally assumed that not all applicants will be able to meet all specifications. Instead, it is frequently assumed that candidates will be able to acquire the necessary skills in due time while learning on the job. This, in part, explains why some unemployed in Germany have become chronic unemployed because these people had originally been trained in vocations for which there are no longer sufficient jobs available since these occupations have been superseded by new technology and/or outsourced to countries with lower wages. At the same time, Germany lacks skilled employees in other job fields—typically in newly created high-tech vocations for which the educational system has not been able to generate sufficient graduates yet.

GERMAN BUSINESS CULTURE

The above excursion into German culture provides an explanation and understanding of German business culture since both are intimately entwined with one another. It is, thus, not surprising that most German businesses tend to have a fairly strict division among its staff into blue and white collar employees, and also between white collar clerical positions and management posts (Hofstede & Hofstede, 2005). Trompenaars and Hampden-Turner (1998), therefore, classify German corporations as bureaucratic organizations in which personal relations play a minor role because the focus is on the tasks at hand. According to Trompenaars and Hampden-Turner (1998), German corporate careers are based on professional qualifications. "Manpower planning, assessment centers, appraisal systems, training schemes and job rotation all have the function of helping to classify and produce resources to fit known roles" (Trompenaars & Hampden-Turner, 1998, p. 174). Since one of the tasks of education is to provide the right training of potential employees for the job market, it becomes clear why the German educational system pursues a highly segmented educational approach so that these specific occupations can be filled with employees meeting precisely those specified qualifications.

Problem Solving

The problem solving methods conveyed in German schools focus not so much on finding a solution; instead, emphasis is placed on outlining and following the proper steps to a solution. Thus, the actual solution to a math problem, for example, will be awarded with only a small percentage of the points for the right answer while the majority of the points will go to the application of the right steps.[14] This explains why in a business context, so much emphasis is put on finding the right steps to a solution. Americans tend to get irritated because Germans take considerable time for deliberations and reaching decisions. But Germans feel that it is necessary to consider and discuss at length all variables before reaching any decisions. After all, most Germans are interested in finding long-term solutions. Americans, in contrast, tend to be more interested in getting short-term results; hence, explaining why American corporations publish quarterly results and German companies traditionally annual results.[15] And if a plan does not work, it is quickly replaced by a new one. This may be best illustrated by the approach to house building. While many houses in the United States are built with frame construction, dry walls, and asphalt roof shingles in a relatively short period of time, most German houses are built with reinforced concrete, bricks, and cement roof tiles. Consequently, house construction typically takes much longer in Germany than in the United States. In Germany, most people still feel that a house has to be built to last for a long time so that future generations can continue to live in it as well. From a German perspective, this makes sense since the marked regional differences traditionally led many people to stay close to their home because it is there where people speak the same dialect and practice the same religion. While this has been changing, most Germans would still prefer to stay in the home region if given a choice.[16]

Business Organizations

German corporations, not surprisingly, have a different organizational structure than U.S. corporations. Traditionally, stock markets played a minor role in the acquisition of capital in Germany. Consequently, only a small proportion of businesses in Germany are organized as a corporation (Wentges, 2002). Other reasons for the relatively small percentage of corporations in Germany include the many corporate regulations, the partial loss of control, tax disadvantages, and considerable codetermination of employees in Germany (Nassauer, 2000). Most of the capital for German businesses is provided by banks (Emmons & Schmid, 1998). It was actually the German banks which provided the capital to the growing industrial enterprises in the nineteenth century when German industrialization began. Since private citizens did not have the capital, and well developed stock markets did not yet exist, banks were the only source of capital in Germany at that time (Nassauer, 2000). Consequently, banks often

have direct influence on German companies that goes well beyond the typical American creditor–company relationship. That is why it is not surprising for banks to be represented in virtually all of the large German corporations (Emmons & Schmid, 1998).

German Corporations

German corporations are controlled by two boards, the *Vorstand*, i.e., management board, which is responsible for managing the company, and the *Aufsichtsrat*, i.e., supervisory board, which exercises control over the management. According to German corporate law, management and control of a company must be exercised separately in companies having more than 500 employees (*Facts about Germany,* 1998; Nassauer, 2000). The assumption is that management does not necessarily pursue the interests of shareholders and, therefore, requires an independent board which acts as a counterbalance to management's power (*Facts about Germany,* 1998; Nassauer, 2000); thus, applying the principle of parity.

The *Vorstand* is empowered to run the business and, thus, formulates and implements the business strategies. It also represents the company externally (Conyon & Schwalbach, 1999; *Facts about Germany,* 1998; Wentges, 2002). The *Vorstand* can consist of one or more executives. Generally, all members of the *Vorstand* are jointly responsible for decisions or actions of a corporation. In practice, though, each member of the *Vorstand* has special duties and competencies in specific business sectors (Wentges, 2002) which conforms to the German desire to segment everything according to areas of expertise. The members of the *Vorstand* are appointed by the *Ausichtsrat* for a maximum term of five years (Conyon & Schwalbach, 1999; Emmons & Schmid, 1998). Reappointments are possible (Emmons & Schmid, 1998). Once a year, the *Vorstand* has to report to the *Ausichtsrat* on the current state and the intended business policy (Conyon & Schwalbach, 1999).

The *Ausichtsrat* monitors the activities of the *Vorstand.* In order to match the requirements of separating the decision-making process and control, the *Aufsichtsrat* is not empowered to run a business (*Facts about Germany,* 1998; Wentges, 2002). Nevertheless, some activities by the management do require approval of the *Aufsichtsrat*. The *Aufsichtsrat* consists of 3 to 21 members, depending on the size of the corporation (*Facts about Germany*, 1998; Nassuer, 2000). While the members of the *Aufsichtsrat* are classified as non-executives, many former CEOs of the company usually chair the *Aufsichtsrat* (Emmons & Schmid, 1998).

The *Mitbestimmungsgesetz*, i.e., the codetermination act, of 1976 introduced the requirement to have employees in the *Aufsichtsrat*. In corporations of more than 500 employees, one-third of the *Aufsichtsrat* have to be employees; in corporations of more than 2,000 employees, that number increases to half (Conyon & Schwalbach, 1999; *Facts about Germany*, 1998; Nassauer, 2000).[17] The remaining members of the *Aufsichtsrat* are elected by the shareholders at the annual shareholder's meeting. This principle of including employees in corporate governance conforms once again to the German principle of consensus and parity. The main duties of the *Aufsichtsrat* are the nomination and discharge of the members of the *Vorstand* and the appointment of the corporate auditor (Wentges, 2002). The *Aufsichtsrat* has considerable rights to receive information in order to effectively monitor the *Vorstand's* activities and fixes the compensation of the corporate executives (Nassauer, 2000).

In contrast, American corporations do not have a two-tier board system in which corporate management and control are separated; instead, a single board of directors is responsible for running the company (Wentges, 2002). Corporations make up about 20 percent of all business types in the United States which is a much higher proportion than in Germany (Nassauer, 2000). This is primarily due to the fact that no minimum capital is needed to found a corporation in the United States (Nassauer, 2000). In addition, it is quite common for private individuals to risk investing in businesses or even business ideas in the United States. Consequently, banks play a smaller role for and in U.S. American corporations than they do in Germany (Nassauer, 2000).

In the United States, the board of directors is responsible for running a corporation. The board is responsible for both the management of the company and the control of the management; it typically consists of eleven to thirteen members (Nassauer, 2000). The board is elected at the annual shareholders' meeting, but it is an independent entity that can reach decisions without following the instructions of the shareholders (Wentges, 2002). The board is responsible for setting the corporation's strategies, controlling the executive officers, nominating the Chief Executive Officer (CEO), and determining executive compensation (Wentges, 2002). The management team of a U.S. corporation is headed by the chief executive officer (CEO) who is superior to all the other managers and usually chairs the board (Witt, 2002). The CEO is usually also the center of public attention since the CEO is typically identified with the corporation (Witt, 2002). Thus, the CEO has a very powerful and encompassing position when compared to the head of a German corporation.

Wages and Salaries

Wages and salaries of German employees are typically fixed by so-called collective tariff agreements which are negotiated between trade union representatives and the representatives of the employers' association of a particular industrial and/or service branch; for example, the metal industry which includes the automobile industry (*Facts about Germany,* 1998). These agreements regulate, for example, the wages and salaries, the working hours, holidays, minimum notice, overtime rates, and apply them to all enterprises of that particular branch in that particular region of Germany (*Facts about Germany*, 1998), thus, establishing parity among all employees in the same sector. This system essentially serves to keep employees tied to a particular employer since it would make little sense to switch employers because one would continue to earn the same pay for the same occupation elsewhere. And since German employees are typically qualified for a specific job field, it is not easy to switch to another job field without proper qualifications as noted above. Likewise, the tariff system reduces the need for strikes which helps reduce uncertainty for both sides. Compared to other European countries, Germany has relatively few strikes. This is usually ascribed to the collective tariff system and the principle of codetermination (*Facts about Germany*, 1998), i.e., consensus.

Thus, it is not surprising that German business culture reflects many aspects of German culture. Indeed, national culture often serves as a model for corporate culture. So it is not surprising that German corporations are headed by two distinct governing bodies which mirrors the division of power in the German executive branch while U.S. American corporations only have one governing body which reflects the single executive branch. And it is also not surprising that the notion of parity and consensus is incorporated into German corporate governance, i.e., the representation of the employees in the *Aufsichtsrat*, since it is a fundamental principle of the German Basic Law.

THE INTERRELATIONSHIP OF CULTURE AND BUSINESS CONDUCT

While some people might notice some differences in corporate structure and organization, few would assume that work routines and thinking processes differ across cultures—after all, business is business no matter where it is conducted on the globe. Yet, it is precisely these subtle differences that lead to misunderstandings, frustration, and even anger in many international business alliances (Harris & Moran, 1996; Hofstede & Hofstede, 2005; Trompenaars & Hampden-Turner, 1998).

Task Oriented

Germans, like U.S. Americans, are very task oriented. But, in Germany, as noted above, the specific expertise of individuals is also considered to be very important because it is assumed that such expertise leads to the best possible results. Consequently, Germans will usually argue and try and convince others with facts and data (Schroll-Machl, 2002). This explains why German presentations (and applications) will contain as many facts and as much data as possible because the more facts and data one presents, the more convincing one will be. Germans do not like to make mistakes because they are expected to be experts in their field of specialization. Should, therefore, someone present the wrong facts and figures, then that person will be disrespected because that person occupies a position for which he or she does not have sufficient expertise. Consequently, most Germans do not like to admit to having made a mistake (Lord, 1998) because mistakes result in uncertainty—something most Germans would like to avoid. While Americans will also use facts and figures, they will appeal to people's ideals and emotions

as well; especially if they are attempting to motivate others (Lewis, 2000). Germans, in contrast, consider emotions to be unprofessional in a business context because emotions are neither tangible nor objective and, thus, distort the facts.

Relationships

Germans tend to strictly separate business relationships from private relationships. A friendly atmosphere at work and getting along with others in a business context is considered to be a nice side effect, but it is not really essential for a successful interaction in Germany (Schroll-Machl, 2002). Indeed, it is not uncommon for German colleagues to use the formal *Sie* and the last name with title when addressing and conversing with one another even though they may have worked together for many years. The use of titles is another expression of uncertainty avoidance and also of a larger power distance. If someone has a title or titles, then that person will be addressed by that/those title(s). Titles appear on bank cards, driver's licenses, and ID cards, etc. Titles identify a person's status and background; thus, identifying a person's qualifications, competence, and rank within a corporate and social hierarchy at a glance.

Time Management

Germans are very punctual and tend to be very monochronic in their work routine. In business appointments, most Germans would expect an apology if one is more than one minute late.[18] That is why most Germans will make an effort to actually arrive ahead of the appointed time. Time is considered to be very important like in the United States, but it also leads most Germans to consider small talk to be a waste of time in a business context since it has nothing to do directly with the task at hand. Presentations and meetings, consequently, will commence immediately with the business at hand (Lewis, 2000). When Germans make appointments, they do not reconfirm them—even if the appointment is made half a year in advance; this reinforces reliability and avoids uncertainty. One usually only contacts the other party if one needs to cancel or postpone the appointed meeting. Germans tend to first finish a particular task or assignment completely before commencing with another task or assignment (Lewis, 2000). This tenacious approach is often also found in product development which translates into product improvement in Germany. The aim is to achieve absolute perfection and precision in any product or product family. This, in part, explains the excellent reputation German precision products and engineering have in many parts of the world.

Information Flow

Another typical German characteristic is the monopolization of information. Consequently, there is little free flow of information between departments of a company, i.e., horizontal communication, and between the various hierarchical levels, i.e., vertical communication.[19] German companies are traditionally very compartmentalized and often closed to outsiders. This might also explain why office doors are usually closed in German companies unlike American companies where employees walk down the hall to exchange information with their colleagues (Lewis, 2000). In fact, this different "door policy" illustrates how cultural patterns influence people's thinking and behavior. When, for example, American visitors enter a typical German office building and encounter closed doors, the Americans might assume that the office doors have been closed because no one is to overhear the conversations inside the offices as is often the case in the United States. If those American visitors came to the German company to negotiate a deal, then the visitors may think that the Germans are deliberately trying to hide something from them. Consequently, the Americans may assume that the negotiations will be difficult, troublesome, and tricky. During the subsequent meeting, this negative predisposition of the Americans could result in a negative interpretation of everything the Germans say or seem to say and do even though that is not the intention of the Germans. Hence, this makes for a difficult meeting because the Americans will be wary and suspicious while the Germans will be wondering why the Americans are behaving so strangely. This could, in turn, make the Germans wary and suspicious of the Americans' intentions; thus, creating a detrimental chain reaction.

Business Meetings and Negotiations

As noted above, Germans like to be well prepared for a meeting which often, though, translates into a lack of spontaneity. Not surprisingly, brainstorming sessions are quite rare in Germany (LeMont Schmidt, 2001). Because Germans have researched a subject and prepared themselves in great detail for a meeting, they are often inflexible in responding to unanticipated questions. When, for example, it comes to negotiating the price, most Germans are only willing to consider a divergence of ten percent from the asking price since they will have considered all aspects and determined precisely the exact price of an item in advance and, thus, see no reason to continue haggling over the price (Otte, 1996; Hill, 1998). This reduces the uncertainty of a bargaining session and saves precious time.

German American Group Work

The following example describes the different approaches typically employed by Germans and Americans when they work together in a group. Germans like to have an initial and comprehensive understanding of all aspects associated with a problem. This means that any and all details, including potential possibilities and possible unintended consequences are considered. Hence, existing approaches and solutions play an important role while new ideas are considered and evaluated critically. This evaluation process is carried out within a group. When it is assumed that all aspects have been considered and discussed, then tasks will be assigned to the group members according to their field of expertise and experience. This ends the planning phase (Schroll-Machl, 1995). Next follows the execution phase during which everyone works alone with little or no exchange of information. There is little or no need to meet and talk because everything had been discussed during the initial planning phase, including anticipated possibilities. Therefore, repetition would be a waste of valuable time. And since everyone is a specialist in their own field, there is little need to talk with others because the others would not be able to make a valuable contribution as they lack expertise outside their field of specialization. Subsequent meetings are, thus, only necessary if an intermediate meeting had been scheduled previously, or if there is an unanticipated problem. But alterations to any previously fixed details are rarely done and not liked since it indicates that the initial planning had been insufficient and, therefore, inexpert (Schroll-Machl, 1995; Gibson, 2000).

Americans, in contrast, like to focus on the goal after having been assigned a task. This is usually done in the form of brainstorming in which the group members present their thoughts and ideas. Once the goal has been determined, the group decides on a plan of action to solve the problem at hand. The group leader assigns the various tasks to the group members which ends the planning phase. The execution of the plan begins when every group member creates a detailed work plan. The experiences of the group members are applied in solving the problem. The group members often consult with one another on how to best solve the problem. This results in very active communication and a lively exchange of information among all group members while there is constant feedback on whether or not a solution leads to the desired goal. The exchange of information occurs also with one's superiors. The initial plan of action can be changed any time if it proves to be necessary and the goal becomes untenable (Schroll-Machl, 1995; Gibson, 2000).

The above example clearly illustrates that Germans and Americans use different approaches in tackling problems despite the fact that they are actually much closer to each other culturally than to Chinese or Japanese culture, for example. The brainstorming session would probably cause difficulties for German group members since it is not typically applied in Germany while the detailed discussion of possible and anticipated problems would seem to be too detailed for American group members. This attitude would be frowned upon by the German group members who would consider Americans to be too superficial and imprecise. The isolated work environment with little or no contact to other group members and virtually no feedback from one's supervisors would seem problematic to Americans because information exchange and communication are of paramount importance in solving any problem. To the Germans, this need for communication and feedback would simply signify that either the initial planning was faulty and superficial, or that the American colleagues are not as expert as they claim to be; otherwise, they should have been able to solve the problem

at hand. Consequently, both Germans and Americans would be frustrated because the group work did not lead to any concrete results. But the reasons for these feelings would be different as indicated above.

CONCLUDING REMARKS

The more one studies German and American business cultures, the more one will notice differences that become apparent not only in the artifacts of both business cultures, but also in their respective sociofacts and mentifacts. That is why one needs to be aware of these subtle, but decisive cultural differences. If, however, someone lacks this awareness, then it can result in frustration because that person does not know why the others are behaving and/or communicating the way they are. Viewed and evaluated from one's own cultural perspective, the behavior of the others can be seen as inefficient and ineffective, even wrong. So awareness can foster understanding. Understanding, though, is only possible if one is aware of the fact that cultural differences exist also in the world of business and that these cultural differences influence the way people conduct their business. With proper understanding, though, it is possible to overcome these differences and to foster mutually profitable business relationships across diverse cultures.

Notes

1. It should also be remembered that most business partners seek contact with potential partners because each side hopes to benefit in some form from this relationship. This beneficial end goal tends to also have an impact on the interpretation and evaluation of the communicated messages by both sides, i.e., it tends to make the initial interpretation positive as long as you assume that you are not being cheated. In fact, this positive association is usually applied to the general transactional relationship that is in the process of being established.

2. These American English words were taken from *Webster's New World College Dictionary* (2001), 4th edition.

3. These German words were taken from *Duden* (2006), 6th edition.

4. VW even tried to improve the lagging sales by changing the car's name in Germany from Jetta to initially Vento and later Bora, but without success. In the USA, VW kept the name for all Jetta generations.

5. It will be assumed that the reader is somewhat familiar with American culture, but not German culture. In fact, Samovar et al.'s *Communication between Cultures* makes numerous references to and includes many examples taken from American history. That is why the focus will be on German culture which will, though, be compared to and contrasted with American culture to illustrate the differences in both.

6. Interestingly, some of the stereotypes associated with *Wessis* parallel those associated with Yankee carpetbaggers during Reconstruction in the American South.

7. It will be recalled that Chancellor Merkel is herself a native of East Germany.

8. This is actually a bit ironic because the communist party wants to transcend class and national barriers; after all, their party anthem is *The Internationale*.

9. This principle of economic parity reaches down all the way to local municipalities in counties where richer communities have to help finance poorer communities (*Sächsische Zeitung*, March 27, 2007).

10. A legal code refers to laws, statutes, and regulations that have been enacted and are codified in books whereas legal cases refer to court cases that establish a legal precedent and tradition on which the law of the land is based—these cases may, though, also be recorded in books.

11. This can create a dilemma as a recent case of cannibalism illustrates. The German criminal code does not expressly forbid cannibalism since no one had thought this would happen in modern Germany. Consequently, when a person actually did commit an act of cannibalism recently, it was not possible to convict the person of cannibalism since it had not been declared illegal. The criminal court could only rule on manslaughter.

12. This regional difference is particularly noticeable at the secondary level since the states have different curricula. Consequently, it is difficult for children to overcome this gap which is why most German parents are wary of moving their families to a different state.

13. This is also expressed in the application documents. German application documents are very different from typical American application documents. A German resume contains detailed personal information including a photograph of the candidate, the date of birth and place of birth, marital status as well as the occupation of the parents, and even the religion of the applicant. The education section describes in detail all school types starting with the primary school while the employment section only mentions the dates of employment, the place of employment, and the occupation. A detailed job description, so typical of American resumes, is not needed because the job title suffices since German

employers will know exactly what qualifications and skills that job entails. In addition to the resume and cover letter, German applications need to also include certified copies of any and all relevant documents, certificates, degrees, letters of reference, etc.

14. This information is based on what the author was told in a number of conversations with German students.

15. German corporations listed, for example, on the New York Stock Exchange have to, of course, conform to American law when it comes to financial statements and their publication.

16. This information is based on information ascertained from a number of conversations with Germans in various regions. All expressed a strong attachment to their home region; in part, due to linguistic and religious reasons as well as due to close ties to family and friends.

17. In fact, all German companies need to have works councils, i.e., *Betriebsrat*, which are a permanent fixture in the companies. These works councils have to approve "all matters concerning personnel, such as hiring, job classifications, departmental restructuring and transfers" (*Facts about Germany*, 1998, p. 393).

18. This maximum of one minute was confirmed in many conversations with German executives.

19. Proudfoot Consulting calculated lost productivity due to improper or lack of communication in German corporations at $223.1 billion in 2001 which translates into 14.9% of the German GDP (see Optiz, 2003, for details). The figures are similar even today.

References

Adler, R. B., & Rodman, G. (2003). *Understanding human communication*. 8th ed. New York: Oxford University Press.

ARD.de (2009). Die Ergebnisse der Bundeswahl im Überblick. Retrieved from the World Wide Web on February 18, 2010: www.tagesschau.de/wahl

Chen, G-M., & Starosta, W. J. (1998). *Foundations of intercultural communication*. Boston: Allyn and Bacon.

Conyon, M. J., & Schwalbach, J. (1999). Corporate governance, executive pay and performance in Europe. In J. Carpenter & D. Yermack (Eds.), *Executive compensation and shareholder value: Theory and evidence* (pp. 13–33). Dordrecht: Kluwer Academic Publishers.

De Mooij, M. (2007). The reflection of culture in a global business and marketing strategy. In M. B. Hinner (Ed.), *The influence of culture in the world of business* (pp. 343–356). Frankfurt am Main: Peter Lang.

Duden. (2006). Mannheim: Dudenverlag.

Edmunds Auto Observer. (2007, May 17). Daimler-Chrysler: Why the marriage failed. Retrieved from the World Wide

Web on August 18, 2008: www.autoobserver.com/2007/05/daimler-chrysler-why-the-marriage-failed.html

Emmons, W. R., & Schmid, F. A. (1998). Universal banking, control rights, and corporate finance in Germany. *Federal Reserve Bank of St. Louis Review* 80.

Facts about Germany. (1998). Frankfurt am Main: Societäts Ver.

Gibson, R. (2000). *Intercultural business communication.* Berlin: Cornelsen & Oxford University Press GmbH & Co.

Gudykunst, W. B., & Kim, Y. Y. (1997). *Communicating with strangers: An approach to intercultural communication.* 3rd ed. Boston: McGraw Hill.

Harris, P. R., & Moran, R. T. (1996). *Managing cultural differences: Leadership strategies for a new world of business.* 4th ed. Houston: Gulf Publishing Company.

Herrmann, J., ed. (1988). *Deutsche Geschichte in 10 Kapiteln.* Berlin: Akademie-Verlag.

Hill, R. (1998). *EuroManagers & Martinis.* Brussels: Europlublic SA/NV.

Hinner, M. B. (1998). The importance of intercultural communication in a globalized world. *Freiberger Arbeitspapiere der Fakultät für Wirtschaftswissenschaften* 06.

Hinner, M. B. (2004). Culture and product integration. *German American Trade* 15(7), pp. 19–21.

Hinner, M. B. (2005). Can quality communication improve business relationships? In M. B. Hinner (Ed.), *Introduction to business communication* (pp. 15–40). Frankfurt am Main: Peter Lang.

Hinner, M. B., & Rülke, T. (2002). Intercultural communication in business ventures illustrated by two case studies. *Freiberger Arbeitspapiere der Fakultät für Wirtschaftswissenschaften* 03.

Hofstede, G. (2005). The universal and the specific in 21st century management. In M. B. Hinner (Ed.), *Introduction to business communication* (pp. 273–286). Frankfurt am Main: Peter Lang.

Hofstede, G., & Hofstede, J. G. (2005). *Cultures and organizations: Software of the mind.* New York: McGraw Hill.

Homburg, C. & Krohmer, H. (2003) *Marketing Management: Strategie. Instrument-Umsetzung-Unternehmensführung.* Wiesbaden: Gabler Verlag.

Howard, L. B. (1965). *Business law: An introduction.* Woodbury: Barron's Educational Series, Inc.

Jankuhn, H., Boockmann, H., & Treue, W., eds. (1983). *Deutsche Geschichte in Bildern von der Urzeit bis zur Gegenwart.* Wiesbaden: Verlag für Wissenschaft und Forschung – AULA GmbH.

Klopf, D. W. (1998). *Intercultural encounters: The fundamentals of intercultural communication.* 4th ed. Englewood: Morton Publishing Company.

König, W. (1989). *Dtv-Atlas zur deutschen Sprache.* 7th ed. Munich: Deutscher Taschenbuch Verlag.

LeMont Schmidt, P. (2001). *Die amerikanische und die deutsche Wirtschaftskultur im Vergleich: Ein Praxisbuch für Manager.* 3rd ed. Göttingen: Hainholz Verlag.

Lewis, R. D. (2000). *Handbuch internationale Kompetenz: Mehr Erfolg durch den richtigen Umgang mit Geschäftspartnern weltweit.* Frankfurt am Main: Campus Verlag.

Lord, R. (1998). *Culture shock! Germany: Guide to customs and etiquette.* Portland: Graphic Arts Center Publishing Company.

Lustig, M. W., & Koester, J. (2006). *Intercultural competence: Interpersonal communication across cultures.* 5th ed. Boston: Pearson Education, Inc.

Martin, J. N., & Nakayama, T. K. (1997). *Intercultural communication in contexts.* Mountain View: Mayfield Publishing Company.

Meffert, H. (2000). *Marketing-Grundlagen Marktorientierter Unternehmensführung.* Wiesbaden: Gabler Verlag.

Nassauer, F. (2000). *Corporate Governance und die Internationalisierung von Unternehmungen.* Frankfurt am Main: Peter Lang.

Oetzel, J. G. (2009. *Intercultural communication: A layered approach.* New York: Pearson Education, Inc.

Opitz, I. (2003). Good internal communication increases productivity. *Freiberger Arbeitspapiere der Fakultät für Wirtschaftswissenschaften* 07.

Otte, M. (1996). *Amerika für Geschäftsleute: Das Einmaleins der ungeschriebenen Regeln.* Frankfurt am Main: Campus Verlag.

Sächsische Zeitung. (2007, March 22). Uno kritisiert das deutsche Schulsystem, pp. 1 + 4.

Sächsische Zeitung. (2007, March 27). Firmen zahlen kräftig Steuern, p. 13.

Sächsische Zeitung. (2008, March 26). Im Osten ist die Hälfte unzufrieden, p. 2.

Samovar, L. A., Porter, R. E., & Stefani, L. A. (1998). *Communication between cultures.* 3rd ed. Belmont: Wadsworth Publishing Company.

Schroll-Machl, S. (1995). Die Zusammenarbeit in internationalen Teams–Eine interkulturelle Herausforderung dargestellt am Beispiel USA–Deutschland. In J. M. Scholz (Ed.), *Internationales Change-Management: Internationale Praxiserfahrungen bei der Veränderung von Untenehmen und Humanressourcen* (pp. 201–222). Stuttgart: Schäffer-Poeschel Verlag.

Schroll-Machl, S. (2002). *Die Deutschen–Wir Deutsche: Fremdwahrnehmung und Selbstsicht im Berufsleben.* Göttingen: Vandenhoeck & Ruprecht.

Schuler, R. (2010, February 19). Wie geschmacklos ist der Osten? *Sächsische Zeitung,* p. 5.

Siemon, P. (2007, March 22). Langzeitstudie in Sachsen: Nostalgische Rückkehr zu sozialistischen Idealen. In

Dresdener Morgenpost. Retrieved from the World Wide Web on March 26, 2007: www.wiedervereinigung.de/sls/PDF/mopo220307.pdf

Trompenaars, F., & Hampden-Turner, C. (1998). *Riding the waves of culture: Understanding diversity in global business.* 2nd ed. New York: McGraw Hill.

Waterman, J. T. (1976). *A history of the German language.* Revised ed. Seattle: University of Washington Press.

Welt Online. (2010, January 19). Ost-West-Debatte: Lafontaine warnt vor Spaltung der Linken. Retrieved from the World Wide Web on February 18, 2010: www.welt.de/politik/Deutschland/artikel5911997/Lafontaine-warnt-vor-Spaltung-der-Linken.html

Wentges, P. (2002). *Corporate Governance und Stakeholder Ansatz: Implikationen für die betriebliche Finanzierung.* Wiesbaden: Deutscher Universitätsverlag.

Witt, P. (2002). Grundeprobleme der corporate governance und international unterschiedliche Lösungsansätze. In M. Nippa, K. Petzold, & W. Kursten (Eds.), *Corporate governance: Herausforderungen und Lösungsansätze* (pp. 41-72). Heidelberg: Physica-Verlag.

Zentner, C. (1980). *Geschichtsführer in Farbe: Weltgeschichte in Bildern, Daten, Fakten.* München: Delphin Verlag GmbH.

Concepts and Questions

1. How might the similarities between American and German business cultures affect intercultural communication?

2. What does Hinner mean when he writes about external and hidden cultural differences? How can these differences affect product marketing?

3. How does the history of Germany influence the culture of German business organizations?

4. In what ways does the tradition of regional autonomy influence German business culture?

5. How do the bases of American and German law compare? How do these differences contribute to the distinct business cultures found in each country?

6. In what ways does the German educational system differ from that of the United States? How does the German education system support German business?

7. Describe how German culture's emphasis on order and hierarchy is displayed in the division of employees in business organizations.

8. What are the differences between German and American corporate organization? How do these differences affect communication within and between German and American businesses?

9. List the advantages and disadvantages of the German corporate system of simultaneously operating under two different boards of directors. Would such a system be effective in the United States?

THE EDUCATION CONTEXT

Intercultural Communication in the University Classroom

LISA M. SKOW

LAURIE STEPHAN

INTRODUCTION

The university is a setting in which, for the first time in their lives, most students will encounter a community comprising people from many different countries and ethnic communities in the United States. Many of your own classmates may be from Japan, Denmark, Poland, India, or Australia, or from areas of the United States about which you've only heard or read. You might be an international student studying in the United States as a member of the multinational university community on your campus. Some of your instructors, too, may be from diverse countries and cultural communities, and they often bring to their classrooms a host of experiences and views that contribute in significant and unique ways to your learning. It is nearly impossible that university students in the United States would finish their degrees without meeting and interacting with people from countries and cultures other than their own.

With such a diverse community of learners and teachers, communication in the classroom can be exhilarating and yet sometimes problematic. At times, the best intentions of teachers to reach their students are ineffective because their methods of instruction may not reach certain groups in multicultural

Courtesy of Lisa M. Skow and Laurie Stephan. This original essay has appeared in several past editions of this book. All rights reserved. Permission to reprint must be obtained from the authors and the publisher. Lisa M. Skow is Clinical Assistant Professor in the Department of Health Service, School of Public Health, University of Washington. Laurie Stephan is Program Manager, Biosource-based Energy for Sustainable Societies at the University of Washington.

classrooms. And of equal concern is when students lack an understanding of the teaching methods or communication style used by international college instructors. Culture strongly influences how we learn and teach, and it is a significant factor in shaping how students and teachers communicate to accomplish teaching and learning. Educational systems are developed based on norms of communication practiced by individual societies. In an international and multicultural classroom, students and teachers may disagree on appropriate ways of engaging in discussion, or even about whether to discuss at all. Rules of formality versus informality (i.e., raising hands to speak) or nonverbal ways of signaling confusion to the teacher (i.e., silence or inquisitive looks) are often culturally determined. Thus, although the international and multicultural university classroom offers a variety of benefits to students, students and teachers need to make greater efforts to understand how cultural differences influence communication and learning processes. This article has been written with this goal in mind.

Note that we have included increasing understanding for both students and teachers in our objective. As with any form or context of communication, the classroom is a place where communication occurs among many people and, therefore, the communication that is created and the relationships that are built are the responsibility of all members of a classroom. Each day in the multicultural classroom is an intercultural event that includes teachers and students trying to teach and learn from one another; when we are involved in an event, we each have a stake in the outcome. So as you read this article, think about your own role in the intercultural events you engage in each time you walk into a college classroom. What is happening communicatively to promote or hinder learning? Are there cultural ways of understanding what is taking place among students and teachers? What are you doing to contribute to this cross-cultural understanding?

First, we will take a look at the trends in the United States that have seen increasing numbers of international graduate students and international teaching faculty on U.S. campuses. You will notice that it is increasingly likely that undergraduates at major universities will have instructors from other countries at some point during their educational careers. Then we

will move into a discussion of the variety of dynamics that can come into play in the intercultural classroom and provide opportunities for you to apply what you've learned to actual intercultural scenarios.

THE INTERNATIONAL PRESENCE ON U.S. CAMPUSES

We've stated the importance of examining intercultural communication in university classrooms because of the strong likelihood that undergraduates will have teachers from other cultures and nations. But just how internationalized are our universities in the United States? From what countries and cultures do international instructors arrive?

In the past twenty-five years, there has been a general increase in the number of international students studying at U.S. universities. Whereas 489,000 international students were enrolled during the 1992–93 academic year, only slightly more than 34,000 international students were studying in the United States in 1955 (Institute of International Education, 1992–93). Although this may sound like a substantial increase, international students today represent only approximately 3 percent of the total U.S. university student population (Goodman, 1996). When we compare this figure to France, where international students make up approximately 12 percent of the total university student population, the United States can be seen overall to have a significantly lower international student body attending its universities (Crossing pedagogical oceans, 1991). Still, a crucial, undeniable international presence is evident on university campuses throughout the United States. "From the perspective of a teacher...foreign students are vital to the quality of teaching and to the learning process itself" (Goodman, 1996, p. A52).

During the 1992–93 academic year, approximately 44 percent of the international students in the United States were enrolled in graduate programs. Furthermore, more than 65 percent of these graduate students come from the Asian countries of China, Japan, Taiwan, and Korea. European graduate students from Germany, France, Spain, and Greece make up the second largest group of international graduate students. With the number of U.S. citizens studying for advanced degrees in business administration, mathematics, and the sciences steadily decreasing, international graduate students have filled the resulting gaps. For example, the number of U.S. citizens receiving doctorates in mathematics has decreased by 50 percent in the last twenty years; as a result, "in 1989, most of the Ph.Ds in mathematics awarded by U.S. universities went to citizens of other countries" (Crossing pedagogical oceans, 1991, p. 3). Undergraduates will take the majority of their introductory courses in the sciences and mathematics at the same institutions where international graduate students are studying, and many of these graduate students will teach as international teaching assistants (ITAs) while engaged in their studies. Although most of the courses undergraduates take will be with native English-speaking instructors, they "are likely to have comparatively limited but intensely important contact with ITAs" (Crossing pedagogical oceans, 1991, pp. 6–7).

Another important part of the international presence on U.S. university campuses is the hiring of faculty members from other countries. U.S. colleges and universities are hiring greater numbers of faculty members from other countries, especially in the areas of mathematics and engineering. In 1987, 40 percent of the assistant professors teaching mathematics and 35 percent of those assistant professors teaching engineering were graduates of foreign universities. Again, these international professors have filled the gap left by the decreasing number of U.S. citizens studying for advanced degrees in mathematics and engineering, because only approximately 40 percent of new engineering Ph.Ds granted by U.S. universities from 1983 to 1985 were U.S. citizens (Crossing pedagogical oceans, 1991). That number might be even lower today.

All of these statistics combine to mean that at some point in the academic careers of most undergraduates, they will have classes and communicate with instructors who are from other countries and cultures. Although we cannot generalize about these experiences because international instructors have a wide diversity of backgrounds and experiences, one thing is certain: The university has become an intercultural environment. And within such an environment, each day in the college classroom is an intercultural event. The experience of learning and communicating in an intercultural environment is an exciting one with rich possibilities, and improving communication skills and learning to work with people from diverse backgrounds are just two of the benefits. But to succeed in and benefit from the numerous intercultural events of which you will be a part while studying for your degree, it is helpful to have some knowledge of the dynamics that are often present in intercultural classrooms. These dynamics are often grounded in differences in cultural values, learning and teaching styles, and verbal and nonverbal ways of speaking.

CULTURE AND CLASSROOM COMMUNICATION

Although the presence of culture is pervasive in any educational setting, as people interested in studying intercultural communication, we cannot examine everything in the classroom. We are most interested in those particular aspects of culture that greatly influence classroom communication. We will first look at how values influence intercultural communication. Then we will examine how culture can determine the different learning and teaching styles found in multicultural classrooms. The two final issues we will discuss will be how culture-specific verbal and nonverbal ways of speaking influence communication between students and teachers.

The Influence of Values on Classroom Communication

One of the primary ways that culture can influence teaching and learning is through the communication of cultural values and attitudes in the classroom. Although Maslow (1971) described a value system as simply a big container of miscellaneous, vague things, values are quite specific and dominant in our lives. Derived from the deep philosophical underpinnings that shape a culture, values are organized rules that help individuals in a given culture make choices and reduce conflicts (Samovar & Porter, 1997). Although we each hold a unique set of values that characterizes us as individuals, we all carry with us a set of values that we share with others within our culture (Minnick, 1968). Value systems are sets of strong preferences held by cultures that assist their members in knowing right from wrong, appropriate versus inappropriate behavior, and how the world should be. For example, four dominant U.S. cultural values can be seen clearly in the development of its current educational system (Robinson, 1992). The U.S. values *individualism* and *competition* among individuals, a value that is manifested in its system of grading and its focus on independent learning and thinking. The *philosophy of knowledge* that shapes our concerns about plagiarism and the emphasis we place on students completing individual course work reflect our concerns about individualism and individual competition as well. U.S. values associate knowledge with the individual, as opposed to other cultures that may assign knowledge to the public domain, and concerns about plagiarism and sharing knowledge in study sessions or on tests are of much less concern.

Equal access to education, the use of multiple forms of evaluation, and the often relaxed relationship between teachers and students demonstrate the values of equality and informality within U.S. society. This tendency to see education as something equally due to all and that encourages equality in the classroom is quite different from most educational systems in the world. Crittenden (1994) explains this more common approach to higher education:

> The elite systems that typify much of higher education in the world . . . are intended to perpetuate or develop a small elite in society. Selection of students is by birth or more typically by merit, usually defined in terms of scores on competitive exams. Admission requires extreme talent and/or extreme prior investment in the education process on the part of the student. (p. 6)

In such a system, where students are privileged to be selected for higher education and accustomed to working extremely hard to gain that privilege, student responsibility for acquiring knowledge overshadows the role of teacher. Students seem to take much more responsibility for their learning and accomplishment in such a system than they do in a more egalitarian educational system. This means that teachers in these systems may have very different attitudes about teacher and student responsibilities and roles than those of U.S. teachers.

The American educational system is one that tends to emphasize the pragmatic application of learning to real world examples. Thus, many students and teachers in the United States may expect that lessons relate to real world situations and require creative, critical thinking on the part of the individual. Educational systems in other parts of the world may be less focused on individuals applying their knowledge critically to problems in the real world and more focused on imparting a great deal of information, with groups of students working together to learn as much of the information as possible.

Although students are certainly studying and learning practical information and using creative, critical thinking in these systems, these learning goals and methods may take on different forms with quite different functions. For example, learning how to work collaboratively to solve problems may sometimes be more practical and important within particular cultures than having students work independently to accomplish the same kind of task.

Other culturally derived values help shape and maintain educational systems. The work of Geert Hofstede (1986) lends insight into the influence that cultural values has on communication between students and teachers. Based on his well-known study on work-related values in more than 50 countries, Hofstede applied his four-value scheme to the educational setting. He described cultural differences in teacher–student and student–student interaction according to four dimensions: individualism—collectivism, power distance, uncertainty avoidance, and masculinity-femininity (see Table 1). Each of these values manifests itself in culturally specific ways in the classroom. Hofstede claims that, to a large extent, these four values influence the nature of the relationship that develops between teachers and students and help to shape the communication that goes on in classroom settings. We suggest that Hofstede's model should be applied to intercultural classroom communication using a critical lens. As you read our overview of this model, be aware of places where you do not agree with his description of what you have experienced or know about various cultures and their ways of learning and communicating, including your own. We believe that the value of models such as Hofstede's lie less in telling us what cultures are and more in helping us develop sets of

Table 1 *Value Differences in Teaching and Learning*

Collectivistic Societies (Arab countries, African, Mexico, Portugal, Taiwan, Japan)	Individualistic Societies (Great Britain, United States, Norway, Germany, Spain, France)
• Young should learn; adults cannot accept student role. • Students will speak only when called upon by teacher; harmony in learning situations should be maintained at all times. • Education is a way of gaining prestige, getting into higher social class. • Teachers expected to give preferential treatment to some students.	• One is never too old to learn. • Individual students will speak up in response to general invitation of teacher. • Education is a way of improving economic worth and self-respect based on ability and competence. • Teachers expected to be strictly impartial.

Small Power Distance Societies (Costa Rica, Sweden, United States, Australia, Canada, Netherlands)	Large Power Distance Societies (France, South Africa, African countries, Arab countries, Japan, Korea, Thailand)
• Teachers should respect independence of students. • Student-centered education. • Teacher expects students to find their own paths. • Students allowed to contradict teacher. • Effectiveness of learning related to amount of two-way communication in class. • Outside class, teachers are treated as equals.	• Teacher merits the respect of students. • Teacher-centered education. • Students expect teacher to outline paths to follow. • Teacher is never contradicted. • Effectiveness of learning related to excellence of teacher. • Respect for teachers shown outside of class; they maintain authority.

Weak Uncertainty Avoidance Societies (Canada, Hong Kong, India, Sweden, Philippines)	Strong Uncertainty Avoidance (Japan, Greece, Peru, Korea, Austria, Equador)
• Students feel comfortable in unstructured learning situations. • Teachers are allowed to say "I don't know." • Good teacher uses plain language. • Students rewarded for innovative approaches to problem solving.	• Students feel comfortable in structured learning situations (precise objective, detailed assignments, strict timetables). • Teachers expected to have all the answers. • Good teacher uses academic language. • Students rewarded for accuracy in problem solving.

Feminine Societies (Sweden, Denmark Costa Rica, Chile, Spain, France, Finland)	Masculine Societies (Jamaica, Austria, Mexico, Japan, Ireland, United States, Australia, Venezuela)
• Teachers avoid openly praising students. • Teachers use average student as the norm. • System rewards students' social adaptation. • Students admire friendliness in teachers. • Students try to behave modestly. • Male students may choose traditionally feminine academic subjects.	• Teachers openly praise good students. • Teachers use best students as the norm. • System rewards students' academic performance. • Students admire brilliance in teachers. • Students try to make themselves visible. • Male students avoid traditional feminine academic subjects.

From G. Hofstede's "Cultural Differences in Teaching and Learning," 1986, *International Journal of Intercultural Relations, 10,* 301–319.

questions about cultures. We especially encourage you to use Hofstede's model to help you formulate questions about your own cultural values and expectations in relation to learning and classroom communication.

Collectivism versus Individualism. Hofstede described strong individualistic societies such as Great Britain, the United States, and Germany as those that tend to believe that one is never too old to learn and encourage individual students to speak up freely in class. Strong collectivist societies such as Taiwan, Mexico, and many African countries, however, tend to believe that it is the young who should learn because adults cannot accept the less powerful role of the student, and students are often encouraged to speak only when called upon. How societies conceive of the individual has a profound effect on how educational systems are structured. For example, educational theories and practices developed by the Chinese are much less interested in individual differences of students; they focus more of their attention on those educational procedures that will transform whole groups of students (Munro, 1977). In the United States, the focus or center of teaching is the individual learner, whereas within Chinese society the collective or a classroom of students is the focal point. This focus on the individual student in U.S. education mirrors the strong cultural value of personal autonomy and individual rights so deeply entrenched in the American psyche. Although traditional Chinese philosophies may mention individual freedoms and rights, these are "subordinate to ideas of duty, ethical conduct, public benefit, and social responsibility—all in pursuit of social harmony" (Pratt, 1991, p. 298). How Chinese college students perceive themselves is also in line with a strong collectivist society as they tend to describe themselves with significantly more collectivist characteristics (e.g., family, ethnicity, occupational groups) than U.S. students (Triandis, 1989).

Communication in the classroom is greatly shaped according to whether a culture tends to be more collectivistic or individualistic. Teachers from individualistic cultures teaching in China or Japan may find it difficult to get their students to discuss their ideas in class because to do so would be to spotlight one's individuality and autonomy by expressing a personal opinion. Whereas American students might feel comfortable

and even encouraged to ask a question if they have not understood something a teacher has said, Japanese students are much less likely to do so because of their desire "to secure harmony and to save their face as well as that of their instructor" (Neuliep, 1997, p. 448). Indeed, when students do not ask questions in the United States, it may be seen as a sign of indifference or disinterest (Althen, 1988). Again, in educational settings the focus for more collectivist cultures is being a member of a class and teaching a group of students, whereas classrooms are a typical feature of the U.S. educational system as a whole. However, before we assume that these are typical features of individual U.S. classrooms, we should note that these approaches to classroom teaching and learning have gained in popularity only in the last thirty years. More "loosely structured" learning methods such as collaborative groups and class discussion are greatly debated in academic circles, and they regularly pose difficulties for U.S. teachers and students who are not used to such open-ended teaching methods and who may not agree about the benefits of such approaches. It is therefore wise to state that, although the United States might as a society rate low in uncertainty avoidance using Hofstede's findings, uncertainty avoidance may be very high for students and teachers within many classroom settings throughout the United States.

Keep in mind that Hofstede's four-value system for describing differences in educational practices across cultures is only one way to describe how cultures tend to be and is not meant to pigeonhole entire societies as masculine versus feminine, or collectivistic versus individualistic. His scheme does, however, provide us with a set of possible perspectives from which to think about how values can shape the kind of educational system and classroom communication a society chooses to adopt.

Learning and Teaching Styles

A learning style is a preference for how we go about the business of internalizing and understanding ideas and concepts. Learning styles can be individual, with some people preferring to read about news events and others choosing to learn about the day's happenings by watching Tom Brokaw on NBC or by listening to National Public Radio. Our preferences for learning can also reflect the dominant learning style that our society has sanctioned and used to develop and implement its educational system. Thus, while we may have our own ways of learning, we also have those culturally defined ways of learning that influence us just as profoundly. In the multicultural classroom, especially when a teacher is from another country, teaching methods and ways of communicating in the classroom do not always mesh with the mode of learning to which most students might be accustomed.

Let's take the example of Mr. Chou. Mr. Chou was described by his students as being unexpressive in his ways of explaining material and that he did not explain what he was writing on the board. In China, a dominant style of learning is one in which students are expected to wrestle with the incompleteness of a lesson because "if one is to gain as much knowledge as the mentor [teacher], one must accept the need to piece it together for oneself through collective effort with one's peers" (Christy & Rittenberg, 1988, p. 118). Given this view of how students are expected to learn in China, if Mr. Chou thoroughly explained what he was writing on the board, he would not be allowing his students to struggle with the material but would be, in a sense, giving them the answers. This method of teaching would prevent students from learning as much as possible. Mr. Chou's noble intentions, however, have the opposite effect with his students in the United States because the majority of them are accustomed to instructors who attempt to explain concepts as thoroughly as possible and allow for questions if students do not understand.

Within the United States, there are equally diverse culturally determined ways of learning that can help us explain the problems that students and teachers often have when their methods of teaching and learning do not blend amicably. Traditional Native American styles of learning often do not match university faculty ways of communicating; most of them are of various Anglo-American heritages (Scollon, 1981). Native students at an Alaskan university, for example, described the deductive way of presenting a point (beginning with a general, abstract theory and then moving to specific examples) often used by non-Native teachers as "often misunderstood (by students) as not getting to the point" (Scollon, 1981, p. 10). Whereas a typical Anglo style of presenting an argument or point of view resembles a debate—in which a position is directly stated, the opposing side is described as incorrect, supporting evidence is provided, and a conclusion offered—other cultures may neither seek combat nor come to the point directly (Condon & Yousef, 1988). One method of teaching and a preferred way of learning for some societies is to weave stories as a way to present one's "argument." The first author of this article witnessed such a style during a debate in a small village high school in Nairagi Enkare, Kenya. One of the finest speakers in the school was a first year Maasai student named Obote Uka. Obote would pace at the front of the auditorium and "argue" his point by telling a story or legend that illustrated the point he was trying to make. Few speakers were able to catch the students' attention or persuade them toward their side like Obote, because many of them attempted to mirror the style of argument that their Anglo-American teacher tended to emphasize.

Although there is not one specific way of learning for Native Americans, common patterns of learning have been found across tribal groups (More, 1989). In some exciting work done by Susan Phillips (1983) on the Warm Spring Indian Reservation in Oregon, Native American children tended not to respond when their Anglo teachers asked them questions in front of their peers but did so more frequently when the children initiated conversation with the teacher. How can we explain this according to the cultural ways of learning and communicating amongst the Warm Springs Indian community? In addition to Phillips's work with the Warm Springs children, studies examining the learning styles of children from the Navajo (Longstreet, 1978), Oglala Sioux (Brewer, 1977), and Yaqui (Appleton, 1983) tribes have come to a similar conclusion. Children from these Native American groups tend to develop a learning style in the home that corresponds to the following pattern:

1. Child watches parent, grandparent, or elder sibling do a task.
2. Child receives minimal verbal instruction but self-reflects on the proper way to accomplish the task.
3. Child tries to accomplish the task through self-testing, often alone.
4. Child is ready to perform task in front of others.

Compared to the question-and-response method of teaching and learning carried out by Warm Springs teachers, the above process differs greatly. Observation is the first and most important step, with attempts to accomplish the task taking place only within the safe confines of solitude, not in front of one's peers where a student may not be prepared to perform competently for others. Instead of using the trial-and-error and "If at first you don't succeed, try, try, again" method of learning, children from many Native American communities prefer to follow the watch-and-do and "If at first you don't think, and think again, don't bother trying" philosophy of learning (More, 1989; Werner & Begishe as cited in Swisher & Deyhle, 1989).

Verbal Ways of Speaking in the Classroom

The most obvious cultural difference that can be found in any multicultural classroom, especially on a university campus with a significant international student and faculty presence, is in the area of language. But identifying language differences among culturally diverse peoples is not as obvious as one might think. Unless you are in a foreign language class, English is usually spoken in every university classroom in the United States; thus people are typically speaking the same language in multicultural university classrooms. It is the nuances of language, those less obvious linguistic subtleties that can both enhance and make problematic the teaching and learning that takes place in college multicultural classrooms. In the following section we will examine how culture influences such language issues as idiomatic expressions, rules for politeness, and communication content. As you read, think about your own experiences with language differences in the classroom. How did they manifest themselves? How did you react?

Idiomatic Expressions. A Middle Eastern student attempted to use the idiom "laid back" and ended up mistranslating the phrase from Turkish, causing himself embarrassment as a result. Another student from the Middle East had learned to greet his U.S. friends with "Hey!" followed by the person's last name. When he tried out this idiom to get his instructor's attention during an examination, he exclaimed,

"Hey, Smith!" Mr. Smith was not amused and was offended by the rather exuberant, informal greeting during a very serious occasion (Magrath, 1981). Even regional differences in the English language can cause moments of confusion in the classroom. When one of the authors of this article (born and raised on the West Coast) was teaching in Terre Haute, Indiana, one of her students used the idiom "honked off"[1] while relaying an experience. The phrase "honked off" is a decidedly Midwestern phrase, and she had to ask for a definition before the class could continue. These are all examples of how the use of idioms can cause confusion when they are used improperly or in the presence of someone who is not privy to their definition. Usually, any confusion surrounding idioms can be addressed quite easily and swiftly by defining them for the person who does not understand or using contextual cues to interpret them. In addition, those of us who hear idioms that are being used incorrectly can be more understanding of others who may not know the "rules" surrounding particular idiomatic phrases. More than any aspect of language, idioms and metaphors probably make the point most clearly that language is developed and constructed by a people for their own particular purposes and based on objects and experiences specific to a nation, culture, or region. Halliday (1970) has suggested that "the nature of language is closely related to the demands that we make on it, the functions it has to serve. In the most concrete terms, these functions are specific to a culture" (p. 141). It is their culturally specific function that often explains why idioms do not always translate well and are oftentimes difficult to decipher by outsiders. For example, directly translating the English "Forgive me" to Arabic is problematic because such a phrase spoken in Arabic means "May God forgive." Idioms are not just words strung together; they carry with them the cultural preferences and beliefs held by the people who speak them. In the multicultural classroom setting, translation problems may occur because idioms are being spoken by people from different cultural vantage points and they are therefore not necessarily privy to their intended definitions (Bentahila & Davies, 1989).

Rules of Politeness. Language difficulties can also manifest themselves in multicultural situations when people use their own cultural rules instead of applying the rules of the culture in which they are communicating. For example, an ITA in chemistry was very diligent about checking with students to see how their experiments were progressing. She would approach each group of students and ask, "What are you doing?" Students were startled at what they perceived as an abrupt, even accusatory statement, a message that she did not intend to convey (Hoekje & Williams, 1992). A U.S. American TA would probably have said something like, "So, how are things going?" as a way to find out where the students were in the experiment. Sometimes what appears to be a perfectly acceptable question can actually be interpreted as accusatory and combative given a particular situation. Although this can happen in monocultural situations, intercultural communication settings are especially susceptible to such misunderstandings. An opposite dilemma is often faced by many ITAs from Asian cultures such as Japan who might use roundabout, indirect ways of expressing an opinion and go to great lengths to be polite and maintain harmony (Kuroda, 1986). The more direct style of speaking used by U.S. students may appear offensive to these instructors. To U.S. students unaccustomed to extreme efforts to be polite, communication by Japanese teachers may be perceived as inarticulate, disingenuous, or even deceptive.

Translating requests from one language to the next can be problematic when different rules of politeness are working. For example, British English emphasizes what Brown and Levinson (1978) describe as "negative politeness," or a concern for not being an imposition on another person. Thus, British and Americans speaking English might say, "Would you like some more?" But Moroccans use "positive" politeness, which displays a concern for another's welfare and therefore they might use the imperative "Take some more." Although the same message is conveyed ("I would like you to have some more"), whether the message is communicated using a question or an imperative, and how the message is interpreted, depends on the cultural background of the speaker and listener. The necessity of teaching the culturally specific aspects of a language is something with which foreign language instructors often struggle. What cultural rules do they teach students about when to speak and how? In a Spanish class, a teacher could choose to teach the communication rules of Mexico, Spain, or many other

South or Central American countries, and each set of rules might be different from the others. Students need to understand that learning a language does not necessarily mean they have learned the rules for communicating in that language in every society that speaks it.

Content of Communication. A U.S. university professor was talking in his office with a visiting student from Russia. The student noticed pictures of the professor's family on his desk and asked, "Why make your family pictures available? You devalue your family and experiences and memories by doing this" (Carbaugh, 1993, p. 169). The student went on to explain that people in Russia do not discuss personal experiences in public, "whatever they are . . . love, sex, relations with God, we cannot express these in words. You make it shallow if you speak it in public." This student's mild admonishment of Professor Carbaugh's display of personal artifacts and his follow-up explanation do much toward our understanding that what we talk about in public settings, including classroom time and office hours, is partially culturally determined. Although we have our own preferences for how much to reveal within educational contexts, what is defined as "public" and "private" in the classroom is not the same across cultures. It may be appropriate to discuss politics in the United States, but in less open societies, such talk in a classroom might mean the loss of a job. Thus, even though talk is a universal occurrence found in every culture, what students and teachers talk about in the classroom depends on where that classroom is in the world and who's doing the talking.

Nonverbal Ways of Speaking in the Classroom

Qiong-ying is a TA from the People's Republic of China. Qiong-ying does not look at her students during the class period and speaks in a voice that students must strain to hear. In the United States, these nonverbal ways of speaking communicate a message to students that is quite different than if Qiong-ying were teaching in China. Confucian standards of hierarchy have strongly influenced the nature of relationships among students and teachers, and Qiong-ying is using nonverbal ways of communicating to her students that maintain the social distance prescribed by such standards. In addition, using communication that may draw attention toward her physical self could reduce the focus on her intellectual abilities (Christy & Rittenberg, 1988). But status differences between students and teachers are much more relaxed in U.S. classrooms, and not to look at someone or speak using an adequate amount of volume are seen as signs of disinterest and even rudeness by Qiong-ying's students. This example points dramatically to the vastly different interpretations our nonverbal behavior can communicate to people who do not share our cultural experiences and philosophies, and the problems it can create for students and teachers when engaged in the intercultural event of teaching and learning in a multicultural classroom.

Nonverbal ways of speaking encompass a wide array of communicative behaviors, from tones of voice and eye contact to our use of hand gestures and the physical environment in which we communicate. In this section, we will examine how tone of voice, pronunciation, accent, and silence influence communication in the multicultural university classroom.

Paralinguistics. *Paralinguistics* refer to qualities of our voice such as tone, volume, rate of speech, and intonation. These characteristics of our voices also include pronunciation of words and accent. The paralinguistic characteristics of our communication is such a major part of how a message is interpreted that sometimes it overwhelms the words we are uttering and misunderstanding can result. Middle Eastern students may find that others believe they are angry or hostile because their way of speaking appears loud and their intonation similar to what a person would use if they were angry in another culture. This misunderstanding is a function of others' unfamiliarity with the intonation patterns of Arabic and Turkish (Magrath, 1981). When we "hear" another language with the same cultural ear we use to hear our own language, the rules do not always transfer. This dynamic of listening with our own language ear can result in some uncomfortable situations. For instance, in one classroom, an East Indian instructor would call on his students frequently because he wanted to encourage participation in the classroom. However, the intonation of his voice made students feel like he was calling on them in a scolding manner and talking down to them. The instructor was

appalled when he found this out, and worked very hard to try and change his intonation so that his positive intentions of wanting to help the students learn could become more apparent. Learning about differences in intonation would have been a very valuable lesson for everyone in this classroom.

How we pronounce our words is also included in the paralinguistic qualities of our voice. As those who have studied a second or third language know, learning a language is not just about picking up vocabulary and using correct grammatical structure. It also involves the vocalized stress we put on certain syllables and the sounds of letters. Even the slightest variations in pronunciation can lead to miscommunication. For example, Hardjo, an Indonesian student learning English, lamented to his tutor, "What is my problem?" because he was having an increasingly difficult time learning the language. Hardjo was having difficulty in part because his mouth was simply unaccustomed to forming certain sounds. Sounds like "g" and "k" were indistinguishable to his ear, which prevented him from pronouncing "dog" and "dock" as two different words (Hoven, 1987).

The accent of our speech—that is, those qualities that can often indicate what country or region a person is from—is also a nonverbal characteristic of communication that can influence classroom communication. When hearing an accent with which we are unfamiliar, it can be difficult to adjust immediately to this new sound of speaking. Just as English speakers may never become native-like in their ability to speak other languages, Hardjo's accent may never become native-like simply because he grew up without utilizing the muscles required to make certain consonantal or vocalic sounds. However, this does not mean that Hardjo's English is inaccurate or inadequate. In fact, as English increasingly becomes the lingua franca throughout the world, there are growing numbers of what are becoming known as "world Englishes." These are developing in normative English speaking countries where the majority of official educational systems and international business transactions are increasingly conducted in English. As this transition occurs, new brands of English are developed that adhere to grammatical and pronunciation rules that are an amalgamation of the native language of that country and a particular type of English (be it British English, Australian, U.S., or other). Thus, English is no longer seen as only that type of English spoken in Canada or New Zealand. In this increasingly international world in which we must all have some knowledge of each others' ways of speaking to ensure effective communication, native English speakers are finding themselves becoming more familiar with world Englishes from around the globe. The university classroom is a place in which such familiarity can be learned and an appreciation of world Englishes can be celebrated.

Silence. Although silence may be commonly understood as the absence of communication, such a conceptualization ignores silence as the definitive form of nonverbal expression. Western cultures largely view silence as asocial or even antisocial (Johannesen, 1974). The significance of silence among many people in the United States is best exemplified in the U.S. Constitution's Fifth Amendment, which guarantees every citizen the right to remain silent. And yet when this right is invoked, there is usually suspicion and the assumption of wrongdoing. Simply put, silence is suspect in individualistic cultures, "something to be filled in conversations" (Gudykunst, 1994, p. 140). Silence among the Japanese, however, is thought to convey truthfulness because spoken words can often involve distortion and deception (Lebra, 1987).

In the intercultural classroom, silence may be used by a teacher in ways that are useful yet sometimes problematic. In her study of the characteristics of successful classroom discourse, Patricia Rounds (1987) identified three categories of silence in the classrooms of ITAs teaching mathematics: administrative, strategic, and empty. Administrative silences included times when a teacher was reading a math problem in the book, writing on the chalkboard, erasing the chalkboard, and handing out papers. Strategic silences were those moments when a teacher wanted to create "a certain rhetorical or dramatic effect...such as the pregnant pause that comes just before a punch line is delivered or a major point is made" (Rounds, 1987, p. 653). It was the use of empty silences that proved problematic for students and ITAs. For example, when Rounds analyzed "Lee's" talk in the classroom, she found that sometimes his pauses occurred in the middle of sentences and created a haphazard effect. In the following example of Lee's communication, the periods in parentheses represent untimed pauses:

"And because this (.) concept (.) are very important (.) so (.) we give (.) some (.) names (.) for the (.) quotient (.) and of the limit" (Rounds, 1987, p. 654). Rounds suggests that such uses of silence, unlike administrative and strategic silences, serve to "diffuse attention rather than focus it" (p. 654). Some students in this classroom explained that they had difficulty concentrating on what Lee was saying because his use of silence made it difficult to maintain their train of thought.

Was Lee not communicating effectively with his math students because of his use of empty pauses? Obviously, for some of them this particular use of silence was problematic, whereas other forms of silence were helpful to their learning. As a nonnative English speaker, Lee's frequent use of silence can be understood as a struggle to find the right words to convey a thought. These linguistic challenges can be common events in intercultural classrooms, and although they may be cause for frustration among students, they are even more so for nonnative English-speaking instructors.

IMPROVING COMMUNICATION IN THE INTERCULTURAL CLASSROOM

Remember that our goal in writing this article was to help students and teachers understand the influence that culture and national origin can have on classroom communication dynamics. We would like to end this essay by challenging you to analyze some intercultural classroom situations on your own. Each scenario below is based on actual experiences of university ITAs and their students. We invite you to read them and consider the following four questions:

1. How is culture influencing the perspectives of education held by the students and ITAs in these scenarios?
2. How is culture influencing the teaching and learning styles described in the scenarios?
3. How is culture being manifested through the verbal and nonverbal behavior and communication of the students and ITAs?
4. What suggestions do you have for the ITAs and students in these scenarios that would positively influence or even improve the classroom communication?

Intercultural Classroom Scenario One: Conflicting Expectations

Imagine that you are an instructor from Russia who teaches entry-level calculus to undergraduates at a large U.S. university. You are frustrated with your students and feel as if you cannot help them. Your students are at all different levels of background knowledge, many of them don't do their homework, and some of them ask the most simplistic questions in class that they could have answered if they'd just done their homework. They've also asked for homework solution handouts with the solutions all carefully worked out and reviews for the tests that have problems on them that look like those that are likely to be on the test. You can't decide if giving all this extra help will really contribute to their learning. In addition, it tends to keep you much busier than you can afford to be, what with all of the demands being placed on you with your rigorous graduate work. You wonder if there is a way to determine which students really belong in the classroom and if there is a way to get them to do more of their own problem solving on the homework.

You invite one of your colleagues to visit the class and ask the students questions about how the course is going. There seems to be a split opinion about your teaching among the students. About half of them think that you are working hard to help them learn calculus. The other half, however, feels that you are condescending and move too quickly through some of the problems. These students are afraid to ask questions, and some are even afraid of visiting your office hours for fear that you'll make them feel less capable. All of the students feel that you could spend more time letting them solve problems and ask questions in class. Right now, you tend to just write all the problems on the board and go through the solutions without giving them enough time to ask questions. What could you do to address the students' concerns without compromising your own teaching standards?

Intercultural Classroom Scenario Two: Issues of Privacy

You are a student in a German conversation class. Your instructor, Anna, is an ITA from Germany. Anna handed out everybody's grades on the last day of class and proclaimed, "Now let's discuss your grades." There was absolute silence in the classroom.

"What? What's wrong?" Anna asked.

"We don't do that here. We don't share our grades," said one of your classmates.

"Well in Germany you do. In Germany you hand out the grades and you discuss it as a class and you negotiate with the professor whether you can change it or not. If you don't think it's fair, you challenge the professor and the whole class decides whether it's fair or not."

No one in the class said a word. "So, anybody not happy with their grade?" Anna asked.

One of the students raised her hand and said, "I don't think that's gonna work here."

"Well, just pretend like it's Germany. This is a class on German. . . . We'll just pretend like it's in Germany," explained Anna.

"I just don't think it's gonna work," said one student.

It was a tense situation and no one was sure what to say next. How could this classroom interaction continue in a more positive direction?

Intercultural Classroom Scenario Three: Voices in the Classroom

Raj was a mathematics teacher who had taught for a few years in India before coming to the United States. He was now a teaching assistant for a math quiz section at the same university in which he was studying for his doctoral degree. When he asked his students for feedback during the middle of the quarter, Raj received complaints about his classroom communication. Many students said that it was difficult to understand what he was saying and a handful believed his accent was the primary problem. Others said that he rarely looked at them and often spoke toward the board as he was explaining problems. But almost all of them described him as knowledgeable and willing to answer questions throughout the class period. Raj was perplexed. He had no idea that his students were having a problem understanding him; no one had mentioned it until now. He didn't know what he could do about his accent, or even if he wanted to change that part of his Indian heritage. He had been speaking English since he was five years old and was a fluent English speaker. No one in his life had ever said they could not understand his communication. Why didn't they understand him?

SUGGESTIONS FOR STUDENTS IN INTERCULTURAL CLASSROOMS

It was our intent to provide you with some insight into the communication dynamics of intercultural and international university classrooms. You may have already experienced some of the issues we have identified, and perhaps you have developed your own ways of adapting to the changes and adjustments that are often needed in your own classes. We applaud such efforts to raise awareness of possible communication differences and to improve interactions in what can be challenging—but exciting circumstances for learning. The following are some ideas that we hope will assist you further as you continue to learn and communicate in intercultural classrooms.

First, we suggest that you try analyzing the communication in your classes to find out how culture might be influencing interactions among students and teachers. By taking a second look at what is happening in your own classrooms, you might come to understand more fully how culture influences teaching and learning. Two questions to ask yourself as you reflect on classroom interaction are: (1) What comes "naturally" for you? (2) How does this contribute to what you expect in the class? Answers to these questions can help you understand how your own ways of learning and communicating might not be considered natural or even desirable to others. Your reflections can also help you form a wisdom you will be able to rely on for successful intercultural interactions in the future. Second, we suggest you focus on listening to a way of speaking with which you might be unfamiliar. Be patient with the unfamiliar accents, body language, or intonation of your teachers and fellow students. It might take a few weeks until your ear and your expectations have adjusted to new ways of communicating. The payoff, however, is improved communication not only in the present, but also in the future when you meet others who have similar ways of communicating. Our third suggestion is related to the second: Do not hesitate to ask your instructor to repeat information or questions. This is one of the primary ways that teachers of any nationality have of finding out if they have been understood. Fourth, we suggest that you ask your international instructors about their home countries. It has been our experience that most ITAs like to talk about life in their home countries and appreciate the show of interest in their background and experience. A final suggestion we have is probably the most important idea to remember when studying and taking part in any communication situation, but of particular importance in intercultural interactions: Remember that communication in any classroom setting requires people to work together to reach understandings. Sometimes that work is a bit more challenging when people are trying to negotiate their own cultural notions of teaching and learning.

Note

1. The idiom "honked off" is similar to the more crude idiom "pissed off" and means to get angry or upset.

References

Althen, G. (1988). *American ways: A guide for foreigners in the United States*. Yarmouth, ME: Intercultural Press.

Appleton, N. (1983). *Cultural pluralism in education*. New York: Longman.

Bail, F. T., & Mina, S. S. (1981). Filipino and American student perceptions of teacher effectiveness. *Research in Higher Education, 14*, 135–145.

Bentahila, A., & Davies, E. (1989). Culture and language use: A problem for foreign language teaching. *IRAL, 27*, 99–112.

Brewer, A. (1977). On Indian education. *Integrateducation, 15*, 21–23.

Brown, P., & Levinson, S. (1978). Universals in language use: Politeness phenomena. In E. N. Goody (Ed.), *Questions and politeness*. Cambridge, UK: Cambridge University Press.

Carbaugh, D. (1993). Competence as cultural pragmatics: Reflections on some Soviet and American encounters. In R. L Wiseman & J. Koester (Eds.), *Intercultural communication competence* (pp. 168–183). Newbury Park, CA: Sage.

Christy, F. E., & Rittenberg, W. (1988). Some typical problems in the training of Chinese teaching assistants: Three case studies. In J. C. Constantinides (Ed.), *Wyoming NAFSA Institute on Foreign TA Training: Working papers* (pp. 111–127). Washington, DC: National Association for Foreign Student Affairs.

Collier, J. J., & Powell, R. (1990). Ethnicity, instructional communication and classroom systems. *Communication Quarterly, 38*, 334–349.

Condon, J. C., & Yousef, F. (1988). *An introduction to intercultural communication*. New York: Macmillan.

Crittenden, K. S. (1994). The mandate to internationalize the curriculum. *Teaching Sociology, 2*, 1–9.

Crossing pedagogical oceans: International teaching assistants in U.S. undergraduate education. (1991). *ASHEERIC Higher Education Report No. 8*. Washington, DC: The George Washington University School of Education and Human Development.

Goodman, A. E. (1996, February 16). What foreign students contribute. *The Chronicle of Higher Education*, p. A52.

Gudykunst, W. B. (1994). *Bridging differences: Effective intergroup communication* (2nd ed.). Thousand Oaks, CA: Sage.

Halliday, M. A. K. (1970). Language structure and language function. In J. Lyons (Ed.), *New horizons in linguistics*. Harmondsworth, UK: Penguin Books.

Hoekje, B., & Williams, J. (1992). Communicative competence and the dilemma of international teaching assistant education. *TESOL Quarterly, 26*, 243–269.

Hofstede, G. (1986). Cultural differences in teaching and learning. *International Journal of Intercultural Relations, 10*, 301–319.

Hoven, D. (1987, August). *"What is my problem?" A case study of an adult Indonesian ESL learner in Australia*. Paper presented at the conference of the International Association of Applied Linguistics, New South Wales, Australia.

Institute of International Education. (1993). *Open doors 1992-93*. New York: Author.

Johannesen, R. L. (1974). The functions of silence: A plea for communication research. *Western Journal of Speech Communication, 38*, 25–35.

Kuroda, T. (1986). Overcoming the conflict between Asian TAs and Americans. In J. L. Gburek & S. C. Dunnett (Eds.), *The foreign TA: A guide to teaching effectiveness* (pp. 16–17). Buffalo: State University of New York Press.

Lebra, T. S. (1987). The cultural significance of silence in Japanese communication. *Multilingua, 6*, 343–357.

Longstreet, E. (1978). *Aspects of ethnicity*. New York: Teachers College Press.

Magrath, D. (1981). *Culture and language learning: Middle Eastern students*. Paper presented at the TESOL summer meeting, New York, NY.

Maslow, A. H. (1971). *The farther reaches of human nature*. New York: Viking Press.

Minnick, W. C. (1968). *The art of persuasion* (2nd ed.). Boston: Houghton Mifflin.

More, A. J. (1989). Native Indian learning styles: A review for researchers and teachers. *Journal of American Indian Education, Special Issue*, 15–28.

Munro, D. (1977). *The concept of man in contemporary China*. Ann Arbor: University of Michigan Press.

Neuliep, J. W. (1997). A cross-cultural comparison of teacher-immediacy in American and Japanese college classrooms. *Communication Research, 24*, 431–451.

Phillips, S. (1983). *The invisible culture: Communication in classroom and community on the Warm Springs Indian Reservation*. New York: Longman.

Pratt, D. D. (1991). Conceptions of self within China and the United States: Contrasting foundations for adult education. *International Journal of Intercultural Relations, 15*, 285–310.

Robinson, J. (1992, October). *International students and American university culture: Adjustment issues*. Paper presented at Washington Area Teachers of English to Speakers of Other Languages, Arlington, VA.

Rounds, P. L. (1987). Characterizing successful classroom discourse for NNS teaching assistant training. *TESOL Quarterly, 21*, 643–671.

Samovar, L. A., & Porter, R. E. (1997). An introduction to intercultural communication. In L. A. Samovar & R. E. Porter (Eds.), *Intercultural communication: A reader* (8th ed.) (pp. 5–27). Belmont, CA: Wadsworth.

Sanders, J. A., & Wiseman, R. L. (1990). The effects of verbal and nonverbal teacher immediacy on perceived cognitive, affective, and behavioral learning in the multicultural classroom. *Communication Education, 39*, 341–353.

Scollon, S. B. K. (1981, April). *Professional development seminar: A model for making higher education more culturally sensitive*. Paper presented at the National Association of Asian and Pacific American Education, Honolulu, HI.

Swisher, K., & Deyhle, D. (1989). The styles of learning are different, but the teaching is just the same: Suggestions for teachers of American Indian youth. *Journal of American Indian Education, Special Issue*, 1–14.

Triandis, H. (1989). The self and social behavior in differing cultural contexts. *Psychological Review, 96*, 506–520.

Twale, D. J., Shannon, D. M., & Moore, M. S. (1997). NGTA and IGTA training and experience: Comparisons between self-ratings and undergraduate student evaluations. *Innovative Higher Education, 22*, 61–77.

Wood, J. T. (1997). Gender, communication, and culture. In L. A. Samovar & R. E Porter (Eds.), *Intercultural communication: A reader* (8th ed.) (pp. 164–174). Belmont, CA: Wadsworth.

Concepts and Questions

1. Describe several ways in which the international presence on U.S. university campuses has affected the learning process.

2. What differences might you find between collective and individualistic cultures in the structure of the classroom and the learning process?

3. How might a student from a culture in which hierarchies and respect for elders are strong cultural values perceive the relaxed relationship between teachers and students often reflected in U.S. universities?

4. What role does power distance play in determining the forms of communication that are appropriate to the teaching and learning process?

5. How does the gender orientation of a culture affect the forms of communication in the classroom?

6. How might a student from a culture that is high in uncertainty avoidance react to a U.S. professor who answers a student question by saying, "I don't know"?

7. Based on your own observations, detail as many learning styles as you can. How do these various styles merge in a college classroom environment?

8. In what ways do cultural differences in ways of speaking affect learning in a multicultural learning environment?

9. How does cultural diversity in nonverbal behavior affect interactions in a multicultural learning setting.

Culture and Communication in the Classroom

Geneva Gay

A semiotic relationship exists among communication, culture, teaching, and learning, and it has profound implications for implementing culturally responsive teaching. This is so because "what we talk about; how we talk about it; what we see, attend to, or ignore; how we think; and what we think about are influenced by our culture . . . [and] help to shape, define, and perpetuate our culture" (Porter & Samovar, 1991, p. 21). Making essentially the same argument, Bruner (1996) states that "learning and thinking are always situated in a cultural setting and always dependent upon the utilization of cultural resources" (p. 4). Culture provides the tools to pursue the search for meaning and to convey our understanding to others. Consequently, communication cannot exist without culture, culture cannot be known without communication, and teaching and learning cannot occur without communication or culture.

INTRODUCTION

The discussions in this article explicate some of the critical features and pedagogical potentials of the culture—communication semiotics for different ethnic groups of color. The ideas and examples presented are composites of group members who strongly identify and affiliate with their ethnic group's cultural traditions. They are not intended to be descriptors of specific individuals within ethnic groups, or their

Reprinted by permission of the publisher from Geneva Gay, *Culturally Responsive Teaching* (New York: Teachers College Press, © 2000 by Teachers College, Columbia University. All rights reserved), 77–110. Geneva Gay is Professor Emerita at the University of Washington.

behaviors in all circumstances. If, how, and when these cultural characteristics are expressed in actual behavior, and by whom, are influenced by many different factors. Therefore, the ethnic interactional and communication styles described in this article should be seen as general and traditional referents of group dynamics rather than static attributes of particular individuals.

Students of color who are most traditional in their communication styles and other aspects of culture and ethnicity are likely to encounter more obstacles to school achievement than those who think, behave, and express themselves in ways that approximate school and mainstream cultural norms. This is the case for many highly culturally and ethnically affiliated African Americans. In making this point, Dandy (1991) proposes that the language many African Americans speak "is all too often degraded or simply dismissed by individuals both inside and outside the racial group as being uneducated, illiterate, undignified or simply non-standard" (p. 2). Other groups of color are "at least given credit for having a legitimate language heritage, even if they are denied full access to American life" (p. 2). Much of educators' decision making on the potential and realized achievement of students of color is dependent on communication abilities (their own and the students'). If students are not very proficient in school communication and teachers do not understand or accept the students' cultural communication styles, then their academic performance may be misdiagnosed or trapped in communicative mismatches. Students may know much more than they are able to communicate, or they may be communicating much more than their teachers are able to discern. As Boggs (1985, p. 301) explains, "The attitudes and behavior patterns that have the most important effect upon children . . . [are] those involved in communication." This communication is multidimensional and multipurposed, including verbal and nonverbal, direct and tacit, literal and symbolic, formal and informal, grammatical and discourse components.

The discussions of culture and communication in classrooms in this article are organized into two parts. The first outlines some key assertions about culture and communication in teaching and learning in general. These help to anchor communication within culturally responsive teaching. In the second part of the article, some of the major characteristics of the communication modes of African, Native, Latino, Asian, and European Americans are presented. The focus throughout these discussions is on discourse dynamics—that is, who participates in communicative interactions and under what conditions, how these participation patterns are affected by cultural socialization, and how they influence teaching and learning in classrooms.

RELATIONSHIP AMONG CULTURE, COMMUNICATION, AND EDUCATION

In analyzing the routine tasks teachers perform, Smith (1971) declares that "teaching is, above all, a linguistic activity" and "language is at the heart of teaching" (p. 24). Whether making assignments, giving directions, explaining events, interpreting words and expressions, proving positions, justifying decisions and actions, making promises, dispensing praise and criticism, or assessing capability, teachers must use language. And the quality of the performance of these tasks is a direct reflection of how well teachers can communicate with their students. Smith admonishes educators for not being more conscientious in recognizing the importance of language in the performance and effectiveness of their duties. He says, "It could be that when we have analyzed the language of teaching and investigated the effects of its various formulations, the art of teaching will show marked advancement" (p. 24). Dandy (1991) likewise places great faith in the power of communication in the classroom, declaring that "teachers have the power to shape the future, if they communicate with their students, but those who cannot communicate are powerless" (p. 10). These effects of communication skills are especially significant to improving the performance of underachieving ethnically different students.

Porter and Samovar's (1991) study of the nature of culture and communication, the tenacious reciprocity that exists between the two, and the importance of these aspects to intercultural interactions provides valuable information for culturally responsive teaching. They describe communication as "an intricate matrix of interacting social acts that occur in a complex social environment that reflects the way people live and how they come to interact with and get along in their world. This social environment is culture, and if we are to truly understand communication, we must also understand culture" (p. 10). Communication is dynamic, interactive, irreversible, and invariably contextual. As such, it is a continuous, ever-changing activity that takes place between people who are trying to influence each other; its effects are irretrievable once it has occurred, despite efforts to modify or counteract them.

Communication is also governed by the rules of the social and physical contexts in which it occurs (Porter & Samovar, 1991). Culture is the rule-governing system that defines the forms, functions, and content of communication. It is largely responsible for the construction of our "individual repertoires of communicative behaviors and meanings" (p. 10). Understanding connections between culture and communication is critical to improving intercultural interactions. This is so because "as cultures differ from one another, the communication practices and behaviors of individuals reared in those cultures will also be different," and "the degree of influence culture has on intercultural communication is a function of the dissimilarity between the cultures" (p. 12).

Communication entails much more than the content and structure of written and spoken language, and it serves greater purposes than the mere transmission of information. Sociocultural context and nuances, discourse logic and dynamics, delivery styles, social functions, role expectations, norms of interaction, and nonverbal features are as important as (if not more so than) vocabulary, grammar, lexicon, pronunciation, and other linguistic or structural dimensions of communication. This is so because the "form of exchange between child and adult and the conditions in which it occurs will affect not only what is said, but how involved the child will become" (Boggs, 1985, p. 301). Communication is the quintessential way in which humans make meaningful connections with each other, whether in caring, sharing, loving, teaching, or learning. Montague and Matson (1979, p. vii) suggest that it is "the ground of [human] meeting and the foundation of [human] community."

Communication is also indispensable to facilitating knowing and accessing knowledge. This is the central idea of the Sapir–Whorf hypothesis about the relationship among language, thought, and behavior.

It says that, far from being simply a means for reporting experience, language is a way of defining experience, thinking, and knowing. In this sense, language is the semantic system of meanings and modes of conveyance that people habitually use to code, analyze, categorize, and interpret experience (Carroll, 1956; Hoijer, 1991; Mandelbaum, 1968). In characterizing this relationship, Sapir (1968) explains that "language is a guide to 'social reality'. . . [and] a symbolic guide to culture. . . . It powerfully conditions all of our thinking about social problems and processes" (p. 162). People do not live alone in an "objectified world" or negotiate social realities without the use of language. Nor is language simply a "mechanical" instrumental tool for transmitting information. Instead, human beings are "very much at the mercy of the particular language which has become the medium of expression for their society" (p. 162). The languages used in different cultural systems strongly influence how people think, know, feel, and do.

Whorf (1952, 1956; Carroll, 1956), a student of Sapir, makes a similar argument that is represented by the "principle of linguistic relativity." It contends that the structures of various languages reflect different cultural patterns and values, and, in turn, affect how people understand and respond to social phenomena. In developing these ideas further, Whorf (1952) explains that "a language is not merely a reproducing instrument for voicing ideas but rather is itself the shaper of ideas, the program and guide for the individual's mental activity, for his analysis of impressions, for his synthesis of his mental stock in trade" (p. 5). Vygotsky (1962) also recognizes the reciprocal relationship among language, culture, and thought. He declares, as "indisputable fact," that "thought development is determined by language . . . and the sociocultural experience of the child" (p. 51).

Moreover, the development of logic is affected by a person's socialized speech, and intellectual growth is contingent on the mastery of social means of thought, or language. According to Byers and Byers (1985), "the organization of the processes of human communication in any culture is a template for the organization of knowledge or information in that culture" (p. 28). This line of argument is applied specifically to different ethnic groups by theorists, researchers, and school practitioners from a variety of disciplinary perspectives, including social and developmental psychology, sociolinguistics, ethnography, and multiculturalism. For example, Ascher (1992) applied this reasoning to language influences on how mathematical relationships are viewed in general. Giamati and Weiland (1997) connected it to Navajo students' learning of mathematics, concluding that the performance difficulties they encounter are "a result of cultural influences on perceptions rather than a lack of ability" (p. 27). This happens because of the reciprocal interactions among language, culture, and perceptions. Consistently, when these scholars refer to "language" or "communication," they are talking more about discourse dynamics than structural forms of speaking and writing.

Thus, languages and communication styles are systems of cultural notations and the means through which thoughts and ideas are expressively embodied. Embedded within them are cultural values and ways of knowing that strongly influence how students engage with learning tasks and demonstrate mastery of them. The absence of shared communicative frames of reference, procedural protocols, rules of etiquette, and discourse systems makes it difficult for culturally diverse students and teachers to genuinely understand each other and for students to fully convey their intellectual abilities. Teachers who do not know or value these realities will not be able to fully access, facilitate, and assess most of what these students know and can do. Communication must be understood to be more than a linguistic system.

CULTURALLY DIFFERENT DISCOURSE STRUCTURES

In conventional classroom discourse, students are expected to assume what Kochman (1985) calls a *passive-receptive* posture. They are told to listen quietly while the teacher talks. Once the teacher finishes, then the students can respond in some prearranged, stylized way—by asking or answering questions; validating or approving what was said; or taking individual, teacher-regulated turns at talking. Individual students gain the right to participate in the conversation by permission of the teacher. The verbal discourse is accompanied by nonverbal attending behaviors and speech-delivery mechanisms that require maintaining eye contact with the speaker and using little or no physical movement. Thus, students are expected to be silent and look at teachers when they are talking and wait to be acknowledged before they take their turn at talking. Once permission is granted, they should follow established rules of decorum, such as one person speaking at a time, being brief and to the point, and keeping emotional nuances to a minimum (Kochman, 1981; Philips, 1983).

These structural protocols governing discourse are expressed in other classroom practices as well. Among them are expecting students always to speak in complete sentences that include logical development of thought, precise information, appropriate vocabulary, and careful attention to grammatical features such as appropriate use of vocabulary and noun–verb agreement. Student participation in classroom interactions is often elicited by teachers asking questions that are directed to specific individuals and require a narrow range of information-giving, descriptive responses. It is important for individuals to distinguish themselves in the conversations, for student responses to be restricted to only the specific demands of questions asked, and for the role of speaker and audience to be clearly separated.

In contrast to the passive–receptive character of conventional classroom discourse, some ethnic groups have communication styles that Kochman (1985) describes as *participatory–interactive*. Speakers expect listeners to engage them actively through vocalized, motion, and movement responses *as they are speaking*. Speakers and listeners are action-provoking partners in the construction of the discourse. These communicative styles have been observed among African Americans, Latinos, and Native Hawaiians. As is the case with other cultural behaviors, they are likely to be more pronounced among individuals who strongly identify and affiliate with their ethnic groups and cultural heritages. For example, low-income and minimally educated members of ethnic groups are likely to manifest group cultural behaviors more thoroughly than those who are middle class and educated. This is so because they have fewer opportunities to interact with people different from themselves and to be affected by the cultural exchanges and adaptations that result from the intermingling of a wide variety of people from diverse ethnic groups and varied experiential backgrounds.

ETHNIC VARIATIONS IN COMMUNICATION STYLES

Among African Americans, the participatory–interactive style of communicating is sometimes referred to as *call-response* (Asante, 1998; Baber, 1987; Kochman, 1972, 1981, 1985; Smitherman, 1977). It involves listeners' giving encouragement, commentary, compliments, and even criticism to speakers *as they are talking*. The speaker's responsibility is to issue the "calls" (making statements), and the listeners' obligation is to respond in some expressive, and often auditory, way (e.g., smiling, vocalizing, looking about, moving around, "amening") (Dandy, 1991; Smitherman, 1977). When a speaker says something that triggers a response in them (whether positive or negative; affective or cognitive), African American listeners are likely to "talk back." This may involve a vocal or motion response, or both, sent directly to the speaker or shared with neighbors in the audience. Longstreet (1978) and Shade (1994) describe the practice as "breaking in and talking over." This mechanism is used to signal to speakers that their purposes have been accomplished or that it is time to change the direction or leadership of the conversation. Either way, there is no need for the speaker to pursue the particular discourse topic or technique further.

African Americans "gain the floor" or get participatory entry into conversations through personal assertiveness, the strength of the impulse to be involved, and the persuasive power of the point they wish to make, rather than waiting for an "authority" to grant permission. They tend to invest their participation with personality power, actions, and emotions. Consequently, African Americans are often described as verbal performers whose speech behaviors are fueled by personal advocacy, emotionalism, fluidity, and creative variety (Abrahams, 1970; Baber, 1987). These communication facilities have been attributed to the oral/aural nature of African American cultural and communal value orientations (Pasteur & Toldson, 1982; Smitherman, 1977). Many teachers view these behaviors negatively, as "rude," "inconsiderate," "disruptive," and "speaking out of turn," and they penalize students for them.

Native Hawaiian students who maintain their traditional cultural practices use a participatory–interactive communicative style similar to the call-response of African Americans. Called "talk-story" or "co-narrative," it involves several students working collaboratively, or talking together, to create an idea, tell a story, or complete a learning task (Au, 1980, 1993; Au & Kawakami, 1985, 1991, 1994; Au & Mason, 1981; Boggs, Watson-Gegeo, & McMillen, 1985). After observing these behaviors among elementary students, Au (1993) concluded that "what seems important to Hawaiian children in talk-story is not individual . . . but group performance in speaking" (p. 114). These communication preferences are consistent with the importance Native Hawaiian culture places on individuals' contributing to the well-being of family and friends instead of working only for their own betterment (Gallimore, Boggs, & Jordon, 1974; Tharp & Gallimore, 1988).

A communicative practice that has some of the same traits of call-response and talk-story has been observed among European American females. Tannen (1990) calls it "cooperative overlapping" and describes it as women "talking along with speakers to show participation and support" (p. 208). It occurs most often in situations where talk is casual and friendly. This *rapport-talk* is used to create community. It is complemented by other traditional women's ways of communicating, such as the following:

- Being "audience" more often than "speaker" in that they are recipients of information provided by males
- Deemphasizing expertise and the competitiveness it generates
- Focusing on individuals in establishing friendships, networks, intimacy, and relationships more than exhibiting power, accomplishment, or control
- Negotiating closeness in order to give and receive confirmation, support, and consensus
- Avoiding conflict and confrontation (Belensky, Clinchy, Goldberger, & Tarule, 1986; Klein, 1982; Maltz & Borker, 1983; Tannen, 1990)

While these habits of "communal communication and interaction" are normal to the users, they can be problematic to classroom teachers. On first encounter, they may be perceived as "indistinguishable noise and chaos" or unwholesome dependency. Even after the shock of the initial encounter passes, teachers may still consider these forms of communication socially deviant, not conducive to constructive intellectual engagement, rude, and insulting. They see them as obstructing individual initiative and preempting the right of each student to have a fair chance to participate in instructional discourse. These assessments can prompt attempts to rid students of the habits and replace them with the rules of individualistic, passive-receptive, and controlling communication styles predominant in classrooms.

Teachers may not realize that by doing this they could be causing irreversible damage to students' abilities or inclinations to engage fully in the instructional process. Hymes (1985) made this point when he suggested that rejecting ethnically different students' communication styles might be perceived by them as rejection of their personhood. Whether intentional or not, casting these kinds of aspersions on the identity and personal worth of students of color does not bode well for their academic achievement.

Problem Solving and Task Engagement

Many African American, Latino, Native American, and Asian American students use styles of inquiry and responding that are different from those employed most often in classrooms. The most common practice among teachers is to ask convergent (single-answer) questions and use deductive approaches to solving problems. Emphasis is given to details, to building the whole from the parts, to moving from the specific to the general. Discourse tends to be didactic, involving one student with the teacher at a time (Goodlad, 1984). In comparison, students of color who are strongly affiliated with their traditional cultures tend to be more inductive, interactive, and communal in task performance. The preference for inductive problem solving is expressed as reasoning from the whole to parts, from the general to the specific. The focus is on the "big picture," the pattern, the principle (Boggs et al., 1985; Philips, 1983; Ramirez & Castañeda, 1974; Shade 1989).

Although these general patterns of task engagement prevail across ethnic groups, variations do exist. Some teachers use inductive modes of teaching, and some students within each ethnic group of color learn deductively. Many Asian American students seem to prefer questions that require specific answers but are proposed to the class as a whole. Many Latino students may be inclined toward learning in group contexts, but specific individuals may find these settings distracting and obstructive to their task mastery.

In traditional African American and Latino cultures, problem solving is highly contextual. One significant feature of this contextuality is creating a "stage" or "setting" prior to the performance of a task. The stage setting is invariably social in nature. It involves establishing personal connections with others who will participate as a prelude to addressing the task. In making these connections, individuals are readying themselves for "work" by cultivating a social context. They are, in effect, activating their cultural socialization concept that an individual functions better within the context of a group. Without the group as an anchor, referent, and catalyst, the individual is set adrift, having to function alone.

These cultural inclinations may be operating when Latino adults begin their task interactions with colleagues by inquiring about the families of other participants and their own personal well-being or when African American speakers inform the audience about their present psychoemotional disposition and declare the ideology, values, and assumptions underlying the positions they will be taking in the presentation (i.e., "where they are coming from"). This "preambling" is a way for the speakers to prime the audience and themselves for the subsequent performance. Students of color may be setting the stage for their engagement with learning tasks in classrooms (e.g., writing an essay, doing seatwork, taking a test) when they seem to be spending unnecessary time arranging their tests, sharpening pencils, shifting their body postures (stretching, flexing their hands, arms, and legs, etc.), or socializing with peers rather than attending to the assigned task. "Preparation before performance" for these students serves a similar purpose in learning as a theater performer doing yoga exercises before taking the stage. Both are techniques the "actors" use to focus, to get themselves in the mood and mode to perform.

Those Asian Americans who prefer to learn within the context of groups use a process of *collaborative and negotiated problem solving*. Regardless of how minor or significant an issue is, they seek out opinions and proposed solutions from all members of the constituted group. Each individual's ideas are presented and critiqued. Their merits are weighed against those suggested by every other member of the group. Discussions are animated and expansive so that all parties participate and understand the various elements of the negotiations. Eventually, a solution is reached that is a compromise of several possibilities. Then more discussions follow to ensure that everyone is in agreement with the solution and understands who is responsible for what aspects of its implementation. These discussions proceed in a context of congeniality and *consensus building* among the many, not with animosity, domination, and the imposition of the will of a few.

A compelling illustration of the positive effects of this process on student achievement occurred in Treisman's (1985; Fullilove & Treisman, 1990) Mathematics Workshop Program at the University of California, Berkeley. He observed the study habits of Chinese Americans to determine why they performed so well in high-level mathematics classes and if he could use their model with Latinos and African Americans. He found what others have observed more informally—the Chinese American students always studied in groups, and they routinely explained to each other their understanding of the problems and how they arrived at solutions to them. Treisman attributed their high achievement to the time they devoted to studying and to talking through their solutions with peers. When he simulated this process with African Americans and Latinos, their achievement improved radically. Treisman was convinced that "group study" made the difference. Given other evidence that compatibility between cultural habits and teaching/learning styles improves student performance, this is probably what occurred. Communal problem solving and the communicative impulse were evoked, thus producing the desired results.

These are powerful but challenging pedagogical lessons for all educators to learn and emulate in teaching students of color. Collective and situated performance styles require a distribution of resources (timing, collective efforts, procedures, attitudes) that can collide with school norms; for instance, much of how student achievement is assessed occurs in tightly scheduled arrangements, which do not accommodate stage setting or collective performance. Students of color have to learn different styles of performing, as well as the substantive content, to demonstrate their achievement.

This places them in potential double jeopardy—that is, failing at the level of both procedure and substance. Pedagogical reform must be cognizant of these dual needs and attend simultaneously to the content of learning and the processes for demonstrating mastery. It also must be bidirectional—that is, changing instructional practices to make them more culturally responsive to ethnic and cultural diversity while teaching students of color how to better negotiate mainstream educational structures.

Organizing Ideas in Discourse

In addition to mode, the actual process of discourse engagement is influenced by culture and, in turn, influences the performance of students in schools. Several elements of the dynamics of discourse are discussed here to illustrate this point: organizing ideas, taking positions, conveying imagery and affect through language, and gender variations in conversational styles. How ideas and thoughts are organized in written and spoken expression can be very problematic to student achievement. Two techniques are commonly identified—*topic-centered* and *topic-associative,* or *topic-chaining,* techniques. European Americans seem to prefer the first while Latinos, African Americans, Native Americans, and Native Hawaiians (Au, 1993; Heath, 1983) are inclined toward the second.

In *topic-centered* discourse, speakers focus on one issue at a time; arrange facts and ideas in logical, linear order; and make explicit relationships between facts and ideas. In this process, cognitive processing moves deductively from discrete parts to a cumulative whole with a discernible closure. Quality is determined by clarity of descriptive details, absence of unnecessary or flowery elaboration, and how well explanations remain focused on the essential features of the issue being analyzed. The structure, content, and delivery of this discourse style closely parallel the expository, descriptive writing and speaking commonly used in schools. A classic example of topic-centered discourse is journalistic writing, which concentrates on giving information about who, what, when, where, why, and how as quickly as possible. Its purpose is to convey information and to keep this separate from other speech functions, such as persuasion, commentary, and critique. Another illustration is the thinking and writing associated with empirical inquiry, or critical problem solving. Again, there is a hierarchical progression in the communication sequence—identifying the problem, collecting data, identifying alternative solutions and related consequences, and selecting and defending a solution. There is a clear attempt to separate facts from opinions, information from emotions.

A *topic-associative style* of talking and writing is episodic, anecdotal, thematic, and integrative. More than one issue is addressed at once. Related explanations unfold in overlapping, intersecting loops, with one emerging out of and building on others. Relationships among segments of the discourse are assumed or inferred rather than explicitly established (Cazden, 1988; Lee & Slaughter-Defoe, 1995). Thinking and speaking appear to be circular and seamless rather than linear and clearly demarcated. For one who is unfamiliar with it, this communication style sounds rambling, disjointed, and as if the speaker never ends a thought before going to something else.

Goodwin (1990) observed topic-chaining discourse at work in a mixed-age (4- to 14-year-olds) group of African Americans in a Philadelphia neighborhood as they told stories, shared gossip, settled arguments, and negotiated relationships. She noted the ease and finesse with which a child could switch from a contested verbal exchange to an engaging story and dramatically reshape dyadic interactions into multiparty ones. Using a single utterance, the children could evoke a broad history of events, a complex web of identities and relationships that all participants understood without having elaborate details on any of the separate segments. The talk-story discourse style among Native Hawaiians operates in a similar fashion, which explains why Au (1993) characterizes it as a "joint performance, or the cooperative production of responses by two or more speakers" (p. 113).

Two other commonplace examples are indicative of a topic-chaining or associative discourse style. One is used by many African Americans, who literarily try to attach or connect the sentences in a paragraph to each through the prolific use of conjunctive words and phrases—for example, frequently beginning sentences with "consequently," "therefore," "however," thus," "moreover," "additionally," and "likewise." These sentences are in close proximity to each other—sometimes as often as four of every five or six.

The second example illuminates the storytelling aspect of topic-chaining discourse. African Americans (Kochman, 1981, 1985; Smitherman, 1977) and Native Hawaiians (Boggs, 1985) have been described as not responding directly to questions asked. Instead, they give narratives, or tell stories. This involves setting up and describing a series of events (and the participants) loosely connected to the questions asked. It is as if ideas and thoughts, like individuals, do not function or find meaning in isolation from context. A host of other actors and events are evoked to assist in constructing the "stage" upon which the individuals eventually interject their own performance (i.e., answer the question). This narrative-response style is also signaled by the attention given to "introductions" and preludes in writing. They are extensive enough to prompt such comments from teachers as "Get to the point" or "Is this relevant?" or "More focus needed" or "Too much extraneous stuff" or "Stick to the topic." The students simply think that these preludes are necessary to setting the stage for the substantive elements of the discourse.

Storytelling as Topic-Chaining Discourse

Speaking about the purposes and pervasiveness of storytelling among African Americans, Smitherman (1977) surmises that they allow many different things to be accomplished at once. These include relating information, persuading others to support the speaker's point of view, networking, countering opposition, exercising power, and demonstrating one's own verbal aestheticism. She elaborates further:

An ordinary inquiry [to African American cultural speakers] is likely to elicit an extended narrative response where the abstract point or general message will be couched in concrete story form. The reporting of events is never simply objectively reported, but dramatically acted out and narrated. The Black English speaker thus simultaneously conveys the facts and his or her personal sociopsychological perspective on the facts.... This meandering away from the "point" takes the listener on episodic journeys and over tributary rhetorical routes, but like the flow of nature's rivers and streams, stories all eventually lead back to the source. Though highly applauded by Blacks, this narrative linguistic style is exasperating to Whites who wish you'd be direct and hurry up and get to the point. (pp. 161, 148)

It takes African American topic-chaining speakers a while to get to the point—to orchestrate the cast of contributors to the action. The less time they have to develop their storylines, the more difficult it is for them to get to the substantive heart of the matter. Frequently in schools, the time allocated to learning experiences lapses while African Americans are still setting up the backdrop for "the drama"—their expected task performance—and they never get to demonstrate what they know or can do on the proposed academic task.

Posed to an African American student who routinely uses a topic-chaining discourse style, a simple, apparently straightforward question such as "What did you do during summer vacation?" might prompt a response such as the following:

> Sometimes, especially on holidays, you know, like July 4, or maybe when a friend was celebrating a birthday, we go to the amusement park. It's a long ways from where I live. And, that is always a big thing, because we have to get together and form car caravans. Jamie and Kelly are the best drivers, but I preferred to ride with Aisha because her dad's van is loaded, and we be just riding along, chilling, and listening to tapes and stuff. Going to the amusement park was a kick 'cause we had to drive a long way, and when we got there people would stare at us like we were weird or something. And we would just stare right back at them. All but Dion. He would start to act crazy, saying things like "What you lookin' at me for? I ain't no animal in no zoo. I got as much right to be here as you do." You see, Dion gets hyped real quick about this racist thing. And we be telling him, "Man, cool it. Don't start no stuff. We too far from home for that." Then, we just go on into the park and have us a good time. We try to get all the rides before everything closes down for the night. Then, there's the trip home. Everybody be tired but happy. We do this three or four times in the summer. Different people go each time. But, you know something—we always run into some kind of funny stuff, like people expecting us to make trouble. Why is that so? All we doing is out for a good time. Dion, of course, would say it's a racist thing.

The narrator does eventually answer the question, but it is embedded in a lot of other details. In fact, there are stories within stories within stories (e.g., celebration rituals, friendships, drivers, the drive, racism, risk taking, activities at the amusement park, similarities and differences, continuity and change, etc.). These elaborate details are needed to convey the full meaning of the narrator's answer to the initial question. But to culturally uninitiated listeners or readers, such as many classroom teachers, the account sounds like rambling and unnecessarily convoluted information, or Smitherman's (1977) notion of "belabored verbosity" (p. 161).

Teachers seeking to improve the academic performance of students of color who use topic-associative discourse styles need to incorporate a storytelling motif into their instructional behaviors. This can be done without losing any of the substantive quality of academic discourses. Gee (1989) believes topic-associative talking is inherently more complex, literary, and enriching than topic-centered speech. The assertions are verified by the success of the Kamehameha Early Elementary Program, which produced remarkable improvement in the literacy achievement of Hawaiian students by employing their cultural and communication styles in classroom instruction. Boggs (1985) found that the performance of Native Hawaiian students on the reading readiness tests correlated positively with narrative abilities. The children who told longer narratives more correctly identified the picture prompts than those who responded to individually directed questions from adults.

Yet topic-associative discourse is troubling to many conventional teachers. Michaels and Cazden's (1986) research explains why. The European American teachers who participated in their study found this discourse style difficult to understand and placed little value on it. African American teachers gave equal positive value to topic-centered and topic-associative discourse. We should not assume that this will always be the case. Some African American teachers are as troubled by topic-chaining discourse among students as teachers from other ethnic groups. The ethnicity of teachers is not the most compelling factor in culturally responsive teaching for ethnically diverse students. Rather, it is teachers' knowledge base and positive attitudes about cultural diversity, and their recognition of diverse cultural contributions, experiences, and perspectives, that enhance their ability to teach ethnically diverse students effectively.

Taking Positions and Presenting Self

In addition to significant differences in the *organization* of thinking, writing, and talking, many ethnically diverse students *relate* differently to the materials, issues, and topic discussed or analyzed. Most of the information available on these patterns deals with African and European Americans. Not much research has been done on the discourse dynamics of Latinos and Native Americans. Deyhle and Swisher (1997) concluded their historical view of research conducted on Native Americans with a strong conviction that there are fundamental and significant linkages among culture, communication, and cognition that should help shape classroom instruction for ethnically diverse students. But they do not provide any descriptions of the discourse dynamics of various Native American groups. Fox (1994) examined the thinking, writing, and speaking behavior of international students from different countries in Africa, Asia, Latin America, and the Middle East studying in U.S. colleges and universities. She found that their cultural traditions valued indirect and holistic communication, wisdom of the past, and the importance of the group. Their cultural socialization profoundly affects how these students interact with professors and classmates, reading materials, problem solving, and writing assignments. How they write is especially important to their academic performance because, according to Fox (1994), "writing touches the heart of a student's identity, drawing its voice and strength and meaning from the way the student understands the world" (p. xiii).

Personalizing or Objectifying Communications

Kochman (1972, 1981, 1985), Dandy (1991), and Smitherman (1977) point out that African Americans (especially those most strongly affiliated with the ethnic identity and cultural heritage) tend to take positions of advocacy and express personal points of view in discussions. Facts, opinions, emotions, and reason are combined in presenting one's case.

The worth of a particular line of reasoning is established by challenging the validity of oppositional ideas and by the level of personal ownership of the individuals making the presentations. Declaring one's personal position on issues, and demanding the same of others, is also a way of recognizing "the person" as a valid data source (Kochman, 1981). Publication is not enough to certify the authority of ideas and explanations, or the expertise of the people who author them. They must stand the test of critical scrutiny and the depth of personal endorsement.

Consequently, Kochman (1981) proposes that African Americans are more likely to challenge authority and expertise than students from other ethnic groups. He suggests the following reason for this:

> Blacks . . . consider debate to be as much a contest between individuals as a test of opposing ideas. Because it is a contest, attention is also paid to performance, for winning the contest requires that one outperform one's opponents; outthink, outtalk, and outstyle. It means being concerned with art as well as argument. . . . [B]lacks consider it essential for individuals to have personal positions on issues and assume full responsibility for arguing their validity. Otherwise, they feel that individuals would not care enough about truth or their own ideas to want to struggle for them. And without such struggle, the value of ideas cannot be ascertained. (pp. 24–25)

According to Kochman (1981), the discourse dynamics of European Americans are almost the opposite of African Americans. He says they relate to issues and materials as spokespersons, not advocates, and consider the truth or merits of an idea to be intrinsic, especially if the person presenting it has been certified as an authority or expert. How deeply individuals personally care about the idea is irrelevant. Their responsibility is to present the facts as accurately as possible. They believe that emotions interfere with one's capacity to reason and quality of reasoning. Thus, European Americans try to avoid or minimize opposition in dialogue (especially when members of ethnic minority groups are involved) because they assume it will be confrontational, divisive, and lead to intransigence or the further entrenchment of opposing viewpoints. They aim to control impulse and emotions, to be open-minded and flexible, and to engage a multiplicity of ideas. Since no person is privy to all the answers, the best way to cull the variety of possibilities is to ensure congeniality, not confrontation, in conversation. As a result of these beliefs and desires, the European American style of intellectual and discourse engagement "weakens or eliminates those aspects of character or posture that they believe keep people's minds closed and make them otherwise unyielding" (Kochman, 1981, p. 20).

Playing with and on Words

African American cultural discourse uses repetition for emphasis and to create a cadence in speech delivery that approximates other aspects of cultural expressiveness such as dramatic flair, powerful imagery, persuasive effect, and polyrhythmic patterns (Baber, 1987; Kochman, 1981; Smitherman, 1977). Some individuals are very adept at "playing on" and "playing with" words, thereby creating a "polyrhythmic character" to their speaking. It is conveyed through the use of nonparallel structures, juxtaposition of complementary opposites, inclusion of a multiplicity of "voices," manipulation of word meanings, poetic tonality, creative use of word patterns, and an overall playfulness in language usage. Although decontextualized, this statement written by a graduate student illustrates some of these tendencies: "The use of culturally consistent communicative competencies entails teachers being able to recognize the multitude of distinct methods of communication that African American students bring to the classroom." Another example of these discourse habits is the frequent use of verb pairs. Following are some samples selected from the writings of students:

- A number of public issues to be explored and represented
- Numerous factors have impacted and influenced
- Make an attempt to analyze and interpret
- No model is available to interpret and clarify
- Many ways of explaining and understanding
- A framework that will enable and facilitate
- Validity was verified and confirmed
- He will describe and give account

Two other examples are helpful in illustrating the dramatic flair and poetic flavor of playing with words

that characterize African American cultural discourse. One comes from Smart-Grosvenor (1982), who describes African American cultural communication as "a metaphorical configuration of verbal nouns, exaggerated adjectives, and double descriptives" (p. 138).

She adds (and in the process demonstrates that which she explains) that "ours is an exciting, practical, elegant, dramatic, ironic, mysterious, surrealistic, sanctified, outrageous, and creative form of verbal expression. It is a true treasure trove of vitality, profundity, rhythm—and, yes, style" (p. 138). Smitherman (1972) provides a second example of African American discourse style and aestheticism. She writes:

> The power of the word lies in its enabling us to translate vague feelings and fleeting experiences into forms that give unity, coherence, and expression to the inexpressible. The process of composing becomes a mechanism for discovery wherein we may generate illuminating revelations about a particular idea or event. (p. 91)

Ambivalence and Distancing in Communication

Classroom experiences and personal conversations with Asian international and Asian American college students and professional colleagues reveal some recurrent communication features. These individuals tend not to declare either definitive advocacy or adversarial positions in either oral or written discourse. They take moderate stances, seek out compromise positions, and look for ways to accommodate opposites. They are rather hesitant to analyze and critique but will provide factually rich descriptions of issues and events. They also use a great number of "hedges" and conciliatory markers in conversations—that is, "starts and stops," affiliative words, and apologetic nuances interspersed in speech, such as "I'm not sure," "maybe . . . ," "I don't know, but . . . ," "I may be wrong, but . . ." These behaviors give the appearance of tentative, unfinished thinking, even though the individuals using them are very intellectually capable and thoroughly prepared academically. And many Asian and Asian American students are virtually silent in classroom discussions.

I have observed Asian and Asian American students frequently interjecting laughter into conversations with me about their academic performance. This happens in instructional and advising situations in which students are having difficulty understanding a learning task that is being explained by the teacher. Rather than reveal the full extent of their confusion, or lack of understanding, students will interject laughter into the conversations. It functions to defuse the intensity of their confusion and give the impression that the problem is not as serious as it really is. Teachers who are unaware of what is going on may interpret these behaviors to mean the students are not taking their feedback or advice seriously. Or they may assume that the students understand the issue so completely that they have reached a point in their intellectual processing where they can relax and break the mental focus (signaled by laughter). When queried about this practice, students invariably say "It's cultural" and often add an explanation for it that invokes some rule of social etiquette or interpersonal interaction that is taught in their ethnic communities. Interestingly, Japanese, Chinese, Korean, Taiwanese, and Cambodians offer similar explanations about the motivation behind and meaning of this shared behavior. These students explain that "ritualized laughter" is a means of maintaining harmonious relationships and avoiding challenging the authority or disrespecting the status of the teacher.

These communication behaviors among students of Asian origin are consistent with those reported by Fox (1994). Hers were gleaned from observations, interviews, and working with students from non-Western cultures and countries (Fox refers to them as "world majority students") on their analytical writing skills in basic writing courses at the Center for International Education at the University of Massachusetts. Data were collected over three years. Sixteen graduate students from several different disciplines participated in the formal interviews. They represented 12 countries: Korea, Japan, the People's Republic of China, Nepal, Indonesia, Brazil, India, Chile, Sri Lanka, Cote d'Ivoire, Somalia, and Cape Verde. Faculty members who worked closely with these students were also interviewed. Additional information was derived from informal conversations and interactions with other students; analysis of writing samples; the teacher's notes about how she and the students worked through writing difficulties; and students' explanations about what they were trying to say in their writing, why assignments were misunderstood, and connections among language, culture, and writing.

Among these students from different countries, several common writing habits emerged that conflict with formal writing styles of academe, known variously as academic argument, analytical or critical writing, and scholarly discourse (Fox, 1994). The characteristics and concerns included:

- Much background information and imprecise commentary
- Exaggeration for effect
- Prolific use of transitional markers, such as "moreover," "nevertheless," and "here again"
- Preference for contemplative instead of action words
- Much meandering around and digressions from the primary topic of discussion
- Emphasis on surrounding context rather than the subject itself
- Being suggestive and trying to convey feelings instead of being direct and concise and providing proof or specific illustrations, as is the expectation of academic writing in the United States
- Tendency to communicate through subtle implications
- Great detail and conversational tonality
- Elaborate and lengthy introductions
- Reticence to speak out, to declare personal positions, and to make one's own ideas prominent in writing

Although all the students shared these communication tendencies, according to Fox's (1994) study, how they were expressed in actual behaviors varied widely. Culturally different meanings of "conversational tone" illustrate this point. Fox notes:

> In Spanish or Portuguese . . . speakers and writers may be verbose, rambling, digressive, holistic, full of factual details, full of feeling, sometimes repetitious, sometimes contradictory, without much concern for literal meanings. In many Asian and African languages

and cultures, metaphor, euphemism, innuendo, hints, insinuation, and all sorts of subtle nonverbal strategies—even silence—are used both to spare the listeners possible embarrassment or rejection, and to convey meanings that they are expected to grasp. (p. 22)

These descriptions of Asian American and non-Western student discourse are based on observations and conversations with a small number of people, in college classes and professional settings. How widespread they are across other educational settings, ethnic groups, generations of immigrants, and social circumstances is yet to be determined. Much more description and substantiation of these communicative inclinations are needed.

The explanation of Asian students that their discourse styles are cultural is elaborated by Chan (1991), Kitano and Daniels (1995), and Nakanishi (1994). They point to traditional values and socialization that emphasize collectivism, saving face, maintaining harmony, filial piety, interdependence, modesty in self-presentation, and restraint in taking oppositional points of view. Leung (1998) suggests some ways these values translate to behavior in learning situations, which underscore the observations made by Fox. Students socialized in this way are less likely to express individual thoughts, broadcast their individual accomplishments, and challenge or disagree with people in positions of authority, especially in public arenas. These interpretations echo the connections between Asian American culture and communicative styles provided by Kim (1978). She suggests that one of their major functions is to promote social harmony and build community. Consequently, many Asian American students may avoid confrontations as well as the expression of negative feelings or opinions in classroom discourse.

GENDER VARIATIONS IN DISCOURSE STYLES

Most of the detailed information on gender variations in classroom communication involves European Americans. Some inferences can be made about probable gender discourse styles among African, Latino, Native, and Asian Americans from their cultural values and gender socialization, since culture and communication are closely interrelated.

Females Communicate Differently from Males

Lakoff (1975) was among the first to suggest that different lexical, syntactical, pragmatic, and discourse features existed for females and males. She identified nine speech traits prolific among females that are summarized by L. Crawford (1993) as specialized vocabulary for homemaking and caregiving, mild forms of expletives, adjectives that convey emotional reactions but no substantive information, tag comments that are midway between questions and statements, exaggerated expressiveness, super polite forms, hedges or qualifiers, hypercorrect grammar, and little use of humor.

Other research indicates that European American females use more affiliating, accommodating, and socially bonding language mechanisms, while males are more directive, managing, controlling, task focused, and action oriented in their discourse styles. Girls speak more politely and tentatively, use less forceful words, are less confrontational, and are less intrusive when they enter into conversations. By comparison, boys interrupt more; use more commands, threats, and boast of authority; and give information more often (Austin, Salem, & Leffler, 1987; Crawford, 1995; Grossman & Grossman, 1994; Hoyenga & Hoyenga, 1979; Maccoby, 1988; Simkins-Bullock & Wildman, 1991; Tannen, 1994). Because of these gender patterns, Maccoby (1988) concludes that "speech serves more egotistic functions among boys and more socially binding functions among girls" (p. 758).

These general trends were substantiated by Johnstone (1993) in a study of spontaneous conversational storytelling of men and women friends. The women's stories tended to be about groups of people (women and men) engaged in supportive relationships and the importance of community building. The men's stories were more about conquests (physical, social, nature) in which individuals acted alone. Invariably, the characters were nameless men who did little talking but engaged in some kind of physical action. More details were given about places, times, and things than about people. Based on these findings, Johnstone suggests that women are empowered through cooperation, interdependence, collaboration, and community. For men, power comes from individuals "conquering" and acting in opposition to others.

Research by Gray-Schlegel and Gray-Schlegel (1995–1996) on the creative writing of third- and sixth-grade students produced similar results. They examined 170 creative writing samples of eighty-seven students to determine if differences existed in how control, outcomes, relationships, and violence were used. Clear gender patterns emerged. Both boys and girls placed male characters in active roles more often than females, but this tendency increased with age only for the males. Females were more optimistic about the fate of their characters, while males were inclined to be cynical. Boys usually had their protagonists acting alone, while girls had them acting in conjunction with others. Regardless of age or the gender of the story character, boys included more crime and violence in their narratives.

Gender Communication Patterns Established Early in Life

These kinds of gender-related discourse patterns are established well before third grade, as research by Nicolopoulou, Scales, and Weintraub (1994) revealed. They examined the symbolic imagination of four-year-olds as expressed in the kinds of stories they told. The girls' stories included more order and social realism. These concepts were conveyed through the use of coherent plots with stable characters, continuous plot lines, and social and familial relationships as the primary topics of and contexts for problem solving. Their stories emphasized cyclical patterns of everyday domestic life, along with romantic and fairy tale images of kings and queens, princesses and princes. They were carefully constructed, centered, and coherent, with elaborate character and theme development, and were invariably directed toward harmonious conflict resolution.

Whenever threatening disruptive situations occurred, the girls were careful to reestablish order before concluding their stories. The boys' stories contained much more disorder and a picaresque, surrealistic aesthetic style. These traits were apparent in the absence of stable, clearly defined characters, relationships, and plots; large, powerful, and frightening characters; violence, disruption, and conflict; and a series of loosely associated dramatic images, actions, and events.

The boys were not concerned with resolving conflicts before their stories ended. Instead, action, novelty, excess, defiance, destruction, and often escalating and startling imagery drove their plots.

In summarizing differences between how boys and girls construct stories, Nicolopoulou and associates (1994) made some revealing observations that should inform instructional practices. They noted that the stories produced by girls focused on "creating, maintaining, and elaborating structure." In comparison, the stories boys told emphasized "action and excitement" and involved a restless energy that is often difficult for them to manage (p. 110). Furthermore, the boys and girls dealt with danger, disorder, and conflict very differently. The girls' strategy was *implicit avoidance* while the boys' technique was *direct confrontation*.

Another fascinating verification of theorized gender differences in communication is provided by Otnes, Kim, and Kim (1994). They analyzed 344 letters written to Santa Claus (165 from boys and 179 from girls). Although the age of the authors was not specified, they were probably eight years old or younger, since children stop believing in Santa Claus at about this time. The content of the letters was analyzed to determine the use of six kinds of semantic units, or meaning phrases: (1) polite or socially accepted forms of ingratiation, (2) context-oriented references, (3) direct requests, (4) requests accompanied by qualifiers, (5) affectionate appeals, and (6) altruistic requests of gifts for someone other than self. For the most part, results of the study confirmed the hypothesized expectations. Girls wrote longer letters, made more specific references to Christmas, were more polite, used more indirect requests, and included more expressions of affection. By comparison, boys made more direct requests. There were no differences between boys and girls in the number of toys requested or the altruistic appeals made. Findings such as these provide evidence about the extent and persistence of patterns of culturally socialized communicative behaviors.

Early gender patterns of communication may transfer to other kinds of social and educational interactions. They also can entrench disadvantages that will have long-term negative effects on student achievement. Interventions to achieve more comparable communications skills for male and female students should begin early and continue throughout the school years. Efforts should also be undertaken in both research and classroom situations to determine if or how communicative styles are differentiated by gender in ethnic groups other than European Americans. Undoubtedly some differences do exist, since discourse styles are influenced by cultural socialization, and males and females are socialized to communicate differently in various ethnic groups.

Problems with Gendered Communication Styles

The "gendered" style of communication may be more problematic than the gender of the person involved in the communication. If this is so, then a female who is adept at using discourse techniques typically associated with males will not be disadvantaged in mainstream social interactions. Conversely, males who communicate in ways usually ascribed to females will lose their privileged status. Hoyenga and Hoyenga (1979) offer some support for this premise. In their review of research on gender and communication, they report that "feminine communication styles" are associated with less intelligence, passivity, and submissiveness, while "masculine styles" evoke notions of power, authority, confidence, and leadership.

However, Crawford (1995) suggests that some of the claims about female–male communication differences need to be reconsidered. For example, indirectness and equivocation in communication are not inherently strategies of female subordination or dominance. They can be tools of power or powerlessness as well. Interpretations of speech behaviors may depend more on the setting, the speaker's status and communicative ability, and the relationship to listeners rather than the person's gender per se (Tannen, 1994). Sadker and Sadker (1994) propose that males may be at greater *emotional risk* than females because of their role socialization. Girls are encouraged to be caring and emotionally expressive, but boys are taught to deny their feelings and to be overly cautious about demonstrating how deeply they care. Thus, male advantages in conventional conceptions of academic discourse may be countered somewhat by the psychoemotional and social advantages that females have in interpersonal relations.

CONCLUSION

Communication is strongly culturally influenced, experientially situated, and functionally strategic. It is a dynamic set of skills and performing arts whose rich nuances and delivery styles are open to many interpretations and instructional possibilities. Ethnic discourse patterns are continually negotiated because people talk in many different ways for many different reasons. Sometimes the purpose of talking and writing is simply to convey information. It is also used to persuade and entertain; to demonstrate sharing, caring, and connections; to express contentment and discontentment; to empower and subjugate; to teach and learn; and to convey reflections and declare personal preferences. In imagining and implementing culturally responsive pedagogical reform, teachers should not merely make girls talk more like boys, or boys talk more like girls, or all individuals within and across ethnic groups talk like each other. Nor should they assume that all gender differences in communication styles are subsumed by ethnicity or think that gender, social class, and education obliterate all ethnic nuances. Instead, we must be mindful that communication styles are multidimensional and multimodal, shaped by many different influences. Although culture is paramount among these, other critical influences include ethnic affiliation, gender, social class, personality, individuality, and experiential context.

The information in this essay has described some of the patterns, dynamics, and polemics of the discourse styles of different ethnicities and groups. Since communication is essential to both teaching and learning, it is imperative that it be a central part of instructional reforms designed to improve the school performance of underachieving African, Native, Asian, and European American students. The more teachers know about the discourse styles of ethnically diverse students, the better they will be able to improve academic achievement. Change efforts should attend especially to discourse dynamics as opposed to linguistic structures. The reforms should be directed toward creating better agreement between the communication patterns of underachieving ethnically diverse students and those considered "normal" in schools.

Knowledge about general communication patterns among ethnic groups is helpful, but it alone is not enough. Teachers need to translate it to their own particular instructional situations. This contextualization might begin with some self-study exercises in which teachers examine their preferred discourse modes and dynamics, and determine how students from different ethnic groups respond to them. They should also learn to recognize the discourse habits of students from different ethnic groups. The purposes of these analyses are to identify (1) habitual discourse features of ethnically diverse students; (2) conflictual and complementary points among these discourse styles; (3) how, or if, conflictual points are negotiated by students; and (4) features of the students' discourse patterns that are problematic for the teacher. The results can be used to pinpoint and prioritize specific places to begin interventions for change.

Whether conceived narrowly or broadly, and expressed formally or informally, communication is the quintessential medium of teaching and learning. It is also inextricably linked to culture and cognition. Therefore, if teachers are to better serve the school achievement needs of ethnically diverse students by implementing culturally responsive teaching, they must learn how to communicate differently with them. To the extent they succeed in doing this, achievement problems could be reduced significantly.

References

Abrahams, R. D. (1970). *Positively Black*. Englewood Cliffs, NJ: Prentice-Hall.

Asante, M. K. (1998). *The afrocentric idea* (Rev. and exp. ed.). Philadelphia: Temple University Press.

Ascher, M. (1992). *Ethnomathematics*. New York: Freeman.

Au, K. R. (1980). Participation structures in a reading lesson with Hawaiian children: Analysis of a culturally appropriate instructional event. *Anthropology and Education Quarterly, 11*, 91–115.

Au, K. R. (1993). *Literacy instruction in multicultural settings*. New York: Harcourt Brace.

Au, K. R., & Kawakami, A. J. (1985). Research currents: Talk story and learning to read. *Language Arts, 62,* 406–411.

Au, K. R., & Kawakami, A. J. (1991). Culture and ownership: Schooling of minority students. *Childhood Education, 67,* 280–284.

Au, K. R., & Kawakami, A. J. (1994). Cultural congruence in instruction. In E. R. Rolling, J. E. King, & W. C. Hayman (Eds.), *Teaching diverse populations: Formulating a knowledge base* (pp. 5–23). Albany: State University of New York Press.

Au, K. P., & Mason, I. M. (1981). Social organizational factors in learning to read: The balance of rights hypothesis. *Reading Research Quarterly, 17,* 115–152.

Austin, A. M. B., Salem, M., & Leffler, A. (1987). Gender and developmental differences in children's conversations. *Sex Roles, 16,* 497–510.

Baber, C. R. (1987). The artistry and artifice of Black communication. In G. Gay & W. L. Baber (Eds.), *Expressively Black: The cultural basis of ethnic identity* (pp. 75–108). New York: Praeger.

Belensky, M. F., Clinchy, B. M., Goldberger, N. R., & Tarule, I. M. (1986). *Women's ways of knowing: The development of self, voice, and mind.* New York: Basic Books.

Boggs, S. T. (1985). The meaning of questions and narratives to Hawaiian children. In C. B. Cazden, V. H. John, & D. Hymes (Eds.), *Functions of language in the classroom* (pp. 299–327). Prospect Heights, IL: Waveland.

Boggs, S. T., Watson-Gegeo, K., & McMillen, G. (1985). *Speaking, relating, and learning: A Study of Hawaiian children at home and at school.* Norwood, NJ: Ablex.

Bruner, I. (1996). *The culture of education.* Cambridge, MA: Harvard University Press.

Byers, P., & Byers, H. (1985). Nonverbal communication and the education of children. In C. B. Cazden, V. P. John, & D. Hymes (Eds.), *Functions of language in the classroom* (pp. 3–31). Prospect Heights, IL: Waveland.

Carroll, J. B. (Ed.). (1956). *Language, thought, and reality: Selected writings of Benjamin Lee Whorf.* Cambridge, MA: MIT Press.

Cazden, C. B. (1988). *Classroom discourse: The language of teaching and learning.* Portsmouth, NH: Heinemann.

Chan, S. (Ed.). (1991). *Asian Americans: An interpretative history.* Boston: Twayne.

Crawford, L. W. (1993). *Language and literacy learning in multicultural classrooms.* Boston: Allyn & Bacon.

Crawford, M. (1995). *Talking difference: On gender and language.* Thousand Oaks, CA: Sage.

Dandy, E. B. (1991). *Black communications: Breaking down the barriers.* Chicago: African American Images.

Deyhle, D., & Swisher, K. (1997). Research in American Indian and Alaska native education: From assimilation to self-determinations. In M. W. Apple (Ed.), *Review of research in education* (Vol. 22, pp. 113–194). Washington, DC: American Educational Research Association.

Fox, H. (1994). *Listening to the world: Cultural issues in academic writing.* Urbana, IL: National Council of Teachers of English.

Fullilove, R. E., & Treisman, P. U. (1990). Mathematics achievement among African American undergraduates at the University of California, Berkeley: An evaluation of the Mathematics Workshop Program. *Journal of Negro Education, 59,* 463–478.

Gallimore, R., Boggs, J. W., & Jordon, C. (1974). *Culture, behavior and education: A study of Hawaiian Americans.* Beverly Hills, CA: Sage.

Gee, J. P. (1989). What is literacy? *Journal of Education, 171,* 18–25.

Giamati, C., & Weiland, M. (1997). An exploration of American Indian students' perceptions of patterning, symmetry, and geometry. *Journal of American Indian Education, 36,* 27–48.

Goodlad, J. I. (1984). *A place called school: Prospects for the future.* New York: McGraw-Hill.

Goodwin, M. H. (1990). *He-said she-said: Talk as social organization among Black children.* Bloomington: Indiana University Press.

Gray-Schlegel, M. A., & Gray-Schlegel, T. (1995–1996). An investigation of gender stereotypes as revealed through children's creative writing. *Reading Research and Instruction, 35,* 160–170.

Grossman, H., & Grossman, S. H. (1994). *Gender issues in education.* Boston: Allyn & Bacon.

Heath, S. B. (1983). *Ways with words: Language, life, and work in communities and classrooms.* Cambridge, England: Cambridge University Press.

Hoijer, H. (1991). The Sapir–Whorf hypothesis. In L. A. Samovar & R. E. Porter (Eds.), *Intercultural communication: A reader* (6th ed., pp. 244–251). Belmont, CA: Wadsworth.

Hoyenga, K. B., & Hoyenga, K. T. (1979). *The question of sex differences: Psychological, cultural, and biological issues.* Boston: Little Brown.

Hymes, D. (1985). Introduction. In C. B. Cazden, V. P. John, & D. Hymes (Eds.), *Functions of language in the classroom* (pp. xi–xvii). Prospect Heights, IL: Waveland.

Johnstone, B. (1993). Community and contest: Midwestern men and women creating their worlds in conversational storytelling. In D. Tannen (Ed.), *Gender and conversational interaction* (pp. 62–80). New York: Oxford University Press.

Kim, B. L. (1978). *The Asian Americans: Changing patterns, changing needs.* Montclair, NJ: Association for Korean Christian Scholars of North America.

Kitano, H., & Daniels, R. (1995). *Asian Americans: Emerging minorities* (2nd ed.). Englewood Cliffs, NJ: Prentice-Hall.

Klein, S. S. (Ed.). (1982). *Handbook for achieving sex equity through education.* Baltimore: Johns Hopkins University Press.

Kochman, T. (Ed.). (1972). *Rappin' and stylin' out: Communication in urban Black America.* Urbana: University of Illinois Press.

Kochman, T. (1981). *Black and White styles in conflict.* Chicago: University of Chicago Press.

Kochman, T. (1985). Black American speech events and a language program for the classroom. In C. B. Cazden, V. P. John, & D. Hymes (Eds.), *Functions of language in the classroom* (pp. 211–261). Prospect Heights, IL: Waveland.

Lakoff, R. (1975). *Language and women's place.* New York: Harper & Row.

Lee, C. D., & Slaughter-Defoe, D. T. (1995). Historical and sociocultural influences on African American education. In J. A. Banks & C. A. M. Banks (Eds.), *Handbook of research on multicultural education* (pp. 348–371). New York: Macmillan.

Leung, B. P. (1998). Who are Chinese American, Japanese American, and Korean American children? In V. O. Pang & L-R. L. Cheng (Eds.), *Struggling to be heard: The unmet needs of Asian Pacific American children* (pp. 11–26). Albany: State University of New York Press.

Longstreet, W. (1978). *Aspects of ethnicity: Understanding differences in pluralistic classrooms.* New York: Teachers College Press.

Maccoby, E. E. (1988). Gender as a social category. *Developmental Psychology, 24,* 755–765.

Maltz, D. N., & Borker, R. A. (1983). A cultural approach to male-female miscommunication. In J. J. Gumperz (Ed.), *Communication, language, and social identity* (pp. 196–216). Cambridge, England: Cambridge University Press.

Mandelbaum, D. G. (Ed.). (1968). *Selected writings of Edward Sapir in language, culture and personality.* Berkeley: University of California Press.

Michaels, S., & Cazden, C. B. (1986). Teacher/child collaboration as oral preparation for literacy. In B. B. Schietfelin & P. Gilmore (Eds.), *The acquisition of literacy: Ethnographic perspectives* (pp. 132–154). Norwood, NJ: Ablex.

Montague, A., & Matson, F. (1979). *The human connection.* New York: McGraw-Hill.

Nakanishi, D. (1994). *Asian American educational experience.* New York: Routledge.

Nicolopoulou, A., Scales, B., & Weintraub, J. (1994). Gender differences and symbolic imagination in the stories of four-year-olds. In A. H. Dyson & C. Genishi (Eds.), *The need for story: Cultural diversity in classroom and community* (pp. 102–123). Urbana, IL: National Council of Teachers of English.

Otnes, C., Kim, K., & Kim, Y. C. (1994). Yes, Virginia, there is a gender difference: Analyzing children's requests to Santa Claus. *Journal of Popular Culture, 28,* 17–29.

Pasteur, A. B., & Toldson, I. L. (1982). *Roots of soul: The psychology of Black expressiveness.* Garden City, NY: Anchor Press/Doubleday.

Philips, S. U. (1983). *The invisible culture: Communication in classroom and community on the Warm Springs Indian Reservation.* Prospect Heights, IL: Waveland.

Porter, R. E., & Samovar, L. A. (1991). Basic principles of intercultural communication. In L.A. Samovar & R. E. Porter (Eds.), *Intercultural communication: A reader* (6th ed., pp. 5–22). Belmont, CA: Wadsworth.

Ramirez, M., III, & Castañeda, A. (1974). *Cultural democracy, bicognitive development and education.* New York: Academic Press.

Sadker, M., & Sadker, D. (1994). *Failing at fairness: How our schools cheat girls.* New York: Touchstone.

Sapir, E. (1968). The status of linguistics as a science. In D. G. Mandelbaum (Ed.), *Selected writings of Edward Sapir in language, culture and personality* (pp. 160–166). Berkeley: University of California Press.

Shade, B. J. (Ed.). (1989). *Culture, style, and the educative process.* Springfield, IL: Thomas.

Shade, B. J. (1994). Understanding the African American learner. In E. R. Hollins, J. E. King, & W. C. Hayman (Eds.), *Teaching diverse populations* (pp. 175–189). Albany: State University of New York Press.

Simkins-Bullock, J. A., & Wildman, B. G. (1991). An investigation into the relationship between gender and language. *Sex Roles, 24,* 149–160.

Smart-Grosvenor, V. (1982). We got a way with words. *Essence, 13,* 138.

Smith, B. O. (1971). On the anatomy of teaching. In R. T. Hyman (Ed.), *Contemporary thought on teaching* (pp. 20–27). Englewood Cliffs, NJ: Prentice-Hall.

Smitherman, G. (1972). Black power is Black language. In G. M. Simmons, H. D. Hutchinson, & H. E. Summons (Eds.), *Black culture: Reading and writing Black* (pp. 85–91). New York: Holt, Rinehart & Winston.

Smitherman, G. (1977). *Talkin' and testifyin': The language of Black America.* Boston: Houghton Mifflin.

Tannen, D. (1990). *You just don't understand: Women and men in conversation.* New York: Morrow.

Tannen, D. (1994). *Gender and discourse.* New York: Oxford University Press.

Tharp, R. G., & Gallimore, R. (1988). *Rousing minds to life: Teaching, learning, and schooling in social context.* Cambridge, England: Cambridge University Press.

Treisman, P. U. (1985). *A study of the mathematics achievement of Black students at the University of California, Berkeley.* Unpublished doctoral dissertation, University of California, Berkeley.

Vygotsky, L. S. (1962). *Thought and language.* Cambridge, MA: MIT Press.

Whorf, B. L. (1952). *Collected papers on metalinguistics.* Washington, DC: Department of State, Foreign Service Institute.

Whorf, B. L. (1956). Language, mind, and reality. In J. B. Carroll (Ed.), *Language, thought and reality: Selected writings of Benjamin Lee Whorf* (pp. 246–270). Cambridge, MA: MIT Press.

Concepts and Questions

1. How do students' communication abilities affect teachers' perceptions of students?

2. Beyond the transmission of information, what other purposes does Gay suggest that language serves?

3. What does Gay mean when she says, "languages and communication styles are systems of cultural notations and the means through which thoughts and ideas are expressively embodied"?

4. What does Gay mean when she uses the term "discourse structures"?

5. Distinguish between *passive–receptive* and *participatory–interactive* styles of discourse.

6. Describe the methods employed by many African American students to gain entry into conversations. How does this style differ from the communication styles of Native Hawaiian students?

7. Describe differences in problem-solving styles among African Americans, Latinos, Native Americans, and Asian American students.

8. Distinguish between *topic-centered* and *topic-associative* (or *topic-chaining*) techniques in organizing ideas in discourse. Which method is associated with which cultural groupings of students?

9. How does the African American storytelling style function as topic-chaining discourse?

10. Distinguish between female and male communication styles.

THE HEALTH CARE CONTEXT

Negotiating Cultural Understanding in Health Care Communication

PATRICIA GEIST-MARTIN

While knowledge and appreciation of cultural diversity are growing in all types of contexts, providers in the health care setting have more to learn about the effects of culture on individuals' perception and expression of their symptoms. The white coat and high technology image of modern medicine dominating American medicine coincides with what many people see as an excessive medical emphasis on disease and a biological understanding of illness (Littlewood, 1991). The reality of our contemporary society is that it is a culturally diverse community of individuals with many different national, regional, ethnic, racial, socioeconomic, and occupational orientations that influence interactions in health care settings (Kreps & Thornton, 1992).

This article examines the complex and dynamic features of communication in a health care context challenged by the culturally diverse expectations and behaviors of individuals seeking health care. In the last decade, with increasing numbers of immigrants admitted to the United States, greater attention has been paid to cross-cultural caring, cultural sensitivity, and transcultural care. The article begins with a discussion of the long-standing interest in considering sociocultural backgrounds of patients in health care delivery. What we discover is that the movement to communicate in culturally sensitive ways is constrained by the Western emphasis on the biomedical model and its inherent progressive ideology. The

article continues by presenting specific case examples where providers and patients face difficulties when the culturally specific beliefs and practices of patients are not discussed or considered in diagnosing and determining appropriate treatment. Finally, the article concludes with avenues for overcoming the obstacles revealed in the case examples and for expanding our notions of culture and culturally sensitive health care.

LINKING CULTURE, HEALTH, AND COMMUNICATION

In 1989 the United States admitted over one million immigrants from all over the world (see Table 1). In fact, California is expected to be the first mainland state with a nonwhite majority in the coming decades (Howe-Murphy, Ross, Tseng, & Hartwig, 1989). With the diversity of individuals entering the United States comes increasing diversity in health care beliefs and practices of persons seeking health care. However, medical education, generally, has failed to integrate intercultural communication training into its curriculum.

Sectors of health care education have long been concerned with cultural influences upon health care delivery. Three decades ago, the field of transcultural nursing was established, and with it an emphasis on culture-specific care, culturally congruent care, and

Table 1 *Immigrants to the United States in 1989*

Country or Region	Number of Immigrants	Percent of Immigrants
Mexico	405,660	37%
Asia	296,420	27%
Central America	101,273	9%
Europe	94,338	9%
Caribbean	87,597	8%
South America	59,812	5%
Africa	22,486	2%
Canada	18,294	2%
Oceania*	4,956	<1%

*Includes Australia, Fiji, New Zealand, Tonga, and Western Samoa

culturally sensitive care (Leininger, 1991). Transcultural nursing, a humanistic and scientific area of formal study and practice, focuses upon differences and similarities among cultures with respect to human care, health (or well-being), and illness based upon the people's cultural values, beliefs, and practices (Leininger, 1991). Operating from this philosophy, nurses work to avoid imposing their cultural beliefs on their patients, and provide them with cultural-specific or culturally congruent care.

Transcultural nursing has been criticized for its limited notion of culture. One criticism is that it views culture as a unified whole with a direct cause and effect relationship upon behavior. Instead, in viewing culture as dynamic, and the experiences of individuals from similar cultures as varied, we begin to focus on the unique requirements of individuals—their feelings, opinions, and experiences (Mason, 1990). Second, critics believe that transcultural nursing must include more of a global perspective (Lindquist, 1990), one that goes beyond traditional cultural beliefs and practices to the history and political situation in the country from which individuals have immigrated. Finally, culturally sensitive care needs to address the stressful and traumatic experiences of immigrants in adapting to their new home in the United States (Boyle, 1991).

Today, the significant influence of culture on perceptions, treatment, and interaction is being recognized and written about in a wide array of texts, including *Patients and Healers in the Context of Culture* (1980), *Medicine and Culture* (1988), *Culture, Health and Illness* (1990), *Caring for Patients from Different Cultures: Case Studies from American Hospitals* (1991), and *Cross-Cultural Caring* (1991), to name a few. What is clear in just about every examination of health and culture is that "miscommunication, noncompliance, different concepts of the nature of illness and what to do about it, and above all different values and preferences of patients and their physicians limit the potential benefits of both technology and caring" (Payer, 1989, p. 10). Cross-cultural caring considers health care a social process in which professionals and patients bring a set of beliefs, expectations, and practices to the medical encounter (Waxler-Morrison, Anderson, & Richardson, 1991). The task of negotiating an understanding of the problem, diagnosis, or treatment often is complicated by these cultural differences.

In the United States, the emphasis on technological progress and the biomedical model complicates the task of communicating to negotiate understanding even further. A progressive ideology has produced a society of experts who possess the technical knowledge, not social knowledge, and whose communication to the public places priority on the "body," not the "person" (Hyde, 1990). This progressive ideology places great emphasis on the functioning and malfunctioning of the human machine. One physician points out that this emphasis permeates medical education.

> Disease, we were told [in medical school] was caused by a malfunction of the machine, the body.
>
> …The emphasis began and ended with the body…. For this reason the modern medical model is called the molecular theory of disease causation…. (Dossey, 1982, pp. 6–8)

But, as a growing number of providers are discovering, this model does not account for the part of the human psyche that is most centrally involved in the cure of illness, namely varying perceptions of what constitutes health, illness, treatment, and the appropriate interaction between provider and patient (Lowenberg, 1989; Needleman, 1985). In fact, many would argue as Lowenberg (1989) does, that the single, most overriding conflict in the health care system is the polarization between humanistic and technological advances in health care. Fisher (1986) suggests that crosscutting all interactions between providers and patients is an ideology that supports the authority of the medical perspective over the patient's perspective. Consequently, the asymmetry of the medical relationship creates difficulties for patients in raising topics of interest to them and/or providing information they see as relevant (Fisher, 1986; Mishler, 1984).

Negotiating cultural understanding in the health care context necessitates willingness on the part of providers and patients to communicate honestly; to build a supportive, trusting relationship—"a relationship based not on unrealistic certainty, but on honesty in facing the uncertainty in clinical practice" (Inlander, Levin, & Weiner, 1988, p. 206). We need to understand illness and care as embedded in the social and cultural world (Kleinman, 1980). For Kleinman, "medicine is a cultural system, a system of symbolic meanings anchored in particular arrangements of social institutions and patterns of interpersonal interactions" (p. 24). He uses the term *clinical reality* to describe health-related aspects of social reality—especially attitudes and norms concerning sickness and health, clinical relationships, and treatment or healing activities (p. 37).

Increasing immigration of individuals from diverse cultures brings with it an amalgam of modern and traditional beliefs, values, and institutions that often conflict and contradict (Kleinman, 1980). The call to expand our understanding and appreciation of clinical realities implies that we need to acknowledge our ethnocentrism in dictating the proper way to provide care (Leininger, 1991); internationalize our professional education system (Lindquist, 1990); consider the sociocultural background of patients (Boyle, 1991; Giger & Davidhizar, 1991); develop our cultural sensitivity (Waxier-Morrison et al., 1991); understand traditional (folk-healing) health care beliefs and incorporate them into care (Krajewski-Jaime, 1991); and generally communicate interculturally, recognizing the problems, competencies, prejudices, and opportunities for adaptation (Barna, 1994; Brislin, 1991; Kim, 1991; Spitzberg, 1991).

EXPANDING CULTURAL SENSITIVITY IN THE HEALTH CARE CONTEXT

A growing crisis in the U.S. health care system is the culture gap between the medical system and the huge number of ethnic minorities it employs and serves (Galanti, 1991). Assessment is a clinical art that combines sensitivity, clinical judgment, and scientific knowledge (Anderson, Waxier-Morrison, Richardson, Herbert, & Murphy, 1991). Rather than using phrases like "taking the history," "physical examination," or "case management," health care providers negotiate a plan that will be acceptable to both themselves and their patients. The following cases reveal the difficulties that providers and patients face negotiating appropriate care. Differences in beliefs about health and illness, perceptions of appropriate treatment, and expectations about interaction in the medical setting complicate the communication process in health care delivery.

CULTURAL DIFFERENCES IN PERCEPTIONS, TREATMENT PRACTICES, AND RELATIONSHIPS

All cultures have beliefs about health and illness that have been passed down from generation to generation (Galanti, 1991; Krajewski-Jaime, 1991). The difference between the belief system of the Western biomedical model and that of other cultures can result in inappropriate assessment or complications in treatment and communication in the provider-patient relationship. The research investigating the intersection of health and culture abounds with vivid examples of these challenges and the successes and failures in negotiating understandings acceptable to both providers and patients.

One source of misunderstanding in health care delivery stems from the practice of folk-healing medicine. Some practices can result in misdiagnosis; others simply contradict scientific medicine; and still others can result in improper medical treatment (Galanti, 1991). Curanderismo, a Hispanic folk-healing belief system originating in Europe, is the treatment of a variety of ailments with a combination of psychosocial interventions, mild herbs, and religion (Chesney, Thompson, Guevara, Vela, & Schottstaedt, 1980; Comas-Diaz, 1989; Krajewski-Jaime, 1991; Maduro, 1983). The three most common beliefs about the causes of disease are (a) natural and supernatural forces; (b) imbalances of hot and cold; and (c) emotions (Krajewski-Jaime, 1991, p. 161). Three practices central to this belief system are: (a) the role of the social network, particularly kin, in diagnosing and treating illness; (b) the relationship between religion and illness, which includes the use of religious ritual in many healing processes; and (c) consistency (but not uniformity) of beliefs among Hispanic communities about symptoms and regimens of healing (Krajewski-Jaime, 1991, p. 160).

Knowledge of folk-healing beliefs and practices enables providers to communicate with empathy, sensitivity, and open-mindedness. Social workers, physicians, and nurses who receive special training in interviewing and communication may build trust and mutual sharing of cultural information in their relationships with their patients (Krajewski-Jaime, 1991).

When this training has not been part of medical education, differences in health beliefs between predominant-culture providers and minority patients may result in inappropriate assessment. Providers may interpret folk-healing beliefs and practices as ignorance, superstition, abuse, or neglect because patients do not follow prescribed treatments. In the following case, described by Krajewski-Jaime in her research on folk-healing beliefs and practices among Mexican-American families, she reveals how a non-Hispanic caseworker's recommendations could have resulted in the unnecessary removal of a Mexican-American child from his caring and nurturing family.

The assessment indicated that the child in question was ill and in need of medical care, but the mother had obvious emotional problems and appeared to be irrational; the mother had kept on saying in broken English, that she could not allow any evil spirits to come near her child and had locked the child in his room; hung from the ceiling a pair of sharp scissors just above his head, and would not allow anyone, including the caseworker and the doctor, to enter the child's room. The caseworker's supervisor, who had some knowledge of the folk-healing practices among some of the agency's Mexican-American clients, asked a Mexican-American child protective service worker to reinvestigate the case. The worker visited the mother, who, while upset about the child's illness, welcomed someone who spoke Spanish. The mother explained that she had used several home remedies to help her child's fever go away, but evil spirits had already taken possession of her child and the usual remedies no longer helped. The only thing left to do was to prevent new spirits from entering the child's body. The scissors would immediately cut any spirits that would try to enter the child's body. Since evil spirits could attach to anyone who entered the room, she could not allow anyone to enter the room, thus preventing any further harm to her child. The Mexican-American worker, although familiar with folk-healing practices had not seen this particular cure before. She understood the validity of this belief within the client's cultural context, but to successfully obtain the mother's permission to see the child, to remove the dangerous scissors, and to see that the child received medical attention, she had to validate the mother's beliefs and gain her trust. She told the mother that although she had not seen anyone use this cure before, she had heard her grandmother talk about it. To protect the patient and his or her entire surrounding, however, the grandmother usually nailed the scissors on the room's entrance door. The worker explained that, should the spirits attach themselves to anyone who wished to enter the room, the scissors on the entrance door would immediately prevent them from doing so and thus provided stronger protection to the patient. The Mexican-American worker went on to ask the mother if this made sense to her. She asked the mother if she thought this would be more beneficial since it would allow her child to be seen by the caseworker and the doctor. The mother agreed and emphasized that she wanted only what was best for her child. She changed the location of the scissors and welcomed the caseworker and the doctor to examine the child (pp. 158–159).

As Krajewski-Jaime points out, although this is an extreme example because of the dangerousness of the practice, most folk-healing practices are harmless. This case demonstrates how folk-healing, if understood, can become a resource on which to capitalize in building rapport in relationships with patients or families and negotiating appropriate diagnosis and treatment.

Similar to curanderismo, Chinese folk medicine bases many of its beliefs on maintaining a harmonious balance between the two opposing forces of "hot" and "cold," often substituted for yang and yin (Lai & Yue, 1990). Illness may be seen as an imbalance in hot or cold foods and thus people may seek cures from food substances they associate with their own deficiency.

For instance, a traditional Chinese may eat animals' brains in order to grow wiser. A diabetic may eat an animal's pancreas in hope of cure. People thought to be anemic often eat red foods. These examples illustrate why traditional Chinese may have difficulty in regarding plastic capsules as a cure (Lai & Yue, p. 80).

These beliefs and practices provide evidence of the Chinese people's great concern about questions of health and healthcare, more so than Americans (Kleinman, 1980). However, along with this emphasis comes a belief in self-medication that may cause serious health problems.

Three specific examples of health practices reveal the problems that may develop with a patient's self-medication. First, Chinese, embracing the maxim of "all things in moderation," may believe that taking medicine over an extended period of time may weaken their bodies (Li, 1987). As a result, they often feel that:

> Western medicine is too potent for them or their small bodies and they may reduce dosages to a quantity they believe suitable. For example, an elderly Chinese with diabetes may reduce his insulin because it is "foreign" and jeopardizes his health (Lai & Yue, 1990, pp. 83–84).

In fact, Chinese may refuse blood tests, believing that loss of blood will weaken their bodies or that the tests are too invasive (Lai & Yue). Second, dual use of Western medicine and folk medicine is common in the Korean, Bahamian, Haitian, Puerto Rican, Cuban, and Southern U.S. black cultures (Scott, 1974). However, Western prescriptions may contain the same chemical ingredients as herbal prescriptions patients are presently consuming; consequently patients may experience overdose or adverse reactions (Park & Peterson, 1991). Finally, in this third example, we see how the beliefs of a Guatemalan patient's husband led to double dosages of birth control pills:

> One couple that came together for family planning counseling returned in only two weeks asking for more pills. The husband responded to all the questions for his wife regarding how she felt, if she was experiencing any irregular bleeding or pain, without consulting her even though she did understand enough Spanish to know what was being asked. She sat next to him silently as he explained that apparently the woman had taken two pills a day, thinking that they work better if the dosage is doubled. During the initial counseling the husband also responded to all the questions by the female nurse and translator and stated he understood the procedures required for use of the Pill. However, the subsequent visit indicated that he did not fully understand why he had to take extra precaution during the first few weeks, and thus he had encouraged his wife to double the dosage (Miralles, 1989, pp. 102–103).

In these three examples, the significance of communication in the provider–patient relationship is pronounced. And it is clear that providers who lack knowledge of health care beliefs and practices must negotiate and construct understanding during their interactions with patients.

The advice to health care providers in communicating with individuals from diverse cultures is to ask specifically about their beliefs and practices concerning herbal medicines or folk-healing practices (Park & Peterson, 1991). Asking these questions directly, rather than waiting for patients to volunteer the information or to ask about such issues, is especially important considering that Chinese and other immigrant groups generally have been taught to respect doctors and not to ask questions (Lai & Yue, 1990). In fact, for many Chinese, agreement and use of the word "yes" help to avoid the embarrassment of saying "no," as the following case illustrates:

> Link Lee, a sixty-four-year-old Chinese woman [was] hospitalized for an acute evolving heart attack. At discharge, her physician suggested that she come back in two weeks for a follow-up examination. She agreed to do so, but never returned. It is likely that she never intended to do so but agreed because he was an authority figure. Chinese are taught to value accommodation. Rather than refuse to the physician's face and cause him dishonor, Mrs. Lee agreed. She simply did not follow through, sparing everyone embarrassment. When Nancy, her Chinese American nurse, saw her in Chinatown several weeks later, Mrs. Lee was very cordial and said she was feeling fine (Galanti, 1991, p. 21).

In a case such as this we find that negotiating an agreed upon "yes" cannot be taken at face value. Providers who understand how cultural values can lead patients to communicate in prescribed ways will be sensitive to different communication styles in order to avoid the difficulties created by situations such as the one described above.

One additional factor complicating efforts to construct understanding in the provider–patient relationship is the common problem of patients not possessing English language competence. And although the use of translators can help to mitigate this problem, for a variety of reasons, translators, patients, or family members can complicate and obstruct efforts to negotiate understanding (Fitzgerald, 1988; Galanti, 1991; Hartog & Hartog, 1983; Miralles, 1989).

Miscommunication is a frequent problem with the use of translators (Fitzgerald, 1988; Galanti, 1991; Miralles, 1989). Even with expert translation, problems such as linguistic differences between the terms in English and other languages can present difficulties, especially languages such as Vietnamese which includes diverse dialects.

> [Vietnamese] words that translate "feeling hot" don't mean "fever." What they mean is "I don't feel well" and generalized malaise. And if you should ask your Vietnamese patients, "Have you ever had hepatitis?" the translator [may] translate that into "liver disease," and liver disease in Vietnam means itching. . . . Similarly, the kidney is the center of sexual potency to Indochinese and Vietnamese, and therefore "kidney trouble" may really mean decreased libido or other sexual difficulty (Fitzgerald, 1988, p. 67).

In addition, translators sometimes choose not to translate exactly what the patient says for any number of reasons—embarrassment, desire to portray the culture in a certain light, or lack of understanding:

> [Translators] are sometimes reluctant to translate what they think is ignorance or superstition on the part of the patient. So they are sophisticated and tell you what they think rather than what the patient said. [Or the provider may ask] "How do you feel?" The translator then spends five to ten minutes in discussion with the patient and comes back and says, "Fine" (Fitzgerald, 1988, p. 65).

Linguistic variations, slang, and culturally specific terminology existing within any culture can create communication difficulties even for an excellent translator. In addition, translators often selectively choose what to communicate from the patient's or provider's narratives, giving a synopsis of what the patient says or grossly altering the meaning of the communication (Anderson et al., 1991).

A translator's use of medical jargon and technical vocabulary also may contribute to communication difficulties. In the following case, the provider and patient *appeared* to have negotiated understanding, but unfortunately this was not the case:

> Jackie, an Anglo nurse, was explaining the harmful side effects of the medication [that] Adela Samillan, a Filipino patient, was to take at home after her discharge. Although Mrs. Samillan spoke some

English, her husband, who was more fluent, served as interpreter Throughout Jackie's explanation, the Samillans nodded in agreement and understanding and laughed nervously. When Jackie verbally tested them on the information, however, it was apparent that they understood very little. What had happened? Dignity and self-esteem are extremely important for most Asians. Had the Samillans indicated they did not understand Jackie's instructions, they would have lost their self-esteem for not understanding or they would have caused Jackie to lose hers for not explaining the material well enough. By pretending to understand, Mr. and Mrs. Samillan felt they were preserving everyone's dignity. Jackie's first clue should have been their nervous laughter. Asians usually manifest discomfort and embarrassment by giggling. Once Jackie realized they had not understood the material, she went over it until they were able to explain it back to her (Galanti, 1991, p. 20).

This case, as well as other previous cases, demonstrates how important it is not to take smiles and nods of agreement as understanding when communicating with Asian patients. The nurse in this case communicated with the patients in order to assess their understanding and it was only through her continued time, patience, and effort that they were able to negotiate understanding.

And still another complicating factor is the fact that often professional translators are not available in the medical setting and the patient's friends or family members are asked to serve as translators. For a wide variety of reasons, these circumstances can contribute to miscommunication. In the following case, we begin to understand how awkward, embarrassing, or difficult it might be for family members to communicate what they are being asked to translate.

> A Hispanic woman, Graciela Garcia, had to sign an informed consent for a hysterectomy. Her bilingual son served as the interpreter. When he described the procedure to his mother, he appeared to be translating accurately and indicating the appropriate body parts. His mother signed willingly. The next day, however, when she learned that her uterus had been removed and that she could no longer bear children, she became very angry and threatened to sue the hospital. What went wrong? Because it is inappropriate for

a Hispanic male to discuss private parts with his mother, the embarrassed son explained that a tumor would be removed from her abdomen and pointed to that general area. When Mrs. Garcia learned that her uterus had been removed, she was quite angry and upset because a Hispanic woman's status is derived in large part from the number of children she produces (Galanti 1991, p. 15).

There is a whole set of issues complicating communications in the health care setting when children serve as translators. In the case above, cultural rules dictate who can discuss what with whom (Galanti, 1991). In other cases, asking a patient's child to interpret can undermine the patient's competence in the eyes of the child, creating tensions in their relationship (Anderson et al., 1991). Once again we find that selection and use of translators is a complex issue that can interfere with providers' and patients' efforts to negotiate cultural understanding. In the final section of this article we discuss avenues for overcoming the obstacles faced in negotiating cultural understanding and for expanding our notions of culturally sensitive health care.

CULTURALLY SENSITIVE HEALTH CARE

The past ten years have seen a growing body of literature offering advice for increasing cultural sensitivity in health care delivery. Although, many of these suggestions focus on what actions providers should take, it is possible to see the implications these ideas have for anyone's efforts to increase their sensitivity to and understanding of other culture's health care beliefs and practices.

One useful starting point for health professionals is training that assists individuals in examining their own cultural beliefs and values as a basis for understanding and appreciating other cultural beliefs and values (Gorrie, 1989). At the University of Southern California, a course in cross-cultural communication sensitizes physician assistants to their personal biases and prejudices through videotaped mock interviews. Believing that self-awareness of personal discomfort can become a tool for promoting sensitive cross-cultural communication, the curriculum is based on

the model, "Differences + Discomforts = Discoveries." Critiquing the interviews, students are encouraged to investigate their own feelings of prejudice and bias and to use their sensitivity to discomfort as "a cue that they are perceiving a difference and to inquire further rather than seek safety in the harbor of fear and prejudice" (Stumpf & Bass, 1992, p. 115).

In a system-wide approach, Howe-Murphy et al. (1989) describe the Multicultural Health Promotion Project, a multidisciplinary, multicultural, and participative model designed to address the need for changes in allied health service delivery to minority populations. Their training efforts are focused on faculty from three allied health departments (Health Science, Nutrition and Food Science, and Occupational Therapy), students preparing for careers in these three professions, and community health care practitioners— all of whom face issues of health promotion in the multicultural environment.

Viewing cultures as dynamic, and not static unified wholes, means that variations exist among individuals of any one culture. Accordingly, health care providers need to assess each patient individually before deciding on a plan of care (Park & Peterson, 1991). Taking a more holistic approach, concentrating on an "individual's own experience and understanding of illness" may assist in this assessment (Littlewood, 1991). Providers should acquire a knowledge of the specific language of distress utilized by patients and providers' diagnosis and treatment must make sense to patients, acknowledging patients' experience and interpretation of their own condition (Heiman, 1990). Individuals from similar cultural groups often share metaphors (sayings or idioms) that express their perspective on situations, problems, and dilemmas. Providers may use these metaphors in the form of anecdotes, stories, or analogies to build rapport in relationships with patients and to magnify the patient's need to make the changes recommended in treatment plans (Zuniga, 1992).

Listening to the patient's stories (Kreps & Thornton, 1992), soliciting their illness narratives (Kleinman, 1988), and building partnerships (Geist & Dreyer, 1993) will facilitate negotiation of cultural understanding in provider–patient relationships. Since relationships among patients and providers inevitably are shaped by the health care context (Geist & Hardesty,

1992), the complexities and uncertainties of cultural diversity in medical work must continually be negotiated as patients and providers communicate in ways to meet their needs.

References

Adams, R., Briones, E. H., & Rentfro, A. R. (1992). Cultural Considerations: Developing a Nursing Care Delivery System for a Hispanic Community. *Nursing Clinics of North America, 27,* 107–117.

Alexander, F. (1965). *Psychosomatic Medicine.* New York: Norton.

Anderson, J. M., Waxler-Morrison, N., Richardson, E., Herbert, C., & Murphy, M. (1991). Conclusion: Delivering Culturally Sensitive Health Care. In N. Waxler-Morrison, J. M. Anderson, and E. Richardson (Eds.), *Cross-Cultural Caring: A Handbook for Health Professionals in Western Canada.* Vancouver: University of British Columbia.

Balch, J. F., & Balch, P. A. (1990). *Prescription for Nutritional Healing.* Garden City Park, NY: Avery.

Barna, L. M. (1994). Stumbling Blocks in Intercultural Communication. In L. A. Samovar and R. E. Porter (Eds.), *Intercultural Communication: A Reader,* 7th ed. (pp. 345–353). Belmont, CA: Wadsworth.

Boyle, J. S. (1991). Transcultural Nursing Care of Central American Refugees. *Imprint, 38,* 73–79.

Brislin, R. W. (1991). Prejudice in Intercultural Communication. In L. A. Samovar and R. E. Porter (Eds.), *Intercultural Communication: A Reader,* 6th ed. (pp. 366–370). Belmont, CA: Wadsworth.

Bulger, R. J. (1989). The Modern Context for a Healing Profession. In R. J. Bulger (Ed.), *In Search of the Modern Hippocrates* (pp. 3–8). Iowa City: *University of Iowa* Press.

Chesney, A. P., Thompson, B. L, Guevara, A., Vela, A., & Schottstaedt, M. F. (1980). Mexican-American Folk Medicine: Implications for the Family Physician. *The Journal of Family Practice, 11,* 567–574.

Comas-Dias, L. (1989). Culturally Relevant Issues and Treatment Implications for Hispanics. In D. R. Kowlow and E. P. Salett (Eds.), *Crossing Cultures in Mental Health* (pp. 31–48). Washington, DC: Sietar.

Corea, G. (1985). *The Hidden Malpractice: How American Medicine Mistreats Women.* New York: Harper & Row.

Coward, R. (1989). *The Whole Truth: The Myth of Alternative Health.* Boston: Faber & Faber.

Dossey, L. (1982). *Space, Time, and Medicine.* Boston: New Science.

Fisher, S. (1986). *In the Patient's Best Interest: Women and the Politics of Medical Decisions.* New Brunswick, NJ: Rutgers University Press.

Fitzgerald, F. T. (1988). How They View You, Themselves, and Disease. *Consultant, 28,* 65–77.

Galanti, G. (1991). *Caring for Patients from Different Cultures: Case Studies from American Hospitals.* Philadelphia: University of Pennsylvania Press.

Geist, P., & Dreyer, J. (1993). Juxtapositioning Accounts: Different Versions of Different Stories in the Health Care Context. In S. Herndon and G. Kreps (Eds.), *Qualitative Research: Applications in Organizational Communication* (pp. 79–105). Cresskill, NJ: SCA. Applied Communication Series/Hampton Press.

Geist, P., & Hardesty, M. (1992). *Negotiating the Crisis: DRGs and the Transformation of Hospitals.* Hillsdale, NJ: Lawrence Erlbaum.

Giger, J. N., & Davidhizar, R. E. (1991). *Trans-cultural Nursing: Assessment and Intervention.* St. Louis: Mosby-Year Book.

Gorrie, M. (1989). Reaching Clients Through Cross Cultural Education. *Journal of Gerontological Nursing* 15 (10), 29–31.

Gould, R. (July 7,1989). Dissident Doctoring. *The Times Literary Supplement,* D 748.

Hartog, J., & Hartog, E. A. (1983). Cultural Aspects of Health and Illness Behavior in Hospitals. *The Western Journal of Medicine, 139,* 106–112.

Heiman, C. G. (1990). *Culture, Health, and Illness: An Introduction for Health Professionals.* Boston: Wright.

Howe-Murphy, R., Ross, H., Tseng, R., & Hartwig, R. (1989). Effecting Change in Multicultural Health Promotion: A Systems Approach. *Journal of Allied Health, 18,* 291–305.

Howze, E. H., Broyden, R. R., & Impara, J. C. (1992). Using Informal Caregivers to Communicate with Women about Mammography. *Health Communication, 4,* 171–181.

Hyde, M. J. (1990). Experts, Rhetoric, and the Dilemmas of Medical Technology: Investigating a Problem of Progressive Ideology. In M. J. Medhurst, A. Gonzalez, and T. R. Peterson (Eds.), *Communication and the Culture of Technology* (pp. 115–136). Pullman, WA: Washington State University.

Inlander, C. B., Levin, L. S., & Weiner, E. (1988). *Medicine on Trial: The Appalling Story of Medical Ineptitude and the Arrogance that Overlooks It.* New York: Pantheon.

Jones, J. A., & Phillips, G. N. (1988). *Communicating with Your Doctor.* Carbondale, IL: Southern Illinois University Press.

Kim, Y. Y. (1991). Communication and Cross-Cultural Adaptation. In L. A. Samovar and R. E. Porter (Eds.), *Intercultural Communication: A Reader,* 6th ed. (pp. 401–411). Belmont, CA: Wadsworth.

Kleinman, A. (1980). *Patients and Healers in the Context of Culture: An Exploration of the Borderland Between*

Anthropology, Medicine, and Psychiatry. Berkeley: University of California Press.

Kleinman, A. (1988). *The Illness Narratives: Suffering Healing and the Human Condition.* New York: Basic Books.

Kleinman, A. (1992). Local Worlds of Suffering: An Interpersonal Focus for Enthographies of Illness Experience. *Qualitative Health Research, 2,* 127–134.

Krajewski-Jaime, E. R. (1991). Folk-Healing Among Mexican American Families as a Consideration in the Delivery of Child Welfare and Child Health Care Services. *Child Welfare, 70,*157–167.

Kreps, G. L., & Thornton, B. C. (1992). *Health Communication: Theory and Practice* (2nd ed). New York: Longman.

Lai, M. C., & Yue, K. K. (1990). The Chinese. In N. Waxler-Morrison, J. A. Anderson, and E. Richardson (Eds.), *Cross-Cultural Caring: A Handbook for Health Professionals in Western Canada* (pp. 68–90). Vancouver: University of British Columbia Press.

Leininger, M. (1991). Transcultural Nursing: The Study and Practice Field. *Imprint, 38*(2), 55–66.

Li, K. C. (February 1987). *The Chinese Perspective Towards Mental Illness and Its Implications in Treatment.* Paper presented at Haughnessy Hospital, Vancouver.

Lindquist, G. J. (1990). Integration of International and Transcultural Content in Nursing Curricula: Process for Change. *Journal of Professional Nursing, 6,* 272–279.

Littlewood, R. (1991). From Disease to Illness and Back Again. *The Lancet, 337,* 1013–1015.

Lowenberg, J. S. (1989). *Caring and Responsibility: The Crossroads Between Holistic Practice and Traditional Medicine.* Philadelphia: University of Pennsylvania Press.

Maduro, R. (1983). Curanderismo and Latino View of Disease and Curing. *The Western Journal of Medicine, 139,* 868–874.

Mason, C. (1990). Women as Mothers in Northern Ireland and Jamaica: A Critique of the Trans-cultural Nursing Movement. *International Journal of Nursing Studies, 27,* 367–374.

Miralles, M. A. (1989). *A Matter of Life and Death: Health-Seeking Behavior of Guatemalan Refugees in South Florida.* New York: AIMS Press.

Mishler, E. G. (1984). *The Discourse of Medicine: Dialectics of Medical Interviews.* Norwood, NJ: ABLEX.

Needleman, J. (1985). *The Way of the Physician.* San Francisco: Harper & Row.

Northouse, P. G., & Northouse, L. L. (1985). *Health Communication: A Handbook for Health Professionals.* Englewood Cliffs, NJ: Prentice-Hall.

O'Brien, M. E. (1981). Transcultural Nursing Research: Alien in an Alien Land. *Image, 13,* 37–39.

Park, K. Y., & Peterson, L. M. (1991). Beliefs, Practices, and Experiences of Korean Women in Relation to Childbirth. *Health Care for Women International, 12,* 261–267.

Payer, L. (1989). *Medicine and Culture: Notions of Health and Sickness in Britain, the US., France, and West Germany.* London: Victor Gallancz LID.

Scott, C. (1974). Health and Healing Practices Among Five Ethnic Groups in Miami, Florida. *Public Health Report, 89,* 524–532.

Siegel, B. S. (1986). *Love, Medicine, and Miracles: Lessons Learned About Self-Healing from a Surgeon's Experience with Exceptional Patients.* New York: Harper & Row.

Simon, S. (June 25 1992). A Dose of Their Own Medicine. *Los Angeles Times,* Al, 9.

Sirott, L., & Waitzkin, H. (1984). Holism and Self-Care: Can the Individual Succeed Where Society Fails. In V. W. Sidel and R. Sidel (Eds.), *Reforming Medicine: Lessons from the Last Quarter Century* (pp. 245–264). New York: Pantheon.

Spitzberg, B. H. (1991). Intercultural Communication Competence. In L. A. Samovar and R. E. Porter (Eds.), *Intercultural Communication: A Reader,* 6th ed. (pp. 353–365). Belmont, CA: Wadsworth.

Stumpf, S. H., & Bass, K. (1992). Cross Cultural Communication to Help Physician Assistants Provide Unbiased Health Care. *Public Health Records, 107,*173–115.

U.S. Bureau of the Census. (1991). *Statistical Abstract of the U.S.:1991* (11th ed.). Washington, DC.

Wallis, C. (November 4, 1991). Why New Age Medicine Is Catching On. *Time,* 68–76.

Waxler-Morrison, N., Anderson, J., & Richardson, E. (1991). *Cross-Cultural Caring: A Handbook for Health Professionals in Western Canada.* Vancouver: University of British Columbia.

Zuniga, M. E. (1992). Using Metaphors in Therapy: Dichos and Latino Clients. *Social Work, 37,* 55–60.

Concepts and Questions

1. How does the type of communication between caregivers and patients affect a patient's recovery?
2. What is required of health practitioners in order for them to develop a cultural understanding of health?
3. How might cultural diversity in the ideologies of quality of life influence decisions regarding whether or when to withdraw life support?
4. What are "dialogic dialectics," and how are they employed in health care communication?
5. How should a caregiver make use of the "dialectics of self" in establishing an initial communicative relationship with a patient?

6. In what manner is the term "patient" a problem-laden word?
7. How does the practice of folk-healing medicine influence communication in the health care setting?
8. Discuss some of the problems inherent in the use of language translators in the health care setting. How can these problems be minimized?
9. What recommendations would you make to a health care provider who encounters a situation in which a male family member assumes the role of speaking for a female patient?
10. What recommendations about communication would you make to a health care provider who encounters a Hmong family with an ill child whom the parents claim is afflicted by a *qaug dap peg*, that is, a spirit that catches you and makes you fall down?

"Half-Truths" in Argentina, Brazil, and India: An Intercultural Analysis of Physician–Patient Communication

NAGESH RAO

Mr. Akbar Ali, a 60-year-old Muslim from Pakistan, has been diagnosed as having insulin-dependent diabetes. Dr. Martin has prescribed insulin for him and instructed his family on how to administer it. However, when Mr. Ali returns for a checkup, Dr. Martin notices little improvement. Careful questioning of Mr. Ali's son reveals that Mr. Ali has not been taking his insulin, and when asked why, Mr. Ali sternly replies, "I am an Orthodox Muslim and would rather die than disobey Islam." Dr. Martin is puzzled and has no idea what Mr. Ali means. (Gropper, 1996)

Such instances are not uncommon when physicians[1] in the United States treat patients from diverse cultural backgrounds. In this case, it is likely that Mr. Ali has heard that insulin is made from the pancreas of a pig. A Muslim is expected to avoid any product of swine because it is considered unclean. Dr. Martin needs to explain that insulin can come from sheep or oxen too, and she would take care to make sure the insulin is not from a pig. This kind of problem, however, is not limited to situations where the caregiver and the patient speak different languages and come from two different countries.

Helman (1994) aptly notes that, "Physicians and patients, even if they come from the same social and cultural background, view ill-health in very different ways. Their perspectives are based on very different premises, employ a different system of proof, and assess the efficacy of treatment in a different way" (p. 101). The following anecdote narrated by a patient named "Chris" is not uncommon even when the physician and patient perceive the other as having the same cultural background[2]:

> I was a sergeant in the army. I had been in the hospital, sick with fever for a week. I had lost 24 pounds (15% of my body weight) and the physicians could not find the cause of the illness. The physician read the results of some blood work that had been run the day before. Without preparing me for it, he casually said, "hmm…people with your white blood count normally have leukemia." He then started walking away. When I tried to stop him to ask questions, he reprimanded me for not calling him "sir!"

In this paper, we argue that the interaction between a physician and patient is inherently an *intercultural*[3] encounter even when the two parties *perceive* they are from the same culture. The distinction between illness and disease helps explain why every encounter between a physician and patient is intercultural. Rosen et al. (1982) define disease "as the malfunctioning of biological and/or psychological processes whereas illness may be defined as the perception, evaluation, explanation, and labeling of symptoms by the patient and his family and social network" (p. 496). Traditionally, physicians focus on the disease while patients are concerned with the illness. As du Pré (2000) adds, patients are operating with feelings while physicians are addressing evidence. Thus, in our anecdote, the physician is keen to diagnose the disease (possibly leukemia), while "Chris" is dealing with the psychological implications of having leukemia. This disparity in the physician's and patient's beliefs and value structures could create miscommunication between them and lead to ineffective medical care.

Recent research on physician–patient interaction also suggests the need to study the intercultural aspects of physician–patient communication. Physician–patient research generally falls into one of two broad areas: (1) research focusing on the interpersonal communication aspects of physician–patient interactions and identifying specific interpersonal skills for physicians to learn (e.g., see Burgoon, et al., 1991; O'Hair, 1989;

Ong De Haes, Hoos, & Lammes, 1995; Roter, 2000; Sharf, 1990), and (2) scholarship focusing on the cross-cultural aspects of physician–patient communication to assist caregivers in being more culturally sensitive toward their patients (e.g., see Baylav, 1996; Greengold & Ault, 1996; Rosenbaum, 1995; Young & Klingle, 1996). Both of these areas of research, however, fail to bring communication and culture together; the first area of research concentrates on communication and not culture, and the second area focuses on culture, but cross-culturally rather than interculturally. Kim Klingle, Sharkey, Park, Smith, & Cai (2000) begin the quest to create an intercultural approach to physician–patient communication by analyzing how a patient's self-construal impacts his or her verbal communication with a physician. Further, Geist (2000) offers an insightful analysis of the health challenges faced in dealing with co-cultural differences in the United States. In this chapter, as part of a five-year study to develop an *intercultural* model of physician–patient communication, we offer data from our interviews with physicians in Argentina, Brazil, and India.

In this essay, we begin with a literature review on the impact of culture on physician–patient communication and summarize the key findings. After offering a brief description of our methodology (see Rao and Beckett, 2000, for further information), we offer three key findings from our interviews with 91 physicians in Argentina, Brazil, and India. Finally, we highlight our main findings and discuss the implications for future research.

IMPACT OF CULTURE ON PHYSICIAN–PATIENT COMMUNICATION

Traditional medical literature increasingly stresses the importance of good physician communication skills (Burgoon et al., 1991; Cegala, McGee, & McNeils, 1996; O'Hair, 1989; Ong et al., 1995; Roter, 2000). Many factors that inhibit physician–patient communication have previously been documented. Although time limitations remain the number one reason given by providers for lack of communication, some posit that the qualities that earn respect from colleagues are very different from those that earn respect from patients (Welsbacher, 1998). With the exception of several key areas (e.g., care for refugees, using interpreters), the influence of culture(s) in health-related interactions has been largely glossed over. Considering the high rates of global migration, physicians from many different sociocultural backgrounds will find themselves serving an increasingly diverse patient population. Thus, it would seem that a major gap exists within mainstream medical literature.

However, there is one notable exception within the medical arena. Researcher–practitioners within the field of nursing have long advocated that health care providers become familiar with how patients of different cultures conceptualize the notions of "health" and "care." In particular, Madeline Leininger (1991) has been at the forefront of research dedicated to extrapolating these differences. According to her Theory of Culture Care Diversity and Universality, all cultures express care but attach different meanings to health-related practices. Within the health care context, meaning is shaped by technology, religion, cultural norms, economics, and education. Her work is critical in reminding providers that there is far more to culture than simple geography.

Several themes emerge from the nursing research. We are reminded that just as diversity exists across cultures, it also exists within cultural groups (Rosenbaum, 1995). These differences can be intensified by factors such as ethnicity, religion, education, age, sex, and acculturation. As Herselman (1996) aptly states, perceptions are influenced by individual experiences as well as cultural background. Thus, there is a great danger in relying on excessive generalizations (Meleis, 1996). For example, Denham (1996) explains that medical practitioners tend to believe that rural Appalachians are fatalistic in their outlook and in their health practices. However, Denham (1996) adds that a lot of variability occurs in rural Appalachians' fatalistic beliefs and health practices. Finally, if a health care provider is to understand how these variables influence a patient's ways of thinking and behaving, he or she must first be familiar with the patient's cultural background. One must also be aware of how the patient's cultural heritage intersects with the culture of the particular health care organization.

Language can provide a major barrier to culturally appropriate care because exploring goals and expectations can become difficult (Baylav, 1996). In her thesis, "When Yes Means No," Katalanos (1994) argues convincingly that South-East Asian (SEA) patients who are recent immigrants have health beliefs that are different from those held by the health care professionals in the United States, and these differences are manifested in the communication behaviors of the two parties. Katalanos's (1994, p. 31) analyses of the communication patterns (see following section) show that there is significant misunderstanding between SEA patients and U.S.-trained health care providers, sometimes with serious consequences.

PHYSICIAN ASSISTANT: "Are you happy here in America?"

VIETNAMESE PATIENT: "Oh yes" [meaning: I am not happy at all, but I do not want to hurt your feelings. After all, your country took me in].

Further, "yes" may simply mean, "I hear you, and I will answer your question," as the following exchange illustrates:

PHYSICIAN ASSISTANT: "Did you take your medicine?"

VIETNAMESE PATIENT: "Yes [I hear you]. No [I did not take it]."

PHYSICIAN ASSISTANT: "You did not take your medicine?"

VIETNAMESE PATIENT: "Yes [I hear you]. Yes [I did not take it. The medicine was too strong]."

PHYSICIAN ASSISTANT: "Ah, so you did not take it!"

VIETNAMESE PATIENT: "Yes. No."

These responses leave both the health care provider and the patient frustrated, as each person is operating out of her or his own paradigm—the U.S. provider paradigm of diagnosing the specific cause of illness and providing medication, and the SEA paradigm of being polite and not wanting to hurt the provider's feelings.

Medical jargon exacerbates linguistic barriers even further. Some measures that nurses have taken to compensate for these barriers include the use of interpreters, health education sessions run in conjunction with local service providers, ethnic recruiting, alternative medical services, cultural sensitivity training, multicultural videos/fliers, and cultural health care fairs (Baylav, 1996; Kothari & Kothari, 1997).

Research in nursing has also acknowledged the importance of culture in understanding a patient's attitudes toward birth, death, sex, relationships, and ritual (Mullhall, 1996). Treatments that are based on assumptions of how a patient regards such issues could potentially result in miscommunication, if not outright noncompliance. Spitzer Kesselring, Ravid, Tamir, Granot, & Noam (1996) assert that expecting a patient to conform to a health care provider's orders is simply a cultural imposition rather than a joint process of discovering the best ways to treat certain ailments. Charonko (1992) also argues that the term "noncompliant" is biased toward preserving the power of the health care provider at the expense of his or her patient. From Charonko's perspective, it is the provider's responsibility to help patients live as productively as possible within *their* choices. Patient satisfaction, which depends heavily on communication, has been strongly correlated with compliance (Eraker, Kirscht, & Becker, 1984).

The traditional medical literature in the United States, however, is beginning to acknowledge the increasing diversity of the United States. Between 1990 and 1996, growth in Latino, African American, and Asian American populations accounted for almost two-thirds of the increase in the U.S. population (Bureau of the Census, 1996). While the patient population in the United States is growing more diverse, there is little being done to prepare our physicians to work more effectively with these patients (Baylav, 1996; Greengold & Ault, 1996; Rao & Beckett, 2000; Rosenbaum, 1995). For example, Drake and Lowenstein (1998) hold that California is an interesting case study because "minorities" (e.g., Latinos, Asians) will soon outnumber Caucasians.[4] Texas has also attracted attention as of late because of its ranking as the fifth most culturally diverse state (Kothari & Kothari, 1997). In either case, pronounced disparities exist between ethnicity and level of access to health care. The researchers do note that education, language, and literacy are major reasons why access to health care is limited among certain populations. Studies such as this dance around the issue of culture but stop short of providing culturally specific care based on systematic research.

One area of medical research where culture is central, however, concerns health care for refugees. Although Kang, Kahler, and Tesar (1998) assert that there are 26 million refugees in the world, the crisis in Kosovo has surely increased these numbers. And the current problems in Afghanistan are creating additional refugees. Keeping this in mind, physicians will find themselves dealing with these issues increasingly often. Similarly, Obmans, Garret, and Treichel (1996) write that immigrants and refugees are often over-represented in emergency room care. Interpreters are often necessary for physicians to provide care for refugees, yet many communication problems have been documented from this activity. Regardless of strategy, Obmans et al. (1996) write that negotiation and compromise will remain critical to culturally appropriate treatment.

Our succinct review suggests that culture impacts physician–patient communication in several significant ways. The key findings from research on physician–patient communication can be summarized as follows. First, most physicians follow the biomedical approach where they focus more on the disease rather than on the person. Roter (2000) argues, rather persuasively, that as molecular and chemistry-oriented sciences gained prominence in the 20th century, the focus on communication as a central tenet in physician–patient relationships has declined. Second, there has been considerable research emphasizing the importance of several communication skills like empathy, active listening, and so on in physician–patient communication (Burgoon, et al., 1991; Ong et al., 1995; Roter & Hall, 1992). Third, research in nursing and counseling has emphasized the usefulness of focusing on the patient's culture in creating more effective encounters (Leininger, 1991). Fourth, patients are most satisfied when both task and relational dimensions of the relationship are addressed effectively in the physician–patient communication (Helman, 1991; Lochman, 1983; Stewart, 1995). Fifth, while most medical students enter medical school with an idealism to save lives, they often leave with "detached concern" because of the biomedical nature of the training (Miller, 1993). Finally, some medical schools train their students to communicate more effectively with their patients, but such models still focus on general communication and not on intercultural communication (Marshall, 1993).

It can be argued, therefore, that the research on physician–patient communication has focused on how to improve a physician's interpersonal and cross-cultural skills. Since there is limited research on the intercultural nature of this encounter, we are working on a systematic research program to create an intercultural communication model of physician–patient communication. In this next section, we focus on the first phase of our research project to answer the following research question: How do physicians in different countries communicate with culturally diverse patients? We administered the Medical Provider Questionnaire (MPQ) to 29 physicians in Campinas, Brazil; 30 physicians in Madras, India; and 32 physicians in Cordoba, Argentina.[5] Each interview was tape recorded and ranged between 45 to 90 minutes in length. The MPQ had several parts: (1) What motivated these physicians to join this profession; (2) What they liked and disliked about this profession; (3) How they communicated with culturally diverse patients; (4) The physician's response to the case study described in the first part of this article; (5) How physicians defined a successful encounter with a patient; and (6) What the physicians would change in the medical system if they were to go through medical school again. In this next section, we focus on the physicians' responses to questions 3 and 4. We first begin with how physicians defined cultural diversity in their context. Then, we focus on the three key findings—"half-truths," family as patient, and how physicians defined success.

Physicians' Definition of Culture

Almost without exception, the physicians in Argentina, Brazil, and India saw their countries as heterogeneous. This was not surprising by itself. However, what was surprising was how physicians defined diversity in these three countries. In Brazil, a few physicians divided patients along traditional race, ethnic, and national origin lines. One of our respondents, a resident in cardiology, explained:

> Oh, of course. No doubt about it because mainly the kind of settlement of people here in Brazil was in periods over these five centuries. So in the South region you have mostly a European settlement in the

last century so Italians, Germans, many of these people. So in the North and Northeast mainly Portuguese and Indians and the slaves that were brought from Africa, so they are totally different. Most of our Brazilian respondents, however, felt that their main cultural diversity was based on socioeconomic status. Brazil, according to them, had two distinctive cultures, the rich and the poor. For example, a cardiology resident summarized it rather succinctly: Oh, no, we have many cultures here. We have a statesman, a former minister of industry, economics, I don't know, and he always said Brazil is—was Belindia, I don't know if you ever heard of it—it's part of Belgium and part of India. You have many countries inside a country. I don't know if you have traveled for many states here. I don't know if you know the state of Maranhao. The Northeast region is the poorest region in the country. So our country is a mosaic, so if we are having problems here, you can imagine what they are having in the Northeast or the North region where we have the Amazon forest and many people don't have hospitals, don't have many roads because all of the transport system is water, it's rivers and boats and all of this, so the country is extremely, it's not homogeneous like you said.

Similarly, the physicians in Argentina saw their culture as heterogeneous. One senior female cardiologist noted:

> It [Argentina] is heterogeneous. People who formed this country have different origins, different customs, different traditions, and at the same time there were people who were from here.

Most Argentinean physicians focused primarily on education and socioeconomic status to describe the diversity in their country. One internist explained:

> No, it is heterogeneous. We have people very intellectual and with a lot of knowledge and people with a complete lack of education.

An ophthalmologist described Argentina with passion:

> I would say that it is heterogeneous but mainly because we have a huge difference between social classes. Instead of paying 20 dollars to go to a theater, you just think that you need food and clothing. There are many people here who are right now experiencing those kinds of problems.

Physicians in India also saw their country as diverse, but focused on different aspects of diversity—religion, language, socioeconomic status, north–south differences, and so on. A senior female general practitioner described India in the following manner:

> We have patients from all spectrums of life. When the patient's language is different, it is almost like they are from a different country. Their dress is different, language is different, and habits are different. The people in the south are much more humane.

A senior oncologist, working for a large private hospital, explained:

> In our setup here, we see really a cross section both geographically and culturally and even to some extent economically. It is not that only rich people come here. Here patients know that there is better treatment available. So people come here selling all their belongings. Secondly, we see a lot of patients from the northeast. At least 30% of the patients come from that region.

It is intriguing that while Argentina, Brazil, and India have significant diversity based on immigration patterns, religion, languages, and so on, the physicians in Argentina and Brazil focused mainly on socioeconomic status and education as the main indicators of diversity. The Indian physicians represented the various aspects of India's diversity, including language, socioeconomic status, and the like. A physician in Brazil explained that because they speak Portuguese throughout the country, even though there is diversity, the common language takes care of cultural differences. This explanation is also viable in Argentina where Spanish is spoken throughout the country.

India, however, has 18 official languages, and it is difficult to ignore the cultural diversity. An Indian colleague often uses this analogy, "Think of India as a mini-Europe. You can travel 100 miles and speak a completely new language!" Thus, it is not surprising that the physicians in these cultures focused on different aspects of their country's diversity. These cultural differences also played a significant role in how they communicated with their patients.

"Half-truths"

As part of the interview, we asked our respondents to read the following case study (cited previously)

and asked them if the physician had responded appropriately.

> I was a sergeant in the army. I had been in the hospital, sick with fever for a week. I had lost 24 pounds (15% of my body weight) and the physicians could not find the cause of the illness. The physician read the results of some blood work that had been run the day before. Without preparing me for it, he casually said, "hmm . . . people with your white blood count normally have leukemia." He then started walking away. When I tried to stop him to ask questions, he reprimanded me for not calling him "sir!"

All 91 respondents indicated that the physician in this case study had responded inappropriately. We then asked the physicians to explain what they would have done if they had to tell a patient that he or she is terminally ill. Our data suggest that 90 percent of the physicians in these three countries engaged in what we have termed "half-truths," where physicians did not disclose the diagnosis immediately, described the diagnosis in doses over several visits, or informed a family member of the diagnosis first before telling the patient. In all these cases, the physicians explained that hearing such life-threatening news immediately would psychologically harm the patient, which, in turn, would reduce the patient's ability to fight the illness. In other words, the type of "half-truth" used was based on the psychological readiness of the patient. In 10 percent of the cases, the physicians insisted that they would tell the patient directly and immediately because that is what they would have liked. A cardiologist from India described his strategy:

> If I knew a patient had a terminal illness like leukemia, I would tell him that we have to do more tests before we can really be sure. If I tell him directly, he could die of the shock. If I think he is stronger, I may tell him that there are several possibilities and one could be cancer. If he is not strong, I would see which family member he has come with and take them aside to tell them the news. We are very family oriented, and he has to get their support. So, better to tell them first. Also, they may have to make preparations.

A Brazilian physician, in response to the case study, offered a more direct example of "half-truths":

It's completely crazy—unacceptable. First of all, because a blood exam is not enough to make a diagnosis of leukemia. It's more complicated; there are no justifications to answer this question in this way. I think the physician could hide the diagnosis in the start. If I was the physician I would try to hide my scared face. I would try not to reveal to the patient the situation and I would think more about it. I would ask for more tests, and when the diagnosis was certain, I would talk to the patient about the disease and about the treatment. Leukemia is not lethal and can be cured through chemotherapy.

A rheumatologist from Argentina described what he would do in this situation:

One patient never comes alone, so I think that if I know the background and I recognize that the patient is unable to hear anything about himself, I first talk with the family if the background allows me to do that. If there is no family here, in the case of leukemia, sometimes you have to wait, just one day, two days, one week until you say to the patient, to know him better to know which words to use.

One Argentinean doctor, however, indicated that he would prefer to tell the patient directly:

You have to tell the truth to a patient and tell what the patient wants to know. If the patient has leukemia, you have to explain to him that if you follow the treatment, you will be better. The patient knows that because you tell him about the several studies on this topic. You have to motivate the patient to do the treatment and keep on living.

In each of these cases, most of the physicians from Argentina, Brazil, and India chose to use "half-truths" to tell a patient that he or she is terminally ill. This phenomenon can be best explained by understanding collectivism and face-saving behaviors. Argentina, Brazil, and India are collective cultures where "[a] 'we' consciousness prevails: Identity is based on the social system; the individual is emotionally dependent on organizations and institutions; the culture emphasizes belonging to organizations; organizations invade private life and the clans to which individuals belong; and individuals trust group decisions even at the expense of individual rights"

(Samovar & Porter, 2001, pp. 67–68). In these three cultures, the physicians are thinking of the patient's well-being within the context of his or her family and the larger community.

It is common to use face-saving behaviors like "half-truths" to comfort the patient and sustain the harmony of the group. Face-saving behaviors focus less on the veracity of a statement than what is culturally appropriate for the context. In our preliminary interviews in the United States, physicians were clear that they would tell only the patient and tell him or her directly. This is consistent with the individualistic nature of the United States where direct and explicit communication is preferred. Du Pré (2000) notes that therapeutic privilege was a practice in the United States when physicians withheld information if they thought sharing the information would hurt the patient. However, Veatch (1991) argues that if we wish for patients to be informed partners in their health care, therapeutic privilege is counterproductive. Consistent with current legal expectation in medicine, there is an expectation that physicians in the United States inform the patient as soon as they know the diagnosis.

Family as Patient

Our analysis of "half-truths" indicated that physicians often chose to tell a family member rather than tell the patient. Further investigation suggested that even in regular health care visits, the physician had to treat the "family as patient," rather than focus just on the patient. When a patient was ill, the family members felt ill. When a patient recovered, the family members felt better too. We had explained earlier that Argentina, Brazil, and India are collectivistic cultures. People from these cultures also tend to have an interdependent self-construal (Markus & Kitayama, 1991) where a person's identity is intrinsically connected with his or her family's identity. A person with an interdependent self-construal often makes decisions taking into consideration the needs of his or her family members, and family members often make decisions for him or her. Physicians described this interconnectedness in several ways. A cardiologist in India noted:

Patients rarely come alone to the clinic. There are always two or three family members with them. I have to be careful to understand the family dynamics and understand how I should share the information. I will share certain kinds of information with the wife, some with the son, and may decide not to share anything with the uncle. I also know that the wife and the son feel the pain the patient is suffering from. When the patient feels better, I feel good too.

A senior cardiologist in Brazil explained how he would include the family so that they can make decisions for the patient:

If the family were there, I would tell them together. If it were just the patient, I would contact the family. Why? The patient may not need to say anything. I would try to talk to the patient's spouse or child or parents. I would say, your son, your husband, your wife has this illness and we are going to treat it. In this situation, I would tell because the family has to prepare, there is going to be therapy, days when the patient is not feeling well, his diet will change, his hair will fall out. He needs the family's help.

An obstetrician in Argentina described how he would share the news with a patient that the baby in her womb is dead:

The most common situation is to tell the news that the baby inside of the womb is dead. If I made the diagnosis, I won't tell her immediately. I will take a patient aside and, if she is alone, I will try to call the family so she begins to suspect something is wrong. I allow that to happen because it helps me. If you tell her directly her baby is dead, she will be very hurt. Now she guesses and asks if her baby is dead. So the baby is dead, but that word might come from her mouth and not mine. Then I stay with her, I hold her arms and help her cry for a little while. If the husband comes later, which happens very often, I repeat the same exercise. In all these cases, the family is an integral part of the healing process, being constantly present, making decisions, seeking advice, and protecting the patient.

Our initial conversations with physicians in the United States suggest that patients generally come alone and, if family members are present, they respect the patient's space. Occasionally, the family member may seek clarification on behalf of the patient on certain issues.

Defining Success

We asked the physicians to explain when they had a successful interaction with a patient. In about two-thirds of our interviews, we asked the physician if it was a failure if their patient died. Every one of these physicians indicated that it was not a failure if the patient died, as long as they had done everything possible for the patient. Our preliminary conversations with physicians in the United States suggest that they would see it as a failure if the patient died. It is likely that the U.S. physicians trained in the biomedical perspective are focusing on curing the disease. If they cannot cure the patient, they have failed. Death is the ultimate failure with this perspective. Physicians in Argentina, Brazil, and India focused mostly on relational issues or relational plus task issues to define success, with a limited few focusing only on task-related issues (curing the patient). An emergency room physician summarized the task-oriented perspective by saying:

I think I am always successful because I always give them a favorable solution. I try to help them. For example, when I am in the emergency room, I am there to give all I can so that a patient can leave the hospital with a treatment or with any response to her problem.

Most physicians, however, described the importance of building trust and strengthening the relationship with a patient as a key part of being successful. A second-year nuclear resident in Brazil defined success as follows:

When he comes back with another patient. When he brings his uncle or daughter or wife. They would come over and say, "Oh, I knew that you were here; that is why I brought my grandmother. I wanted you to take a look at her." Probably the grandmother didn't have anything, but he wanted me to look at her. That is when I know a patient likes me.

A family practice physician in Madras described how she looked at both task and relational issues to define success:

Early diagnosis. When we are able to pick up on traits and/or behaviors that might possibly cause illness. Success is also when a patient comes to you and says that they are happy with the treatment you have given them. You are building trust with a patient that will definitely help with the cure.

A senior physician of legal medicine in Argentina summarized the need to be aware of the patient's multiple needs by defining success as follows:

In many moments, but especially when you have to transmit [to] a patient the information of an incurable disease, but not terminal. When sharing this information with the patient, if it ends up in improving the patient's wish to fight for his/her life and it has given the patient the possibility of living wonderful experiences that s/he has never lived before, I have allowed the patient a certain quality of life.

THE INTERCULTURAL JOURNEY CONTINUES

"The doctor is mean and the patient is dumb" (du Pré, 2000, p. 48) is a common response in the United States. In this essay, we have argued that it is not fruitful to assign blame to the physician or the patient when communication fails between these two parties. While there is significant research on the interpersonal and cross-cultural aspects, there is little focus on the *intercultural* aspects of physician–patient communication. Our overall goal is to create such an intercultural model, drawing on literature from several disciplines and from original research. Our interviews with physicians in Argentina, Brazil, and India suggest that their collective orientation influences them to use unique communication strategies to deal with culturally diverse patients. They use "half-truths" to share challenging diagnoses, treat the family as the patient, and define success mostly along relational or relational and task objectives. Our results have several significant implications for studying the role of culture in physician–patient communication.

First, as Lienenger (1991) pointed out in her work, there is more to culture than just geography. Our respondents in Argentina and Brazil defined their country's cultural diversity mainly through socio-economic and educational differences. Many of our respondents noted that having a common language (Portuguese or Spanish) reduced the impact of other cultural differences such as gender, age, ethnicity, religion, and so on. This is a particularly important finding since Bennett (1998) points out that people from most countries generally tend to focus on race, ethnicity, religion, and language when discussing cultural diversity. Second, it is important to understand the communication strategies used by physicians in individualistic cultures. Toward this end, we are presently interviewing physicians in the United States to understand how they communicate with patients from culturally diverse backgrounds. Finally, since there are at least two people involved in a physician–patient communication, there are at least two cultural perspectives interacting in their communication. Therefore, it is no longer sufficient to conduct research from only the physician's or the patient's perspective; rather, the physician–patient communication must be analyzed as an *intercultural* phenomenon.

To achieve this goal, in addition to our interviews with physicians, we have administered our Multicultural Health Beliefs Inventory (MBHI) to 600 patients in Argentina, Brazil, India, and the United States to explicate how they define good health (Rao, Beckett, & Kandath, 2000). The MBHI assesses respondents' perceptions of good health along five dimensions of health—physical, psychological, relational, spiritual, and lifestyle/environmental. Du Pré (2000) explains how the physician and the patient bring two opposing worldviews when they interact; the physician focuses on the disease (task) only, while the patient focuses on the illness (task plus relational dimension). By combining our data from physicians and patients from several cultures, our goal is to create an *intercultural* model of physician–patient communication that will have both theoretical and practical implications.

Notes

1. In our paper, the term *physicians* includes only Doctors of Medicine trained in the allopathic tradition.
2. We used this case study as a part of our Medical Provider Questionnaire to interview physicians.
3. Lustig and Koester (1999) explain that the term *intercultural* "denotes the presence of at least two individuals who are culturally different from each other on such important attributes as value orientations, preferred communication codes, role expectations and perceived rules of social relationships" (p. 60).

4. Since this research was conducted, Caucasians have become a minority in California.
5. We chose these three countries to compare how physicians in collectivistic cultures treated their patients as compared to physicians in the United States, an individualistic culture. For a more detailed explanation of our methodology, see Rao and Beckett (2000).

References

Baylav, A. (1996). Overcoming culture and language barriers. *The Practitioner, 240,* 403–406.

Bennett, M. J. (1998). *Basic concepts of intercultural communication.* Yarmouth, ME: Intercultural Press.

Bureau of the Census. (1996). *Statistical abstract of the United States* (116th ed.). Washington, DC: Author.

Burgoon, M., Birk, T. S., & Hall, J. R. (1991). Compliance and satisfaction with the physician-patient communication: An expectancy theory interpretation of gender differences. *Human Communication Research, 18,* 177–208.

Cegala, D. J., McGee, D. S., & McNeils, K. S. (1996). Components of patients' and physicians' perceptions of communication competence during a primary care medical interview. *Health Communication, 8,* 1–27.

Charonko, C. V. (1992). Cultural influences in "noncompliant" behavior and decision making. *Holistic Nursing Practice, 6,* 73–78.

Denham, S. (1996). Family health in a rural Appalachian Ohio county. *Journal of Appalachian Studies, 2,* 299–310.

Drake, M. V., & Lowenstein, D. H. (1998). The role of diversity in the health care needs of California. *Western Journal of Medicine, 168,* 348–354.

du Pré, A. (2000). *Communicating about Health.* Mountain View, CA: Mayfield Publishing Company.

Eraker, S. A., Kirscht, J. P., & Becker, M. H. (1984). Understanding and improving patient compliance. *Annals of Internal Medicine, 100,* 258–268.

Geist, P. (2000). Communicating health and understanding in the borderlands of co-cultures. In L. A. Samovar & R. E. Porter (Eds.) *Intercultural communication: A reader* (9th ed., pp. 341–354). Belmont, CA: Wadsworth.

Greengold, N. L., & Ault, M. (1996). Crossing the cultural physician-patient barrier. *Academic Medicine, 71,* 112–114.

Gropper, R. C. (1996). *Culture and the clinical encounter: An intercultural sensitizer for the health professions.* Yarmouth, ME: Intercultural Press.

Helman, C. G. (1991). Limits of biomedical explanation. *Lancet, 337,* 1080–1083.

Helman, C. G. (1994). *Culture, health and illness.* Boston: Butterworth–Heinemann.

Herselman, S. (1996). Some problems in health communication in a multi-cultural clinical setting: A South African experience. *Health Communication, 8,* 153–170.

Kang, D. S., Kahler, L. R., & Tesar, C. M. (1998). Cultural aspects of caring for refugees. *American Family Physician, 57,* 1245–1255.

Katalanos, N. L. (1994). "When yes means no: Verbal and nonverbal communication of southeast Asian refugees in the New Mexico health care system" (pp. 10–54). Unpublished Master's Thesis. Albuquerque: University of New Mexico.

Kim, M., Klingle, R. S., Sharkey, W. F., Park, H., Smith, D. H., & Cai, D. (2000). A test of a cultural model of patients' motivation for verbal communication in physician-patient interactions. *Communication Monographs, 67,* 262–283.

Kothari, M. P., & Kothari, V. K. (1997). Cross-cultural health-care challenges: An insight into small American community hospitals. *Journal of Hospital Marketing, 12,* 23–32.

Leininger, M. (1991). *Culture care diversity and universality: A nursing theory.* New York: National League for Nursing Press.

Lochman, J. E. (1983). Factors related to patients' satisfaction with their medical care. *Journal of Community Health, 9,* 91–109.

Lustig, M. W., & Koester, J. (1999). *Intercultural competence: Interpersonal communication across cultures* (3rd ed.). New York: Longman.

Markus, H. R., & Kitayama, S. (1991). Culture and the self: Implications for cognition, emotion, and motivation, *Psychological Review, 98,* 224–253.

Marshall, A. A. (1993). Whose agenda is it anyway? Training medical residents in patient-centered interviewing techniques. In E. B. Ray (Ed.), *Case Studies in Health Communication* (pp. 15–30). Hillsdale, NJ: Lawrence Erlbaum.

Meleis, A. I. (1996). Culturally competent scholarship: Substance and rigor. *Advances in Nursing Science, 19,* 1–16.

Miller, K. I. (1993). Learning to care for others and self: The experience of medical education. In E. B. Ray (Ed.), *Case Studies in Health Communication* (pp. 3–14). Hillsdale, NJ: Lawrence Erlbaum.

Mullhall, A. (1996). The cultural context of death: What nurses need to know. *Nursing Times, 92,* 38–40.

Obmans, P., Garrett, C., & Treichel, C. (1996). Cultural barriers to health care for refugees and immigrants: Provider perceptions. *Clinical and Health Affairs, 79,* 26–30.

O'Hair, D. (1989). Dimensions of relational communication control during physician-patient interactions. *Health Communication, 1,* 97–115.

Ong, L. M. L., De Haes, J. C. J. M., Hoos, A. M., & Lammes, F. B. (1995). Physician-patient communication: A review of the literature. *Social Science and Medicine, 40,* 903–918.

Rao, N., & Beckett, C.S. (2000). "Half-truths" and analogies in doctor-patient communication: Dealing with culturally diverse patients in Brazil. Paper presented at the Health Communication Division of the International Communication Association Conference, Washington, DC.

Rao, N., Beckett, C. S., & Kandath, K. (2000). What is good health? Exploratory analyses of a multidimensional health beliefs scale in Brazil and in India. Paper presented at the Health Communication Division of the National Communication Association Conference, Seattle, Washington.

Rosen, G., Kleinman, A., & Katon, W. (1982). Somatization in family practice: A biopsychosocial approach. *Journal of Family Practice, 14,* 493–502.

Rosenbaum, J. N. (1995). Teaching cultural sensitivity. *Journal of Nursing Education, 4,* 188–198.

Roter, D. (2000). The enduring and evolving nature of patient-physician relationship. *Patient Education and Counseling, 39,* 5–15.

Roter, D., & Hall, J. A. (1992). *Physicians talking with patients, patients talking with physicians.* Westport, CT: Auburn House.

Samovar, L. A., & Porter, R. E. (2001). *Communication between cultures* (4th ed.). Stamford, CT: Wadsworth Thomson Learning.

Sharf, B. (1990). Physician-patient communication as interpersonal rhetoric: A narrative approach. *Health Communication, 2,* 217–231.

Spitzer, A., Kesselring, A., Ravid, C., Tamir, B., Granot, G., & Noam, R. (1996). Learning about another culture: Project and curricular reflections. *Journal of Nursing Education, 35,* 323–328.

Stewart, M. A. (1995). Effective physician-patient communication and health outcomes: A review. *Canadian Medical Association Journal, 152,* 1423–1433.

Veatch, R. M. (1991). *The patient-physician relation: The patient as partner* (Part 2). Bloomington: Indiana University Press.

Welsbacher, A. (1998). The give and take of physician-patient communication: Can you relate? *Minnesota Medicine, 81,* 15–20.

Young, M., & Klingle, R. S. (1996). Silent partners in medical care: A cross-cultural study of patient participation. *Health Communication, 8,* 29–53.

Concepts and Questions

1. How does Rao distinguish between the dynamics of illness and disease? In what manner may these dynamics be influenced by culture and affect physician–patient communication?

2. Describe several ways culture might inhibit physician–patient communication.

3. In what ways might cultural diversity in language affect physician–patient communication?

4. Rao makes the argument that effective physician–patient communication requires both cultural knowledge and well-developed interpersonal communication skills. What justification is there for this position?

5. How do physician perceptions of cultural diversity in Argentina and Brazil seem to differ from those evident in India?

6. What effect does the cultural dynamic of collectivism have on physician–patient communication in Argentina, Brazil, and India?

7. How does the collectivistic concept of family as patient differ from the individualistic approach most common in the United States?

8. In what way does building trust between physician and patient in Argentina, Brazil, and India differ from how it is achieved in the United States?

9. What does Rao mean when he refers to the intercultural aspects of physician–patient communication?

10. In what ways do the communication strategies of physicians in collectivistic cultures seem to differ from those of physicians in individualistic cultures?

Communicating Interculturally: Becoming Competent

We can rarely see things from the point of view of another person because we look at the facts through the screen of an impression or an interest which distorts our view; and then there are accusations, quarrels and misunderstanding.

BARRY LONG

The obstacles to cross-cultural understanding may be conceptualized as differences in cultural assumptions and values.

EDWARD C. STEWART

The fish only knows that it lives in the water after it is already on the river bank. Without our awareness of another world out there, it would never occur to us to change.

SOURCE UNKNOWN

One of the main purposes of this book over the last forty years has been to improve our readers' communication with members of cultures different from their own. The three opening quotations serve as a fitting transition for us to develop this point while at the same time introduce this chapter. We call your attention to the words *misunderstanding*, *obstacles*, and *change* in the three opening quotations. These three words highlight the major goal of this chapter, to increase your fund of knowledge about intercultural communication competence by stressing the importance of (1) being sensitive to the potential *misunderstanding* that often plagues the intercultural encounter, (2) learning how to recognize cross-cultural *obstacles* created by cultural differences, and (3) discovering ways to *change your behavior* in a positive manner that will contribute to cultural understanding. Although the chapter uses the term "Becoming Competent" in its title, this entire book is concerned with helping you become a competent intercultural communicator.

Each of the preceding chapters introduced you to diverse cultures and settings to demonstrate how people from a variety of cultures view the world and communicate as participants in that world. By observing these cultural differences, you have collected a fund of knowledge that will assist you in understanding people from a variety of cultures. However, our examination to this point has been more theoretical than practical. Knowing about other cultures and people is only the first step in attempting to understand how intercultural communication operates in the real world. Taking part in intercultural communication requires reciprocal and complementary participation by you and your communication partner(s). This means that intercultural communication becomes an activity in which participants must make simultaneous inferences, not only about their own roles but also about the roles of other(s) in the interaction. This act of mutual role-taking must exist before people can achieve a level of communication that results in shared understanding. In intercultural communication this means that you must recognize your own culture and the culture of the other person(s) as well.

Communication is something people do—a shared activity that involves action. Regardless of how much you may understand another culture or person on an intellectual level, even if you have a clear picture of them in your head, in the final analysis communication means interaction. This generalization implies that you are part of a behavioral exchange and must be prepared to adjust your communicative behaviors to the specific situation. The series of readings in this chapter are intended to improve the way you connect to others by providing some of the information needed to develop and improve your intercultural communication competence.

As previously noted, three common threads link all the selections in this chapter: cultural misunderstanding, intercultural obstacles, and your power to change the way you communicate with others. Being alert to potential problems, and knowing how to solve them, is a major step toward achieving intercultural communication competence.

Our opening essay was one of the first to expand the theory of communication competence to the field of intercultural communication. In "A Model of Intercultural Communication Competence," Brian H. Spitzberg offers a profile of the effective intercultural communicator. Spitzberg suggests a course of action that is likely to enhance your competence when you are in an intercultural setting. His advice takes the form of a series of ten propositions that have been well documented by numerous studies in communication. Spitzberg believes that by understanding and acting on these propositions you can become a more successful intercultural communicator. He guides you through these propositions as he asks you, when engaging in an intercultural exchange, to (1) be motivated, (2) be knowledgeable, (3) practice using effective interpersonal skills, (4) be credible, (5) try to meet the expectations of your communication partner, (6) strike a balance between autonomy needs and intimacy needs, (7) reflect similarities, (8) manifest trust, (9) offer social support, and (10) have access to multiple relationships.

Our next selection, much like Spitzberg's, is yet another piece that was instrumental in moving a major communication construct into the intercultural arena.

Prior to "Managing Intercultural Conflicts Effectively" by Stella Ting-Toomey, most communication scholars examined the issue of conflict only as it applied to a single culture. Ting-Toomey believes that "Conflict is inevitable in all social and personal relationships"; therefore, any analysis of its elements needs to be applied to intercultural communication settings. As a starting point to her approach, Ting-Toomey identifies some of the problems created by interpersonal disharmony in the intercultural setting. To help you improve your capacity to clarify and regulate conflict, Ting-Toomey explains three significant features of intercultural conflict. First, a framework that uses low-context versus high-context and monochronic and polychronic time is advanced to demonstrate why and how cultures are different and similar. Second, some basic assumptions and factors that contribute to conflict are discussed. Finally, she offers a series of skills that can help individuals manage conflict when it develops in the intercultural encounter.

Our next selection, by Mary Jane Collier, seeks to promote and facilitate the practice of intercultural communication. Collier's position is that improving a person's intercultural communication skills is not an easy assignment because of multifaceted variables that compose an intercultural interaction. She states that "The study of intercultural communication is complex and dynamic; occurs in broad historical, economic, political, and social contexts; and is characterized by distinctive social norms and practices in the particular situation." To help you understand the complicated nature of communication and culture, Collier offers a "Ten-Step Inventory" in the form of ten relevant questions. Not only does Collier pose the questions, she answers each question by reviewing the important literature in the field and illuminating the issues that must be considered by anyone attempting to improve their intercultural communication skills. In addition, Collier encourages you to take the information in her article and apply it to current social problems and your own intercultural experiences. Collier's approach offers a blueprint for improving your intercultural skills.

The final selection in this chapter appeared in this reader for the first time nearly thirty years ago, and it is as relevant today as it was when it first appeared. It was one of the earliest attempts to address the often neglected topic of how people adapt to a new culture. Today approximately 40 million immigrants live in the United States, and nearly two million more are added each year. How these people adapt to their new culture is at the core of Young Yun Kim's essay, "Adapting to a New Culture." Kim is concerned with the communication approaches used by immigrants as they try to adjust to a new culture. These approaches, which are internalized from early childhood, may prove troublesome in the new communication environment. To counter some of these difficulties, Kim discusses both the problems and the solutions facing anyone who seeks to adapt to a new culture. Her central thesis is that one learns to communicate by interacting with others. She suggests that immigrants need to find ways to communicate with members of the dominant culture. Kim advances some specific recommendations for immigrants trying to adapt to a new culture. She suggests they study other languages, learn to expect differences in nonverbal communication, and expose themselves to other cultures so they do not feel threatened by these cultures.

A Model of Intercultural Communication Competence

Brian H. Spitzberg

The world we live in is shrinking. Travel that once took months now takes hours. Business dealings that were once confined primarily to local economies have given way to an extensively integrated world economy. Information that once traveled through error-prone and time-consuming methods now appears in the blink of an eye across a wide range of media. People in virtually all locations of the globe are more mobile than ever and more likely to traverse into cultures different from their own. Literally and figuratively, the walls that separate us are tumbling down. Though we may not have fully become a "global village," there is no denying that the various cultures of the world are far more accessible than ever before, and that the peoples of these cultures are coming into contact at an ever-increasing rate. These contacts ultimately comprise interpersonal encounters. Whether it is the negotiation of an arms treaty, or the settlement of a business contract, or merely a sojourner getting directions from a native, cultures do not interact, people do.

The purpose of this essay is to examine the concept of interactional competence in intercultural contexts. For the purposes of this essay, *intercultural communication competence is considered very broadly as an impression that behavior is appropriate and effective in a given context*. Normally, competence is considered to be an ability or a set of skilled behaviors. However, any given behavior or ability may be judged competent in one context, and incompetent in another.

Consequently, competence cannot be defined by the behavior or ability itself. It must instead be viewed as a social evaluation of behavior. This social evaluation comprises the two primary criteria of appropriateness and effectiveness.

Appropriateness means that behavior is viewed as legitimate for, or fitting to, the context. To be appropriate ordinarily implies that the valued rules, norms, and expectancies of the relationship are not violated significantly. Under some circumstances, however, a person violates existing norms to establish new norms. A colleague with whom you work and almost exclusively exchange task information may one day take you aside to talk about a personal problem. This violation of norms, however, may not seem inappropriate as you come to see this person as a friend rather than just a colleague.

Effectiveness is often equated with competence (Bradford, Allen, & Beisser, 1998). Here *effectiveness* is viewed as the accomplishment of valued goals or rewards relative to costs and alternatives. Effectiveness is relative to the available options. For example, effectiveness often implies satisfaction, but there are times when all reasonable courses of action are dissatisfying or ineffective. In such a context, the most effective response may be simply the least dissatisfying. For example, many people find virtually all conflict dissatisfying. If your partner breaks up with you, you may find there is no "effective" response (i.e., something that would "win" this person back). But there are reactions that may be more or less effective in achieving other objectives (e.g., maintaining a friendship, getting your compact discs back, etc.). Effectiveness is also related to, but distinct from, efficiency. *Efficiency*, or expediency, is concerned with communication that is "direct, immediate, and to the point" (Kellerman & Shea, 1996, p. 151). Generally, more efficient communication is considered more effective because it presumes less effort. However, obviously efficient behavior is not always the most effective in obtaining preferred outcomes.

Communication in an intercultural context, therefore, is competent when it accomplishes the objectives of an actor in a manner that is appropriate to the context. *Context* here implies several levels, including culture, relationship, place, and function (Spitzberg & Brunner, 1991). The chapters of this book all illustrate the importance of culture to the use and evaluation of behavior. The competence of behavior also depends significantly on the type of relationship between the interactants. What is appropriate for spouses is not always appropriate for colleagues or friends. Competence also depends on place, or the physical environment. Behavior appropriate for fans at a sporting event will rarely be appropriate at a funeral. Finally, the competence of behavior is influenced by function, or what the communicators are attempting to do. Behavior appropriate for a conflict is often quite different from behavior appropriate for a first date.

The two standards of appropriateness and effectiveness also depend on interaction quality. Quality can be defined by these two criteria by examining the four possible communication styles that result. Communication that is inappropriate and ineffective is clearly of low quality and is referred to as *minimizing*. Communication that is appropriate but ineffective suggests a social chameleon who does nothing objectionable but also accomplishes no personal objectives through interaction. This suggests a *sufficing* style, or one that is sufficient to meet the minimum demands of the situation but accomplishes nothing more. Communication that is inappropriate but effective includes such behaviors as lying, cheating, coercing, forcing, and so forth, which are messages that are ethically problematic. This *maximizing* style reflects a person who attempts to achieve everything, even if it is at the expense of others. While there may be instances in which such actions could be considered competent, they are rarely the ideal behaviors to employ in any given circumstance. Interactants who achieve their goals in a manner that is simultaneously appropriate to the context are competent in an *optimizing* way.

A MODEL OF INTERCULTURAL COMPETENCE

Most existing models of intercultural competence have been fairly fragmented (Lustig & Spitzberg, 1993; Martin, 1993). Typically, the literature is reviewed and a list of skills, abilities, and attitudes is formulated to summarize the literature (Spitzberg & Cupach, 1989). Such lists appear on the surface to reflect useful guidelines for competent interaction and adaptation. For example, Spitzberg's (1989) review of studies reveals dozens of skills, including ability to deal with stress, understanding, awareness of culture, cautiousness, charisma, cooperation, conversational management, empathy, frankness, future orientation, flexibility, interest, managerial ability, opinion leadership, task persistence, self-actualization, self-confidence, self-disclosure, and strength of personality. Although each study portrays a reasonable list of abilities or attitudes, there is no sense of integration or coherence across lists. It is impossible to tell which skills are most important in which situations, or even how such skills relate to each other. In addition, such lists become cumbersome, as it is difficult to imagine trying to learn dozens of complex skills to become competent.

A more productive approach would be to develop an integrative model of intercultural competence that is both consistent with the theoretical and empirical literatures and provides specific predictions of competent behavior. This approach is reflected in basic form in Figure 1 and elaborated by means of a series of propositions below. The propositions are broken down into three levels of analysis: the individual system, the episodic system, and the relational system. The *individual system* includes those characteristics an individual possesses that facilitate competent interaction in a normative social sense. The *episodic system* includes those features of a particular Actor that facilitate competent interaction on the part of a specific Co-actor in a specific episode of interaction. The *relational system* includes those components that assist a person's competence across the entire span of relationships rather than in just a given episode of interaction. Each successive system level subsumes the logic and predictions of the former. The propositions serve both to provide an outline of a theory of interpersonal competence in intercultural contexts and offer practical advice. To the extent interactants analyze intercultural situations sufficiently, each proposition suggests a course of action that is likely to enhance their competence in the situation encountered.

By way of overview, the model portrays the process of dyadic interaction as a function of two individuals' *motivation* to communicate, *knowledge* of

Figure 1 *An Integrative Model of Intercultural Competence*

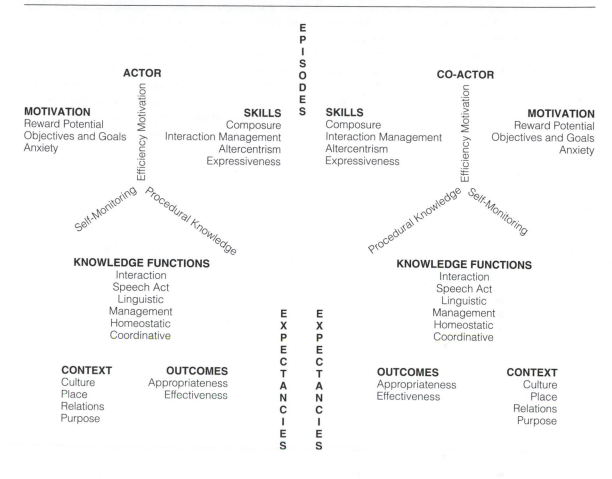

communication in that context, and *skills* in implementing their motivation and knowledge. Over the course of the interaction both within and across episodes, behavior is matched to expectancies each person has of the other and of the interaction process. If expectancies are fulfilled in a rewarding manner, then interactants are likely to perceive both self and other as communicatively competent and feel relatively satisfied that objectives were accomplished. Interactants may be seen as incompetent because they lack motivation to perform competently, lack knowledge of the competent lines of action in the context concerned, or simply lack the communication skills to carry off a deft interaction. Also, interactants may be viewed as incompetent because their partner has unrealistic expectancies for the person or episode.

INDIVIDUAL SYSTEM

1. As Communicator Motivation Increases, Communicative Competence Increases

Very simply, the more a person wants to make a good impression and communicate effectively, the more likely it is that this person will view self, and be viewed by others, as competent. What constitutes or leads to high levels of motivation? The following propositions address this question.

1a. As communicator confidence increases, communicator motivation increases. Confidence results from several individual experiences. For example, a person who is nervous meeting strangers is likely to be less confident when encountering a new person from a different culture. Further, the more unfamiliar a person is with a given type of situation, the less confident that person is regarding what to do and how to do it. Finally, some situations carry more significant implications and are more difficult to manage than others. For example, getting directions to a major urban landmark is likely to permit greater confidence than negotiating a multimillion dollar contract for your company. Thus, social anxiety, familiarity with the situation, and the importance or consequences of the encounter all influence a person's confidence in a social context.

1b. As reward-relevant communicator efficacy beliefs increase, communicator motivation increases. Efficacy beliefs are self-perceptions of ability to perform a given set of behaviors (Bandura, 1982). Basically, the more actors believe they are able to engage in a set of valued or positive actions, the more prone they are to do so. A professional arbitrator is likely to have much higher efficacy beliefs in negotiating disputes or contracts than the average person. However, this arbitrator might not have any greater confidence than the average person in developing friendships with others in a different culture. Efficacy beliefs are therefore usually task-specific and depend on familiarity with tasks and contexts.

1c. As communicator approach dispositions increase, communicator motivations increase. Approach dispositions refer to personality characteristics that prompt someone to value communicative activity. Several dispositions have been found to influence motivation. People who are higher in self-esteem, who consistently seek relatively high levels of sensory stimulation, who believe they have high levels of control over their environment, who are low in social anxiety (Neuliep & McCroskey, 1997), and who are generally well adjusted psychologically, are likely to seek out communication encounters and find them positively reinforcing. Furthermore, people who are more interculturally tolerant are more likely to engage in competent interaction across cultures (Mendleson, Bures, Champion, & Lott, 1997).

1d. As the relative cost–benefit ratio of a situation increases, communicator motivation increases. Very simply, every situation can be viewed as having certain potential costs and benefits. Even in no-win situations (e.g., "true" conflicts), the behavior that leads to the least costly or painful outcome is considered the most preferable or beneficial. Likewise, in a win-win situation, the least desirable outcomes are also the most costly. As the perception of potential benefits increases relative to the potential costs of a course of action, the more motivated a person is to pursue that particular course of action. Obviously, the weighing of costs and benefits must always be done relative to alternatives. Asking directions from someone who does not speak your language may be considered too effortful, but only relative to the alternatives of consulting a map, trial-and-error exploration, seeking someone who speaks your language who might be familiar with the locale, or getting hopelessly lost.

2. As Communicative Knowledge Increases, Communicative Competence Increases

A stage actor needs to be motivated to give a good performance to be viewed as a competent actor. However, merely wanting to perform well and being unhampered by stage fright are rarely sufficient to produce a competent performance. The actor also needs to know the script, the layout of the stage, the type of audience to expect, and so forth. Similarly, the more an interactant knows about how to communicate well, the more competent that person is likely to be.

Knowledge of interaction occurs at several microscopic levels (Greene, 1984). As identified in Figure 1, an actor needs to know the basic goals or *interaction* functions being pursued. These interaction behaviors are combined to fulfill *content* functions, which include the production of speech acts such as asking questions, asserting opinions, and making promises. To perform speech acts in turn requires knowledge of semantics, syntax, and the constituents of a meaningful sentence. In other words, grammatical sentences are formed to fulfill a *linguistic* function. Actual performance of these actions requires adaptation of this behavior to the other person. Such adaptation includes achieving coherence, continuity of topic, and relatively smooth flow of speaking turns (i.e., *management* function), a relative balance of physiological activity level (i.e., *homeostatic* function), and an individual matching of verbal and nonverbal components (i.e., *coordinative* function). Several predictions help specify the relevance of knowledge to competent interaction.

2a. As task-relevant procedural knowledge increases, communicator knowledge increases. Procedural knowledge concerns the "how" of social interaction rather than the "what." For example, knowing the actual content of a joke would be considered the substantive knowledge of the joke. Knowing how to tell it, with all the inflections, subtle timing, and actual mannerisms, are all matters of the procedural knowledge of the joke. This knowledge is typically more "mindless" than other forms of knowledge. Many skill routines are overlearned to the point that the procedures are virtually forgotten, as in driving a familiar route home and not remembering anything about the drive upon arrival. You "know" how to drive, but you can use such knowledge with virtually no conscious attention to the process. Thus, the more a person actually knows how to perform the mannerisms and behavioral routines of a cultural milieu, the more knowledgeable this person is likely to be in communicating with others in this culture. In general, as a person's exposure to a culture increases, his or her stores of relevant subject matters, topics, language forms, as well as procedural competencies, are likely to increase.

2b. As mastery of knowledge acquisition strategies increases, communicator knowledge increases. A person who does not already know how to behave is not necessarily consigned to incompetence. People have evolved many means for finding out what to do, and how to do it, in unfamiliar contexts. The metaphor of international espionage illustrates some of the strategies by which people acquire information about others, such as interrogation (e.g., asking questions), surveillance (e.g., observing others), information exchange (e.g., disclosing information to elicit disclosure from others), posturing (e.g., violating some local custom and observing reactions to assess value of various actions), bluffing (e.g., acting as if we know what we are doing and letting the unfolding action inform us and define our role), or engaging

double agents (e.g., using the services of a native or mutual friend as informant). The more of these types of strategies actors understand, the more capable they are in obtaining the knowledge needed to interact competently in the culture.

2c. As identity and role diversity increases, communicator knowledge increases. In general, the more diverse a person's exposure to distinct types of people, roles, and self-images, the more this person is able to comprehend various roles and role behaviors characteristic of a given cultural encounter. Some people live all their lives in a culture within very narrow ranges of contexts and roles. Others experience a wide variety of societal activities (e.g., jobs, tasks), roles (e.g., parent, worshiper, confidant), groups (e.g., political party, religious affiliation, volunteer organization, cultures and co-cultures). A person who has a highly complex self-image reflecting these social identities (Hoelter, 1985) and has interacted with a diversity of different types of persons and roles (Havighurst. 1957) is better able to understand the types of actions encountered in another culture.

2d. As knowledge dispositions increase, communication knowledge increases. Many personality characteristics are related to optimal information processing. Specifically, persons higher in intelligence, cognitive complexity, self-monitoring, listening skills, empathy, role-taking ability, nonverbal sensitivity, perceptual accuracy, creativity, and problem-solving ability, are more likely to know how to behave in any given encounter. In short, while mere possession of information may help, a person also needs to know how to analyze and process that information.

3. As Communicator Skills Increase, Communicator Competence Increases

Skills are repeatable, goal-oriented actions or action sequences. A person who is motivated to perform well and knows the script well still may not possess the acting skills required to give a good performance. All of us have probably encountered instances in which we knew what we wanted to say but just could not seem to say it correctly. Such issues concern the skills of performing our motivation and knowledge.

Research indicates that there are four specific clusters of interpersonal skills and one more general type of skill.

Before specifying the nature of skills that facilitate intercultural communication competence, an important qualifier needs to be considered. There are probably no specific behaviors that are universally competent. Even if peoples from all cultures smile, the smile is not always a competent behavior. However, there may be skills that are consistently competent according to standards of appropriate usage within each culture. For example, probably all cultures value the smooth flow of conversation, even though they may differ in the specific behaviors and cues used to accomplish such interaction management. All cultures apparently value eye contact and the use of questions, even if they vary greatly in the *way* in which these skills are appropriately used. Any skill or ability is constrained by its own contextual rules of expression. Thus, skills are always assessed relative to their *contextual frame*. It is in this sense that the following propositions are developed regarding communication skills.

3a. As conversational altercentrism increases, communicator skill increases. *Altercentrism* ("alter" means other, "centrism" means to focus upon) involves those behaviors that reveal concern for, interest in, and attention to another person or persons. Behaviors such as eye contact, asking questions, maintenance of others' topics, appropriate body lean and posture, and active listening all indicate responsiveness to the other person.

3b. As conversational coordination increases, communicator skill increases. Conversational coordination involves all those behaviors that assist in the smooth flow of an encounter. Minimizing long response delays, providing for smooth initiation and conclusion of conversational episodes, avoiding disruptive interruptions, providing transitions between themes or activities, and providing informative feedback cues all assist in managing the interaction and maintaining appropriate pacing, rhythms, and punctuation of a conversation.

3c. As conversational composure increases, communicator skill increases. To be composed in a conversation is to reflect calmness and confidence in

demeanor. Composure consists of avoiding anxiety cues such as nervous twitches, tapping of feet, lack of eye contact, and breaking vocal pitch. Conversely, composure also implies behaviors such as a steady volume and pitch, relaxed posture, well-formulated verbal statements, and self-assured tones of verbal and nonverbal expression. The composed communicator tends to appear in control of his or her own behavior.

3d. As conversational expressiveness increases, communicator skill increases. Expressiveness concerns those skills that provide vivacity, animation, intensity, and variability in communicative behavior. Expressiveness is revealed by such behaviors as vocal variety, facial affect, opinion expression, extensive vocabulary usage, and gestures. Expressive communication is closely associated with the ability to display culturally and contextually appropriate affect and energy level through speech and gesture.

3e. As conversational adaptation increases, communicator skill increases. Adaptation is a commonly noted attribute of the competent intercultural communicator. It typically suggests several characteristics. First, rather than radical chameleon-like change, adaptation implies subtle variation of self's behavior to the behavioral style of others. Second, it implies certain homeostatic or consistency-maintaining, regulatory processes—that is, verbal actions are kept relatively consistent with nonverbal actions. Similarly, amounts of personal altercentrism, coordination, composure, and expressiveness are kept relatively consistent with personal style tendencies. Third, adaptation suggests accommodation of both the actions of the other person as well as one's own goal(s) in the encounter. Rather than implying completely altercentric or egocentric orientations, adaptation implies altering and balancing self's goals and intentions to those of the other person. Thus, the skill of adaptation implies such behaviors as shifts of vocal style, posture, animation, and topic development, as the behaviors of the other person vary and as changes in self's goals change over the course of a conversation.

The propositions in this section have examined three basic individual components of interculturally competent communication. In general, the more motivated, knowledgeable, and skilled a person is, the more competent this person is likely to be. It is possible that a person can be viewed as highly competent if high in only one or two of these components. For example, a person who is very motivated may compensate for lack of knowledge and skill through perseverance and effort alone. Likewise, someone who is extremely familiar with a given type of encounter may be able to "drift" through an interaction with minimal access to his or her motivation. A salesperson might claim to have "written so many contracts in my life I can negotiate one in my sleep." Nevertheless, across most encounters, the more of each of these components a person possesses or demonstrates, the more competent this person's interaction is likely to be.

EPISODIC SYSTEM

The first three primary propositions represented factors that increase the likelihood an actor will produce behaviors that are normatively competent. However, given that competence is an impression, there is no guarantee that a person who has performed behaviors that normally would be viewed as competent will be viewed as competent by a particular conversational partner in a particular relational encounter. The propositions in this section address this latter issue. These propositions are episodic in the sense that characteristics of an actor influence the impressions of the co-actor in a specific episode of interaction. The statements concern those characteristics of an actor that predict co-actor's impression of actor's competence.

4. As Actor's Communicative Status Increases, Co-Actor's Impression of Actor's Competence Increases

Communicative status is meant here to represent all those factors that enhance this person's positive evaluation. Competence is, after all, an evaluation. Generally, as a person's status goes, so goes his or her competence. There are obvious exceptions, but it is instructive to consider those status characteristics particularly relevant to communicative competence.

4a. As actor's motivation, knowledge, and skills increase, co-actor's impression of actor's competence increases. The logic of the individual system also applies to the episodic system—that is, the factors that lead a person to behave competently in a normative sense will usually lead to a competent relational performance as well (Imahori & Lanigan, 1989; Spitzberg & Cupach, 1984). This is true in two slightly different senses. In one sense, norms comprise the majority of people's views and behaviors, so a person who is normatively competent will usually be viewed as competent in any given encounter. In another sense, an actor who is motivated to interact competently with a particular co-actor, knowledgeable about this particular co-actor, and skilled in interacting with this particular co-actor also is more likely to communicate better and be viewed as competent by this co-actor in a given encounter.

Factors that facilitate motivation, knowledge, and skill in a particular episodic system are likely to be logical extensions of the individual system components. For example, motivation is likely to increase as attraction to co-actor increases and as positive reinforcement history with co-actor increases. Knowledge of co-actor is likely to increase with duration of relationship, and depth and breadth of self-disclosure between actor and co-actor increase. Skill in interacting with co-actor is likely to increase as adaptation and refinement increase over the lifetime of the relationship.

4b. As contextual obstruction of actor's performance increases, co-actor's impression of actor's competence increases. When forming an impression of an actor, a co-actor is left to determine the extent to which the actor's outcomes are due to the actor's own abilities and effort, rather than the context or other factors. For example, a physically unattractive actor who consistently makes friends and has dates is likely to be viewed as more communicatively competent than a person who is physically attractive. The reasoning is that the social context is weighted against the unattractive actor and in favor of the attractive actor. Thus, the attractive actor would achieve the same outcomes due to attractiveness rather than his or her competence, whereas the unattractive actor must overcome the contextual barriers through more competent action. In essence, all other things being equal, an actor's competence is "discounted" if there are obvious alternative explanations for the actor's good fortune. Similarly, an actor's incompetence is "forgiven" if there are many apparent alternative reasons for his or her failure.

4c. As actor's receipt of valued outcomes increases, co-actor's impression of actor's competence increases. While the discounting effect discussed above influences impressions of competence, it is not likely to outweigh other factors entirely. If an actor is perceived as consistently achieving positive outcomes, a co-actor is likely to assume that the actor has something to do with this success (Kaplowitz, 1978). The negotiator who consistently presides over significant agreements is likely to be viewed as more communicatively competent as a simple result of the tangible outcomes, almost regardless of extenuating circumstances.

4d. As actor's extant attributed communicative status increases, co-actor's impression of actor status increases. An actor who comes into an encounter with an established high level of status is more likely to be viewed as competent in subsequent interactions. In addition, an actor who has established a satisfying relationship with a particular co-actor has, in effect, established a reserve of competence in the co-actor's views. Thus, Nelson Mandela, Boris Yeltsin, or even Bill Gates enter any communicative situation with considerable communicative status in tow. In essence, then, the impression we initially have of an actor is likely to be the basis for our later impressions until such time that significant events alter these impressions. Furthermore, certain cultures develop higher regard for other cultures generally. The mutual regard that Americans and Japanese-Americans may share is probably quite different from that which the South African blacks and whites may share.

5. Co-Actor's Impression of Actor's Competence Is a Function of Actor's Fulfillment of Co-Actor's Expectancies

Over time, interactants develop expectations regarding how interpersonal interaction is likely to and should occur in particular contexts. Not surprisingly, therefore, a person's competence in a given relationship

is due partly to expectancy fulfillment and violation. Research indicates that expectancies generally develop along the three fundamental EPA dimensions: *evaluation, potency,* and *activity* (Osgood, May, & Miron, 1975; Spitzberg, 1989); that is, most contexts are viewed in terms of their valence (e.g., good versus bad), power (e.g., dominant versus passive), and animation (e.g., noisy versus quiet). A traditional, noncharismatic church service typically is expected to be good (valence), with the audience passive (potency) and relatively quiet (activity). A typical party, in contrast, is expected to be good (valence), strong (potency), fast, and noisy (activity). Upon being fired, an exit interview is expected to be unpleasurable (valence), and the interviewee as weak (potency) and relatively passive (activity). The point is that experience with interpersonal encounters produces expectancies and evaluations about both anticipated and appropriate behavior. The propositions below elaborate the influence of these expectancies.

5a. As actor's fulfillment of positive co-actor expectancies increases, co-actor's impression of actor's competence increases. To the extent that co-actor expects an encounter with actor to be positive, then actor is likely to be viewed as competent to the extent that he or she fulfills these expectancies. Because the expectancies typically form a consistent system in a co-actor's mind, an actor needs to fulfill each of the EPA dimensions. If an interviewer expects interviews to be good (E), his or her own role to be relatively powerful and the role of the interviewee to be relatively powerless (P), and the encounter to be generally quiet but quick (A), then the actor is well advised to behave according to these expectancies. Because the interviewer has developed these expectancies along all three dimensions, they tend to be "set" in relationship to each other. Thus, part of what makes the interview "good" in the interviewer's opinion is that the interviewer's role is typically powerful, and the interviews tend to go quietly and quickly.

5b. As actor's normative violation of co-actor's negative expectancies increases, co-actor's impression of actor's competence increases. The logic of the former proposition reverses itself when a co-actor expects an encounter to be negative. Consider the previous interview example from the interviewee's perspective. An interviewee may find interviews highly anxiety-producing, threatening, and difficult. As such, the interview context is expected to be uncomfortable, the interviewee's role as submissive, and the encounter as generally slow and inactive. So, if the interviewer wants to make a good impression, then he or she needs to violate the interviewee's expectations in an appropriate manner. Such an interviewer might change the setting to a less formal lunchroom context, dress more casually, tell some stories and initially discuss topics unrelated to the position, and generally spend time putting the interviewee in a good mood. Such an encounter violates the interviewee's expectancies, but does so in a way that is normatively acceptable and positive.

5c. As actor's fulfillment of co-actor's competence prototype expectancies increases, co-actor's impression of actor's competence increases. A prototype in this usage is basically a cognitive outline of concepts, analogous to a mental map of the competence territory. The prototype of a competent person is likely to consist of several levels of concepts varying in their abstraction. A simplified example of a competent communicator prototype is displayed in Figure 2.

At the highest level is the category label that determines what types of inferences are relevant to a given set of observed behavior. For example, observing someone changing the oil in a car is not relevant to the category of "competent communicator." At the next level are types of inferences or impressions that collectively constitute the label of competent communicator. In this hypothetical example, a competent communicator is someone who is believed to be friendly, trustworthy, and assertive. Each inference, in turn, is based on certain types of behavior. To the extent that these behaviors are observed, the inferences follow. Observed behaviors are matched or compared to those that over time have come to occupy the position of category indicators. If there is a good match, then the inferences and evaluations that make up the label of competent communicator (in this case, friendly, trustworthy, assertive) are attributed to the person observed. If only some of the behaviors match, then the inference of competence is diminished proportionately. Certain behaviors in any given encounter also may be weighted in their importance to the impression. When judging whether or not someone is being deceptive, for example, many people would rely most heavily on that person's eye contact, relative to other behaviors, in assessing his or her competence.

5d. As actor's normative reciprocity of positive affect and compensation of negative affect increases, co-actor's impression of actor's competence increases. Reciprocity implies a matching or similarity of response, whereas compensation suggests an opposite or homeostatic response. Research indicates that across most types of relationships and encounters, interactants are generally considered more competent when they reciprocate positive affect and feel more competent when they compensate for negative affect (Andersen, 1998; Spitzberg, 1989). To the extent that the co-actor expresses positive affect, the actor's response in kind is likely to produce more positive impressions. When the co-actor expresses negative affect, the actor is likely to be more competent, responding with more neutral or positive affect.

Figure 2 *A Simplified Cognitive Prototype of a Competent Communicator*

Prototype Category	The Competent Communicator		
Intermediate Inferences	Friendly	Trustworthy	Assertive
Behavioral Indicators	Smiles Talkative	Reliable Honest	Gestures Animated
	Socializes	Keeps Secrets	Expresses Opinions

5e. As actor's normative compensation of power relations increases, the more co-actor's impression of actor's competence increases. Across most types of interpersonal relationships, complementary power relationships tend to produce higher impressions of competence. This is obviously an overstatement in many ways. For example, optimal negotiation outcomes tend to result when parties begin with a competitive and end up in a cooperative orientation. Still, this principle is useful in most types of relations.

Specifically, dominance is more competently met with passivity, and passivity with dominance, than vice versa. The validity of this proposition is best illustrated by considering its alternative. Imagine, for example, reciprocal dominance in work relationships in which every time a superior gives a subordinate orders, the superior is met with counter orders or refusal. Imagine symmetric passivity in married couples in which neither person ever actually makes a decision. In other words, relationships and encounters tend to work more smoothly and comfortably when dominant moves are responded to with complementary passive moves, and passive moves are met with more directive moves. This does not imply that people should adopt a role of passivity or dominance, but that, in general, on a statement-by-statement basis, most interaction will be viewed as competent to the extent that its power balance is complementary rather than reciprocal.

This section has examined the episodic system of intercultural competence. Specifically, the propositions in this section have involved those characteristics of an actor that increase the likelihood that co-actor views actor as competent in a given episode of interaction. The following section concerns an abbreviated excursion into the relational system, in which characteristics that facilitate competence across the life span of a relationship are considered.

RELATIONAL SYSTEM

Relationships are not simply sums of episodes over time. Certainly, the more competent the average episode of interaction, the more relationally stable and satisfying the relationship is likely to be. In this sense, the logic of the individual system and episodic system also extends to the relational system. However, other factors are at work, and the following section examines some of these features. In this discussion, the phrase "relational competence" refers to the level of communicative quality in an established relationship.

6. As Mutual Fulfillment of Autonomy and Intimacy Needs Increases, Relational Competence Increases

Autonomy and intimacy are two fundamental human needs (McAdams, 1988). Typically, they exist in a form of dialectical tension: Both "struggle" for dominance over the other at any given time, but both are ever-present to some degree. The need for intimacy involves the desire for human contact, connection, belonging, inclusion, camaraderie, communal activity, and nurturance. The need for autonomy, in contrast, is a need for self-control, independence, power, privacy, and solitude. Individuals seem to fluctuate between these two needs over time. And, as with virtually all needs, as each need is fulfilled, it ceases to dominate the individual's behavior. A lonely person continuously thinks about companionship. Once companionship is found, other needs begin to influence this person's thoughts and actions. It follows that if a relationship is competent over the course of its life span, then the members need to fulfill the needs of each other as these dialectical needs fluctuate (Spitzberg, 1993).

7. As Mutual Attraction Increases, Relational Competence Increases

This highly intuitive proposition simply indicates that as partners grow more and more attracted to each other, the more this is likely to reflect and result in mutually competent interaction over time (Eagly, Ashmore, Makhijani, & Longo, 1991). This proposition gains support from the consistent finding that attraction is closely associated, at least initially, with interpersonal similarity (Feingold, 1988). Highly similar persons provide a worldview of similar values and orientations, as well as similar communication skills that facilitate interaction (Burleson & Denton, 1992). In general, we enjoy interacting with those who are similar because they seem to "speak our language." One implication is that initial interactions with culturally dissimilar others should focus on areas of similarity that can support sufficient motivation and reinforcement for continued interaction. This is not to imply that differences are always negatively reinforcing. However, differences tend to make the *process* of communication more effortful and difficult, and thereby generally less rewarding.

8. As Mutual Trust Increases, Relational Competence Increases

Similar to the above proposition, the more partners trust one another, the more competent interaction is likely to be, and the more competent the relationship is likely to be (Canary & Spitzberg, 1989). Trust provides a context in which interaction can be more honest, spontaneous, direct, and open. Over time, such a trusting climate is likely to be mutually reinforcing and lead to a productive and satisfying communicative relationship.

9. As Access to Social Support Increases, Relational Competence Increases

Social support is anything offered by another that assists a person in coping with problematic or stressful situations. Types of support range from the tangible (e.g., lending money) to the informational (e.g., offering advice) to the emotional (e.g., comforting words). Because stresses stimulate personal and often relational crises, anything that diminishes the effects of these stresses is likely to enhance the person's ability to manage the relationship itself. One of the common problems of sojourner couples or families is that the stresses of being in a new culture often cannot be resolved by the social support of a friendship network because it has yet to be established in the new culture.

10. As Relational Network Integration Increases, Relational Competence Increases

When discussing relationships, it is ironically easy to forget that individuals are always simultaneously members of multiple relationships. When two people come together and form a relationship, part of what determines the competence of this relationship is the extent to which each member's personal network integrates with the other person's network of social relationships. Increasingly, as businesses become multinational and move entire management teams to work with labor in other countries, the problems of social network integration will become substantial. The development of common activities and goals that require cooperation or interaction across social networks, and the development of easier access to the network, are likely to facilitate this aspect of intercultural competence.

CONCLUSIONS

Before examining the implications of this essay, an important qualification needs to be considered. Specifically, most of the propositions presented here have what can be considered upper limits. Basically, too much of a good thing can be bad. For example, someone can be too motivated, be too analytical or knowledgeable, use too much expressiveness, or be too composed. Virtually any piece of advice, when carried to extremes, tends to lose its functional value. This can be viewed as a *curvilinearity principle*. In essence, as motivation, knowledge, and skill increase, so do impressions of competence, to a point, after which the relationship reverses, and competence impressions decrease.

Sir Karl Popper, an eminent philosopher of science, has warned that theories are only useful if they are in danger of failing. Theories that tell us what we already know must be true, tell us nothing. The point is that theories are only valuable to the extent they make risky predictions that may be disproved. It is in this sense that this essay must be viewed with caution.

Within this cautionary frame, one of the obvious, yet often ignored, lessons is the interdependence of adaptation. It is often assumed, for example, that host cultures possess a position of dominant status, and that visitors or immigrants must bear the responsibility of adapting to the host culture. Ultimately, however, competence in any encounter is contingent on all parties to the interaction. You can be highly motivated, knowledgeable, and skilled, and if the co-actors of another culture reject your legitimacy, there may be little chance of a competent interaction (Bourhis, Moise, Perreault, & Senécal, 1997). The responsibility of adaptation is best shared if competence is a preferred mode of interaction.

The predictions offered in this essay represent statements that, in the daily interplay of lives, are often in danger of being false. None of the predictions should be considered absolutely true or an infallible view of the complex canvas of intercultural relations. Nevertheless, progress in the development of knowledge results from such risky propositions, and this essay has attempted to chart a path to progress. In doing so, I have attempted to paint with broad brush strokes the outline of a theory of intercultural competence. The lines of this theory are strained by their abstraction to the point of no longer resembling the vibrant landscape they are meant to represent. Thus, like any theory or work of abstract art, the key is that the benefactor will find some significant personal meaning in it and be ever mindful that the symbol is not the thing to which it refers.

References

Andersen, P. A. (1998). The cognitive valence theory of intimate communication. In M. T. Barnett & G. A. Barnett (Eds.), *Progress in communication sciences* (Vol. 14, pp. 39–72). Stamford, CT: Ablex.

Bandura, A. (1982). Self-efficacy mechanism in human agency. *American Psychologist, 37,* 122–147.

Bourhis, R. Y., Moise, L. C., Perreault, S., & Senécal, S. (1997). Towards an interactive acculturation model: A social psychological approach. *International Journal of Psychology, 32,* 369–386.

Bradford, L., Allen, M., & Beisser, K. (1998, April). *An evaluation and meta-analysis of intercultural communication competence research.* Paper presented at the Central States Communication Association Conference, Chicago, IL.

Burleson, B. R., & Denton, W. H. (1992). A new look at similarity and attraction in marriage: Similarities in social-cognitive and communication skills as predictors of attraction and satisfaction. *Communication Monographs, 59,* 268–287.

Canary, D. J., & Spitzberg, B. H. (1989). A model of the perceived competence of conflict strategies. *Human Communication Research, 15,* 630–649.

Eagly, A. H., Ashmore, R. D., Makhijani, M. G., & Longo, L. C. (1991). What is beautiful is good. But. . . . A meta-analytic review of research on the physical attractiveness stereotype. *Psychological Bulletin, 110,* 109–128.

Feingold, A. (1988). Matching for attractiveness in romantic partners and same-sex friends: A meta-analysis and theoretical critique. *Psychological Bulletin, 104,* 226–235.

Greene, J. O. (1984). A cognitive approach to human communication: An action assembly theory. *Communication Monographs, 51,* 289–300.

Havighurst, R. J. (1957). The social competence of middle-aged people. *Genetic Psychology Monographs, 56,* 297–375.

Hoelter, J. W. (1985). A structural theory of personal consistency. *Social Psychology Quarterly, 48,* 118–129.

Imahori, T. T., & Lanigan, M. L. (1989). Relational model of intercultural communication competence. *International Journal of Intercultural Relations, 13,* 269–286.

Kaplowitz, S. A. (1978). Towards a systematic theory of power attribution. *Social Psychology, 41,* 131–148.

Kellerman, K., & Shea, B. C. (1996). Threats, suggestions, hints, and promises: Gaining compliance efficiently and politely. *Communication Quarterly, 44,* 145–165.

Lustig, M. W., & Spitzberg, B. H. (1993). Methodological issues in the study of intercultural communication competence. In R. L. Wiseman & J. Koester (Eds.), *Intercultural communication competence* (pp. 153–167). Newbury Park, CA: Sage.

Martin, J. N. (1993). Intercultural communication competence: A review. In R. Wiseman & J. Koester (Eds.), *Intercultural communication competence* (International and Intercultural Communication Annual, Vol. 16, pp. 16–31). Newbury Park, CA: Sage.

McAdams, D. P. (1988). Personal needs and personal relationships. In S. Duck (Ed.), *Handbook of personal relationships: Theory, research and* interventions (pp. 7–22). New York: John Wiley & Sons.

Mendleson, J. L., Bures, A. L., Champion, D. L., & Lott, J. K. (1997). Preliminary development of the intercultural tolerance scale. *Psychological Reports, 80,* 867–876.

Neuliep, J. W., & McCroskey, J. C. (1997). The development of intercultural and interethnic communication apprehension scales. *Communication Research Reports, 14,* 145–156.

Osgood, C. E., May, W. H., & Miron, S. (1975). *Cross-cultural universals of affective meaning.* Urbana: University of Illinois Press.

Spitzberg, B. H. (1989). Issues in the development of a theory of interpersonal competence in the intercultural context. *International Journal of Intercultural Relations, 13,* 241–268.

_____ (1993). The dialectics of (in)competence. *Journal of Social and Personal Relationships, 10,* 137–158.

_____, & Brunner, C. C. (1991). Toward a theoretical integration of context and competence inference research. *Western Journal of Speech Communication, 55,* 28–46.

_____, & Cupach, W. R. (1984). *Interpersonal communication competence.* Beverly Hills, CA: Sage.

_____, & Cupach, W. R. (1989). *Handbook of interpersonal competence research.* New York: Springer-Verlag.

Concepts and Questions

1. What does Spitzberg mean when he says intercultural competence must be viewed as the social evaluation of behavior?
2. What are the individual, episodic, and relational systems of analysis?
3. What is the relationship between communicator motivation and intercultural communication competence?
4. What is communicator approach disposition? How is it related to intercultural communication competence?
5. What is task-relevant procedural knowledge, and how does it relate to communication competence?
6. What are valued outcomes, and how do they affect the entire communication encounter?
7. What is relational competence?
8. How does mutual attraction affect relational competence?
9. How can you make use of the Spitzberg model if you seek to improve the manner in which you communicate?

Managing Intercultural Conflicts Effectively

STELLA TING-TOOMEY

Conflict is inevitable in all social and personal relationships. The Latin root words for conflict, *com* and *fligere,* mean "together" and "to strike," or more simply, "to strike together." Conflict connotes a state of dissonance or collision between two forces or systems. This state of dissonance can be expressed either overtly or subtly. In the context of intercultural encounters, *conflict* is defined in this article as the perceived and/or actual incompatibility of values, expectations, processes, or outcomes between two or more parties from different cultures over substantive and/or relational issues. Such differences are often expressed through different cultural conflict styles. Intercultural conflict typically starts off with miscommunication. Intercultural miscommunication often leads to misinterpretations and pseudoconflict. If the miscommunication goes unmanaged or unclarified, however, it can become actual interpersonal conflict.

This article is developed in three sections: (1) A cultural variability perspective that emphasizes identity construal variations, low-context versus high-context, and monochronic and polychronic time patterns is presented; (2) assumptions and factors leading to conflict induced by violations of expectations are explained; and (3) effective conflict management skills in managing intercultural conflicts are discussed.

A CULTURAL VARIABILITY PERSPECTIVE

To understand differences and similarities in communication across cultures, it is necessary to have a framework to explain why and how cultures are

Courtesy of Stella Ting-Toomey. This original essay first appeared in the seventh edition. All rights reserved. Permission to reprint must be obtained from the author and the publisher. Stella Ting-Toomey is Professor in the Department of Human Communication Studies at California State University, Fullerton.

different or similar. A cultural variability perspective refers to how cultures vary on a continuum of variations in accordance with some basic dimensions or core value characteristics. Although cultures differ on many dimensions, one that has received consistent attention from both cross-cultural communication researchers and psychologists around the world is individualism–collectivism. Countless cross-cultural studies (Chinese Culture Connection, 1987; Gudykunst & Ting-Toomey, 1988; Hofstede, 1980, 1991; Hui & Triandis, 1986; Schwartz & Bilsky, 1990; Triandis, Brislin, & Hui, 1988; Wheeler, Reis, & Bond, 1989) have provided theoretical and empirical evidence that the value orientations of individualism and collectivism are pervasive in a wide range of cultures. Ting-Toomey and associates (Ting-Toomey, 1988, 1991; Ting-Toomey et al., 1991; Trubisky, Ting-Toomey, & Lin, 1991) have related individualism–collectivism to conflict styles, providing clear research evidence that the role of cultural variability is critical in influencing the cross-cultural conflict negotiation process.

The cultural socialization process influences individuals' basic assumptions and expectations, as well as their process and outcome orientations in different types of conflict situations. The dimension of individualism–collectivism, as a continuum of value tendency differences, can be used as a beginning point to understand some of the basic differences and similarities in individual-based or group-based cultures. Culture is defined as a system of knowledge, meanings, and symbolic actions that is shared by the majority of the people in a society.

Individualism–Collectivism Value Tendencies

Basically, *individualism* refers to the broad value tendencies of a culture to emphasize the importance of individual identity over group identity, individual rights over group rights, and individual needs over group needs. In contrast, *collectivism* refers to the broad value tendencies of a culture to emphasize the importance of the "we" identity over the "I" identity, group obligations over individual rights, and in-group-oriented needs over individual wants and desires. An *in-group* is a group whose values, norms, and rules are deemed salient to the effective functioning of the group in the society, and these norms serve as the guiding criteria for everyday behaviors. On the other hand, an *out-group* is a group whose values, norms, and rules are viewed as inconsistent with those of the in-group, and these norms are assigned a low priority from the in-group standard. Macro-level factors such as ecology, affluence, social and geographic mobility, migration, cultural background of parents, socialization, rural or urban environment, mass media exposure, education, and social change have been identified by Triandis (1988, 1990) as some of the underlying factors that contribute to the development of individualist and collectivistic values. High individualistic values have been found in the United States, Australia, Great Britain, Canada, the Netherlands, and New Zealand. High collectivistic values have been uncovered in Indonesia, Colombia, Venezuela, Panama, Ecuador, and Guatemala (Hofstede, 1991). In intercultural communication research (Gudykunst & Ting-Toomey, 1988), Australia, Canada, and the United States have been consistently identified as cultures high in individualistic value tendencies, while strong empirical evidence has supported that China, Taiwan, Korea, Japan, and Mexico can be clearly identified as collectivistic, group-based cultures. Within each culture, different ethnic communities can also display distinctive individualistic and collectivistic value tendencies. For example, members of first-generation Asian immigrant cultures in the United States may retain some basic group-oriented value characteristics. The core building block of individualism–collectivism is its relative emphasis on the importance of the "autonomous self" or the "connected self" orientation.

In using the terms *independent construal of self* and *interdependent construal of self* to represent individualist versus group-oriented identity, Markus and Kitayama (1991) argue that the placement of our self-concept in our culture has a profound influence on our communication with others. They argue that the sense of individuality that accompanies the independent construal of self includes a sense of oneself as an agent, as a producer of one's actions.

One is conscious of being in control over the surrounding situation, and of the need to express one's own thoughts, feelings, and actions to others. Such acts of standing out are often intrinsically rewarding because they elicit pleasant, ego-focused emotions (e.g., pride) and also reduce unpleasant ones (e.g., frustration). Furthermore, the acts of standing out themselves form an important basis of self-esteem. (p. 246)

Conversely, the self-concept that accompanies an interdependent construal of self includes an attentiveness and responsiveness to others that one either explicitly or implicitly assumes will be reciprocated by these others, as well as the willful management of one's other-focused feelings and desires so as to maintain and further the reciprocal interpersonal relationship.

One is conscious of where one belongs with respect to others and assumes a receptive stance toward these others, continually adjusting and accommodating to these others in many aspects of behavior. Such acts of fitting in and accommodating are often intrinsically rewarding, because they give rise to pleasant, other-focused emotions (e.g., feeling of connection), while diminishing unpleasant ones (e.g., shame) and, furthermore, because the self-restraint required in doing so forms an important basis of self-esteem. (p. 246)

Thus, the cultural variability of independent versus interdependent construal of self frames our existential experience and serves as an anchoring point in terms of how we view our communicative actions and ourselves. For example, if we follow an independent construal of self orientation, our communicative action will tend to be more self-focused, more ego-based, and more self-expressive. Concurrently, the value we place on our particular self-conception also influences the criteria we use to perceive and evaluate others' communicative actions. To illustrate, if we follow an interdependent construal of self orientation, we will tend to use group norms, group interests, and group responsibilities to interpret and evaluate others' conflict behaviors. Overall, the cultural variability dimension of individualism–collectivism and the independent and interdependent construal of self help us to "make sense" or explain why people in some cultures are more likely to prefer certain approaches or modes of conflict negotiation than people in other cultures.

Low Context and High Context

In addition to individualism–collectivism, Edward T. Hall's (1976, 1983) low-context and high-context communication framework helps enrich our understanding of the role of communication in individualistic and collectivistic cultures. According to Hall (1976), human transaction can be basically divided into low-context and high-context communication systems:

HC [high-context] transactions feature preprogrammed information that is in the receiver and in the setting, with only minimal information in the transmitted message. LC [low-context] transactions are the reverse. Most of the information must be in the transmitted message in order to make up what is missing in the context. (p. 101)

Although no culture exists exclusively at one extreme of the communication context continuum, in general, low-context communication refers to communication patterns of a linear logic interaction approach, direct verbal interaction style, overt intention expressions, and sender-oriented value (Ting-Toomey, 1985). High-context communication refers to communication patterns of a spiral logic interaction approach, indirect verbal negotiation mode, subtle nonverbal nuances, responsive intention inference, and interpreter-sensitive value (Ting-Toomey, 1985). Low-context (LC) communication patterns have typically been found in individualistic cultures, and high-context (HC) communication patterns have typically been uncovered in collectivistic cultures.

For individualistic, LC communicators, the bargaining resources in conflict typically revolve around individual pride and self-esteem, individual ego-based emotions, and individual sense of autonomy and power. For collectivistic, HC interactants, the negotiation resources in conflict typically revolve around relational "face" maintenance and group harmony, group-oriented status and self-esteem, face-related emotions, and a reciprocal sense of favors and obligations. For individualistic, LC negotiators, conflict typically arises because of incompatible personalities, beliefs, or goal orientations. For collectivistic, HC negotiators, conflict typically arises because of incompatible facework or relational management.

The concept of face is tied closely to the need people have to a claimed sense of self-respect in any social interactive situation (Ting-Toomey, 1985, 1988, 1994; Ting-Toomey & Cole, 1990). As human beings, we all like to be respected and feel approved in our everyday communicative behaviors. However, how we manage face and how we negotiate "face loss" and "face gain" in a conflict episode differ from one culture to the next. As Cohen (1991) observes:

> Given the importance of face, the members of collectivistic cultures are highly sensitive to the effect of what they say on others. Language is a social instrument—a device for preserving and promoting social interests as much as a means for transmitting information. [Collectivistic], high-context speakers must weigh their words carefully. They know that whatever they say will be scrutinized and taken to heart. Face-to-face conversations contain many emollient expressions of respect and courtesy alongside a substantive element rich in meaning and low in redundancy. Directness and especially contradiction are much disliked. It is hard for speakers in this kind of culture to deliver a blunt "no." (p. 26)

M-Time and P-Time

Finally, the concept of time in the conflict-negotiation process also varies in accordance with the individualism–collectivism dimension. Time is reflective of the psychological and the emotional environment in which communication occurs. Time flies when two friends are enjoying themselves and having a good time. Time crawls when two enemies stare at each other and have nothing more to say to one another. Time influences the tempos and pacings of the developmental sequences of a conflict-negotiation session. It also influences the substantive ideas that are being presented in a conflict bargaining episode.

Hall (1983) distinguished two patterns of time that govern the individualistic and collectivistic cultures: monochronic time schedule (M-time) and polychronic time schedule (P-time). According to Hall (1983):

> P-time stresses involvement of people and completion of transactions rather than adherence to preset

schedules. Appointments are not taken as seriously and, as a consequence, are frequently broken. P-time is treated as less tangible than M-time. For polychronic people, time is seldom experienced as "wasted" and is apt to be considered a point rather than a ribbon or a road, but that point is often sacred. (p. 46)

For Hall (1983), Latin American, Middle Eastern, African, Asian, French, and Greek cultures are representatives of P-time patterns, whereas northern European, North American, and German cultures are representatives of M-time patterns. M-time patterns appear to predominate in individualistic, low-context cultures, and P-time patterns appear to predominate in group-based, high-context cultures. People who follow individualistic, M-time patterns usually compartmentalize time schedules to serve individualistic-based needs, and they tend to separate task-oriented time from socioemotional time. In addition, they are more future conscious of time than centered in the present or the past. People who follow collectivistic, P-time patterns tend to hold more fluid attitudes toward time schedules, and they tend to integrate task-oriented activity with socioemotional activity. In addition, they are more past and present conscious than future oriented.

Members of individualistic, M-time cultures tend to view time as something that can be possessed, drained, and wasted, while members of collectivistic, P-time cultures tend to view time as more contextually based and relationally oriented. For individualistic, M-time people, conflict should be contained, controlled, and managed effectively within certain frames or within certain preset schedules. For collectivistic, P-time people, the clock time in resolving conflict is not as important as is taking the time to really know the parties who are involved in the dispute. For P-time individuals, the time spent in synchronizing the implicit interactional rhythms between people is much more important than any preset, objective timetable.

In sum, in individualistic cultures, people typically practice "I" identity-based values, low-context direct interaction, and M-time negotiation schedules. In collectivistic cultures, people typically treasure "we" identity-based values, high-context indirect interaction, and P-time negotiation rhythms.

VIOLATIONS OF CONFLICT EXPECTATIONS

Drawing from the key ideas of the cultural variability perspective, we can now apply these concepts to understanding the specific conflict assumptions, conflict issues and process factors, and the conflict interaction styles that contribute to intercultural miscommunication or intercultural conflict. When individuals from two contrastive cultures meet one another, especially for the first time, they typically communicate out of their culturally based assumptions and beliefs, stereotypical images of each other, and habitual communication patterns. These assumptions create expectations for others' conflict behavior.

It is inevitable that we hold anticipations or expectations of how others should or should not behave in any communicative situation. These expectations, however, are grounded in the social norms of the culture and also depend on the symbolic meanings individuals assign to behaviors (Burgoon, 1991). Intercultural miscommunication or intercultural conflict often occurs because of violations of normative expectations in a communication episode. Expectation violations occur frequently, especially if one party comes from an individualistic-based culture and the other party comes from a collectivistic-based culture.

Cultural Conflict Assumptions

Different cultural value assumptions exist as the metaconflict issues in framing any intercultural conflict episode. Based on the individualism–collectivism dimension, we can delineate several cultural assumptions concerning LC and HC communicators' basic attitudes toward conflict. For individualistic, LC communicators, conflict typically follows a "problem-solving" model: (1) Conflict is viewed as an expressed struggle to air out major differences and problems; (2) conflict can be both dysfunctional and functional; (3) conflict can be dysfunctional when it is repressed and not directly confronted; (4) conflict can be functional when it provides an open opportunity for solving problematic issues; (5) substantive and relational issues in conflict should be handled separately; (6) conflict should be dealt with openly

and directly; and (7) effective management of conflict can be viewed as a win-win problem-solving game.

For the collectivistic, HC interactants, their underlying assumptions of conflict follow a "face maintenance" model: (1) Conflict is viewed as damaging to social face and relational harmony and should be avoided as much as possible; (2) conflict is, for the most part, dysfunctional; (3) conflict signals a lack of self-discipline and self-censorship of emotional outbursts, and hence, a sign of emotional immaturity; (4) conflict provides a testing ground for a skillful facework negotiation process; (5) substantive conflict and relational face issues are always intertwined; (6) conflict should be dealt with discreetly and subtly; and (7) effective management of conflict can be viewed as a win-win face negotiation game.

In the conflict as a "problem-solving" model, conflict is viewed as potentially functional, personally liberating, and an open forum for "struggling against" or "struggling with" one another in wrestling with the conflict issues at hand. In the conflict as a "face maintenance" model, conflict is viewed as primarily dysfunctional, interpersonally embarrassing and distressing, and a forum for potential group-related face loss and face humiliation. These fundamental cultural conflict assumptions influence the mind-sets and attitudinal level of the conflict parties in terms of how they should approach an interpersonal conflict episode. Appropriate and inappropriate conflict behaviors, in short, are grounded in the basic value assumptions of the cultural conflict socialization process.

Conflict Issues and Process Violations

Every conflict entails both substantive and relational issues. Individualistic conflict negotiators typically attend to the objective, substantive issues more than the relational, socioemotional issues. Collectivistic conflict negotiators, in contrast, typically attune to the relational, affective dimension as the key issue in resolving task-related or procedural-related conflict.

When collectivistic communicators are in sync with one another and their nonverbal rhythms harmonize with one another, peaceful resolutions can potentially follow. When individualistic communicators are able to rationalize the separation of the people from the problems, and emphasize compartmentalizing affective issues and substantive issues, conflict can be functional.

In reviewing diplomatic negotiation case studies between individualistic, low-context (United States) and collectivistic, high-context (China, Egypt, India, Japan, and Mexico) cultures, Cohen (1991) concludes:

> Individualistic, low-context negotiators can be described as primarily problem oriented and have the definition of the problem and the clarification of alternative solutions uppermost in their thoughts; [collectivistic] high-context negotiators are seen to be predominantly relationship oriented. For them, negotiation is less about solving problems (although, obviously, this aspect cannot be dismissed) than about attending a relationship. For interdependent cultures it is not a conflict that is resolved but a relationship that is mended.... In international relations the consequence is concern both with the international relationship and with the personal ties between the interlocutors. (p. 51)

In individualistic, LC cultures such as Australia and the United States, control of one's autonomy, freedom, territory, and individual boundary is of paramount importance to one's sense of self-respect and ego. In collectivistic, HC cultures such as Japan and Korea, being accepted by one's in-group members and being approved by one's superiors, peers, and/or family members is critical to the development of one's sense of self-respect. Thus, conflict issues in individualistic cultures typically arise through the violation of autonomous space, privacy, individual power, and sense of individual fairness and equity. In collectivistic cultures, conflict issues typically revolve around the violation of in-group or out-group boundaries, norms of group loyalty and commitment, and reciprocal obligations and trust.

In terms of different goal orientations in intercultural conflict, individualists' conflict management techniques typically emphasize a win-win goal orientation and the importance of a tangible outcome action plan. For collectivists, typically time and energy are invested in negotiating face loss, face gain, and face protection issues throughout the various developmental phases of conflict. Whereas individualists tend to be highly goal or result oriented in conflict

management, collectivists tend to emphasize heavily the relational or facework process of conflict resolution. This collectivistic conflict facework negotiation process can also take place beyond the immediate conflict situation.

Several writers (Cohen, 1991; Leung, 1987, 1988; Ting-Toomey, 1985) indicate that collectivists tend to display a stronger preference for informal third-party conflict mediation procedure than individualists. For example, in the Chinese culture, conflict is typically defused through the use of third-party intermediaries. However, there exists a key difference in the use of third-party mediation between the individualistic, Western cultures and the collectivistic, Asian cultures. In the Western cultures, conflict parties tend to seek help from an impartial third-party mediator (such as a professional mediator or family therapist). In many Asian cultures, conflict parties typically seek the help of an older (and hence assumed to be wiser) person who is related to both parties. It is presumed that the informal mediator has a richer database to arbitrate the conflict outcome. Expectations may be violated when an individualistic culture sends an impartial third party to arbitrate an international conflict with no prior relationship-building sessions. Conflict process violations also arise if an individualistic culture sends an intermediary who is perceived to be of lower rank or lower status than the representative negotiators of the collectivistic culture. Conversely, a collectivistic culture tends to violate the individualistic fairness norm when it sends an "insider" or in-group person to monitor or arbitrate the conflict outcome situation.

The concept of power in a conflict negotiation situation also varies from an individualistic culture to a collectivistic culture. Power, in the context of individualistic culture, often means tangible resources of rewards and punishments that one conflict party has over another. Power, in the context of collectivistic culture, often refers to intangible resources such as face loss and face gain, losing prestige or gaining reputation, and petty-mindedness versus benevolent generosity as displayed in the conflict anxiety-provoking situation.

Finally, the interpretation of conflict resolution rhythm also varies along the individualism–collectivism dimension. For individualistic, M-time people, conflict resolution processes should follow a clear agenda of opening, expressing conflicting interests, negotiating, and closing sequences. For collectivistic, P-time people, conflict facework processes have no clear beginning and no clear end. For M-time individuals, conflict resolution time should be filled with decision-making activities. For P-time individuals, time is a "being" construct that is governed by the implicit rhythms in the interaction between people. Whereas M-time negotiators tend to emphasize agenda setting, objective criteria, and immediate, future-oriented goals in the conflict negotiation process, P-time negotiators typically like to take time to engage in small talk, to delve into family or personal affairs, and also to bring in the historical past to shed light on the present conflict situation. As Cohen (1991) observes:

> [North] Americans, then, are mostly concerned with addressing immediate issues and moving on to new challenges, and they display little interest in (and sometimes little knowledge of) history. The idea that something that occurred hundreds of years ago might be relevant to a pressing problem is almost incomprehensible.... In marked contrast, the representatives of non-Western societies possess a pervasive sense of the past.... This preoccupation with history, deeply rooted in the consciousness of traditional societies, cannot fail to influence diplomacy. Past humiliations for these societies (which are highly sensitive to any slight on their reputations) are not consigned to the archives but continue to nourish present concerns. (p. 29)

The arbitrary division of clock time or calendar time holds little meaning for collectivistic, P-time people. For them, a deadline, in one sense, is only an arbitrary human construct. For P-time individuals, a deadline is always subject to revision and renegotiation. Graceful handling of time pressure is viewed as much more important than a sense of forceful urgency. In sum, people move with different conflict rhythms in conflict negotiation sessions. For M-time individuals, a sense of timeline and closure orientation predominate in their mode of conflict resolution. For P-time individuals, a sense of the relational commitment and synchronized relational rhythm signal the beginning stage of a long-term, conflict-bargaining process.

Expectation violations often occur when a person from an individualistic culture engages a person from a collectivistic culture in an interpersonal conflict situation. Different cultural conflict assumptions lead to different attitudes toward how to approach a basic conflict episode. Miscommunication often gives rise to escalatory conflict spirals or prolonged misunderstandings. Although common feelings of anxiety, frustration, ambivalence, and a sense of emotional vulnerability typically exist in individuals in any conflict situation, how we go about handling this sense of emotional vulnerability varies from one culture to the next.

Individualists and collectivists typically collide over their substantive orientation versus relational face maintenance orientation, goal orientation versus process orientation, formal versus informal third-party consultation process, tangible versus intangible power resources, and different time rhythms that undergird the conflict episode. In addition, the verbal and nonverbal messages they engage in, and the distinctive conflict styles they carry with them, can severely influence the overall outcome of the conflict dissonance process.

Cross-Cultural Conflict Interaction Styles

In a conflict situation, individualists typically rely heavily on direct requests, direct verbal justifications, and upfront clarifications to defend their actions or decisions. In contrast, collectivists typically use qualifiers ("Perhaps we should meet this deadline together"), tag questions ("Don't you think we might not have enough time?"), disclaimers ("I'm probably wrong but..."), tangential responses ("Let's not worry about that now"), and indirect requests ("If it won't be too much trouble, let's try to finish this report together") to make a point in the subtle, conflict face-threatening situation. From the collectivistic orientation, it is up to the interpreter of the message to pick up the hidden meaning or intention of the message and to respond either indirectly or equivocally. In addition, in an intense conflict situation, many collectivists believe that verbal messages can often compound the problem. However, by not using verbal means to explain or clarify a decision, collectivists are often viewed as "inscrutable."

Silence is viewed as demanding immense self-discipline in a collectivistic conflict situation. On the other hand, silence can be viewed as an admission of guilt or incompetence in an individualistic culture. In addition, whereas open emotional expression during a stressful conflict situation is often viewed as a signal of caring in an individualistic culture, proper emotional composure and emotional self-restraint are viewed as signals of a mature, self-disciplined person in most collectivistic Asian cultures. In comparing verbal and nonverbal exchange processes in Japan and the United States, Okabe (1983) summarizes:

> The digital is more characteristic of the [North] American mode of communication.... The Japanese language is more inclined toward the analogical; its use of ideographic characters...and its emphasis on the nonverbal aspect. The excessive dependence of the Japanese on the nonverbal aspect of communication means that Japanese culture tends to view the verbal as only a means of communication, and that the nonverbal and the extra-verbal at times assume greater importance than the verbal dimension of communication. This is in sharp contrast to the view of Western rhetoric and communication that the verbal, especially speech, is the dominant means of expression. (p. 38)

In short, in the individualistic cultures, the conflict management process relies heavily on verbal offense and defense to justify one's position, to clarify one's opinion, to build up one's credibility, to articulate one's emotions, and to raise objections if one disagrees with someone else's proposal. In collectivistic conflict situations, ambiguous, indirect verbal messages are often used with the intention of saving mutual face, saving group face, or protecting someone else's face. In addition, subtle nonverbal gestures or nonverbal silence is often used to signal a sense of cautionary restraint toward the conflict situation. The use of deep-level silence can also reflect a sense of resignation and acceptance of the fatalistic aspect of the conflict situation. The higher the person is in positional power in a collectivistic culture, the more likely she or he will use silence as a deliberate, cautionary conflict strategy.

In terms of the relationship between the norm of fairness and cross-cultural conflict interaction style, results from past research (Leung & Bond, 1984; Leung & Iwawaki, 1988) indicate that individualists typically prefer to use the equity norm (self-deservingness norm) in dealing with reward allocation in group conflict

interaction. In comparison, collectivists often prefer to use the equality norm (the equal distribution norm) to deal with in-group members and thus avoid group disharmony. However, like their individualistic cohorts, collectivists prefer the application of the equity norm (the self-deservingness norm) when competing with members of out-groups, especially when the conflict involves competition for scarce resources in the system.

Findings in many past conflict studies also indicate that individuals do exhibit quite consistent cross-situational styles of conflict negotiation in different cultures. Although dispositional, relationship, or conflict salient factors also play a critical part in conflict management patterns, culture assumes the primary role in the conflict style socialization process. Based on the theoretical assumptions of the "I" identity and the "we" identity, and the concern of self-face maintenance versus mutual face maintenance in the two contrasting cultural systems, findings across cultures (China, Japan, Korea, Taiwan, Mexico, and the United States) clearly indicate that individualists tend to use competitive control conflict styles in managing conflict, whereas collectivists tend to use integrative or compromising conflict styles in dealing with conflict. In addition, collectivists also tend to use more obliging and avoiding conflict styles in task-oriented conflict situations (Chua & Gudykunst, 1987; Leung, 1988; Ting-Toomey et al., 1991; Trubisky et al., 1991).

Different results have also been uncovered concerning in-group and out-group conflict in the collectivistic cultures. For example, Cole's (1989) study reveals that Japanese students in the United States tend to use obliging strategies more with members of in-groups than with members of out-groups. They also tend to use more competitive strategies with out-group members than with in-group members. In addition, the status of the in-group person plays a critical role in the collectivistic conflict process.

Previous research (Ting-Toomey et al., 1991) suggests that status affects the conflict management styles people use with members of their in-group. For example, in a collectivistic culture, although a high-status person can challenge the position or opinion of a low-status person, it is a norm violation for a low-status person to directly rebut or question the position or the opinion of the high-status person, especially in the public arena. Again, the issue of face maintenance becomes critical in high- versus low-status conflict interaction. The low-status person should always learn to "give face" or protect the face of the high-status person in times of stressful situations or crises. In return, the high-status person will enact a reciprocal face protection system that automatically takes care of the low status person in different circumstances.

Overall, the preferences for a direct conflict style, for the use of the equity norm, and for the direct settlement of disputes reflect the salience of the "I" identity in individualistic, HC cultures; whereas preferences for an indirect conflict style, for the use of the equality norm, and for the use of informal mediation procedures reflect the salience of the "we" identity in collectivistic, HC cultures. In individualistic, LC cultures, a certain degree of conflict in a system is viewed as potentially functional and productive. In collectivistic, HC cultures, in which group harmony and consultative decision making are prized, overt expressions of interpersonal conflict are highly avoided and suppressed. Instead, nonverbal responsiveness, indirect verbal strategies, the use of informal intermediaries, and the use of cautionary silence are some of the typical collectivistic ways of dealing with interpersonal conflict.

EFFECTIVE CONFLICT MANAGEMENT

Effective conflict management requires us to communicate effectively, appropriately, and creatively in different conflict interactive situations. Effective conflict management requires us to be knowledgeable and respectful of different worldviews and ways of dealing with a conflict situation. It requires us to be sensitive to the differences and similarities between low-context and high-context communication patterns and to attune to the implicit negotiation rhythms of monochronic-based and polychronic-based individuals.

Effective conflict management also requires the awareness of the importance of both goal-oriented and process-oriented conflict negotiation pathways, and requires that we pay attention to the close relationship between cultural variability and different conflict communication styles. For both individualists and collectivists, the concept of "mindfulness" can serve as the first effective step in raising our awareness of the differences and similarities in cross-cultural conflict negotiation processes. Langer's (1989) concept of mindfulness helps individuals to tune in conscientiously to their habituated mental scripts and expectations. According to Langer, if mindlessness is the "rigid reliance on old categories, mindfulness means the continual creation of new ones. Categorization and re-categorization, labeling and relabeling as one masters the world are processes natural to children" (p. 63). To engage in a mindfulness state, an individual needs to learn to (a) create new categories, (b) be open to new information, and (c) be aware that multiple perspectives typically exist in viewing a basic event (Langer, 1989, p. 62).

Creating new categories means that one should not be boxed in by one's rigid stereotypical label concerning cultural strangers. One has to learn to draw out commonalties between self and cultural strangers and to appreciate the multifaceted aspects of the individuals to whom the stereotypical label is applied. In order to create new categories, one has to be open to new information. New information relies strongly on responsible sharing and responsive listening behavior.

Some specific suggestions can be made based on differences in individualistic and collectivistic styles of conflict management. These suggestions, however, are not listed in order of importance. To deal with conflict effectively in the collectivistic culture, individualists need to:

1. Be mindful of the face maintenance assumptions of conflict situations that take place in this culture. Conflict competence resides in the strategic skills of managing the delicate interaction balance of humiliation and pride, shame, and honor. The face moves of one-up and one-down in a conflict episode, the use of same-status negotiators, and the proprieties and decorum of gracious "face fighting" have to be strategically staged with the larger group audience in mind.

2. Be proactive in dealing with low-grade conflict situations (such as by using informal consultation or the "go-between" method) before they escalate into runaway, irrevocable, mutual face loss episodes.

Individualists should try to realize that by helping their opponent to save face, they might also enhance their own face. Face is, intrinsically, a bilateral concept in the group-based, collectivistic culture.

3. "Give face" and try not to push their opponent's back against the wall without any room for maneuvering face loss or face recovery. Learn to let their opponent find a gracious way out of the conflict situation if at all possible, without violating the basic spirit of fundamental human rights. They should also learn self-restraint and try not to humiliate their opponent in the public arena or slight her or his public reputation. For collectivists, the concept of "giving face" typically operates on a long-range, reciprocal interaction system. Bilateral face giving and face saving ensure a continuous, interdependent networking process of favor giving and favor concessions—especially along a long-term, historical timeline.

4. Be sensitive to the importance of quiet, mindful observation. Individualists need to be mindful of the historical past that bears relevance to the present conflict situation. Restrain from asking too many "why" questions. Since collectivistic, LC cultures typically focus on the nonverbal "how" process, individualists need to learn to experience and manage the conflict process on the implicit, nonverbal pacing level. Use deep-level silence, deliberate pauses, and patient conversational turn taking in conflict interaction processes with collectivists.

5. Practice attentive listening skills and feel the co-presence of the other person. In Chinese characters, hearing or *wun* means "opening the door to the ears," and listening or *ting* means attending to the other person with your "ears, eyes, and heart." Listening means, in the Chinese character, attending to the sounds, movements, and feelings of the other person. Patient and deliberate listening indicates that one person is attending to the other person's needs, even if it is an antagonistic conflict situation.

6. Discard the Western-based model of effective communication skills in dealing with conflict situations in collectivistic, HC cultures. Individualists should learn to use qualifiers, disclaimers, tag questions, and tentative statements to convey their point of view. In refusing a request, learn not to use a blunt "no" as a response because the word "no" is typically perceived as carrying high face threat value in the collectivistic culture. Use situational or self-effacing accounts ("Perhaps someone else is more qualified than I am in working on this project"), counter questions ("Don't you feel someone else is more competent to work on this project?"), or conditional statements ("Yes, but . . .") to convey the implicit sense of refusal.

7. Let go of a conflict situation if the conflict party does not want to deal with it directly. A cooling period may sometimes help to mend a broken relationship, and the substantive issue may be diluted over a period of time. Individualists should remember that avoidance is part of the integral, conflict style that is commonly used in the collectivistic, LC cultures. Avoidance does not necessarily mean that collectivists do not care to resolve the conflict. In all likelihood, avoidance is strategically used to avert face-threatening interaction and is meant to maintain face harmony and mutual face dignity.

In sum, individualists need to learn to respect the HC, collectivistic ways of approaching and handling conflicts. They need to continuously monitor their ethnocentric biases on the cognitive, affective, and behavioral reactive levels; learn to listen attentively; and observe mindfully and reflectively.

Some specific suggestions also can be made for collectivists in handling conflict with individualists. When encountering a conflict situation in an individualistic, LC culture, collectivists need to:

1. Be mindful of the problem-solving assumptions. The ability to separate the relationship from the conflict problem is critical to effective conflict negotiation in an individualistic, LC culture. Collectivists need to learn to compartmentalize the task dimension and the socioemotional dimension of conflict.

2. Focus on resolving the substantive issues of the conflict, and learn to openly express opinions or points of view. Collectivists should try not to take the conflict issues to the personal level, and learn to maintain distance between the person and the conflict problem. In addition, try not to be offended

by the upfront, individualistic style of managing conflict. Learn to emphasize tangible outcomes and develop concrete action plans in implementing the conflict decision proposal.

3. Engage in an assertive, leveling style of conflict behavior. Assertive style emphasizes the rights of both individuals to speak up in a conflict situation and to respect each other's right to defend her or his position. Collectivists need to learn to open a conflict dialogue with an upfront thesis statement and then develop the key points systematically, with examples, evidence, figures, or a well-planned proposal. In addition, collectivists need to be ready to accept criticisms, counterproposals, and suggestions for modification as part of the ongoing group dialogue.

4. Own individual responsibility for the conflict decision-making process. Owning responsibility and using "I" statements to describe feelings in an ongoing conflict situation constitute part of effective conflict management skills in an individualistic, LC culture. Collectivists need to learn to verbally explain a situation more fully and learn not to expect others to infer their points of view. Assume a sender-based approach to resolving conflict; ask more "why" questions, and probe for explanations and details.

5. Provide verbal feedback and engage in active listening skills. Active listening skills, in the individualistic, LC culture, means collectivists have to engage in active verbal perception checking and ensure that the other person is interpreting points accurately. Collectivists need to use verbal paraphrases, summary statements, and interpretive messages to acknowledge and verify the storyline of the conflict situation. Learn to occasionally self-disclose feelings and emotions; they cannot rely solely on nonverbal, intuitive understanding to "intuit" and evaluate a situation.

6. Use direct, integrative verbal messages that clearly convey their concern over both the relational and substantive issues of a conflict situation. Collectivists should also not wait patiently for clear turn-taking pauses in the conflict interaction because individualistic conversation typically allows overlap talks, simultaneous messages, and floor-grabbing behavior. Collectivists also may not want to engage in too many deliberate silent moments because individualists will infer incompetence or an inefficient use of time.

7. Commit to working out the conflict situation with the conflict party. Collectivists should learn to use task-oriented integrative strategies and try to work out a collaborative, mutual goal dialogue with the conflict party. Work on managing individual defensiveness and learn to build up trust on the one-to-one level of interaction. Finally, confirm the conflict person through explicit relationship reminders and metacommunication talks, while simultaneously working on resolving the conflict substantive issues, responsibly and constructively.

In sum, collectivists need to work on their ethnocentric biases as much as the individualists need to work on their sense of egocentric superiority. Collectivists need to untangle their historical sense of cultural superiority—especially in thinking that their way is the only "civilized" way to deal appropriately with conflict. Both individualists and collectivists need to be mindful of the cognitive, affective, and behavioral blinders they bring into a conflict mediation situation. They need to continuously learn new and novel ideas in dealing with the past, present, and the future for the purpose of building a peaceful community that is inclusive of all ethnic and cultural groups.

In being mindful of the potential differences between individualistic, LC and collectivistic, HC conflict styles, the intercultural peacemaking process can begin by affirming and valuing such differences as diverse human options in resolving some fundamental human communication phenomena. Although it is not necessary to completely switch one's basic conflict style in order to adapt to the other person's behavior, mutual attuning and responsive behavior in signaling a willingness to learn about each other's cultural norms and rules may be a major first step toward a peaceful resolution process. In addition, conflicting parties from diverse ethnic or cultural backgrounds can learn to work on collaborative task projects and strive toward reaching a larger-than-self, community goal.

To be a peacemaker in the intercultural arena, one has to be first at peace with oneself and one's style. Thus, the artificial switching of one's style may only bring artificial results. Creative peacemakers must learn first to affirm and respect the diverse values that exist as part of the rich spectrum of the basic human experience. They may then choose to modify their behavior to adapt to the situation at hand. Finally, they may integrate diverse sets of values and behaviors, and be able to move in and out of different relational and cultural conflict boundaries. Creative peacemakers can be at ease and at home with the marginal stranger in their search toward common human peace. Peace means, on a universal level, a condition or a state of tranquility—with an absence of oppressed thoughts, feelings, and actions, from one heart to another, and from one nation state to another nation state.

References

Burgoon, J. (1991). Applying a comparative approach to expectancy violations theory. In J. Blumer, J. McCleod, & K. Rosengren (Eds.), *Communication and culture across space and time.* Newbury Park, CA: Sage.

Chinese Culture Connection. (1987). Chinese values and search for culture-free dimensions of culture. *Journal of Cross-Cultural Psychology, 18,* 143–164.

Chua, E., & Gudykunst, W. (1987). Conflict resolution style in low- and high-context cultures. *Communication Research Reports, 4,* 32–37.

Cohen, R. (1991). *Negotiating across cultures: Communication obstacles in international diplomacy.* Washington, DC: U.S. Institute of Peace.

Cole, M. (1989, May). Relational distance and personality influence on conflict communication styles. Unpublished master's thesis, Arizona State University, Tempe.

Gudykunst, W., & Ting-Toomey, S. (1988). *Culture and interpersonal communication.* Newbury Park, CA: Sage.

Hall, E. T. (1976). *Beyond culture.* New York: Doubleday.

Hall, E. T. (1983). *The dance of life.* New York: Doubleday.

Hofstede, G. (1980). *Culture's consequences: International differences in work-related values.* Beverly Hills, CA: Sage.

Hofstede, G. (1991). *Cultures and organizations: Software of the mind.* London: McGraw-Hill.

Hui, C., & Triandis, H. (1986). Individualism–collectivism: A study of cross-cultural researchers. *Journal of Cross-Cultural Psychology, 17,* 225–248.

Langer, E. (1989). *Mindfulness.* Reading, MA: Addison-Wesley.

Leung, K. (1987). Some determinants of reactions to procedural models for conflict resolution: A cross-national study. *Journal of Personality and Social Psychology, 53,* 898–908.

Leung, K. (1988). Some determinants of conflict avoidance. *Journal of Cross-Cultural Psychology, 19,* 125–136.

Leung, K., & Bond, M. (1984). The impact of cultural collectivism on reward allocation. *Journal of Personality and Social Psychology, 47,* 793–804.

Leung, K., & Iwawaki, S. (1988). Cultural collectivism and distributive behavior. *Journal of Cross-Cultural Psychology, 19,* 35–49.

Markus, H., & Kitayama, S. (1991). Culture and the self: Implications for cognition, emotion, and motivation. *Psychological Review, 2,* 224–253.

Okabe, R. (1983). Cultural assumptions of East-West: Japan and the United States. In W. Gudykunst (Ed.), *Intercultural communication theory.* Beverly Hills, CA: Sage.

Schwartz, S., & Bilsky, W. (1990). Toward a theory of the universal content and structure of values. *Journal of Personality and Social Psychology, 58,* 878–891.

Ting-Toomey, S. (1985). Toward a theory of conflict and culture. In W. Gudykunst, L. Stewart, & S. Ting-Toomey (Eds.), *Communication, culture, and organizational processes* (pp. 71–86). Beverly Hills, CA: Sage.

Ting-Toomey, S. (1988). Intercultural conflict styles: A face negotiation theory. In V. Kim & W. Gudykunst (Eds.), *Theories in intercultural communication.* Newbury Park, CA: Sage.

Ting-Toomey, S. (1991). Intimacy expressions in three cultures: France, Japan, and the United States. *International Journal of Intercultural Relations, 15,* 29–46.

Ting-Toomey, S. (Ed.). (1994). *The challenge of face-work: Cross-cultural and interpersonal issues.* Albany: State University of New York Press.

Ting-Toomey, S., & Cole, M. (1990). Intergroup diplomatic communication: A face-negotiation perspective. In F. Korzenny & S. Ting-Toomey (Eds.), *Communicating for peace: Diplomacy and negotiation.* Newbury Park, CA: Sage.

Ting-Toomey, S., et al. (1991). Culture, face maintenance, and styles of handling interpersonal conflict: A study in five cultures. *International Journal of Conflict Management, 2,* 275–296.

Triandis, H. (1988). Collectivism vs. individualism: A reconceptualization of a basic concept in cross-cultural psychology. In G. Verma & C. Bagley (Eds.), *Cross-cultural studies of personality, attitudes and cognition.* London: Macmillan.

Triandis, H. (1990). Cross-cultural studies of individualism and collectivism. In J. Berman (Ed.), *Nebraska Symposium on Motivation.* Lincoln: University of Nebraska Press.

Triandis, H., Brislin, R., & Hui, C. H. (1988). Cross-cultural training across the individualism–collectivism divide. *International Journal of Intercultural Relations, 12,* 269–289.

Trubisky, P., Ting-Toomey, S., & Lin, S. L. (1991). The influence of individualism–collectivism and self-monitoring on conflict styles. *International Journal of Intercultural Relations, 15,* 65–84.

Wheeler, L., Reis, H., & Bond, M. (1989). Collectivism–individualism in everyday social life: The middle kingdom and the melting pot. *Journal of Personality and Social Psychology, 57,* 79–86.

Concepts and Questions

1. How does Ting-Toomey define conflict?
2. In what way does the cultural socialization process relate to different forms of intercultural conflicts?
3. From the perspective of intercultural conflict, how may in-group and out-group differences contribute to such conflict?
4. How can differences between high- and low-context cultures contribute to intercultural conflict?
5. How can an awareness of expectations help mediate intercultural conflict?
6. How do differences along the individualistic–collectivist scale of cultural differences contribute to intercultural conflict? What would you suggest to minimize these influences?
7. In what ways can differences in cross-cultural conflict interaction styles affect intercultural communication?
8. What role does silence play in intercultural conflict reduction?
9. What differences are there between individualistic and collectivist conflict?

Understanding Cultural Identities in Intercultural Communication: A Ten-Step Inventory

Mary Jane Collier

Let me begin by introducing myself and characterizing my experiences and background. We are beginning a conversation about intercultural communication, so becoming familiar with the fundamental assumptions I'm making about it will help you better understand why I'm making particular arguments, as well as help you evaluate the utility of my approach for your own views and conduct.

My orientation to intercultural communication is based on where I come from and where I have been—just as yours is. I am a European American, white, middle-class, middle-aged female, and I've lived on a Navajo reservation in Arizona, in small towns, and in large cities in the United States. I have been a sojourner in South Africa. I have studied national, ethnic, and gender identity and intercultural communication dealing with ethnically diverse South Africans, various British ethnic groups in England, Israelis and Palestinians in the Middle East, and African, Asian, and Latino Americans in the United States. I have participated in protests and marched for political causes. My M.A. and Ph.D. in Communication are from the University of Southern California in Los Angeles.

I have come to believe that ignoring our cultural and intercultural communication processes has profound consequences. Unless we commit our hearts, minds, and spirits to understanding what happens when people with different group identities come together, we will be doomed to approach protracted conflicts such as those in the Middle East, Bosnia, and Northern Ireland through violence and military action. U.S. Americans will continue political and social violence against recent immigrants and marginalized groups in California in the name of "native-born Americans," as I heard recently, and forget that the United States was founded by immigrants who took the land and destroyed the lives and cultures of the indigenous peoples. We'll go on denying the kind of racism, classism, and sexism that have become more insidious and damaging now that they are hidden behind language that we call "politically correct," and those of us who are more conservative will denounce "the liberals," while those of us who are more liberal will denounce "the conservatives." We'll continue to believe that our truth is the one and only truth, rather than remembering that truths are created and molded and shaped by individuals within religious, political, and social contexts and histories.

REQUEST TO ENGAGE THE DIALOGUE

Some things you read here and then talk about will validate and confirm your ideas and identities. Some things you read here will challenge your views of yourselves and the world.

When we begin inquiry about intercultural communication, we are studying how we do, be, and know ourselves and others as cultural beings. Communication, however, is a process that occurs unconsciously or mindlessly (Langer, 1989) much or at least some of the time. Learning about things we take for granted and seeing our lives from the perspective of people who don't live the same way or value the same things can teach us about alternative ways of interpreting and being in the world, and increase our own options. In this way, we can also know better how to engage in talk and actions that will be viewed as moral and ethical.

Please enter into this reading as if we are having a dialogue; agree, disagree, and note alternative views and examples in the margins as you read. Also, talk about the claims you read here and add or modify ideas in and outside of class.[1] Search for alternative interpretations, examples, and reactions as you discuss these issues. Please think about how your behavior looks and sounds to strangers or outsiders, and take the time to develop an understanding of the words and actions of strangers until they become more familiar. I encourage you to continue the dialogue with each other as well as with me by using e-mail to send me your reactions and thoughts (mjc@unm.edu).

In this essay, I outline an inventory,[2] a series of steps you can use to build your understanding of an intercultural event that you observed or heard about, improve the quality of an intercultural relationship, work toward solving a social problem that is based in intercultural communication, or conduct a systematic research study. The inventory will help you focus on how people construct their cultural identities in particular situations. Some of the questions on the inventory may be more relevant to particular situations and events than others, but all questions apply and affect what you conclude.

A TEN-STEP INVENTORY

The inventory is a series of questions designed to help you understand and critically evaluate diverse intercultural situations. The questions can be asked before, during, or after an intercultural experience and can be applied to public or group meetings, interpersonal conversations, and what you see and hear in films or television shows, read in newspapers or magazines, or come across on the Internet. The following questions can be thought of as steps that are interrelated but not necessarily sequential. In other words, when you answer the questions in Step 7 about the context of your intercultural issue, you may need to go back and revise how you answered an earlier step about cultural identities. Each step in the inventory has to do with questions that you, the "problem solver," need to ask.

1. What do I believe about communication and culture?
2. What intercultural communication question do I want to answer? Specifically, what do I want to know, understand, or change?
3. What cultural identity issues are relevant to the intercultural communication problem in which I'm interested?

4. How do power and ideology emerge and affect the intercultural communication problem in which I'm interested?
5. What intergroup and interpersonal relationship processes are relevant to my intercultural problem?
6. What kind of communication messages will I examine? What will be my "data"?
7. What is the context? What situational, historical, institutional, and social factors affect my intercultural problem?
8. What perspective and procedures should I use to analyze or interpret the communication messages?
9. What are my preliminary interpretations and findings? What are alternative views and interpretations?
10. How can I apply my interpretations to improve the quality of my own and others' intercultural experiences?

To show how the inventory can be applied, each step will be explained and then examples will be given. Each step will be applied first to a particular intercultural problem, one based on one or more recent conflicts on college campuses across the United States. The inventory can be applied not only to analyzing a current social problem or issue but also to helping you answer a question about your own intercultural experiences or to guide a research project you conduct.

To apply the inventory to our specific campus problem, you need a little background. The current debate regarding affirmative action and policies regarding immigrants in the United States is evident in political campaigns, town meetings, television talk shows, and campus organizations. On many university campuses, the debate is fueling discussion regarding the need for ethnic studies and women's studies programs, a higher percentage of faculty from underrepresented groups, separate ethnic cultural centers or international houses on campus, and separate residence halls for international students. The debate is based on whether it is best to have programs and places in which students who have particular ethnic backgrounds or backgrounds from countries outside the United States may meet, socialize, and study in a safe environment of support; or whether it is best to offer traditional programs that emphasize how to be successful in the United States; hire faculty without attention to race, ethnicity, or sex; close the cultural centers; and streamline funding by devoting resources only to student activities that welcome all students.

This issue is complex, and each campus is different depending on the demographics and the mission of the institution. On many campuses, funding for maintaining the cultural centers and student programs comes from both administrative sources and student fees. On many campuses, costs are increasing and administrators are looking for places to downsize and save money. Take a minute to think about your own campus. Is there an ethnic studies department or program? Is there a women's studies department or program? Are there cultural centers? If you have residence halls, are any designated only for international students?

Here is the specific problem to work with and apply the steps in the inventory. An administrator on your campus has proposed closing all the cultural centers (black student alliance, Hispanic center, Native American longhouse) and international house, as well as the women's studies program and the ethnic studies program, and opening the residence hall previously designated for international students to all students. The administrator argues that separatist organizations do not prepare students to live in a culturally diverse, global society, and the centers and programs are too costly to maintain.

Answering the inventory of questions about this campus problem can help you make sense of the multiple points of view and perhaps better understand why some group members feel as they do. In the rest of this essay, each step in the inventory will be illustrated by systematically analyzing the campus problem; it will also be applied by explaining similar steps in research studies about a range of cultural groups.

STEP 1: WHAT DO I BELIEVE ABOUT COMMUNICATION AND CULTURE?

There are many ways we all commonly think of culture, and each may be more or less useful to help us understand a certain process, event, or relationship.

Approaches to Culture

Culture as Place. Often when you meet someone, the first question asked is "Where are you from?" Sometimes this refers to a question about where the person grew up, and other times it's a question about where the person lived previously. Groups also are described in print and broadcast media, literature, and academic texts as people who are from or reside in a country or region of a country. These references become evident in everyday discourse as well when an individual says, "I'm from L. A. (Los Angeles), so . . ." implying that who she or he is can be understood through knowing where she or he lives—in this case, in Southern California, which is known for the entertainment industry, wealth, freeway commuting, and a warm coastal climate.

Places of origin or residence bring to mind different social hierarchies and norms, class distinctions, political orientations, and communication styles. Without thinking about it, we assume that people who are raised or live in a particular place probably speak the same language, hold many of the same values, and communicate in similar ways.

Culture as Ancestry and People. Another common way we think about culture is to define culture as the group of people who share the same ancestry. Ethnicity is often used as an indicator of culture. For instance, Japanese Americans are understood as a people who live in the United States whose Japanese ancestors or relatives taught them Japanese language, values, and traditions. During the Second World War, U.S. government representatives assumed that ancestry was a powerful enough force to determine their cultural alliance with Japan, and U.S. citizens of Japanese ancestry were evicted from their homes, their businesses were closed or taken over, and they were imprisoned in internment camps for the duration of the war.

An approach to culture that is also based on ancestry is that which is exemplified by linking race with culture. When people remark, "He's the white guy who lives next door to me," or when writers of newspaper accounts of crimes, for instance, include a description of the race of the alleged perpetrator, then the speaker and writer are making assumptions about racial appearance and ancestry as apparent indicators

of character and identity. Scholars point out that race is a social construct and that we cannot predict behavior, values, or beliefs—let alone the content of one's character—by skin color or hair texture (Martin, 1997; Omi & Winant, 1986; Webster, 1992). As a social construct, however, racial appearance is an everyday shorthand way to stereotype others.

Culture as Art and Artifact. Creative endeavors and expressions that represent the heart, spirit, emotions, or philosophies of a group at a particular time and place are another way we think of culture. Examples include not only what can be seen in museums and galleries, but also the artifacts and remnants of pottery, jewelry, tools, weapons left behind by groups such as the Anasazi Indians, and what is left of their dwellings in Mesa Verde.

Culture as Capital or Economic Resource. Many countries and organizations are based on economic principles of capitalism. We often come to think of areas of the world in terms of their economic status and relative wealth. More specifically, countries or regions are thought of in terms of their buying power and developing markets; the CBS television network program "60 Minutes," for example, featured a segment on investment opportunities and expanding wealth in Russia. Approaching groups as buyers or as producers of products is to think of culture as an economic resource.

Culture as Product. We think about cultures as commodities or products when we think of the numerous toys, foods, films, videos, and music that are internationally exported and imported. The Barbie doll produced by Mattel in the United States is sold to young women all over the world. A colleague of mine who visited Beijing last year commented that the department store mannequins advertising women's clothing and accessories were, more often than not, tall and blond replicas of Barbie. When the same colleague lived with a single mother and two children in Costa Rica who were extremely poor, the daughter wanted a Barbie doll more than any other gift for the Christmas holiday.

Culture as Politics and Ideology. Another way to think of culture is to associate a country with a political ideology. In the United States, the Peace Corps was created in 1961 to give people in areas such as Central America and Africa new technologies, agricultural techniques, and democratic values. More recently, the export of U.S. democratic values through the Peace Corps has been criticized as actually exporting imperialism and colonialism.

Halualani (1998) notes that culture can be approached as the structures, ideologies, and master narratives of groups in power that are created through mediated and public forms to maintain and extend their power. The press coverage of U.S. involvement in the Persian Gulf War in 1991 has been cited as an example of government and military control of the press, and thus the coverage reflected a public-relations emphasis. The news featured the success of the United States and its allies, the spectacle of the missiles and technology, and the lack of casualties (Sturken, 1995); it did not include references to deaths caused by friendly fire or civilian casualties.

Culture as Psychology, Worldview, or Style of Thinking and Speaking. One of the ways in which we come to know who we are is to compare our own group identities with the character of other groups (Tajfel, 1978). Our everyday talk often includes references to *they* and *we*. We learn and attribute to others, based on their group memberships, particular styles of thinking and feeling. In short, we may begin to stereotype other group members by attributing particular psychological tendencies to them (Brislin, 1986). Katz (1960) found that stereotypes become prejudiced, evaluative prejudgments about group members so that we can knowledgeably predict or explain the conduct of people in other groups, as well as serving an ego-defensive function that allows us to blame others for the outcomes of events. For example, when a European American friend of mine called to tell me he was not hired for a job at a fire station, he blamed affirmative action policies that favored members of ethnic minority groups.

Culture as Performance. Sometimes we think of culture as a kind of role we are acting in a play. Goffman (1967) created a theory of communication as performance and noted that some of our identities are "front stage" and others are more "back stage" or private. The audience affects the quality of the

performance as well. Many groups such as Native American Indians have a long-standing tradition of elders sharing the oral histories and origin myths of their people at social gatherings and celebrations.

Culture as Group Identity. We have experienced an exponential increase in access to international information because of computer technology and the Internet; far-away places and people have become more accessible through more affordable and available travel; corporations are told to be multinational to be successful; and our nations and communities have become characterized by increasing diversity. In winter 1998, we could see the tired faces and nonverbal cues of frustration during televised interviews with United Nations representatives and national leaders as they discussed the possibility of a U.S. military strike in Iraq. Through such public and private contact with others, we come to define ourselves as members of cultural groups.

When we approach culture as group character or identity, it is essential to recognize that each group is made up of a multitude of individuals and voices, and each individual has a range of group identities. McPhail (1997), for instance, discusses the range of voices and political standpoints and values making up the African American community. Halualani (1998) argues that the "American Dream" is an idealized myth that is not available to people like her who are Japanese, Hawaiian, and female. Thus, we need to recognize that cultural identities are complex and created, sustained, challenged, and contested in our contact with each other.

Culture and the Campus Problem

Stereotyping occurs on the basis of linking culture to ancestry or race, so students who experience discrimination on the basis of race may argue that they need separate cultural centers in order to have a place to meet where they can feel safe and know that people who look like them are welcome. On the other hand, European American students may argue that cultural centers or ethnic studies programs are not necessary because these students may not value ethnicity or see why ancestry and past traditions are more important than the current American orientation.

Defining culture as ideology and politics may help you understand why members of different groups are so committed to maintaining their own cultural centers and programs, or why they wish to replace such programs. The programs are not only a source of identity reinforcement but also a source of empowerment. Finally, consider that the resources allocated to groups and programs—as well as courses focused on ethnic history, philosophy, and art—are an acknowledgment of the contribution and legitimacy of ethnic members of the U.S. American community. Thus, such programs and designated places are the site in which cultural identities are reinforced, contested, modified, and celebrated.

In my own research, I combine several approaches to culture. Currently, I define *culture* as a historically based, interpretive, constitutive, creative set of practices and interpretive frames that demonstrate affiliation with a group. Culture as group identity is the way I most often think of culture, although I also study the politics and ideology and the performance of the enacted group identities. A communication event or interaction becomes intercultural when different cultural identities emerge in the text or talk of interactants. I'll give several examples of the cultural groups and identity issues I study throughout the remainder of this article.

STEP 2: WHAT INTERCULTURAL COMMUNICATION QUESTION DO I WANT TO ANSWER?

Specifically, what do you want to know about the communicative event, contact, discourse, text, and situation? What problem do you want to address? You may have had a personal experience or an intercultural conversation that left you puzzled or intrigued. Have you witnessed or been a part of an intercultural conflict that you might want to manage? Do you want to explain why members of one group seem to adapt to a new country more quickly than members of another group? Do you wish to critique how multinational corporations in developed countries influence developing nations by introducing technology and products and creating dependency? For the campus problem, you may ask: How does the social history of each "ethnic

minority" group affect the standpoint taken by spokespersons of that group in the campus newspaper? How can understanding the perspective of the administrator (who has more than one cultural identity) and the perspective of the women's studies faculty and students (who also have many cultural identities) help you identify common goals?

This is the step in which you should narrow your interests to a question that you can answer by analyzing specific messages, what you can read, see, and hear in mediated or person-to-person communication. You need to be able to answer your question through systematic empirical observation or analysis or critique of communication messages in conversations, groups, public venues, and all forms of print and broadcast media. You are acting on the premise that people construct their identities and relationships through their communication, and the study of communication messages can help us not only understand what is going on in our communication with each other, but also potentially how to improve the quality of our intercultural relationships.

STEP 3: WHAT CULTURAL IDENTITY ISSUES ARE RELEVANT?

The third set of questions points to cultural identities and how they are enacted, produced, reproduced, reinforced, contested, constructed, and reconstructed in your selected problematic situation. Listed as follows are several principles or assumptions about cultural identities that you may find helpful as you think about the campus problem and your own experiences and research.

Multiple Cultural Identity Types (CITs)

Many groups (although not all) form cultural systems. In some cases, shared history or geography provides commonality of worldview or lifestyle that helps create and reinforce a cultural system of communication. To create a culture, a group must first define itself as a group. This may be on the basis of nationality, ethnicity, gender, profession, geography, organization, community, physical ability or disability, or type of relationship, among others. Once the group defines itself as a unit, then a cultural system may develop. For instance, U.S. Americans define themselves as a group based on use of English as a shared code; reinforcement of democracy through political discussion and action; individual rights and freedoms of speech, press, religion, and assembly being explicitly described in the Bill of Rights and enforced in the courts; and so forth. Attorneys or sales clerks or homemakers may be linked by similarities in daily activities and standard of living.

National and Ethnic Cultures. To better understand the many different types of cultures, we can categorize them from the more general and more common to the more specific. National and ethnic cultures are fairly general. These kinds of groups base membership on heritage and history that have been handed down for generations. Their histories are based on traditions, rituals, codes of language, and norms.

Persons who share the same nationality were born in a particular country or spent a significant number of years and period of socialization in that country. Such socialization promotes and reinforces particular values, beliefs, and norms. Many people contribute to the creation of a national culture's symbols, meanings, and norms, so national culture is fairly abstract and predictions about language use and what symbols mean must be general. For instance, Japanese national culture has been described as collectivistic, high-context, high on power distance, and other-face-oriented (Gudykunst & Ting-Toomey, 1988). Not all Japanese people follow these norms in every situation; comparing Japanese to Germans, however, the Japanese as a group are more group-oriented and emphasize status hierarchies more than do the Germans as an overall group (Hofstede, 1980).

Ethnicity is a bit different in that ethnic groups share a sense of heritage and history, as well as origin from an area outside of or preceding the creation of the current nation-state of residence (Banks, 1984). In some but not all cases, ethnic groups share racial characteristics, and many have a specific history of having experienced discrimination. In the United States, ethnic groups include African Americans, Asian Americans (e.g., Japanese Americans, Chinese Americans, Vietnamese Americans), Mexican Americans, German Americans, Irish Americans, Native American Indians, and Jewish Americans.

Sex and Gender. Another common cultural group is that based on biological sex or socially constructed gender. There are many subcategories of gender cultures. Groups create, reinforce, and teach what it means to use a gender style and what is interpreted as feminine or masculine. Groups also reinforce what is appropriate or inappropriate for a good husband, good wife, feminist, chauvinist, heterosexual, gay, or lesbian. Parents, religious leaders, teachers, and what we read and see in the media all provide information about how to be a member of a particular gender culture.

Remember that nationality, ethnicity, race, and sex are cultural group affiliations based on citizenship, heritage, and biology, and such broad memberships do not guarantee that members of those groups will automatically behave or interpret messages in the same ways. Many individuals have parents and grandparents with different backgrounds and heritages and claim more than one ethnicity and may have lived in several different countries. From the CIT perspective, cultural identity is created when a group affiliation is enacted, when an individual or group members claim membership in one or more groups. Cultural identity is based on what members of a group or community say and do and think and feel as they affiliate with others who share their history, origins, or biology. For a cultural identity to be recognized, the identity needs to be claimed and communicated in some way.

Profession. Groups of professionals sometimes create their own culture. Politicians, physicians, field workers, sales personnel, maintenance crews, bankers, and consultants share common ways of spending time, earning money, communicating with others, and sharing norms about how to be a member of their profession. For instance, most health care professionals share a commitment to health, to helping others, and to improving others' quality of life. They also share educational background, knowledge about their aspect of health care, and standards of practicing their profession.

Geographic Area. Geographic area is sometimes a boundary that contributes to the formation of a cultural group. In South Africa, the area surrounding Cape Town has its own version of spoken Afrikaans, has a higher population of coloureds (those of mixed race), and is viewed by many as a cosmopolitan area in South Africa. The South in the United States has its own traditions, historical orientation, and Southern drawl.

Corporation. Organizational culture is yet another type of culture. The most common type is that created in large corporations such as IBM, Nike, and Xerox. Here individuals are taught the corporate symbols; the corporate myths, heroes, and legends; and what it means to be an employee. In addition, individuals are taught the proper chain of command, procedures, policies, and schedules. Finally, they are taught the norms in the corporation, who to talk to about what and at which time. Some corporations value "team players," whereas others value "individual initiative." Some corporations have mottoes like "Never say *no* to an assignment" or "Never be afraid to speak up if you don't have what you need."

Support groups also have their own version of organizational culture. Alcoholics Anonymous, Overeaters Anonymous, and therapy and support groups, among others, have their own sets of symbols and interpretations and norms. For example, "Let go and let God" is an important requirement in the anonymous groups, emphasizing that relinquishing individual control to a higher power is a tool in managing one's addictions. Social living groups also often create their own cultures, such as sororities and fraternities, international dormitories, and the like.

Physical Ability and Disability. Physical ability and disability is still another category of group that can become a basis for culture. Professional athletic teams teach rookies how to behave and what to do to be accepted members of the team. Persons who have physical handicaps share critical life experiences, and groups teach individuals how to accept and overcome their disabilities, as well as how to communicate more effectively with those who do not have the disability (Braithwaite, 1991).

Cultural Identification as Constituted in Communication

Cultural identity is the particular character of the group communication system that emerges when people claim group membership in a particular situation, event, or communication context. Cultural identities are negotiated, co-created, reinforced, and challenged through communication (Hecht, Collier, & Ribeau, 1993). In CIT, identity is approached from a communication perspective, which views identity as located in the communication process in which messages are constructed, reinforced, contested, and challenged. A communication perspective also includes attention to the creation of cultural identities through products or words and images that are transmitted through media or technological channels. Group affiliation and membering occurs in multiple contexts in which insiders and outsiders enact what membership looks and sounds like. All cultures that are created are influenced by a host of social and psychological and environmental factors as well as by institutions, history, and context. Latinos who wish to maintain their cultural center may argue their position more strongly at private meetings attended by members of their group and change the intensity of their tone and persuasive appeals when interacting with community representatives on their board of advisors. Identities therefore are co-created in relationship to other people. Who we are and how we are differs and emerges depending on who we are with, the cultural identities that are important to us and others, the context, the topic of conversation, and our interpretations and attributions.

Multivocality and Interpellated Cultural Identities

From an individual perspective, each person has a range of groups and cultures to which she or he belongs in a constantly changing environment. Each individual participates in many cultural systems each day, week, and year. Cultures are affected not only by changing socioeconomic and environmental conditions, but also by other cultures. As poet and writer bell hooks (1989) reminds us, she is not only an African American, but also a woman and a college professor. To understand her conduct, one must recognize her multiple identities and voices, just as someone else must recognize *your* multiple voices and identities. It is also important to recognize that not all voices within a group sound alike.

Morgan (1996) uses the term *feminisms* to recognize multivocality within feminists as a group; some voices are more radical, some more conservative, and some both radical and conservative. *Interpellation* refers to the interrelationships among such cultural identities as sex, race, and class, and the point that one cannot understand sex without also studying race and class.

Several months ago, on my way to work, I drove by a local seminary. For several days I saw on the outside lawn a small group of women leading another larger group in prayer. I also read in the newspaper that these women were on a hunger strike and were protesting discrimination toward women faculty who were denied tenure or a voice in determining policy in the seminary. If I want an accurate picture of the issues and group standpoints, then identifying how the women leading the protest, the staff, the students, and the administrators of the seminary were defining religion, feminism, and political voice would be important, as would noticing that the individuals within each group constructed their identities and position on the issues in a unique way.

Avowal and Ascription Processes

I have used the term *multivocality* to point out that groups are made up of individuals with unique as well as similar voices. In addition, each individual may enact various cultural identities over the course of a lifetime, not to mention over the course of a day. Identities are enacted across contexts through *avowal* and *ascription* processes. Avowal has to do with what an individual portrays to others and is analogous to the face or image shown to others. In a way, avowal is the individual showing to others "This is who I am" as a member of this group or these groups.

Ascription is when individuals or group members come to know that others attribute particular identities to them as members of a group. Stereotypes and attributions that are communicated are examples. In part, identity is shaped by others' communicated views of us. For example, a black Zulu female's cultural identities in South Africa are not only shaped by her definition and image of what it means to be a black Zulu female but also by the communicated views of the white Afrikaners for whom she works, her Zulu family and relatives, the township in which she lives in poverty, her white teachers who speak Afrikaans and English, and so forth.

Another way of thinking about this concept is to say that cultural identities have both subjective and ascribed meanings. Some cultures emphasize ascription or an orientation toward others. In Japan, a traditional philosophy sometimes reflected in practice is that of *amae*. Amae represents an other orientation and a sense of obligation to the group; an individual is expected to sacrifice individual needs and give to others, and others are expected to reciprocate. Thus, the harmony and cohesiveness of the group is maintained (Doi, 1989; Goldman, 1992).

Information about avowal and ascription can be useful in understanding the role others play in developing your own cultural identities. If you feel you are a member of a group that is marginalized and discriminated against or has a high need for status, then those aspects of identity may be influenced by the stereotypes or conceptions held and communicated by other groups.

Salience and Intensity Differences

Identities differ in their salience in particular contexts, and identities are enacted with different intensities at different times. The intensities provide markers of strong involvement and investment in the identity. As a white U.S. American female professor visiting Australia and being taken on a dream time walk by a male aborigine, at different times throughout the walk, I was aware of being a white minority, a U.S. American tourist who was stereotyped somewhat negatively, a college professor who was interested in culture, and an honored guest.

Salience refers to featuring one or more particular identities more strongly than others, and it certainly does not mean individuals have split personalities or need to give up one cultural identity to feature another. Some people also have less choice about what cultural identities they can feature. I have come to see that I have certain unearned privileges and choice about whether or not I choose to share my British German ethnic heritage.

Enduring and Changing Property of Identity

Cultural identities are both enduring and changing. As already mentioned, cultures have a history that is continually constructed and reconstructed with new members over time. Cultural identities change because of economic, political, social, psychological, and contextual factors, not to mention the influence of other cultural identities.

Enacting the cultural identity of being gay or lesbian in the 1990s has certain things in common with being gay in the 1980s and 1970s. Individuals who "come out of the closet" encounter similar stereotypes and ascriptions to those in earlier centuries. However, the political climate in some areas of the country in which ballot initiatives sought to limit the rights of gays or link gays with other groups such as sadomasochists also affects the cultural identity of the group. Sometimes context changes how one manifests identity and how intensely one avows an identity. For example, not all members of a gay, lesbian, and bisexual alliance may avow that identity outside of their support group.

STEP 4: WHAT IS THE ROLE OF POWER AND IDEOLOGY?

This leads us to the fourth set of questions you will want to ask about power and ideology. These include: What is power? Is it a process, a commodity, a perception or impression of influence, access, or ability to distribute resources? How do people lose or gain power?

I have noticed in my classes that members of marginalized groups are more likely to make statements such as "All intercultural communication is political" or "Power is always an issue in intercultural communication." The newer theoretical perspectives point us to identifying the extent to which power is constructed through history, institutions, and social practices; and for some of us to interrogate previous assumptions and benefits we accrue on the basis of being white or male or upper class.

There are days when individually I feel somewhat powerless, and yet I, as a white, middle-class professional, benefit from institutional practices in higher education and the broader political system that maintain my rights and privileges and lead me to expect to be hired, treated with respect by staff, or waited on in a department store without being shadowed or suspected of being a shoplifter. Even with affirmative-action policies, across the United States I am more

likely to be hired for a corporate position or a position in higher education than my Latina, African American, or Native American Indian counterparts.

On the other hand, assuming that groups are either "all powerful" and totally "imperialist" or "powerless" and "colonized" can be an inappropriate oversimplification. Consider international contexts in which new products or ideologies are introduced by corporate representatives from developed nations to people in less developed nations. When parents in a village in Nicaragua take a Barbie doll that was a gift from a U.N. visitor and stain the skin to be darker, dress her in indigenous clothing, and create a new ritual in which she is the voice of the ancestors sharing their stories, this is a redefinition of power.

As both group members and problem solvers, we ought to recognize that those who have some degree of power will seek to maintain it, and that there are many collective interpretations of power and resistance. McClintock (1995) notes that there exists a "diverse politics of agency, involving the dense web of relations between coercion, negotiation, complicity, refusal, dissembling, mimicry, compromise, affiliation, and revolt" (p. 15). There are also benefits to becoming aware of presumed sources of power that have become somewhat invisible to some of us, as well as engaging in what hooks calls intercultural dialogue between those who feel oppressed and those who "exploit, oppress and dominate" (1989, p. 129) because this opens opportunities and spaces for understanding of the structures and functions of domination (Foss, 1998).

There are many related questions you may ask about power and what has endured in order to understand the historical, social, and ideological context of your intercultural problem. Such questions may address the importance of the environment, history, and institutions such as education and religion in determining how cultural identities emerge. Our own socioeconomic class affects what we deem appropriate and what we expect from others, and histories of racism, sexism, and classism, for example, influence how we all behave.

The importance of acknowledging the historical and social context in which power emerges is illustrated by the following comments. On a visit to the Middle East in spring 1998, a young Palestinian woman asked me, "What do you think? I am Palestinian and I live in Gaza. The Israeli government laws deny me and my brothers the right I.D. [identity] card, so I can't work in Israel, visit my aunts and uncles, or visit holy sites in Jerusalem. How can this be?" A young Israeli woman told me, "We were raised to hate them [Palestinians], to think that the men are all terrorists and the women are abused by their husbands because of Islam."

You may want to ask a more specific set of questions with regard to the power and ideology of different cultural groups in their intercultural contact. Who makes important decisions in the group, determines when and where meetings or social gatherings will take place, or speaks for the rest of the group in intercultural meetings or in public presentations? How are decisions made to allocate resources or create policy and procedures? What kinds of values and ideologies are handed down to new members?

STEP 5: WHAT ARE THE INTERGROUP AND INTERPERSONAL RELATIONSHIP PROCESSES?

Our cultural identities are constructed in relationships with others inside our own groups and with members of other groups. *Relationship process* refers to the quality of connection or bond that emerges in communication. When persons communicate with each other, their messages carry not only information, but also cues about the relationship between individuals and groups. These cues indicate who is dominant or submissive throughout the conversation or event, how much intimacy or hostility is felt, how much each partner or party trusts one another, and how much they feel included or excluded.

You could analyze the campus newspaper coverage of the debate about closing the campus centers and programs, or attend the public forum on campus where students articulate their views. Using the newspaper articles or transcriptions of the public meeting or both, you could look for relational messages that constitute the relationship, phrases that indicate friendliness such as "We support the need for safe places to meet and are open to designating additional spaces for intercultural dialogue"; or control, "How can redefining what used to be a separatist place into a place where all

students can go possibly be a bad thing?"; or exclusion in the press headline "Provost Says, 'Student Input Has No Place in Closing Cultural Centers.'" You could ask intercultural friends to tape-record their informal talk about the campus problem and look for what Baxter and Montgomery (1996) and Martin, Nakayama, and Flores (1997) describe as dialectic tensions in the dialogue. For instance, intercultural friends may experience contradictory tendencies to be both independent and connected, private and public, and dominant and submissive. Looking for dialectic tensions may help you guard against making overly simplistic generalizations about a group's preferred mode of communication.

Sometimes people use their in-group language to reinforce their in-group status and establish distance from the out-group (Giles, Coupland, & Coupland, 1991). At other times, they may use the language of the out-group in order to adapt and align with the out-group. Some Mexican Americans speak Spanish when in neighborhood communities in order to preserve their history and roots and to reinforce their identification and bond as a people. The same persons may speak English at work because the supervisor and executives of the company demand it. They may also choose to speak Spanish in meetings to plan their response to close their cultural center, and choose English when meeting with the provost.

STEP 6: WHAT KINDS OF COMMUNICATIVE MESSAGES SHOULD I EXAMINE IN MY STUDY?

What kind of data or communication messages do you need to answer your questions? What types or forms of messages may be important? Are you interested in analyzing a series of meetings between diplomats over several years, or the speeches of one political figure in a particular period of time, or a relationship you have, or a conversation that took place yesterday? It is also important to think about what you need to examine in the way of functions or outcomes of those forms.

This set of questions deals with what kind and how much communicative data you wish to understand or explain. Some scholars study the rhetoric that is common in a century or decade, or in the letters written by an international traveler during his or her lifetime. Others choose a much more specific focus on a particular event in time or critical point in a relationship. For the campus problem, if you want to interview people from various groups, you must decide who you want to interview, what you want to ask, if you want answers to specific questions or you want to have more of a collaborative dialogue, and how many times you want to meet with them. Whether you are addressing a concrete problem or conducting a research study, you need to think about the breadth and scope of your data and what it will take to answer your question appropriately.

Form and Function of Discourse Texts

The form and function of talk with friends was the focus of a study of adolescent members of various ethnic groups in London, England (Collier & Thompson, 1997). We found that discourse among friends served dual functions: (1) maintaining traditional and previous home cultural identity, language, and norms; and (2) developing a new national or ethnic identity. Using in-depth group interviews, we asked questions about three contexts: home, school, and socializing with friends, and the national and ethnic identities constructed in each. We asked respondents in each context to think of a situation in which they were aware of being from different cultural backgrounds. Then we asked about who was there, what was discussed, what activities took place, and the purpose and outcome of the contact.

The adolescents were most aware of their shared national identity as British citizens at school, and they were most aware of their different ethnic backgrounds at home because that was where home language was often spoken and where narrative rituals recalling history and people were most often seen. Several respondents pointed out that these family gatherings and storytelling episodes by grandparents served to bring the family together, remind them of their past and roots, and provide a way of reinforcing transcendent values and extended family ties.

Message Patterns and Themes

Another way to analyze communication texts is to look for message patterns and themes. For example, you may wish to see how often a particular phrase or idea such as feminism comes up, around what topics, and with which conversational partners. You may also want to analyze narratives or stories and look for themes that may emerge. For example, Hecht and Ribeau (1987) and Hecht, Ribeau, and Alberts (1989) analyzed recalled conversations of African Americans with European Americans and distinguished several improvement strategies such as asserting point of view and positive self-presentation.

Modes of Expression: Labels and Norms

Labels are a way of establishing identity. The same label may vary widely in its interpretation. The term *American* is perceived as acceptable and common by many residents of the United States, as ethnocentric and self-centered by residents of Central America and Canada, and as associated with a group that is privileged, wealthy, and powerful by some developing countries. Labels used in the discourse of people involved in the campus problem can potentially reveal a great deal about identities ascribed to outsiders.

For example, *Hispanic* is a general term that many social scientists use to describe "persons of Mexican, Puerto Rican, Cuban, Central or South American or other Spanish culture of origin, regardless of race" (Marin & Marin, 1991, p. 23). Persons may choose to describe their own ethnicity with a much more specific label such as Mexican American or Chicano or Chicana. The individuals may differ on their ideas about what it means to be a member of that culture. Whether the label was created by members of the group or members of another group (e.g., *Hispanic* is a term that was originally generated by the U.S. government) provides useful information about what the label means and how it is interpreted.

Norms are explicit or inferred prescriptions of modes of appropriate and effective communication. Norms are prescriptive or evaluative because they specify appropriate and acceptable behavior, moral standards, and expectations for conduct. Norms provide cultural group members with a criteria to decide to what degree another is behaving in a competent manner. Reviewing the historical, political, and ideological context of norms and expectations that group members may bring to the public forum on campus can be helpful when assigning interpretations to the chanting and loud interruptions by members of one group.

Cultural groups create and reinforce standards for "performing the culture" appropriately and effectively. An individual is successful at enacting identity when one is accepted as a competent member of the group. For example, all those who are registered as members of Native American Indian tribes in the United States are defined as "real Indians" only when they conduct themselves in ways that insiders judge to be appropriate and acceptable for Indians (Weider & Pratt, 1990). Norms and standards for acceptable conduct are general trends at best; they are constructed by group members and interpreted by individuals, and they change across contexts.

Affective, Cognitive, and Spiritual Components

Throughout history, many groups have felt strongly enough about the supremacy of their beliefs to conquer and convert outsiders. For instance, Jerusalem is a holy city to three of the world's largest religions, and Israeli control is contested by Muslim and Christian groups. Emotions and feelings are attached to identities, and these change across situation, historical context, political climate, and relationship with others. Sometimes, the avowal or featuring of a particular identity more strongly and more violently is a signal of the importance of that identity and the degree to which that identity is perceived to be threatened. When a colleague and I (Collier & Bowker, 1994) asked women friends who had different cultural identities what made a good intercultural ally, two of the African American women said that their European American friends needed to be able to hear their anger and rage about daily experiences with oppression, while their European American women friends said their feelings about the value of the friendship needed to be reciprocated.

The cognitive component of identity relates to the beliefs we have about that identity. Persons have a range of premises about each culture group to which they belong, but certain similarities become evident when you ask people to talk about what it means to be U.S. American or Thai or a member of the environmentalist group Earth First! Members of Earth First! share beliefs in the value of ancient forests, distrust executives who run the logging companies and politicians who support the lumber industry, and view spiking trees and sabotaging logging equipment as sometimes necessary forms of protest. Such beliefs can be summarized into a core symbol, here the name of the organization—Earth First!

STEP 7: WHAT IS THE CONTEXT OF THE INTERCULTURAL PROBLEM?

How we construct identities occurs in a broad context of history, power dynamics, social norms, and specific situations. Thus, it is important to ask questions such as: What factors outside of the messages can help me understand the intercultural communication? What is the physical environment? What histories and institutions (e.g., political, religious, educational) are relevant?

The site of one of my first exploratory studies of culture and communication was the Navajo reservation in Chinle, Arizona. I lived with a family and taught high school classes. I became interested in how Navajos developed and strengthened their cultural identities through family rituals and community events, and how their identities were threatened by institutions such as the Bureau of Indian Affairs schools in which students were forced to speak English.

Context includes the physical environment, for instance, where persons with different cultural identities have contact, or the location or place in which a media text, cultural product, or speech is produced, distributed, and interpreted by audiences or consumers, as well as a social and historical place in time. For example, in the campus problem, if someone argues that curriculum as well as programs of study should be based on the canons of traditional Greek knowledge as a foundation, it may be important to consider that Aristotle's ideas about rhetoric, for example, were created in a time in which women were excluded from political participation and in a place in which wealth and power were concentrated in the hands of a few of the elite.

In one of my studies, I wished to understand how young people from different cultural groups in South Africa in 1992 approached and experienced interpersonal, intercultural relationships. We (Collier & Bornman, in press) discovered, for instance, that interethnic and interracial friendships were more common among nonwhite group members and more common in private than in public contexts. We also found that blacks, Asian Indians, and coloureds (those of mixed race) emphasized the need to acknowledge history and the consequences of the apartheid system of government, while the Afrikaners and British we interviewed emphasized the need to be present- and future-oriented.

STEP 8: WHAT PERSPECTIVES AND PROCEDURES SHOULD I USE TO STUDY THE DATA?

Epistemological Perspectives

How can you best study the communication messages in which you're interested? Whether you are trying to understand an intercultural problem, an event, or asking a research question, you will need to decide if you should be as objective as possible, ask others how they make sense of their subjective experiences, be an engaged participant, or be a more distant but knowledgeable critic. Many perspectives to doing research are available to you as you approach inquiry about a particular intercultural communication situation or text. Becoming familiar with them will give you a better basis from which to choose one or more perspectives in answering your own question.

I describe three broad perspectives to epistemology, or what and how we know what we do, as follows.[3] We will talk about these types as epistemological perspectives because each is a way in which we can view knowledge building in intercultural communication. Although I emphasize research examples, you may also adapt these approaches to practical problems from your own experience.

Positivist and Objectivist Perspectives

Positivist approaches have the longest legacy in communication because of their origins in social science. Anderson (1996) notes that objectivist theories are based in principles of empiricism (observation), materialism, determinism (cause–effect relationships), and objectivity. Assumptions made by researchers taking this perspective are that a material reality "out there" can be discovered, observed, measured, and operationalized, and causal relationships proven. A common assumption is that psychological states such as beliefs, feelings, attitudes, and values can be discovered and quantified through behavioral assessments such as scaled questionnaires. Further, it is assumed that behaviors (actions that can be seen and categorized) are authentic representations of psychological states (what individuals are thinking or feeling).

Perhaps as you listen to people talk about the campus problem, you begin to hypothesize that students who have friends from other cultures or who have traveled in other countries are more likely to voice their support for keeping the cultural centers and various programs. You decide to test this relationship. You could develop a set of questions that measure the extent of previous intercultural contact (e.g., living in another country, number of friends who have a different nationality or ethnicity) and measure the likelihood that a person might make or agree with someone who makes such comments as, "Programs like ethnic studies are valuable for all students" or "Women's studies courses teach issues that can be useful for men and women to learn." You would be assuming that such questions would be interpreted and mean the same things to all students, and the extent to which they agreed or disagreed with each question would represent their overall attitude. You, like social science scholars who use positivism, would want to be able to predict, for example, particular kinds of communication behavior and partly explain that behavior by looking at the variable of previous intercultural contact.

Another example of positivist research is that of Gudykunst (1994), who proposed that because Japanese people are more collectivistic and group-oriented and emphasize contextual factors such as silence in interpretation more highly than do U.S. Americans, Japanese individuals communicating with strangers will experience a higher level of anxiety than will U.S. Americans. Assumptions made in anxiety and uncertainty management theory (Gudykunst, 1994) include that national culture is a predictor and explanatory variable for intergroup behavior and that relationships among such variables as uncertainty, anxiety, and mindfulness can predict and explain strangers' intergroup behavior.

Critical Deconstructionist Perspectives

As scholars in communication, the ways we come to know have changed dramatically over the last few centuries. One of the characteristic turns is the emergence of skepticism and questions about what we know, how we know, and who we are as scholars and people.

Certain overarching assumptions are shared by scholars aligned with a critical perspective. Scholars are primarily concerned with *exploitation, power, empowerment,* and the development of rhetorical tools to *deconstruct* and *critique* discourse and media texts and provide alternative interpretations. Prus (1996) characterizes the critical voice as "extreme skepticism in the viability of all forms of knowing" (p. 217).

One group of critical scholars describes the work it does as *postcolonialist.* These scholars not only criticize the use and misuse of power by particular groups, but they also point out that scholars may exert power and influence on the cultural identities and conduct of the masses by deciding what is important to study and how to describe groups and social issues.

An example of the *critical perspective* is the work of van Dijk (1993) on social cognition and racism. He examines the social, political, and cultural reproduction of racism by giving attention to what he calls *microlevel interactions* and *everyday conversational talk,* along with macrostructures, socially shared strategies and representations of power, dominance, and access. He has investigated forms of racism and sexism in television news reports as well as in newspaper articles and examined how institutions are represented, how political points of view are articulated, and how economic and social policies are challenged or reinforced. Similarly, you could take a critical perspective in analyzing the newspaper reports about the campus problem and identify who is being interviewed, whose voices are featured most, what kind of examples are being quoted by members of particular groups, and the overall portrayal of particular groups.

Interpretive and Reconstructive Perspectives

A third type of epistemological perspective can be called *interpretive* because the goal is understanding. In most interpretive approaches, the goal of the researcher is to build an understanding of how respondents come to do, be, and know (Sachs, 1984) their cultural identities. Many scholars use interpretive approaches to build an understanding about the negotiation and enactment of cultural identities in particular interactional contexts.

One example of an *interpretive perspective* is CIT (Collier, 1998a, 1998b; Collier & Thomas, 1988; Hecht, Collier, & Ribeau, 1993), which I've featured throughout this article. To review, one of the major premises I make is the assumption that we align with various groups, and part of what we do when we communicate with others is define who we are and distinguish ourselves as members of groups. We also construct our cultural identities as a way of developing relationships, increasing or contesting our lack of power in various situations, and creating a history that can transcend situations, periods of time, and lifetimes.

In a CIT approach, cultural identities are historical, contextual, and relational constructions; we create to some degree through our communication, our pasts, and what we hand down to new members and teach in our institutions. The historical, social, political, economic, and relational context, as well as our physical surroundings, affect who we are and who we come to be with one another. Cultural identities are commonly intelligible and accessible to group members (Carbaugh, 1990). Cultural identities emerge in everyday discourse as well as in social practices, rituals, norms, and myths that are handed down to new members. Each perspective is based on a set of assumptions about inquiry and knowledge building. Just as our social world is characterized by rapid and complex change, so our perspectives should be open to interrogation and modification.

Researcher Perspective

Identities are constructed by and can be studied as constructions of individuals, relational partners, or group members of a community. In addition to selecting an epistemological perspective, you'll also need to select a researcher perspective. You may wish to focus on the point of view of individuals. Each person has individual interpretations of what it means to be U.S. American or Austrian or Indian, for example, and each person enacts his or her cultural identities slightly differently. If we want to understand why an individual behaves in a particular way, then we can ask the individual to talk about his or her cultural identity and experiences as a group member.

You can also study culture from a relational point of view. You can observe interaction between people, friends, co-workers, or family members who identify themselves as members of a relationship and with different groups. Collier (1988) found that Mexican American friends emphasized the importance of their relationship in their descriptions of what is appropriate and effective (e.g., meeting frequently and spending a significant portion of time together). They also described the most important characteristics of friendship to be support, trust, intimacy, and commitment to the relationship.

You may also study culture in terms of its communal properties. This is giving attention to public communication contexts and activities in communities and neighborhoods. Rituals, rites of passage, and holiday celebrations are other sources of information about how people use cultural membership to establish community.

STEP 9: WHAT ARE MY PRELIMINARY AND ALTERNATIVE INTERPRETATIONS AND CONCLUSIONS?

The ninth set of questions has to do with your interpretations. What patterns are you observing? What are your preliminary answers to your research questions? What are your tentative conclusions?

After you formulate preliminary conclusions and answers to your questions, it will be useful to ask: What are alternative interpretations and conclusions? Who might disagree with these findings? Would your respondents (people you interviewed) or the audience for the film or newspaper articles agree or disagree with your findings? Can you ask them for further information? Have any voices or views been heretofore silent and unspoken? It is also important to ask yourself: To what extent are my personal history, socialization, preferred norms of conduct, and cultural identities affecting my interpretations and conclusions? What are my personal biases that need to be identified? In

the campus problem, would a student who had taken courses in women's studies, ethnic studies, or international studies have alternative interpretations of my data that might change my overall conclusions?

STEP 10: HOW CAN I APPLY MY INTERPRETATIONS?

Finally, the last set of questions asks you to pinpoint how you can apply what you learned from the intercultural problem to your own cultural identities and intercultural communication, as well as broader community, national, and international issues. Essentially, you should propose how your findings could be useful to improve your own intercultural relationships and ability to analyze critically what you read and hear, as well as how your findings may be useful for members of the cultural communities you studied or the wider community.

Sometimes what we learn has implications for similar cultural groups or intercultural interactions in a wide variety of contexts even from one country to another. How has what you learned changed how you [are what you] do, [and what you] know about intercultural communication? With whom should you share your findings? What are ethical or moral insights that you might have developed? How can you apply what you learned about the campus problem to comprehend better current political discourse about affirmative action? What do you still need to know or study?

CONCLUSIONS

The study of intercultural communication is complex and dynamic; occurs in broad historical, economic, political, and social contexts; and is characterized by distinctive social norms and practices in the particular situation. My goal is for the inventory to become a useful guide for you to build knowledge about how we co-create our cultural identities and relationships through our contact with one another. I hope the steps indicate some of the major issues that emerge in intercultural communication, such as cultural identities, power, quality of relationship, and context, as well as point you toward the many options you have to study and potentially manage intercultural problematics. Finally, I hope that the examples from the communication discourse of people in my classes and research studies encourage you to think about perspectives that are different from your own in a new way.

Learning about intercultural communication is a lifelong endeavor. It is a commitment to improving the quality of what exists now and transcends our lifetimes. Let the dialogue continue.

Notes

1. Melissa McCalla, Jennifer Thompson, and Charlene Belitz, doctoral students at the University of Denver, assigned a draft of this chapter in their undergraduate intercultural communication courses. The student feedback and recommendations were insightful and helpful.
2. I am grateful to Melissa McCalla for suggesting this term.
3. Please see Anderson (1996), Deetz (1994), and Mumby (1997) for additional reading about how these particular categories of knowing emerged.

References

Anderson, J. A. (1996). *Communication theory: Epistemological foundations*. New York: Guilford Press.

Banks, J. (1984). *Teaching strategies for ethnic studies* (3rd ed.). Boston: Allyn & Bacon.

Baxter, L., & Montgomery, B. (1996). *Relating: Dialogues and dialectics*. New York: Guilford Press.

Braithwaite, D. (1991). "Just how much did that wheelchair cost?" Management of privacy boundaries by persons with disabilities. *Western Journal of Speech Communication, 55,* 254–274.

Brislin, R. (1986). Prejudice and intergroup communication. In W. Gudykunst (Ed.), *Intergroup communication* (pp. 74–85). Baltimore: Edward Arnold.

Carbaugh, D. (1990). Intercultural communication. In D. Carbaugh (Ed.), *Cultural communication and intercultural contact* (pp. 151–176). Hillsdale, NJ: Lawrence Erlbaum.

Collier, M. J. (1988). A comparison of conversations among and between domestic culture groups: How intra- and intercultural competencies vary. *Communication Quarterly, 36,* 122–144.

Collier, M. J. (1998a). Researching cultural identity: Reconciling interpretive and post-colonial perspectives. In D. Tanno & A. Gonzalez (Eds.), *Communication and identity across cultures (International and Intercultural Communication Annual, Vol. XXI,* pp. 122–147). Thousand Oaks, CA: Sage.

Collier, M. J. (1998b). Intercultural friendships as interpersonal alliances. In J. Martin, T. Nakayama, & L. Flores (Eds.), *Readings in cultural contexts* (pp. 370–378). Mountain View, CA: Mayfield.

Collier, M. J., & Bornman, E. (In press). Core symbols in South African intercultural friendships. *International Journal of Intercultural Relations.*

Collier, M. J., & Bowker, J. (1994, November). *U.S. American women in intercultural friendships.* Paper presented at the annual Speech Communication Association conference, New Orleans.

Collier, M. J., & Thomas, M. (1988). Cultural identity: An interpretive perspective. In Y. Y. Kim & W. Gudykunst (Eds.), *Theories in intercultural communication* (pp. 99–122). Newbury Park, CA: Sage.

Collier, M. J., & Thompson, J. (1997, May). *Intercultural adaptation among friends: Managing identities across contexts and relationships.* Paper presented at the International Conference of Language and Social Psychology, Ottawa, Canada.

Deetz, S. (1994). The future of the discipline: The challenges, the research and the social contribution. In S. Deetz (Ed.), *Communication yearbook 17* (pp. 115–147). Thousand Oaks, CA: Sage.

Doi, T. (1989). *The anatomy of dependence.* Tokyo: Kodansha Publishers.

Foss, S. K. (1998). bell hooks. In S. K. Foss, K. A. Foss, & C. L. Griffin (Eds.), *Feminist rhetorical theories.* Thousand Oaks, CA: Sage.

Giles, H., Coupland, N., & Coupland, J. (1991). Accommodation theory: Communication, contexts and consequences. In J. Giles, N. Coupland, & J. Coupland (Eds.), *Contexts of accommodation: Developments in applied sociolinguistics.* Cambridge, England: Cambridge University Press.

Goffman, E. (1967). *Interaction ritual: Essays on face-to-face interaction.* Garden City, NY: Doubleday.

Goldman, A. (1992). *The centrality of "Ningensei" to Japanese negotiating and interpersonal relationships: Implications for U.S.–Japanese communication.* Paper presented at Speech Communication Association conference, Chicago.

Gudykunst, W. B. (1994). Anxiety/uncertainty management (AUM) theory: Current status. In R. Wiseman (Ed.), *International and Intercultural Communication Annual, Vol. XIX* (pp. 170–193). Thousand Oaks, CA: Sage.

Gudykunst, W. B., & Ting-Toomey, S. (1988). *Culture and interpersonal communication.* Newbury Park: Sage.

Halualani, R. T. (1998). Seeing through the screen: A struggle of "culture." In J. Martin, T. Nakayama, & L. Flores (Eds.), *Readings in cultural contexts* (pp. 264–274). Mountain View, CA: Mayfield.

Hecht, M., & Ribeau, S. (1987). Afro-American identity labels and communicative effectiveness. *Journal of Language and Social Psychology, 6,* 319–326.

Hecht, M., Collier, M. J., & Ribeau, S. (1993). *African American communication.* Newbury Park: Sage.

Hecht, M., Ribeau, S., & Alberts, J. K. (1989). An Afro-American perspective on interethnic communication. *Communication Monographs, 56,* 385–410.

Hofstede, G. (1980). *Culture's consequences.* Newbury Park, CA: Sage.

hooks, b. (1989). *Talking back: Thinking feminist, thinking black.* Boston: South End.

Katz, E. (1960). The functional approach to the study of attitudes. *Public Opinion Quarterly, 24,* 164–204.

Langer, E. (1989). *Mindfulness.* Reading, MA: Addison-Wesley.

Marin, G., & Marin, B. V. (1991). *Research with Hispanic populations.* Newbury Park, CA: Sage.

Martin, J. (1997). Understanding whiteness in the United States. In L. Samovar & R. Porter (Eds.), *Intercultural communication: A reader* (8th ed., pp. 54–62). Belmont, CA: Wadsworth.

Martin, J., Nakayama, T. K., & Flores, L. A. (1997). A dialectical approach to intercultural communication. In J. Martin, T. Nakayama, & L. Flores (Eds.), *Readings in cultural contexts* (pp. 5–14). Mountain View, CA: Mayfield.

McClintock, A. (1995). *Imperial leather.* New York: Routledge.

McPhail, M. (1997). (Re)constructing the color line: Complicity and black conservatism. *Communication Theory, 7,* 162–177.

Morgan, R. (1996). Introduction. *Sisterhood is global.* New York: The Feminist Press.

Mumby, D. (1997). Modernism, postmodernism, and communication studies: A rereading of an ongoing debate. *Communication Theory, 7,* 1–28.

Omi, M., & Winant, H. (1986). *Racial formation in the United States.* New York: Routledge & Kegan Paul.

Prus, R. (1996). *Symbolic interaction and ethnographic research.* Albany: State University of New York Press.

Sachs, H. (1984). On doing "being ordinary." In J. M. Atkinson & J. Heritage (Eds.), *Structures of social action: Studies in conversation analysis* (pp. 413–429). Cambridge, UK: Cambridge University Press.

Sturken, M. (1995). The television image and collective amnesia: Dis(re)membering the Persian Gulf war. In P. d'Agostino & D. Tafler (Eds.), *Transmission: Toward a post-television culture* (2nd ed., pp. 135–150). Thousand Oaks, CA: Sage.

Tajfel, H. (1978). Interindividual and intergroup behaviour. In H. Tajfel (Ed.), *Differentiation between social groups* (pp. 27–60). London: Academic Press.

van Dijk, T. (1993). *Discourse and elite racism.* London: Routledge.

Webster, Y. (1992). *The racialization of America.* New York: St. Martin's Press.

Weider, D. L., & Pratt, S. (1990). On being a recognizable Indian among Indians. In D. Carbaugh (Ed.), *Cultural communication and intercultural contact* (pp. 45–64). Hillsdale, NJ: Lawrence Erlbaum.

Concepts and Questions

1. What is the central purpose of the "series of steps" presented by Collier?

2. Which one of Collier's "approaches to culture" do you believe most directly relates to intercultural communication?

3. How would you answer the following question: What do I want to know about the communicative event, contact, discourse, text, and situation?

4. What does Collier mean by the phrase "multiple types of cultural identities"?

5. Why is power an important variable in intercultural communication?

6. How would you answer the following question: What kinds of communicative messages should I examine to study intercultural communication?

7. How is Collier using the word *context*?

8. In what specific ways do you believe Collier's 10 steps can be applied to your personal study of intercultural communication?

Adapting to a New Culture

YOUNG YUN KIM

One of the dramatic changes we are witnessing today is the enormous interface of different cultures in human affairs—from politics and economics to the arts and leisure activities. At the forefront of this global reality are the countless people who are on the move across cultural boundaries. Each year, millions of immigrants and refugees change homes. Driven by natural disaster or economic need, or hoping for freedom, security, or social and economic betterment, people uproot themselves from their homes and embark on a new life in an alien and sometimes hostile milieu. In addition, numerous temporary sojourners, such as diplomats, military personnel, and other governmental and intergovernmental agency employees, are on overseas assignments. Peace Corps volunteers have worked in nearly 100 nations since inception of the program in 1960. Researchers, professors, and students visit and study at foreign academic institutions; missionaries carry out religious endeavors. Many business employees are given overseas assignments; and a growing number of accountants, teachers, construction workers, athletes, artists, musicians, and writers find employment in foreign countries.

These individuals and many others like them are, indeed, contemporary pioneers opening new frontiers. They face, at least temporarily, the drastic and all-encompassing challenge of having to construct a new life. This essay presents a brief account of their experiences in confronting the difficult task of adapting to a new cultural and communication system. (For a fuller discussion of this topic, see Kim, 1988, 1995, in press; Kim & Ruben, 1988).

STRESS, ADAPTATION, AND GROWTH

Individuals move to another country for varied reasons, under differing circumstances, and with differing levels of commitment to the host society. Most immigrants plan the move as permanent in the sense that they now expect the host society to be the primary setting for their life activities. For many short-term sojourners, on the other hand, contacts with new cultures are mostly peripheral, requiring less overall engagement. Foreign students, for example, can limit their adaptation to the bare minimum required to fulfill their role as students and can confine their informal social contact to fellow students from their home country. A similar pattern of self-imposed social isolation is seen among seasonal migrant workers and military personnel and their families in foreign countries. (See Berry, 1990; Brislin, 1981; Dyal & Dyal, 1981; Furnham, 1988; Volkan, 1993, for discussions of various situations of cross-cultural migration.)

Despite such differences in the degree of adaptive demands, most people in a foreign land begin life in the host society as *strangers* (Gudykunst & Kim, in press; Simmel, 1950/1908). Many of their previously held beliefs, taken-for-granted assumptions, and routine behaviors are no longer relevant or appropriate. Faced with things that do not follow their unconscious "cultural script," strangers must cope with a high level of uncertainty and anxiety (Gudykunst, 1995). They are challenged to learn at least some new ways of thinking, feeling, and acting—an activity commonly called *acculturation* (Berry, 1990; Broom & Kitsuse, 1955; Padilla, 1980; Shibutani & Kwan, 1965; Spicer, 1968). At the same time, they go through the process of *deculturation* (Bar-Yosef, 1968; Eisenstadt, 1954), of unlearning some of their previously acquired cultural habits, at least to the extent that new responses are adopted in situations that previously would have evoked old ones.

The experience of acculturation and deculturation inevitably produces *stress* (Barna, 1983; Dyal & Dyal, 1981; Kim, 1988, 1995, in press; Moos, 1976) in the form of temporary psychic disturbance or even a "breakdown" in some extreme cases. Stress experiences are particularly acute during the initial phase of relocation, when strangers face the severe difficulties and disruptions amply documented in studies of "culture shock" and related issues (Adler, 1975, 1987; Furnham, 1984, 1988; Furnham & Bochner, 1986; Oberg, 1960; Taft, 1977; Torbiorn, 1982). Internally, strangers are temporarily in a state of disequilibrium—undergoing an inner struggle between the desire to retain their original identity and the desire to forge a new identity more in harmony with the changed milieu (Boekestijn, 1988; Chan & Lam, 1987; Ford & Lerner, 1992). Strangers often cope with such a state of flux through various "defense mechanisms," such as selective attention, denial, hostility, cynicism, avoidance, and withdrawal (Lazarus, 1966).

Yet the stress strangers experience also works as the very impetus for their *adaptation*. In time, most strangers manage to achieve a new level of learning and self-adjustment that helps them accommodate to the demands of the host environment and work out new ways of handling their daily activities. In the ongoing relationship with the environment, strangers gradually modify their cognitive, affective, and behavioral habits and acquire increasing proficiency in expressing themselves, understanding new cultural practices, and coordinating their actions with those of the local people. The interplay of stress and adaptation gradually leads to an internal *growth*—a transformation in the direction of increased functional fitness and psychological health vis-à-vis the host environment.

Stress, then, is part and parcel of a stranger's adaptation and growth experiences over time. Together, the three elements—stress, adaptation, and growth—help define the nature of strangers' psychological movement in the direction of an increased chance of success in meeting the demands of the host environment. As shown in Figure 3, the *stress-adaptation-growth dynamic* plays out not in a smooth, arrow-like linear progression, but in a cyclic and continual "draw-back-to-leap" pattern similar to the movement of a wheel. Each stressful experience is responded to with a "draw back" (temporary disintegration and disengagement), which then activates adaptive energy to help strangers reorganize themselves and "leap forward" (temporary integration or engagement). This internal process reflects a dialectic relationship between new cultural learning (acculturation) and the unlearning of old cultural habits (deculturation). As strangers work through the setbacks, they come out "victorious," with an increased capacity to see others, themselves, and situations in a new light and to face challenges yet to come. Failure to work through this process results in prolonged feelings of inadequacy and frustration.

Figure 3 *Stress-Adaptation-Growth Dynamics of Adaptive Transformation*

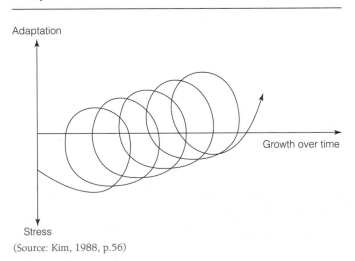

(Source: Kim, 1988, p.56)

THE ROLE OF COMMUNICATION

Given the basic process of cross-cultural adaptation described above, we now turn to the question of differential adaptation rates (speeds at which different strangers adapt). Even though most strangers in alien cultures have demonstrated an impressive capacity to manage cross-cultural challenges successfully without damaging their overall integrity, some do suffer more intensely and for a longer period due to an extreme inability to find ways to overcome the challenges of the host environment. Some may strongly resist the idea of having to change their old cultural habits, thereby raising psychological barriers that work against adaptation. Others may be ill-equipped to deal with states of panic, causing a prolonged psychological disequilibrium that leads to greater alienation from, and bitterness toward, the natives or even to a decision to return to their home country prematurely.

The fact that individual strangers differ in adaptation rate leads to the question "Why do some strangers adapt faster than others?" or "Given the same length of time, why do some strangers attain a higher level of adaptation?" To explain differential adaptive changes among individual strangers, we need to focus on the process in and through which such changes take place—that is, the communication process. Communication activities of encoding and decoding verbal and nonverbal information lie at the heart of cross-cultural adaptation by serving as the essential mechanism that connects strangers and the host society. Just as natives acquire their capacity to function properly in their society through communicative interactions, strangers come to organize their own and others' activities by learning the significant symbols of the host culture and by participating in various communication activities of the host society.

Strangers' communication activities can be categorized into two basic, inseparable dimensions—personal communication and social communication. According to Ruben (1975), *personal communication* involves "private symbolization" activities—all the internal mental activities that dispose and prepare people to act and react in certain ways in actual social situations. Personal communication is linked to *social communication* when two or more individuals interact

with one another, knowingly or not. Ruben (1975) defines social communication as the process underlying "intersubjectivization," a phenomenon that occurs as a consequence of "public symbolization." In Geyer's (1980) terms, the personal communication process can be compared to the "off-line functions" of a computer system, which interfaces with the environment through "on-line functions" involving input-output transactions of messages (p. 32).

Personal Communication

Personal (or intrapersonal) communication refers to the mental processes by which we organize ourselves in and with our sociocultural milieu, developing ways of seeing, hearing, understanding, and responding to the environment. In Ruben's (1975) words, "Personal communication can be thought of as sensing, making-sense-of, and acting toward the objects and people in one's milieu. It is the process by which the individual informationally fits himself into . . . his environment" (pp. 168–169). In the context of cross-cultural adaptation, then, personal communication can be examined in terms of *host communication competence*—that is, the overall internal capacity of a stranger to decode and encode information in accordance with the communication practices of the host culture. Natives begin to acquire this competence early in life, and it is so internalized in their personal communication system that, by and large, it operates automatically and unconsciously. For strangers, however, many elements of the same competence must be acquired, often painstakingly, through trial and error. Until strangers have acquired a sufficient level of host communication competence, they are handicapped in their ability to function and relate to the system of host cultural pragmatics. The degree to which a given stranger acquires host communication competence should be reflected in his or her overall ability to fit in the host society, while the lack of such competence manifests itself in various forms of "miscommunication" (Banks, Gao, & Baker, 1991; Gass & Varonis, 1991).

The many elements of host communication competence—from knowledge about the host language and social norms to ability to manage interpersonal relationships and solve impending problems at work—can be grouped into three categories commonly employed in the study of communication competence: cognitive, affective, and operational (or behavioral) (Kim, 1991; Spitzberg & Cupach, 1984). The primary element of *cognitive competence* that strangers must develop is knowledge of the host language and culture, including the knowledge of the history, institutions, laws and regulations, worldviews, beliefs, norms, and rules of social conduct and interpersonal relationships. Knowledge of the host language means not just linguistic knowledge (such as phonetics, syntax, and vocabulary) but also knowledge about the pragmatic uses of the language in everyday life (such as the many subtle nuances in the way the language is used and interpreted by the natives in various formal and informal social engagements).

Linguistic and cultural knowledge is accompanied by development of cognitive complexity (Kelly, 1955; Schroder, Driver, & Streufert, 1967). Cognitive complexity refers to the structural differentiation and integration in an individual's information-processing capacity. During the initial phase of adaptation, strangers' perceptions of the host environment tend to be overly simplistic and based on gross stereotypes. As strangers learn more about the host language and culture, however, their perceptions become increasingly more refined and complex, enabling them to engage in more effective social interactions.

Affective competence facilitates cross-cultural adaptation because it provides the emotional and aesthetic sensibilities that raise communication experiences with the natives from a level that is merely technical to one that is more meaningful and thus more fulfilling. Affective competence allows strangers to empathize with the natives—to share their experiences of joy, excitement, humor, triumph, and beauty, as well as sadness, boredom, sarcasm, despair, and ugliness. The strangers' affective competence thus leads to a sense of belonging and a positive regard for the natives, which, in turn, brings the strangers closer to the local people and their culture. Conversely, strangers who lack affective competence are likely to feel alienated and marginalized, for they cannot show genuine interest in local cultural experiences or in developing close relationships with the natives. In Mansell's (1981) words:

> The concept of aesthetic awareness is linked with ineffable, intuitive feelings of appreciation and celebration. This form of awareness creates a consciousness which

transforms individuals' perceptions of the world and imparts a sense of unity between self and surrounding.... It is in this transformative mode of experiencing that many people create access to the momentary peaks of fulfillment which makes life meaningful. (p. 99)

Closely linked with cognitive and affective competence is *operational competence*, or "enactment tendencies" (Buck, 1984, p. vii). This dimension of host communication competence refers to strangers' capacity to express their cognitive and affective experiences outwardly when communicating with others. As strangers try to come up with a mental plan for action, they must base the decision on their current knowledge about the host culture and language; the decision depends also on the degree of sophistication in their information-processing capacity and on their ability and motivation to appreciate the emotional and aesthetic experiences of the natives. Operational competence thus enables strangers to choose the "right" combination of verbal and nonverbal actions to meet the demands of everyday interactions—managing face-to-face encounters, initiating and maintaining relationships, seeking appropriate information sources, solving various problems they may encounter, and finding ways to succeed in accomplishing their goals.

Social Communication

Strangers' host communication competence is directly and reciprocally linked to their participation in the social communication activities of the host society. On the one hand, their social communication activities are constrained by their capacity to communicate in the host cultural context. On the other hand, each communication encounter with the host society offers strangers an opportunity to cultivate host communication competence cognitively, affectively, and operationally.

Central to the domain of social communication is *interpersonal communication*, or direct face-to-face interaction in the context of interpersonal relationships with others. As Fogel (1993) argues, individuals develop through their relationships. Interpersonal communication activities help strangers to secure vital information and insight into the mind-sets and behaviors of the local people. In interacting with the natives face-to-face, strangers also learn about themselves—how they think, express themselves, and respond to others. As a result, strangers' interpersonal communication activities not only enable them to carry out their daily tasks, but also provide them with needed emotional support and points of reference for checking and validating their own thoughts and actions (Adelman, 1988; Kim, 1986, 1987; McPherson, 1991; Pescosolido, 1992; Wellman, 1992).

In addition to interpersonal communication, strangers' participation in the host social communication process occurs as they are exposed to the *mass communication* activities of the host society. These activities involve a wide range of public media, large and small, from radio, television, newspapers, magazines, and movies to art, music, and drama. By engaging in such communication activities, strangers interact with their host milieu without direct involvement with specific individuals; they expand the scope of their adaptive learning beyond the immediate social context with which they have contact. In transmitting messages that reflect the aspirations, myths, work, and play, as well as the issues and events of the host society, the various mass communication media explicitly or implicitly convey the worldviews, myths, beliefs, values, mores, and norms of the culture. Of the various forms of mass communication experiences, exposure to information-oriented messages such as those found in newspapers, magazines, television and radio news, and documentaries has been found to be particularly helpful to adaptation, when compared with exposure to more entertainment-oriented media contents (Kim, Lee, & Jeong, 1982; Kim, 1976, 1979b).

The effect of mass communication on adaptation should be particularly significant during the initial phase of resettlement (Kim, Lee, & Jeong, 1982; Kim, 1976, 1979b). During this phase, strangers have not yet developed a level of host communication competence sufficient to forge meaningful interpersonal relationships with local people. Direct communication experiences with the natives can be intensely frustrating or intimidating to many strangers. They may feel awkward and out of place in relating to others, and the immediate negative feedback from another person may be too overwhelming for them to have pleasurable face-to-face encounters with the natives. Under such circumstances, the strangers naturally tend to withdraw from direct contacts and instead prefer mass media as an alternative, pressure-free channel through which elements of the host culture can be experienced (Kim, 1979b; Ryu, 1978; Walker, 1993; Yang, 1988).

THE ROLE OF THE ENVIRONMENT

The adaptation function of personal and social (interpersonal and mass) communication cannot be fully understood in isolation from the conditions of the new sociocultural milieu. Societies and communities present different environments for strangers, particularly in three key areas: (1) host receptivity, (2) host conformity pressure, and (3) ethnic group strength. Together, these factors help define the relative degree of "push and pull" that a given stranger is likely to face in a host environment.

Host Receptivity

The receptivity of a host environment refers to the degree to which the environment is open to, welcomes, or accepts strangers into its social communication networks and offers them various forms of informational, technical, material, and emotional support. The term *host receptivity* incorporates the meaning of other similar terms, such as *interaction potential* (Kim, 1979a) and *acquaintance potential* (Cook, 1962), that have been employed to refer to the access that strangers have to the host social communication processes.

A given environment can be receptive toward certain groups of strangers and unwelcoming toward certain others. For example, Canadian visitors arriving in a small town in the United States are likely to find a largely receptive environment. Yet the same town may show less receptivity toward visitors from lesser known and vastly different cultures such as Turkey or Iran. Such differences in host receptivity toward strangers can be attributed to a number of plausible reasons, including (1) the nature of the relationship, friendly or hostile, between the host country and the stranger's home country, (2) the degree of cultural and ideological difference and incompatibility between the two cultures, (3) the perceived or actual status or power of the stranger's home country and culture, (4) the perceived or actual economic, social, and political standing (or merit) of the stranger's ethnic group within the host society, (5) the perceived or actual economic, social, and political threat to the host society posed by the stranger's ethnic group, and (6) the racial/ethnic prejudice predominantly held by the society against certain groups.

Host Conformity Pressure

Societies (and communities) also vary in the degree of "conformity pressure" (Zajonc, 1952) they exert—that is, the extent to which the natives exert conscious or unconscious pressure on strangers to change their original patterns of behavior and adopt those of the new culture. Conversely, societies (and communities) differ in the degree to which local people are able or willing to permit, tolerate, accommodate, or appreciate cultural practices that strangers bring with them and to allow strangers to deviate from the hosts' normative expectations. Host conformity pressure should be distinguished from host receptivity in that a society that strongly expects strangers to conform to its cultural life may or may not welcome strangers with distinct cultural and ethnic characteristics.

The conformity pressure of a given host environment is not uniformly applied to all strangers. It is often more acutely felt by those strangers whose livelihood is dependent on communicating well with and being accepted by the natives (De Vos & Suarez-Orozco, 1990, p. 253). Proficiency in the host language and culture is particularly vital to immigrants whose success or failure in pursuing personal goals is dependent on the acceptance and approval of at least the relevant segments of the host population. Even some temporary sojourners, such as employees of multinational companies, Peace Corps volunteers, diplomats, and international students, are subject to some degree of host conformity pressure as they try to carry out their tasks and develop good working relationships with local people. By comparison, other sojourner groups, such as American military personnel stationed overseas, whose daily activities are largely independent of the workings of the host society, are subject to only a minimal level of host conformity pressure.

Another factor influencing the degree of host conformity pressure is the ethnic homogeneity or heterogeneity of a given environment. Societies (and communities) that are more pluralistic in ethnic profile and mainstream political ideology (such as metropolitan centers in democratic societies like Australia, Canada, England, and the United States) tend to manifest a greater accommodation of foreign-born individuals as well as native-born ethnic minorities. A stricter imposition of dominant linguistic and cultural patterns on all people can be seen in more traditional societies with authoritarian political systems (such as China, Iran, and Saudi Arabia). In such monolithic societies, foreign-born visitors or immigrants are likely to be subject to a greater pressure to follow local customs.

Ethnic Group Strength

Another environmental condition affecting strangers' adaptation is the strength of their ethnic group relative to the host society at large. Ethnic groups differ in their relative status within the host society. A useful insight into ethnic group strength has been provided by sociologists Clarke and Obler (1976), who proposed a three-stage theory of ethnic group development. The first is the stage of the economic adjustment, which begins upon arrival of the group and continues until the group becomes an integral part of the permanent economy. The second stage is community building, which involves the development of community leadership and institutional resources that are used to assert the ethnic group's identity and interests. This stage of ethnic community development corresponds to the concept of "institutional completeness" (Breton, 1964, 1991; Goldenberg & Haines, 1992). The third stage is the period of political growth and aggressive self-assertion, which serves to strengthen the collective ethnic identity and common interests of the group.

The phenomenon of ethnic group strength has been discussed in social psychology in terms of ethnolinguistic vitality (Giles & Johnson, 1987). In research on the influences of the social milieu and the consequences of fluency in a second language, Giles, Bourhis and Taylor (1977) suggested that the influence of ethnolinguistic vitality on individual behavior can be defined in terms of three structural variables: (1) the status of a language in a community, (2) the absolute and relative number of its locuters, and (3) the institutional support (such as governmental services, schools, mass media) for the ethnic language.

Ethnolinguistic vitality as an objective environmental condition has been linked to what Giles and his associates (1977) term "subjective ethnolinguistic vitality," or the perceived legitimacy of the position of one's ethnic group. For example, speakers who perceive the subordinate position of their group as legitimate are likely to adjust their communication behaviors to "converge" with those of the dominant outgroup.

The preceding two views on ethnic group strength offer implications for the role of ethnic group strength in a stranger's adaptation to the host society. Integrating these views allows us to describe the strength of an ethnic group in terms of one or more of the following elements: (1) ethnolinguistic vitality, (2) economic status, (3) institutional completeness, and (4) ethnic political activism. Frequently, these community characteristics are closely associated with the size of the ethnic population and the historical "maturity" of the community in the host society. From this perspective, the Cuban Americans in Miami, Florida, for example, have an ethnic community that is stronger than the smaller Russian community in Chicago. Exceptions can be seen in a small ethnic group such as that of the Americans who recently began working and living in the former Czechoslovakia. Despite this group's small size, the fact that it is American gives it political and economic status and prestige that render it a strong ethnic group.

Because a stronger ethnic group provides its members with a stronger subculture and offers many vital services to its members, it is likely to facilitate the cross-cultural adaptation of strangers during the initial phase. In the long run, however, a strong ethnic community tends to discourage the adaptation of strangers to the host society because it encourages ethnolinguistic maintenance. A strong ethnic community is further likely to exert subtle or even explicit pressure to conform to the ethnic community norms; it thereby discourages an active participation in the host social communication activities. Empirical evidence supporting this observation is provided by Rosenthal and Hrynevich (1985), who found that the Greek immigrant community in Australia is more cohesive and organized than is the Italian; they also reported that Greek Australian adolescents placed more emphasis than did Italian Australian adolescents on their ethnic identity and maintenance of their heritage. In addition, according to the investigators, the Greek Australian adolescents placed less emphasis on adapting to the dominant Australian culture. Similar results were reported by Driedger (1976), who found, in Canada, that an ethnic group's status within the host society correlated with its institutional completeness; groups high on both status and institutional completeness (the French and Jewish groups) had the strongest sense of ethnic identity.

THE ROLE OF PREDISPOSITION

The adaptation of strangers is influenced not only by the conditions of the host environment, but also by the traits that the strangers themselves bring to the adaptive journey. Each stranger begins the adaptation process with a different set of preexisting internal characteristics that help set the parameters for their own subsequent changes. Some begin with enthusiasm and determination, while others find themselves forced into change by unavoidable circumstances. Some may be wide open to new experiences, while others may feel they are too old to make changes in their lifetime habits. The various ways in which strangers differ in their internal conditions can be organized into three categories: (1) preparedness, (2) ethnicity, and (3) personality. Together, these predispositional factors constitute a stranger's "adaptive potential" (Kim, 1979a) or "permeability" (De Vos, 1990) with respect to the host environment.

Preparedness

Strangers come to their new environment with differing levels of preparedness, or readiness, for dealing with that environment. Specifically, their preparedness is reflected in the level of host communication competence they have acquired prior to moving to the host culture. As previously discussed, host communication competence includes the cognitive, affective, and operational abilities to participate in the social communication activities of the host society—from knowledge of the new language and culture and ability to empathize with the local people's emotional and aesthetic experiences to the capacity to perform appropriately and effectively in various social situations.

Strangers' preparedness is raised when they have realistic expectations and knowledge about the host society, shaped by formal and informal learning (Brabant, Palmer, & Gramling, 1990). Included in such learning activities are schooling and training in, as well as media exposure to, the host language and culture. Education in particular, regardless of its cultural context, helps expand our mental capacity for new learning and for meeting the challenges of life in general. Many cross-cultural training and orientation programs emphasize familiarizing trainees with their host culture (Brislin & Yoshida, 1994; Landis & Bhagat, 1995). For some strangers, an even more effective source of language and culture learning occurs through personal contacts with members of the host society prior to actually entering the host society. Peace Corps volunteers are among the best-prepared sojourners because they go through an intensive screening process and extensive language and cultural training before being given an overseas assignment.

Strangers' preparedness is also influenced by whether their cross-cultural move is voluntary or involuntary and by how long they intend to stay in the host society. Voluntary, long-term immigrants, for example, are likely to enter the host society with greater readiness and willingness to make necessary changes in themselves than are temporary visitors who relocate for reasons (such as wars or natural disasters) other than their own volition.

Ethnicity

Strangers vary not only in their preparedness but also in their ethnicity (McGuire, McGuire, Child, & Fujioka, 1978). The term *ethnicity* is used here as an inclusive term to refer to various inherited characteristics that strangers have as members of a distinct ethnic group. Japanese sojourners and immigrants, for example, bring to a given host society common physical, linguistic, and cultural features that are different from, say, features of Mexican or French sojourners. Such ethnic characteristics play a crucial role in the cross-cultural adaptation process by affecting the ease or difficulty with which strangers develop communication competence in a given host society and participate in its social communication activities.

The ethnicity of a given stranger influences his or her adaptation process in two interrelated ways. First, each ethnic background presents certain linguistic and cultural barriers for the stranger to overcome before developing host communication competence and being able to participate in host social communication activities. Second, each individual ethnicity creates a certain psychological barrier (or affinity) in the minds of the natives, which, in turn, affects the natives' receptivity toward the stranger. Strangers embark on their cross-cultural adaptation process with certain advantages (or handicaps) due simply to their ethnic characteristics (Phinney & Rosenthal, 1992, p. 145). Japanese business executives in the United States, for example, are likely to face a greater challenge in overcoming language barriers than are their British counterparts. Their physical features (such as height, skin color, and facial structure) may add to the challenge they face by accentuating the psychological gap between them and their American hosts.

Personality

Strangers differ from one another not only in ethnicity but also in personality—a set of more or less enduring traits and sensibilities. Each stranger meets the challenges of the new environment within the context of his or her own personal psychological tendencies. Of particular importance are three personality factors—openness, strength, and positivity—that interactively facilitate strangers' adaptation by enabling them to endure stressful challenges and maximize new learning.

Openness is defined as an internal posture that is receptive to new information (Gendlin, 1962, 1978). Openness, like a child's innocence, allows strangers to minimize their resistance and to maximize their willingness to attend to the new and changed circumstances. Openness further enables strangers to perceive and interpret various events and situations in the new environment, as they occur, with less rigid, ethnocentric judgments. It is a dimension of personality that encourages strangers to continually seek new cultural learning, to cultivate greater emotional and aesthetic sensitivity, and to expand the range of their behavioral repertoire—all of which are vital to actively participating in and accommodating to the demands of the host milieu. This term incorporates other similar but more specific concepts such as "flexibility," "open-mindedness," and "tolerance for ambiguity."

Strength is an additional personality trait that bears significance for cross-cultural adaptation. Closely related to openness, strength of personality serves as a type of inner resolve that empowers strangers to take on intercultural challenges without losing their basic integrity. Personality strength, unlike stubbornness, includes the quality of flexibility—that is, the ability to "bend," to empathize with others while believing in oneself, and to let go of anxiousness (MacKinnon, 1978). While stubbornness discourages adaptation, strength facilitates creative and effective responses to impending problems. The strength of personality thus represents a personal capacity to cope with various difficulties presented in an alien culture and to find what is best in each potentially problematic situation. It allows strangers to fix their sights and chart a course without depending heavily on, or blaming, external forces because they are equipped with a solid sense of self as the main agent of action and responsibility.

Personality strength, in this sense, is a broad concept that represents a range of interrelated personality attributes such as resilience, risk taking, hardiness, persistence, patience, elasticity, and resourcefulness. It represents all of the inner qualities that help an individual to absorb shocks from the environment and bounce back without being seriously damaged by them. Strangers with a high level of personality strength tend to be stimulated by new challenges and remain effervescent and confident. On the other hand, low levels of personality strength are manifested in tendencies to be shy, fearful, and easily distressed by uncertain or stressful situations.

The open and strong personality tends to be a positive one as well. *Positivity* refers to an affirmative and optimistic outlook and to the capacity to defy negative prediction (Dean & Popp, 1990). Positivity does not mean blind romanticism or far-fetched idealism. It means, instead, the enduring tendency to see the bright side of things while recognizing their dark side. When directed inward, positivity reflects a fundamental confidence in one's ability to overcome obstacles. Positivity helps one to find what is best in each problematic situation and to discover what can be learned from it (Maslow, 1969; Zurcher, 1977).

Positivity, together with openness and strength, helps define the personality predispositions that serve as inner resources. These attributes help strangers "push" themselves in their adaptation process. Strong, open, and positive individuals are less likely to give up easily and more likely to take risks willingly under challenging situations in the host society. They are better equipped to work toward developing host communication competence because they continually seek new learning and new ways to handle their life activities. In doing so, they become better able to make necessary adjustments in themselves. Serious lack of these qualities, on the other hand, weakens an individual's adaptive capacity and works as a self-imposed barrier against adaptive development (Hettema, 1979).

SUMMARY AND INTEGRATION

In this essay, I have described the cross-cultural adaptation process as a joint, interactive venture: The strangers and the host environment co-influence the dynamic and fluctuating experiences of stress, adaptation, and growth. The adaptation process is essentially a manifestation of the ever present human capacity to face challenges, learn from them, and arrive at a greater level of self-integration. Few individuals in an alien environment can entirely escape the necessity to adapt. Adaptation occurs naturally and most, if not all, strangers welcome it as long as they are engaged in direct and continual interactions with the host environment.

At the heart of the adaptation process are communication activities that link strangers and the host environment. As strangers undergo continual interaction of push and pull with the new environment, they become more functionally fit and psychologically healthier. These adaptive changes hinge on the psychic movement of the stress-adaptation-growth dynamic strangers experience as they cope with the challenges of the environment. As a result, they acquire new cultural elements (acculturation) and unlearn at least some of their old cultural habits (deculturation). Because of the central role of communication in the adaptation process, the quantity and quality of strangers' interpersonal and mass communication activities contribute critically to, and are facilitated by, the development of their host communication competence. The strangers' host communication competence serves as the internal "engine" that carries them along the adaptive journey, while their participation in host social communication processes serves as the very "fuel" that ignites the engine. Realistically, few strangers can ever adapt completely, no matter how long and how extensive their communication with the host environment. Most of them, nonetheless, do make a workable adaptation given sufficient time and are gradually able to attain a higher level of proficiency in managing their daily affairs.

As strangers participate in various forms of interpersonal and mass communication activities, they are both encouraged and pressured by the host society as well as by their ethnic community. The three environmental conditions—host receptivity, host conformity pressure, and ethnic group strength—help define the "push and pull" dynamics that a receiving society offers strangers. An environment influences stranger adaptation optimally when the native population welcomes and supports the strangers (receptivity), while expecting them to conform to the local norms (host conformity pressure). In facing these environmental forces, the strangers' own predisposition plays an important role. Strangers who are better prepared for the new environment, whose ethnic backgrounds are more similar to the dominant ethnicity of the local people, and whose personality is more open, stronger, and more positive are better able to facilitate their own adaptation process.

Should strangers choose successful adaptation, they must be prepared and willing to face the stressful experiences of coping with the uncertainties and anxieties in the host society. They must concentrate on acquiring new communication habits and putting aside some of the old ones. They must recognize the importance of host communication competence as the fundamental mechanism by which they adapt successfully, and they must work to develop it to the fullest extent possible. They must also take maximum advantage of opportunities to participate in the interpersonal and mass communication processes of the host society. Finally, they must work toward achieving a greater openness, strength, and positivity in their personal disposition.

However, strangers cannot accomplish their adaptive goals alone. Adaptation is an interactive process involving both strangers and the new environment. Indeed, members of the host society can help facilitate strangers' adaptation by maximizing receptivity toward the strangers—by accepting their original ethnicity and providing them with a supportive interpersonal environment. The host society can actively encourage strangers to adapt through communication training programs. Such programs should facilitate the strangers' acquisition of host communication competence. In addition, the ethnic community can provide a significant adaptive service for the strangers in their early stages of resettlement. Ethnic communities can provide support systems to assist new arrivals in coping with stresses and initial uncertainties and can guide them toward effective adaptation. At the same time, however, strangers must realize that exclusive and prolonged reliance on their ethnic community will delay and eventually limit opportunities for them to adapt to the host milieu.

Ultimately, the adaptation of strangers, particularly long-term immigrants, is of vital interest to the host society as well. Through communication, the host society is able to engender mutual trust and goodwill among its diverse ethnic and cultural groups (Amir, 1969) and thereby maintain the necessary societal unity and integrity. As long as common channels of communication remain, consensus and patterns of concerted action will persist in the society (Mendelsohn, 1964). Communication, then, makes it possible to merge the incoming new members into a cohesive social organization of commonly shared ideas and values.

References

Adelman, M. (1988). Cross-cultural adjustment: A theoretical perspective on social support. *International Journal of Intercultural Relations,* 12(3), 183–204.

Adler, P. (1975). The transition experience: An alternative view of culture shock. *Journal of Humanistic Psychology,* 15(4), 13–23.

Adler, P. (1987). "Culture Shock and the Cross-cultural Learning Experience." In L. Luce and E. Smith (Eds.), *Toward Internationalism,* 24–35. Cambridge, Mass.: Newbury.

Amir, Y. (1969). Contact hypothesis in ethnic relations. *Psychological Bulletin,* 7(5), 319–342.

Banks, S., Gao, G., & Baker, J. (1991). "Intercultural Encounters and Miscommunication." In N. Coupland, H. Giles, and J. Wiemann (Eds.), *"Miscommunication" and Problematic Talk,* 103–120. Newbury Park, Calif.: Sage.

Bar-Yosef, R. (1968). Desocialization and resocialization: The adjustment process of immigrants. *International Migration Review,* 2, 27–42.

Barna, L. (1983). "The Stress Factor in Intercultural Relations." In D. Landis and R. Brislin (Eds.), *Handbook for Intercultural Training: Vol. II. Issues in Training Methodology,* 19–49. New York: Pergamon Press.

Berry, J. (1990). "Psychological Acculturation: Understanding Individuals Moving Between Cultures." In R. Brislin (Ed.), *Applied Cross-Cultural Psychology,* 232–253. Newbury Park, Calif.: Sage.

Boekestijn, C. (1988). Intercultural migration and the development of personal identity: The dilemma between identity maintenance and cultural adaptation. *International Journal of Intercultural Relations,* 12(2), 83–105.

Brabant, S., Palmer, C., & Gramling, R. (1990). Returning home: An empirical investigation of cross-cultural reentry. *International Journal of Intercultural Relations,*14(4), 387–404.

Breton, R. (1964). Institutional completeness of ethnic communities and the personal relations of immigrants. *American Journal of Sociology,* 70, 193–205.

Breton, R. (1991). *The Governance of Ethnic Communities: Political Structures and Processes in Canada.* Westport, Conn.: Greenwood Press.

Brislin, R. (1981). *Cross-Cultural Encounters.* Elmsford, NY.: Pergamon Press.

Brislin, R., & Yoshida, T. (1994). *Intercultural Communication Training: An Introduction.* Thousand Oaks, Calif.: Sage.

Broom, L., & Kitsuse, J. (1955). The validation of acculturation: A condition to ethnic assimilation. *American Anthropologist,* 62, 44–48.

Buck, R. (1984). *The Communication of Emotion.* New York: Guilford Press.

Chan, K., & Lam, L. (1987). "Psychological Problems of Chinese Vietnamese Refugees Resettling in Quebec." In K. Chan and D. Indra (Eds.), *Uprooting, Loss and Adaptation: The Resettlement of Indochinese Refugees in Canada,* 27–41. Ottawa: Canadian Public Health Association.

Clarke, S., & Obler, J. (1976). "Ethic Conflict, Community-Building, and the Emergence of Ethnic Political Traditions in the United States." In S. Clarke and J. Obler (Eds.), *Urban Ethnic Conflict: A Comparative Perspective,* 1–34. Chapel Hill, N.C.: University of North Carolina.

Cook, S. (1962). The systematic analysis of socially significant events. *Journal of Social Issues,* 18(2), 66–84.

De Vos, G. (1990). "Self in Society: A Multilevel, Psychocultural Analysis." In G. De Vos and M. Suarez-Orozco (Eds.), *Status Inequality: The Self in Culture,* 17–74. Newbury Park, Calif.: Sage.

De Vos, G., & Suarez-Orozco, M. (1990). "Ethnic Belonging and Status Mobility." In G. De Vos and M. Suarez-Orozco (Eds.), *Status Inequality: The Self in Culture,* 246–264. Newbury Park, Calif.: Sage.

Dean, O., & Popp, G. (1990). Intercultural communication effectiveness as perceived by American managers in Saudi Arabia and French managers in the U.S. *International Journal of Intercultural Relations,* 14(4), 405–424.

Driedger, L. (1976). Ethnic self-identity: A comparison of ingroup evaluations. *Sociometry,* 39, 131–141.

Dyal, J., & Dyal, R. (1981). Acculturation, stress and coping. *International Journal of Intercultural Relations,* 5(4), 301–328.

Eisenstadt, S. (1954). *The Absorption of Immigrants.* London: Routledge & Kegan Paul.

Fogel, A. (1993). *Developing Through Relationships: Origins of Communication, Self, and Culture.* Chicago: University of Chicago Press.

Ford, D., & Lerner, R. (1992). *Developmental Systems Theory: An Integrative Approach.* Newbury Park, Calif.: Sage.

Furnham, A. (1984). Tourism and culture shock. *Annals of Tourism Research,* 11(1), 41–57.

Furnham, A. (1988). "The Adjustment of Sojourners." In Y. Kim and W. Gudykunst (Eds.), *Cross-cultural Adaptation,* 42–61. Newbury Park, Calif.: Sage.

Furnham, A., & Bochner, S. (1986). *Culture Shock: Psychological Reactions to Unfamiliar Environments.* London: Methuen.

Gass, S., & Varonis, E. (1991). "Miscommunication in Non-native Speaker Discourse." In N. Coupland, H. Giles, and J. Wiemann (Eds.), *"Miscommunication" and Problematic Talk,* 121–145. Newbury Park, Calif.: Sage.

Gendlin, E. (1962). *Experiencing and the Creation of Meaning.* New York: Free Press.

Gendlin, E. (1978). *Focusing.* New York: Everest House.

Geyer, R. (1980). *Alienation Theories: A General Systems Approach.* New York: Pergamon Press.

Giles, H., Bourhis, R., & Taylor, D. (1977). "Towards a Theory of Language in Ethnic Group Relations." In H. Giles (Eds.), *Language, Ethnicity, and Intergroup Relations,* 307–348. London: Academic Press.

Giles, H., & Johnson, P. (1987). Ethnolinguistic identity theory: A social psychological approach to language maintenance. *International Journal of the Sociology of Language,* 68, 69–99.

Goldenberg, S., & Haines, V. (1992). Social networks and institutional completeness: From territory to ties. *Canadian Journal of Sociology,* 17(3), 301–312.

Gudykunst, W. (1995). "Anxiety/Uncertainty Management (AUM) Theory: Current Status." In R. Wiseman (Ed.), *Intercultural Communication Theory*, 8–58. Thousand Oaks, Calif.: Sage.

Gudykunst, W., & Kim, Y. (in press). *Communicating with Strangers: An Approach to Intercultural Communication*, 3d ed. New York: McGraw-Hill

Hettema, P. (1979). *Personality and Adaptation*. New York: North-Holland.

Kelly, G. (1955). *The Psychology of Personal Constructs: Vol. 1. A Theory of Personality*. New York: W. W. Norton.

Kim, J., Lee, B., & Jeong, W. (1982). *Uses of Mass Media in Acculturation: Dependency, Information Preference, and Gratification*. Paper presented at the annual meeting of the Association for Education in Journalism, Athens, Ohio, May.

Kim, Y. (1976). *Communication Patterns of Foreign Immigrants in the Process of Acculturation: A Survey Among the Korean Population in Chicago*. Unpublished doctoral dissertation, Northwestern University, Evanston, Illinois.

Kim, Y. (1979a). "Toward an Interactive Theory of Communication-Acculturation." In B. Ruben (Ed.), *Communication Yearbook III*, 435–453. New Brunswick, N.J.: Transaction Books.

Kim, Y. (l979b). *Mass Media and Acculturation*. Paper presented at the annual conference of the Eastern Communication Association, Philadelphia, May.

Kim, Y. (1986). "Understanding of the Social Context of Intergroup Communication: A Personal Network Approach." In W. Gudykunst (Ed.), *Intergroup Communication*, 86–95. London: Edward Arnold.

Kim, Y. (1987). "Facilitating Immigrant Adaptation: The Role of Communication and Interpersonal Ties." In T. Albrecht and M. Adelman (Eds.), *Communicating Social Support*, 192–211. Newbury Park, Calif.: Sage.

Kim, Y. (1988). *Communication and Cross-Cultural Adaptation: An Integrative Theory*. Clevedon, England: Multilingual Matters.

Kim, Y. (1991). "Intercultural Communication Competence: A Systems-Theoretic View." In S. Ting-Toomey and F. Korzenny (Eds.), *Cross-Cultural Interpersonal Communication*, 259–275. Newbury Park, Calif.: Sage.

Kim, Y. (1995). "Cross-Cultural Adaptation: An Integrative Theory." In R. Wiseman (Ed.), *Intercultural Communication Theory*, 170–193. Thousand Oaks, Calif.: Sage.

Kim, Y. (in press). *Becoming Intercultural: An Integrative Theory of Cross-Cultural Adaptation*. Thousand Oaks, Calif.: Sage.

Kim, Y., & Ruben, B. (1988). "Intercultural Transformation." In Y. Kim and W. Gudykunst (Eds.), *Theories in Intercultural Communication*, 299–321. Newbury Park, Calif.: Sage.

Landis, D., & Bhagat, R. (Eds.). (1995). *Handbook of Intercultural Training*, 2nd ed. Thousand Oaks, Calif.: Sage.

Lazarus, R. (1966). *Psychological Stress and the Coping Process*. St. Louis: McGraw-Hill.

MacKinnon, D. (1978). *In Search of Human Effectiveness*. Buffalo, N.Y.: Creative Education Foundation.

Mansell, M. (1981). Transcultural experience and expressive response. *Communication Education, 30*, April, 93–108.

Maslow, A. (1969). "A Theory of Metamotivation: The Biological Rooting of the Value-Life." In H. Chiang and A. Maslow (Eds.), *The Healthy Personality*, 35–56. New York: Van Nostrand Reinhold.

McGuire, W., McGuire, C., Child, P., & Fujioka, T. (1978). Salience of ethnicity in the spontaneous self-concepts as a function of one's ethnic distinctiveness in the social environment. *Journal of Personality and Social Psychology, 36*, 511–520.

McPherson, J. (1991). *Opportunities for Contact and Network Diversity: Further Explorations of Homophily in Voluntary Organizations*. Paper presented at the annual meeting of the International Sunbelt Social Network Conference, Tampa, Florida, February.

Mendelsohn, H. (1964). "Sociological Perspective on the Study of Mass Communication." In L. Dexter and D. White (Eds.), *People, Society, and Mass Communication*, 29–36. New York: Free Press.

Moos, R. (1976). *Human Adaptation: Coping with Life Crisis*. Lexington, Mass.: D. C. Heath.

Oberg, K. (1960). Culture shock Adjustment to new cultural environments. *Practical Anthropology, 7,* 170–179.

Padilla, A. (Ed.). (1980). *Acculturation: Theory, Models and Some New Findings*. Washington, D.C.: Westview.

Pescosolido, B. (1992). Beyond rational choice: The social dynamics of how people seek help. *American Journal of Sociology, 97*(4), 1096–1138.

Phinney, J., & Rosenthal, M. (1992). "Ethnic Identity in Adolescence." In G. Adams, T. Gullota and R. Montemayor (Eds.), *Adolescent Identity Formation*, 145–172. Newbury Park, Calif.: Sage.

Rosenthal, D., & Hrynevich, C. (1985). Ethnicity and ethnic identity: A comparative study of Greek-, Italian-, and Anglo-Australian working-class adolescents. *Journal of Youth and Adolescence, 12*, 117–135.

Ruben, B. (1975). "Intrapersonal, Interpersonal, and Mass Communication Process in Individual and Multi-Person Systems." In B. Ruben and J. Kim (Eds.), *General Systems Theory and Human Communication*, 164–190. Rochelle Park, N.J. Hayden.

Ryu, J. (1978). *Mass Media's Role in the Assimilation Process: A Study of Korean Immigrants in the Los Angeles Area*.

Paper presented at the annual meeting of the International Communication Association, Chicago, May.

Schroder, H., Driver, M., & Streufert, S. (1967). *Human Information Processing: Individuals and Groups Functioning in Complex Social Situations*. New York: Holt, Rinehart and Winston.

Shibutani, T., & Kwan, K. (1965). *Ethnic Stratification: A Comparative Approach*. New York: Macmillan.

Simmel, G. (1950/1908). "The Stranger." In K. Wolff (Ed. and Trans.), *The Sociology of Georg Simmel*. New York: Free Press.

Spicer, E. (1968). "Acculturation." In D. Sills (Ed.), *International Encyclopedia of the Social Sciences*, 21–27. New York: Macmillan & Free Press.

Spitzberg, B., & Cupach, W. (1984). *Interpersonal Communication Competence*. Beverly Hills, Calif.: Sage.

Taft, R. (1977). "Coping with Unfamiliar Cultures." In N. Warren (Ed.), *Studies in Cross-Cultural Psychology: Vol. 1*, 121–153. London: Academic Press.

Torbiorn, I. (1982). *Living Abroad: Personal Adjustment and Personnel Policy in the Overseas Setting*. New York: Wiley.

Volkan, V. (1993). Immigrants and refugees: A psychodynamic perspective. *Mind & Human Interaction*, 4(2), 63–69.

Walker, D. (1993). *The Role of the Mass Media in the Adaptation of Haitian Immigrants in Miami*. Unpublished doctoral dissertation, Indiana University, Indianapolis.

Wellman, B. (1992). Which type of ties and networks provide what kinds of social support? *Advances in Group Processes*, 9, 207–235.

Yang, S. (1988). *The Role of Mass Media in Immigrants' Political Socialization: A Study of Korean Immigrants in Northern California*. Unpublished doctoral dissertation, Stanford University, Stanford, Calif.

Zajonc, R. (1952). Aggressive attitude of the "stranger" as a function of conformity pressures. *Human Relations*, 5, 205–216.

Zurcher, L. (1977). *The Immutable Self: A Self Concept for Social Change*. Beverly Hills, Calif.: Sage.

Concepts and Questions

1. What does Kim mean when, speaking of new immigrants and refugees, she states that they are like "pioneers"?
2. What are some "defense mechanisms" immigrants and refugees employ as a way of coping?
3. How would you explain the idea that stress is part of the adaptation process?
4. Why do some "individual strangers" adapt faster than others?
5. What does Kim mean when she writes of "cognitive complexity"?
6. How do mass communication activities help the adaptation process? Can they also hinder the process? If so, in what ways?
7. How does Kim explain host receptivity, host conformity pressure, and ethnic group strength?
8. What happens when "strangers" arrive with unrealistic expectations regarding the host culture?
9. Does Kim believe that "strangers" can accomplish their adaptation process alone? If not, why not?

Ethical Considerations: Changing Behavior

Our behavior toward each other is the strangest, most unpredictable, and most entirely unaccountable of all the phenomena with which we are obliged to live.

LEWIS THOMAS

Whenever two good people argue over principles, they are both right.

MARIE VON EBNER-ESCHENBACH

Moral systems are interlocking sets of values, virtues, norms, practices, identities, institutions, technologies, and evolved psychological mechanisms that work together to suppress or regulate self-interest and make cooperative societies possible.

JONATHAN HAIDT

Since the inaugural edition of this book we have stressed the idea that communication is an instrumental endeavor. By this we mean that the act of communication involves some degree of action. And more important, that action creates a response within another individual. Whether it is purchasing an automobile, finding a mate, getting elected to public office, teaching a friend a foreign language, or simply seeking directions, you and another person are engaged in an activity. That activity, be it significant or insignificant, always has an impact. Put in slightly different terms, something happens when you send someone a message. Your words and actions can change behavior, attitudes, perception, a person's self-concept, and even his or her mood. Imagine if you were feeling sad and all at once a good friend appears and places an arm around you and utters the words, "Don't worry, everything will be okay." Most likely that seemingly simple act would change you. The change might be short term or long term, immediate or delayed, public or private, but you would experience some degree of change.

Our example illustrates the fact that an ethical component is built into every communication act. For thousands of years cultures have recognized this ethical dimension of communication. Every one of the traditional world religions advances an ethical doctrine to its members. Recognition regarding the importance of ethics to society exists at both the legal and the interpersonal level. For example, in the United States legal recognition of communication ethics is manifested in libel, slander, truth-in-advertising, and political campaign practice laws. At the interpersonal level there is an inherent need to be accountable for your communication behavior and avoid malicious and cruel speech. The reason for these formal and informal "cultural rules," as noted, is that the consequences of your actions affect other people. As Shakespeare wrote in his *Comedy of Errors*, "Every why hath a wherefore." This chapter asks you to reflect on the "why" and "wherefore"—to think about your actions and the results those actions produce.

There is an ethical responsibility built into every communication, and your "responsibility" is more difficult to assess within the intercultural context. Brazilian anthrophilosopher Valdemar W. Setzer presented this difficulty when he stated, "Ethics is not definable, is not implementable, because it is not conscious; it involves not only our thinking, but also our feeling." This chapter asks you to be aware of those feelings, and your responsibilities, as you engage in intercultural communication. Specifically, we offer four selections that focus on what you need to consider as you communicate within the intercultural arena.

We begin with an essay that is as relevant today as it was when it first appeared in this reader. In addition, it returns us to an issue discussed throughout this book: What problems are brought about by an increase in cultural contact at home and abroad? Harlan Cleveland examines some of the ramifications of that contact in "The Limits of Cultural Diversity." Cleveland begins with a blunt assertion about intercultural contact in today's world and the negative results of many of the contacts: "Ethnic and religious diversity is creating painful conflicts around the world." News events fill our days with accounts of how these conflicts turn one culture against another in ideological disputes. When this happens, according to Cleveland, "culture is being used as an instrument of repression, exclusion, and extinction." Cleveland fears that when people see the chaos created by alien cultures they "believe that their best haven of certainty and security is a group based on ethnic similarity, common faith, economic interest, or political like-mindedness." What makes Cleveland's point of view provocative and relevant is that he rejects the "single culture" hypothesis that is popular among many scholars even today. He recommends a counterforce of wider views, global perspectives, and more universal ideas. This universal view, according to Cleveland, rests in a philosophy that has civilization (universal values, ideas, and practices) as the basic core for all humanity. In this analysis, culture represents the "substance and symbols of the community," and civilization is rooted in compromise and built on "cooperation and compassion." With this orientation, people can deal with each other in ways that respect cultural differences while granting essential overarching values. Cleveland's optimism is clearly stated in his conclusion: "For the twenty-first century, the cheerful acknowledgment of differences is the alternative to a global spread of ethnic cleansing and religious rivalry."

"Intercultural Personhood: An Integration of Eastern and Western Perspectives," by Young Yun Kim, has been included in many past editions of this reader. Kim's analysis is based on one of the central themes of effective intercultural communication—the idea that today's interconnected and fast-changing world demands that you change your assumptions about culture and your individual place within that culture. Recognizing these changes, Kim advances a philosophical orientation that she calls "intercultural personhood." For Kim, intercultural personhood combines the key attributes of Eastern and Western cultural traditions. She presents a model that uses these attributes and considers the basic modes of consciousness, cognitive patterns, personal and social values, and communication behavior.

In "A Communicative Approach to Intercultural Dialogue on Ethics," Richard Evanoff first describes two normative models specifying how sojourners should interact with people from their host culture. In the first, visitors adapt themselves to the norms of their hosts—sort of a "when in Rome do as the Romans do" approach. In the second, individuals maintain their own norms while respecting those of the host culture. Neither of these approaches has proven to be sufficiently satisfactory to foster effective intercultural relations. Evanoff, therefore, proposes an alternative model "in which common ground between people with different ethical norms can be actively constructed through a process of intercultural dialogue." The end goal of his proposal is the integration of ethical norms across cultures that results in a new ethic to govern relationships between individuals in cross-cultural situations.

The underlying assumption of Evanoff's integration process is that "persons who have undergone the experience of learning how other cultures perceive the world acquire an intercultural mindset." He focuses on the multiple frames of reference inherent in all cultures. In presenting his integration principle, Evanoff identifies three specific forms of integration. He begins with a discussion of integrating multiple frames of reference to develop an intercultural mindset that leads to a wider view of the world and of human possibilities. Next, he discusses the difference between integration and adaptation. He sees adaptation as the process whereby individuals adapt their personal norms to the norms of the host culture. Integration, on the other hand, concerns itself both with the psychological process by which individuals begin to incorporate values from the host culture into their own system of values and the process by which the host culture may be influenced by the values of the sojourner.

Evanoff ends his essay with a discussion of integration at the formal level in which critical dialogue ensues to evaluate the value system of the sojourner and the host culture. He proposes models for this form of dialogue and draws examples from Western and Asian cultures to demonstrate this form of integration.

We conclude this chapter with yet another selection that has appeared in numerous editions of this book. In "Peace as an Ethic for Intercultural Communication," David W. Kale sets forth a series of specific challenges. Kale begins by acknowledging that most people feel uncomfortable addressing cultural beliefs about what is right and wrong. He reminds readers that most of these beliefs are at the foundation of your lives and culture. Despite this uneasiness, increased contact with diverse cultures, combined with the problems that can occur when cultures clash, demands examination of the issues associated with questions of right and wrong. To help in that examination, Kale asks you to look at five inter-related issues directly associated with any evaluation of intercultural ethics: (1) a definition of communication ethics, (2) cultural relativity versus universal ethics, (3) the concept of spirit as a basis for intercultural ethics, (4) peace as the fundamental value in intercultural ethics, and (5) a universal code of ethics in intercultural communication. Kale amplifies the fifth issue by urging us to follow a specific code that is predicated on four principles that should guide the actions of ethical communicators: (1) address people of other cultures with the same respect that you would like to receive yourself; (2) seek to describe the world as you perceive it as accurately as possible; (3) encourage people of other cultures to express themselves in their uniqueness; and (4) strive for identification with people of other cultures.

The selections included in this chapter provide a small sampling of the many issues confronting those involved in intercultural communication. This field is relatively new, and the challenges are so varied that accurately predicting future directions is impossible. Our intent in this chapter, therefore, is simply to introduce you to a few of the concepts that await further discussion as you move through the twenty-first century.

One final note: Much of what we offer in this chapter is subjective and may even appear naive to some of you. We do not apologize for our belief that in intercultural contacts each person should aim for the ideal. We have introduced you to new ways of perceiving yourself and others. In so doing, our aim is to help make this complex and shrinking planet a more habitable and peaceful place for all of its more than seven billion residents.

The Limits of Cultural Diversity

HARLAN CLEVELAND

I'm engaged just now in an effort to think through the most intellectually interesting, and morally disturbing, issue in my long experience of trying to think hard about hard subjects. I call it The Limits of Cultural Diversity. If that seems obscure, wait a moment.

After the multiple revolutions of 1989, it began to look as if three ideas we have thought were Good Things would be getting in each other's way, which is not a Good Thing. What I have called the "triple dilemma," or "trilemma," is the mutually damaging collision of individual human rights, cultural human diversity, and global human opportunities. Today the damage from that collision is suddenly all around us.

In 1994, in the middle of Africa, ethnicity took over as an exclusive value, resulting in mass murder by machete. In ex-Yugoslavia (and too many other places), gunpowder and rape accomplish the same purpose: trampling on human rights and erasing human futures. Even on the Internet, where individuals can now join global groups that are not defined by place-names or cordoned off by gender or ethnicity, people are shouting at each other in flaming, capital-letters rhetoric.

Look hard at your hometown, at the nearest inner city; scan the world by radio, TV, or newspapers and magazines. What's happened is all too clear: Just when individual human rights have achieved superstar status in political philosophy, just when can-do information technologies promise what the U.N. Charter calls "better standards of life in larger freedom," culture and diversity have formed a big, ugly boulder in the road called Future.

From *The Futurist*, March–April 1995, pp. 23–26. Reprinted by permission of the World Future Society. The late Harlan Cleveland was a U.S. Assistant Secretary of State, Ambassador to NATO, President of the University of Hawaii, and President of the World Academy of Art and Science.

"If we cannot end now our differences, at least we can help make the world safe for diversity." That was the key sentence in the most influential speech of John F. Kennedy's presidency: his commencement address at American University on June 10, 1963. That speech led directly (among other things) to the first nuclear test ban treaty. For most of the years since then, we were mesmerized by the threat of strategic nuclear war, but now a big nuclear war has become the least likely eventuality among the major threats to human civilization. And that brings us face to face with the puzzle identified in Kennedy's speech: how to make diversity safe.

But is "cultural diversity" really the new Satan in our firmament? Or does it just seem so because "culture" is being used—as Culture has been used in other times and places—as an instrument of repression, exclusion, and extinction?

AN EXCESS OF CULTURAL IDENTITY

In today's disordered world, the collision of cultures with global trends is in evidence everywhere. Ethnic nations, fragmented faiths, transnational businesses, and professional groups find both their inward loyalties and their international contacts leading them to question the political structures by which the world is still, if tenuously, organized. The results are sometimes symbolic caricatures ("In Rome, can a Moslem minaret be built taller than St. Peter's dome?") and sometimes broken mosaics like the human tragedy in what used to be Yugoslavia.

More people moved in 1994 than ever before in world history, driven by fear of guns or desire for more butter and more freedom. (This was true even before a couple of million Rwandans left their homes in terror—and some were floated out of the country as cadavers.) This more-mobile world multiplies the incentives for individuals to develop "multiple personalities," to become "collages" of identities, with plural loyalties to overlapping groups. Many millions of people believe that their best haven of certainty and security is a group based on ethnic similarity, common faith, economic interest, or political like-mindedness.

Societies based on fear of outsiders tend toward "totalitarian" governance. Fear pushes the culture beyond normal limits on individuals' behavior. "To say

that you're ready to *die* for cultural identity," said one of my colleagues at a workshop of the World Academy of Art and Science in Romania last year, "means that you're also ready to kill for cultural identity." Said another: "The ultimate consequence of what's called 'cultural identity' is Hutus and Tutsis murdering each other."

The fear that drives people to cleave to their primordial loyalties makes it harder for them to learn to be tolerant of others who may be guided by different faiths and loyalties. But isolating oneself by clinging to one's tribe is far from a stable condition; these days, the tribe itself is highly unstable. Differences in birthrates and pressures to move will continue to mix populations together. So ethnic purity isn't going to happen, even by forcible "cleansing."

Besides, cultures keep redefining themselves by mixing with other cultures, getting to know people who look, act, and believe differently. In today's more-open electronic world, cultures also expose themselves to new faiths and fashions, new lifestyles, work ways, technologies, clothing, and cuisines.

The early stage of every realization of "cultural identity," every assertion of a newfound "right" of differences, does create a distinct group marked by ethnic aspect ("black is beautiful"), gender ("women's lib"), religion ("chosen people"), or status as a political minority. But when members of a group insisting on the group's uniqueness do succeed in establishing their own personal right to be different, something very important happens: They begin to be treated *individually* as equals and tend to integrate with more inclusive communities. Traditions of separateness and discrimination are often persistent, but they are never permanent and immutable. The recent history of South Africa bears witness.

Before the fighting in Yugoslavia, the most-tolerant people in that part of the world were seen by their close neighbors to be the Serbs, Croats, and Moslems living together in Bosnia and Herzegovina, with the city of Sarajevo as a special haven of mutual tolerance. The problem does not seem to be culture itself, but cultural over enthusiasm. Cultural loyalties, says one European, have the makings of a runaway nuclear reaction. Without the moderating influence of civil society—acting like fuel rods in a nuclear reactor—the explosive potential gets out of hand. What's needed is the counterforce of wider views, global perspectives, and more-universal ideas.

Post-communist societies, says a resident of one of them, have experienced a loss of equilibrium, a culture shock from the clash of traditional cultures, nostalgia for the stability of Soviet culture, and many new influences from outside. What's needed, he thinks, is cultural richness without cultural dominance, but with the moderating effect of intercultural respect.

CULTURE AND CIVILIZATION

We have inherited a fuzzy vocabulary that sometimes treats *culture* as a synonym for *civilization*. At a World Academy workshop, my colleagues and I experimented with an alternative construct.

In this construct, *civilization* is what's universal—values, ideas, and practices that are in general currency everywhere, either because they are viewed as objectively "true" or because they are accepted pragmatically as useful in the existing circumstances. These accepted "truths" offer the promise of weaving together a civitas of universal laws and rules, becoming the basis for a global civil society.

What is sometimes called "management culture" appears to be achieving this kind of universal acceptance, hence becoming part of global "civilization." But nobody has to be in charge of practices that are generally accepted. For instance, the international exchange of money—a miracle of information technologies—is remarkably efficient, daily moving more than a trillion dollars' worth of money among countries. Yet, no one is in charge of the system that makes it happen. Recently, the puny efforts of governments to control monetary swings by buying and selling currencies have only demonstrated governments' incapacity to control them.

If civilization is what's universal, *culture* is the substance and symbols of the community. Culture meets the basic human need for a sense of belonging, for participating in the prides and fears that are shared with an in-group. Both culture and civilization are subject to continuous change. In our time, the most-pervasive changes seem to be brought about by the spread of knowledge, the fallout of information science and information technologies.

Civil society consists of many structures and networks, cutting across cultural fault lines, brought into being by their ability to help people communicate. They are not very dependent on public authority for their charters or their funding, increasingly taking on functions that used to be considered the responsibility of national governments.

Many of these "nongovernments"—such as those concerned with business and finance, scientific inquiry, the status of women, population policy, and the global environmental commons—have become effective users of modern information technologies. In consequence, they are providing more and more of the policy initiative both inside countries and in world affairs.

Civilization is rooted in compromise—between the idea of a democratic state and a strong state, between a free-market economy and a caring economy, between "open" and "closed" processes, between horizontal and vertical relationships, between active and passive citizenship. The required solvent for civilization is *respect for differences*. Or, as one of my World Academy colleagues puts it, we need to learn *how to be different together*.

Civilization will be built by cooperation and compassion, in a social climate in which people in differing groups can deal with each other in ways that respect their cultural differences. "Wholeness incorporating diversity" is philosopher John W. Gardner's succinct formulation. The slogan on U.S. currency is even shorter, perhaps because it's in Latin: *E pluribus unum* ("from many, one").

LESSONS FROM AMERICAN EXPERIENCE

We Americans have learned, in our short but intensive 200-plus years of history as a nation, a first lesson about diversity: that it cannot be governed by drowning it in "integration." I came face to face with this truth when, just a quarter century ago, I became president of the University of Hawaii. Everyone who lives in Hawaii, or even visits there, is impressed by its residents' comparative tolerance toward each other. On closer inspection, paradise seems based on paradox: Everybody's a minority. The tolerance is not despite the diversity but because of it.

It is not through the disappearance of ethnic distinctions that the people of Hawaii achieved a level of racial peace that has few parallels around our discriminatory globe. Quite the contrary. The glory is that Hawaii's main ethnic groups managed to establish the right to be separate. The group separateness in turn helped establish the rights of individuals in each group to equality with individuals of different racial aspect, different ethnic origin, and different cultural heritage.

Hawaii's experience is not so foreign to the trans-atlantic migrations of the various more-or-less-white Caucasians. On arrival in New York (passing that inscription on the Statue of Liberty, "Send these, the homeless, tempest-tost, to me"), the European immigrants did not melt into the open arms of the white Anglo-Saxon Protestants who preceded them. The reverse was true. The new arrivals stayed close to their own kind, shared religion and language and humor and discriminatory treatment with their soul brothers and sisters, and gravitated at first into occupations that did not too seriously threaten the earlier arrivals.

The waves of new Americans learned to tolerate each other—first as groups, only thereafter as individuals. Rubbing up against each other in an urbanizing America, they discovered not just the old Christian lesson that all men are brothers, but the hard, new, multicultural lesson that all brothers are different. Equality is not the product of similarity; it is the cheerful acknowledgment of difference.

What's so special about our experience is the assumption that people of many kinds and colors can together govern themselves without deciding in advance which kinds of people (male or female, black, brown, yellow, red, white, or any mix of these) may hold any particular public office in the pantheon of political power. For the twenty-first century, this "cheerful acknowledgement of difference" is the alternative to a global spread of ethnic cleansing and religious rivalry. The challenge is great, for ethnic cleansing and religious rivalry are traditions as contemporary as Bosnia and Rwanda in the 1990s and as ancient as the Assyrians who, as Byron wrote, "came down like a wolf on the fold" but says the biblical Book of Kings, were prevented by sword-wielding angels from taking Jerusalem.

In too many countries there is still a basic if often unspoken assumption that one kind of people is anointed to be in general charge. Try to imagine a Turkish chancellor of Germany, an Algerian president of France, a Pakistani prime minister of Britain, a Christian president of Egypt, an Arab prime minister of Israel, a Jewish president of Syria, a Tibetan ruler in Beijing, anyone but a Japanese in power in Tokyo.

Yet in the United States during the twentieth century, we have already elected an Irish Catholic as president, chosen several Jewish Supreme Court justices, and racially integrated the armed forces right up to chairman of the Joint Chiefs of Staff. We have not yet adjusted—as voters in India, Britain, and Turkey have done—to having a woman atop the American political heap. But early in the twenty-first century, that too will come. And during that same new century, which will begin with "minorities" as one in every three Americans, there is every prospect that an African American,[1] a Latin American, and an Asian American will be elected president of the United States.

I wouldn't dream of arguing that we Americans have found the Holy Grail of cultural diversity when in fact we're still searching for it. We have to think hard about our growing pluralism. It's useful, I believe, to dissect in the open our thinking about it, to see whether the lessons we are trying to learn might stimulate some useful thinking elsewhere. We do not yet quite know how to create "wholeness incorporating diversity," but we owe it to the world, as well as to ourselves, to keep trying.

Note

1. As Cleveland predicted in 1995, an African American was elected president in November 2008.

Concepts and Questions

1. What does Cleveland mean when he speaks of making diversity safe?
2. What does Cleveland imply when he refers to "an excess of cultural identity"?
3. How does loyalty to one's own cultural identity make it difficult to be tolerant of others?
4. What is meant by the term *cultural over enthusiasm*? How does it affect intercultural relations?
5. How does Cleveland differentiate between the concepts of *culture* and *civilization*?
6. What are the hallmarks of civilization? How can they be maintained?
7. What does Cleveland imply when he states that diversity cannot be governed by drowning it in integration?
8. What does Cleveland mean when he argues that there are limits to diversity?

Intercultural Personhood: An Integration of Eastern and Western Perspectives

YOUNG YUN KIM

We live in a time of clashing identities. As the tightly knit communication web has brought all cultures closer than ever before, rigid adherence to the culture of our youth is no longer feasible. Cultural identity in its "pure" form has become more a nostalgic concept than a reality. As Toffler (1980) noted, we find ourselves "[facing] a quantum leap forward. [We face] the deepest social upheaval and creative restructuring of all time. Without clearly recognizing it, we are engaged in building a remarkable new civilization from the ground up" (p. 44). Yet the very idea of cultural identity, coupled with rising nationalism and xenophobic sentiments, looms over much of today's fractious world landscape. Can the desire for some form of collective uniqueness be satisfied without resulting in divisions and conflicts among groups? Can individuals who are committed to communal values and responsibilities transcend allegiance to their own people?

This essay addresses these issues by proposing the concept of *intercultural personhood*—a way of life in which an individual develops an identity and a definition of self that integrates, rather than separates, humanity. Intercultural personhood projects a kind of human development that is open to growth—a growth beyond the perimeters of one's own cultural upbringing.[1] In making a case for the viability of intercultural personhood, we will first survey some of the core elements in the two seemingly incompatible cultural traditions of the East and the West. We will focus on the cultural apriority, or "root ideas" that define these philosophical perspectives. An argument will be made that certain aspects of these two traditions, often considered unbridgeably incompatible, are profoundly complementary and that such complementary elements can be creatively integrated into a ground-level consideration of human conditions. We will then examine how the process of building an intercultural personhood is actually played out in the lives of people whose life experiences span both cultural worlds.

The current discussion of intercultural personhood owes much to the writings of several prominent thinkers of the twentieth century who have explored ideologies larger than national and cultural interests and that embrace all humanity. One such work is Northrop's *The Meeting of East and West* (1966), in which an "international cultural ideal" was presented as a way to provide intellectual and emotional foundations for what he envisioned as "partial world sovereignty." Inspiration has also been drawn from the work of Thompson (1973), which explored the idea of "planetary culture," or how Eastern mysticism was integrated with Western science and rationalism. The primary sources for the current analysis of Eastern and Western cultural traditions also include Nakamura's *The Ways of Thinking of Eastern Peoples* (1964), Campbell's *The Power of Myth* (1988), Gulick's *The East and the West* (1963), Oliver's *Communication and Culture in Ancient India and China* (1971), Capra's *The Tao of Physics* (1975), and Hall's *Beyond Culture* (1976) and *The Dance of Life* (1983).

EASTERN AND WESTERN CULTURAL TRADITIONS

Traditional cultures throughout Asia—including India, Tibet, Japan, China, Korea, and those in Southeast Asia—have been influenced by such religious and philosophical systems as Buddhism, Hinduism, Taoism, and Zen. On the other hand, Western Europe has mainly followed the Greek and Judeo-Christian traditions. Of course, any attempt to present the cultural assumptions of these two broadly categorized civilizations inevitably sacrifices specific details and the uniqueness of variations within each tradition. No two individuals or groups hold identical beliefs and manifest uniform behaviors, and whatever characterizations we make about one culture or cultural group must be thought of as normative tendencies that vary rather than monolithic and uniform attributes. Nevertheless, several key elements distinguish each group from the other. To specify these elements is to indicate the general interconnectedness of different nations that constitute either the Eastern or the Western cultural world.

Universe and Nature

A fundamental way in which culture shapes human existence is through the explicit and implicit teachings about our relationships to the nature of the universe and the human and nonhuman realms of the world. Traditional Eastern and Western perspectives diverge significantly with respect to basic premises about these relationships. As Needham (1951) noted in his article "Human Laws and the Laws of Nature in China and the West," people in the West have conceived the universe as having been initially created and, since then, externally controlled by a Divine power. As such, the Western worldview is characteristically dualistic, materialistic, and lifeless. The Judeo-Christian tradition sets "God" apart from this reality; having created it and set it into motion, God is viewed as apart from "His" creation. The fundamental material of the universe is conceived to be essentially nonliving matter, or elementary particles of matter, that interact with one another in a predictable fashion. It is as though the universe is an inanimate machine wherein humankind occupies a unique and elevated position among the life-forms that exist. Assuming a relatively barren universe, it seems only rational that humans make use of the lifeless material universe (and the "lesser" life-forms of nature) on behalf of the most intensely living—humankind itself.

Comparatively, the Eastern worldview is more holistic, dynamic, and inwardly spiritual. From the Eastern perspective, the entirety of the universe is viewed as a vast, multidimensional, living organism consisting of many interdependent parts and forces. The universe is conscious and engaged in a continuous dance of creation: The cosmic pattern is viewed as self-contained and self-organizing. It unfolds itself because of its own inner necessity and not because it is "ordered" by any external volitional power. What exists in the universe are manifestations of a divine life force. Beneath the surface appearance of things, an "Ultimate Reality" is continuously creating, sustaining, and infusing our worldly experience. The all-sustaining life force that creates our manifest universe is not apart from humans and their worldly existence. Rather, it is viewed as dynamic and intimately involved in every aspect of the cosmos—from its most minute details to its grandest features.

The traditional Eastern worldview, then, reveres the common source out of which all things arise. As Campbell (1990) noted, "people in Eastern cultures—whether they are Indians, Japanese, or Tibetans—tend to think that the real mystery is in yourself.... Finding the divine not only within you, but within all things.... And what the Orient brings is a realization of the inward way. When you sit in meditation with your hands in your lap, with your head looking down, that means you've gone in and you're coming not just to a soul that is disengaged from God: you're coming to that divine mystery right there in yourself" (p. 89).

This perspective recognizes that everything in this world is fluid, ever-changing, and impermanent. In Hinduism, all static forms are called *maya*, that is, existing only as illusory concepts. This idea of the impermanence of all forms is the starting point of Buddhism. Buddhism teaches that "all compounded things are impermanent," and that all suffering in the world arises from our trying to cling to fixed forms—objects, people, or ideas—instead of accepting the world as it moves. This notion of impermanence of all forms and the appreciation of the aliveness of the universe in the Eastern worldview contrasts with the Western emphasis on the definitive forms of physical reality and their improvement through social and material progress.

Knowledge

Because the East and the West have different views of cosmic patterns, we can expect them to have different approaches to knowledge. In the East, because the universe is seen as a harmonious organism, there is a corresponding lack of dualism in epistemological patterns. The Eastern view emphasizes perceiving and knowing things synthetically, rather than analytically. The ultimate purpose of knowledge is to transcend the apparent contrasts and "see" the interconnectedness of all things. When the Eastern mystics tell us that they experience all things as manifestations of a basic one-ness, they do not mean that they pronounce all things to be the same or equal. Instead, they emphasize that all differences are relative within an all-encompassing phenomenon. Indeed, the awareness that all oppo-sites are polar and, thus, a unity, is one of the highest aims of knowledge. As Suzuki (1968) noted: "The fundamental idea of Buddhism is to pass beyond the world of opposites, a world built up by intellectual distinctions and emotional defilements, and to realize the spiritual world of non-distinction, which involves achieving an absolute point of view" (p. 18).

Because all opposites are interdependent, their con-flict can never result in the total victory of one side but will always be a manifestation of the interplay between the two sides. A virtuous person is not one who undertakes the impossible task of striving for the "good" and eliminating the "bad," but rather one who is able to maintain a dynamic balance between the two. Transcending the opposites, one becomes aware of the relativity and polar relationship of opposites. One realizes that good and bad, pleasure and pain, life and death, winning and losing, light and dark, are not absolute experiences belonging to different categories, but merely two sides of the same reality—extreme parts of a single continuum. The Chinese sages in their symbolism of the archetypal poles, yin and yang, have emphasized this point extensively. And the idea that opposites cease to be opposites is the very essence of *Tao.* To know the Tao, the illustrious way of the universe, is the highest aim of human learning.

This holistic approach to knowledge in the East is pursued by means of "concepts by intuition," a sense of the aesthetic components of things. A concept by intuition is something immediately experienced, apprehended, and contemplated. Northrop (1966) described it as the "differentiated aesthetic continuum" within which there is no distinction between subjec-tive and objective. The aesthetic continuum is a single all-embracing continuity. The aesthetic part of the self is also an essential part of the aesthetic object, whether the object is a flower or a person. Taoism, for example, pursues an undifferentiated aesthetic continuum as it is manifested in the differentiated, sensed aesthetic qualities in nature. The Taoist claim is that only if we take the aesthetic continuity in its all-embracingness as ultimate and irreducible, will we properly understand the meaning of the universe and nature. Similarly, Confucianism stresses the all-embracing aesthetic con-tinuum with respect to its manifestations in human nature and its moral implications for human society: Only if we recognize the all-embracing aesthetic mani-fold to be an irreducible part of human nature will we have compassion for human beings other than ourselves.

As such, the undifferentiated aesthetic continuum is the Eastern conception of the constituted world. The differentiations within it—such as particular scenes, events, or persons—are not irreducible atomic identities, but merely arise out of the undifferenti-ated ground-level reality of the aesthetic continuum. Sooner or later, they fade back into it again. They are transitory and impermanent. Thus, when Eastern sages insist that one must become *selfless,* they mean that the self consists of two components: one, a differentiated, unique element, distinguishing one person from any other person, and the other the all-embracing, aestheti-cally immediate, compassionate, and undifferentiated component. The former is temporary and transitory, and the cherishing of it, the desire for its immortality, is a source of suffering and selfishness. The part of the self that is not transitory is the aesthetic component of the self, which is identical not merely in all persons, but in all aesthetic objects throughout the universe.

While the Eastern knowledge tradition has con-centrated its mental processes on the holistic, intui-tive, aesthetic continuum, the Western pursuit of knowledge has been based on a doctrinally formu-lated dualistic worldview. In this view, because the world and its various components came into exist-ence through the individual creative acts of a god, the fundamental question is, "How can I reach out to the external inanimate world or to other people?" In this question, there is a basic dichotomy between the knower and the things to be known. Accompa-nying this epistemological dualism is the emphasis on rationality in the pursuit of knowledge. Since the Greek philosopher Plato "discovered" reason, virtually all subsequent Western thought—its themes, questions, and terms—relies on an essential rational basis (Wei, 1980).

Even Aristotle, the great hero of all anti-Platonists, was not an exception. Although Aristotle did not propose, as Plato did, a realm of eternal essences ("really real") to justify the primacy of reason, he was by no means inclined to deny this primacy. This is an indication that, while the East has tended to emphasize the direct experience of oneness via intuitive concepts and contemplation, the West has viewed the faculty of the intellect as the primary instrument of worldly mastery. While Eastern thought tends to conclude in more or less vague, imprecise statements, consistent with its existential flexibility, Western thought emphasizes clear and distinct categorization and the linear, analytic logic of syllogism. While the Eastern cultural drive for human development is aimed at spiritual attainment of oneness with the universe, the Western cultural drive finds its expression in its drive for material and social progress.

Time

Closely parallel to differences between the two cultural traditions regarding the nature of knowledge are differences in the perception and experience of time. Along with the immediate, undifferentiated experiencing of here and now, the Eastern time orientation can be portrayed as a placid, silent pool within which ripples come and go. Historically, the East has tended to view worldly existence as cyclical and has often depicted it with metaphors of movement such as a wheel or an ocean: The "wheel of existence" or the "ocean of waves" appears to be in a continual movement but is "not really going anywhere." Although individuals living in the world may experience a rise or fall in their personal fortunes, the lot of the whole is felt to be fundamentally unchanging. As Northrop (1966) noted, "the aesthetic continuum is the greater mother of creation, giving birth to the ineffable beauty of the golden yellows on the mountain landscape as the sun drops low in the late afternoon, only a moment later to receive that differentiation back into itself and to put another in its place without any effort" (p. 343).

Because worldly time is not experienced as going anywhere and because in spiritual time there is nowhere to go but the eternity within the now, the future is expected to be virtually the same as the past. Recurrence in both cosmic and psychological realms is very much a part of the Eastern thought. Thus, the individual's aim is not to escape from the circular movement into linear time, but to become a part of the eternal through the aesthetic experience of the here and now and the conscious evolution of spirituality to "know" the all-embracing, undifferentiated wholeness. In contrast, the West has represented time either with an arrow or as a moving river that comes out of a distant place and past (which are not here and now) and that goes into an equally distant place and future (which also are not here and now). In this view of time, history is conceived of as goal-directed and gradually progressing in a certain direction (toward the universal salvation and second coming of Christ or, in secular terms, toward an ideal state such as boundless freedom or a classless society).

Closely corresponding to the above comparison is Hall's (1976, 1983) characterization of Asian cultures as "polychronic" and Western cultures as "monochronic" in their respective time orientations. Hall explained that individuals in a polychronic system are less inclined to adhere rigidly to time as a tangible, discrete, and linear entity; instead, they emphasize completion of transactions in the here and now, often carrying out more than one activity simultaneously. Comparatively, according to Hall, a monochronic system emphasizes schedules, segmentation, promptness, and standardization of activities. We may say that the Eastern polychronic time orientation is rooted in the synchronization of human behavior with the rhythms of nature, whereas the Western time orientation is driven by the synchronization of human behavior with the rhythms of the clock or machine.

Communication

The historical ideologies examined so far have shaped the empirical content of the East and the West. The respective Eastern and Western perspectives on the universe, nature, knowledge, and time are reflected in many of the specific activities of individuals as they relate themselves to fellow human beings—how individuals view self and the group, and how they use verbal and nonverbal symbols in communication.

First, the view of self and identity cultivated in the Eastern tradition is embedded within an immutable social order. People tend to acquire their sense of identity from an affiliation with, and participation in, a virtually unchanging social order. As has been pointed out in many of the contemporary anthropological studies, the self that emerges from this tradition is not the clearly differentiated existential ego of the West, but a less distinct and relatively unchanging *social ego*. Individual members of the family tend to be more willing to submit their own self-interest for the good of the family. Individuals and families are often expected to subordinate their views to those of the community or the state.

The Eastern tradition also accepts hierarchy in social order. In a hierarchical structure, individuals are viewed as differing in status, although all are considered to be equally essential for the total system and its processes. A natural result of this orientation is the emphasis on authority—the authority of the parents over the children; of the grandparents over their descendants; of the official head of the community, the clan, and the state over all its members. Authoritarianism is an outstanding feature of Eastern life, not only in government, business, and family, but also in education and in beliefs. The more ancient a tradition, the greater is its authority.

The Eastern view further asserts that who "we" are is not limited to our physical existence. Consciousness is viewed as the bridge between the finite and differentiated (one's sense of uniqueness) and the infinite and undifferentiated (the experience of wholeness and eternity). With sufficient training, each person can discover that who he or she is correlates with nature and the divine. All are one and the same in the sense that the divine, undifferentiated, aesthetic continuum of the universe is manifested in each person and in nature. Through this aesthetic connection, individuals and nature are none other than the Tao, the Ultimate Reality, the divine life force, Nirvana, God.

Comparatively, the Western view, in which God, nature, and humans are distinctly differentiated, fosters the development of autonomous individuals with strong ego identification. The dualistic worldview is manifested in an individual's view of his or her relationship to other persons and nature. Interpersonal relationships are essentially egalitarian—cooperative arrangements between two equal partners in which the personal needs and interests of each party are more or less equally respected, negotiated, or resolved by compromise. Whereas the East emphasizes submission (or conformity) of the individual to the group, the West encourages individuality and individual needs to drive the group. If the group no longer serves the individual needs, then it (not the individual) must be changed. The meaning of an interpersonal relationship is decided on primarily by the functions that each party performs in satisfying the needs of the other. A relationship is regarded as healthy to the extent that it serves the expected function for all parties involved. As extensively documented in anthropology and cross-cultural psychology (e.g., Hsu, 1981; Kluckhohn & Strodtbeck, 1960; Triandis, 1995), individualism is the central theme of the Western personality distinguishing the Western world from the collectivistic non-Western world.

This pragmatic interpersonal orientation of the West can be contrasted with the Eastern tradition, in which group membership is taken as given and therefore unchallenged, and in which individuals must conform to the group in case of conflicting interest. Members of the group are encouraged to maintain harmony and minimize competition. Individuality is discouraged, while moderation, modesty, and the bending of one's ego are praised. In some cases, both individual and group achievement (in a material sense) must be forsaken to maintain group harmony. In this context, the primary source of interpersonal understanding is the unwritten and often unspoken norms, values, and ritualized mannerisms pertinent to a particular situation. Rather than relying heavily on explicit and logical verbal expressions, the Eastern communicator grasps the aesthetic essence of the communication dynamic by observing subtleties in nonverbal and circumstantial cues. Intuition, rather than rational thinking, plays a central role in the understanding of how one talks, how one addresses the other, under what circumstances, on what topic, in which of various styles, with what intent, and with what effect.

These implicit communication patterns are reflected in the Eastern fondness for verbal hesitance and ambiguity—out of fear of disturbing or offending others (Cathcart & Cathcart, 1982; Doi,

1982; Kincaid, 1987). Even silence is sometimes preferred to eloquent verbalization in expressing strong compliments or affection. Easterners are often suspicious of the genuineness of excessive verbal praises or compliments because, to their view, truest feelings must be intuitively apparent and therefore do not need to be, and cannot be, articulated. As a result, the burden of communicating effectively is shared by both the speaker and the listener, who is expected to "hear" the implicit messages through empathic attentiveness. In contrast, the Western communicative mode is primarily direct, explicit, and verbal, relying on logic and rational thinking. Participants in communication are viewed as distinctly different individuals, and their individuality has to be expressed through accurate verbal articulation. Inner feelings are not to be intuitively understood but to be honestly and assertively verbalized and discussed. Here, the burden of communicating effectively lies primarily with the speaker.

The preceding characterization of Eastern and Western communication patterns is largely consistent with observations made by other scholars such as Kincaid (1987), Yum (1994), and Hall (1976, 1983). Hall, in particular, has depicted Asian cultures as *high-context* in comparison with the low-context cultures of the West. The focal point of Hall's cross-cultural comparison is "contexting," that is, the act of taking into account information that is either embedded in physical or social context (which includes nonverbal behaviors) or internalized in the communicator. In this scheme, low-context communication, which is more prevalent in the West, is observed when most interpersonal information is expressed by explicit, verbalized codes.

BEYOND CULTURAL DIFFERENCES

As has been pointed out, many of the specific differences that we observe between Eastern and Western societies hinge upon their respective worldviews. Based on an organic, holistic, and cyclic worldview, the East has followed an epistemology that emphasized direct, immediate, and aesthetic components in human experience of the world. The ultimate aim of human learning was to transcend the immediate,

differentiated self and to develop an integrative perception of the undifferentiated universe. The goal is to be spiritually one with the universe and to find the eternal within the present moment, which is a reflection of the eternal. Alternatively, the eternal resides in the present moment. The Western tradition, in contrast, is rooted in the cosmology of dualism, determinism, and materialism. It engenders an outlook that is rational, analytic, and indirect. History is conceived as a linear progression from the past into the future. The pursuit of knowledge is not so much a pursuit of spiritual enhancement as a quest to improve the human condition.

These different worldviews, in turn, are reflected in the individual's conception of the self, the other, and the group. While the East has stressed the primacy of the group over the individual, the West has stressed the primacy of the individual over the group. Interpersonally, the East views the self as deeply merged in the group ego, while the West encourages distinct and autonomous individuality. Explicit, clear, and logical verbalization is a salient feature in the Western communication system, as compared to the emphasis on implicit, intuitive, and nonverbal messages in the Eastern tradition.

The cultural premises of the East and the West that we have examined suggest the areas of vitality, as well as areas of weakness, that are characteristic of each civilization. The Western mechanistic and dualistic worldview has helped to advance scientific efforts to describe systematically and explain physical phenomena, leading to extremely successful technological advancements. The West has learned, however, that the mechanistic worldview and the corresponding communication patterns are often inadequate for understanding the rich and complex phenomena of human relationships and that this lack of understanding can cause alienation from self and others. The West has seen that its dualistic distinction between humanity and nature brings about alienation from the natural world. The analytical mind of the West has led to modern science and technology, but it also has resulted in knowledge that is often compartmentalized, fragmented, and detached from the fuller totality of reality.

In comparison, the East has not experienced the level of alienation that the West has. At the same time, however, the East has not seen as much material and social development. Its holistic and aesthetic worldview has not been conducive to the development of science or technology. Its hierarchical social order and binding social relationships have not fostered the civic-mindedness, worldly activism, humanitarianism, and volunteerism that flourish in the West. Many of the Asian societies continue to struggle to bring about democratic political systems that are based on the rights and responsibilities of individuals.

It should be stressed at this time that the Western emphasis on logical, theoretic, dualistic, and analytic thinking does not suggest that it has been devoid of intuitive, direct, purely empirical, aesthetic elements. Conversely, emphasizing the Western contributions of sociomaterial development is not meant to suggest that the East has been devoid of learning in these areas. The differences that have been pointed out do not represent diametric opposition, but rather differences in emphasis that are nonetheless significant and observable. Clearly, the range of sophistication of Western contributions to the sociomaterial domain far exceeds that of contributions from the East. However, the Eastern emphasis on aesthetic and holistic self-mastery has offered a system of life philosophy that touches on the depth of human experience vis-à-vis other humans, the natural world, and the universe.

Indeed, many have expressed an increasing realization of the limitations in the Western worldview. Using the term "extension transference," for instance, Hall (1976) pointed out the danger of the common intellectual maneuver in which technological "extensions"—including language, logic, technology, institutions, and scheduling—are confused with or take the place of the process extended. We observe the tendency in the West to assume that the remedy for problems arising from technology should be sought not in the attempt to rely on an ideal minimum of technology, but in the development of even more technology. Burke (1974) called this tendency "technologism": "[There] lie the developments whereby 'technologism' confronts its inner contradictions, a whole new realm in which the heights of human rationality, as expressed in industrialism, readily become 'solutions' that are but the source of new and aggravated problems" (p. 148).

Self-criticisms in the West have also been directed to the rigid scientific dogmatism that insists on the discovery of truth based on mechanistic, linear causality, and objectivity. In this regard, Thayer (1983) commented:

What the scientific mentality attempts to emulate, mainly, is the presumed method of laboratory science. But laboratory science predicts nothing that it does not control or that is not otherwise fully determined.... One cannot successfully study relatively open systems with methods that are appropriate only for closed systems. Is it possible that this is the kind of mentality that precludes its own success? (p. 88)

Similarly, Hall (1976) has pointed out that the Western emphasis on logic as synonymous with the "truth" denies that part of human self that integrates. Hall sees that logical thinking is only a small fraction of our mental capabilities and that there are many different and legitimate ways of thinking that have tended to be less emphasized in Western cultures (p. 9).

The criticisms raised by these and other critics of scientific epistemology do not deny the value of the rational, inferential knowledge. Rather, they are directed to the error of Western philosophy in regarding concepts that do not adhere to its mode as invalid. They refer to the arrogance or overconfidence in believing that scientific knowledge is the only way to discover truth, when, in reality, the very process of doing science requires an immediate, aesthetic experience of the phenomenon under investigation. Without the immediately apprehended component, the theoretical hypotheses proposed could not be tested empirically with respect to their truth or falsity and would lack the relevance to the corresponding reality. As Einstein once commented:

Science is the attempt to make the chaotic diversity of our sense-experience correspond to a logically uniform system of thought. In this system single experiences must be correlated with the theoretic structure in such a way that the resulting coordination is complete and convincing. (Quoted in Northrop, 1966, p. 443)

In this description of science, Einstein is careful to indicate that the relation between the theoretically postulated component and the immediately experienced aesthetic component is one of correspondence. The wide spectrum of our everyday life activities demands both scientific and aesthetic modes of apprehension: critical analysis as well as perception of wholes; doubt and skepticism as well as unconditional appreciation; abstraction as well as concreteness; perception of the general and regular as well as the individual and unique; the literalism of technical terms as well as the power and richness of poetic language, silence, and art; relationships with casual acquaintances as well as intimate personal engagement. If we limit ourselves to the dominant scientific mode of apprehension and do not value the aesthetic mode, then we would be making an error of limiting the essential human to only a part of the full span of life activities.

As such, one potential benefit of incorporating the Eastern aesthetic orientation into Western cultural life is a heightened sense of freedom. The aesthetic component of human nature is in part indeterminate, and the ambiguity of indetermination is the basis of our freedom. We might also transcend the clock-bound worldly time to the "Eternal Now," the "timeless moment" that is embedded within the center of each moment. By occasionally withdrawing into the indeterminate, aesthetic component of our nature, away from the determinate, transitory circumstances, we could overcome the pressures of everyday events into a basis for renewal of our human spirit. The traditional Eastern practice of meditation is designed primarily for the purpose of moving one's consciousness from the determinate to the indeterminate, freer state.

Second, incorporation of the Eastern view could bring the West to a greater awareness of the aliveness and wholeness of the universe we inhabit and the life we live. The universe is engaged in a continuous dance of creation at each instant of time. Everything is alive—brimming with a silent energy that creates, sustains, and infuses all that exists. With the expanded perspective on time, we would increase our sensitivity to the rhythms of nature—such as the seasons and the cycles of birth and decay. This integrative worldview is one that pacifies us. Because of its all-embracing oneness and unity, the indeterminate aesthetic continuum helps us to cultivate compassion and intuitive sensitivity—not only for other humans but also for all of nature's creatures. In this regard, Maslow (1971) referred to Taoistic receptivity or "let-be" as an important attribute of self-actualizing persons:

We may speak of this respectful attention to the matter-in-paradigm as a kind of courtesy or deference (without intrusion of the controlling will) which is akin to "taking it seriously." This amounts to treating it as an end, something per se, with its own right to be, rather than as a means to some end other than itself; i.e., as a tool for some extrinsic purpose (p. 68).

Such aesthetic perception is an instrument of intimate human meeting, a way to bridge the gap between individuals and groups. In dealing with each other aesthetically, we do not subject ourselves to a rigid scheme, but do our best in each new situation, listening to the silence as well as the words, and experiencing the other person as a whole living entity with less infusion of our own egocentric and ethnocentric demands. A similar attitude can be developed toward the physical world, as is witnessed in the rising interest in the West in ecological integrity and holistic medicine (see Brody, 1997; Wallis, 1996).

What the preceding considerations suggest is that many Eastern and Western philosophical premises offer views of reality that are not competitive, but complementary. Of course, the entire values, norms, and institutions of the West cannot, and should not, be substituted for their Eastern counterparts, and vice versa. The West may no more adopt the worldview of the East than the East may adopt the worldviews of the West. Rather, we need to recognize that a combination of rational and intuitive modes of experiencing life leads to a life that is more real and more meaningful. With this understanding, we see the interrelatedness and reconciliation of the two seemingly incompatible perspectives.

Our task, then, is to reach for the unity in human experiences and simultaneously to express diversity. A general synthesis of East and West is neither possible nor desirable: The purpose of evolution is not to create a homogeneous mass, but to continuously unfold an ever diverse and yet organic whole. Yet knowledge of differing cultural traditions can help each society move toward greater collective self-understanding—especially by revealing blind spots that can be illuminated only by adopting a vastly different way of seeing. Each tradition can play a necessary and integral part in the continuing evolution of humanity, out of which another birth, a higher integration of human consciousness, may arise.

EMERGENCE OF INTERCULTURAL PERSONHOOD

The task of synthesizing elements of Eastern and Western cultural traditions is taken not merely to satisfy an esoteric academic curiosity but also out of keen relevance to the everyday realities of numerous individuals whose life experiences extend beyond their primary cultural world. Through extensive and prolonged experiences of interfacing with other cultures, they have embarked on a personal evolution, creating a new culture of their own, fusing diverse cultural elements into a single personality. As Toffler (1980) noted, they have created a new personal culture that is "oriented to change and growing diversity" that attempts "to integrate the new view of nature, of evolution and progress, the new, richer conceptions of time and space, and the fusion of reductionism and wholism, with a new causality" (p. 309).

Identity Transformation

The emergence of intercultural personhood is a direct function of dramatically increasing intercultural communication activities—from the personal experiences of diverse people and events through direct encounters to observations via various communication media such as books, magazines, television programs, movies, magazines, art museums, music tapes, and electronic mail. Communicating across cultural identity boundaries is often challenging because it provokes questions about our presumed cultural premises and habits, as well as our inevitable intergroup posturing and the us-and-them psychological orientation (Kim, 1991). Yet it is precisely such challenges that offer us openings for new cultural learning, self-awareness, and personal growth (Adler, 1982; Kim, 1988, 1995, 2001). The greater the severity of intercultural challenges, the greater the potential for reinvention of an inner self that goes beyond the boundaries of our original cultural conditioning. In this process, our

identity is transformed gradually and imperceptibly from an ascribed or assigned identity to an achieved or adopted identity—an emergent intercultural personhood at a higher level of integration (Grotevant, 1993). Such an identity transformation takes place in a progression of stages. In each stage, new concepts, attitudes, and behaviors are incorporated into an individual's psychological makeup. As previously unknown life patterns are etched into our nervous systems, they become part of our new psyches.

The evolution of our identity from cultural to intercultural is far from smooth or easy. Moments of intense stress can reverse the process at any time because individuals may indeed regress toward re-identifying with their origins, having found the alienation and malaise involved in maintaining a new identity too much of a strain (De Vos & Suárez-Orozco, 1990). Such strain may take various forms of an identity crisis (Erickson, 1968) and cultural marginality (Stonequist, 1964; Taft, 1977). Yet the stress experience also challenges individuals to accommodate new cultural elements and become more capable of making deliberate and appropriate choices about action as situations demand.

The emerging intercultural personhood, then, is a special kind of mindset that promises greater fitness in our increasingly intercultural world (Kim, 1995, 2001; Kim & Ruben, 1988). It represents a continuous struggle of searching for the authenticity in self and others within and across cultural groups. It is a way of existence that transcends the perimeters of a particular culture and is capable of embracing and incorporating seemingly divergent cultural elements into one's own unique worldview. The process of becoming intercultural affirms the creative courage and resourcefulness of humans because it requires discovering new symbols and new patterns of life. This creative process of identity development speaks to a uniquely human plasticity, "our relative freedom from programmed reflexive patterns...the very capacity to use culture to construct our identities" (Slavin & Kriegman, 1992, p. 6). It is the expression of normal, ordinary people in the act of "stretching" themselves out of their habitual perceptual and social categories. In Adler's (1982) words, the development of an intercultural identity and personhood places strangers at a position of continually "negotiating ever new formations of reality" (p. 391).

This kind of human development echoes one of the highest aims of humans in the spiritual traditions of the Eastern cultures. Suzuki (1968) writes: "The fundamental idea of Buddhism is to pass beyond the world of opposites, a world built up by intellectual distinctions and emotional defilements, and to realize the spiritual world of non-distinction, which involves achieving an absolute point of view" (p. 18). A virtuous person in this tradition is not one who undertakes the impossible task of striving for the good and eliminating the bad, but rather one who is able to maintain a dynamic balance between good and bad. This Eastern notion of dynamic balance is reflected in the symbolic use by Chinese sages of the archetypal poles of *yin* and *yang*. These sages call the unity lying beyond *yin* and *yang* the *Tao* and see it as a process that brings about the interplay of the two poles. Yoshikawa (1988) described this development as a stage of "double-swing" or "transcendence of binary opposites" (p. 146). With this transcendental understanding, intercultural persons are better able to conciliate and reconcile seemingly contradictory elements and transform them into complementary, interacting parts of a single whole.

An Illustration

Indeed, many people have been able to incorporate experiential territories that have seldom been thought possible, attainable, or even desirable. In doing so, they have redrawn the lines of their original cultural identity boundary to accommodate new life patterns. They remind us of the fact that we humans are active, if not always successful, strategists of our own development in a world of competing and overlapping interests. Although few theories and empirical studies have systematically examined the phenomenon of identity development, many firsthand accounts are available that bear witness to the reality of intercultural personhood. Such accounts have appeared in case studies, memoirs, biographical stories, and essays of self-reflection and self-analysis (see, for instance, Ainslie, 1994; Copelman, 1993; Keene, 1994; O'Halloran, 1994). Many of these accounts present vivid insights into the emotional ebb and flow of the progress toward an eventual realization of intercultural transformation.

One example of a personal fusion of Eastern and Western cultural elements can be seen in the canvases of the artist C. Meng. Since leaving Shanghai in 1986, Meng has earned a Master of Fine Arts degree in the United States and has been teaching at a university in Texas. In response to Meng's recent exhibit in Dallas, art critic and reporter C. Mitchell characterized Meng's paintings as masterful expressions of "the contrast between Eastern and Western modes of thought." Mitchell (1992) noted the unique synthesis of the two sensibilities in Meng's method, which used both Chinese calligraphy and Western-style abstraction techniques.

An illustration of intercultural synthesis is also offered by Duane Elgin, who was born and raised in the United States as a Christian and studied Buddhism in Tibet and Japan for many years. In his book *Voluntary Simplicity* (1981), Elgin integrated the philosophical ideas of Eastern and Western worldviews into his concept of voluntary simplicity. He presented this idea as global common sense and as a practical lifestyle to reconcile the willful, rational approach to life of the West with the holistic, spiritual orientation of the East. Examining historical trends, cycles of civilizations, and related ecological concerns, Elgin proposed voluntary simplicity as a goal for all of humanity. The main issue Elgin addresses is how humans can find ways to remove, as much as possible, the nonessential clutter of life. He suggests, for example, that one owns or buys things based on real need and consider the impact of one's consumption patterns on other people and on the earth. Before purchasing nonessential items, one should ask oneself if these items promote or compromise the quality of one's nonmaterial life. One could also consciously simplify communications by making them clearer, more direct, and more honest, eliminating idle, wasteful, and manipulative speech. One should also respect the value of silence and nonverbal actions.

Perhaps one of the most succinct and eloquent testimonials to the present conception of intercultural personhood was offered by Muneo Yoshikawa (1978). As one who had lived in both Japan and the United States, Yoshikawa offered the following insight into his own psychic development—an insight that captures the essence of what it means to be an intercultural person:

I am now able to look at both cultures with objectivity as well as subjectivity; I am able to move in both cultures, back and forth without any apparent conflict.... I think that something beyond the sum of each [cultural] identification took place, and that it became something akin to the concept of "synergy"—when one adds 1 and 1, one gets [3], or a little more. This something extra is not culture-specific but something unique of its own, probably the emergence of a new attribute or a new self-awareness, born out of an awareness of the relative nature of values and of the universal aspect of human nature.... I really am not concerned whether others take me as a Japanese or an American; I can accept myself as I am. I feel I am much freer than ever before, not only in the cognitive domain (perception, thoughts, etc.), but also in the affective (feeling, attitudes, etc.) and behavioral domains. (p. 220)

Emerging from these and other personal stories are common patterns associated with the development of intercultural personhood. One such pattern is a mindset that is less parochial and more open to different perspectives. This outlook has been referred to as a "third-culture" orientation that enables us to transcend the "paradigmatic barrier" (Bennett, 1976) between divergent philosophical perspectives. Development of an intercultural personhood leads to a cultural relativistic insight (Roosens, 1989) or moral inclusiveness (Opotow, 1990) that is based on an understanding of the profound similarities in human conditions as well as recognition of important differences between and among human groups.

In becoming intercultural, then, we can rise above the hidden grips of our childhood culture and discover that there are many ways to be good, true, and beautiful. In this process, we attain a *wider circle of identification,* approaching the limits of many cultures and, ultimately, humanity itself. This process is not unlike climbing a mountain. As we reach the mountaintop, we see that all paths below lead to the same summit and that each path offers unique scenery. Likewise, the process of becoming intercultural leads to an awareness of ourselves as being part of a larger, more inclusive whole and gives us a greater empathic capacity to "step into and imaginatively participate in the other's world view" (Bennett, 1977, p. 49).

Such developments, in turn, endow us with a special kind of *freedom* and *creativity,* with which we can make deliberate choices about action in specific situations rather than to have these choices simply be dictated by habitual conventions of thought and action. This psychic evolution presents the potential for achieving what Harris (1979) defined as "optimal communication competence." An optimally competent communicator, according to Harris, has a sophisticated "meta system" for critiquing his or her own managing system and interpersonal system. The very existence of the meta system makes the difference between the optimal level and the other two levels of competence a qualitative one (p. 31).

In the end, people such as Meng, Elgin, and Yoshikawa constitute the sustaining core or cross-links of our intercultural world. They provide an infrastructure of moral cement that helps hold together the human and planetary community, and discourage excessive identity claims at the exclusion of other identities. They are the ones who can best meet the enormous challenge that confronts us all—that is, "to give not only yourself but your culture to the planetary view" (Campbell, 1990, p. 114).

Note

1. The term "intercultural personhood" represents other similar terms such as "multicultural man" (Adler, 1982), "universal man" (Tagore, 1961; Walsh, 1973), "international man" (Lutzker, 1960), and "species identity" (Boulding, 1990), as well as "meta-identity" and "transcultural identity."

References

Adler, P. (1982). Beyond cultural identity: Reflections on cultural and multicultural man. In L. Samovar & R. Porter (Eds.), *Intercultural communication: A reader,* 3rd ed. (pp. 389–408). Belmont, CA: Wadsworth.

Ainslie, R. (1994, May). Notes on the psychodynamics of acculturation: A Mexican-American experience. *Mind and Human Interaction,* 5(2), 60–67.

Bennett, J. (1976). *The ecological transition: Cultural anthropology and human adaptation.* New York: Pergamon.

Boulding, E. (1990). *Building a global civic culture.* Syracuse, NY: Syracuse University Press.

Brody, J. (1997, November 6). U.S. panel on acupuncture calls for wider acceptance. *The New York Times,* p. A10.

Burke, K. (1974). Communication and the human condition. *Communication, 1,* 135–152.

Campbell, J. (1988). *The power of myth* (with B. Moyers). New York: Doubleday.

Campbell, J. (1990). *An open life* (in conversation with M. Toms). New York: Harper & Row.

Capra, F. (1975). *The Tao of physics.* Boulder, CO: Shambhala.

Cathcart, D., & Cathcart, R. (1982). Japanese social experience and concept of groups. In L. Samovar & R. Porter (Eds.), *Intercultural communication: A reader,* 3rd ed. (pp. 120–127). Belmont, CA: Wadsworth.

Copelman, D. (1993, April). The immigrant experience: Margin notes. *Mind and Human Interaction,* 4(2), 76–82.

De Vos, G., & Suárez-Orozco, M. (1990). *Status inequality: The self in culture.* Newbury Park, CA: Sage.

Doi, T. (1982). The Japanese patterns of communication and the concept of amae. In L. Samovar & R. Porter (Eds.), *Intercultural communication: A reader,* 3rd ed. (pp. 218–222). Belmont, CA: Wadsworth.

Elgin, D. (1981). *Voluntary simplicity.* New York: Bantam Books.

Erickson, E. (1968). *Identity, youth, and crisis.* New York: Norton.

Grotevant, H. (1993). The integrative nature of identity: Bridging the soloists to sing in the choir. In J. Kroger (Ed.), *Discussions on ego identity* (pp. 121–146). Hillsdale, NJ: Lawrence Erlbaum.

Gulick, S. (1963). *The East and the West.* Rutland, VT: Charles E. Tuttle.

Hall, E. (1976). *Beyond culture.* Garden City, NY: Anchor Books.

Hall, E. (1983). *The dance of life: The other dimension of time.* Garden City, NY: Anchor Press.

Harris, L. (1979, May). *Communication competence: An argument for a systemic view.* Paper presented at the annual meeting of the International Communication Association, Philadelphia, PA.

Hsu, F. (1981). *The challenges of the American dream.* Belmont, CA: Wadsworth.

Keene, D. (1994). *On familiar terms: A journey across cultures.* New York: Kodansha International.

Kim, Y. (1988). *Communication and cross-cultural adaptation: An integrative theory.* Clevedon, UK: Multilingual Matters.

Kim, Y. (1991). Intercultural communication competence. In S. Ting-Toomey & F. Korzenny (Eds.), *Cross-cultural interpersonal communication* (pp. 259–275). Newbury Park, CA: Sage.

Kim, Y. (1995). Cross-cultural adaptation: An integrative theory. In R. Wiseman (Ed.), *Intercultural communication theory* (pp. 170–193). Thousand Oaks, CA: Sage.

Kim, Y. (2001). *Becoming intercultural: An integrative theory of communication and cross-cultural adaptation.* Thousand Oaks, CA: Sage.

Kim, Y., & Ruben, B. (1988). Intercultural transformation. In Y. Kim & W. Gudykunst (Eds.), *Theories in intercultural communication* (pp. 299–321). Newbury Park, CA: Sage.

Kincaid, L. (1987). Communication East and West: Points of departure. In L. Kincaid (Ed.), *Communication theory: Eastern and Western perspectives* (pp. 331–340). San Diego: Academic Press.

Kluckhohn, F., & Strodtbeck, F. (1960). *Variations in value orientations.* New York: Row, Peterson.

Lutzker, D. (1960). Internationalism as a predictor of cooperative behavior. *Journal of Conflict Resolution, 4,* 426–430.

Maslow, A. (1971). *The farther reaches of human nature.* New York: Viking.

Mitchell, C. (1992, June 15). Review. *The Dallas Morning News,* p. C6.

Nakamura, H. (1964). *Ways of thought of Eastern peoples.* Honolulu: University of Hawaii Press.

Needham, J. (1951). Human laws and the laws of nature in China and the West. *Journal of the History of Ideas,* XII.

Northrop, F. (1966/1946). *The meeting of the East and the West.* New York: Collier Books.

O'Halloran, M. (1994). *Pure heart, enlightened mind.* Boston: Charles E. Tuttle.

Oliver, R. (1971). *Communication and culture in ancient India and China.* Syracuse, NY: Syracuse University Press.

Opotow, S. (1990). Moral exclusion and inclusion. *Journal of Social Issues,* 46(1), 1–20.

Roosens, E. (1989). *Creating ethnicity: The process of ethnogenesis.* Newbury Park, CA: Sage.

Slavin, M., & Kriegman, D. (1992). *The adaptive design of the human psyche.* New York: Guilford.

Stonequist, E. (1964). The marginal man: A study in personality and culture conflict. In E. Burgess & D. Bogue (Eds.), *Contributions to urban sociology* (pp. 327–345). Chicago: University of Chicago Press.

Suzuki, D. (1968). *The essence of Buddhism.* Kyoto, Japan: Hozokan.

Taft, R. (1977). Coping with unfamiliar culture. In N. Warren (Ed.), *Studies in cross-cultural psychology,* Vol. 2 (pp. 121–153). London: Academic Press.

Tagore, R. (1961). *Toward universal man.* New York: Asia Publishing House.

Thayer, L. (1983). On "doing" research and "explaining" things. *Journal of Communication,* 33(3), 80–91.

Thompson, W. (1973). *Passages about earth: An exploration of the new planetary culture.* New York: Harper & Row.

Toffler, A. (1980). *The third wave.* New York: Bantam Books.

Triandis, H. (1995). *Individualism and collectivism*. Boulder, CO: Westview Press.

Wallis, C. (1996, June 24). Healing. *Time,* pp. 58–64.

Walsh, J. (1973). *Intercultural education in the community of man*. Honolulu: University of Hawaii Press.

Wei, A. (1980, March). *Cultural variations in perception*. Paper presented at the 6th Annual Third World Conference, Chicago, IL.

Yoshikawa, M. (1978). Some Japanese and American cultural characteristics. In M. Prossor, *The cultural dialogue: An introduction to intercultural communication* (pp. 220–239). Boston: Houghton Mifflin.

Yoshikawa, M. (1988). Cross-cultural adaptation and perceptual development. In Y. Kim & W. Gudykunst (Eds.), *Cross-cultural adaptation: Current approaches* (pp. 140–148). Newbury Park, CA: Sage.

Yum, J. (1994). The impact of Confucianism on interpersonal relationships and communication patterns in East Asia. In L. Samovar & R. Porter (Eds.), *Intercultural communication: A reader,* 7th ed. (pp. 75–86). Belmont, CA: Wadsworth.

Concepts and Questions

1. What is meant by the term "intercultural personhood"?
2. How do Eastern and Western teachings about humankind's relationship to the nature of the universe differ?
3. In what major ways do Eastern and Western approaches to knowledge differ?
4. How do Eastern time orientations differ from those found in the West?
5. How do differences in Eastern and Western views of self and identity affect intercultural communication?
6. What are the major differences between Eastern and Western modes of communication?
7. What strengths and weaknesses are found in Eastern and Western worldviews?
8. How could an integration of Eastern and Western perspectives benefit both Eastern and Western cultural life?
9. What conditions are required for the emergence of intercultural personhood?
10. What benefits accrue to both society and the individual from the development of an intercultural personhood perspective?

A Communicative Approach to Intercultural Dialogue on Ethics

Richard Evanoff

The aim of this essay is to develop a communicative approach to intercultural dialogue on ethics. For this purpose ethics will be defined as critical reflection on behavior in relation to ourselves (personal ethics), others (social ethics), and the world in which we live (environmental ethics).

Three basic methodological approaches are utilized in the field of intercultural communication: (1) *empirical approaches*, which attempt to describe cultures as they are, employing both qualitative and quantitative methods; (2) *theoretical approaches*, which attempt to construct models and make generalizations about cultures based on empirical data; and (3) *normative approaches*, which attempt to solve problems in intercultural situations.

Empirical and theoretical approaches gather facts and make generalizations about, for example, how people from different cultures view marriage or conduct business. Such knowledge does not indicate, however, how problems which arise in intercultural marriages or international joint ventures might be resolved. Normative approaches involve imagining creative solutions to such problems rather than simply describing or analyzing existing values and norms. The main problem for intercultural ethics, therefore, is how normative solutions can be arrived at across cultures, given the fact that different cultures have different values and norms—a problem which is receiving increased attention both among interculturalists and in the emerging field of global ethics (see the references).

Courtesy of Richard Evanoff. This original essay was written for an earlier edition of this reader. Permission to reprint must be obtained from the author and the publisher. Richard Evanoff is Professor in the School of International Politics and Economics, Aoyama Gakuin University, Tokyo, Japan.

Traditional approaches to intercultural ethics can be divided into two types: *Universalist* and *Particularist*. Universalist approaches attempt to ground ethics variously in religion, nature, history, reason, etc. These approaches largely fail, however, because there is no agreement about what is religiously authoritative, natural, historical, or reasonable. Moreover, universalists often simply regard their own particular culture as "universal"—a stance which is especially prevalent in Western cultures ("global standards," for example, are frequently simply American standards writ large). Universalist approaches are connected with objective, foundational approaches to ethics, as well as to modernism, globalization, and a unilinear model of cultural development which sees all cultures as proceeding along a single line of development and converging on a single universal set of values and norms (*cf.* Fukuyama's "end of history").

Particularist approaches to intercultural ethics deny that there can be a single universal set of values and norms, and instead relativize values and norms to particular individuals and/or groups. Ethical individualism—one example of which is the notion that economic decisions should be made on the basis of individual preferences rather than on the basis of some form of collective decision-making—contends that individuals are the final arbiters of value. Such a stance may be acceptable when deciding flavors of ice cream but may be less acceptable when applied to the health, safety, and environmental impact of particular products. Cultural relativism similarly contends that since different cultural groups have different values and norms, it is impossible to formulate any values and norms which are valid across cultures. Particularism is connected with subjective, skeptical approaches to ethics, as well as to postmodernism, the preservation of local cultures and ethnic identities, and a multilinear model of cultural development which sees all cultures as proceeding along separate lines of development and diverging with respect to values and norms (*cf.* Huntington's "clash of civilizations").

It is clear that neither the universalist nor the particularist approach offers an adequate framework for intercultural ethics. While universalist tendencies can still be widely found in the fields of international politics and economics, they have been largely discredited in the field of intercultural communication, where the emphasis has been on recognizing and preserving cultural differences rather than on creating a single, homogenous "global culture." Nonetheless, cultural relativism, which is widely accepted in the field of intercultural communication, is also problematic. Although it is obvious that various cultures construct ethical systems in ways which are often incommensurable, cultural relativism does not answer the question of how conflicts between people from cultures with different values and norms can be resolved. The solution most often proposed is that we should simply "understand" and "respect" different cultures—"When in Rome do as the Romans do."

A distinction can be made, however, between cultural relativity (the fact that cultures are different) and cultural relativism (the value judgment that different cultures must simply be accepted as they are). Descriptive ethics (what is *actually* done in a particular culture) cannot be equated with normative ethics (this is what *should* be done). To equate the two commits the naturalistic fallacy, i.e., the attempt to derive an *ought* from an *is*. Hatch writes, "The fact of moral diversity no more compels our approval of other ways of life than the existence of cancer compels us to value ill-health" (1983, p. 68). Cultural relativism seems progressive but is in fact conservative and tradition-bound because it obligates us to simply accept the values and norms of other cultures rather than giving us the opportunity to critically reflect on them and make considered decisions about which values and norms are worthy of adoption. It regards culture in "essentialist" terms (cultures have certain "essential" features which are fixed and unchanging) rather than in constructivist terms (cultures are human *constructs* and therefore susceptible to creative change). From a purely practical perspective relativism offers no solution to intercultural conflicts. Simply contending that "you have your way and I have mine" makes it impossible for people from different cultures to work together cooperatively on problems of mutual concern.

A communicative approach to intercultural ethics may offer a viable alternative to both universalism and particularism. The communicative approach recognizes that while we are each situated in a particular culture and socialized into certain norms, we are nonetheless able to reflect back on those norms and change them if necessary. We are also able to critically reflect on the norms of other cultures and to selectively adopt (or reject) those norms which seem plausible (or implausible) to us. Such reflection results in greater objectivity, although never in pure, absolute objectivity—as humans we never have access to a "Gods-eye" view of the world. Dialogue on intercultural ethics can thus be seen as taking place between specific people from specific cultures in specific contexts and in relation to specific problems. Although the context can be widened to include more than one culture, there are no "universals."

A communicative approach to intercultural ethics is also relational, seeing individuals as having relationships both with others in society and with one's natural environment (*cf.* Watsuji 1961). Ethical dialogue can take place at a variety of different levels: at the personal level there is intrapersonal communication through which decisions are made with respect to how we live our lives as individuals; at the social level there is interpersonal and intergroup communication through which decisions are made with respect to how we live together with others; at the global level there is international communication through which decisions are made with respect to the relations which exist between nations and wider cultural groups (*cf.* the distinction made in Apel 1980 between micro-, meso-, and macro-domains and in Singer 1987 between the interpersonal, intergroup, and international levels). Decisions are most appropriately made at the appropriate level. At the interpersonal level, for example, it is not necessary to formulate universal norms with respect to international marriages; such norms are more appropriately made by the marriage partners themselves and will vary from couple to couple. At the global level, however, it may be necessary to construct norms which are universal or near-universal in scope in order to address problems which cross cultural and national boundaries, such as global warming.

It can be suggested that the main principle for deciding the level at which norms should be created is related to the scope of the consequences which a particular action has. Dower has suggested the following maxim for intercultural ethics: ". . . where the lines of cause and effect run across nation-states, so do the lines of moral responsibility" (1998, p. 165). If my action only affects myself, then the decision should be purely personal. If my action affects others, then those who are affected should have the right to participate in the process by which a decision is reached regarding that action (this is a simplified statement of Habermas's discourse ethics; see Habermas 1989; 1993). For example, it may be alright for me to smoke in my own room, but not in a room full of people who find smoking objectionable; driving a car may no longer be appropriately regarded as a personal decision if the carbon dioxide emitted from my car contributes to global warming.

Finally, a communicative approach to intercultural ethics is pragmatic in that it is concerned, as mentioned previously, with solving particular problems faced by particular people in particular situations. As new problems emerge, new ethical solutions must be found; we cannot simply fall back on past ethical traditions for guidance. Ethical systems can be both abandoned and created. We no longer find slavery acceptable, for example, and we are constantly in the process of creating new ethical norms to deal with emergent problems, such as advances in medical technology and increased contact across cultures. Rather than see ethics as fixed and unchanging, a communicative approach sees ethics as dynamic and creative. It can be associated with an ecological model of cultural development which recognizes that cultures may proceed along different lines of development but nonetheless co-evolve through the communicative relations they have with other cultures.

A communicative approach to cross-cultural dialogue on ethics recognizes that intercultural situations are by their very nature anomic (*a-nom:* "without law") because the norms to govern behavior in such situations have not yet been created. The ethical norms we are socialized into accepting as individuals usually tell us how to deal with people in our own cultures, not how to deal with people from other cultures. The question for intercultural ethics, therefore, is: given a particular problem, what should people from different cultures with differing ethical traditions actually *do* about it? Various solutions are possible: (1) *avoidance:* we can avoid having contact with people from different cultures; (2) *adaptation:* one side is obliged to conform to the norms of the other side; (3) *confrontation:* each side insists that it alone is right: (4) *domination:* one side attempts to impose its view on the other; or

(5) *dialogue:* the two sides communicate with each other about which norms should be adopted in a particular situation.

If dialogue is the preferred method for dealing with issues related to intercultural ethics, how can such dialogue be conducted? Ethnocentric approaches to cross-cultural dialogue typically take their own cultural values and norms as correct and view those of the opposite side as incorrect. Such a view rests on an Aristotelian logic which holds that if a given proposition is true, its opposite cannot be true at the same time. If individualism is "true," for example, then collectivism must be "false."

A more Hegelian, dialectical approach, however, would contend that within any point of view there are "positive" and "negative" features which can be differentiated from each other. It may be agreed that a positive feature of individualism is its emphasis on self-reliance; a negative feature is its tendency towards egoism. A positive feature of collectivism is its emphasis on cooperation; a negative feature is its tendency towards conformity. What often happens in cross-cultural criticism, of course, is that the positive side of one position is used to criticize the negative side of the other position. Self-reliance is seen as being superior to conformity and cooperation is seen as being superior to egoism. It should, however, be possible to integrate the positive features of each of the positions into a new synthesis, while discarding the negative features. Self-reliance can be combined with cooperation without contradiction, while egoism and conformity can be discarded. This new synthetic position constitutes a "third culture" which combines aspects from each of the original cultures but also transforms them in creative ways. Third cultures have the potential to provide a common ground for coordinated action across cultures and can be applied to a wide variety of cultural disputes related to value differences.

ACKNOWLEDGMENTS

This essay is based on a paper originally presented at the Aoyama Symposium on International Communication, held at Aoyama Gakuin University in Tokyo, Japan on March 5, 2005. The article summarizes research further elaborated in Evanoff 1996; 1998; 1999; 2000; 2001; 2004; 2006a; 2006b. Slightly different versions of this article have appeared in Evanoff 2005 and 2007.

References

Apel, K. O. (1980). *Towards a transformation of philosophy,* G. Adey & D. Frisby, Trans. (London: Routledge and Kegan Paul).

Appiah, K. A. (2006). *Cosmopolitanism: Ethics in a world of strangers.* (London: Allen Lane).

Asuncio-Lande, N. C. (Ed.). (1979). *Ethical perspectives and critical issues in intercultural communication.* (Falls Church, VA: Speech Communication Association).

Barnlund, D. C. (1979). The cross-cultural arena: An ethical void. In L. A. Samovar & R. E. Porter (Eds.), *Intercultural communication: A reader,* 4th ed. (Belmont, CA: Wadsworth), 394–399.

Booth, K., T. Dunne, & M. Cox (Eds.). (2001). *How might we live? Global ethics in the new century.* (Cambridge: Cambridge University Press).

Casmir, F. L. (Ed.). (1997). *Ethics in intercultural and international communication.* (London: Lawrence Erlbaum).

Commers, M. S. R., W. Vandekerckhove, & A. Verlinden, eds. (2008). *Ethics in an era of globalization.* (Aldershot: Ashgate).

Cook, J. W. (2002). *Morality and cultural differences.* (New York: Oxford University Press).

Dower, N. (1998). *World ethics: The new agenda.* (Edinburgh: Edinburgh University Press).

Eade, J., & D. O'Byrne (2005). *Global ethics and civil society.* (Farnham: Ashgate).

Evanoff, R. (1996). Intercultural ethics: New ways of learning to get along with each other. In *Language and Culture in International Communication* (Tokyo: Aoyama Gakuin University Press), 145–225.

Evanoff, R. (1998). A constructivist approach to intercultural ethics. *Eubios Journal of Asian and International Bioethics,* 8, 84–87.

Evanoff, R. (1999). Towards a constructivist theory of intercultural dialogue. In N. Honna & Y. Kano (Eds.), *International Communication in the 21st Century.* (Tokyo: Sanseido), 109–153.

Evanoff, R. (2000). The concept of 'third cultures' in intercultural ethics. *Eubios Journal of Asian and International Bioethics,* 10, 126–129.

Evanoff, R. (2001). Discussion paper on intercultural dialogue and education. UNU Workshop on the Contribution of Education to the Dialogue of Civilizations at the United Nations University, Tokyo, Japan, May 3–5. Available at http://www.unu.edu/dialogue/papers/evanoff-s5.pdf

Evanoff, R. (2004). Universalist, relativist, and constructivist approaches to intercultural ethics. *International Journal of International Relations, 28*, 439–458.

Evanoff, R. (2005). A communicative approach to intercultural dialogue on ethics. Human Dignity and Humiliation Studies website. Available at http://www.humiliationstudies.org/documents/EvanoffInterculturalEthics.pdf

Evanoff, R. (2006a). Integration in intercultural ethics. *International Journal of International Relations, 30*, 421–437.

Evanoff, R. (2006b). Intercultural ethics: A constructivist approach. *Journal of Intercultural Communication, 9*, 89–102.

Evanoff, R. (2007). A communicative approach to intercultural dialogue on ethics. In *Gaikokugo kyouiku sentaa daiichirui FD katsudou kirokushu 2003–2005*. (Hiratsuka: Tokai University Press), 14–16.

Fukuyama, F. (1992). *The end of history and the last man*. (New York: Free Press).

Habermas, J. (1989). *Moral consciousness and communicative action*, C. Lenhardt & S. W. Nicholsen, Trans. (Cambridge: Polity Press).

Habermas, J. (1993). *Justification and application*, C. Cronin, Trans. (Cambridge: MIT Press).

Hatch, E. (1983). *Culture and morality*. (New York: Columbia University Press).

Hopkins, W. E. (1997). *Ethical dimensions of diversity*. (Thousand Oaks: Sage).

Huntington, S. P. (1996). *The clash of civilizations and the remaking of world order*. (New York: Simon and Schuster).

Johannesen, R. (2002). *Ethics in human communication*, 5th ed. (Prospect Heights: Waveland Press).

Kale, D. W. (1991). Ethics in intercultural communication. In L. A. Samovar & R. E. Porter (Eds.), *Intercultural communication: A reader*, 6th ed. (Belmont: Wadsworth), 421–426.

Lange, H., A. Löhr, & H. Steinmann (Eds.). (1998) *Working across cultures: Ethical perspectives for intercultural management*. (Dordrecht: Kluwer Academic Publishers).

Makau, J. M., & R. C. Arnett (Eds.) (1997). *Communication ethics in an age of diversity*. (Urbana: University of Illinois Press).

Morgan, E. (1998). *Navigating cross-cultural ethics: What global managers do right to keep from going wrong*. (Boston: Butterworth-Heinemann).

Singer, M. R. (1987). *Intercultural communication: A perceptual approach*. (Englewood Cliffs: Prentice-Hall).

Watsuji, T. (1961). *Climate and culture*, G. Bownas, Trans. (Tokyo: Hokuseido).

Wiredu, K. (1996). *Cultural universals and particulars: An African perspective*. (Bloomington: Indiana University Press).

Wiredu, K. (2005). On the idea of a global ethic. *Journal of Global Ethics, 1*, 45–51.

Concepts and Questions

1. Differentiate between *empirical*, *theoretical*, and *normative* methodological approaches to solve problems in intercultural ethics. How do their methodologies differ?

2. Evanoff asserts that attempts to ground ethics variously in religion, nature, history, or reason largely fail. Why is this?

3. What is the fundamental assumption of the particularist approach to intercultural ethics?

4. How does Evanoff differentiate between cultural relativity and cultural relativism? Give an example of each of these approaches to ethics.

5. How does a communicative approach to intercultural ethics differ from earlier approaches?

6. Evanoff suggests that ethical dialogue can take place at a variety of levels: the interpersonal, the social, and the global. How do these levels differ in terms of the types of ethical issues with which they deal? Give examples from your own experiences that reflect ethical issues you might consider at each of these levels.

7. Evanoff poses the question for developing intercultural ethics in the following manner: given a particular problem, what should people from different cultures with different ethical traditions actually *do* about it? What is your answer to this question?

8. How would you engage in an intercultural dialogue to resolve issues related to intercultural ethics? What underlying assumptions would you make about the conduct of the dialogue?

9. What does Evanoff mean when he suggests that the result of communicative dialogue to establish an intercultural ethic constitutes a "third culture"?

Peace as an Ethic for Intercultural Communication

DAVID W. KALE

A Ford Foundation executive with more than 20 years of experience in overseas travel has been quoted as saying that "most problems in cross-cultural projects come from different ideas about right and wrong" (Howell, 1981, p. 3). This executive's statement refers to two problem areas that have caused a great deal of difficulty in intercultural communication. First, many people have been in the uncomfortable position of doing something completely acceptable in their own country, while unknowingly offending the people of the culture they were visiting. This problem arose when I took a group of university students to Guyana in South America. In that warm climate, our students wore the same shorts they would have worn at home, but the Guyanese were offended by what they considered to be skimpy clothing, particularly when worn by the women. A second problem that arises in intercultural situations results when we try to get the rest of the world to live according to our culture's ideas about right and wrong. Interestingly, we get rather upset when people of another culture tell us how to behave. We like to believe that the way our culture chooses to do things is the right way, and we do not appreciate people of other cultures telling us we are wrong.

Both of these problems have a bearing on ethics in intercultural communication. Discussing this topic causes stress to people of all cultures. Bonhoeffer suggests this is because we get the feeling that the basic issues of life are being addressed. When that happens, some of our most cherished beliefs may be challenged.

When our cultural beliefs about right and wrong are being threatened, we feel that the very foundation of our lives may be under attack (Bonhoeffer, 1965, pp. 267–268).

While such a discussion may be threatening, it must be undertaken nonetheless. With contact among people of various cultures rapidly on the rise, an increase in the number of conflicts over matters of right and wrong is inevitable. This essay addresses the ethics of intercultural communication by developing the following points: (1) a definition of communication ethics, (2) cultural relativity versus universal ethics, (3) the concept of spirit as a basis for intercultural ethics, (4) peace as the fundamental value in intercultural ethics, and (5) a code of ethics in intercultural communication.

A DEFINITION OF COMMUNICATION ETHICS

Richard Johannesen (1978, pp. 11–12) has said that we are dealing with an ethical issue in human communication when:

1. People voluntarily choose a communication strategy.
2. The communication strategy is based on a value judgment.
3. The value judgment is about right and wrong in human conduct.
4. The strategy chosen could positively or negatively affect someone else.

It is important to note in this definition that values are the basis for communication ethics. For example, we place a value on the truth, and therefore it is unethical to tell a lie to another person. Without this basis in values, we have no ethical system whatsoever.

We face a major problem in our society because some people think they can decide right and wrong for themselves with no regard for what others think. Such a mindset shows that these people really don't understand ethics at all. If they did they would know that ethics are based on values, and values are determined by culture. Thus, there can be no such thing as a totally individual system of ethics. Such an approach would eventually result in the total destruction of human society (Hauerwas, 1983, p. 3; Weaver, 1971, p. 2).

Within a culture there is a continual dialogue about the things that are the most meaningful and important to the people of that culture. As a result, cultures are continually in a state of change. When cultures change, so do the values that culture holds. Thus, we must acknowledge that there is no fixed order of values that exists within a culture (Brummett, 1981, p. 293). This does not mean, however, that we are free to determine right and wrong for ourselves. It is much more accurate to say that we are shaped by the values of our culture than to say that we shape the values of our culture (Hauerwas, 1983, p. 3).

CULTURAL RELATIVISM VERSUS UNIVERSAL ETHICS

Because the values on which our ethics are built are generated by dialogue within a culture, the question must then be asked whether a person of one culture can question the conduct of a person in another culture. The concept of cultural relativity would suggest that the answer to this question is generally "No." Cultural relativity suggests that a culture will develop the values it deems best for the people of that culture. These values depend on the context in which the people of that culture go to work, raise their children, and run their societies. As such, those who are from a different context will develop a different set of cultural values and therefore have no basis on which to judge the conduct of people in any culture other than their own.

Few people would be willing to strictly follow the concept of cultural relativity, however. To do so would suggest that it was alright for Hitler to murder six million innocent people because the German people did nothing to stop it (Jaska & Pritchard, 1988, p. 10). At the same time, few are willing to support the idea that people of all cultures must abide by the same code of ethics. We know that cultures develop different value systems and thus must have different ethical codes.

Both Brummett (1981, p. 294) and Hauerwas (1983, p. 9) have argued that because values are derived through dialogue, there is nothing wrong with attempting to persuade people of other cultures to accept our values. Before we do that, however, we must be convinced that our values are worthy and not based on limited self-interest. We must also be

willing to work for genuine dialogue; too often these discussions tend to be monologues. We are generally far more willing to present the case for our own value system than we are to carefully consider the arguments for those of other cultures.

At the time of this writing, for example, people of many cultures are attempting to get the people of Brazil to stop cutting down their rainforests. As long as these persuasive efforts are based on a genuine concern for the negative effect cutting these trees is having on the global climate, there is nothing unethical about them. We must, however, also be willing to understand what is motivating the Brazilians' behavior and accept some responsibility in helping them to solve the serious economic problems their country is facing.

SPIRIT AS THE BASIS FOR ETHICAL UNIVERSALS

To develop the next point, how we are to make ethical decisions in intercultural communication, let me suggest that there is a concept on which we can base a universal code of ethics: the human spirit (Eubanks, 1980, p. 307). In the words of Eliseo Vivas:

> The person deserves unqualified respect because he (or she) is not merely psyche but also spirit, and spirit is, as far as we know, the highest form of being. It is through the human spirit that the world is able to achieve cognizance of its status as creature, to perceive its character as valuable, and through human efforts to fulfill a destiny, which it freely accepts. (p. 235)

It is this human spirit that people of all cultures have in common that serves as a basis of belief that there are some universal values on which we can build a universal code of ethics in intercultural communication.

We have watched dramatic changes take place in the world as people in Eastern Europe and the Commonwealth of Independent States (the former Soviet Union) have attempted to improve the quality of life for themselves and their offspring. We identify with their efforts because we share a human spirit that is the same regardless of cultural background. It is this spirit that makes us people who value in the first place. It is from this spirit that the human derives the ability to make decisions about right and wrong, to decide what makes life worth living, and then to make life the best it can possibly be. Therefore, the guiding principle of any universal code of intercultural communication should be to protect the worth and dignity of the human spirit.

PEACE AS THE FUNDAMENTAL HUMAN VALUE

There is a strong temptation for those of us in Western democracies to identify freedom of choice as the fundamental human value. Hauerwas (pp. 9–12) has convincingly argued that freedom of choice is an unachievable goal for human endeavor. He notes that it is not possible for everyone to have freedom of choice. At the time of this writing, some people in Czechoslovakia want to have the country stay together as a whole, while others want it to divide into two separate countries, with each being the home of a different ethnic group. It cannot be that both parties will have their choice.

A goal that is possible to achieve, however, is to direct our efforts toward creating a world where people of all cultures are living at peace with one another. This goal consists of three different levels: minimal peace, moderate peace, and optimal peace:

- *Minimal peace* is defined as merely the absence of conflict. Two parties in conflict with each other are at minimal peace when they would be involved in violent conflict if they felt free to act out their hostile feelings. Perhaps there are U.N. peacekeeping forces restraining the two sides from fighting. Perhaps both sides know that continual fighting will bring condemnation from the rest of the world community. Whatever the reason, the peace is only superficial.
- *Moderate peace* results when two conflicting parties are willing to compromise on the goals they want to achieve. In this case, each party has major concessions it is willing to make to reach agreement, but considerable irritation still exists with the opposing party in the conflict. Each party considers its own goals as worthy and justifiable, and any of the other party's goals that conflict with its own are clearly unacceptable.

Moderate peace describes the situation that exists today between Israel and its Arab neighbors.

Negotiations are proceeding in Washington between Israel and countries such as Syria, Jordan, and Egypt. The fact that these countries are at least willing to sit down at the same table and negotiate indicates that their relationship has developed beyond that of minimal peace. If those negotiations break off and hostile feelings intensify, they could be back to a relationship of minimal peace in a short period of time.

- *Optimal peace* exists when two parties consider each other's goals as seriously as they do their own. This does not mean that their goals do not ever conflict. The United States and Canada have a relationship that could be considered as optimal peace, yet there is considerable disagreement over the issue of whether acid rain from U.S. factories is destroying Canadian woodlands. Each side pursues its own goals in negotiations, but considers the other party's goals as worthy and deserving of serious consideration.

At the current time the Soviet republics of Armenia and Azerbaijan are locked in a bitter ethnic conflict over a territory within the republic of Azerbaijan that is populated mostly by Armenians. Because the territory is in their republic, the people of Azerbaijan say they should control it; because largely Armenians populate it, the Armenians say they should control it. Both groups cannot have freedom of choice in this situation, but they can live in peace if they are willing to submit to reasonable dialogue on their differences.

The concept of peace applies not only to relations between cultures and countries, but also to the right of all people to live at peace with themselves and their surroundings. As such it is unethical to communicate with people in a way that violates their concept of themselves or the dignity and worth of their human spirit.

A UNIVERSAL CODE OF ETHICS IN INTERCULTURAL COMMUNICATION

Before launching into the code itself, a "preamble" should first be presented based on William Howell's suggestion that the first step to being ethical in any culture is the intent to do what one knows is right (1982, p. 6). All societies set out rules of ethical conduct for people to follow based on cultural values.

The foundation of ethical behavior is that people intend to do what they know is right. To choose to do something that you know to be wrong is unethical in any culture.

Principle #1—Ethical communicators address people of other cultures with the same respect that they would like to receive themselves.

It is based on this principle that I find ethnic jokes to be unethical. Some people may argue that ethnic jokes are harmless in that they are "just in fun," but no one wants to be on the receiving end of a joke in which their own culture is demeaned by people of another culture (LaFave & Mannell, 1978). Verbal and psychological abuse can damage the human spirit in the same way that physical abuse damages the body. Verbal and psychological violence against another person, or that person's culture, is just as unacceptable as physical violence. People of all cultures are entitled to live at peace with themselves and the cultural heritage that has had a part in shaping them. It is, therefore, unethical to use our verbal and/or nonverbal communication to demean or belittle the cultural identity of others.

Principle #2—Ethical communicators seek to describe the world as they perceive it as accurately as possible.

While in our culture we might call this telling the truth, what is perceived to be the truth can vary greatly from one culture to another. We know that reality is not something that is objectively the same for people of all cultures. Reality is socially constructed for us by our culture; we live in different perceptual worlds (Kale, 1983, pp. 31–32).

The point of this principle is that ethical communicators do not deliberately set out to deceive or mislead, especially since deception is damaging to the ability of people of various cultures to trust each other. It is only when people of the world are able to trust one another that we will be able to live in peace. That trust is only possible when the communication that occurs between those cultures is devoid of deliberate attempts to mislead and deceive (Bok, 1978, pp. 18–33; Hauerwas, 1983, p. 15).

Principle #3—Ethical communicators encourage people of other cultures to express themselves in their uniqueness.

This principle is reflected in Article 19 of the Universal Declaration of Human Rights as adopted by the United Nations. It states: "Everyone has the right to freedom of opinion and expression; this right includes the freedom to hold opinions without interferences and to seek, receive and impart information and ideas through any media and regardless of frontiers" (Babbili, p. 9).

In his book, *I and Thou,* Martin Buber (1965) cogently discusses the need for us to allow the uniqueness of the other to emerge if genuine dialogue is to take place. We often place demands on people of other cultures to adopt our beliefs or values before we accept them as full partners in our dialogue.

Is it the right of the U.S. government to demand that Nicaragua elect a non-communist government before that country is granted full partnership in the intercultural dialogue of this hemisphere? It is certainly possible that the people of that country will elect a communist government, and if they do, they are still entitled to equal status with the other governments of Central America. At the same time, we celebrate the fact that in central Europe people of several countries are finally being allowed to express themselves by throwing off the stranglehold of communist ideology imposed on them by forces outside their culture. Ethical communicators place a high value on the right of cultures to be full partners in the international dialogue, regardless of how popular or unpopular their political ideas may be. It is the height of ethnocentrism, and also unethical, to accord people of another culture equal status in the international arena only if they choose to express themselves in the same way we do.

Principle #4—Ethical communicators strive for identification with people of other cultures.

Identification is achieved when people share some principles in common, which they can do while still retaining the uniqueness of their cultural identities (Burke, 1969, p. 21). This principle suggests that ethical communicators encourage people of all cultures to understand each other, striving for unity of spirit. They do this by emphasizing the commonalities among cultural beliefs and values, rather than their differences.

At the present time we are, unfortunately, seeing an increasing number of racial incidents occurring on our college and university campuses. Many times these take the form of racist slogans appearing on the walls of campus buildings. The purpose of these actions is often to stir up racial animosity, creating wider divisions among ethnic groups. Such behavior is unethical according to this principle in that it is far more likely to lead to conflict than it is to peace.

ACKNOWLEDGMENT

The author wishes to thank Angela Latham-Jones for her critical comments on an earlier version of this essay.

References

Babbili, A. S. (1983). *The problem of international discourse: Search for cultural, moral and ethical imperatives.* Paper presented at the convention of the Association for Education in Journalism and Mass Communication, Corvallis, Oregon.

Bok, S. (1978). *Lying: Moral choice in public and private life.* New York: Random House.

Bonhoeffer, D. (1965). *Ethics.* Eberhard Bethge, ed. New York: Macmillan.

Brummett, B. (1981). A defense of ethical relativism as rhetorically grounded. *Western Journal of Speech Communication, 45*(4), 286–298.

Buber, M. (1965). *I and thou.* New York: Peter Smith.

Burke, K. (1969). *A rhetoric of motives.* Berkeley: University of California Press.

Eubanks, R. (1980). Reflections on the moral dimension of communication. *Southern Speech Communication Journal, 45*(3), 240–248.

Hauerwas, S. (1983). *The peaceable kingdom.* South Bend, IN: University of Notre Dame.

Howell, W. (1981). *Ethics of intercultural communication.* Paper presented at the 67th convention of the Speech Communication Association, Anaheim, California.

Howell, W. (1982). *Carrying ethical concepts across cultural boundaries.* Paper presented at the 68th convention of the Speech Communication Association, Louisville, Kentucky.

Jaska, J., & Pritchard, M. (1988). *Communication ethics: Methods of analysis.* Belmont, CA: Wadsworth.

Johannesen, R. (1978). *Ethics in human communication.* Wayne, NJ: Avery.

Kale, D. (1983, September). In defense of two ethical universals in intercultural communication. *Religious Communication Today, 6,* 28–33.

LaFave, L., & Mannell, R. (1978). Does ethnic humor serve prejudice? *Journal of Communication,* Summer, 116–124.

Vivas, E. (1963). *The moral life and the ethical life.* Chicago: Henry Regnery.

Weaver, R. (1971). *Ideas have consequences.* Chicago: University of Chicago Press.

Concepts and Questions

1. How do culturally different concepts of right and wrong affect intercultural communication?
2. What conditions constitute an ethical issue in human communication?
3. Why does Kale suggest that there can be no such thing as a totally individual system of ethics?
4. Given the cultural relativity of ethics, under what conditions is it permissible for people of one culture to attempt to persuade people of other cultures to accept their values?
5. How may the human spirit serve as a basis for a universal ethic?
6. What is minimal peace? How does it differ from moderate peace?
7. Under what circumstances does optimal peace exist? Is optimal peace a realistic goal in international relations?
8. What is the first step to being ethical in any culture?
9. What is the main point associated with the ethical principle that communicators should seek to describe the world as they perceive it as accurately as possible?
10. How can individuals develop the capability to fulfill the ethical principle that ethical communicators strive for identification with people of other cultures?

New Perspectives: Prospects for the Future

All things are daily changing.

PLUTARCH

*To me there is something thrilling and
exalting in the thought that we are drifting
forward in a splendid mystery—into
something that no mortal eye hath yet seen,
and no intelligence has yet declared.*

E. H. CHAPIN

*Because things are the way they are, things
will not stay the way they are.*

BERTOLT BRECHT

A principal objective of this fortieth anniversary edition has been to look backward to see where the discipline of intercultural communication began and to examine how it has progressed over the past four decades. That perspective guided the construction and content of the initial eight chapters. The retrospective offered in the preceding essays clearly demonstrates the growth, complexity, and increased necessity of intercultural communication competency in the current era of globalization. Drawing on that philosophy, we felt it important to consider the road ahead, the future of the discipline. Accordingly, we asked six noted scholars from the field to offer their insights on the continuing evolution and growth of intercultural communication. Their visions are contained in the following five essays written specifically for this fourteenth edition of the reader.

This chapter's first essay, "From Culture to Interculture: Communication, Adaptation, and Identity Transformation in the Globalizing World," echoes an implicit topic in this volume's selections from early editions and an explicit topic in those from later editions—globalization and cultural change. Kim perceptively points out that globalization has transformed, and continues to transform, the many and variant aspects of human interaction. She contends that "culture in its pure form has become more a nostalgic concept than a reality." In other words, in contemporary society, change, not stability, has become the norm.

Quite naturally, these dynamic and near constant changes are corrosive to social continuity and stressful for the individual, and both are subjected to a process of adaption through communication. Of particular interest to Kim is the stress created when individuals are confronted with frictions arising from the "interface of differing cultural traditions." The successful management of, and adaptation to, these circumstances carries the very real promise of transforming one's identity from being "cultural" to becoming "intercultural." The process is explained through the "stress-adaptation-growth dynamic" model, which illustrates how successful adaptation to stress, such as that produced by cultural change, can ultimately bring about a transformation from "cultural" to "intercultural." The insight offered by Kim in this essay is especially timely and relevant to the dynamic societal changes arising from globalization. She presents a path for understanding and successfully adapting to contemporary cultural changes, one which also portends societal and personal advancement.

As was discussed in Chapter 1, intercultural communication is not a new phenomenon. It has been a factor throughout history. However, as Bernard Saint-Jacques points out in "The Multiculturalism Dilemma," the past fifty years have witnessed a dramatic rise in the number of people taking residence in countries outside their native lands. This cultural mixing has produced societies more ethnically, culturally, linguistically, and religiously diverse than at any time in the past. This cultural mixing has made obsolete the traditional concept of nation-states being predominantly homogeneous. According to Saint-Jacques, we are now living in an age of "super diversity."

In some cases, the growing number of immigrants has given rise to negative perceptions of multiculturalism. This is often the case when dominant cultural groups have felt threatened by the new arrivals, who usually bring alien values, languages, customs, and behaviors. According to Saint-Jacques, the reality of "super diversity" has given rise to a basic question—how can people with contrasting ethnic, cultural, and linguistic backgrounds live harmoniously and communicate effectively? His answer is *multiculturalism*, which is discussed from three different perspectives: (1) introducing courses on different cultures into the educational system, (2) multicultural education, and (3) multiculturalism as an ideology or political system.

Saint-Jacques contends that because the United States and Canada are the products of large numbers of immigrants, the two countries offer a rich selection of materials addressing multiculturalism from both a critical and a positive vantage point. His essay examines both sides of "immigrant multiculturalism" in the United States and Canada as presented in contemporary literature. From this comparison, Saint-Jacques concludes that successful multiculturalism requires that immigrants learn the language and acquiesce to the cultural and societal variations of their new homes while keeping their own language and culture alive. In addition, he calls for governments to view citizens "as individuals rather than as groups."

The third essay, "Asiacentricity and Shapes of the Future," is a thought-provoking, broad-based examination of intercultural communication that provides a constructive critique of the discipline's past. Recommendations also are provided to help guide future directions in a globalized society. Yoshitaka Miike and Jing Yin contend that intercultural communication "still suffers from comparative Eurocentricism" (the tendency to view the world, and other people, from the perspective of European cultural values). To overcome this problem, the authors advocate examining the culturally embedded contrastive styles and goals of communication usage in different cultures. This is illustrated through an examination of intercultural communication from Afro-centric and Asiacentric perspectives, which are then contrasted to the Eurocentric viewpoint. An objective of Miike and Yin is to demonstrate the necessity of viewing intercultural communication through a variety of culturally based lenses. They effectively use Hinduism, Buddhism, Confucianism, and Islam to illustrate that contention.

The essay purports that globalization demands scholars in the field of intercultural communication rethink the traditional approaches that have been part of this field since its inception. Specifically, the authors advocate using fresh perspectives to help understand identity, community, and communication ethics. More broadly, they call for communication researchers to advance a new and comprehensive "philosophy and policy of intercultural communication." Miike and Yin conclude their examination of intercultural communication by pointing out the discipline's extraordinary growth—both domestically and internationally—over the past forty years and underscore the ever-increasing importance of competent communication between cultures.

The last couple of decades have seen a dramatic growth in China's economic and geopolitical importance on the world stage. The potential for tensions between China and the United States, as well as other nations in the near region of China, has grown in concert with Beijing's rising desire to assume a greater international role. In the fourth essay of this chapter, Guo-Ming Chen offers his insight and recommendations on how to bring about more harmonious and effective East–West communication. He begins by contrasting and discussing differences between the United States and China using the philosophical contexts of (1) ontology, (2) axiology, (3) epistemology, and (4) methodology. Chen cogently points out that cultural awareness and an understanding of differences alone do not guarantee successful intercultural communication interaction—a tolerance or acceptance of differences is also required. He proposes using a process termed "boundary wisdom" as a means of enhancing effective intercultural communication in a globalized world. This process can be visualized as drawing on outside differences to challenge one's personal core values. The *tai chi* model of *yin* and *yang* (equal but opposing forces) is used to illustrate the boundary wisdom process. Chen ends with the observation that globalization is irreversible, and to function successfully in contemporary multicultural society one must learn to accept intercultural differences.

Our final essay examines a topic that is particularly relevant in the contemporary globalized society—new media. The digital revolution has, in a very short period, enabled people around the world to communicatively interact across national and cultural borders. Whether it be email, Twitter, Skype, or some other form of media, people from different cultures are now commonly communicating for professional, social, and recreational purposes. Emergent new media forms are transforming traditional intercultural communication by expanding the communication context far beyond the limits of face-to-face interaction. Robert Shuter asserts that culture and new media are interwoven. Culture influences societal use of new media, and new media concomitantly bring change to culture. To meet the challenges and help understand the transformation produced by new media innovation, a new area of communication investigation is proposed—Intercultural New Media Studies (INMS). The objective of INMS is to "identify new digital theories of intercultural contact as well as refine and expand twentieth-century theories of intercultural communication." In this comprehensive essay, Shuter conceptualizes the parameters of the two major areas of INMS: (1) new media and intercultural communication theory and (2) culture and new media. He concludes with a call for a reexamination and reconfiguration of major intercultural communication theories to make them more applicable to the digital age.

From Culture to Interculture: Communication, Adaptation, and Identity Transformation in the Globalizing World

Young Yun Kim

When the skies grow dark, the stars begin to shine.

Charles Austin Beard (1874–1948)

We are all migrants now. We are in the throes of a worldwide integration of cultures, a tectonic shift of habits and dreams called globalization—the communicative integration of the world in which human activities that used to be bounded by culture now play out on the world's stage. The all-encompassing changes in human affairs that globalization renders are no longer a choice, but a pervasive and compelling reality.

All changes are stress-producing, and the contemporary world is under tension. Many feel lost, resist change, and fight for the old ways in search of authenticity in a world of clashing traditions and identities. The very forces that diminish physical boundaries exacerbate ethnic and national rivalries, rendering alarming daily news headlines and a deeply unsettling political landscape. From long-festering prejudices and hatreds to the more recent acts of violent rage and terror, people in all corners of the world are witnessing the rapid escalation of angry words, hurt, and destruction. In many countries, the relatively simple civic consensus in the vision of a diverse, but

peaceful and democratic, society is being challenged by one that upholds a particular cultural identity in place of the larger identity of citizenry. The seemingly innocent banner of cultural identity is often a compelling sore spot and a rallying point, galvanizing people into us-against-them posturing. Largely absent in such identity polemics are the main ideals of diversity and multiculturalism itself, that is, people with different roots can coexist, they can learn from each other, and they can, and should, look across and beyond the frontiers of traditional group boundaries with minimum prejudice or illusion.

Against this landscape of clashing identities, this essay addresses another unfolding reality of globalization that is largely hidden from daily news headlines—the adaptation of individuals to the increasing interface of differing cultural traditions. At the forefront of this phenomenon are the numerous individuals who change homes each year crossing cultural boundaries—from immigrants and refugees resettling in search of a new life, to temporary sojourners finding employment overseas, governmental agency employees, Peace Corps volunteers, military personnel, exchange students, and the like. Physical distance no longer dictates the extent of exposure to the images and sounds of once distant cultures. Many urban centers present their own contexts of new cultural learning and adaptation as the natives are routinely engaging in face-to-face contacts with people of differing ethnic and cultural backgrounds.

The author's main interest in discussing the phenomenon of cross-cultural adaptation is to highlight its potential for transforming an individual's identity from a cultural to an increasingly intercultural one. The author seeks to demonstrate that, through extensive and prolonged experiences of intercultural communication and adaptation to a new and changing cultural environment, an individual's identity orientation is likely to undergo a gradual and largely unconscious process of reaching beyond the parameters of a single culture. With this aim, the author offers in this essay some new insights she has gained since the 1980s when she wrote the two essays that appear elsewhere in this anniversary volume: "Adapting to a New Culture" and "Intercultural Personhood: An Integration of Eastern and Western Perspectives." Reflecting on these two previous essays, and based on the integrative theory of communication and cross-cultural adaptation developed and refined since the early 1980s (Kim, 1988, 2001, 2005, 2011), the author puts forth an argument that intercultural transformation of an individual's identity is not only a theoretical possibility, but also an achievable goal toward which we may strive as we search for a constructive way of being engaged in the globalizing world.

THE PROCESS OF CROSS-CULTURAL ADAPTATION

Adaptation is one of the fundamental life-sustaining and life-enhancing activities, one that is deeply rooted in the self-organizing, self-regulating, or integrative capacity in all living systems, particularly humans (Jantsch, 1980; Kauffman, 1995). Through adaptation, we are able to learn and be changed by new learning. This basic adaptive capacity is a built-in biological feature of the human mind and is manifested in the plasticity we enjoy, including the relative freedom to free ourselves from archaic and unnecessary constraints, and to negotiate the complexities of the cultural environment. We humans are "active, if not always successful, strategists of their own development and synthesizers of their own 'inclusive self-interest' in a world of deceptively competing and overlapping interests" (Slavin & Kriegman, 1992, p. 11). Cross-cultural adaptation, then, can be understood as a special case of the natural human tendency of self-organizing in response to a new or changing cultural environment.

ADAPTATION AS A COMMUNICATION PHENOMENON

Grounded in the General Systems perspective (Bertalanffy, 1956; Ruben, 1972), this author regards each person as an "open system" that exchanges information with the environment through communication, and co-evolves with the environment. As such, a person's internal constitution undergoes changes throughout life. At the intersection of the person and the environment, adaptation is a process that occurs in, and through, communication activities. Adaptive change takes place as long as individuals are engaged in a given sociocultural environment through the exchange of messages. The input and output messages are not limited to linguistic or other explicitly coded symbols such as traffic signs and mathematical symbols. The messages also include more spontaneous and expressive nonverbal messages that are often unintentional and implied, that is, all actions and events (as well as non-actions and non-events).

In the words of Watzlawick, Beavin, and Jackson (1967), "One cannot not communicate." As communicators, we as individuals "record, monitor, and promote a dialectical process in which the ambiguous, deception-filled web of competing and overlapping interests in the relational world is continuously negotiated and renegotiated" (Slavin & Kriegman, 1992, p. 12). Underscored in this view is that communication is the necessary vehicle without which adaptation cannot take place, and that adaptation occurs as long as the individual remains in interaction with the environment. Accordingly, cross-cultural adaptation is defined as the communication process in which individuals strive to establish and maintain a relatively stable, reciprocal, and functional relationship with a changing or changed cultural environment. At the core of this definition is the goal of achieving an overall person-environment "fit" between an individual's internal conditions and the conditions of the environment. Adaptation, thus, is an activity that is "almost always a compromise, a vector in the internal structure of culture and the external pressure of environment" (Sahlins, 1964, p. 136).

ACCULTURATION AND DECULTURATION

The activities of intercultural contact, communication, and new cultural learning is the essence of *acculturation,* that is, the acquisition of the new cultural patterns and practices in wide-ranging areas including the learning of a new language, norms, and practices. An equally significant aspect of the learning entails the acquisition of new cultural aesthetic and emotional sensibilities, from a new way of appreciating beauty, fun, joy, as well as despair, anger, and the like.

Acculturation does not occur randomly or automatically following intercultural exposures. New cultural elements are not simply added to prior internal conditions. Rather, it is a process over which each individual has a degree of freedom or control, based on his or her predispositions, pre-existing needs, and interests. Such an ego-protective and ego-centric psychological principle is demonstrated, for example, in Chang's (2001) finding, in a study of Asian immigrants in Singapore, of relatively higher levels of acculturation in workplace-related and public norms and values compared to private realms and home life. Nevertheless, the experience of acculturation, over time, brings about the development of cognitive complexity, that is, the structural refinement in an individual's information-processing capacity with respect to the newly encountered cultural milieu.

As new learning occurs, *deculturation* or unlearning of at least some of the old cultural elements has to occur, in the sense that new responses are adopted in situations that previously would have evoked old ones. Deculturation is an experience that is seldom intentional or deliberate. Rather, it is a natural phenomenon that takes place in individuals engaged in the acculturative activity of acquiring something new and of the suspending of the old habit, at least temporarily. "No construction without destruction," as Burke (1974) put it. This interplay of acculturation and deculturation underlies the psychological evolution individuals undergo—from changes in "surface" areas such as outwardly expressive behaviors, for example, choices of music, food, and dress, to deeper-level changes in social role-related behaviors and fundamental values.

THE STRESS-ADAPTATION-GROWTH DYNAMIC

As acculturation and deculturation continue, each experience of adaptive change inevitably accompanies *stress* in the individual psyche—a kind of identity conflict rooted in resistance to change and the instinctive desire to retain old habits in keeping with the original identity, on the one hand, and the necessity to change behavior in seeking harmony with the new milieu, on the other. This conflict is essentially between the need for acculturation and the resistance to deculturation, that is, the "push" of the new culture and the "pull"

of the old. The internal disequilibrium created by such conflicting forces can be manifested in intense emotional "lows" of uncertainty, confusion, and anxiety. Such intense situations can generate moments of "crises" in which our mental and behavioral habits are brought into awareness and called into question.

Stress, indeed, is an expression of the instinctive human desire to restore homeostasis, that is, to hold constant a variety of variables in internal structure to achieve an integrated whole. Some people may attempt to avoid or minimize the anticipated or actual "pain" of disequilibrium by selective attention, denial, avoidance, and withdrawal, as well as by compulsively altruistic behavior, cynicism, and hostility toward the new or changed external reality. Others may seek to regress to an earlier state of existence in the familiar "old" culture, a state in which there is no feeling of isolation, no feeling of separation. Even in the form of anguish and tribulations, however, stress presents us with an opportunity to search deeply inside ourselves for new possibilities to recreate ourselves. Stress, in this regard, is intrinsic to the complex human psychological system and essential in the adaptation process—one that allows for self-(re)organization and self-renewal. Over time, such internal conflicts make individuals susceptible to external influence and compel them to acquire new habits. For most people, internal changes take hold as they embrace environmental challenges and strive to stabilize themselves by overcoming the predicament and partake in the act of *adaptation*.

What follows a long-term and cumulative experience and successful management of the stress-adaptation disequilibrium is a subtle and often imperceptible psychological *growth*, that is, an increased complexity in an individual's internal system. Periods of stress pass as an individual works out new ways of handling problems, owing to the creative forces of self-reflexivity of human mentation. Together, the concepts of stress, adaptation, and growth constitute three-pronged experiences of the *stress-adaptation-growth dynamic*—a psychological movement in the forward and upward direction of increased chances of success in a changing or changed environment (see Figure 1). In this process of personal evolution, individuals experience varying degrees of "boundary-ambiguity syndromes" (Hall, 1976, p. 227), in which the original cultural identity begins to lose its

Figure 1 *The Stress-Adaptation-Growth Dynamic*

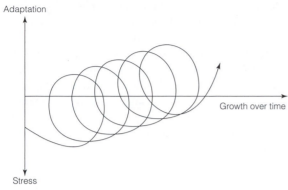

Adaptation

Growth over time

Stress

Source: Kim, 2001, p. 59

distinctiveness and rigidity while an expanded and more flexible self-definition emerges.

As depicted in Figure 1, the stress-adaptation-growth dynamic does not play out in a smooth, steady, and linear progression, but in a continual and cyclic "draw-back-to-leap" pattern. Each stressful experience is responded to with a "draw back" (or a state of "regression"), which, in turn, activates adaptive energy to help individuals reorganize themselves and "leap forward." As growth of some units always occurs at the expense of others, the adaptation process follows a pattern that juxtaposes integration and disintegration, progression and regression, and novelty and confirmation. This systems-theoretic explanation echoes Dubos' (1965) view of human adaptation as "a dialectic between permanence and change" (p. 2).

The stress-adaptation-growth transformative process continues as long as there are new environmental challenges, with the overall forward and upward movement in the direction of greater adaptation and growth. In this process, as shown in Figure 1, large and sudden changes are more likely to occur during the initial phase of exposure to a new or changing cultural milieu. Such drastic changes are themselves indicative of the severity of difficulties and disruptions. Over a long period of undergoing internal change, the diminishing fluctuations of stress and adaptation become less intense or severe, leading to an overall "calming" of our internal condition.

IDENTITY TRANSFORMATION: INDIVIDUATION AND UNIVERSALIZATION

Emerging from the experiences of acculturation, deculturation, and the stress-adaptation-growth dynamic is an *intercultural identity*—an open-ended, adaptive, and transformative self-other orientation. One of the two key elements of intercultural identity development is *individuation* that involves a clear self-definition and definition of the other as a singular individual rather than a member of a conventional social category. With this capacity, one is better able to see oneself and others on the basis of unique individual qualities rather than categorical stereotypes. Individuation, thus, fosters a mental outlook that exhibits greater cognitive differentiation and particularization (Oddou & Mendenhall, 1984). Accompanying individuation is *universalization* in self-other orientation, a parallel development of a synergistic cognition "of a new consciousness...born out of an awareness of the relative nature of values and of the universal aspect of human nature" (Yoshikawa, 1978, p. 220).

As we advance in this identity transformation process, we are, at once, more likely to see the individual particularities of cultural strangers we encounter beyond their group generalities and stereotypes, as well as the common humanity we share with them beyond the cultural differences between us and them. The two interrelated identity development processes, individuation and universalization, enable us to overcome parochialism and form a vital outlook that is not locked in a provincial interest of our own group membership, but one in which we are better able to locate the points of consent and complementarity beyond the points of difference and contention.

Existing terms similar to the present theoretical concept, intercultural identity, include "meta-identity" and "cosmopolitan" or "transcultural" identity. These concepts, while not addressing the phenomenon of individuation, signify a less dualistic and more meta-contextual, universalized outlook on self and others than the rigid boundedness of conventional social categories such as ethnicity or culture. Intercultural identity, however, is to be differentiated from other terms that represent various forms of additions of specific cultural components such as bicultural, multicultural, or hybrid identity. While incorporating the common thrust of these terms, intercultural identity goes beyond them, highlighting one of the well-known central maxims for all living systems: The whole is greater than the sum of its parts. The cultural base of an individual identity is not going to disappear until the end of one's life, even if one wanted to remove it. What does happen in the process of intercultural transformation is a juxtaposition of deculturation and acculturation—one loses some and gains some—in doing so becomimg something else, as represented by a formula, A + B = A′ + B′ + X, with A′ and B′ representing modifications in some of the original (A) and new (B) cultural patterns and X representing the extra dimension of individuation and universalization in an individual's identity and personhood.

EMPIRICAL EVIDENCE

A broad array of research studies provides direct and indirect support for the present theoretical accounts of acculturation and deculturation, and of the interrelationship of intercultural stress and subsequent adaptation and growth leading to a gradual intercultural transformation. Such empirical evidence comes largely from more than half a century of social scientific studies of immigrants and of temporary sojourners conducted largely in the United States and, more recently, in other parts of the world. (See Kim, 2001, for an extensive documentation of empirical evidence.) Eaton and Lasry (1978), for example, reported that the stress level of more upwardly mobile immigrants was greater than of those who were less upwardly mobile. Among Japanese-Americans (Marmot & Syme, 1976) and Mexican-American women (Miranda & Castro, 1977), the better adapted immigrants had initially experienced a somewhat greater frequency of stress-related symptoms (such as anxiety and a need for psychotherapy) than the less adapted group. In addition, Suro (1998) reported that Hispanics in the United States showed diminished Hispanic cultural patterns in their judgments and increased social interactions with non-Hispanics. Another study by Dasgupta (1983) indicated that Asian-Indian immigrants were able to resolve the conflict between their traditional value of holism

and ascription and the American cultural values of individualism, achievement, and competition by dichotomizing and attaining a healthy balance between primary ingroup relationships and achievement in their occupational lives in the larger society.

Data from studies of temporary sojourners have shown similar patterns of relationship between stress, adaptation, and growth. Findings from Ruben and Kealey's (1979) study of Canadian technical advisors in Nigeria, for example, suggested that those who were the most effective in their new environment underwent the most intense culture shock during the initial transition period. Similarly, in a study in Japan among college students from the United States and a number of other countries, Milstein (2005) concluded that the sojourn experience resulted in increased levels of "self-efficacy." Employing the present theoretical account of the stress-adaptation-growth dynamic, Milstein showed further that the increase in self-efficacy was linked positively to the level of challenge the students reported to have experienced and to the eventual perceived success of their sojourn. In another study employing 15-month ethnographic fieldwork among American exchange students studying in a college in France, Pitts (2009) has described in detail how, at various stages of the sojourn, the stress-adaptation-growth dynamic plays out in the college students' intercultural experiences and in their own verbal accounts thereof. Likewise, intercultural identity development and emergence of intercultural personhood have been observed by Shearer (2003) in native-born "mainstream" individuals. Using a biographical case study method, Shearer examined two white Australians' intercultural communication experiences over the years. Through an in-depth biographical-interpretive analysis, Shearer reported that the cases of two mainstream Australians show some evidence of intercultural personhood and make identity claims comparable with immigrants and minority ethnic individuals.

CASE ILLUSTRATIONS

Further evidence for the present theoretical account of cross-cultural adaptation and intercultural transformation can be found in a variety of publicly available first-hand personal accounts told in biographical stories. Such accounts have appeared in case studies, memoirs, biographical stories, and essays of self-reflection. These personal accounts bear witness to concrete realities that illuminate the aforementioned theoretical explication of intercultural identity in terms of individuation and universalization.

One of the most pointed testimonials to the present formulation of individuation and universalization in intercultural identity transformation was offered by Mueno Yoshikawa (1978). As someone who had lived in Japan and in the United States, Yoshikawa offered the following insight into his own personal evolution—an insight that captures the very essence of what it means to be an intercultural person:

I am now able to look at both cultures with objectivity as well as subjectivity; I am able to move in both cultures, back and forth without any apparent conflict. . . . I think that something *beyond the sum of each [cultural] identification* took place, and that it became something akin to the concept of "*synergy*"—when one adds 1 and 1, one gets three, or a little more. This something extra is not culture specific but something unique of its own, probably the *emergence of a new attribute or a new self-awareness*, born out of an awareness of the relative nature of values and of the universal aspect of human nature. . . . I really am not concerned whether others take me as a Japanese or an American; I can accept myself as I am. I feel I am much *freer* than ever before, not only in the cognitive domain (perception, thoughts, etc.), but also in the affective (feeling, attitudes, etc.) and behavioral domains. (Italics added; p. 220)

The creative insight into human conditions rooted in the life of intercultural personhood appears to have been also the driving passion for the 2006 winner of the Nobel Prize in Literature, the Turkish novelist Orhan Pamuk. Pamuk is recognized for having captured in his writings new symbols for the interlacing of cultures. In an interview with National Public Radio following the Nobel Prize announcement (National Public Radio, October 12, 2006), Pamuk was reminded by the interviewer that he had talked previously about "coming from one of those countries...on the periphery of the Western world where the art was developed, and being one of those writers who is grabbing that art from the center to the periphery and then *producing something new* to show the world" (Italics added). Pamuk reaffirmed this intercultural theme in his work and suggests the intercultural nature of his own identity as follows:

My whole book, my whole life, is a testimony to the fact that East and West actually *combine, come together gracefully and produce something new*. That is what I have been trying to do all my life.... I don't believe in clashes of civilization. I think that was a fanciful idea which, unfortunately, is sometimes coming to be true. But no, I think that East and West meet. I think that my whole work is a testimony to the fact that *we should find ways of looking, combining East and West without any clash, but with harmony, with grace, and produce something new for humanity*. (Italics added)

Another illustration of intercultural identity development is found in an essay written by an African-American economist Glenn Loury (1993). In the following excerpt, Loury (1993) reflects on his own identity evolution that is no longer defined by his race, but by his individual and human conditions.

I no longer believe that the camaraderie engendered among blacks by our collective experience of racism constitutes an adequate basis for any person's self-definition....The most important challenges and opportunities that confront me derive *not from my racial condition, but rather from my human condition*. I am a husband, a father, a son, a teacher, an intellectual, a Christian, a citizen. In none of these roles is my race irrelevant, but neither can racial identity alone provide much guidance for my quest to adequately discharge these responsibilities. The particular features of my social condition, the external givens, merely set the stage of my life, they do not provide a script. *That script must be internally generated*....In my view, a personal identity wholly dependent on racial contingency falls tragically short of its potential because it embraces too parochial a conception of what is possible, and of what is desirable. (pp. 7–10)

TOWARD INTERCULTURAL PERSONHOOD

The tightly knit system of communication and transportation continues to bring differing cultures, nationalities, races, religions, and linguistic communities closer than ever before in a web of interdependence and a common fate. In this intercultural world, the business-as-usual ways of doing things are fast losing their relevance, as culture in its pure form has become more a nostalgic concept than a reality. They are challenged to face one another's various differences and search for human similarities, so as to be able to move beyond their customary imagination in search of creative solutions to problems. Such routine encounters compel everyone involved to put aside and even unlearn at least some of the original cultural patterns.

Indeed, globalization has made cross-cultural adaptation and intercultural transformation the "business of our time" (Kim, 2001, p. 234). Whether at home or on foreign soil, numerous people the world over are being challenged to undergo at least some degree of acculturation, deculturation, and the experience of the stress-adaptation-growth dynamic. To the individuals, social organizations, communities, and nations that are nostalgic for the age of certainty, permanence, and a fixed and unitary cultural identity, this changing global reality can represent a particularly unsettling discontinuity and malaise. One may refuse to admit this reality, but only at the cost of the immense effort of spending one's life resisting or denying it. Although such a psychological posture may help one to "feel better," at least temporarily, about oneself and one's group, it is also likely to engender a further refusal to adapt.

Yet, the dynamic nature of cross-cultural adaptation and intercultural identity development points to an alternative way of living in the world. It is a journey that compels us to make choices and to be accountable for the outcomes. Those who have successfully crossed cultural boundaries are likely to be those who chose to adapt and to be changed by that choice. It shows us that we can strive to embrace and incorporate seemingly divergent cultural elements into something new and unique—something that conjoins and integrates, rather than separates and divides. It projects the real possibility of cultivating a special kind of mindset in which cross-borrowing of identities is not an act of "surrendering" one's personal and cultural integrity, but an act of appreciation for, and a creative integration of, cultural differences that leaves neither the lender nor the borrower deprived.

It is, in the end, up to each of us to decide how we wish to relate to the changing global environment. Meanwhile, the earlier testimonials of Yoshikawa, Pamuk, and Loury bring the theoretical explication of intercultural identity development to a tangible reality, with their own words affirming the possibility that the experiences of going through adaptive challenges bring about a special privilege and freedom—to think, feel, and act creatively beyond the confines of any single culture in our increasingly interconnected world.

References

Bertalanffy, L. (1956). General systems theory. *General Systems,* 1, 1–2.

Burke, K. (1974). Communication and the human condition. *Communication,* 1. United Kingdom: Gordon and Breach Science Publishers, 135–52.

Chang, W. C. (2001, April). *A model of situation-specific multiculturalism of Asian immigrants in Singapore.* Paper presented at the 2nd biennial congress of the International Academy for Intercultural Research, Oxford, Mississippi.

Dasgupta, S. (1983). *Indian immigrants: The evolution of an ethnic group.* Unpublished doctoral dissertation, University of Delaware, Newark, New Jersey.

Dubos, R. (1965). *Man adapting.* New Haven, CT: Yale University Press.

Eaton, W., & Lasry, J. (1978). Mental health and occupational mobility in a group of immigrants. *Science and Medicine,* 12, 53–58.

Hall, E. (1976). *Beyond culture.* Garden City, NY: Anchor.

Jantsch, E. (1980). *The self-organizing universe: Scientific and human implications of the emerging paradigm of evolution.* New York: Pergamon.

Kauffman, S. (1995). *At home in the universe: The search for the laws of self-organization and complexity.* New York: Oxford University Press.

Kim, Y. Y. (1988). *Communication and cross-cultural adaptation: An integrative theory.* Clevedon, United Kingdom: Multilingual Matters.

Kim, Y. Y. (2001). *Becoming intercultural: An integrative theory of communication and cross-cultural adaptation.* Thousand Oaks, CA: Sage.

Kim, Y. Y. (2005). Adapting to a new culture: An integrative communication theory. In W. Gudykunst (Ed.), *Theorizing about intercultural communication* (pp. 375–400). Thousand Oaks, CA: Sage.

Kim, Y. Y. (2011). Beyond categories: Communication, adaptation, and transformation. In J. Jackson (Ed.), *Handbook of language and intercultural communication* (pp. 229–243). New York: Routledge.

Loury, G. C. (1993). Free at last? A personal perspective on race and identity in America. In G. Early (Ed.), *Lure and loathing: Essays on race, identity, and the ambivalence of assimilation* (pp. 1–12). New York: Penguin.

Marmot, M., & Syme, S. (1976). Acculturation and coronary heart disease in Japanese-Americans. *American Journal of Epidemiology,* 104(3), 225–247.

Milstein, T. J. (2005). Transformation abroad: Sojourning and the perceived enhancement of self-efficacy. *International Journal of Intercultural Relations,* 29(2), 217–238.

Miranda, M., & Castro, F. (1977). Culture distance and success in psychotherapy with Spanish speaking clients. In J. Martinez Jr. (Ed.), *Chicano Psychology* (pp. 249–262). New York: Academic Press.

National Public Radio (October 12, 2006). Once resented, Pamuk takes solace in Nobel. Interview transcript from *All Things Considered.* Retrieved from http://www.npr.org/templates/story/story.php?storyId=625630

Oddou, G., & Mendenhall, M. (1984). Person perception in cross-cultural settings. *International Journal of Intercultural Relations,* 8(1), 77–96.

Pitts, M. (2009). Identity and the role of expectations, stress, and talk in short-term student sojourner adjustment: An application of the integrative theory of communication and cross-cultural adaptation. *International Journal of Intercultural Relations* 33(6), 450–462.

Ruben, B. D. (1972). General system theory: An approach to human communication. In R. Budd & B. D. Ruben (Eds.), *Approaches to human communication* (pp. 120–144). Rochelle Park, NJ: Hayden Books.

Ruben, B., & Kealey, D. (1979). Behavioral assessment of communication competency and the prediction of cross-cultural adaptation. *International Journal of Intercultural Relations,* 3(1), 15–27.

Sahlins, M. (1964). Culture and environment: The study of cultural ecology. In S. Tax (Ed.), *Horizons of anthropology* (pp. 132–147). Chicago: Aldine.

Shearer, H. E. (2003, December). *Intercultural personhood: A 'mainstream' Australian biographical case study.* Unpublished doctoral dissertation, Griffith University, Mt Gravatt, Queensland, Australia.

Slavin, M., & Kriegman, D. (1992). *The adaptive design of the human psyche.* New York: Guilford.

Suro, R. (1998). *Strangers among us: How Latino immigration is transforming America.* New York: Alfred A. Knoff.

Watzlawick, P., Beavin, J. H., & Jackson, D. D. (1967). *Pragmatics of human communication: A study of interaction patterns, pathologies, and paradoxes.* New York: W. W. Norton.

Yoshikawa, M. (1978). Some Japanese and American cultural characteristics. In M. Prosser, *The cultural dialogue: An introduction to intercultural communication* (pp. 220–239). Boston, MA: Houghton Mifflin.

Concepts and Questions

1. Implicit in Kim's essay is the idea that through the exposure to globalization one's original cultural values and behaviors evolve. Provide an empirical example of this concept.

2. According to the essay, in order to become functional in the "globalizing world," one's identity needs to undergo a process of transformation. In your opinion, is this necessary and how may it be achieved?

3. Cross-cultural adaption, according to Kim, is a "communication process." Explain this concept and provide examples.

4. Think about the meaning of "deculturation." Since entering college, what aspects of your identity have undergone deculturation?

5. The change from high school to college life is similar to entering a new culture and normally involves some degree of stress. Explain some of the changes that created stress for you and how you adapted. What role did communication play?

6. Use an experience from your own life to explain how Kim's stress-adaptation-growth dynamic model works.

7. Kim asserts that "culture in its pure form has become more a nostalgic concept than a reality." What does she mean by this? Do you agree? Why?

8. The essay concludes with the observation that the changes brought about by globalization can be disquieting to those "individuals, social organizations, communities, and nations that are nostalgic for the age of certainty." Identify some instances where cultural change brought about by globalization is creating conflict between groups and organizations in the United States. What are the ways these conflicts are being communicated?

The Multiculturalism Dilemma

BERNARD SAINT-JACQUES

INTRODUCTION

There is a phenomenon in the modern world which has never happened with similar intensity and importance: people from poor countries, or countries dominated by cruel dictators, or again countries where ethnic wars are constant, escaping and migrating to richer and more peaceful countries. In recent years there is even a new type of migration—people from very affluent and wealthy countries moving to other countries where they feel life is more agreeable and where they will be allowed more freedom. This is the case of the second economic power in the world, modern China: "Money has been flooding out of China in streams of tens of billions of dollars a year as wealthy Chinese look for safe havens for their assets and for themselves in the United States, Europe, and Canada, especially in Vancouver and Toronto. Recent surveys (in 2011) have agreed that about 60% of wealthy Chinese are either in the process of emigrating or intend to do so" (Manthorpe, 2012).

In the last five decades the global number of people living outside the country where they were born has reached a number higher than at any time in history. This massive immigration has taken place in all continents of the world. Many societies in Europe, North and South America, and Asia have entered the age of "super diversity." The most important result of this massive immigration is that societies have become ethnically, culturally, linguistically, and religiously far more diverse. The traditional assumption of the nation-state where ethnicity, culture, language, and religion are homogeneous constituents of the nation is obsolete. The enormous flow of immigrants and refugees in the so-called "rich and peaceful countries" creates important economic and social problems for these countries. The people of these "rich and peaceful countries" often believe that the newcomers in their country do not integrate sufficiently, do not respect the various aspects of the culture and society of their country, and are a threat to the social and cultural identity of their country. Racism is often born and extreme-right political groups exert pressure on their governments to stop immigration. Unsurprisingly, many states have started perceiving diversity as a problem, potentially threatening national unity, while anti-immigration and xenophobic attitudes have experienced a rapid surge. The basic question arising from the reality of this super diversity of most nations in the world is how people from very different ethnic, cultural, and linguistic origins can live peacefully and communicate in a particular nation. The whole problem can be summarized in one word: *multiculturalism*. The term multiculturalism is used in two broad ways, either descriptively or normatively. As a descriptive term, it refers to the simple fact of diversity: in nations, cities, businesses, schools, etc. As a normative term, it refers to ideologies or policies that promote diversity or its political institution.

There are in the world two countries which were developed and are basically constituted by immigration, two countries which moreover offer an extremely rich, extensive, and abundant literature on multiculturalism, literature either favorable or critical of multiculturalism: The United States of America and Canada. The first section of this essay will present a comprehensive survey of studies on multiculturalism in the United States from its historical beginnings to the present, discussing the positive and negative opinions of the many authors. In the second section, a similar survey will be done for Canada. The third section will evaluate several aspects of multiculturalism comparing and contrasting multiculturalism in the two countries. The examination and analyses of multiculturalism in this essay, although based on the United States and Canada, certainly have some important relations to world multiculturalism.

The focus of this essay is "immigrant multiculturalism." The recognition of the rights of indigenous and native people cannot be equated with problems related to immigrant multiculturalism. Before entering into the three main sections of this essay, it is important to mention briefly that multiculturalism can be discussed from three different perspectives: (1) The introduction of multicultural courses (courses about various cultures) in the education system, (2) Multicultural education as the way to prepare future citizens to be able to understand and accept people in their society who are from different ethnicities and cultures and live peacefully with them, treating them as equals, (3) The third aspect, the most controversial, is multiculturalism as a political system or ideology. It refers to a set of ideas or ideals by which cultural differences in a given state are celebrated for personal and societal enrichment.

1. The introduction of courses about various cultures in the education system

The implementation of these courses was in response to the ethnic revitalization movements and to answer the needs of immigrant groups. The main purpose of these courses was to make the educational system more suited to minority groups by including programs dealing with the cultures and histories of various ethnic groups in a given society. This has been particularly evident in the United States where the general educational failure and the large number of dropouts among blacks and certain minority group students were attributed to a curriculum dominated by a white Anglo-Saxon European perspective, alien to the needs and aspirations of these students.

There are several controversial and questionable aspects of these programs. First, although these courses should present cultures in an objective way, that is not always the case. Many of these courses do not attach equal importance and objectivity to all cultures. "They commonly portray Western or Euro-American culture in a negative light and selectively ignore prominent cultural contributions made by groups that are out-of-favor with their ideology" (Schmidt, 1997, p. 11). Moreover, many of these courses offer a very simplistic view of cultures. Students are exposed to a variety of cultures as part of an enrichment experience. However, the "enrichment model," sometimes called

the "museum approach," which entails the study of artifacts and factual material about food, dress, and so on, studying diverse cultures at the level of material culture, stripping these cultures of their historical context, discussing them from an outsider's point of view, has negative results for both the ethnic minorities and the white majority. Emma LaRoque illustrates this problem after seeing a film about the Cree Indians: "We went into a teepee. We saw a drum, a moccasin, a snowshoe. Then we saw a canoe, a horse, and Indian clothes." These types of courses will simply reinforce the negative stereotypes of the majority and the inferiority complex of the minority groups (Saint-Jacques, 1999, p. 47; Fleras & Elliott, 1992, pp. 190–191).

A more tendentious aspect of some of these courses was the tendency to equate culture with race or skin color. The message was that people of different skin colors represent different cultures. "Such presentations give a distorted picture of culture; one might even call such attempts racist. Culture does not stem from people's genes or skin color. Rather, culture consists of society's institutionalized values, beliefs, and practices that are learned through human interaction, not biologically inherited. There is no such thing as a white, black, brown, or yellow culture" (Schmidt, 1997, p. 15).

Moreover, many of these programs are based on a problematic view of culture and of the individual's relationship to culture. "Globalization has changed the notion of culture. Culture can no longer be described as the property of a single ethnic group or nation. Globalization stands for the overlapping of global and local factors" (Saint-Jacques, 2011, p. 45). People in most parts of the world live within cultures that are already cosmopolitan and characterized by cultural hybridity. One cannot but agree with Waldron (1995) who rejects the premise that the options available to an individual must come from a particular culture; meaningful options may come from a variety of cultural sources (quoted in *Stanford Encyclopedia of Philosophy*, 2010). Finally, there is an evident practical problem with the selection of cultures to offer in these courses. With the extremely large number of ethnic groups, both in the United States and Canada, on what criteria can a given culture rather than another be selected? No education program could accommodate all cultures!

2. Multicultural education

Multicultural education may be defined as education reform proposals whose purposes are to "make students appreciative of diversity and respectful of all cultures" (Webster, 1997, p. 3). In other words, the main goal of multicultural education is to foster intercultural sensitivity in students. This sensitivity is evidently closely related to interpersonal sensitivity which is the ability to distinguish how others differ in their behavior, perceptions, or feelings in one's own ethnic group (Bronfenbrener et al., 1958). According to Bennett (1984), intercultural sensitivity is the development process in which one is able to transform oneself affectively, cognitively, and behaviorally from ethnocentric stages to ethnorelative stages. Seen from this objective point of view, multicultural education has very few opponents. However, an idealistic or over-simplistic interpretation of multicultural education is often the reason for its failure or rejection. One must clearly distinguish between multicultural education as an ideal, a school program, and its *possible effects on society*. To prescribe multicultural education as a sure, infallible panacea for various problems in society, whether it is racism, inequality, or discrimination, is based on a deep misunderstanding of education. The education system on its own cannot bring fundamental changes in society. The education system is only one of many societal institutions reflecting the values and attitudes of a society. "It is a universal experience—and hence one of education's few truly scientific laws—that primary and secondary schools do not lead society. They are led by it. Only a decadent society relies on schools to maintain languages, morals, ethnic identity, and religion. The fate of them is determined outside the schools and the most we can expect of schools is that they support society in its stated or unstated ambitions, or at any rate the nobler ones among them" (MacNamara, 1974).

3. Multiculturalism as an ideology or political system

It cannot be denied that in certain countries multiculturalism has some kind of reference or relevance to the political system of these countries or to a prevalent ideology. This political ideology has powerful repercussions on the national identity and collective image of a nation. In recent years this third aspect of multiculturalism has been the object of virulent polemics. The main purpose of this essay is the detailed study of multiculturalism as a political ideology in the United States and Canada.

MULTICULTURALISM IN THE UNITED STATES

The earliest reference to the American "melting pot" image is found in Hector St. John Crevecoeur's *Letters from an American Farmer,* published in London in 1782. In this monograph, de Crevecoeur, himself a naturalized American from France, writes to his friends overseas, describing Americans and their culture in the following words: "They are a mixture of English, Scotch, Irish, Dutch, Germans, and Swedes. From this promiscuous breed, that race now called Americans has arisen.... Here [in the U.S.] individuals of all nations are melted in a new race" (Schmidt, 1997, p. 106). The French observer, Alexis de Tocqueville, in 1830, was fascinated by this power of assimilation: "How does it happen that in the United States where the inhabitants have only immigrated to the land they now occupy... where, in short, the instinctive love of country can scarcely exist; how does it happen that everyone takes as zealous an interest in the affairs of his township, his country, and the whole state as if they were his own" (de Tocqueville, 1945, p. 250). This assimilation ideology, pervasive near the turn of the century and during World War I, was embodied and expressed in the play, *The Melting Pot,* by Israel Zangwill. The son of a Jewish immigrant, Zangwill illustrated in this play the melting pot reality by portraying the life of a Jewish immigrant in New York, absorbing American culture and the English language. The play opened in 1908 and became a tremendous success.

The first serious opponent of America's great melting pot was Horace Kallen, the son of a German rabbi. He advocated and coined the term, cultural pluralism, which was diametrically opposed to the melting pot ideology. Kallen harbored a strong dislike for the assimilated culture of the United States (Schmidt, 1997, p. 106). America "did not have a single national culture," wrote Kallen (1924), rather it had many different cultures: "the peculiarity of our nationalism is its internationalism....Democracy involves, not the elimination of differences, but the perfection and conservation of differences." Thanks to immigration, "the United States are in the process of becoming a federal state, not merely as a union of geographical and administrative unities, but also as a cooperation of cultural diversities, as a federation or commonwealth of national cultures" (Kallen, 1924, pp. 132, 61, 116). For Kallen, the toleration of ethnic differences was not sufficient, the social affirmation of these differences was necessary. It is tempting to establish a parallel with former Canadian Prime Minister Pierre Trudeau's declaration in the House of Commons, October 8, 1971: "I am sure that there cannot be one cultural policy for Canadians of British and French origins, another for the original peoples, and yet a third for all others. For although there are two official languages, there is no official culture, nor does any ethnic group take precedence over any other" (Saint-Jacques, 1976, p. 20).

Kallen was the first interculturalist in the United States. Although his ideas had little impact at the time, they became enormously influential later in the century. Recent proponents of Kallen's ideas in the United States have been quite prolific and the number of books defending some forms of multiculturalism is most impressive: Asante, 1989; Dathorne, 1994; Fish, 1994; Lind, 1995; Nelson et al., 1993; Takaki, 1993, are only a few examples.

At the same time demographic trends in immigration started to change dramatically. The large numbers of immigrants from Asia and Latin America became a challenge to the comfortable majority held by the white population, more specifically the Euro-American white population. Euro-Americans are already minorities in several American cities and are destined to become a minority in the state of California. The United States is the fourth largest Spanish-speaking country in the world (Vincent, 1997, p. 24).

These developments, both political and demographic, provoked nervousness within the American society of European ancestry. Allan Bloom, in his book *The Closing of the American Mind* (1987), lashes out against cultural and ethnic diversity. He stresses the importance of Western civilization for America. Arthur Schlesinger, in *The Disuniting of America: Reflections on a Multicultural Society* (1992), condemns

the cult of ethnicity—the shift from assimilationism to separatism—which is contrary to the American melting pot tradition. American history has been shaped more than anything else by British tradition and culture. In *Alien Nation: Common Sense about Immigration Disaster,* Peter Brimelow (1995) argues that the majority of immigrants coming from Asia and Latin America do not fit the traditional ideal of an American.

It is quite evident that the underlying themes of these three books are the opposition to the new demographic patterns of immigration as well as the reluctance of the traditional white Anglo-Saxon population to give up its majority status. It would be more informative, however, to focus on "multiculturalism" versus "the melting pot ideology" from the points of view of nationhood and the related concepts of unity, identity, and culture within a nation or state. For this purpose, I will discuss two books: *The Menace of Multiculturalism—Trojan Horse in America* (Schmidt, 1997) and *The Unmaking of Americans: How Multiculturalism Has Undermined the Assimilation Ethic* (Miller, 1998).

According to Miller, the United States is losing or has lost its national sense of purpose. If multiculturalism tendencies go unchecked, the result can only be the fragmentation, resegregation, and tribalization of American life. The struggle to become American is the process of assimilation, and assimilation is a vital part of keeping this nation of immigrants whole. The motto on the United States seal is *E pluribus unum* (out of many, one). Without assimilation, the *pluribus* threatens to drown out the *unum,* imperiling the very concept of American nationhood (Miller, 1998, pp. 5–7). In America the sense of peoplehood derives not from a common lineage, but from their adherence to a set of core principles about equality, liberty, and self-government. Before the founding of the United States, insists Miller, kinship—or at least the perception of kinship—was the most important element in nation building. Bloodlines united nations (Miller, 1998, p. 24). Quoting G. K. Chesterton (1923), Miller writes that "America is the only nation in the world that is founded on a creed. That creed is set forth with dogmatic and even theological lucidity in the Declaration of Independence" (1998, p. 27). For Miller, assimilation or Americanization is a constitutive aspect of nationhood in America. Paraphrasing Margaret Mead's famous passage: "George Washington does not represent the past to which one belongs by birth, but the past to which one tries to belong by effort" (1942, p. 49), Miller asserts again that "Americanization was not awarded from on high to the lucky few. It was achieved through effort, and open to people from all sorts of backgrounds" (1998, p. 93).

One more important criticism of multiculturalism developed by Miller relates to the fact that multiculturalism encourages immigrants to think of themselves as members of groups rather than as individuals. "It is very important that the government treats its citizens as individuals rather than as groups. Americanization says that membership in any particular racial or ethnic group is a private matter" (1998, p. 125). To illustrate this point, Miller recalls the testimony of a young Pakistani immigrant, named Ali Raza, who appeared before the California legislature in 1991 to testify against a proposed law which would have required schools to make their graduation classes reflect the state's racial and ethnic composition. Raza said: "When I was young [in Pakistan] my father would tell us stories at the dinner table. He would open the story by identifying the family from which the character of the story came. One day I asked him: 'Dad, what's the difference whether or not a person comes from or belongs to a particular family?' My father replied: 'Son, it matters in Pakistan what family one comes from.' And then he added: 'If you want to be judged on the basis of your individual performance, you should go to America'" (1998, p. 119).

Schmidt's epigraph to his book *The Menace of Multiculturalism* (1997) leaves no doubt about his opposition to multiculturalism: "To my dear sons, Timothy and Mark, may they do their part in keeping multiculturalism from destroying their great nation and their future." The main theme of the book is that multiculturalism in the United States promotes the importance of race, ethnicity, and cultural separateness. Quoting Martin Luther King, Schmidt writes that Americans must judge each other not by the color of their skin, but the content of their character (1997, p. xii). After all, as its name suggests, multiculturalism is a doctrine of culture. However, when multiculturalists use the word "multicultural" they fail to define what they mean by "culture." They ignore longstanding definitions of culture presented by anthropologists and sociologists.

They apply the word "culture" to almost any group that has some behavioral variations from that of another. A group that has some behavioral variations vis-à-vis another is not necessarily a separate culture, any more than some behavioral variations on the part of family members make them another family. They fail to distinguish between the culture of a country and that of its subcultures. Thus multiculturalists talk about the culture of minority groups as though they were entities separate from their country's culture at large, when in fact they are only subcultural groups, and thus still part of their nation's common culture. The United States is a multiethnic, not a multicultural country. The former Yugoslavia and the former Soviet Union were multicultural societies (Schmidt, 1997, pp. 18–21). The former Yugoslavia has long rejected cultural assimilation, retained ethnic consciousness, and kept multiculturalism alive.

In light of the Balkan disaster, Schmidt asks why intelligent people still promote multiculturalism. "Why do they not see that multiculturalism does not work? It never has, and it never will, for as long as human nature remains what it always has been, multiculturalism will produce more ills than it will cure" (Schmidt, 1997, p. 17).

Language being an important part of culture, Schmidt naturally disagrees with the Bilingual Education Act of 1968: "The greatest hindrance to a nation's assimilation process is, of course, the implementation of nationwide bilingualism. It never failed to divide a country" (1997, p. 111). Canada, The Balkans, and Belgium are typical examples. Referring to these countries, Schmidt quotes the following from Mauro Mujica, an immigrant from Chile, "All you have to do is look at these places to see what can happen. Our national unity and national prosperity depend on a shared language" (1997, p. 126).

MULTICULTURALISM IN CANADA

In the United States, multiculturalism stems from the initiatives of individuals and minority/ethnic groups. In Canada, it is a policy of the government. Until the 1960s the Canadian government restricted immigration to those who could be deemed assimilable into the dominant British and French groups.

The purpose of this restriction was to exclude those who were considered unassimilable, the visible minorities: Chinese, Japanese, South Asians, Blacks. The policy regarding Native people was related to a similar principle: gradual assimilation. In the 1960s the Canadian government reversed its policy toward immigration, particularly toward visible minorities. The main reason for this change stems from the powerful nationalistic movement in Quebec, where Canadians of French origin no longer considered themselves a minority in Canada, but a majority in the province of Quebec, and they no longer referred to Quebec as a province, but as a country, a nation "le pays du Québec." Their language was not "Canadian French" but "le québécois" (Saint-Jacques, 1976, p. 59). The separatist movement was born.

In 1963, in response to this situation, the government of Canada appointed the "Royal Commission on Bilingualism and Biculturalism." The basic mandate of the Commission was to study the existing state of bilingualism and biculturalism in Canada and make recommendations regarding the steps necessary for developing the Canadian confederation on the basis of an equal partnership between the two founding races, English and French. However, in their studies, the Commissioners could not ignore the other people living in Canada who were not English or French Canadians, that is, ethnic minorities and native Indians. Book 4 of the Commission was therefore devoted to the ethnic groups of Canada other than French or English.

The policy of multiculturalism continued to figure more prominently over the years and, in 1971, Prime Minister Trudeau declared that although there were two official languages in Canada, there was no official culture, and no ethnic group took precedence over any other. A Ministry of Multiculturalism was created in 1973 to monitor the implementation of multiculturalism. In 1988 Canada became the first country in the world to pass a national multiculturalism law—The National Multiculturalism Act—which acknowledges multiculturalism as a fundamental characteristic of Canadian society. This Act was created to enhance multiculturalism in Canada through the preservation of cultures and languages. The Act seeks to preserve, enhance, and incorporate cultural differences into the functioning of Canadian Society.

The multicultural policy of the Canadian government is now under attack, perhaps more than at any time since 1971. In particular, multiculturalism is said to be undermining the historical tendency of immigrant groups to integrate, encouraging ethnic separation, putting "cultural walls" around ethnic groups, and thereby eroding the ability to act collectively as citizens (Kymlicka, 1998, p. 15). Many myths were born from the multicultural Canadian ideology. Not all of them are favorable. Many Canadians think that multiculturalism is expensive, unnatural, and counterproductive. They believe that multiculturalism keeps Canadians apart and that without a common identity, national unity is impossible. Some Canadians suggest that multiculturalism policies are only a way for politicians to obtain votes from the always increasing ethnic population. (Although the Canadian population is the smallest among the G8 countries, percentage-wise, every year Canada takes in the greatest number of immigrants. Canada's population is growing faster than any other G8 nation's, fueled primarily by immigration. In the last five years, the growth rate was 5.9 per cent, which exceeds the United States growth rate of 4.4 per cent). Others point out that the problems of some ethnic minorities are not cultural, but economic and, therefore, their solutions lie beyond what multiculturalism can offer (Porter, 1965; Li & Singh, 1983).

As in the United States, many Canadian authors have entered the debate on multiculturalism. Bissondath's *Selling Illusions: The Cult of Multiculturalism in Canada* (1994) and Gwyn's *Nationalism Without Walls: The Unbearable Lightness of Being Canadian* (1995) both denounce the Canadian policy on multiculturalism. According to Bissondath, multiculturalism has led to undeniable ghettoization. Instead of promoting integration, it encourages immigrants to form "self-contained" ghettos alienated from the mainstream. He agrees with Arthur Schlesinger's (1992) claim that multiculturalism reflects a cult of ethnicity that exaggerates differences, intensifies resentments and antagonism, and drives even deeper the wedges between races and nationalities. Multiculturalism policy does not encourage immigrants to think of themselves as Canadians; even the children of immigrants continue to see Canada through the eyes of foreigners (Bissondath, 1994, pp. 110–111, 98, 133). Gwyn, for his part, argues that official multiculturalism encourages apartheid and/or ghettoism. Multiculturalism encourages ethnic leaders to keep their members apart from the mainstream. As a result, Canadian policy supports ethnic groups in maintaining an apartheid form of citizenship (Gwyn, 1995, pp. 234, 274).

Canada's commitment to diversity has been idealized in repeated references to the "cultural mosaic," a metaphor that has also come under severe criticism. As Susan Crean (1986, p. 9) has noted, the mosaic image has become ingrained in Canadian society. Is it an accurate image of diversity in Canada? As Palmer (1976) and Porter (1979) have argued, mosaic is an over simplification and distortion. It has romanticized the approach to diversity and has denigrated that of the United States as crass. The mosaic metaphor overstates Canada's commitment to diversity by ignoring the pervasiveness of intolerance and assimilationist forces in the past and present. At the same time, the melting pot metaphor understates the degree to which diversity and segregation are maintained in the United States. These metaphors, the mosaic and the melting pot, are inaccurate descriptions of intergroup relations. "That is, Canada is not a pluralist heaven where diversity is celebrated and minorities integrated as full and equal participants. By the same token, American life does not conform to its cliché either. Reality, it seems, lies somewhere in between these visionary—and illusory—ideals" (Fleras & Elliott, 1992, p. 66).

Fleras and Elliott (1992, pp. 132–140) have summarized the various critiques of multiculturalism under the following headings.

Multiculturalism is socially divisive. Concern is expressed over the potential divisiveness inherent in the promotion of cultural diversity. There is even less justification for this divisiveness when officially condoned and publicly funded. "Canada is an accommodating country, and ethnic Canadians are free to keep alive their families' ethnic identity. But they should do so by their private efforts, not expect governments to support attempts to counter the natural nation building processes of integration and assimilation" (Editorial, *Kitchener-Waterloo Record*, 13 July 1987). Fleras and Elliott quote Prof. Rais Khan, Chair of the Political Science Department at the University of Winnipeg: "I did not come to Canada to be labeled as an ethnic or member of the multicultural community, to be coddled with preferential treatment, nurtured with special grants, and then to sit on the sidelines and watch the world go by. In fact I came here to be a member of the mainstream of Canadian society. I do not need paternalism; I need opportunity. I do not want affirmative action; I expect fairness. I do not desire special consideration. I wish to be treated equally."

Multiculturalism is regressive. Minority concerns over equality and justice are displaced by government-funded efforts to enliven the cultural landscape through quaint ethnic festivals and customs (Nunziata, 1989). Multiculturalism reinforces the marginal status of certain minorities and this is accomplished through a veneer of cultural accommodation. Porter in *The Vertical Mosaic* (1965) and Clement in *The Canadian Corporate Elite* (1975) have strongly criticized this particular aspect of multiculturalism.

Multiculturalism is decorative. In fact it is disguised assimilation. Federal multiculturalism is not interested in promoting ethnic cultures in the substantive sense of the term, which is the complex range of beliefs and values: culture in the anthropological sense.

Multiculturalism is impractical. Multiculturalism begins with the premise that social unity can be constructed from cultural diversity whenever minorities are secure in their cultural heritage. However, there is ample evidence that positive ingroup attitudes do not automatically foster receptivity toward outgroups. Moreover, there is no reliable proof that awareness of one's culture will always foster intercultural communication or understanding, particularly in situations of competition and inequality.

Not all Canadian authors have a negative view of multiculturalism. Kymlicka, in his book *Finding Our Way* (1998), finds that multiculturalism is coherent, defensible, and a successful approach to immigration. "Multiculturalism is working well, and fears of ethnocultural separatism are misplaced" (p. 10). "In the field of ethnocultural relations, Canada is a recognized leader. Countries like Spain, Belgium, South Africa, and Russia look to Canada as a model" (pp. 1–3). It is to be wondered if Kymlicka knows anything about the countries "which look to Canada as a model for ethnocultural relations"! In Belgium, for generations the two ethnic groups, Walloon and Flemish, have been fighting each other. Three years ago some politicians of the Walloon side were discussing the possibility of becoming part of France. In 2012 many Flemish politicians talked openly about the northern part of Belgium (the Flemish part) becoming an independent country. In Spain, the Catalonians, who a few years ago obtained official recognition of their language, are now advocating the total political separation from Spain. Canada would be a very poor model!! In terms of ethnocultural relations, it is not necessary to even discuss the cases of South Africa and Russia.

Another aspect of Kymlicka's enthusiasm for the Canadian multiculturalism model is also erroneous: "Multiculturalism is working well, and fears of ethnocultural separatism are misplaced." The history of Canadian immigration is predominantly urban. "The vast majority of immigrants move to Toronto, Vancouver, and Montreal, in that order. In each of these major cities immigrants have been increasingly creating ethnic enclaves. Canada had only six ethnic enclaves in 1976. Now Metro Vancouver alone has more than 110. Many neighbourhoods in Richmond (a suburb of Vancouver) are more than 70% Chinese" (Todd, 2011, p. D4). When an ethnic enclave reaches more than 70%, like the Chinese enclaves in Richmond, in scientific language it is no longer called an enclave, but a ghetto, culturally and linguistically separated. This is ethnocultural separatism. These types of economic enclaves where immigrants can have social, economic, banking, and entertainment facilities without knowledge of one of the official languages of Canada (English or French) are one of the greatest obstacles to the most basic aspect of integration in the Canadian society.

A great number of Chinese immigrants move to these enclaves because they feel more comfortable and protected in such a familiar Chinese environment and where they do not have to struggle with English. However, life in these enclaves reduces immigrants' sense of belonging to Canada. Consequently, many of the residents of enclaves who cannot adequately speak English or French struggle in the labor market and often end up working in enclave immigrant communities. A federally funded 2009 research paper by University of British Columbia geography professor Daniel Hiebert looking at immigrant enclaves in Vancouver, Toronto, and Montreal found that many

enclave residents had higher unemployment levels. Moreover, the noted Harvard sociologist Robert Putnam is among many researchers who are finding that trust levels tend to decline when a city is composed of enclaves (quoted in Todd, 2011).

Concerning the Chinese ethnic minority, it is important (although unexpected) that the majority group in the greater Vancouver area bears some responsibility for the increase of Chinese enclaves by reinforcing the importance of the Chinese language and, therefore, making it possible that one can manage without the knowledge of English. Some examples among many others: One is always surprised when going to the opera at the Queen Elizabeth Theatre to find that some pages are written in Chinese! Why Chinese? Or again when phoning the most important cable TV company to hear the following recording: "For English, press 1, for other languages, press 2." If you press 2, you are told that 'other languages' are Mandarin and Cantonese. Why Chinese? Some local newspapers have commercials in Chinese! Why Chinese? In a Richmond construction zone one can see the following sign for drivers: SLOW DOWN translated into Chinese! Why Chinese? There are so many other minority languages spoken in British Columbia. The reason is very simple: financial. There are many wealthy Chinese immigrants! (See the introduction of this essay.)

EVALUATING MULTICULTURALISM

Whether it is multiculturalism as a policy of government, Canadian style, or multiculturalism resulting from the efforts of minority or pressure groups and/or the writings of individual authors, American style, assimilation is taking place in both countries. From the point of view of linguistic assimilation, there is no difference between the Canadian mosaic and the U.S. melting pot: "Surveys with various ethnic groups have showed that second generation members do not have any more active mastery of their parents' mother tongue. Third generation members who can speak it are the exception" (Saint-Jacques, 1979, p. 210). "There is also a strong and consistent increase in the percentages reporting no knowledge of the language as generation level increases" (O'Bryan, Reitz,

Kuplowska, 1974, p. 12). There is no evidence to show that assimilation of ethnic groups is occurring faster in the United States than in Canada.

Gregory Rodriguez (1999) demonstrated in a very convincing way that the "melting pot" in the United States, that is, assimilation, is surviving. The proper measure of assimilation is not whether ethnic groups have cut their ties to their homeland completely, but whether they have put down roots in the United States. He argues that if you look at the four most important measures of "roots"—citizenship, home ownership, language acquisition, and intermarriage—assimilation is proceeding much as it always has. The longer immigrants stay in the United States, the more likely they are to become citizens. In 1996, there was a 212% increase over the previous years of Mexican immigrants who became citizens. In 1996, 75% of immigrants who had been in the United States for at least 25 years owned their own homes compared with 70% of native-born Americans. The figure for inter-marriage and language-acquisition are equally heartening from an assimilationist point of view. By the third generation, a third or more of Latino and Asian women are marrying outside their ethnic group. Many of the children of Asian immigrants can speak only English. *The Economist* (July 3, 1999), commenting on Rodriguez's book, observed: "Much of what Mr. Rodriguez has to say is common sense. The United States is the most culturally powerful nation in the world, striking terror into chauvinists from Paris to Tehran; it is hardly surprising that it should be able to absorb people within its own borders, particularly since most people come to the U.S. with the express purpose of getting ahead" (p. 30).

Similar assimilation patterns are taking place in Canada. Kymlicka has pieced together some of the elements that are crucial in integration or assimilation: adopting a Canadian identity rather than clinging exclusively to one's ancestral identity; participating in broader Canadian institutions, for instance, political participation, rather than participating solely in ethnic specific institutions; learning an official language rather than relying solely on one's mother tongue; mixed marriages (1998, pp. 16–21). In fact, Canada fares better than the United States on virtually every dimension of integration and assimilation. Its naturalization rates are almost double those of the United States. Canadians show much greater approval for intermarriages. In 1998, when 72% of Canadians approved of interracial marriages, only 4% of Americans approved (Kymlicka, 1998, p. 21). Looking at these patterns of integration and assimilation both in the United States and Canada, one is reminded of Oliver Wendell Holmes, an American author and physician, who once wrote: "We are the Romans of the modern world—the great assimilating people" (1957, p. 133), and also of Schmidt who was born in Canada, the son of a German immigrant family, who wrote that it was natural and normal for him to learn the Canadian majority culture: "Assimilation was a blessing, not an oppressive evil" (1997, p. xii).

When one considers the similar patterns of integration and assimilation in the United States and Canada, one can wonder about the official multiculturalism policy of the Canadian government. What is it for? However politically appealing, is official multiculturalism simply an exercise with little positive application? As Bullivan (1981) asserts, multiculturalism in the purest sense could only be devised in a utopian setting. What perhaps is more realistically attainable in a country like Canada is a commitment to the principle of diversity against a strong setting of shared values, priorities, and rights. *Interculturalism*—as multiculturalism is called by the Quebec government—is equally concerned with the acceptance of cultural communities as a reality within Quebec, but only within a framework that establishes the unquestioned supremacy of French as the language and culture of Quebec (Fleras & Elliott, 1992, p. 83). There must be a limit for a state to accommodate its customs, institutions, and traditions to the demands of immigrant groups. The demand that Sikh men be exempted from the requirement to wear the ceremonial Royal Canadian Mounted Police (RCMP) headgear created quite an uproar in Canada. Kymlicka called the decision of the Canadian government to allow Sikh men in the RCMP to wear the turban "integrative accommodation" (1998, p. 45). *I entirely disagree.* Moreover, following Miller's opinion (1998, p. 125), I firmly believe that the Canadian government's multiculturalism policy puts far too much emphasis on Canadians as members of groups, rather than as individuals.

Canada's population consists of two founding nations, France and England, numerous First Nations (Aboriginal bands), and immigrants from over 200 countries and territories (1996 census). What is Canadian identity? National identity has been a quintessential issue in Canada. There is no ideology of Canadianism. Canadian identity is certainly an elusive concept. Northon Frye cannot find any positive characteristics: "There is no Canadian way of life, no one hundred per cent Canadian, no ancestral figure corresponding to Washington or Franklin or Jefferson..." (1982, p. 48). Louis Sabourin puts it this way: "L'Américain ne sent pas le besoin de définir son identité alors que le Canadien passe son temps à la chercher" [The American does not feel the need to define his own identity. The Canadian is always looking for it] (1992, p. 50). One might say that Canadian ideals are a matter of individual choice; they are not identified in any explicit or formal way with nationality (Saint-Jacques, 1996, p. 300). Recently, Canadian government representatives commented that they felt people around the world understood what it meant to be "American," but that Canada lacked a similar sense of identity. They believe the federal government may have gone too far in encouraging diversity through the Canadian "mosaic" (Press, 2011, B2).

One aspect of Canadian identity which meets the universal approval of a great number of Canadians is "Un-Americanism." When questioned about defining Canadian identity, many Canadians answer in the negative way: "I am not American!" *The Economist* in a special survey of Canada concludes the article with the following remark: "Being American is not a bad thing—but neither is being un-American" (July 24, 1999, p. 16).

CONCLUSION

In a globalized world where the massive immigration of populations is taking place, there is no doubt that multiculturalism will continue to increase, not only in the United States and Canada, but in most countries of the world. Even Japan, where non-Japanese represent less than 2% of the population, a country with a falling birthrate and a large number of elderly people, will have to open its doors to immigrants for the lack of young people in the workforce. With massive immigration, nations have become ethnically, culturally, linguistically, and religiously far more diverse. The basic question

arising from this diversity of most nations in the world is how people from very different ethnic, cultural, and linguistic origins can live peacefully and communicate together in a particular nation. Multiculturalism in the United States and Canada can provide us with some elements of a solution. First, immigrants, while keeping their mother tongue and culture in their private lives, must learn the language of their new nation and accept some cultural and societal aspects which might be different from their own. Secondly, governments must treat their citizens as individuals rather than as groups. The most important aspect of multiculturalism is a commitment to the principle of diversity against a strong setting of shared values, priorities, and rights.

It is a fact that the cultures of immigrants and the cultures of nations receiving immigrants will change. Cultures are not static, they are dynamic processes, changing constantly and indefinitely renewable. People in most parts of the world live within cultures that are already cosmopolitan and characterized by cultural hybridity. Meaningful options for an individual and a nation may come from a variety of cultures.

The observation by Alexis de Tocqueville in 1830, quoted earlier, could very well be a prophetic explanation of successful multiculturalism and bears repeating as we advance into the era of globalization.

> How does it happen that in the United States where the inhabitants have only immigrated to the land they now occupy,... how does it happen that everyone takes as zealous an interest in the affairs of his township, his country and the whole state as if they were his own?

References

Asante, M. K. (1989) *Afrocentricity*. Trenton, NJ: Africa World Press.

Bennet, M. J. (1984) *Towards Ethnorelativism: A Development Model of Intercultural Sensitivity*. Paper presented at the annual conference on International Exchange, Minneapolis, Minnesota.

Bissondath, N. (1994) *Selling Illusions: The Cult of Multiculturalism in Canada*. Toronto: Penguin.

Bloom, A. (1987) *The Closing of the American Mind*. New York: Simon and Schuster.

Brimelow, P. (1995) *Alien Nation: Common Sense about America's Immigration Disaster*. New York: Random House.

Bronfenbrener, U., Harding, J., & Gallwey, M. (1958) "The Measurement of Skill in Social Perception," in McClelland, D. C. (Ed.) *Talent and Society.* New York: Van Nostrand.

Bullivan, B. (1981) "Multiculturalism: Pluralist Orthodoxy or Ethnic Hegemony," *Canadian Ethnic Studies,* 13(2) 1–22.

Chesterton, G. K. (1923) *What I Saw in America.* London: Hodder and Stoughton.

Clement, W. (1975) *The Canadian Corporate Elite.* Toronto: McClelland & Stewart.

Crean, S. (1986) "Cracks in the Mosaic," *Border Crossings* 5(4) 9–11.

Dathorne, O. R. (1994) *In Europe's Image: The Need for American Multiculturalism.* Westport, Conn.: Bergin and Garvey.

de Tocqueville, A. (1945) *Democracy in America.* Vol. 1. New York: Vintage Books.

Fish, S. (1994) *There is no such Thing as Free Speech, and it's a Good Thing.* New York: Oxford University Press.

Fleras, A. & Elliott, J. L. (1992) *Multiculturalism in Canada.* Scarborough: Nelson Canada.

Frye, N. (1982) *Divisions on a Ground: Essays on Canadian Culture.* Toronto: Anansi Press.

Gwyn, R. (1995) *Nationalism without Walls :The Unbearable Lightness of Being Canadian.* Toronto: McClelland and Stewart.

Holmes, O. W. (1957) quoted in Franklin, F. G. *American Nationalism: An Interpretive Essay.* New York: MacMillan.

Kallen, H. (1924) *Culture and Democracy in the United States.* (reprint, 1970) New York: Arno Press.

Kymlicka, W. (1998) *Finding our Way.* Toronto: Oxford University Press.

Li, P. S. & Singh, B. (1983) *Racial Minorities in Multicultural Canada.* Toronto: Garamond Press.

Lind, M. (1995) *The Next American Nation: The New Nationalism.* New York: Free Press.

MacNamara, J. (1974) "What can be expected from a Bilingual Program?" *Travaux de recherches sur le bilinguisme, no 4.*

Manthorpe, J. (2012) "China Fears unrest at home more than foreign war," *The Vancouver Sun,* March 7, p. 1.

Mead, M. (1942) *And Keep your Powder Dry: An Anthropologist looks at America.* New York: William Morrow and Company.

Miller, J. J. (1998) *The Unmaking of America; How Multiculturalism has Undermined the Assimilation Ethics.* New York: The Free Press.

Nelson, D. et al. (1993) *Multicultural Mathematics.* Oxford: Oxford University Press.

Nunziata, J. (1989) "Multicultural Policy Feeds Discrimination," *Toronto Star,* October 31.

O'Bryan, K. G., Reitz, J., Kuplowska, O. (1974) *Non-Official Languages Study—Synopsis of Draft Report.* Department of the Secretary of State.

Palmer, H. (1976) "Mosaic versus Melting Pot? Immigration and Ethnicity in Canada and United States," *International Journal,* Summer, 488–522.

Porter, J. (1965) *The Vertical Mosaic.* Toronto: University of Toronto Press.

Porter, J. (1979) *The Measure of Canadian Society: Education, Equality and Opportunity.* Toronto: Gage Publishing.

Press, J. (2011) "Mosaic doesn't give Canadians identity," *The Vancouver Sun,* Sept. 7, p. B2.

Rodriguez, G. (1999) *From Newcomers to Americans: The Successful Integration of Immigrants into American Society.* Washington, D.C.: National Immigration Forum.

Sabourin, L. (1992) *Le Dilemme Québec-Canada dans un Univers en Mutation.* Montréal.

Saint-Jacques, B. (1976) *Aspects Sociolinguistiques du Bilinguisme Canadien.* Quebec: International Centre for Research on Bilingualism.

Saint-Jacques, B. (1979) "The Language of Immigrants: Aspects of Immigration in Canada," *The Languages of Canada.* Montreal: Didier 207–225.

Saint-Jacques, B. (1996) "Identity and Nationalism in Canadian Literature," *Nationalism vs Internationalism* (Zach, W. & Goddwin, L. eds.) Tübingen: Stauffenburg Verlag, 299–307.

Saint-Jacques, B. (1999) "Tayoosei wo oshieru koto (Teaching Diversity)," *Intercultural Communication Studies,* Vol. 2, February, Nagoya.

Saint-Jacques, B. (2011) "Intercultural Communication in a Globalized World," *Intercultural Communication. A Reader* (L. Samovar, R. Porter, & E. McDaniel, eds.) Boston: Wadsworth, 45–56.

Schlesinger, A. (1992) *The Disuniting of America: Reflections on a Multicultural Society.* Knoxville: Norton.

Schmidt, A. J. (1997) *The Menace of Multiculturalism: Trojan Horse in America.* Westport, Connecticut: Praeger.

Stanford Encyclopedia of Philosophy (2010).

Takaki, R. A. (1993) *Different Mirror: A History of Multicultural America.* Boston: Little Brown.

Todd, D. (2011) "As Metro Ethnic Enclaves Expand, will Residents' Trust Hold?" *The Vancouver Sun,* October 20, p. A15.

Vincent, P. (1997) "An Overview of Multiculturalism in the US Today," *The Bulletin of Seitaku University,* Vol. 2.

Waldron, J. (1995) "Minority Cultures and the Cosmopolitan Alternative," *The Rights of Minority Cultures.* Oxford: Oxford University Press.

Webster, Y. O. (1997) *Against the Multicultural Agenda. A Critical Thinking Alternative.* Westport, Connecticut: Praeger.

Concepts and Questions

1. What does the word "multiculturalism" mean to you personally?
2. List five advantages and five disadvantages of multiculturalism. Discuss the pros and cons of each.
3. Saint-Jacques describes three different perspectives for discussing multiculturalism. Which of the three perspectives is most effective for you personally? Why?
4. What are some of the differences and similarities behind the history of immigration in the United States and Canada? Were some aspects more effective than others? If so, which and why?
5. Saint-Jacques identifies four critiques of multiculturalism. Select one of the four and provide your personal opinion; include why the critique is either correct or incorrect.
6. Do you agree or disagree that immigrants should learn the language of their new nation? Why?
7. What does Saint-Jacques mean when he says that governments must treat citizens "as individuals rather than as groups"?

Asiacentricity and Shapes of the Future: Envisioning the Field of Intercultural Communication in the Globalization Era

YOSHITAKA MIIKE

JING YIN

people can know their base so well that from it they can connect to other worlds past and present, far and wide, and assess and evaluate. The question of one's base should never be underestimated. It is the basis of all knowledge and human development. A person must know where they stand in order to know in what directions they must proceed. A clarity of destiny and of direction to it are dependent on a knowledge of where one is. (Ngũgĩ wa Thiong'o, 1997, p. 32)

Maulana Karenga (2010), the founding theorist of African *Kawaida* philosophy, defined multiculturalism as "thought and practice organized around respect for human diversity" (p. 51) and laid out four basic premises of multiculturalism: (1) mutual respect for each people and culture as an equally valid and valuable way of being human in the world; (2) mutual respect for each people's right and responsibility to speak their special cultural truths and make their unique contributions to the local community and the global society; (3) mutual commitment to the sustained search for common ground in the midst of human diversity; and (4) mutual commitment to an ethics of sharing in order to build the world in which we all desire

Courtesy of Yoshitaka Miike and Jing Yin. This original essay appears here for the first time. All rights reserved. Permission to reprint must be obtained from the authors and publisher. Yoshitaka Miike is Associate Professor and Chair of the Department of Communication, University of Hawaii, Hilo. Jing Yin is Associate Professor, Department of Communication, University of Hawaii, Hilo.

and deserve to live. Karenga (2006) postulated that "despite claims of multiculturalism and respect for one's culture, if one's culture is never or insufficiently used as a source of reflective problematics—the hub around which both the philosophical and educational enterprises revolve—the claims have little or no validity" (p. 247).

According to Prosser (1974), the Speech Communication Association (SCA) founded the Commission for International and Intercultural Communication in December 1970. The International and Intercultural Communication Division of the National Communication Association (formerly the SCA) thus celebrated its 40-year history of scholarly contributions in 2010. The first edition of *Intercultural Communication: A Reader*, whose planning and preparation began in 1967, was published in 1972. It is not too much to say, therefore, that the present pioneering anthology has been with the emergence and evolution of the international and intercultural communication fields (see Martin, Nakayama, & Carbaugh [2012], Mowlana [2012], Prosser & Kulich [2012], and Weaver [2013b] for the historical development of these fields). Indeed, the past thirteen editions (1972–2012) have nurtured the phenomenal growth of cross-cultural and intercultural communication research. The field today is very diverse in its theoretical approaches and methodological orientations (Chen & Starosta, 2004; Martin & Nakayama, 2008, 2010; Shuter, 2013; Starosta & Chen, 2005). It is extremely difficult to reflect on the current status of the field and propose its future directions without taking a certain paradigmatic stance.

For this fortieth anniversary edition, then, our modest contribution is to assess where the field of intercultural communication is in light of Karenga's thesis of multiculturalism and envision where the field can go from an Asiacentric perspective. More specifically, we will explicate the idea of Asiacentricity along with African *Kawaida* philosophy and the Afrocentric paradigm and outline four future tasks ahead for intercultural communication scholars: (1) to explore multicultural meanings and systems of communication; (2) to redefine cultural similarities and differences through multiple lenses; (3) to rethink identity, community, and ethical implications of communication; and (4) to formulate a public philosophy and policy of intercultural communication. These four lines of

inquiry can be pursued within every culture-centric paradigm but illustrated here primarily within the Asiacentric framework.

AFRICAN *KAWAIDA* PHILOSOPHY, AFROCENTRICITY, AND ASIACENTRICITY

Simply put, *Asiacentricity* is about centering, not marginalizing, Asian languages, religions/philosophies, histories, and aesthetics in theorizing and storytelling about Asian communicative life (see Figure 1). To be Asiacentric is to actively place Asian ideas and ideals as theoretical resources at the center of any analysis of Asian peoples and phenomena. For Asians, Asiacentricity encourages their careful and critical engagements with their own cultural traditions for self-understanding, self-expression, communal development, and intercultural dialogue. For non-Asians, Asiacentricity stimulates their cross-cultural reflections on human ways of being, knowing, and valuing through their non-ethnocentric exposure to Asian versions and visions of humanity and communication. Asiacentricity invites us (1) to see the Asian world from the perspective of Asians, (2) to view Asians as subjects and agents of their own realities rather than as objects of analysis and critique, and (3) to have better understanding and deeper appreciation of Asian worldviews and ways of communication (see Miike, 2010a, 2010b, 2013b; Yin, 2009).

Figure 1 *Asiacentricity*

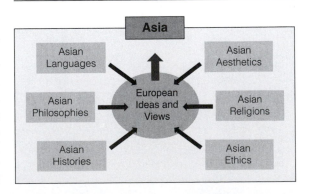

Yoshitaka Miike's vision of Asiacentricity builds on Molefi Kete Asante's legacy of Afrocentricity (see Asante & Miike, 2012), which is, in turn, inspired and influenced by Karenga's (1997, 2006, 2010) African communitarian philosophy of *Kawaida* ("tradition" in Swahili). *Kawaida* philosophy is defined as "an ongoing synthesis of the best of African thought and practice in constant exchange with the world" (Karenga, 2006, p. 245). *Kawaida* philosophy presupposes culture as "a foundation and framework for self-understanding and self-assertion" and submits that Africans should "constantly recover, reconstruct, and bring forth from [their] culture the best of what it means to be African and human in the fullest sense" (Karenga, 2006, p. 245). Karenga (1997) maintained:

> To truly dialogue with African culture means, first of all, using it as a resource rather than as a mere reference. This is the meaning of posing questions and seeking answers within African culture concerning central issues of life and the world. To simply use African culture as a reference is to name things considered important, but never to use it to answer questions, solve problems, or extract and shape paradigms of excellence and possibility in thought and practice. (p. 160)

Furthermore, Afrocentricity posits that Africans have been separated from African linguistic and cultural heritage through physical enslavement and mental colonization and then displaced and peripheralized in the Eurocentric universe of knowledge for the past 500 years, which has deprived Africans of their individual and collective agency (Asante, 2013; Ngũgĩ, 2009). Afrocentricity hence demands that African people be relocated and recentered within the context of their own culture and history and view themselves and be viewed as actors and agents of their cultural world. Ngũgĩ (1997) expounded on the past of colonial dislocation and the future of human knowledge as follows:

> Colonialism distorts [the] basic principle of being. It makes the colonized and their descendants be more familiar first with those experiences that are furthest removed from themselves. Sometimes they are made to remain with just that knowledge of what is distant and which is often against their own interests. They come to identify with the places about which they

have the most knowledge and in our case this means familiarity and therefore identity with the geography, history, culture and language of the colonizer. This mental distortion is the starting point of all the other distortions about ourselves. However, starting with thorough familiarity with the ground on which we stand, we can and should be insatiable in our search of human knowledge. (pp. 32–33)

Asiacentricity shares these cardinal tenets of African *Kawaida* philosophy and the Afrocentric paradigm. Accordingly, Asiacentric studies of Asian communication draw on Asian cultural traditions for describing, interpreting, and evaluating Asian premises and practices of communication. All cultures use language as a common code of communication and a symbolic vehicle of cultural values and epistemologies. Cultural norms, rules, and regulations in a given culture have been largely shaped by its religious-philosophical underpinnings. No culture exists without its own history, from which its members learn important lessons about interpersonal and intercultural ethics and competence. Every culture performs rituals and ceremonies that keep its collectivity and solidarity. When we discern the psychology of Asian communicators and the dynamics of Asian communication, therefore, we should use (1) Asian words as key concepts, (2) Asian religious–philosophical teachings as behavioral principles and codes of ethics, (3) Asian histories as rich contextualization, and (4) Asian aesthetics as analytical frameworks for space–time arrangement, nonverbal performance, and emotional pleasure (Miike, 2013b).

Asiacentricity is neither Asiacentrism (see Figure 2)—an Asian version of Eurocentrism (see Figure 3)—nor ethnocentrism because it does not impose the Asian worldview as the only and best frame of reference on non-Asians. It does not insist that we look at non-Asian cultures and communication from the Asian-centered standpoint. Being Asiacentric in theory and practice has nothing to do with going against other cultures. We can be rooted in our own culture and also open to other cultures by reciprocating the principle of centricity. The concept of center in Afrocentric and Asiacentric paradigms should not be misunderstood as one cultural center diametrically opposed to another. Cultural centers, as defined in Afrocentricity

Figure 2 *Asiacentrism*

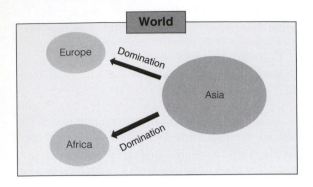

Figure 3 *Eurocentrism*

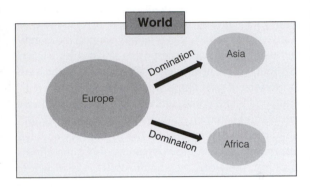

and Asiacentricity, do not allude to mutually exclusive entities in relation to each other (Miike, 2010b). Afrocentricity and Asiacentricity aver that our own culture should be central, not marginal, in our story *without completely ignoring other cultural perspectives on our culture.* Karenga (2012) succinctly stated that "Afrocentricity does not isolate itself or place itself above others, but instead coexists with other-centric pluralism without being hierarchal or subversive" (p. 73). Asante (2010a) further elaborated on the objective and significance of Afrocentricity in the project of multiculturalism without hierarchy and hegemony:

> [T]he aims of Afrocentricity as regards the cultural idea are not hegemonic. Afrocentrists have expressed no interest in one race or culture dominating another; they express an ardent belief in the possibility of diverse populations living on the same earth, without giving

up their fundamental traditions except where those traditions invade other peoples' space. This is precisely why the Afrocentric idea is essential to human harmony. The Afrocentric idea represents a possibility of intellectual maturity, a way of viewing reality that opens new and more exciting doors on human understanding. I do not object to viewing it as a form of historical consciousness, but more than that, it is an attitude, a location, and an orientation. To be centered is to stand somewhere and to come from somewhere; the Afrocentrist seeks for the African person the contentment of a subject, active, agent place. (p. 46)

Asiacentricity is not only descriptive but also prescriptive. In concordance with *Kawaida* philosophy, the Asiacentric enterprise is committed to generating self-defining ideas and taking self-determined actions that underscore ethical visions for human freedom and flourishing and that underline communal solidarity for cultural preservation and integration in Asian societies. Intraculturally, it helps Asians embrace the positive elements of their cultural heritage and transform negative practices according to their ethical ideals. Interculturally, it helps Asians find "a place to stand," so to speak, and provides the basis of equality and mutuality in the global community (Miike, 2012). Asiacentricity is increasingly important in the age of globalization for at least four reasons: (1) the role of culture in regionalism; (2) the initiative to de-colonize the Asian mind; (3) the need to move beyond the Eurocentric structure of knowledge; and (4) the emergence of a dialogical civilization (Miike, 2010a; Mowlana, 1994; Tu, 2007). In the succeeding pages, on the basis of Asiacentricity as an overarching paradigmatic framework, we will delineate four future shapes of the field of intercultural communication in the globalization era.

EXPLORING MULTICULTURAL MEANINGS AND SYSTEMS OF COMMUNICATION

The field of intercultural communication has neither explored nor benefited from multicultural conceptualizations of communication itself in world communities. If we wish to *communicate* interculturally, first and foremost, we must understand the codes, contexts, and complexities of communication in respective cultural terms. It is a widely known fact that many non-European languages do not have words that are exactly equivalent to the English-language word, *communication*. In this regard, *communication* has no universal meaning, although it has become a loanword in non-European languages. Here we suggest four directions for future theorizing and research endeavors: (1) to study etymological origins and semantic implications of communication-related terms in as many languages as possible; (2) to elucidate cultural communication practices and their significance to identity and community; (3) to articulate the inseparable link between worldviews and the purposes of communication; and (4) to examine the totality of cultural communication systems.

Tetsuya Chikushi (2009) compared the English-language term, *expression* with the Chinese-language term, *biaoda* (表达/表達) [surface-reaching] and the Japanese-language term, *hyogen* (表現/表现) [surface-appearing]. *Expression* literally means making things explicitly external, whereas *biaoda* and *hyogen* metaphorically imply making things just sensible and observable. *Biaoda* and *hyogen* also connote natural spontaneity from within and truth-revealing moments. The etymological meanings of these Chinese and Japanese words thus reflect the traditional Asian view that implicitness, subtleness, and ambiguities are important elements of the skillful and sophisticated method of communication, which are ideally complemented by perceptiveness, receptivity, and introspection on the part of emphatic listeners and attentive observers (Chen & Starosta, 2003; Miike, 2012; Yum, 2012).

This Asian emphasis on communication sensitivity, however, does not mean that Asians always employ indirect, subtle, and ambiguous communication styles. Past research findings (e.g., Chen, 2010; Miyahara, 1995; Shim, Kim, & Martin, 2008) concertedly indicated that Asians do use a variety of communication strategies. A careful examination of the totality of communication systems in diverse Asian cultures will unfold a more holistic picture of Asian communication and a more realistic profile of Asian communicators. It is, for example, intriguing to investigate how speaking and writing can complement each other in Asian communication systems especially in the age of new media. Chu (1988) held the view that "the Chinese can be very cordial and friendly in speaking while extremely harsh and tough in writing" (p. 129). He observed that criticism is more likely to be communicated through writing due to the face concern in Chinese culture.

Yoshikawa identified several ways in which Japanese people express *honne* (本音) [true feelings] and discussed the cultural significance of diary writing and *nomication* (drinking-communication). He accounted for what Miike (2003, 2007) theorized as "assertion-acceptance communication" in Japanese organizational settings:

> Subordinates who are conveniently influenced by alcohol occasionally let out the *honne* to their boss. What is expected generally in such a situation is that the boss, who is also conveniently influenced by alcohol, will listen to [her or] his subordinate's *honne* and promise to do something about it. Whether the boss actually fulfills what [she or] he promises [her or] his subordinates is actually irrelevant. What is significant is that [her or] his subordinates release their *honne* or their pent-up emotions and that their boss listens. Although *honne* expressed over drinks is not supposed to be held against the individuals concerned, one must exercise discretion in the degree of disclosure to be made. If one oversteps acceptable limits, his verbal or behavioral demeanor counts against [her or] him. (Yoshikawa, 1988, pp. 163–164)

Lebra (1987) also pinpointed the role of writing as a substitute for speaking and additionally conceptualized "triadic communication" (i.e., communication between the first and second persons through the third person) in Japanese culture. Triadic communication takes two forms: (1) mediation and (2) displacement. Displacement triadic communication is noteworthy in that the first person is expressing her or his true feelings to the third person within the hearing distance of the second person. The first person is talking to the third person, but she or he is actually communicating to the second person.

The rationale, vocabulary, and significance of cultural communication practices are often deeply intertwined with religion, philosophy, and spirituality. Hamid Mowlana (1996), for instance, intimated this nexus in Islamic societies:

> The memorization of the Quran is a common information and communication act that has a long history in all Islamic societies and continues to be practiced

widely in all Muslim countries, an inextricable link between oral and inscriptive modes of communication. Although the Quran is the main source from which Islamic practices and precepts are explained and deduced, the *sunnah* of the Prophet was taken from his deeds and judgments, drawn up and fixed in writing. *Sunna* is the standard of conduct along with the Quran. The word *hadith* means primarily sayings, a communication or narrative transmitted from the Prophet and his companions, *Ahl-ul-bait*, and the Imams. A *hadith* can only be credible when its *isnad* or documentation offers an unbroken series of reliable authorities in oral and written communication. Investigation and study of this whole body of communication is called *ilm-al-hadith*, or the science of transmission of the sayings of the Prophet and his companions. (pp. 46–47)

Of particular relevance to this connection between communication and religious–philosophical foundations is that the purpose of communication is viewed very differently based on different worldviews. Hindu philosophy believes that the ultimate objective of communication is to know the true nature of the relationship between the inner self or *Atman* [the individual soul] and the supreme power or *Brahman* [the universal soul], and that the more a person knows herself or himself, the more she or he is able to know others and nature and hence interact with them fruitfully (Babbili, 2008; Sitaram, 2004). In the Hindu vision, therefore, self-knowledge is the be-all and end-all of communication and *moksa* [spiritual liberation]. According to Buddhist teachings, the aim of communication is to remove all illusionary divisions and distinctions between the self and others toward spiritual enlightenment—the oneness of the universe—and to eliminate the excessive and aggressive ego as a primary source of mental suffering and perceptual barriers (Miike, 2012; Yum, 2012). Compassion emerges from the de-centering of oneself and the realization of *pratitya samutpada* [dependent co-arising]. Confucian thought emphasizes self-cultivation and self-transformation through relational communication. Sensitivity to emotions and feelings of others is central to being and becoming fully human (Shuter, 2003; Tu, 2010b). When individuals of different faiths and worldviews meet and interact, they appear to be communicating toward the same objective on the surface but may be doing so for very different ontological, epistemological, and axiological reasons.

The foregoing discussion exhorts us to apprehend and valorize all cultural systems of communication in a more comprehensive manner because we bring these communicative assumptions into intercultural interactions. If we are not aware of these differences in the meaning and purpose of communication, there is no way for us to truly communicate and connect with the human family for a sustainable future. As power is an overriding concern in critical intercultural communication studies (Halualani, Mendoza, & Drzewiecka, 2009), this research agenda is all the more important for criticality. If we do not grasp the origins, formations, and functions of cultural communication systems in a holistic and historical way, we would easily lose sight of the real interests and needs of people in a particular culture. We would not be able to facilitate social change toward just and democratic communication for bettering their lives. Worse yet, we could run the risk of unknowingly or unintentionally exacerbating power relationships within and between cultures.

REDEFINING CULTURAL SIMILARITIES AND DIFFERENCES THROUGH MULTIPLE LENSES

Yasushi Akashi (2004), Former Under-Secretary-General of the United Nations, tersely stated that "communication is a delicate balance between what unites us and what makes us different from each other" (p. 235). This statement is especially true in communication across cultures. It is hardly surprising, then, that the perception and treatment of cultural similarities and differences are part and parcel of cross-cultural and intercultural communication scholarship (Weaver, 2013a). Chen and Starosta (2003) made the observation that difference and similarity can be a very arbitrary judgment depending on personal interpretation. They quoted Chuang Tzu who quipped that "seeing from the different part, neighbors become far distant; but seeing from the similar part, all myriad are to be a unity" (p. 5). They avowed that the key to successful human communication is "to understand that differences exist in the similarity, and to pursue the unity from the differences" (p. 5). It is precisely because perceived similarities and differences are arbitrary and mutually define each other that we must capture them from truly diverse standpoints and use as many "different mirrors" as possible in order to ruminate on human commonality in cultural communication and cultural diversity in human communication in the globalization era.

Nevertheless, the field of intercultural communication still suffers from comparative Eurocentrism. Many cross-cultural and intercultural communication researchers, albeit unwittingly or unintentionally, normalize and naturalize U.S. European American cultural values and communication styles and contrast them with other dissimilar ones, notably Northeast Asian counterparts (Miike, 2010b). In commenting on early culture and communication research, Weaver (2013a) witnessed: "In many ways, culture was viewed as an obstacle to overcome as the Western world helped the non-West to become more Westernized. Very little research considered communication between people of non-Western cultures or the impact of the non-West on the West" (p. 14). This modernization legacy of Eurocentric development communication scholarship has a long-lasting impact on contemporary cross-cultural and intercultural communication research in the non-Western world. Akira Miyahara (1998) is one of the earliest advocates for Asiacentric comparisons who pointed out this problem of comparative Eurocentrism:

> Researchers from several Asian countries may collaborate in order to identify the emics or culturally equivalent communication concepts of the respective Asian cultures. Similarities in communication behavior tend to be understated, or simply overlooked, in traditional cross-cultural communication studies. Most of the cross-cultural comparisons have been done between such diversely different pairs as: U.S. and Japan, China and France, Korea and Britain, etc., while comparisons between Asians such as Japanese and Chinese, Koreans and Japanese, are still rare to date. (p. 65)

Asian communication specialists, for example, can probe into different cultural manifestations of the same Buddhist doctrine of dependent co-arising (缘起/縁起) by contextualizing and detailing the Chinese concept of *yuan*, the Japanese concept of *en*, and the Korean concept of *yon*. They can also compare Japanese *enryo-sasshi* communication, Korean *saryo-nunchi* communication, and Filipino *pahiwatig-paki-kiramdam* communication to see where these cultural styles converge and diverge. Similarly, it would be fascinating to examine the Japanese *hamani* [cherry-blossom viewing] practice and the Korean *putkott-nori* [cherry-blossom play] practice as similar but different communal and relational performance. A more challenging comparison would be the Indian aesthetics of *rasa* and the Japanese aesthetics of *mono no aware* [the pathos of things]. Of course, as Zhang (2012) pointed out, there are different areas of cross-cultural comparison: (1) the impact of technology use on cultural continuity and change; (2) new media and political participation; (3) group communication dynamics; and (4) religious communication practices.

David I. Hitchcock's (1994) well-known survey for strategic thinkers and policy makers in international relations suggested that, while overall intra-Asia similarities were observable when Asians were compared with U.S. Americans, there were some intriguing differences in cultural values between Northeast Asians (Chinese, Japanese, and South Koreans) and Southeast Asians (Filipinos, Indonesians, Malaysians, Singaporeans, and Thais). In the category of "personal values and qualities," Northeast Asian respondents believed that "self-reliance" and "inner self-fulfillment" were far more important than Southeast Asian respondents did. Northeast Asian participants, however, did not think that they should "follow religious teachings" and "obey their parents" as much as Southeast Asian participants did. In the category of "societal values and qualities," Southeast Asian respondents placed far less importance on "personal freedom" and "individual rights" than Northeast Asian respondents did. Southeast Asian participants, on the other hand, rated higher than Northeast Asian participants on the following items: (1) respect for authority; (2) orderly society; (3) rights of society; (4) openness to new ideas; (5) consensus; and (6) accountability of public officials. Although it is preliminary in nature and twenty years old, Hitchcock's (1994) study can serve as a signpost for Asiacentrists. Cross-cultural communication scholarship needs more of this kind of Asiacentric research that explores intra-Asia differences in cultural values and communication practices.

According to Miike (2010b), comparative Eurocentrism deters the field of intercultural communication from (1) demonstrating internal diversity and complexity within a non-Western region or nation, (2) exploring links and interconnections, and identifying collective identities and common values, among neighboring non-Western cultures, (3) examining similarities and differences from non-Eurocentric perspectives, and (4) projecting non-Western visions of the global village. Miike (2010b) isolated five types of alternative non-Eurocentric comparisons that can enlarge the theoretical horizons of intracultural and intercultural communication studies: (1) continent-diaspora comparisons (e.g., Japanese culture and communication in Japan and Brazil), (2) within-region comparisons (e.g., Indian and Sri Lankan cultures), (3) non-Western comparisons (e.g., Latino/a and Asian cultures), (4) diachronic comparisons (precolonial and postcolonial African cultures), and (5) co-cultural domestic comparisons (Native American and Native Hawai'ian cultures). Native Hawai'ian culture is underrepresented in the current intercultural communication literature. It would be commendable for Native Hawai'ian and Asian communicologists to collaborate and compare, say, the Hawai'ian idea of *lōkahi* and the Chinese notion of *he*, the Hawai'ian method of *ho'oponopono* and the Indonesian practice of *musyawarah-mufakat*, the Hawai'ian worldview of *mana* and the East Asian philosophy of *chi/ki/qi*, and the Hawai'ian thought of *ku* and *hina* and the Taoist principle of *yin* and *yang* (see Meyer [2001] and [2003] for Native Hawai'ian epistemology and conflict resolution).

Martin and Nakayama (2010) problematized that the field of intercultural communication has accorded too much attention to cultural differences. This difference-oriented approach, in their opinion, conceals the way cultures have always been in contact and have already influenced each other. They emphasized the indubitable importance of recognizing both cultural similarities and differences and foregrounding the hybrid and heterogeneous character of all cultures. As a matter of fact, intercultural communication professionals today are challenged anew to attend to cultural hybridity and complexity in every world community.

Nonetheless, it is not so theoretically stimulating and practically instructive for them to merely demonstrate that culture is hybrid and complex (Asante & Miike, 2012). They ought to explain how culture has come to be hybrid and complex and why. To put it another way, they should proffer historical perspectives on each culture's development. It is also essential for intercultural communication critics to assess the consequences of hybridization on each culture. They often scrutinize the impact of West on the rest of the world, but there is a compelling need to study the nature and scope of the impact of the non-West on the West. Have Asian worldviews, values, and ethics, for instance, really merged into the mindset and lifestyle of the mainstream West?

Chikumin Ran's (2002) chronological inquiry into the Japanese concept of *enryo* (遠慮) [literally, distant consideration] may serve as an exemplary historical investigation on cultural hybridity. His study reveals the etymological origin and semantic transformation of *enryo*. The two *kanji* characters of *enryo* simply denote a long-term vision in the Chinese language. It was during the Muromachi period (1392–1603) that the meaning of the word was actually appropriated in Japan. To the Japanese, to think ahead was, and still is, to be modest and considerate in interpersonal interactions. It makes sense, then, that Koreans do not use these two characters to refer to thoughtful consideration because they imported and adopted Chinese characters in their own way. Its equivalent word is *saryo* (思慮) in the Korean language.

The task of redefining cultural similarities and differences takes on added urgency for the future of intercultural communication scholarship in the age of global contact and conflict. The field of intercultural communication must be cautious not to overexaggerate the transformative power of transnationalism and the future prospect of cultural convergence by (1) directing attention only to popular culture, (2) underestimating the realities of geopolitics and international relations, and (3) throwing exclusive light on elite and youth populations in highly industrialized and information societies. Global communication, as Mowlana (1994) proclaimed, is not universal communication. Liu (2012) is surely accurate in saying that "the interconnectivity does not mean that cultural differences are being eradicated and that the whole world is being subsumed into one global culture. Despite the presence of global economy and mass cultural products, people still interpret what they see or have by drawing upon their local beliefs, values, and norms" (p. 269). Asante (2012) forthrightfully asserted that we should first respect one another, even if we are not the same, and then communicate interculturally in such a way that reveals common virtues and possibilities across differences. We should "marvel in that otherness in order to establish genuine communication" (p. 134). Miike (2013b) echoed Asante's assertion:

> Cross-culturalists and interculturalists may remind themselves once again that their pressing mission is not to create a monolingual and monocultural world wherein concrete differences are effaced, and wherein every global citizen is accepted as an abstract individual "just like us." Intercultural communication theory and practice ought to promote a deep respect for otherness, that is, an appreciation of humanity *despite differences and because of differences*.

RETHINKING IDENTITY, COMMUNITY, AND ETHICAL IMPLICATIONS OF COMMUNICATION

Identity has always been a central topos in the study of culture, communication, and intercultural relations. The recent focus of identity research in the field of intercultural communication has concentrated on multidimensional individual identity as opposed to shared collective identity. This proclivity is based on the individualistic assumption that the autonomy of the self can be achieved through a process of separation from all "constraining" social relations (i.e., freeing the self from any external forces, social/cultural structures, or collective identities) (Hsu, 1985; Yin, 2009, 2011). Therefore, dynamic and fluid multicultural identity—the mental capacity to detach from social realities and transcend culturally rooted identities—is celebrated as the most desirable stage of identity development. Notwithstanding the fact that postmodernists, poststructuralists, and postcolonialists have made significant strides in disrupting the notion of static and fixed self in Western

traditions of thought, they uphold the supremacy of sovereignty of the individual in their anti-essentialism thesis. That is, no collective identity is innocent, and all cultural identities need to be deconstructed for critical interrogation (Fraser, 1997). Asante and Miike (2012) posed a poignant question about the *raison d'être* of the intercultural communication field in their Afrocentric–Asiacentric dialogue:

> Should intercultural communication research be concerned only with what the field can do for individual choice and freedom in postmodern spaces, not with what the field can do for the ecology, ethos, and ethics of culture and community? If individuals can be heard in the third space, shouldn't we care for whatever happens to the communal health of culture as a result of intercultural contact? Is intercultural communication essentially for individuals who are "marginals," not for collectives who belong to a community? These are important questions especially for the future of critical intercultural communication studies.
>
> Indeed, the sustainability of local community, let alone global society, through humanistic connection is the paradigmatic problematique of contemporary intercultural communication scholarship. We are so much into multicultural individuality, cosmopolitan mobility, social change, and material progress. We have rarely considered ecological issues in culture and communication. Whereas "intersectionalities" of individual identity, "intercultural personhood" through individuation and universalization, the "third space" through cultural hybridization, and creative "in-between-ness" of marginality may shed light on complex realities in which we all live, they can offer very few insights into actual community building and concrete collective solidarity. (pp. 25–26)

At this critical juncture of identity politics, social disintegration, religious conflicts, and ecological vulnerability, as Chin (2004) stressed, communication should be concerned with "the realization of the moral self in, and for, human collectivities" (p. 69). She noted that "[a]rising from a fundamental need for human connection, communication lies at the heart of constructing, maintaining, and/or transforming communities and societies" (p. 69). As globalization shrinks the world and brings people from different cultures into more contact than ever, it paradoxically highlights cultural differences and heightens the awareness of shared collective identities. It is a *sine qua non* for culture and communication researchers to undertake four projects of theoretical mapping with a view to achieving unity in diversity and building an integrated global community: (1) to envision identity as embedded in the community as well as the formation of the individual; (2) to embrace the community as a unifying and empowering force for human flourishing without sacrificing human diversity; (3) to embody an ethics of communication grounded in duty consciousness without emasculating unique individuality; and (4) to eliminate human insensitivities and expand our network of relationships to encompass the supernatural, humans, and nature.

Tu (2007) went so far as to say that no individual can avoid the issue of cultural identity. For cultural identity is not only what makes the individual a unique and concrete human being, but also what defines a culture and bonds the individual with other members of the culture. Tu (2007) pondered:

> [I]dentity is understood as a personal sense of belonging, the core values that make a group cohesive, the willingness to establish the distinctiveness of an individual and community, and the defining characteristic of an organization, a profession, or an academic discipline. Then how can we avoid "identity" if it is so broadly conceived? (p. 63)

From an Asian vantage point, culture and the individual are not perceived to be in opposition to each other. The Confucian tradition regards the self as a center of relationships in the ever-expanding network (Cheng, 1998). Culture and community are not seen as exclusively constraining forces impeding the realization of individual identity. Rather, they are what make self-actualization possible. Ibn Khaldun, an Islamic philosopher and historian, described society as *assabieh* [solidarity]. The Islamic notion of community, *ummah,* with its religious tenet, goes beyond geopolitical boundaries to include all members of Islam. The primary function of the *ummah* is to provide exemplars and set the highest standards of performance for the development of all its members (Mowlana, 1996). Mahatma Gandhi's vision of *ashram* [village] is a self-sufficient community formed in the movement of *sarvodaya* [the welfare of all] (Pandikattu,

2001). With its primary concern for the interests of disadvantaged members of the society, the principle of *sarvodaya* exemplifies the Asian belief of community as a source of empowerment and enablement for human development and flourishing.

In stark contrast to the ethics of rights-consciousness in the West that insists on natural and absolute rights of the individual, the ethics of duty-consciousness in Asia obligates all parties of a community to work together for the common good and well-being of all members. Confucian wisdom defines rights in terms of duty. Both the individual and the community have mutual obligations of her or his self-cultivation. The community is responsible for securing the environment favorable for each person's self-cultivation, while the person is compelled to fulfill her or his duty to the community by contributing to the social order that makes self-cultivation of others possible. As Cheng (1998) interpreted, "the duty consciousness comes from a vision of the perfect union or unity of self and community in which both their needs are realized" (p. 148). The doctrine of *amr bi al-ma'ruf wa nahy'an al munkar* [commanding to the right and prohibiting from the wrong], the Islamic theory of social responsibility, designates individuals and groups the duty to guide each other to learn and do what is good and ethical (Mowlana, 1996). The Gandhian philosophy of *sarvodaya* also reflects the Asian ethics of duty-consciousness for the welfare of all.

The Asian preference for the collective and the ethics of duty-consciousness should not be understood as an encroachment on human individuality and agency. Tu (2001) eloquently captured the reciprocity between the person and the community in Confucian cultures:

> The self cultivates roots in the family, village, nation, and the world. The feeling of belonging is predicated on a ceaseless spiritual exercise to transcend egotism, nepotism, parochialism, ethnocentrism, and anthropocentrism. The reciprocal interplay between self as center and self for others enables the self to become a center of relationships. As a center, personal dignity can never be marginalized and, as relationships, the spirit of consideration is never suppressed. (p. 26)

In the worldview of many Asian traditional cultures, we are not only recipients and beneficiaries of what was offered by people before us, but also co-creators of the world that we are currently living in and the future that we are striving for (Cheng, 1987). The role of communication is to rediscover and revive our bonds with other human beings, the spirits, and nature and to reduce human insensitivities that preclude us from expanding our network of relationships. The Confucian theme of *tianrenheyi* (天人合一) [the unity of Heaven and humanity] calls for the establishment of an all-encompassing cosmology that includes four inseparable dimensions for sustainable lifeways: (1) self; (2) community; (3) nature; and (4) Heaven (Tu, 2010b). Similarly, the theory of *tawhid* [the unity of God, human beings, nature, and the universe], the eternal guiding principle of Islam, provides meaning for life and commits individuals to ethical actions to maintain unity, coherence, and harmony among all beings of the universe (Mowlana, 1996). The Hindu philosophy of *sarvodaya* is also predicated on the deep awareness of our indebtedness to all beings and the principle of universal kindness, a sense of urgency to reduce the suffering of other beings (Babbilli, 2008). From a Buddhist perspective, Hajime Nakamura (1984) concluded the ideal function of communication about "interrelational existence" as follows:

> Communication need not remain on the external level, in the social, physiological or physical spheres, but more importantly, it should reach into the depths of beings so that people may realize and share the concerns, joys and happiness of one another. Rightly understood and employed, communication is the resolution of the dichotomy in [woman and] man and the revelation of things as they are in their truly inter-penetrative nature. (pp. 151–152)

FORMULATING A PHILOSOPHY AND POLICY OF INTERCULTURAL COMMUNICATION

With an eye on the future, the time is ripe for intercultural communication professionals to actively formulate and propound philosophies and policies of intercultural communication in both local and global contexts. As Chu (1986) illustrated in his cross-cultural comparison of cultural preservation in China and Taiwan, cultural policies significantly influence communication dynamics, cultural continuity, and social change within a given society. For the last decade, largely impacted by the waves of Cultural Studies, poststructuralism, postmodernism, and post-colonialism, the field of intercultural communication has intensively engaged in deconstructive criticism. Such critical inquiries problematize past knowledge about culture as a unitary and static system of shared meanings and communication as a politically neutral means of expression with the aim of uncovering and eliminating contextual constraints and hegemonic practices toward more equal and mutual relations within and across cultures (Halualani, Mendoza, & Drzewiecka, 2009).

Needless to say, deconstruction is extremely important because it broadens and deepens our understanding of the constitutive power of communication by laying bare the mechanism of oppression in the communication process and how our sense of subjectivity is constructed by sociopolitical forces. Deconstructionists typically presume the constitutive capacity of communication as exclusively negative and human subjectivity as an utter product of intersecting discourses. In their criticism, more often than not, this dark side of communication overshadows the bright side that communication has the affirmative, transformative, and emancipatory power to heal, unite, challenge, and expand our awareness. While we are shaped by our particular cultural, social, and historical contexts, we do have the willpower to make collective and individual choices so as to change the course of our lives and future. If we desire to build a global community and a future of our wish, we need public philosophies and cultural policies that can entail positive possibilities of communication and channel human potentials into (re)constructive collective actions.

For a global philosophy and policy, intercultural communication thinkers and activists ought to make concerned efforts to synthesize all cultural traditions and bring forth their best ideas and ideals in order to re-humanize and re-harmonize our troubled and conflict-ridden world. As Asante (2010b) enunciated, "[i]n our attempt to expand the boundaries of communication theory, particularly the ideas of intercultural communication, we should explore every aspect of culture, in every region of the world, in our effort to become truly human" (p. 158). Given the uneven nature of the global society and the ecological crisis of the endangered earth, furthermore, it behooves us to move beyond the Enlightenment mentality of the modern West and cultivate the moral imperative of nonviolence and intercultural dialogue for world peace. Tu (1996) advised us to reconsider the "idealized notion of a human being as a rights-bearing individual motivated by self-interest who attempts to maximize his profits through rational calculation in the market place adjudicated by a legal framework" (p. 70). It is abundantly clear that a global philosophy and policy of intercultural communication must enhance justice, sympathy, civility, and responsibility as well as liberty, rationality, legality, and rights (Tu, 2007) and encourage a culture of peace that "identifies the self significantly with the other, viewing ends and means as a never-ending chain" instead of a culture of violence that "constantly dichotomizes self and others, separating ends and means" (Tehranian, 1994, p. 91).

Asian cumulative wisdom has a great deal to offer for more humane and ethical visions of intercultural communication in the globalization era. Gandhi's idea of *Satyagraha* resistance, for example, took shape from culturally ingrained yet globally shareable values such as self-sacrifice and suffering. As self-sacrifice and suffering are experienced by most underprivileged members of the society, particularly women in this case (Lakshmi, 2007). *Satyagraha* was a form of public philosophy and intervention that turned what was commonly conceived as a weakness like femininity into sources of strength. The underlying assumption of *Satyagraha* was the belief in equal potentiality of women, children, and other vulnerable members of the society. Gandhi's principle of "putting the last first" also has ethical implications for envisioning and changing intercultural communication between the privileged and the disadvantaged in the global village (see Pandikattu, 2001; Singhal, 2010).

For a local philosophy and policy, it is undoubtedly necessary for intercultural communication theoreticians and practitioners to look into local conditions and problems and tap into indigenous cultures for the purpose of extracting ethical ideals that can resonate with the ethos of local people. When we visited Beijing last summer, we were struck by the prevalence of the city slogan called the "Beijing Spirit" (北京精神). Over the image of the splendid historical architecture of the Temple of Heaven, the slogan features: (1) *aiguo* (爱国) [patriotism]; (2) *chuangxin* (创新) [creativity]; (3) *baorong* (包容) [tolerance]; and (4) *houde* (厚德) [development of morals]. This seemingly random collection of words actually reflects social problems facing citizens in Beijing: (1) the deeply-felt unease that China as a country and Beijing as a city are losing their social cohesiveness as the gap between the rich and poor has drastically intensified in the process of privatization and globalization; (2) the wide-spreading concern that China might have become the assembly line for so many transnational corporations and lost the capability of creating or making something of her own; (3) the hard fact of life that people in the city deal with conflicts, disharmony, and discrimination, which were brought by the process of rapid urbanization, and (4) the erosion of morality in the face of ruthless struggle for money and relentless materialism and consumerism. Both the Forbidden City and the Temple of Heaven are the symbols of Beijing. Interesting enough, however, only the Temple of Heaven was showcased in the city slogan. While the Forbidden City signifies the power of the ruler or the government, the Temple of Heaven symbolizes the duty of the ruler to pray to Heaven for blessing for the country and offer moral guidance to people. It is apparent that this choice of the symbol was intended to raise moral consciousness among residents in Beijing.

Cultural recovery from the past and cultural reconstruction for the future is of paramount importance for the formulation of a local philosophy and policy of intercultural communication. From a *Kawaida* philosophical viewpoint, Karenga (2008) specified three stages of cultural recovery: (1) reaching back and studying the past; (2) reconstruction and rebuilding in light of new knowledge and moral reasoning; and (3) putting forth models of excellence as ways to pursue the possible and the good. It goes without saying that, for cultural recovery and reconstruction in such a *Kawaida* sense, cultural traditions ought to be recast in their full complexity as the lived and the living (continuity and change), the indigenous and the hybrid (unity and diversity), and the oppressive and the liberating (the pros and cons). *Chuan-tong* (传统/传統) in Chinese (*den-to* in Japanese and *jeon-tong* in Korean) literally means communicated continuities. Etymologically, this Chinese-language word emanates from the silk-reeling metaphor and symbolizes the unity of those developmental threads that provide cultural continuity across generations. Although it is always debatable how and why certain cultural continuities have been constructed and communicated, it is well worth our while to trace back to each of these threads to understand and appreciate who we are as collective, communal, and cultural beings (Miike, 2013b). A local philosophy and policy must also help the community in question to cope with the dual challenges of identity and adaption and the role of intercultural dialogue that Tu (2010a) articulated:

> A living culture must deal with the dual challenges of identity and adaptation. Without identity, it cannot maintain its internal coherence; without adaptation, it cannot adjust to the changing environment. A fruitful interplay between adaptation and identity is necessary and desirable for cultural renewal and regeneration. Only learning cultures are able to maintain a delicate balance between integrity and flexibility. Intercultural dialogue enables a culture to benefit from taking other cultures as references. (p. 4)

THE CHALLENGE OF INTERCULTURAL COMMUNICATION IN THE GLOBALIZATION ERA

Larry A. Samovar and Richard E. Porter have edited the present groundbreaking anthology, *Intercultural Communication: A Reader*, with their firm belief that "successful intercultural communication is a matter of highest importance if humanity and society are to survive" (Samovar & Porter, 1976, p. iii). Edwin R. McDaniel has affirmed this belief and joined them as the co-editor since the eleventh edition in 2006. In the first edition, recognizing that the field of intercultural communication had not yet been adequately established, Samovar and Porter (1972) wrote: "Up to now, intercultural communication has not been the subject of intensive research by communication scientists. In fact, most of our findings have come from anthropologists and social psychologists" (p. 302). Today, forty years later, the International and Intercultural Communication Division of the National Communication Association (NCA) is one of the largest divisions, with

approximately 1,000 members, in the world-largest organization of communication professionals. Numerous theoretical accounts and empirical assessments now spring from within the discipline of communication (see Miike, 2013a). There is no question among contemporary communication scholars that intercultural communication as a distinct and discrete field of study is well established and well grounded. The full-fledged field is also rapidly expanding all over the world. Yet the ceaseless waves of globalization and the troubling human condition demand that the evolving field answer new questions and solve new problems.

James W. Chesebro (1996) remarked in his presidential address entitled, "Unity in Diversity: Multiculturalism, Guilt/Victimage, and a New Scholarly Orientation," at the 82nd annual meeting of the Speech Communication Association (now NCA) that "multiculturalism deals with some of the most sensitive issues, questions of basic identity, respect for differences, the meaning of minimum rights, and how profound differences can be integrated into a seamless system" (p. 11). He predicted that multiculturalism would function paradoxically and create unity and division and contended that "these dual goals of community and diversity must [be] both our simultaneous—although oxymoronic and contradictory—objectives" (p. 11). Here Chesebro touched on the formidable challenge of intercultural communication in the globalization era. Globalization makes every individual, group, society, nation, and region become acutely aware of similarities and differences in the world of power differentials and impels them to find a balance between identity and community. For such a balance, as Ngũgĩ (1997) opined, each and every one of us needs a more refined sense of who we are, where we came from, and where we stand in relation to others.

Majid Tehranian's (1993) mapped out five major megatrends that characterize the chaotic and convoluted contemporary world: (1) globalism; (2) regionalism; (3) nationalism; (4) localism; and (5) spiritualism. According to him, each of these megatrends can be either constructive or destructive depending on our collective choices and actions. He advocated communitarian globalism, inclusionary regionalism, democratic-benign nationalism, liberal localism, and ecumenical spiritualism. Conversely, he denounced hegemonic globalism, exclusionary regionalism, totalitarian-aggressive nationalism, parochial localism, and fundamentalist spiritualism. Tehranian did not think that the total rejection of these megatrends can be the option and solution to intractable problems confronting both the local community and the global society. He instead urged us to constantly re-direct and re-shape them through international and intercultural communication. In other words, from his communitarian point of view, we are living in the multilayered interactive contexts of globalism, regionalism, nationalism, localism, and spiritualism, and the human future rests in large measure on how we will manage these five megatrends. In short, then, the next frontier of intercultural communication theory and practice is to productively guide and navigate them toward "harmony without uniformity."

References

Akashi, Y. (2004). *Samurai and English* (in Japanese). Tokyo, Japan: Kadokawa Shoten.

Asante, M. K. (2010a). Afrocentricity and Africology: Theory and practice in the discipline. In J. R. Davidson (Ed.), *African American Studies* (pp. 35–52). Edinburgh, Scotland: Edinburgh University Press.

Asante, M. K. (2010b). *Oro-la*: Communicating the person in an African cultural sense. In X. Dai & S. J. Kulich (Eds.), *Identity and intercultural communication: Vol. 1 Theoretical and contextual construction* (pp. 151–159). Shanghai, China: Shanghai Foreign Language Education Press.

Asante, M. K. (2012). Maat and human communication: Supporting identity, culture and history without global domination. *Communication: South African Journal for Communication Theory and Research*, 38(2), 127–134.

Asante, M. K. (2013). Afrocentricity: Toward a new understanding of African thought in the world. In M. K. Asante, Y. Miike, & J. Yin (Eds.), *The global intercultural communication reader* (2nd ed., pp. 101–110). New York, NY: Routledge.

Asante, M. K., & Miike, Y. (2012, November). *Paradigmatic issues in intercultural communication studies: An Afrocentric-Asiacentric dialogue*. Paper presented at the annual meeting of the National Communication Association, Orlando, FL.

Babbili, A. S. (2008). Ethics and the discourse on ethics in postcolonial India. In M. K. Asante, Y. Miike, & J. Yin (Eds.), *The global intercultural communication reader* (pp. 297–316). New York, NY: Routledge.

Chen, G.-M. (2010). *Study on Chinese communication behaviors*. Hong Kong, China: China Review Academic Publishers.

Chen, G.-M., & Starosta, W. J. (2003). Asian approaches to human communication: A dialogue. *Intercultural Communication Studies*, 12(4), 1–15.

Chen, G.-M., & Starosta, W. J. (2004). Communication among cultural diversities: A dialogue. In G.-M. Chen & W. J. Starosta (Eds.), *Dialogue among diversities* (pp. 3–15). Washington, DC: National Communication Association.

Cheng, C. Y. (1987). Chinese philosophy and contemporary human communication theory. In D. L. Kincaid (Ed.), *Communication theory: Eastern and Western perspectives* (pp. 23–43). San Diego, CA: Academic Press.

Cheng, C. Y. (1998). Transforming Confucian virtues into human rights. In W. T. de Bary & W. Tu (Eds.), *Confucianism and human rights* (pp. 154–168). New York, NY: Columbia University Press.

Chesebro, J. W. (1996, December). Unity in diversity: Multiculturalism, guilt/victimage, and a new scholarly orientation. *Spectra: Newsletter of the Speech Communication Association*, 32(12), 10–14.

Chikushi, T. (2009). *To my young friends: Tetsuya Chikushi's last message* (in Japanese). Tokyo, Japan: Shueisha.

Chin, C. B. N. (2004). Communication and the human condition: (Re)calling Adam Smith in the 21st century? *Journal of International Communication*, 10(2), 67–89.

Chu, G. C. (1986). Preservation of traditional culture: A challenge to modernization. In P. Brown Foote, N. Graburn, D. Hibbard, L. Minerbi, & S. Tiwari (Eds.), *Problems and issues in cultural heritage conservation: The proceedings of the 1st HAPI Colloquium on "The Preservation of Traditional Culture"* (pp. 1–3). Honolulu, HI: Heritage of Asia and the Pacific Islands.

Chu, L. L. (1988). Mass communication theory: A Chinese perspective. In W. Dissanayake (Ed.), *Communication theory: The Asian perspective* (pp. 126–138). Singapore: Asian Mass Communication Research and Information Center.

Fraser, N. (1997). *Justice interruptus: Critical reflections on "postsocialist" conduction*. New York, NY: Routledge.

Halualani, R. T., Mendoza, S. L., & Drzewiecka, J. A. (2009). "Critical" junctures in intercultural communication studies: A review. *Review of Communication*, 9(1), 17–35.

Hitchcock, D. I. (1994). *Asian values and the United States: How much conflict?* Washington, DC: Center for Strategic and International Studies.

Hsu, F. L. K. (1985). The self in cross-cultural perspective. In A. J. Marsella, G. DeVos, & F. L. K. Hsu (Eds.), *Culture and self: Asian and Western perspectives* (pp. 24–55). New York, NY: Tavistock.

Karenga, M. (1997). African culture and the ongoing quest for excellence: Dialogue, principles, practice. *The Black Collegian*, 27(2), 160–163.

Karenga, M. (2006). Philosophy in the African tradition of resistance: Issues of human freedom and human flourishing. In L. R. Gordon & J. A. Gordon (Eds.), *Not only the master's tools: African American Studies in theory and practice* (pp. 243–271). Boulder, CO: Paradigm.

Karenga, M. (2008). *Kawaida and the questions of life and struggle: African Americans, Pan-Africanism, and global issues.* Los Angeles, CA: University of Sankore Press.

Karenga, M. (2010). *Introduction to Black Studies* (4th ed.). Los Angeles, CA: University of Sankore Press.

Karenga, M. (2012). Afrocentricity. In J. A. Banks (Ed.), *Encyclopedia of diversity in education* (Vol. 1, pp. 72–74). Thousand Oaks, CA: Sage.

Lakshmi, G. (2007). Gandhi and women's peace movements. *Gandhi Marg: Quarterly Journal of the Gandhi Peace Foundation*, 28(4), 457–469.

Lebra, T. S. (1987). The cultural significance of silence in Japanese communication. *Multilingua: Journal of Cross-Cultural and Interlanguage Communication*, 6(4), 343–357.

Liu, S. (2012). Rethinking intercultural competence: Global and local nexus. *Journal of Multicultural Discourses*, 7(3), 269–275.

Martin, J. N., & Nakayama, T. K. (2008). Thinking dialectically about culture and communication. In M. K. Asante, Y. Miike, & J. Yin (Eds.), *The global intercultural communication reader* (pp. 73–91). New York, NY: Routledge.

Martin, J. N., & Nakayama, T. K. (2010). Intercultural communication and dialectics revisited. In T. K. Nakayama & R. T. Halualani (Eds.), *The handbook of critical intercultural communication* (pp. 59–83). West Sussex, UK: Wiley-Blackwell.

Martin, J. N., Nakayama, T. K., & Carbaugh, D. (2012). The history and development of the study of intercultural communication and applied linguistics. In J. Jackson (Ed.), *The Routledge handbook of language and intercultural communication* (pp. 17–36). London, UK: Routledge.

Meyer, M. A. (2001). To set right: Ho'oponopono, a Native Hawai'ian way of peacemaking. In P. K. Chew (Ed.), *The conflict and culture reader* (pp. 176–181). New York, NY: New York University Press.

Meyer, M. A. (2003). Our own liberation: Reflections on Hawai'ian epistemology. *Amerasia Journal*, 29(2), 139–164.

Miike, Y. (2003). Japanese *enryo-sasshi* communication and the psychology of *amae*: Reconsideration and reconceptualization. *Keio Communication Review*, 25, 93–115.

Miike, Y. (2007). "Not always so": Japanese assertion-acceptance communication. In D. W. Klopf & J. C. McCroskey, *Intercultural communication encounters* (pp. 189–190). Boston, MA: Allyn & Bacon.

Miike, Y. (2010a). An anatomy of Eurocentrism in communication scholarship: The role of Asiacentricity in de-Westernizing theory and research. *China Media Research*, 6(1), 1–11.

Miike, Y. (2010b). Culture as text and culture as theory: Asiacentricity and its *raison d'être* in intercultural communication research. In T. K. Nakayama & R. T. Halualani (Eds.), *The handbook of critical intercultural communication* (pp. 190–215). West Sussex, UK: Wiley-Blackwell.

Miike, Y. (2012). "Harmony without uniformity": An Asiacentric worldview and its communicative implications. In L. A. Samovar, R. E. Porter, & E. R. McDaniel (Eds.), *Intercultural communication: A reader* (13th ed., pp. 65–80). Boston, MA: Wadsworth Cengage Learning.

Miike, Y. (2013a). Intercultural communication as a field of study: A selected bibliography of theory and research. In M. K. Asante, Y. Miike, & J. Yin (Eds.), *The global intercultural communication reader* (2nd ed., pp. 515–556). New York, NY: Routledge.

Miike, Y. (2013b). The Asiacentric turn in Asian communication studies: Shifting paradigms and changing perspectives. In M. K. Asante, Y. Miike, & J. Yin (Eds.), *The global intercultural communication reader* (2nd ed., pp.111–133). New York, NY: Routledge.

Miyahara, A. (1995). Metatheoretical issues in conceptualization of Japanese communication competence. *Keio Communication Review*, 17, 63–82.

Miyahara, A. (1998). Philosophical issues in cross-cultural research on communication competence between Asians and Westerners. In D. R. Heisey & W. Gong (Eds.), *Communication and culture: China and the world entering the 21st century* (pp. 57–70). Amsterdam, Netherlands: Rodopi.

Mowlana, H. (1994). Shapes of the future: International communication in the 21st century. *Journal of International Communication*, 1(1), 14–32.

Mowlana, H. (1996). *Global communication in transition: The end of diversity?* Thousand Oaks, CA: Sage.

Mowlana, H. (2012). International communication: The journey of a caravan. *Journal of International Communication*, 18(2), 267–290.

Nakamura, H. (1984). Interrelational existence. In K. K. Inada & N. P. Jacobson (Eds.), *Buddhism and American thinkers* (pp. 144–152). Albany, NY: State University of New York Press.

Ngũgĩ, T. (1997). *Writers in politics: A re-engagement with issues of literature and society* (Rev. ed.). Oxford, UK: James Currey.

Ngũgĩ, T. (2009). *Something torn and new: An African renaissance*. New York, NY: BasicCivitas Books.

Pandikattu, K. (2001). Global village vs. Gandhian villages: A viable vision. In K. Pandikattu (Ed.), *Gandhi: The meaning of Mahatma for the millennium* (pp. 171–196). Washington, DC: Council for Research in Values and Philosophy.

Prosser, M. H. (1974). Introduction: The birth of a discipline. In N. C. Jain, M. H. Prosser, & M. H. Miller (Eds.), *Intercultural communication: Proceedings of the 10th Speech Communication Association Summer Conference* (pp. 9–13). New York, NY: Speech Communication Association.

Prosser, M. H., & Kulich, S. J. (Eds.). (2012). Early American pioneers of intercultural communication [Special issue]. *International Journal of Intercultural Relations*, 36(6), 743–902.

Ran, C. (2002). *"Enryo" no tsūjitai* [The chronology of "enryo"] (in Japanese). *Kokubungakukō* [*Thoughts on Japanese Literature and Japanese Language*], 174, 1–15.

Samovar, L. A., & Porter, R. E. (Eds.). (1972). *Intercultural communication: A reader*. Belmont, CA: Wadsworth.

Samovar, L. A., & Porter, R. E. (Eds.). (1976). *Intercultural communication: A reader* (2nd ed.). Belmont, CA: Wadsworth.

Shim, T. Y.-J., Kim, M.-S., & Martin, J. N. (2008). *Changing Korea: Understanding culture and communication*. New York, NY: Peter Lang.

Shuter, R. (2003). Ethics, culture, and communication: An intercultural perspective. In L. A. Samovar & R. E. Porter (Eds.), *Intercultural communication: A reader* (10th ed., pp. 449–455). Belmont, CA: Wadsworth.

Shuter, R. (2013). The centrality of culture in the 20th and 21st centuries. In M. K. Asante, Y. Miike, & J. Yin (Eds.), *The global intercultural communication reader* (2nd ed., pp.48–57). New York, NY: Routledge.

Singhal, A. (2010). The Mahatma's message: Gandhi's contributions to the art and science of communication. *China Media Research*, 6(3), 103–106.

Sitaram, K. S. (2004). South Asian theories of speech communication: Origins and applications in ancient, modern, and postmodern times. *Human Communication: A Journal of the Pacific and Asian Communication Association*, 7(1), 83–101.

Starosta, W. J., & Chen, G.-M. (2005). Where to now for intercultural communication: A dialogue. In W. J. Starosta & G.-M. Chen (Eds.), *Taking stock in intercultural communication: Where to now?* (pp. 3–13). Washington, DC: National Communication Association.

Tehranian, M. (1993). Ethnic discourse and the new world dysorder: A communitarian perspective. In C. Roach (Ed.), *Communication and culture in war and peace* (pp. 192–215). Newbury Park, CA: Sage.

Tehranian, M. (1994). World with(out) wars: Moral spaces and the ethics of transnational communication. *Javnost— The Public: Journal of the European Institute for Communication and Culture*, 1(1/2), 77–93.

Tu, W. (1996). Beyond the Enlightenment mentality: A Confucian perspective on ethics, migration, and global stewardship. *International Migration Review*, 30(1), 58–75.

Tu, W. (2001). The global significance of local knowledge: A new perspective on Confucian humanism. *Sungkyun Journal of East Asia Studies*, 1(1), 22–27.

Tu, W. (2007). *Dialogue among civilizations: A study of the modern transformation of Confucian humanism* (in Korean and in English, S. Na, Trans.). Seoul, South Korea: Chunho Jeon.

Tu, W. (2010a). *Intercultural dialogue: Cultural diversity and ecological consciousness*. Keynote address delivered at the UNESCO World Philosophy Day, Tehran, Iran.

Tu, W. (2010b). *The global significance of concrete humanity: Essays on the Confucian discourse in cultural China*. New Delhi, India: Center for Studies in Civilizations and Munshiram Manoharlal Publishers.

Weaver, G. R. (2013a). *Intercultural relations: Communication, identity, and conflict*. Boston, MA: Pearson Learning Solutions.

Weaver, G. R. (2013b). The evolution of international communication as a field of study: A personal reflection. In M. K. Asante, Y. Miike, & J. Yin (Eds.), *The global intercultural communication reader* (2nd ed., pp. 35–47). New York, NY: Routledge.

Yin, J. (2009). Negotiating the center: Towards an Asiacentric feminist communication theory. *Journal of Multicultural Discourses*, 4(1), 75–88.

Yin, J. (2011). Popular culture and public imaginary: Disney vs. Chinese stories of *Mulan*. *Javnost—The Public: Journal of the European Institute for Communication and Culture*, 18(1), 53–74.

Yoshikawa, M. J. (1988). Japanese and American modes of communication and implications for managerial and organizational behavior. In W. Dissanayake (Ed.), *Communication theory: The Asian perspective* (pp. 150–182). Singapore: Asian Mass Communication Research and Information Center.

Yum, J. O. (2012). Communication competence: A Korean perspective. *China Media Research*, 8(2), 11–17.

Zhang, M. (2012). Recent studies in East Asian communication. *Journal of Multicultural Discourses*, 7(3), 263–268.

Concepts and Questions

1. Explain your interpretation of the terms "Eurocentric," "Afrocentric," and "Asiacentric."
2. What are the objectives of "Asiacentricity"?
3. Miike and Yin assert that globalization has increased the importance of an Asiacentric perspective due to the need to "move beyond the Eurocentric structure." What does this mean and do you agree or disagree? Why?
4. The essay discusses "multidimensional individual identity" and "shared collective identity." What are some benefits and disadvantages of each type of identity?
5. Your worldview, according to the essay, influences your perception of the purpose of communication. Examples are given for Hinduism, Buddhism, and Confucianism. Provide an explanation of how values construct one's view of the purpose of communication in Western society.
6. From your reading of the Miike and Yin essay can you isolate what Hinduism, Buddhism, Confucianism, and Islam have in common? Can those commonalities help cultures understand each other?
7. Explain and contrast Western "rights-consciousness" and Asian "duty-consciousness." How can these two ethical approaches bring about misunderstanding and/or conflict in an intercultural communication encounter between a U.S. American and someone from China or Japan?
8. Miike and Yin believe that a culture's worldview is an excellent tool for understanding and appreciating cultural similarities and differences. Can you think of any other cultural characteristics (family interaction, history, etc.) that can serve as a backdrop for studying intercultural communication?
9. Can you think of ways that Hinduism, Buddhism, Confucianism, or Islam might influence face-to-face interaction with people who hold a different worldview?

Seeking Common Ground While Accepting Differences through Tolerance: U.S.–China Intercultural Communication in the Global Community

GUO-MING CHEN

Looking back, I realize the Google China drama was the perfect manifestation of the never-ending China-America chasm. These two great countries and their people are forever trying to understand each other but end up succumbing to stereotypes; hearing the other's words but not comprehending the meaning; endorsing each other in words but undermining each other in deeds; demanding the other to accommodate and empathize but remaining intransigent itself. In my view, these phenomena all boil down to a lack of understanding. (Kai-Fu Lee, 2011)

The quote above from Kai-Fu Lee's autobiography manifests the century's misunderstanding and confrontation between East and West, especially between the United States and China. The description of China as being backward, mysterious, authoritarian, and inscrutable continues to dominate the belief of Western people, even if the Chinese are as similar to Westerners as human beings could be.

The differences and confrontation for the case of Google's withdrawal from China were clearly reflected in the news framing. For example, the *Wall Street*

Journal focused on the reports of China's violation of human rights and government censorship, while *China Daily* accused Google of maneuvering to avoid censoring (Kuang, 2011). The differences in media representation are obviously caused by dissimilar cultural beliefs, because the media's underlying assumptions are embedded in their cultural values, and news agencies tend to reflect their nations' agendas and values. The differences in cultural values often result in the asymmetry of intercultural/international communication and inevitably lead to confrontation not only on the national level, but also in interpersonal and group levels (Chen & Dai, 2012; Entman, 1991).

The media coverage of the 2008 Beijing Olympic Games is another example to illustrate the conflict between the United States and China. As Ni (2008) pointed out, media in the United States mainly portrayed and criticized the Chinese government for political corruption and abusing human rights. In contrast, Chinese media tried to construct a positive national image by setting green Olympics, humanistic Olympics, and scientific Olympics as the three key agendas for the 2008 Olympic Games. The differences in the coverage demonstrate "the Western beliefs in freedom of expression, human rights, individual equality, and social justice, which are in contrast to Chinese cultural values of harmony, face saving, group interest, and social order" (Chen, 2012, p. 7). Moreover, the misunderstanding of China was also shown in Mitt Romney's blame and demonization of China in the 2012 U.S. presidential election. Throughout the campaign, Romney openly criticized China for cheating over the years and constantly hacking into U.S. computers, thereby implying that the U.S. government has the responsibility to keep China playing by the rules.

It is obvious that human society cannot afford any more of this kind of confrontation or potential conflict between the two superpowers in this interconnected global community. The new global community draws together people of differing experiences in terms of race, ethnicity, gender, spirituality, creed, and emotional release. It demands that citizens or groups participate equally and fairly in the construction of a global community, which is defined not by members' racial, political, or geographic boundaries, but by common beliefs, values, and symbolic schemas. Its goal is to promote voluntary pluralism through intercultural communication by integrating different identities and interests to build a global civic culture. In other words, it demands the efforts of members to seek common ground while accepting differences through tolerance in order to develop a "communication reality" in which ideas, beliefs, preferences, qualities, evils, and ideals can be talked about, and through which members can use symbols to recreate themselves and to define why they are a particular kind of human or group in the global community (Thayer, 1987). Hence, a safe space must be found to discuss issues of ethnicity, race, power, gender, and psychological orientation. Ultimately, global citizens must be able to establish their own conscious identities and a total social environment in which they coexist and rationalize their own and others' actions.

The question is how to achieve this goal of global community that can be applied to the case of the U.S.-China entangled relationship. The answers can be found in the research of intercultural communication scholars. That is, to be effective in interaction in the global community one has to possess two abilities: intercultural awareness and intercultural sensitivity.

INTERCULTURAL AWARENESS AND INTERCULTURAL SENSITIVITY

First of all, the lack of intercultural awareness is the culprit for the up and down relationship between the U.S. and China. As Chen and Starosta (1998) indicated, intercultural awareness, representing the cognitive perspective of intercultural communication, refers to knowing the distinct characteristics of one's own and one's counterpart's cultures. Intercultural awareness helps people develop an understanding of cultural dynamics to reduce the level of situational ambiguity and uncertainty in the process of intercultural interaction. Scholars treat human culture as a "map" (Kluckhohn, 1948), and each culture has a "theme" (Turner, 1968) or is regulated by a set of "grammars" (Colby, 1975). In other words, if individuals are able to accurately read the cultural map, to clearly pull out the cultural theme, or to understand the cultural grammars, they are considered to have the ability of intercultural awareness. The map, theme, or grammars of a culture are dictated by its cultural values. Thus, to understand cultural values is the prerequisite for reaching intercultural awareness.

While there are different effective ways to study cultural values (e.g., Condon & Yousef, 1975; Hofstede, 1980; Kluckhohn & Strodbeck, 1961), a more comprehensive approach to the understanding of cultural values is to examine the paradigmatic assumptions of a culture. Figure 1 from Chen (2009a) and Chen and An (2009) was readapted to illustrate the cultural values of the United States vs. China based on paradigmatic assumptions:

Ontologically, Chinese culture treats the universe as a great whole in which, although conflicts exist, human interaction always aims to achieve a holistic or collective goal. In this changing and transforming process, individuals strive for becoming part of and being with nature in order to reach the ultimate state of oneness. Hence, human interaction dictates the interpenetration and identification of the two interactants. In contrast, the United States orients to the atomistic view by emphasizing the importance of individual components in the process of human communication. Reflected on the behavioral level, we can see that Chinese people tend to submerge into the group, which demonstrates the cultural value of collectivism, while U.S. Americans tend to be discrete in the group, displaying the value of individualism.

Axiologically, Chinese culture emphasizes the importance of harmony throughout the universe. As Chen (2006) stated, harmony is the ultimate goal of Chinese communication. The Chinese use harmony to regulate the dynamic process of human communication and consider that only through harmony can people influence each other with dignity in the process of interaction. Harmony is therefore defined by cooperation and fellowship embedded in the process of indirect, subtle, adaptive, consensual, and agreeable communication behaviors. The confrontational stance taken by U.S. Americans reflects the emphasis on directness, expressiveness, dialectic, divisiveness, and being sermonic in interaction. Using confrontation as a tool to solve problems or reach one's communication goal inevitably leads to the stress on competition and opposition. To employ verbal and nonverbal strategies to win over counterparts rather than display a mutually whole-hearted concern through cooperation thus distinguishes the United States from China in terms of axiology orientation.

Epistemologically, interconnectedness is where the Chinese find the real meaning of their existence. Demonstrated by behavioral characteristics, such as reciprocity, group sense, hierarchy, and associative and ascribed relationship, Chinese people believe that to genuinely know the interaction between the

Figure 1 *The Paradigmatic Assumptions of the United States vs. China*

Ontology					
U.S.		China			
Atomistic ←------------------------------------→ Holistic					
discrete individualistic		submerged collectivistic			
Axiology		Epistemology		Methodology	
U.S.	China	U.S.	China	U.S.	China
Confrontational ←---→ Harmonious		Reductionistic ←---→ Interconnected		Logical ←---→ Intuitive	
direct	indirect	independent	reciprocity	objective	subjective
expressive	subtle	l	we	linear	nonlinear
dialectical	adaptive	equal	hierarchical	analytical	ambiguous
divisive	consensual	free will	associative	justificatory	ritual
sermonic	agreeable	achieved	ascribed	manipulative	accommodative

knower and the known, one has to first recognize the interdependent, interfusing, and transformational nature of human communication. Originating from the atomistic ontology assumption, U.S. Americans adopt the reductionistic view of knowing, which is based on the values of independence, I sense, equality, free will, and achievement in the process of interaction. The reductionistic view is greatly different from the Chinese belief in nonduality or identification of opposites through the interconnectedness of interaction.

Methodologically, the Chinese intuitive thinking pattern and problem solving indicate that "many paths can reach the same destination, and in reality no one path is different from the other, because all the paths engage in a mutually-defining and complementary relationship" (Chen, 2006, p. 300). The method mirrors the subjective, nonlinear, ambiguous, ritual, and accommodative styles of the Chinese in the process of interaction. The U.S. American's logical thinking pattern, manifested by objectivity, linearity, analysis, justification, and manipulation in the process of interaction, is in opposition to the Chinese way of thinking. The intuitive way of thinking, intertwined with the subtle and indirect expression style dictated by axiological harmony, may be the main reason why Westerners always claim that China is a mysterious land and Chinese people are inscrutable.

The above paradigmatic assumptions form the essential frame of Chinese and U.S. American cultural values, respectively. Being aware of the distinctions of paradigmatic assumptions between the U.S. and China opens the door for understanding numerous studies by scholars in different disciplines. These show that Chinese behaviors are dictated by such characteristics as intuition, face saving, particularistic relationship, gift giving, moderation, silence, politeness, reciprocity, empathy, emotional control, and avoidance of aggression (e.g., Chen, 2010), while U.S. Americans are seen as aggressive, credible, fair, honest, action oriented, informal, impersonal, having short-term relationships, power driven, noisy, and self-interested (e.g., Stewart & Bennett, 1991).

In addition to the contrast of cultural values based on paradigmatic assumptions between the United States and China, the double-headed arrows between the assumptions (i.e., Holistic ⟷ Atomistic, etc.) in Figure 1 deserve an explanation. As Chen (2009a)

warned, one of the major obstacles for reaching intercultural understanding is to dichotomize cultural values between different groups. Dichotomizing cultural values begets an insurmountable gap of understanding between two cultural groups. The double-headed arrows in Figure 1 infer a continuum between the two opposite values in each paradigmatic assumption. In other words,

> while, for example, holistic is the core value of Chinese culture and atomistic is the core value of U.S. American culture, the dynamic nature and internal variations of the culture will show a range of values regarding the ontological orientation in each culture. Hence, we can only address that the Chinese culture tends to orient to a holistic view of ontology and the U.S. American orients to an atomistic view. More specifically, one should assume that the Chinese culture leans more to the end of holistic or leans less to the end of atomistic, which means that the Chinese culture contains both holistic and atomistic thinking with more towards holistic, and vice versa for the U.S. American culture. (Chen, 2009a, p. 403)

Therefore, the differences between cultures are just in degree rather than in type. This indicates that differences and similarities of cultural values exist at the same time in human societies. Only through this recognition can "Seeking Common Ground While Accepting Differences through Tolerance" specified in the title of this essay be achieved for ending the chasm between the United States and China in their future intercultural communication.

Nevertheless, intercultural awareness, or the understanding of cultural differences and similarities, cannot guarantee the success of intercultural communication, unless it is supplemented by the tolerance or acceptance of differences which is embedded in the ability of intercultural sensitivity. Intercultural sensitivity, representing the affective perspective of intercultural communication, refers to the development of positive emotion that motivates a person or group to willingly understand, acknowledge, respect, tolerate, and accept cultural differences of counterparts (Chen & Young, 2012). As Chen and Starosta (2004) pointed out, intercultural sensitivity requires the ability of empathy that helps people foster the feeling of fellowship "by expanding the self consciousness to the consciousness of one's fellow persons" and "by which the self reaches the state of harmonious interpenetration or expanding and contracting between I and YOU or WE and THEY" (p. 13). Intercultural sensitivity is therefore the best footnote of "Accepting Differences through Tolerance" mentioned previously. It is also the best way to prevent one from taking advantage of the other because of being aware of the other's culture.

INTERCULTURAL COMMUNICATION IN THE GLOBAL COMMUNITY

Effective intercultural communication between the two superpowers discussed above can be used to exemplify the interaction between West and East and should be moved one step further to apply to the global community, which represents the reality of the contemporary human world. Theoretically, the global community is a holistically interconnected network formed by the dynamic interaction of different cultural contexts. In other words, the nature of interaction in the global community is intercultural and multicultural. It demands a dynamic view of cultural multiplicity with flexibility and fluidity in order to reach an effective outcome of communication among diverse cultural groups in the global community.

To put it another way, although cultural context provides a safe and stable space in which members can exercise their social, linguistic, and psychological activities, cultural stability immediately faces challenges when people from different cultures interact in the global community. Thus, to keep the cultural context flexible or fluid for possible negotiation and redefinition of one's cultural identity becomes the key to the success of intercultural communication in the global community. Only cultural flexibility and fluidity can achieve the establishment of the third-culture (Casmir, 1999) or interculturality (Dai, 2010). In this new space of intercultural interaction, participants are able to negotiate and adjust mutually to build a win–win intercultural relationship. It allows interpenetration, interfusion, and transformation of the two different cultural contexts.

Moreover, Chen (2009a) proposed that intercultural or multicultural communication in the global community can be treated as a boundary game. A boundary "represents the limit or border of a space, where a field of contact between two persons/groups is created" (p. 407). No matter that the space is perceived as a center or periphery. The hub of each space is the core area of the person/group, which forms a constant or stronghold place embedded in cultural beliefs and values, and the contact area or the boundary reflects a "degree of ambiguity and uncertainty caused by the impact or counteraction of different ideas from neighboring groups" (p. 407). It is the interaction, either struggling for control or driving for cooperation, of the two parties in this frontier that defines or ascribes one's identity. In other words, the formation, maintenance, and validation of one's identity is based on the discrimination of cultural differences in the boundary. This new synthetic border, which is transformed from an isolated cultural context to a convergent state embedded in the contextual flexibility through interaction, is the state of third-culture or interculturality. This new space can be regarded as the co-center of intercultural/multicultural interaction, and the ideal of global community is to expand this co-center to its maximum level.

Chen (2009a) further advocated that "boundary wisdom" is a way to maximize the space of the co-center of intercultural/multicultural interaction in the global community. According to Chen (2009a), boundary wisdom is "the courage to expand the area of the borderline by acknowledging, recognizing, and accepting the foreign elements, and then integrating them into part of one's own group through an active involvement in the interaction with the different" (p. 407). More specifically,

> boundary wisdom is a process of challenging one's own core values by facing challenges from outside influences. The process reflects an inclusive mindset that keeps enriching one's own culture. The mindset also crystallizes the centricity of the culture through interacting with foreign elements on the basis of pushing and pulling between one's own and other cultural groups. (Chen, 2009a, pp. 407–408)

This multicultural co-existing or cultural flexibility is consistent with the Chinese philosophical thinking of the *tai chi* model specified in the *Book of Changes*. Figure 2 shows the model, which dictates that everything in the universe, including intercultural

Figure 2 *The Chinese Tai Chi Model*

communication, is the product of dynamic interaction between the two opposite forces, i.e., *yin* (the dark side in Figure 2, representing the yielding force) and *yang* (the white side in Figure 2, representing the dominant force). It infers that effective intercultural communication in the global community can only be achieved through the correspondence of the two forces, such as the different cultural values between the United States and China, or West and East, that are opposite, but interdependent, interpenetrated, and mutually interfused and transformative (Chen, 2009b).

The inclusive or multicultural mindset prescribed by boundary wisdom serves as the foundation for the empathic ability required by intercultural sensitivity, which leads to the acceptance of cultural differences through tolerance in the global community. It provides members of the global community, on the basis of intercultural awareness, the ability to share communication symbols, putting feet in others' shoes, showing concern for others' feelings, and establishing an intercultural/multicultural rapport (Barnlund, 1988).

Finally, the multicultural mindset that fosters empathy serves as the foundation for the establishment of a global ethic, referring to a universal set of ethical standards and values followed by members of the global community. Only through this global ethic can members of the global community cross the divide of diversity that causes difference, differentiation, discrimination, dissonance, and demarcation among them. As Tu (1992) indicated, "reciprocity" as stipulated by Confucius requires that one "do not do to others what you do not want them to do to you" and "being able to establish oneself, one should help others to do so" potentially can be treated as the universal principle of ethical communication in the global community. The principle promotes voluntary participation in the interaction, seeking individual focus prior to cultural focus, maintaining the right to freedom from harm, accepting the right to privacy of thought and action, and avoiding imposing personal biases on one's counterparts; and it is embedded in four behavioral standards of an authentic dialogue, namely, mutuality, nonjudgmentalism, honesty, and respect, among members of the global community (Boulding, 1988; Chen & Starosta, 2005).

CONCLUSION

This is not an age of "When Greek meets Greek then comes the tug of war," but an age of "Different approaches contribute to the same end." This essay stipulates that intercultural awareness and intercultural sensitivity are the two major elements for reaching intercultural rapport in the global community, which is not only limited to the relationship between the United States and China, but also to be applied to the interaction between West and East and eventually to all participant cultures in global society. Globalization is a trend that cannot be reversed in contemporary human society. To learn how to "agree to disagree" in order to deepen cooperation among different cultural groups in the global community has become a necessity for a successful and productive life nowadays. It is hoped that the viewpoints proposed in this essay for reaching favorable future U.S.–China intercultural communication can, as well, mirror a beautiful new human world in the coming centuries, or reach the ideal state of "shi jie da tong" (a world of universal harmony) pursued by the Chinese since ancient times.

References

Barnlund, D. C. (1988). Communication in a global village. In L. A. Samovar & R. E. Porter (Eds.), *Intercultural communication: A reader* (7th ed., pp. 5–14). Belmont, CA: Wadsworth.

Boulding, E. (1988). *Building a global civic culture.* Syracuse, NY: Syracuse University Press.

Casmir, F. L. (1999). Foundations for the study of intercultural communication based on a third-culture building model. *International Journal of Intercultural Relations,* 23(1), 91–116.

Chen, G. M. (2006). Asian communication studies: What and where to now. *The Review of Communication*, 6(4), 295–311.

Chen, G. M. (2009a). Beyond the dichotomy of communication studies. *Journal of Asian Communication*, 19(4), 398–411.

Chen, G. M. (2009b). Toward an *I Ching* model of communication. *China Media Research*, 5(3), 72–81.

Chen, G. M. (2010). *Study on Chinese communication behaviors*. Hong Kong: China Review Academic Publishers.

Chen, G. M. (2012). The impact of new media on intercultural communication in global context. *China Media Research*, 8(2), 1–10.

Chen, G. M., & An, R. (2009). A Chinese model of intercultural leadership competence. In D. K. Deardorff (Ed.), *The SAGE Handbook of intercultural competence* (pp. 196–208). Thousand Oaks, CA: Sage.

Chen, G. M., & Dai, X.-D. (2012). New media and asymmetry in cultural identity negotiation. In P. H. Cheong, J. N. Martin, & L. Macfadyen (Eds), *New Media and Intercultural Communication: Identity, Community and Politics*. New York: Peter Lang.

Chen, G. M., & Starosta, W. J. (1998). A review of the concept of intercultural awareness. *Human Communication*, 2, 27–54.

Chen, G. M., & Starosta, W. J. (2004). Communication among cultural diversities: A dialogue. *International and Intercultural Communication Annual*, 27, 3–16.

Chen, G. M., & Starosta, W. J. (2005). *Foundations of intercultural communication*. Lanham, MD: University Press of America.

Chen, G. M., & Young, P. (2012). Intercultural communication competence. In A. Goodboy & K. Shultz (Eds.), *Introduction to communication: Translating scholarship into meaningful practice* (pp. 175–188). Dubuque, IA: Kendall-Hunt.

Colby, B. N. (1975). Culture grammars. *Science*, 187, 913–919.

Condon, J. C., & Yousef, F. (1975). *An introduction to intercultural communication*. Indianapolis: Bobbs-Merrill.

Dai, X.-D. (2010). Intersubjectivity and interculturality: A conceptual link. *China Media Research*, 6(1), 12–19.

Entman, R. M. (1991). Framing U.S. coverage of international news: Contrasts in narratives of the KAL and Iran Air incidents. *Journal of Communication*, 41, 6–27.

Hofstede, G. (1980). *Culture's consequences*. Beverly Hills, CA: Sage.

Kluckhohn, F. K. (1948). *Mirror of man*. New York: Harper Collins.

Kluckhohn, F. K., & Strodbeck, F. L. (1961). *Variations in value orientations*. Evanston, IL: Row, Peterson.

Kuang, K. (2011, November). *Google's withdrawal from China: A case study of news framing through an agenda setting approach*. Paper presented at the annual conference of National Communication. New Orleans, Louisiana.

Lee, K.-F. (2011). *Making a world of difference: An autobiography*. Retrieved January 5, 2013, from http://www.lulijen.com

Ni, J.-P. (2008). *The Beijing Olympics and China's national image building*. Retrieved January 5, 2013, from www.cctr.ust.hk/materials/conference/workshop/14/nizp_olympics.pdf

Stewart, J., & Bennett, M. J. (1991). *American cultural patterns: A cross-cultural perspective*. Yarmouth, ME: Intercultural Press.

Thayer, L. (1987). *On communication: Essays in understanding*. Norwood, NJ: Ablex.

Tu, W.-M. (1992). Core values and the possibility of a fiduciary global community. In K. Tehranian & M. Tehranian (Eds.), *Reconstructing for world peace: On the threshold of the twenty-first century* (pp. 333–345). Cresskill, NJ: Hampton.

Turner, C. V. (1968). The Sinasina "big man" complex: A central cultural theme. *Practical Anthropology*, 15, 16–22.

Concepts and Questions

1. Chen indicates that "Western beliefs in freedom of expression, human rights, individual equality, and social justice" contrast with the Chinese "cultural values of harmony, face saving, group interest, and social order." Give some examples of how these contrasting values can produce conflict within an intercultural setting.

2. Explain how understanding cultural values leads to intercultural awareness.

3. Compare Chinese and U.S. ontological perspectives. How can the contrasts influence intercultural communication?

4. Chen explains that cognitive processing, or thinking patterns, differs sharply between Chinese and U.S. Americans. What cultural values underlie and exemplify these separate styles of thinking?

5. According to Chen, an awareness of cultural differences and similarities will not ensure success in intercultural interactions. Do you agree? Explain?

6. The essay mentions the "state of third-culture or interculturality." Explain what this means.

7. What is "boundary wisdom"?

8. In your opinion, can globalization be reversed? Why or why not?

The Promise of Intercultural New Media Studies

ROBERT SHUTER

New media (ICTs) are ubiquitous, transforming intercultural communication. Contact between individuals and groups from different cultures has increased exponentially due to the Internet (CMC), social network sites (SNSs), mobile phones, Skype, text messaging, online games (MMOGs), virtual worlds, and blogs. People worldwide utilize ICTs to communicate instantaneously with others regardless of geo-political boundaries, time, or space, and hence, are no longer restricted primarily to face-to-face encounters.

Researchers have largely ignored the impact of new media on intercultural communication despite this revolution in cross-cultural contact (Cheong, Martin, & Macfayden, 2012; Shuter, 2011 & 2012). Additional investigations on this topic could challenge more than fifty years of intercultural communication knowledge and theory rooted in the twentieth-century face-to-face paradigm. This article proposes, defines, and sets the research agenda for a new field of study called Intercultural New Media Studies (INMS), which explores the intersection between ICTs and intercultural communication.

INTERCULTURAL NEW MEDIA STUDIES (INMS): PARAMETERS OF A FIELD

Intercultural new media studies primarily examines how ICTs impact communication *between* people who do not share the same cultural backgrounds,

which was often defined as national culture (nation state) and co-culture (i.e., ethnicity and race) in early intercultural communication research, but has been expanded contemporarily to include myriad cultures, both within and across geo-political boundaries, as well as hybridized cultures that have developed transnationally due to migration, diaspora, and time and space reconfigurations in a digital age (Clothier, 2005; Dooly, 2011; McEwan & Sobre-Denton, 2011; Steinkuehler & Williams, 2006). The secondary interest area of INMS is the relationship between culture and new media, which includes how culture impacts the social uses of new media within and across societies, and how new media affect culture.

The primary area of INMS is called new media and intercultural communication theory because it attempts to identify new digital theories of intercultural contact as well as refine and expand twentieth-century theories of intercultural communication. Although there are limited data on the impact of new media on intercultural communication theory, the available research suggests that new media play a major role in the ebb and flow of intercultural encounters, conceivably augmenting twentieth-century theories on communication across cultures.

New Media and Intercultural Communication Theory

This section explores the possible effects of new media, and raises important twenty-first-century suppositions, on five essential areas of intercultural communication and their attendant theories: intercultural dialogue, third culture, acculturation, intercultural competence, and cultural identity.

Intercultural Dialogue, Third Culture, and New Media Intercultural dialogue requires openness and empathy, resulting in a deep understanding of others (Ganesh & Holmes, 2011). Unlike casual contact, intercultural dialogue requires communicators to be aware of, even challenge, their personal values and predispositions—albeit, any aspect of their background—that may prevent a complete understanding of others. To achieve intercultural dialogue, communicators must be open to accepting differences—a deeply rooted principle of dialogue founded on the work of

Buber (1965), Gadamer (1989), and Habermas (1987), all twentieth-century theorists who wrote about dialogue in organic communities. In fact, since theories, models, and strategies for achieving intercultural dialogue emerge from a twentieth-century face-to-face paradigm, it is unclear whether dialogue literature—or dialogue itself—is applicable to a virtual world.

Literature on virtual intercultural dialogue is limited, but the evidence suggests that it is challenged by many of the same factors that affect dialogue in organic communities. Hichang and Jae-Shin (2008) examined computer-mediated groups composed of students from the United States and Singapore and discovered that virtual intercultural collaboration was constrained by preexisting social networks and intergroup boundaries formulated in their respective countries and cultures. They found that the students' willingness to collaborate and share information with others were affected by whether their virtual partners were members of their in-groups and shared their cultural values. Similarly, Pfeil, Zaphiris, and Ang (2006) hypothesized correctly that cultural values influence collaboration, discovering that collaborative authoring patterns of Wikipedia reflected predominant cultural values of French, German, Japanese, and Dutch authors. The researchers concluded that cultural differences found in the physical world are also in play in virtual communities.

Although virtual collaboration may lead to intercultural dialogue, and perhaps is a precursor to dialogue, collaboration is frequently missing requisite dialogic elements like empathy and deep understanding. Hence, the question remains: Is intercultural dialogue possible in the virtual world? Studies of third culture in cyberspace offer some additional insight into this question.

The concept of third culture was originally developed by Fred Casmir (1978, 1997; Casmir & Asuncion-Lande, 1989) who posited that dialogue is necessary to develop a third culture since it cannot be achieved without empathy and deep understanding of others. Starosta and Olorunnisola (1998) add that individuals must be consciously aware of their differences and capable of suspending judgment to build a third culture, a product of convergence, integration, and mutual assimilation. Once achieved, third culture provides an ideal climate to interact because it is mutually accepting, supportive, and cooperative.

Although third cultures are difficult to create in the physical world, some research suggests that they may be more achievable in virtual communities. McEwan and Sobre-Denton (2011) argue that the ease of technological access to cultural others combined with reduced social and economic costs significantly increase the probability of developing third cultures in the virtual world. Virtual communities, unlike organic ones, do not require leaving one's domicile to be an active member, nor are they plagued by face threats due to social errors, according to the authors. In fact, new media provide users with technological tools to manage social distance, which McEwan and Sobre-Denton suggest increase cultural risk-taking and experimentation, leading more readily to virtual third cultures.

There is also evidence, however, that third cultures are difficult to construct in the virtual world. Nelson and Temples (2011) examined graduate students' attempts to negotiate memberships in multiple on-line communities during an international exchange program. The students experienced numerous cultural issues in constructing online relationships in international virtual communities, leading the authors to conclude that the process of what they called "reconciliation," which is comparable to third culture building, is complex and sometimes impossible in cyberspace.

While data are inconclusive on whether intercultural dialogue or third culture can actually occur in virtual communities, the research does suggest that the use of multiple new media technologies in a virtual community may increase the emotional attachment of participants and, hence, the prospect for dialogue. Wang (2012) found that Facebook is a viable platform for building cross-cultural friendships among Taiwanese and American university students; however, to retain these friendships after the completion of a project, other Web 2.0 applications are necessary. Dooly (2011) also discovered that the effectiveness and depth of online cross-cultural relationships between two groups of student teachers in Spain and the United States were affected by the number and nature of communication platforms utilized including Skype, Moodle, Voicethread, and Second Life.

In summary, the following suppositions emerge about intercultural dialogue and third culture building from intercultural new media literature.

1. *Intercultural dialogue and third culture building, as defined in face-to-face literature, may be difficult to achieve in virtual communities.*

   The on-line literature suggests that empathy and deep understanding—prerequisites for dialogue and third culture building—may not be readily achievable in the virtual world.

2. *Intercultural dialogue and third culture building may be governed by different processes in virtual communities and organic ones.*

   The reviewed research suggests that factors like anonymity and controlling social distance, which are inimical to face-to-face dialogue and third culture building, may help produce both outcomes in the virtual world.

3. *It may be necessary to utilize multiple new media platforms to achieve intercultural dialogue and third culture in a virtual world.*

   Research suggests that a mix of new media platforms, including on-line and video chat/conferencing, may increase the chances for achieving intercultural dialogue and third culture in virtual communities.

4. *External factors from the physical world that affect intercultural dialogue and third culture building may also impinge on both outcomes in the virtual world.*

   Social factors from the physical world, including stereotyping, predispositions, and different cultural values, may affect the development of intercultural dialogue and third culture in the virtual world.

Acculturation, Intercultural Competence, and New Media There is a good deal of research on how people adapt to new cultures, and much of the data examine the impact of interpersonal interaction and mass media on acculturation. Young Kim (1988, 2001) found that positive social communication in the host culture, combined with reasonable and successful ethnic support, provide cultural knowledge and skills and emotional stability to acculturate successfully. She also integrates mass media into her model, arguing that acculturation is influenced by the nature, type, and frequency of media consumption patterns. Additional researchers have also found that host culture social communication and mass media play a significant role in acculturation, as do ethnic social support and media from a sojourner's culture of origin

(Durham, 2004; Khan, 1992; Raman & Harwood, 2008). Although there is considerable research on the effects of social communication and mass media on acculturation, there are scant data on new media and acculturation.

Available new media studies suggest that the Internet and selected online communities may facilitate the process of acculturation. For example, Ye (2005) found that Chinese international students who utilize online ethnic support groups composed of Chinese students experience significantly less acculturative stress and more emotional support. Jiali (2006) discovered that Chinese students who received support from both online ethnic groups and interpersonal networks in the host culture tended to experience fewer social difficulties in acculturation. Further, Chen (2010) found that the longer immigrants lived in a host culture, the less likely they surfed home country websites and the more apt they were to communicate online with residents of the host culture, which facilitated their acculturation.

Surprisingly, there are very limited data on the influence of social networking sites on acculturation. Croucher and Cronn-Mills (2011) found that the use of social networking sites among French Muslims reinforced their Islamic identities rather than their French identities, which complicated the adaptation process. In a conceptual essay, Croucher (2011) hypothesized that increased use of social networking sites composed of people from the same culture may serve as an obstacle to acculturation. Croucher's research on social networking sites contrasts with studies on the positive effects of online ethnic support networks on acculturation. Perhaps, social networking sites provide a unique portal for ethnic networking that distinguish them from other types of online ethnic encounters.

Not only is acculturation affected by face-to-face and online support networks, but it is also influenced by the individual's level of intercultural competence, often measured by awareness of and openness to cultural differences as well as the abilities and skills necessary to successfully navigate a new culture (Wiseman & Koester, 1993). While Kim (2001) and others have found that individuals learn about new cultures incrementally, largely through pre-departure preparation, social communication in the host culture, and mass media, there is also evidence that online encounters can increase intercultural competence and enhance acculturation potential.

Studies on Internet mediated second language learning suggest that online international exchanges accelerate language acquisition and intercultural competence. Chun (2011) found that online contact between German and American university students learning each other's language significantly increased their cultural awareness and intercultural communication skills. Belz (2005) reported that Internet mediated language learning between Germans and Americans dramatically improved the participants' ability to use questions to ascertain cultural information, which they argue is an essential component of intercultural competence. While investigating the effect of blogs on second language learning for Spanish and American students, Elola and Oskoz (2008) discovered that blogging in newly acquired languages improved both groups' intercultural competence.

Despite the popularity of virtual gaming worlds like Second Life, World of War Craft, EverQuest, Final Fantasy, and Xbox Live, there is very limited data on whether virtual worlds affect intercultural competence and, hence, acculturation potential. In an important study, Diehl and Prins (2008) explored the cross-cultural exchanges of Second Life participants, evaluating both their real and virtual world interactions. They found that Second Life enhanced the participants' "intercultural literacy" by promoting intercultural friendships, second language acquisition, and openness to diverse cultures, practices, and attitudes. In a related study, Ward (2010) found that the acculturation strategies utilized in the physical world are also employed when participants culturally adapt to virtual gaming worlds, which suggest that this type of cyber-experience may enhance skills that increase acculturation potential.

The data on new media and acculturation raise many provocative suppositions about the role of new media in acculturation and intercultural competence.

1. *Computer-mediated communication (CMC) appears to play a positive role in acculturation and intercultural competence.*
   Available data suggest that online exchanges between members of ethnic groups provide important emotional support and generally play a positive role in acculturation. In contrast, online cross-cultural exchanges during training sessions for second language acquisition can increase intercultural competence, which can improve acculturation potential.

2. *Virtual gaming worlds may play a useful role in improving acculturation potential and increasing intercultural competence.*
   Limited data suggest that participating in Second Life may enhance intercultural skills that are essential for intercultural competence and successful cultural adaptation. Data also suggest that participants of virtual gaming worlds may utilize many of the same acculturation strategies that are used in the physical world.

3. *Social media appear to affect acculturation and intercultural competence, but the data are too limited to speculate on the types of effects.*
   Social media (SNS)—including Facebook, Twitter, and MySpace as well as culturally indigenous brands like QQ (China), Orkut (India), and Weibo (China)—have been virtually unexamined in terms of their effects on acculturation and intercultural competence. Limited data suggest that ethnic social media may negatively affect acculturation, but it is unclear how cross-cultural uses of SNSs affect acculturation and intercultural competence. Do social networking sites increase intercultural contact and, hence, improve acculturation potential or do they merely enable users to communicate with in-groups who share their cultural backgrounds and limit acculturation (Shuter, 2011)?

4. *The interplay between new media, mass media, and acculturation is unexplored and requires careful analysis.*
   Given the interactive and personal nature of new media, could they have more impact on acculturation and intercultural competence than traditional mass media? Does frequency of new media use impact the potential effects of mass media on acculturation and intercultural competence?

5. *The effects of mobile devices on acculturation and intercultural competence has not been explored, and given their omnipresence in the twenty-first century, this new media platform warrants examination.*
   Mobile phones, smart phones, and i-Pads are ubiquitous and powerful. Cell phones are more

plentiful worldwide than are Internet connections, and more people text message and mobile call than engage in computer-mediated communication (Shuter & Chattopadhyay, 2010; Shuter, 2012). Yet, there is no published research on text messaging (SMS), mobile calling—or of any application of a mobile device—and acculturation and intercultural competence.

6. *Since new media are not included in acculturation theories developed in the twentieth century, these theories may not adequately explain how people acculturate in the twenty-first century.*

It's important to revisit and reconfigure major theories of acculturation to ensure that they sufficiently include new media. In addition, how individuals acculturate in online communities and virtual worlds may provide new insights into the process of acculturation in the physical world.

Cultural Identity and New Media According to social identity theory, identity is derived from membership in social groups, an outcome of in-group identification that also influences communication in social groups (Tajfel & Turner, 1986). Collier (2002) argues that identity is co-created and negotiated, impacted by internal and external factors that she calls avowal and ascription, and also affected by communication. This view of cultural identity is rooted in twentieth-century assumptions about the origins of the self in relationship to others; that is, social identity is based on group contact(s) that is fixed in space and time, producing discernible social identity(ies) that varies in salience depending on the social context(s). However, in a new media era of perpetual contact (Katz & Aakhus, 2002), where individuals live in virtual spaces with myriad others, is this perspective relevant and sufficient for explaining the development and maintenance of cultural identity in the twenty-first century?

Available literature on cultural identity and new media raise several important suppositions regarding the salience of past cultural identity research conducted in organic, face-to-face communities.

1. *It is not clear how cultural identities are constructed in virtual communities.*

Cultural identities may not necessarily be co-created or negotiated in virtual communities according to the literature (Beniger,1987; Singh, 2010). Negotiation and co-creation require some degree of parity between parties, which may not be possible in virtual communities since information technology—hardware, software, web design, and new/social media—appear to privilege the West (Chen & Dai, 2012). Moreover, since virtual communities are often pseudo-communities—sometimes anonymous and generally disconnected from physical space and time—intimacy and engagement, which are requisites for co-creation and negotiation, can be quite limited.

2. *It is not clear how virtual and organic communities create hybrid cultural identities.*

While the literature suggests that hybrid cultural identities can emerge in either organic or virtual communities, it is unclear how this process unfolds. If co-created and negotiated, how is hybridity created in virtual and organic communities when traditions, symbols, and icons are co-opted by dominant and powerful cultural forces (Chen & Dai, 2012). Similarly, how is hybridity realized in cyberspace when race, ethnicity, and culture are so pervasive (Grasmuck, Martin, & Shanyang, 2009)?

3. *The dynamics of maintaining cultural identity may be different in virtual communities than organic ones.*

The literature suggests that co-cultures and marginalized individuals may find more and different opportunities for presenting and reinforcing their cultural identities in virtual communities than organic ones. Cyberspace can empower disenfranchised groups in unique and powerful ways that are differentiated from the dynamics of face-to-face interaction (Hu & Leung, 2003; Mehra, Merkel & Bishop, 2004). What are the dynamics of identity preservation in virtual communities and how do they differ from organic communities?

While this section of the essay explored the possible effects of new media on five major areas of intercultural communication, it is not an exhaustive analysis. There are scattered new media studies on other important areas of intercultural communication including stereotyping (Chia-I, 2008; Guéguen, 2008; Nakamura, 2009), high context/low context communication (Pflug, 2011; Richardson & Smith, 2007; Würtz,

2005), culture shock/stress (Karlsson, 2006; Martinez, 2010), intercultural relationship development (Tokunaga, 2009; Young-ok & Hara, 2005), and intercultural conflict (Mollov & Schwartz, 2010; St. Amant, 2002). New media data in these areas are too limited to draw any conclusions except that there is much research to be done to determine whether twentieth-century intercultural communication theories adequately explain our current intercultural transactions. The essay now turns to the impact of culture on the social uses of new media, the secondary research area in intercultural new media studies.

Culture and New Media: Secondary Area of Intercultural New Media Studies

Culture and new media are wedded: Not only does culture affect the social uses of new media, but new media appear to change culture. This is an important dimension of intercultural new media studies and, unlike the previous section on new media and intercultural communication theory, there has been more research conducted here.

Early research on culture and new media focused on computer-mediated communication (CMC) and explored such topics as intercultural communication and CMC (Ma, 1996), country differences in CMC (Yoon, 1996), CMC and the rise of electronic global culture (Ess, 2001; Jones, 2001), and the utilization of CMC in student exchange programs and multicultural classrooms (Meagher & Castanos, 1996; Colomb & Simutis, 1996. More recently, scholars have examined the impact of culture on the social uses of additional new media platforms including mobile phones (Baron & Af Segerstad, 2010; Campbell, 2007; Schroeder, 2010), text messaging (Ling, 2008; Shuter & Chattopadhyay, 2010; Spurgeon & Goggin, 2007), social media (Barker & Ota, 2011; Lin, Peng, M. Kim, S. Kim & LaRose, 2012; Shu-Chuan & Sejung Marina, 2011), blogs (Elola & Oskoz, 2008; Karlsson, 2006), virtual worlds (Diehl & Prins, 2008; Green & Singleton, 2007; Wang, Walther, & Hancock, 2009), and multiplayer on-line games (Chia-I, 2008; Nakamura, 2009; Steinkuehler & Williams, 2006; Ward, 2010).

As new media studies have grown exponentially in the twenty-first century so, too, has research increased on country variations in the social uses of new media, the focal point of most cross-cultural new media investigations. In fact, after an exhaustive analysis of all published studies from 2005–2011 in *New Media and Society* (NMS) and the *Journal of Computer-Mediated Communication* (JCMC)—arguably, the two major communication journals on new media—it was found that both journals published 293 international new media studies, and just forty-one of these included more than one country in the investigation. Since 86% (252) are single country studies, they are overwhelmingly *intracultural* not intercultural examinations of the social uses of new media.

While there are myriad journals that publish new media research, JCMC and NMS are excellent indicators of communication research trends on culture and new media. A close analysis of 293 international new media articles in both journals reveal the following trends for (a) the frequency of research on major platforms and (b) percentage of studies aimed at theory validation, either mass media or new media theories. (1) Most of the international articles (195:66%) are single culture investigations of computer-mediated communication (i.e., online exchanges, websites, Internet, instant messaging). (2) Mobile phone research (calling and text messaging) conducted internationally is the next most frequently researched platform (43:15%), followed by social networking sites (17:6%), multiplayer on-line games (15:5%), blogging (13:4%), and, finally, a few scattered studies on email and YouTube, with zero international articles on virtual worlds. (3) The overwhelming majority of international new media investigations (240:82%) are theory validation studies that primarily attempt to refine new media or mass media theories, with limited analysis of socio cultural implications of new media.

Interestingly, platform research trends identified in JCMC and NMS are also supported by international studies on text messaging (Shuter & Chattopadhyay, 2010; Shuter, 2012) and mobile phones (Shuter & Chattopadhyay, 2012). Recently, communication scholars have also confirmed research trend three—the limited availability of socio cultural critiques of new media, society, and intercultural communication (Cheong, Martin, & Macfadyen, 2012).

Given the research trends on culture and new media, there are many avenues for future investigations to optimize the topic's inclusion in intercultural new media studies. Conceptually, there needs to be significantly more emphasis on intercultural new media research that takes a socio cultural perspective. This translates into new media studies that explore topics such as indigenous (i.e., country, co-culture, hybridity) cultural patterns of new media use, critical analyses of new media and society, and the impact of culture on the social uses of new media. A socio cultural perspective should also produce studies that develop, refine, or extend cultural theories of new media communication including, but not limited to, cultural values and the social uses of new media, co-cultural theory and new media behavior, and socio cultural factors and cultural preferences of new media platforms.

It's also important to conduct significantly more intercultural new media investigations that include two or more cultures and examine a broader range of new media platforms. While single country investigations are important because they reveal intracultural patterns of new media use, multiple culture investigations are also essential for generating comparative cultural data on the social uses of new media. In addition to continuing intercultural research on computer-mediated communication, it is important to examine, with much greater frequency, the social uses of additional new media platforms across cultures, particularly mobile phones, text messaging, social networking sites, multiplayer online games, and virtual worlds. With an abundance of intercultural data on these and other platforms, researchers will have a better understanding of the socio cultural dynamics that drive the social uses of new media.

Lastly, future studies on culture and new media should focus more on generating intercultural theories on the social uses of new media. The current trend of conducting mass media or new media theory validation studies is no substitute for formulating and refining culture-based new media theories that detail and explain socio cultural influences on the social uses of new media. There are a few culture-based new media theories, including Cheong, Martin, and Macfadyen's (2012) critical new media theory and Shuter and Chattopadhyay's (2012) socio cultural values theory of mobile phone activity. Both theories address the inextricable relationship between socio-cultural forces and new media, with Cheong Martin, and Macfadyen focusing on power and new media, and Shuter and Chattopadhyay exploring cultural values and mobile phone activity.

CONCLUSION

This essay conceptualizes the parameters of a new field of inquiry called intercultural new media studies, which consists of two areas: (1) new media and intercultural communication theory and (2) culture and new media. Exploring the intersection of new media and intercultural communication theory has the potential to refine and expand twentieth-century theories of intercultural communication grounded in a face-to-face paradigm. In light of current intercultural new media studies, five major intercultural communication theories (ICC) critiqued in this essay need to be reexamined and reconfigured, resulting in new or modified ICC theories more applicable to a digital era. Area two, culture and new media, focuses on the interdependent relationship between culture and new media, a fertile topic of inquiry delineating the influence of socio cultural forces on the social uses of new media within and across cultures. Intercultural new media studies promises to expand our understanding of intercultural communication in a new media age and is the next frontier in intercultural communication.

GLOSSARY

CMC	Computer-Mediated Communication
INMS	Intercultural New Media Studies
ICT	Information and Communication Technology
MMOG	Massive Multiplayer Online Game
SMS	Short Message Service
SNS	Social Network Site

References

Barker, V., & Ota, H. (2011). Mixi Diary versus Facebook Photos: Social networking site use among Japanese and Caucasian American females. *Journal of Intercultural Communication Research*, 40(1), 39–63. doi:10.1080/17475759.2011.558321

Baron, N. S., & af Segerstad, Y. (2010). Cross-cultural patterns in mobile-phone use: Public space and reachability in Sweden, the USA and Japan. *New Media & Society*, 12(1), 13–34. doi:10.1177/1461444809355111

Belz, J. A. (2005). Intercultural questioning, discovery and tension in Internet-mediated language learning partnerships. *Language & Intercultural Communication*, 5(1), 3–39.

Beniger, J. (1987). Personalization of mass media and the growth of pseudo-community. *Communication Research*, 14(3), 352–371.

Buber, M. (1965). *The knowledge of man*. New York, NY: Harper & Row.

Casmir, F. L. (1978). *Intercultural and international communication*. Washington, DC: University Press of America.

Casmir, F. L. (1997). *Ethics in intercultural and international communication*. Mahwah, NJ: Lawrence Erlbaum.

Casmir, F. L., & Asuncion-Lande, N. (1989). Intercultural communication revisited: Conceptualization, paradigm building, and methodological approaches. In J. A. Anderson (Ed.), *Communication Yearbook* 12 (pp. 278–309). Newbury Park: Sage.

Campbell, S. W. (2007). A cross-cultural comparison of perceptions and uses of mobile telephony. *New Media & Society*, 9(2), 343–363. doi:10.1177/1461444807075016

Chen, G. M., & Dai, X-d. (2012). New media and asymmetry in cultural identity negotiation. In P. H. Cheong, J. N. Martin, & L. Macfadyen (Eds.), *New media and intercultural communication: Identity, community and politics* (pp. 123–138). New York: Peter Lang.

Chen, W. (2010). Internet-usage patterns of immigrants in the process of intercultural adaptation. *Cyberpsychology, Behavior, and Social Networking*, 13(4), 387–399.

Cheong, P. H., Martin. J. N., & Macfadyen, L. (Eds.). (2012). *New media and intercultural communication: Identity, community and politics*. New York: Peter Lang.

Chia-I, H. (2008). A cross-cultural comparison of gender representation in massively multiplayer online role-playing games: A study of Taiwan and the United States. *China Media Research*, 4(2), 13–25.

Chun, D. M. (2011). Developing intercultural communicative competence through online exchanges. *CALICO Journal*, 28(2), 392–419.

Clothier, I. M. (2005). Created identities: Hybrid cultures and the internet. *Convergence: The Journal of Research into New Media Technologies*, 11(4), 44–59. doi:10.1177//1354856505061053

Collier, M. J. (2002). *Intercultural alliances: Critical transformation*. California: Sage Publications.

Colomb, G., & Simutis, J. (1996). Visible conversation and academic inquiry: CMC in a culturally diverse classroom. In S. C. Herring (Ed.), *Computer-mediated communication: Linguistic, social and cross-cultural perspectives* (pp. 203–224). Amsterdam: John Benjamins Publishing Company.

Croucher, S. M. (2011). Social networking and cultural adaptation: A theoretical model. *Journal of International and Intercultural Communication*, 4(4), 259–264.

Croucher, S., & Cronn-Mills, D. (2011). *Religious misperceptions: The case of Muslims and Christians in France and Britain*. New York: Hampton Press.

Dooly, M. (2011). Crossing the intercultural borders into 3rd space culture(s): Implications for teacher education in the twenty-first century. *Language & Intercultural Communication*, 11(4), 319–337. doi:10.1080/14708477.2011.599390

Diehl, W. C., & Prins, E. (2008). Unintended outcomes in second life: Intercultural literacy and cultural identity in a virtual world. *Language & Intercultural Communication*, 8(2), 101–118. doi:10.1080/14708470802139619

Durham, M. G. (2004). Constructing the "new ethnicities:" Media, sexuality, and diaspora identity in the lives of South Asian immigrant girls. *Critical Studies in Media Communication*, 21, 140–161.

Elola, I., & Oskoz, A. (2008). Blogging: Fostering intercultural competence development in foreign language and study abroad contexts. *Foreign Language Annals*, 41(3), 454–477.

Ess, C. (Ed.). (2001). *Culture, technology, communication: Towards an intercultural global village*. Albany, NY: State University of New York Press.

Gadamer, H. G. (1989). *Truth and method*. New York: Crossroads.

Ganesh, S., & Holmes, P. (2011). Positioning intercultural dialogue—theories, pragmatics, and an agenda. *Journal of International and Intercultural Communication*, 4(2), 81–86.

Grasmuck, S., Martin, J., & Shanyang, Z. (2009). Ethno-racial identity displays on Facebook. *Journal of Computer-Mediated Communication*, 15(1), 158–188. doi:10.1111/j.1083-6101.2009.01498.x

Green, E., & Singleton, C. (2007). Mobile selves: Gender, ethnicity and mobile phones in the everyday lives of young Pakistani-British women and men. *Information, Communication & Society,* 10(4), 506–526. doi:10.1080/13691180701560036

Guéguen, N. (2008). Helping on the web: Ethnic stereotypes and computer-mediated communication. *Research Journal of Social Sciences,* 3, 1–3.

Habermas, J. (1987). *The theory of communicative action: Volume 2.* Boston, MA: Beacon Press.

Hichang, C., & Jae-Shin, L. (2008). Collaborative information seeking in intercultural computer-mediated communication groups: Testing the influence of social context using social network analysis. *Communication Research,* 35(4), 548–573.

Hu, S. L. Y., & Leung, L. (2003). Effects of expectancy-value, attitudes, and use of the Internet on psychological empowerment experienced by Chinese women at the workplace. *Telematics and Informatics,* 20(4), 365–382.

Jiali, Y. (2006). Traditional and online support networks in the cross-cultural adaptation of Chinese international students in the United States. *Journal of Computer-Mediated Communication,* 11(3), 863–876. doi:10.1111/j.1083-6101.2006.00039.x

Jones, S. (2001). Understanding micropolis and compunity. In C. Ess (Ed.), *Culture, technology, communication: Towards an intercultural global village* (pp. 53–66). Albany, NY: State University of New York Press.

Karlsson, L. (2006). The diary weblog and the travelling tales of diasporic tourists. *Journal of Intercultural Studies,* 27(3), 299–312. doi:10.1080/07256860600779303

Katz, J. E., & Aakhus, M. (Eds.). (2002). *Perpetual contact: Mobile communication, private talk, public performance.* Cambridge, UK: Cambridge University Press.

Khan, M. (1992). Communication patterns of sojourners in the process of acculturation. *The Journal of Development Communication,* 3, 65–73.

Kim, Y. Y. (1988). *Communication and cross-cultural adaptation: An integrative theory.* Philadelphia, PA: Multilingual Matters.

Kim, Y. Y. (2001). *Becoming intercultural: An integrative theory of communication and cross-cultural adaptation.* Thousand Oaks, CA: Sage.

Lin, J., Peng, W., Kim, M., Kim, S., & LaRose, R. (2012). Social networking and adjustments among international students. *New Media & Society,* 14(3), 421–440. doi:10.1177/1461444811418627

Ling, R. (2008). *New tech, new ties: How mobile communication is reshaping social cohesion.* Cambridge, MA: MIT Press.

Ma, Ringo (1996). Computer-mediated conversations as a new dimension of intercultural communication between East Asian and North American college students. In S. C. Herring (Ed.), *Computer-mediated communication:*

Linguistic, social and cross-cultural perspectives (pp. 173–186). Amsterdam: John Benjamins Publishing Company.

Martinez, V. (2010). University training and education for interculturality in student mobility in Hong Kong. *E-Proceedings of the International Online Language Conference (IOLC),* 60–67.

McEwan, B., & Sobre-Denton, M. (2011). Virtual cosmopolitanism: Constructing third cultures and transmitting social and cultural capital through social media. *Journal of International and Intercultural Communication,* 4(4), 252–258.

Meagher, M. L., & Castanos, F. (1996). Perceptions of American culture: The impact of an electronically mediated cultural exchange program on Mexican high school students. In S. C. Herring (Ed.), *Computer-mediated communication: Linguistic, social and cross-cultural perspectives* (pp. 187–203). Amsterdam: John Benjamins Publishing Company.

Mehra, B., Merkel, C., & Bishop, A. P. (2004). The Internet for empowerment of minority and marginalized users. *New Media & Society,* 6(6), 781–802.

Mollov, M., & Schwartz, D. G. (2010). Towards an integrated strategy for intercultural dialog: Computer-mediated communication and face to face. *Journal of Intercultural Communication Research,* 39(3), 207–224. doi:10.1080/17475759.2010.534905

Nakamura, L. (2009). Don't hate the player, hate the game: The racialization of labor in World of Warcraft. *Critical Studies in Media Communication,* 26(2), 128–144. doi:10.1080/15295030902860252

Nelson, G., & Temples, A. (2011). Identity construction as nexus of multimembership: Attempts at reconciliation through an online intercultural communication course. *Journal of Language, Identity & Education,* 10(2), 63–82. doi:10.1080/15348458.2011.563636

Pfeil, U., Zaphiris, P., & Ang, S. C. (2006). Cultural differences in collaborative authoring of Wikipedia. *Journal of Computer-Mediated Communication,* 12(1), 88–113. doi:10.1111/j.1083-6101.2006.00316.x

Pflug, J. (2011). Contextuality and computer-mediated communication: A cross cultural comparison. *Computers in Human Behavior,* 27(1), 131–137. doi:10.1016/j.chb.2009.10.008

Raman, P., & Harwood, J. (2008). Acculturation of Asian Indian sojourners in America: Applications of the cultivation framework. *Southern Communication Journal,* 73, 295–311.

Richardson, R., & Smith, S. W. (2007). The influence of high/low-context culture and power distance on choice of communication media: Students' media choice to communicate with professors in Japan and America. *International Journal of Intercultural Relations,* 31(4), 479–501. doi:10.1016/j.ijintrel.2007.01.002

Schroeder, R. (2010). Mobile phones and the inexorable advance of multimodal connectedness. *New Media & Society*, 12(1), 75–90. doi:10.1177/1461444809355114

Shu-Chuan, C., & Sejung Marina, C. (2011). Electronic word-of-mouth in social networking sites: A cross-cultural study of the United States and China. *Journal of Global Marketing*, 24(3), 263–281. doi:10.1080/08911762.2011.59246

Shuter, R. (2011). Introduction: New media across cultures—prospect and promise. *Journal of International & Intercultural Communication*, 4(4), 241–245. doi:10.1080/17513057.2011.598041

Shuter, R. (2012). When Indian women text message: Culture, identity, and emerging interpersonal norms of new media. In P. H. Cheong, J. N. Martin, & L. Macfadyen (Eds.), *New media and intercultural communication: Identity, community and politics* (pp. 209–222). New York: Peter Lang.

Shuter, R., & Chattopadhyay, S. (2010). Emerging interpersonal norms of text messaging in India and the United States. *Journal of Intercultural Communication Research*, 39(2), 123–147. doi:10.1080/17475759.2010.526319

Shuter, R., & Chattopadhyay, S. (2012). *Mobile phone activity and community: A cross-national study of socio-cultural values and the social uses of mobile phones.* Paper presented at the National Communication Association, November, 2012.

Singh, C. (2010). New media and cultural identity. *China Media Research*, 6(1), 86–90.

Spurgeon, C., & Goggin, G. (2007). Mobiles into media: Premium rate SMS and the adaptation of television to interactive communication cultures. *Continuum: Journal of Media & Cultural Studies*, 21(2), 317–329. doi:10.1080/10304310701278173

St. Amant, K. (2002). When cultures and computers collide: Rethinking computer-mediated communication according to international and intercultural communication expectations. *Journal of Business and Technical Communication*, 16, 196–214. doi:10.1177/1050651902016002003

Starosta, W. J., & Olorunnisola, A. (1998). A meta model for third culture development. In G. M. Chen, & W. J. Starosta (Eds.), *Foundations in intercultural communication* (pp. 45–63). Boston, MA: Allyn Bacon.

Steinkuehler, C. A., & Williams, D. (2006). Where everybody knows your (screen) name: Online games as "third places." *Journal of Computer-Mediated Communication*, 11(4), 885–909. doi:10.1111/j.1083-6101.2006.00300.x

Tajfel, H., & Turner, J. C. (1986). The social identity theory of intergroup behavior. In H. Tajfel (Ed.), *Social identity and intergroup relations* (pp. 234–256). Cambridge: Cambridge University Press.

Tokunaga, R. S. (2009). High-speed internet access to the other: The influence of cultural orientations on self-disclosures in offline and online relationships. *Journal of Intercultural Communication Research*, 38(3), 133–147. doi:10.1080/17475759.2009.505058

Wang, C. (2012). Using Facebook for cross-cultural collaboration: The experience of students from Taiwan. *Educational Media International*, 49(1), 63–76.

Wang, Z., Walther, J. B., & Hancock, J. T. (2009). Social identification and interpersonal communication in computer-mediated communication: What you do versus who you are in virtual groups. *Human Communication Research*, 35(1), 59–85.

Ward, M. (2010). Avatars and sojourners: Explaining the acculturation of newcomers to multiplayer online games as cross-cultural adaptations. *Journal of Intercultural Communication*, 7(23).

Wiseman, R., & Koester, J. (Eds.). (1993). *Intercultural communication competence.* Thousand Oaks, CA: Sage Publications.

Würtz, E. (2005). Intercultural communication on web sites: A cross-cultural analysis of web sites from high-context cultures and low-context cultures. *Journal of Computer-Mediated Communication*, 11(1), 274–299. doi:10.1111/j.1083-6101.2006.tb00313.x

Ye, J. (2005). Acculturative stress and use of the Internet among East Asian international students in the U.S. *CyberPsychology & Behavior*, 8, 154–161.

Yoon, R. (1996). Yin/yang principles and the relevance of externalism and paralogic rhetoric to intercultural communication. *Journal of Business and Technical Communication*, 11, 297–320.

Young-ok, Y., & Hara, K. (2005). Computer-mediated relationship development: A cross-cultural comparison. *Journal of Computer-Mediated Communication*, 11(1), 133–152. doi:10.1111/j.1083-6101.2006.tb00307.x

Concepts and Questions

1. Robert Shuter claims that the advent of new media forms is transforming intercultural communication. Using examples, explain this claim.
2. What is meant by a "third culture"? How can it be formed through intercultural dialogue?
3. How can new media forms facilitate the acculturation process?
4. Shuter indicates that new media appear to have an impact on culture. Select a new media form (e.g., SNS) and provide an example of how it can facilitate cultural change.
5. Provide an example of intercultural communication you have experienced using new media. What problems were encountered and how did you overcome them?

Index

A

abimsa (nonviolence), 125

accented speech, language difference (awareness), 253

accents, 253

acceptance
  active acceptance, 83
  African American communication, 185
  passive acceptance, 82–83
  white identity development, 82–83

acculturation, 431–432
  concept, 20
  conceptualization, shift, 22
  experience, 385–386
  interplay, 475
  new media
    exclusion, 476
    relationship, 474–476
  research, 93–95
  studies, impact, 94–95

acquaintance potential, 389

active acceptance, 83

actor communicative status, increase, 349–350

actor competence
  function, co-actor impression, 350–352
  increase, co-actor impression, 349–352

actor knowledge, increase, 349

actor motivation, increase, 349

actor normative compensation, 352

actor normative reciprocity, 351

actor performance, contextual obstruction (increase), 349–350

actor skill, increase, 349

actor status, co-actor impression (increase), 350

actual behavior
  indices, research, 178
  perceptions
    confusion, 178–179
    separation, 180

adaptation, 385–386, 419
  impetus, 386
  process, 393–394

adaptive transformation, stress-adaptation-growth dynamics, 386f

aesthetic continuum, 408
  Eastern conception, 407

aesthetic perception, 412

affective competence, 388

affective components, 379

affectiveness, communication feature, 220

affirmative action, 82

African American communication
  acceptance, 185
  assumptions, 183
  authenticity, 185
  authority, challenge, 311
  avoidance, 187
  breaking in and talking over, 306
  confrontation, 188
  education, 187
  effectiveness, 183
  gaining the floor, 306
  genuineness, expression, 187–188
  goal attainment, 186
  improvement strategies, 186–188
  individuals, treatment, 188
  information, 187
  interaction management, 187
  intergroup communication issues, 184–186
  internal management, 188
  intragroup communication issues, 184
  language management, 188
  negative stereotyping, 184–185
  openness/friendliness, 187
  other-orientation, 187
  personal expressiveness, 185
  personalization/objectification, 311–312
  perspective, 182
  point of view, assertion, 186–187
  positive self-presentation, 187
  power dynamics, 186
  problem solving, 307–308
  task engagement, 307–308
  understanding, 186
  word play, 312

African American discourse style
  aestheticism, examples, 312

African American ethnic culture, communicative style, 182

African American listeners, talk back, 306

African American topic-chaining speakers, 310

African *Kawaida* philosophy, 449–452

Afrocentric-Asiacentric dialogue, 457

Afrocentricity, 29, 30f, 450–452
  isolation, 452
  legacy, 451

Afrocentric paradigms, concept, 451–452

aiguo (patriotism), 460

Akashi, Yasushi, 454

Al Aqsa *intifada,* 217

altercentrism, increase, 348

amae, 57

American Indian identity
  focus, 71
  full blood, identity, 71–72
  Indian-ness, communication, 70
  issues, 74–75
  negotiation, 73
  racial/tribal group, 74

Americans. *See* United States
  ethnicity, religion (impact), 88
  experience, lessons, 403–404
  Germans, similarities/differences, 274
  racial/cultural/gendered identity, 72
  tolerance, 404

Americans with Disabilities Act of 1990 (ADA), 162

America, Russia (contrast), 136

Analects, 36

Anaya, Rudolfo, 88

Anderson, Peter, 208, 229

anthropology, discipline, 61–64

anticipatory communication, 117–118

appearances, importance, 226

appropriateness
  meaning, 343
  standards, 344

Arabic
  unity, 131
  worldview, 131–132

Argentina, physician-patient communication, 329

Arias, Ron, 88

Aristotle, 126, 408
  logic, 420

Army of One, 48

Asante, Molefi Kete, 27

ascription process, 56–57, 375

Asiacentric communication ethics/competence, 37

Asiacentricity, 29, 30f, 450–452
  descriptiveness, 452
  flowchart, 450f
  future, 449
  vision, 451

naturalistic fallacy, 418
nature
    universe, 406
    worldview (Maasai), 144–145
Nava, Yolanda, 224
negative stereotyping, African American communication, 184–185
negotiated problem solving, 307–308
nemawashi (informal discussions), 263
    practice, 33
    process, 268
network
    analysis, 100
    reentry, 100
    theory, 98
new media
    acculturation, relationship, 474–476
    cultural identity, relationship, 476–477
    culture, relationship, 477–478
    exclusion, 476
    ICTs, ubiquity, 472
    intercultural communication theory, 472–477
    intercultural dialogue, 472–474
    interplay, 475
New Media and Society (NMS), studies, 477
Nigerians
    culture, accommodation, 102
    transiency, 96–97
ninjo concept, 34
Nishiyama, Kazuo, 262, 266
noise, 8
    physical noise, 8
    physiological noise, 8
    semantic noise, 9
nomini-cation (drink/communicate), 270
nominication (drinking-communication), 453
non-cultural (culturally generic) contract, existence (denial), 100–101
nondisabled culture, disability (redefining), 170–171
nondisabled people
    communication, attempt, 165
    discomfort/stereotypes, overcoming, 165
    people with disabilities, relationships, 164
    researchers, focus (change), 166–167
nondominance
    concept, 157–160
    issues, 154
nondominant groups, impact, 157
nondominant people
    enslavement, 160
    placement, cultural prescription, 159
    suffering, 158

nongovernments, information technology usage, 403
non-heterosexual social identity, development, 193
non-self view, 65
non-separateness, communication (relationship), 32–33
nonverbal behaviors, 12, 13–14
    code, 230
nonverbal codes, 229–231
nonverbal communication
    behavior, culture (influence), 14
    culture, relationship, 229
    verbal communication, combination, 207–208
nonverbal greeting behaviors, 13
nonverbal language, ease, 204
nonverbal processes (Maasai), 147–148
non-Western cultures
    communication, 455
    values, 456
normalcy, belief, 82
norms, 53, 77
    conduct, 57–58
    expression modes, 378–379
    whiteness set, 81–82
North American culture, distinctions, 113
North American orientations, comparison, 112t, 115t
nursing research, themes, 331
Nwosu, Peter O., 51, 92

O

objective truths, mistrust (Russia), 137
oculesics, 208
"Old West" image, 73
olfactics, 208
    nonverbal behavior code, 230–231
omoiyari (empathy), 244
ontology, 429
Onwumechili, Chuka, 51, 92
openness, 392–393
    African American communication, 187
open processes, 403
operational competence, 388
opposite-gender behavior, 191
opposite-sex spouses, similarities, 196
opposites, interdependence, 407
optimal peace, 424
Ordnung, 78
organic communities, hybrid cultural identities, 476
Orkut, 475
other-directedness, 4
Other, image, 30
other-orientation, African American communication, 187

outcastes, 125
outcome-oriented communication, process-oriented communication (contrast), 115
out-group, 356
    distinctions, 113–114
outsiders, 190–191

P

pahiwatig-pakikiramdam dynamics, 34
Palestinians
    argument, 221–222
    culture, emergence, 219
    Israeli-Jews, dialogue/cultural communication, 217
    messages, meaning/significance, 220–221
    peace accords (1993), 217
    speech codes, 217–219
        cultural psychology/sociology, impact, 220
        distinctiveness, 220
        location, 221
    transformative communication, 218
    transformative dialogues, 218–219
Pamuk, Orhan, 435
paradigmatic barrier, 415
paralanguage (Maasai), 147
paralanguage (vocalics), 230
paralanguage, usage (Japan), 246–247
paralinguistics, usage, 297–298
Parents and Friends of Lesbians and Gays (PFLAG), 194
particularistic relationships, universalistic relationships (contrast), 113
passive acceptance, 82–83
passive-receptive posture, 305
Pasupathi, 122
paticcasamupada, law, 65
Paz, Octavio, 224
peace
    fundamental human value, 424
    minimal peace, 424
    moderate peace, 424
    optimal peace, 424
Peace Corps volunteers, preparedness, 392
peace, ethic, 422
Pearson, Judy C., 152, 174
people, development (stages), 175
people of color, cultural difference, 82
perception-13, 12
personal, political relationship, 190–196
personal altercentrism, 348
personal communication, 387–388
personal contacts, maintenance, 270
personal expressiveness, African American communication, 185